HOLT, RINEHART AND WINSTON, INC.
New York · Chicago · San Francisco · Atlanta · Dallas
Montreal · Toronto · London

Warren R. Baller
United States International University

Don C. Charles
Iowa State University

SECOND EDITION

THE PSYCHOLOGY OF HUMAN GROWTH AND DEVELOPMENT

Library of Congress Card Number: 68-16608

03-068940-6

Printed in the United States of America

90123 40 9876543

Preface

The second edition of *The Psychology of Human Growth and Development* perpetuates the main objectives of the earlier edition. Like its predecessor, it is a book primarily for students of education. It is designed to meet their need for sound knowledge of psychology at the level of introductory acquaintance with the subject.

Most of the ideas which governed the writing of the first edition appear to be equally relevant to the revision. Some have been reworded in part at least, better to bring out their meaning. As in the first edition, there are six governing ideas:

1. Human growth and development provides an appropriate context in which to present a beginning psychology course.

2. The subject matter of an introductory course in psychology for teachers should clearly be *a psychology of persons*. The understanding of persons is, therefore, the central theme that runs throughout the sixteen chapters of the book. Deriving from this theme, as interpreted by the authors, is a proposition that will appear with considerable regularity from chapter to chapter. It is the idea that human creatures are, in much of their experience, engaged in *a life-long* effort to achieve self-identity and a sense of meaning in their life.

The authors believe that the theme of the book should help reassure the student that what he is studying draws its meaning from the kinds of experience which are already known to him, though often quite imperfectly. The theme is expected also to supply continuity of discussion from chapter to chapter.

3. The study of human behavior and development must be soundly based in research. The authors have seen no reason to weigh their discussion down under masses of evidence. But, at the same time, they believe that it would be a disservice to students to fail to make clear the dependence which the truth about behavior and development has

on research. They have, therefore, dignified the principal conclusions in the various chapters by showing their research connections.

4. The psychology of human behavior and development is a distinctive study which is not to be confused with an indiscriminate collection of facts from various sciences that study man. The authors have drawn extensively from different behavioral sciences, but always with the intent of showing the relationship of the facts thus selected to the understanding of human beings.

5. A teacher's knowledge of the psychology of human behavior and development should be functional in school situations. We have, therefore, developed ideas and principles in contexts that are well fortified by illustrations and examples from school and other situations vital to the lives of young people.

6. Developmental psychology for teachers must present much of the human life span rather than limited segments of it. We feel that all teachers need to understand their students not only in terms of their present age, but in terms of what has gone before and what awaits them later on in development. Much of a child's behavior is determined by events which occurred before school age—or before birth for that matter. The elementary school child is developing behavior patterns which will flower in adolescence; the adolescent is becoming an adult. Thus, we have examined development from conception to maturity, rather than during childhood or adolescence alone.

The organization and content of this book reflect the authors' experience in teaching introductory psychology courses in a number of universities. Our experience has taught us, for example, that usually, the placement of the course in the curriculum is such that the student will have had little or no previous contact with any of the behavioral sciences. We have kept this circumstance in view as we have drawn upon the various behavioral sciences for our subject matter. Although we have written with the sophomore in mind, we hope that the upperclassman also will find the book both informative and stimulating.

There are four main parts to the book. Some of the parts have titles different from those of the first edition and some of the organization of chapters within the parts has also been altered. *Part 1,* "Orientation to the study of Human Behavior and Development," introduces the basic concepts of the study of behavior and development and the methods of scientific psychology. It also presents for the student some clarification of the central theme of the book. *Part 2,* "The Bio-Social Foundations of Human Behavior," describes the prenatal origins of behavior and the roles, respectively, of perception, motivation, emotion, and cultural experience in the producing and shaping of the behavior of individuals. *Part 3,* "Development and Adjustment," examines the implications for personality and adjustment of physical, mental, cognitive, communicative, and social development. *Part 4,* "Personality and the School's Role in its Development," is intended to examine the formative influence on the life style of the individual of persons close to him. The impact of peers, close relatives and teachers on the personality and self-concept of the individual is the main concern of Part 4. Chapter 15, "Personality and the Self-Concept," should help the student correlate many of the principles and concepts that were developed in the preceding chapters and—to paraphrase an oft-quoted statement—to see the individual steadily and to see him whole. Chapter 16, "Psychology of Teacher-Pupil Relationships," confronts the practical question of how a teacher can effectively apply the psychology of human growth and development to the experiences of the school.

It will be noted that one important topic, learning, has not been allotted a separate chapter or section. As was explained in the first edition, there are two reasons for this circumstance. One is that certain aspects of learning are interlaced with the material of most of the chapters of the book. The second and principal reason for the omission of a chapter on learning is that an extensive treatment of learning, as the present authors view the matter, may best be accorded the major part of a separate course: one that follows the course for which this text is intended.

Supplementary to *The Psychology of Human Growth and Development* is *Readings in the Psychology of Human Growth and Development,* edited by one of the present authors, Warren R. Baller. It is our belief that students benefit greatly from the experience of reading representative selections from published research which relate to the discussion in their textbook. The book of readings contains fifty-two research articles and other scholarly publications; most of these have been quoted in this textbook.

Many persons have in one way or another helped the authors in their preparation of this book. The authors' children and many other children have played an important part. So, too, have the students whom the authors have had in their classes in different universities.

We wish also to acknowledge our indebtedness to present and former staff members of the Department of Educational Psychology and Measurements of the University of Nebraska, from whose experience in the teaching of educational psychology much of the plan and many of the ideas of this book were derived. We are especially appreciative of the encouragement and counsel of Dr. D. A. Worcester, Emeritus Professor, the University of Nebraska, and Dr. C. O. Neidt, Director, Human Factors Research Laboratory, Colorado State University. Both are former chairmen of the Department of Educational Psychology and Measurements of the University of Nebraska. For invaluable suggestions and constructive criticism, we wish to express our gratitude to Dr. Dale B. Harris, Chairman of the Department of Psychology, Pennsylvania State University.

Mentioned in the text and in the references at the end of each chapter are authors and publishers who have generously permitted us to quote or otherwise cite their work. We hope that this mention will convey our feeling of great debt to them.

In the preparation of a book there are many details which only an able secretary and typist can handle well. For their competent assistance with the manuscript, we want to thank Miss Sharon Irmer, Mrs. Linda Hays, Mrs. Donalda Jones, and Mrs. Margaret Heald.

San Diego, California W.R.B.

Ames, Iowa D.C.C.

February 1968

Contents

Orientation to the Study of Human Behavior and Development

PART 1

WHENEVER A PERSON IS INTRODUCED to a new discipline or field of study, he is likely to have at least one simple, but fundamental, question in mind—"What's it about?" This question is particularly appropriate upon beginning the study of psychology and other behavioral sciences.

Popular fiction, the movies, and television often depict psychologists in ways which suggest the occult and mysterious. Chapter 1 of this text is, therefore, designed to tell the learner, "What it's about." It explains the importance of understanding behavior in teaching and working with young people. The concept of growth and development is explored, and the major problem areas in psychology are described. The other chapters of Part I proceed with the question, "What's it about?" where Chapter 1 leaves off.

Most of this book is devoted to study of principles, of concepts, and of suggested application of both. Chapter 2 serves as a forecast of these and tells how the more basic of them will serve as recurrent themes throughout the book. The main purpose of the chapter is to focus the reader's attention on the central idea of the book: the understanding of behavior of children and youth.

The authors' experience in teaching psychology to undergraduates suggests that a major problem lies in the nature of research evidence. It is perfectly natural to reject an idea or statement which is contrary to one's personal (and therefore, limited) experience; as a result the unsophisticated student often disregards or rejects generalizations which it is important to accept. He may, on the other hand, quite uncritically accept statements that derive from nothing more than somebody's strongly worded speculation. The development of habits of curiosity concerning the validity of the conclusions about human behavior and development which one reads or hears is something highly to be desired. In Chapter 3, therefore, the authors attempt to clarify the place, the methods, and the implications of research in the behavioral sciences in order that students will learn to respect *evidence,* as compared to *opinion.*

CHAPTER 1

Psychology's Relationship to Teaching

What knowledge is most important to successful teaching? And what array of capabilities? A warranted answer is that a good many kinds of knowledge and a considerable number of capabilities must be acquired by the person who becomes an effective teacher. To argue that one kind is more important than another is as illogical as to insist that the foundation of a building is more needed than the walls or the floors. All are needed—and other important parts, too.

Nevertheless, to follow the analogy a step further, there can be no argument about the essential function that a firm foundation serves, whether it be buildings or the abilities of teachers that we are talking about. Because the latter is our present concern, let it be stated that among the kinds of knowledge that may be considered foundational is a firm understanding of human behavior and development. To be prepared systematically (not gropingly) to see into the *experience* of the child or the youth as he grows and develops and learns has much to do with a teacher's effectiveness as an instructor, counselor and personal confidant. Such preparation—such an ability—will increase the likelihood that the teacher will do and say the things that help boys and girls develop self-respect, healthy acceptance of other persons, and a genuine *love of learning*. The authors believe that an important foundation for this kind of preparation can be provided by the psychology of human growth and development.

PSYCHOLOGY'S RELATION TO THE UNDERSTANDING OF HUMAN BEHAVIOR AND DEVELOPMENT

The purpose behind the writing of this book is to present the concepts and principles that psychology and other closely related sciences have to offer as means for the deepening and organizing of our understanding of human behavior in general and of human individuals in particular. The purpose—stated a bit differently—is to relate psychology to *teaching* and especially to the very important matter of the teacher's need for insight into the behavior of children and youth.

There is a central theme that runs throughout the book. It is that *persons* are a chief concern of teachers and that helping them to understand themselves and to live well with themselves and others is an important prerequisite to the maturing of the potentialities that are in them. Basically this is a book in psychology. More particularly, it is a book in which psychology is made to lead the way, so to speak, in the refinement of our knowledge of the *experiential accompaniments* of personal growth and development.

But what is psychology? That is, what actually is its subject matter? Also, just where, in the total domain of psychology, should we expect to locate this present kind of study? It is obviously desirable to try to clarify our thinking in these regards as a first step in getting under way with the topics of this book.

PSYCHOLOGY DEFINED AS THE STUDY OF BEHAVIOR

Psychology has frequently and correctly been defined as the study of behavior. One writer comments that the psychologist "takes it for granted . . . that you know he is talking about human and animal behavior, not the behavior of stars or machines or atoms." He then adds, "The person untrained in psychology is usually surprised at the word 'behavior' " and surmises that instead of "behavior" most persons would expect "mind" or "thought" or "feeling" to be specified as the subject matter of psychology (Morgan, 1956) [3].[1]

Morgan, who was just quoted, states in support of his definition that it *is* behavior which we observe when we set out to study another person. "We know very well," he says, "that there are events going on within a person—events that can be called 'thoughts,' 'feelings,' or more generally, 'mental abilities.' We can and do make fairly trustworthy inferences about those events, but we always make them from the way a person behaves. It is what he says, does, and writes that we as scientists can observe and record. Hence it is only behavior that we can study."

This emphasis on behavior should remove one misconception about the subject matter of psychology. It is the notion that psychology is a body of abstract laws and principles which have little if any connection

[1] References thus cited are fully listed and arranged alphabetically at the end of each chapter.

with a student's immediate and personal interest in people and what they do. Psychology is not about data and principles and laws as ends in themselves. Psychology *does* make use of carefully gathered data and the principles that these data suggest, but the significance of the data and principles is in the light they throw on behavior. The student who keeps this explanation in mind as he proceeds with the study of psychology may avoid needless experiences of "losing sight of the forest because of the trees."

A word about what is *not* meant by behavior, as here used, may be helpful. It is not to be equated with what sometimes is meant by "good" or "bad" conduct, or behaving in a conforming or nonconforming way. These are, for psychology, *instances* of behavior. They are by no means the whole of behavior or the whole of what psychology is about. This explanation is made in the present context because occasionally someone in this manner restricts the meaning of "behavior," with the result that he and others have quite different ideas about what they are trying to discuss.

There is probably no term that could be used to describe the subject matter of psychology that would be wholly free from objections, and this goes for the word "behavior." [2] But the term does have the merit of designating something to which we have access, namely, the responses that individuals make. When one tries to understand another person, he will be likely to make some headway only if he is thoughtfully attentive to the things that the person says and does and deliberately lets actions "speak" for themselves.

We have defined one of the terms that make up the title of this book, namely, psychology. Now we may examine three other terms. What is the meaning of the terms "growth" and "development"? And what special significance is there in the use of the word "human" in the title of the book?

MEANING OF HUMAN GROWTH AND DEVELOPMENT

Let us see how the word *human* fits into our discussion. There is a reason for using "human" in the discussions that follow, instead of "child" or "adolescent." The authors wish to take into account as far as possible in this book the entire school-age span of years, plus considerable preschool and even prenatal "biography." And they feel also that much of what the various chapters contain will be applicable to behavior beyond the usual school-age years. Especially are they interested in emphasizing

[2] For a criticism of the statement that psychology's subject matter is behavior, see Waters, Rolland H., "Behavior: Datum or Abstraction" (1958) [6].

that behavior and development are continuous and that no individual can be thought about advantageously without clear regard for the relationship between present and past experience—and even future experience.

In passing it may be noted that the word "human" suggests what has earlier been indicated: that our interest is in the behavior of man rather than that of the lower animals. This is substantially correct, simply because we believe that it is the behavior of persons that teachers most need to understand; we should, therefore, try to build our concepts around that point of reference.

It would, nevertheless, be an unfortunate thing if we were to fail to recognize the very important role that studies of lower animals have in solving the problems of psychology. Much that we understand about man's behavior is the result of the laboratory findings with the not always so lowly white rat or the chimpanzee or some other experimental subject, more manageable than man. These kinds of studies constitute what is called comparative psychology.

Growth and Development

Many of the problems studied in psychology relate closely to the facts about growth and development. Indeed, it is difficult to investigate, interpret, and explain human behavior without viewing it in the context of growth and development—without considering it as something emergent, dynamic, and changing. There is always, in the experience of the individual whose behavior we want to understand, an inescapable reference to changes taking place in him, some of which he tries deliberately to bring about and some of which occur as part of an unfolding natural plan.

The very existence of an organism depends upon change. Old cells are constantly being replaced by new cells; tissues grow and become strengthened as the organism exercises them to meet the increasing demands of life; the fluids of the body and their important constituents are continuously replenished: these and other changes are necessary to an organism's survival.

Development Is More than Change. An individual may be considered changed when, for example, he loses a finger or has a few front teeth extracted and replaced by some the dentist supplies. But no matter how extensive the changes in a person may be they do not necessarily add up to development. Development means a progressive sequence of changes in the organism—a sequence characterized by orderliness and coherent design.

There is still more to development. An adequate description of the development of an organism emphasizes the close relationship between changes in structure and changes in function. The important corollary to the fact that a young robin is growing feathers on its wings is the increasing imminence of the little creature's first flight. Flight is the function of wings. The corollary to the human baby's cumulative strength and length of feet and legs—as well as his improving coordination—is his gradual approach to a level of function that legs serve, namely walking.

Thus it is with every aspect of an organism's structural growth: emergence of related functions is the natural counterpart. And there is another side to the coin. Just as increase in growth is accomplished by new and improved functions, so also, conversely, is decline in growth accompanied by decline in functions.

A definite feature of development is, therefore, the orderly unfolding of the increasingly complex systems of the organism. Growth processes are not capricious; they are lawful and the more we learn about them the more predictable they reveal themselves to be. This is the fact that gives incentive and hope to the researcher's study of the various aspects of human growth and development. And it is the fact that underscores the importance of a close working relationship between those who teach and those who apply their efforts to scientific investigation of growth, development, and behavior.

The term "development" has now been defined. But what does "growth" mean? Does growth have a meaning different from development, or are the two synonymous and quite properly to be used interchangeably? The answer: growth and development do mean different things.

Growth is an increase in magnitude of a living thing or any of its parts; or an increase in the magnitude or scope of something the organism does. The emphasis in this definition is on *increase in magnitude.* Examples of growth are an individual's increase in height or weight; the lengthening of his bodily extremities; the *enlargement* of the organs of his body; the gains (that is, *growth*) made by him in vocabulary or in arithmetic.

Development is more comprehensive than growth. As we consider what was said about development, we may conclude—and correctly so—that development includes growth.

Again, let us make explicit a point that belongs to the central theme of this book. It is that for the teacher these kinds of knowledge (about growth and development) are essential because he must not only know as much as he can about the varying needs of the individual that accompany growth changes but also about *the impact these changes have on the individual's concept of himself.*

AREAS OF STUDY IN PSYCHOLOGY

Psychology has already been defined in this chapter as a study of behavior. This statement may be amplified to the student's advantage by some discussion of the kinds of behavioral phenomena that are studied in psychology.

Often what a person sees as he examines the chapter titles of psychology books are certain key words, such as perception, motivation, emotion, learning, intelligence, and personality. These words are the names of behavioral phenomena about which psychology has much to teach but about which there is still a great deal that has eluded the best efforts of researchers. Frequently when the psychologist uses these key terms, he is designating what to him are psychological *problems* or problem areas—his explanations do not fully cover all the facts that pertain to the phenomena.

Heredity

How much of what one sees in behavior is attributable to gene-controlled inheritance? When and how does heredity begin to collaborate with environment—with the physical-social surroundings of the individual? To what extent does biological inheritance set limits on human growth and development that are not to be transcended by virtue of the kinds of *nurturing* the individual gets?

Such are the kinds of questions for which psychologists as well as biologists have been trying for years to get satisfactory answers. Evidence will be presented in numerous later discussions indicating the extent to which research has given the answers to questions about heredity.

Perception: One's Observation of One's World and One's Self

Every individual has his own special view of his world and himself. When we consider to what extent that which a person does is dependent upon "the way he sees things," we can appreciate the importance that psychologists attach to perception. Does each person have sensations of a given situation that are the same as those of another person? Or does each individual have a "system" all his own for interpreting the data of his sense organs? How could any question be of greater importance to a teacher than that of the way in which an individual develops his particular view of his world and of himself?

Of key importance is the question of how the individual comes to have the special, private, "core" of experience that is revealed in his use of the word "I." What are the ways by which this self-reference comes into being and by which it spreads into the whole of the individual's experience?

These are illustrative of the questions that comprise the study of perception—a topic which will run like a thread through many of the chapters of this book.

Motivation

Psychologists, like teachers, are interested in the "whys" of behavior. Many researches in psychology deal with the relationship between the organism's actions and the events that occur within the organism before, during, and after the observable behavior. Many such studies involve lower animals because of the greater ease with which the factors entering into a behavioral situation can be regulated and accounted for. But classrooms and other "human laboratories" also are used to get data about motivation.

An important aspect of human motivation is that which psychologists refer to as the basic drives and motives. There is considerable agreement among workers in the behavioral sciences that certain fundamental needs are to be found in all individuals. To know what these are, how they are manifested in behavior, and how they can best be satisfied is an important concern of the psychologist—and of the teacher, too.

Feelings and Emotions

The forces that energize behavior are another major interest of psychologists. We have many expressions which we use in our everyday discussions of this aspect of behavior. We say of someone that he shows strong feelings about what he is doing. Or we remark that a person is unusually "stirred up" (emotional) about something. We note that another person is "even tempered," that his behavior is calm and his energies appear to be under good control. Psychologists devote much attention to the investigation of human feelings and emotions and the bearing they have on people's actions and behavior patterns.

Cognition

In recent years, psychologists have been giving increased attention to thinking (cognition) as a phenomenon of special importance. The reason for use of the phrase, "in recent years," is that the psychologist's concern with cognitive processes diminished during the 1920s and 1930s to the point of virtual disappearance from research and publication. The pendulum's direction has been reversed; numerous psychologists, educators and others are now considerably involved in the study of "creative thinking," "divergent thinking," "constructively critical thinking," "productive thinking" and other aspects of cognition.

Learning

No topic is more important to the psychologist, and especially to the educational psychologist, than that of learning. It is a key process, if not indeed, *the* key process in human behavior. The author of the idea just expressed has added, "It pervades everything we do and think. It influences, in one way or another, the language we speak, our customs, attitudes and beliefs, goals, personality traits, both adaptive and maladaptive, and even our perceptions" (Morgan, 1966) [4].

Having underscored the importance of learning as a phenomenon of psychology, the authors must hasten to say—as they did in the Preface—that learning *will not* be accorded special study in this book. Its very importance in educational psychology argues for the provision of book-length (or nearly book-length) treatment of it and its relevance to the work of the school. The authors prefer, therefore, to leave the study of learning for a course following the one for which the present book is intended.

Personality

Whence comes the particular psychophysical organization within an individual that determines his way of relating himself to his environment? Is personality something pretty largely "fixed" by the individual's biological inheritance? Or, is it something which is "made" by his experiences? If the latter, by what kinds of experiences? As will be shown in this book, the problem of trying to conceptualize personality and its development has engaged much of the attention of psychologists and their fellow scientists in closely related fields of study.

Other Problems

It will be evident to the student long before he squarely confronts the problem of personality development (Chapter 15) that much must be understood about how the individual perceives his surroundings—human and physical—and how he deals with them. Because of what sorts of experience does the individual "take on the ways of his people"? Just *how* does an individual acquire the particular attitudes, beliefs, hopes, fears, work preferences, and so forth, that make him recognizable as a member of a given society or segment of some society?

Cultural Influences. The student who develops a special interest in the effect of the culture on the individual will find in this area many researches dealing with child-rearing practices, the impact of these practices on the development of personality, and the relation of both to the make-up of different societies. There are, then, the questions of how the agencies of society (the family, the school, and the peer groups, for example) influence and help shape the behavior pattern (shall we say the "life style") of the individual.

Growth-related Tasks. Individuals *work at* their experiences, especially at the business of growing up—something which does not end with one's twenty-first birthday. There is the aspect of task and everlasting challenge in much of the sweep of one's living with parents, peers, and other people. There is the very real task of learning to live with one's own body and all else that makes up one's own person. There is the element of task in learning to communicate satisfactorily with other persons. Learning the role of male or female has its task implications; so does choosing a mate, and determining one's choice of life work. And, perhaps above all else, there is the "necessity" of growing into the sort of person that is suggested, sometimes faintly, sometimes more clearly, at each step of one's experience.

These are some of the concerns of psychologists and teachers. They are matters that in one form or another we all think about and talk about. Psychologists try systematically to investigate them and to give some consistency to the explanation of them.

There is also another approach to the understanding of what psychology is. That is to examine the applications that are made of psychology to practical work with people.

APPLICATIONS OF PSYCHOLOGY

Psychology is put to work in many places. Business, industry, government, the military agencies: these and many others make use of the methods and knowledge of psychology. But for the purposes of this book, it would seem desirable to give attention largely to the applications of psychology in situations more or less closely related to the school.

Psychology's Alliance with Instruction and Guidance of All Children

Psychology reaches in many ways into the classrooms of schools and colleges where learning, in all its many aspects, takes place. What teachers have learned about individual differences among children in their readiness to master particular skills and concepts and the effectiveness with which teachers can put such knowledge to work is an instance of psychology's wide-ranging application in education. Assisting the teacher in his efforts to understand and help children are various specialists in psychology. Many people feel that the attention of such specialists is confined to children who are not "normal." The fact is that their services are utilized directly or indirectly where *all* children and youth are concerned whether handicapped or not.

Most students have taken tests of learning ability ("IQ" tests they are called by the man on the street), and perhaps they have also had the benefit of various measurements of their specialized abilities and interests and accompanying interviews with consultants trained in counseling psychology. As a consequence of these tests and conferences their programs of schooling were tailored more closely to their abilities and interests; perhaps also they were helped to get a clearer view of their vocational objectives.

Researches by educational psychologists and other psychologists continue to be brought to bear upon virtually every one of the problem phenomena which were mentioned in the preceding section with special reference to their significance in childhood and youth. Improvement of instructional methods and curriculum materials advances in stride with the steps taken by psychological researchers involved in the study of productive thinking and learning in the classroom.

Applications to Work with Exceptional Children

The Handicapped. Many children as well as adults have physical handicaps, mental handicaps, or both. Some of the work of school psychologists is with the problems of handicapped youngsters. School psychologists have played leading roles in the development of methods for determining the learning potentialities of children who are blind, deaf, mentally retarded, or suffering from cerebral palsy or other handicaps. And psychologists, through extensive researches on the learning and adjustment problems of handicappd children, have provided the knowledge for extensive improvements in instructional methods and materials for their schooling. Today, thanks to effective use of these kinds of knowledge, there are thousands of handicapped boys and girls who are learning in school how to become useful, happy citizens rather than unhappy burdens on their relatives and society in general.

The Gifted. The foregoing paragraph relates the work of psychologists to the study of handicapped children and the improvement of their lot in life. There is another category of exceptional children and youth whose education and guidance has been greatly influenced in recent years by the work of psychologists: those who are unusually gifted in their learning aptitudes and talents. We as citizens of a great nation have taken much pride in our virtually unlimited natural resources, but we have been tardy in the recognition that the greatest resource of all is the talents of our youth. Psychology has been of inestimable value in the discovery and development of these talents.

Psychology has, for one thing, raised basic questions about the nature of giftedness and has—particularly during the past thirty years in this country—corrected numerous erroneous ideas to the effect that the very bright and the gifted are likely in other respects to be peculiar or below average in development. The reader will find in Chapter 10 some of the evidence of the contributions of psychology to better understanding of superior intelligence.

Psychology has also provided the methods to locate and study giftedness. The development of tests of mental ability opened the way to the identification of individuals of high academic promise; development and standardization of numerous other tests has greatly improved the chances of early discovery of a wide variety of special abilities and talents.

In addition—as in the case of handicapped children—psychologists have worked closely with school administrators and teachers in planning better educational programs for the gifted. They have also provided expert help in arranging experiments and other studies to prove the values of this or that kind of educational program for the gifted.

Psychological Diagnosis and Therapy

Another thing that many psychologists do is to furnish consultation intended to improve the adjustment of individuals who are emotionally and socially poorly adjusted. This may be done in any one of several different ways. Clinical psychologists, for example, work with persons whose behavior deviates from normal. They are not to be confused with psychiatrists, who are medically trained and medically licensed. Clinical psychologists must be well informed about the conditions that motivate behavior and those that "structure" personality. They must be skilled in the use of methods of analyzing human traits and, especially, in the circumstances that lead to malconditions of personality. They must be expertly trained in methods of counseling clients in order that their interpretations may help the latter to better mental health. Here, in the work of clinical psychologists, we see the application of psychology to the important task of repairing personalities that have been damaged. Increasingly the knowledge that has proved its worth in this connection is being put to use in the *prevention* of personality disorders. This is an especially important development as it pertains to the beginnings of emotional disturbances in children.

Psychological Allies of the Teacher

Closely allied with the nation's teaching force are more than a thousand school psychologists, approximately twenty-two hundred educational psychologists, nearly two thousand counseling and guidance psychologists, over three thousand clinical psychologists, and over eight hundred developmental psychologists.[3] These are accredited psychologists. Many other men and women who are not known primarily as psychologists but who have extensive training in psychology perform roles which overlap

[3] Not eliminating the duplication in membership among its twenty-six divisions, The American Psychological Association lists more than twenty-five thousand members in its *Directory*. Correction for overlap in membership was not made in the figures given for the five divisions mentioned.

with those of the psychologists and result, through collaboration of effort, in the penetration of psychology into almost every activity of the school or college.

OBJECTIVES OF PSYCHOLOGY FOR TEACHERS

The preceding discussion provides the basis for examining the objectives to be attained by the prospective teacher through the study of psychology.

In a monograph entitled *Educational Psychology in Teacher Education,* Rivlin has listed five of these objectives. The present writers believe that Rivlin's statement serves as an exceptionally useful body of criteria by which the prospective teacher may judge his progress in the study of psychology.

1. Educational psychology should develop the student's interest in people, both children and adults, and help him to understand them. The student "should learn why people behave as they do" and how their behavior patterns may be modified. He should try to improve his insight into his own adjustment. He should not only like children but through his increased knowledge of growth and development he should gain increasing respect for them as individuals.

2. Educational psychology should have a favorable effect on the attitudes, behavior, and psychological understanding of students in both personal and professional relationships. This means, for one thing, that educational psychology should develop in the student "a point of view that sees pupils as personalities as well as learners, that regards educational procedures and values as susceptible of objective study and evaluation, and that interprets teaching as being more than a bag of tricks." As the prospective teacher studies the basic patterns and the individual variations of human growth he should become aware of the unique world of each individual child and be "better able to determine the kind of educational environment needed for optimum development of the children with whom he will be in daily contact."

3. Educational psychology should help the prospective teacher to make use of the body of knowledge that is derived from research studies in this field. The student, in gaining this objective, will come to understand "the fundamental facts about human growth and development, learning, personality and adjustment, measurement, and evaluation, and the techniques and methods of educational psychology." Lest these facts remain abstract bits of information it is important that the student gain an understanding of the principles and the theories which make the facts explicable.

4. Increased ability to learn is the fourth objective set forth for the student of educational psychology. The principles that relate to the improvement of learning can be studied advantageously by the student as he applies them to himself as well as to pupils with whom he may work. One aspect of this objective is the development on the part of the student of the habit of reading professional books and articles in the field. Rivlin emphasizes the far-reaching importance of the student's acquisition of self-direction in his study. This is something which the student should get from all his school and college work, but something which in any case it would be most incongruous for him not to acquire from a course in educational psychology.

5. Finally, among the objectives proposed by Rivlin there is appreciation and understanding of research in education. The point is made that "teachers cannot be satisfied to have educational questions decided merely by debate or emotional appeal." Although not many teachers will ever assume major responsibility for the planning of researches and the direction of them, increasingly they are becoming participants in important experiments and investigations, and in all cases they have the right and the obligation to become, as Rivlin says, "intelligent consumers of educational research" (Rivlin, 1953) [5].

In addition to the five objectives already stated, there is another that is deserving of the most serious thought on the part of prospective teachers. Educational psychology shares with other parts of teacher education in the individual's attainment of this objective, which is to become, as a teacher, what Bruner has described as "an immediately personal symbol of the educational process, a figure with whom students can identify and compare themselves" (Bruner, 1960) [2].

For the last-mentioned objective to be achieved, educational psychology must become for the prospective teacher a constant source of help in the attainment of self-acceptance and poise of personality, and a joyous adventure in learning.

THE NEXT STEP

We have examined the meaning and something of the scope of psychology. We have noted the debt that teaching owes to psychology and especially to developmental psychology. And we have found a central theme which we can expect to help us achieve a sense of direction and clear purpose as we proceed to other chapters. The theme, reiterated, is that *persons* are a major concern of teachers; that helping them to understand themselves and to grow in their abilities to get along well with themselves and others is basic to their attainment of a mature personality.

The next step is to examine some basic ideas pertaining to the study of human behavior and development. The authors suggest that as this is done, Chapter 2 be considered essentially an extension of the present one.

Suggested Collateral Readings

Cronbach, L. J., *Educational psychology,* 2d ed. New York: Harcourt, Brace & World, 1963. Chapter 1.

Eson, M. E., *Psychological foundations of education.* New York: Holt, Rinehart and Winston, Inc., 1964. Chapter 1.

Garrison, K. C., A. J. Kingston, and A. S. McDonald, *Educational psychology,* 2d ed. New York: Appleton-Century-Crofts, 1964. Chapters 1 and 2.

Hilgard, E. R., and R. C. Atkinson, *Introduction to psychology,* 4th ed. New York: Harcourt, Brace & World, Inc., 1962. Chapters 1 and 24.

Johnson, D. M., *Psychology: A problem-solving approach.* New York: Harper & Row, Publishers, 1961. Chapter 1.

Morgan, C. T., and R. A. King, *Introduction to psychology,* 3d ed. New York: McGraw-Hill, Inc., 1966. Chapter 1.

Pressey, S. L., F. P. Robinson, and J. E. Horrocks, *Psychology in education.* New York: Harper & Row, Publishers, 1959. Chapter 1.

Skinner, C. E., ed., *Educational psychology,* 4th ed. Englewood Cliffs, N.J.: Prentice-Hall, Inc., 1959. Chapter 1, "Nature and Methods of Educational Psychology" (G. Lester Anderson).

Smith, H. P., *Psychology in teaching,* 2d ed. Englewood Cliffs, N.J.: Prentice-Hall, Inc., 1962. Chapter 1.

Smith, K. U., and W. M. Smith, *The behavior of man: An introduction to psychology.* New York: Holt, Rinehart and Winston, Inc., 1958. Chapter 1.

References

1. American Psychological Association, 1966 *Directory,* Washington, D. C.: American Psychological Association.
2. Bruner, J. S., 1960, *The process of education.* New York: Vintage Books, Random House, Inc. Page 90.
3. Morgan, C. T., 1956, *Introduction to psychology.* New York: McGraw-Hill, Inc. Page 3.
4. ———, and R. A. King, 1966, *Introduction to psychology,* 3d ed. New York: McGraw-Hill, Inc. Page 73.
5. Rivlin, H. N., 1953, The objectives of educational psychology in the education of teachers in *Educational psychology in teacher education, a guide for instructors,* Monograph No. 3. Ann Arbor: National Society of College Teachers of Education. Chapter 1.
6. Waters, R. H., 1958, Behavior: datum or abstraction, *The American Psychologist,* 33: 278–282.

CHAPTER 2

Basic Ideas in Understanding Children and Youth

The study of psychology has for teachers, a definite and preeminent objective. It is an objective that can be achieved only by gaining and organizing a body of facts and principles that relate to human behavior and development. But the objective calls for more than this. A person may have acquired a considerable fund of information about behavior and development without becoming any better prepared to understand the individuals he lives with and works with.

The facts and concepts of psychology can be—and for teachers *must be*—learned in such a manner as will point up their relationship to the behavior of *actual persons.* This is the thesis not only of this chapter but also of the entire book. It is a thesis that was well enunciated by Harold E. Jones, the memory of whom is associated with the planning and direction of certain of the more richly productive researches in human growth and development.

Jones had noted that there had been over a period of years many important accomplishments in educational psychology bearing on such matters as the classification of school children, techniques of learning and teaching, the measurement of skills, and the prediction of readiness in learning. He then remarked, "But it is now realized more clearly than before that this is not enough, for we are more concerned with the implications of the fact that 'persons' go to school, not just an equipment for learning, not just memories, minds, or intellects" (Jones, 1946) [6].

The purpose of this chapter is to present some ideas that together provide such an orientation to psychology as has just been advocated. The purpose, stated figuratively, is to secure early in this book a few good vantage points from which to keep the individual *as a person* continuously in view while we study the facts and principles pertaining to his development and behavior.

One further explanation: the ideas herein discussed will, like the main theme of the book, be recurrent throughout the chapters that follow. Furthermore, like the main theme they should *impart meaning and significance* to the facts and principles learned and also *gain meaning and significance* from them.

ON THE NATURE OF BEING A HUMAN ORGANISM

To emphasize the fact that man is an organism is to emphasize the obvious. But some of the implications of this fact are not so obvious, and certain of these implications have more than a little importance to teachers—to anyone, for that matter, who is concerned with what it means to be a living, functioning thing.

The Organism Is a Living Unity

The word "organism" connotes a *living unity*—a dynamic system whose parts are interrelated and function together. Man as an organism shares with all other creatures this remarkable characteristic of functioning as a unified system. No matter how many parts an organism has and how capable they are of performing their respective operations, the operations are not ends in themselves. The operations "serve" an end, or purpose, which is the maintenance of the system as a whole. Man is a notable creature not simply because he possesses many more parts than various other living things but rather because of the high level of integration that obtains in the functioning of his parts.

We sometimes tend to "dismember" the organic system that a person is as we try to explain separately some aspect of his behavior. This tendency is shown, for example, in the remarks, "his intelligence didn't work well," or "he was carried away by his emotions," or "here we see his physical self." Comments of these kinds are appropriate enough when their purpose is simply to call attention to a particular aspect of someone's behavior at a given moment. But any implication in such comments that the behavior of a person is actually separable into relatively independent functions is a distortion of the very meaning of the term, "organism."

There is no escaping the fact that a growing fund of knowledge about man requires that many different researchers press their inquiries in many different directions. Often this, of necessity, calls for the centering of their attention on one or the other relatively limited part of the total organism. Thus, each of the behavioral sciences contributes facts and principles about certain of the vital processes of the human being. There is no adequate substitute in psychology for the facts about how individuals grow, develop, and learn—a point that was stressed in Chapter 1. By the same token, however, there is for the student of educational psychology no substitute for the concept that the operations of the vital processes analyzed by the different sciences are *interdependent and interactive* in the living unity which is a person. For it is this unity—the child, the youth, and our fellow adults—that we who apply psychology to teaching must know.

The Organism Is a Dynamic Energy System

As an organism the individual is by definition a dynamic energy system. Like any other living thing, man depends upon energy to keep going—to stay alive, to grow and develop, and to remain healthy. Additionally, man depends upon energy to get his work done and to be creative in what he does.

For any one of us, therefore, to abuse any of the parts of his body that engage in the supply and distribution of energy is to invite his own organic destruction.

As a dynamic energy system, the individual is constantly involved in developing the energy required for the increasing range of his activities and interests. There are times when his energy supply may be unequal to the demands being made upon him. This we as teachers must understand if we are to be considerate in the assignments of tasks we impose on youngsters.

Characteristic Modes of Energy Use. Every individual operates with a mode of energy transformation that relates to some individual characteristics he possesses. For example, how a youth catches a ball will depend on such circumstances as the length and strength of his arms, hands, and fingers and also upon the characteristics of the rest of his body which, all together, determine the way energy is employed in a given act. There may be ways of catching a ball that are in general the best ways, but the over-all pattern of characteristics of each individual must be taken into account before the exact "right way" for him can be determined. This applies to the myriad of things that the individual does, inclusive of what he tries to learn in school as well as out of school.

There Is Organizing Force in Human Growth

Remarkable organization and efficiency characterize the growth of the human organism. Its energies are employed in no aimless biological game of chance but in *a process characterized by inherent design and direction.* In any listing of the so-called wonders of the universe surely the regulatory, goal-bent character of an organism's development must rank as one of the most fascinating. Long before a human organism has reached its full growth the cells of its body number in the trillions; yet every living one of them works in harmony with all the rest (except those that on occasion engage in a separate act of malignancy).

Several important facts about the growth of an organism are contained in the statement just made. Important as they all are (for example, the number of cells mentioned and their tendency to *work in harmony*) the one most profound fact is that of *inexorable progress toward a goal*—the goal of producing a complete and fully functioning organism. Apropos of this aspect of an organism's development Sinnott (1950) [7] comments:

> A developing embryo, especially if its growth is speeded up by time-lapse photography, certainly *looks* as if it were moving toward a goal which it is bound to reach in spite of the obstacles which we put in its way to test the intensity and resourcefulness of its "purpose."

Sinnott ends the paragraph just quoted by remarking, "Needham's phrase,[1] 'the striving of a blastula to grow into a chicken,' may be a figure of speech, but to some minds it is not far from actual truth." In any case, there is in the growth of an organism from the moment of its inception to its completed form an element of remarkable accuracy. It is an accuracy that governs the production of all the systems of cells, each on schedule, as well as the kind of creature that was implicit from the very outset in a particular blob of protoplasm.

The meaning of *accuracy* as a characteristic of growth and development is effectively indicated by the following sentences from a description of life before birth.[2]

> The total journey from a speck of watery material to a seven-pound, nineteen-inch-long human being takes 267 days and is a marvel of refinement. One change prepares the way for the next, and the plan, for all its subtlety, is marked by an incredible accuracy, both in running true to form and in staying on schedule.
>
> Speed, subtlety, accuracy—they characterize this growth process. But it is the over-all transformation that really staggers the imagination; this is the unbelievable manner in which one's own, and everybody's, biography begins.

Surely a student of the psychology of human development will not long remain casual about how the facts of biology relate to the facts of psychology once he has really understood the extent to which the story of a life can be read only as science unlocks the secrets of living cells.

Maturation Influences the Organism's Behavior

An individual responds to his surroundings in ways permitted and delimited by his biological equipment. To illustrate, a person can per-

[1] Needham, J. S., *The skeptical biologist.* New York: W. W. Norton & Co., Inc., 1930.

[2] Herbert Thoms and Bruce Blevins in Baller, Warren R., ed., *Readings in the psychology of human growth and development.* New York: Holt, Rinehart and Winston, Inc., 1962. Chapter 4.

ceive his world only from data supplied by his sense organs. How his sense organs function is a basic determinant of his behavior. Do a five-year-old's eyes report a *b* for a *d?* This not unlikely circumstance may simply be a consequence of the immaturity of certain parts of the eyes. Possibly the muscles that control the movement of the eyes have not yet attained the stage of development required for the coordination and precision of so fine a distinction. Does another five-year-old have difficulty in holding a pencil in such a way that he can trace correctly a figure on a page before him? It may very well be that this exercise also demands more precision than can be achieved at the present level of development of his hands and fingers—not to mention the relationship which the eyes have to the total, coordinated action.

What is the meaning of maturation? To say that it is a process of attaining full development does not help much to signify the basic features of the process. A satisfactory definition of maturation puts emphasis upon the refinements in the structure of the various parts of an individual's body—refinements that occur as the individual progresses toward his goal of adulthood. Maturation is an unfolding or "ripening" of potentials that an individual possesses by virtue of his being a member of a given species and by virtue, more specifically, of his biological inheritance from a particular parentage.

There is more to the full meaning of maturation. It is that maturation denotes *change in function* as well as change in the organism's physical equipment. The close relation of function and structure cannot be overemphasized in any description of development and behavior. We can hardly discuss (or think about) the ripening of an organism's potentials without extending the meaning of "potentials" to what the creature does with its more fully matured parts as well as the changes that are occurring in the parts.

Behind the scenes, so to speak, where maturation is taking place are many different instances of ripening potentials. The strengthening and coordination of eye muscles, in the case of a child's readiness to interpret the material on a printed page, has been given as an instance of maturation. But there is more to seeing than simply being able to move the eyes—regardless of the precision with which this is accomplished. There is involved in it also the functioning of the elaborate *sensory mechanism* of the eye, which responds to light stimuli and transmits the resulting impulses to the central nervous system. And there is the complementing "return" system of nerves that carry impulses from the central organs (primarily the brain) to the muscles and tendons to activate them. Maturation enters into the effectiveness of the working of the nervous system.

Also influenced by maturation, as far as the higher organisms are concerned, are the glandular systems. Especially pertinent to the present discussion is the role that maturation plays in the functioning of the glands related to reproduction. Indeed, a concept quite regularly associated with maturation is that of the individual's proximity in growth to the moment when sex acts may result in reproduction. To say that growth has "flowered" into maturity is literally a proper description of this aspect of maturation.

Readiness. The maturing of an individual's physical equipment, accompanied by the activating of related functions, has—as we have indicated—important bearings upon his behavior. Maturation sets limits on the individual's behavior. We observe the evidence of this as we await the moments when the child first walks and first talks. Attempts on the part of parents or others greatly to speed the coming of these moments have little efficacy. A three-month-old baby cannot talk because at that age the maturation of certain of his systems is too limited.

But understanding and patient as we may be about a baby's maturation where walking and talking are concerned, we are not always so sensitive to the role of maturation in certain other aspects of growing up. Most of the things an individual does involve *learning*. Maturation and learning are closely intertwined. (They are, let us note, intertwined in a child's approach to, and ultimate success with, walking and talking.)

When is a child *ready* to read? Certainly not necessarily on his sixth birthday. The answer is not to be found on the calendar, but in his general maturation as described above and the specific experiences he has had. In both of these respects children differ greatly. A child is ready to read, or to write, or to undertake some other learning situation, when his own individual maturation level and relevant experience have opened the way for him. A query of an experienced teacher seems especially pertinent at this point. She was emphasizing the importance of readiness in children's learning and injected rather emotionally the question, "Why, oh why, do we *insist* on a child's trying to learn 'today' what he might well learn by himself 'tomorrow' when he is mature enough?"

If teachers are sensitive not only to the delimiting functions of a child's maturation but also, on the positive side, to the signs of readiness for this or that kind of response, they will increase their effectiveness in helping the child to grow and learn.

DISTINCTIVE FEATURES OF HUMAN BEHAVIOR

It has been emphasized that human beings are organisms and have many characteristics in common with other organisms. Now let us consider certain features of behavior that are distinctive of man.

Man Is a Socially Sensitive Creature

This statement needs some special qualifying. A case might be made for social sensitivity on the part of lower animals. Many lower animals are also social creatures—they live and work together and some enjoy each other's company. In these respects they are socially sensitive.

Man, however, is the one creature that learns to govern his behavior to a large extent by what difference it makes to his fellow humans. He *cares* what other persons think of his actions—what they think of him. There are few decisions that he makes throughout his life that are not governed directly or indirectly by the fact that he shares his life with other people. Their beliefs, purposes, values, and fears make a real difference to what his will be; indeed, to a considerable extent they become his—as will be illustrated in numerous places in the discussions that follow.

Continuity Characterizes Man's Behavior

Behavior does not simply appear at some moment; it develops continuously over a period of time. Continuity unbroken through time is a basic characteristic of human development and behavior. A child does not simply begin to talk at a particular moment without having gone through a series of preparatory experiences. The fact that on a given day whole phrases began to flow—though there had not been even an intelligible word before—does not mean that there were no antecedent behaviors leading up to this moment. Much "work" may have consisted of sounds not clearly articulated; it may have consisted of considerable implicit speech ("saying" the words inaudibly to himself) ; it probably consisted of a combination of these. A failure to understand this unbroken continuity of behavior prevents one from understanding behaviors in another person which, up to a certain moment, he had not observed—behaviors which he might, therefore, consider illogical and capricious.

Some of our thinking about adolescence would be much improved if we could more consistently keep the fact of developmental continuity in mind. Adolescence is not a period of life separate from what has gone before and what is still to come. It is a phase in an unbroken progression that continues throughout the life span. Certainly, it has its characteristic features. And these features we should study and try to understand for what they tell us about the individual (the adolescent) at this moment in his life experience. But even as we study the various physiological, psychological, and social features associated with adolescence we should be mindful of the fact that in them is a connecting trace with what went before and also a preparation for what is to come.

Especially in this latter respect—the preparation for growth phases still to be reached—are we likely in our dealings with adolescents to be shortsighted. Some rather frequently asked questions reveal this lack of adult perceptiveness about the preparatory nature of adolescent behavior. "Why do they need to be so *daring* about many of the things they do?" is such a question. Another is, "What makes teenagers so determined to be independent—to flout grown-up ideas and advice?" Sometimes a question is more specific, such as, "Why this everlasting 'petting'?" or, "Why their boasting about things they say they do when actually they never have done them?" Perhaps the answer is pretty well summed up in the remark of an observant old counselor, "It's just the 'future' in them!" Yesterday, today, and tomorrow are conveniently separated by the calendar on the wall; they are only figures of speech where human growth and development are concerned.

Behavior Is Task-centered

Two four-year-olds are seen alternately constructing "castles" in their sandbox and then, amidst loud threats, destroying each other's work. Several fourteen-year-old boys may be noted teasing some teen-age girls: they snatch at the girls' school books, make seemingly uncomplimentary remarks about them, and laugh loudly at their own pranks. And the girls "endure" the situation without quickly taking their leave. A college sophomore argues cautiously with the instructor in one of his classes over a point that on the face of it seems rather trivial. These situations may very well have one important aspect in common. It is the aspect of *task*.

The behaviors of the four-years-olds may appear to an adult onlooker to be largely capricious—as just so many impulsive actions. Such a view of them fails, however, to identify something these children are working at—the task of acquiring some "know-how" in dealing with their age-level associates. Similarly, the actions of the fourteen-year-olds can easily be misinterpreted. Much of their conduct too may have the aspect of important task about it. How does one act toward individuals of the opposite sex? What is one expected to say and how should it be said? All the advice in the world, good as it may be, is not going to satisfy one's need (if one is of the age of these youngsters) to learn by *trying*, by working at this task.

In similar vein, something of very real importance may be behind the actions of the college sophomore—something such as the need to know how to speak his thoughts in a situation involving another person whose status is different (the status of "older person," or "authority," for example). The subject matter under discussion and the relevance of his remarks to it are of secondary importance to this student at the moment. His task is defined by his need as felt by him. Untactful and irrelevant as his remarks may seem to his listeners, there may be underlying them a very real and personal task to be accomplished.

In thinking of the degree to which "task," thus interpreted, enters into the things people do and say, one person commented, "To ask 'what is he working at' may not be elegant English, but it is very good psychology." We shall return to this idea a few pages hence in a discussion of how to view behavior's causes.

Striving Characterizes Human Behavior

In a sense, striving is a feature of the life of many creatures other than man, as well as of man. But there is a difference in the case of man. Much of his striving is governed by purposes which he has had a hand in choosing. "Aspiration" is a term that would sound out of place in descriptions of the behavior of lower animals. For us to think in terms of "purposes" and "aspirations" is, however, to risk overlooking something very basic about the nature of *striving*. The descriptions of life before birth which were quoted from Thom and Blevin, Sinnott, and Needham give us the feeling that something very special is intended by the expressions "active," "moving toward a goal," "inner drive," and the like. The concepts behind the use of these words deserve our most thoughtful consideration. Let us ponder the ideas in a slightly different context—in one that presents the individual at a bit later date, that is, in infancy.

In a discussion of "The World of the Newborn," Bettelheim (1967) [3] underscores the basic importance of the evidence that far from being a passive, wholly dependent little creature, the infant is "eminently active" as he engages in the main business of his early postnatal experience, sucking. Bettelheim calls attention to our inclination to view the infant as quite helpless and quite lacking in any subjective experience of its own. He then remarks

> . . . I believe that in his nursing, for example, the infant is eminently active in what to him is a central event in his life. At such times he may not feel that he is moving mountains, but as if he were sucking them dry. To regard such an experience as anaclitic, as utterly passive, contradicts the infant's experience. Because to him it is not his real dependence that counts, but the conviction that his efforts are monumental. Fortunately such views are slowly being presented both in psychoanalytic writings and in academic psychology.

The reader is invited to note the regularity and importance with which the idea of *acting with determination* enters, with differing implications, into parts of later chapters. Especially will this aspect of the world of the newborn have relevance to our study of perception and the beginnings of self-awareness.

Individuals Strive to Be Significant

Nothing matters as much as the feeling of self-significance. This statement will be repeated with considerable regularity throughout this book. The achieving and maintaining of self-significance is for every person life's most compelling task.

"How much of striving for self-significance am I able to discern in the behavior of another person?" This is a question we as teachers need especially to ask ourselves. Do we find ourselves making the attempt thus to get at the meaning in someone else's actions? Doubtless, there are times when it is especially difficult to see that striving for self-significance lies behind another person's behavior. Now and then, for example, a youngster's behavior seems so thoroughly "wrong," so completely unsatisfactory, that one finds the actions hard to reconcile with the idea of striving for self-significance. Tom's conduct will illustrate the difficulty.

Tom had been throughout his boyhood a somewhat withdrawn youngster socially. He seemed content simply to keep his own companionship. He was exceptionally bright and appeared to find considerable satisfaction in his solitary preoccupations with books, piano, and his "grade A" preparation of school assignments. Tom was agreeable with other youngsters as well as with grownups. His reticent, withdrawn manner came to be accepted and little noticed by those who knew him.

Tom was "not the kind" to hold up a filling station at night and to make his escape by firing several shots at the attendant. So thought those who knew him. But this he did. And almost everyone who knew him felt shocked and greatly puzzled over such seemingly inexplicable behavior.

Hours of questioning of Tom by various authorities netted a quantity of what appeared to be wholly nonexplanatory information. Nonexplanatory—except to an experienced consultant to whom Tom confided, "I guess I just couldn't stand it any longer to be a nobody. I kept fighting the thought that I didn't 'count' . . . with everybody I was nothing. I guess I took a crazy way to explode my feelings . . . and I don't know why I did it this way."

A "crazy" way to try to escape from feelings of self-dissatisfaction and self-emptiness! But students of human behavior will often need to look deep into a person's actions to find the logic in them.

There is also behavior that seems so thoroughly "right" that it is hard to identify in it an individual's striving for self-significance. It is easier to see in behavior an "outer" goal to be achieved than an inner *something to be*. But we must learn not to separate the two. The one —the first—stands for the other: they are the subjective and objective parts of a single continuum—the individual's striving to make actual that which he wishes to be.

Individuals Seek Meaning and Commitment

Closely meshed with the individual's sense of significance are the elements of meaning and commitment. Probably at no time in history has so much attention been given to the question of what makes the life of the individual truly meaningful and the related questions of how best to provide the essentials by means of which individuals can experience personal growth in meaningfulness. Physical comforts, important as they are (for many of the world's unfortunate they are desperately lacking) are not the guarantee of self-fulfillment. So it is also with escape from work, abundant freedom, or any other of the apparent assurances of "the good life." Gardner in his book, *Self-Renewal* (1964) [4], states that we are "coming to a conception of happiness that differs fundamentally from the storybook version." He notes that the storybook version "tells of desires fulfilled; the truer version involves striving toward meaningful goals—goals that relate the individual to a larger context of purposes."

In some passages located several pages beyond the lines just quoted, Gardner writes

> Man is in his very nature a seeker of meanings. He cannot help being so any more than he can help breathing or maintaining a certain body temperature. . . .
>
> [Man] has throughout history shown a compelling need to arrive at conceptions of the universe *in terms of which he could regard his own life as meaningful.* He wants to know where *he* fits into the scheme of things. . . .
>
> In the individual life, meaning, purpose and commitment are inseparable. When a man succeeds in the search for identity he has found the answer not only to the question "Who am I?" but to a lot of other questions too: "What must I live up to? What are my obligations? To what must I commit myself?" (Gardner, 1964, pp. 102–103) [5]

Each Person Is Unique

Each person's life has its own story, its own particular themes and continuity. The individual's past experiences and his aspirations for the future help to shape his present behavior. In turn, the impact on him of events in the present shape his future. These facts help spell out the uniqueness of every life. Prescott and his associates, in their summation of the values to be derived by teachers from the study of individual children over a period of time, considered their growing awareness of each child's essential uniqueness to be a value of top consequence.

> They came to see that each child has his own particular and selective readiness for new experience, his own established techniques for dealing with his world, his own way of regarding himself, and his own tempo of growth. They observed that some children characteristically acted with an eager confidence rooted in a long-prevailing sense of security and adequacy. They noted others who continually regarded their world as hostile and who had worked out endless ways of protecting themselves from it or of striking back at it. Most of the children they studied were seen to be threading a way through life between these

extremes. Most of them showed areas of confidence and assurance and other areas of anxiety and of antagonism. (*Helping Teachers Understand Children*, 1945) [1]

Social Relationships Involve Social Interactions

The shrewd observer of human behavior views the relationships between individuals in a social situation as reciprocal. He knows that the behaviors of an individual as he is involved with one or more other persons derive from the individual's needs and purposes on the one hand and the particular demands of the social circumstance on the other. The shrewd observer sees each individual as a striving goal-directed organism in dynamic relationship with a "field" of forces—a field that includes other persons and the interests and problems that occupy the attentions of all concerned. The importance in this way of looking at behavior may be seen in the following illustration:

Harold, who is fourteen and in the ninth grade, has for several minutes been engaged in a lively exchange of opinions with his teacher in a science class. He has expressed an idea which the teacher rejects as being unwarranted by the facts. Harold, with a flush showing on his face, retorts that there are some things that a person can learn from personal experience—that he refuses to accept the explanation found in certain books. The implication, as understood by the teacher, is that Harold considers the teacher to be wrongly informed. He, the teacher, also senses an element of disrespect in Harold's tone of voice. A tense situation has developed. What, we may ask, are some of the more important forces at work in this incident?

Harold, like everyone else, is *self-protective*. By the same token, so is the teacher. What the teacher has said about the lack of evidence to support Harold's opinions threatens Harold's self-concept. And Harold's retort may seem to the teacher to jeopardize his (the teacher's) status. The element of threat, we might suppose, is even more pronounced because this is a class situation with other pupils present. The possibility of losing face may, therefore, be a factor, an element of force, in the present field of forces. Whether Harold feels, at the moment, that the teacher is simply rejecting this statement or rejecting *him* as a person may have a bearing on the course of this interactive event. How far Harold's already established code of conduct will permit him to go in challenging the authority of an adult, and more especially a teacher, may also be a factor of consequence.

The point of the illustration, to repeat, is that the causes of behavior will not readily be found by a simple process of isolating the factors that are presumed to be at work and examining them as independent variables. Harold is more than a "whole child"—he is a dynamic part of any given "whole situation" in which he happens at some moment to be.

IDEAS ABOUT BEHAVIOR'S CAUSES

There are ideas and attitudes pertaining to the *causes of behavior* that contribute greatly to a person's chances of understanding or not understanding the behavior of other persons. The ideas and attitudes which will be described in this section are not all that could be included in this category. They are some of the more important, however, and will suggest differing orientations of thinking about human behavior that can variably influence a person's understanding of actual individuals.

Behavior Is Caused

The statement that behavior is caused sounds pretty obvious. But self-evident as it may be, there are few axioms in psychology that are more frequently violated in our everyday dealings with other people. It is when a corollary of this statement is thoughtfully considered that the significance of the statement can be appreciated. The corollary is that *behavior, being caused, is therefore not its own cause.* Some illustrations may help make the point clear.

A parent inquires what to do about her child who bites his fingernails. "How can you cure that sort of thing?" she asks. A teacher states that one of his pupils is inattentive in class and wants to know what to do about such behavior. Another teacher would like some suggestions about how to deal with a certain boy's "persistent teasing of younger children." In each instance the expressed desire is to change behavior; or more accurately, it is to change the observed behavior.

If one of the persons mentioned above were confronted with a child who was running a fever, his interest would probably be centered not so much in getting rid of the fever as in learning what conditions gave rise to it; he would take the fever to be a signal of something wrong—something requiring diagnosis. In this instance fever is the observed behavior. Certainly, it should not be confused with its causes; that is, it should not be treated as if it were its own cause.

Similarly, the biting of fingernails may be considered the signal, or sign, of conditions which lie behind it and which are its causes. It would be as ill-advised, therefore, to "treat" nailbiting as to apply treatment directly to a fever. A better procedure would be to try to discover the causes of the nailbiting. For similar reasons, it would be sounder policy to look for the causes behind a pupil's inattentiveness than to work directly upon such behavior. Likewise, we may assume that persistent teasing is caused; that it is a symptom of important conditions which lie behind it. In general, the sensible rule is not to apply remedies to symptom behavior, but to regard it as a possible clue to the discovery of underlying causes.[3]

It is intended by these statements to make clear that all behavior is caused. What we like, as well as what we do not like, is caused. Calm and even-tempered or fretful and turbulent behavior, cooperative as well as uncooperative conduct, the socially confident manner and its opposite: all these have their causes.

Many of the conditions that combine to give rise to certain behaviors are located within the individual. Many are, of course, outside the individual. But the main thought is that behavior does not just happen; more to the point, we should not make the mistake of confusing behavior itself with the causes that produce it.

The Causes of Behavior Are Complex and Interrelated

Six-year-old Mary has been humming a joyful tune all morning long. Is it because she feels good? This would seem like a safe surmise. But what conditions enter into her "feeling good"? Even if Mary were three times her present age, she would have difficulty answering the question. She might explain that both her mother and her brother said something nice to her when she came to breakfast. But she could hardly know how these remarks helped to give a good tone to her feelings; how, also, certain intricately associated processes of the body had been initiated by the favorable state of affairs. Mary probably would not have identified these conditions with the impression that her breakfast tasted especially good. Nor would she have sensed the connection between these factors and the unusual resonance of her voice which made singing so delightful. Complexity, not simplicity, would certainly be the word to describe Mary's situation. And the fact that the causal conditions were interrelated is also evident.

Failure to understand the biological and psychological laws which are implicit in such behavior as that just mentioned frequently stands between us and our much-desired improvements in human relationships. We permit ourselves to act toward a particular behavior incident as though it were simple and unitary—lacking in connections with any other biological or psychological fact beyond the aspect that is apparent at the moment to our naked eye. "What is the matter?" we inquire of an acquaintance when his conduct seems a bit unusual, or undesirable in our own estimation. If the answer is "I don't know," we may be inclined

[3] The present writers recognize that not infrequently there are behaviors which, though quite clearly symptomatic of underlying causations not evident at the moment, may, nevertheless, wisely be dealt with directly. Especially is this true where some form of behavior persists as a troublesome habit beyond the time when the original precipitating causes have disappeared.

to suspect our friend of some evasiveness. Actually he may be giving the only accurate answer of which he is capable at the moment. One's own maturity is demonstrated when one can be sympathetic and reassuring when another's behavior is at variance with the accepted norm, and when one can share in another's favorable moods without being overly inquisitive as to their origin.

Multiple Causation Is a General Rule with Behavior

If we could know for sure that the factors mentioned in Mary's case were completely and exclusively responsible for her behavior that morning we might expect to reproduce that behavior at will. A little thought on the matter will lead us to see, however, that Mary might behave in the same way on the following morning because of a quite different combination of circumstances. She might give scarcely a thought to her breakfast. She might not notice the pleasant remarks of her family. If she were asked why she was humming a merry tune, she might answer, "Because this is the day for the circus and I am going to it." Here we see the same *outer* behavior. Some of the same external factors exist. But new and different ones are present and are playing a part in Mary's delightful behavior. It would seem, therefore, that there is no simple rule which one can follow in order to elicit a particular kind of desirable behavior or to eliminate a particular kind of undesirable behavior. The writers' intention in this connection however, is *not* to argue against the use of "rules" in the explanation of behavior, but rather to caution against any tendency to oversimplify explanations of causation.

There is another aspect of what is here being referred to as multiple causation. The word portraits of Mary in the situations described above were intended to show that behavior may seem to be much the same on different occasions when the causes are in certain respects dissimilar. A different illustration of the principle of multiple causation is the appearance of similar behavior in two different persons, for reasons which are fundamentally dissimilar. Faulty understanding of this principle leads to the practice of setting up identical plans of action for dealing with behavior in one person which resembles that of another person who presumably responded satisfactorily to the treatment.

"Were your girls ever moody and irritable when they were in their early teens?" asks one mother of another. The first mother has a "moody" teenage daughter. The answer of the second mother is affirmative; whereupon the two women explore the conditions which in retrospect seem to have been at the roots of the disturbing conduct. Their hope is to find in this comparison of experiences certain common factors which would make the one mother's experience throw light on that of the other. That such undertakings do not always prove to be profitable is no mystery to the person who clearly understands the principle we have stated. The behavior of the girls in these two situations may look much the same. But similar behavior does not always mean identical causes.

Multiple Hypotheses Often Best Identify Behavior's Causes

The inclination to seize upon some quite obvious feature of a behavior situation and to hold to it as *the* explanation is widespread—and fraught with danger. Fundamentally, as was pointed out above, it violates the knowledge which we now have about the complexity of behavior: the complexity of human motivation and of the relationships between the human organism and its surroundings.

A good practice, therefore, when one is trying to find an explanation for a particular behavior, is to proceed on the basis of careful and impartial guesses (or hypotheses). Some people have made good use of the expression "could be" in this connection. Instead of jumping quickly to a definite idea about the cause of a certain behavior, they will deliberately pause and try to see what different possibilities of explanation can be found. They may refer to these possibilities as "could be's." "It could be this; but also, might it be that?" is the way their thinking proceeds.

One virtue of this way of thinking—the habit of using "could be" as a reconnoitering tactic—is that the more obvious factors in a situation are not so likely to crowd out other less obvious but more important ones. This point was expressed by a teacher in this way, "Sometimes the real causes of behavior lie hidden from sight; they are 'round the corner' from where you expect to find them. For a person to set up several tentative explanations is a pretty good way for him ultimately to find the real explanation of behavior."

There is another advantage in the practice which was recommended in the paragraphs immediately above. It is that the person who is trying in this way to find reasons for the behavior of someone else *may* include himself as a possible factor of significance. This is often a difficult undertaking for the teacher or the parent. "Am I *really* doing something that is contributing to my pupil's problem?" The question is not an easy one for the teacher to put to himself. And it is still harder to follow the question with an objective, impersonal examination of one's own behavior, in the search for trouble-making causes.

Sometimes an adult's careful evaluation of his own behavior as it may bear on a child's adjustment will bring some condition of neglect into view. A cause behind the child's difficulties will be seen to be not so much what the adult is doing as what he is failing to do. The ability objectively to view oneself as a possible factor in the complication of another person's behavior is a worthy achievement in human relations.

Behavior Frequently Does Not Fit Our Value Judgments and Easy Inferences

It is not unusual for someone to sum up an impression of another person's behavior by calling it "good" or "bad." In telling about Janice, who is in the fourth grade, a teacher may remark "she is a spoiled, ill-tempered child." These are value terms. They serve the purpose of generalizing one's thinking about a variety of traits as seen in another person.

Often it seems easier to convey an impression of another person in such a manner than to relate what that person does and to permit the facts to speak for themselves. But there are objections to this practice which need to be recognized if one is to improve his understanding of behavior and his dealing with it.

An objection to the use of "good," "bad," "stupid," "brilliant," and the like, when referring to behavior, is that different persons may have different ideas about what the words mean. When John's teacher says that he is a "bad" boy, it would be helpful to know in what way he is bad. The explanation probably would be more enlightening were it to consist of some description of what John does, rather than of a number of "labels" attached to him.

Another objection to the uncritical use of a value term in reference to someone's behavior is that frequently the user of the term allows himself to believe that he has in this way *explained* behavior. Actually, he probably has not even described behavior, much less given an explanation of it. On the other hand, simply to tell what someone does or says is a way of giving helpful description; the process of careful description is usually a necessary preliminary to the finding of a sound explanation.

The tendency, mentioned above, of indulging in hasty explanation may take the form of uncritical inference. An illustration may throw some light on this practice. A teacher remarks, "One of my pupils is very lazy, that's the reason why he doesn't learn arithmetic." Were the teacher to describe the way this child acts, he might presently come upon some signs of causes to which the word "lazy" actually would not apply at all.

Uncritical inference may be noted in another kind of setting. The explanation for behavior may be drawn hastily from some fact about an individual's background as in the query, "How would you expect him to act? He comes from the wrong side of the tracks, doesn't he?" The sweeping inference about the kinds of behavior associated with "the wrong-side" can be matched by many others. "All persons of that race are naturally lazy," someone remarks, with the conclusion, "John is probably no exception to that rule." Another person asks, "What would you expect of a child who comes from a home that is so crowded?" Such a question tends to block from view certain very favorable circumstances that may exist in this particular "crowded" situation.

Words with a technical or semitechnical meaning can be especially confusing when used uncritically to explain behavior. Mrs. Jones states that her daughter suffers from an "inferiority complex." Mr. Johnson, a teacher, believes that one of his pupils has "a feeling of insecurity." Another teacher explains confidently, "The trouble with Alice is that she is a nervous child."

These statements leave some important questions unanswered. We very properly might ask concerning Alice, "What does she do that justifies the use of the expression 'nervous child'?" Perhaps when her behavior is *described,* certain symptoms will be noted that will point to underlying causes. Nervousness would not then be considered a cause; at most it can serve as a generalized description of some observed behavior. Likewise, "feelings of insecurity" and "inferiority complexes" and numerous similar expressions must be employed carefully and critically when they are used. Otherwise, they do not point very straight to the real explanations of behavior.

Causes Are Not Explained by Platitudes

The objection to the incautious use of value terms in the discussion of the causes of behavior applies also to another way of "explaining" behavior. It is the practice of invoking a broad generalization—so broad that it cannot miss being true—to explain some instance of behavior. Illustrative of generalizations that explain little by explaining so much is the overworked statement, "The home is the main influence in the shaping of behavior." In similar, naive vein is the remark, "Heredity and environment are the principal forces in determining the way a person will act." Certainly such statements have some truth in them; as worded, their value for pointing the way to the factors involved in a given behavior situation is limited. The effective searcher for the causes of behavior has some notion about what specifically he should look for in the home, in the school, or in the community at large; or for that matter, in the family tree. He will manage, by the use of careful descriptions of the details of a behavior situation, to be explicit, not merely safely general and vague.

Much Behavior Is Desirable

Another tendency which characterizes much of our thinking about behavior is the assumption that the only behavior worth studying is "bad" behavior. It is not uncommon for parents and teachers to devote almost an entire meeting, class, or written report to some example of undesirable behavior. If a group of teachers were to select some of their pupils for intensive study, there is the possibility that someone might select a child whose behavior deviates from "normal," and his reason for doing so might be a belief that the more unusual the behavior the more suitable it is for study.

"I'm afraid there isn't much to say about the child I have selected for my study," reports Mr. Smith to his fellow teachers in a child-study class. "This child hasn't much the matter with him. So my description will have to be pretty short. And it probably won't be very interesting." One might ask, "Isn't the child alive? Isn't that important? Do you know of anything more important than that a child is well and active and free from impairments?" Or one could ask about the child's use of his energy and about the strength of his defenses against illness. And what about his interests, his purposes, and his accomplishments? And what gives him satisfaction and enjoyment? Surely these are fundamental to an understanding of a child's behavior and development.

To report that a child is singing and has sung much for many days may be as revealing about that child's development and behavior as the report of quarrelsomeness with reference to some other child. To tell how seven-year-old Jerry extended a helping hand to a classmate who fell to the floor; to tell how he offered to exchange seats with Michael who was smaller and could not see over Jerry during the school movie; to tell how he runs faster than any other child and how he skips more gracefully; these and similar observations are as genuinely important as any descriptions of a negative kind.

Careful study of the child whose behavior is considered desirable may prove to be very rewarding. Especially may this be true when one holds steadfastly to description and allows behavior to "tell its own story." What story does the merry little song tell? What is the story in the mixture of animated conversation and laughter when several eight-year-old boys get their heads together? The fact is that desirable behavior may have a story to tell which is as important and full of meaning as any that would be revealed by unfavorable behavior. Or, more to the point, there would appear to be no better way to learn how to produce good behavior than to study good behavior and to search out its causes. Good behavior is neither the absence of, nor simply the opposite of, bad behavior. It is positive and it is oriented toward ends or purposes that cannot properly be described in terms implying only the avoidance of something undesirable.

Behavior's Causes Are Definite and Can Be Learned

Much emphasis has been given in this section of the chapter to the importance of an open mind and the avoidance of fixed ideas when one is searching for the causes of behavior. Warning has been given against hasty attempts to explain behavior, and against the temptation to restrict the explanation to single, unrelated, and uncomplicated factors. At this point, some readers may have an impression of indecisiveness and evasiveness in this discussion of behavior's causes. They may feel at this moment like asking, "Doesn't it make sense to try to go as directly as possible to an explanation of a given behavior? Must one always temporize with every situation and prepare to hunt through a maze of complexities before trying any positive plan of action? Doesn't this invite a 'do-nothing' and 'know-nothing' attitude toward behavior?"

The answer to these questions is that the effective (and definite) determination of the causes of the behavior of individuals, together with the making of suitable plans of action, *is* a major goal of psychology and of the writing of this book. The concept here being emphasized is that the successful search for the causes of behavior requires that the searcher have both a good sense of direction in such matters and a way of viewing what he sees that will make *actual* causes evident to him when he comes upon them. He has much to gain by keeping his perspective broad and his ideas flexible.

By the same token he also has much to gain by being alert to the possibility that a given behavior, complex as its "rootage" may be, needs no elaborate, complicated explanation. We run the risk of overlooking valid clues to behavior episodes if we allow ourselves to become habituated in a tendency always to seek out complicated explanations of behavior. "Depth" interpretations are not required for every little action that takes place in the classroom or on the playground. Broad perspective on behavior's causes is not to be confused with explanations-within-explanations virtually ad infinitum.

Ideas that are helpful in the development of a good sense of direction in the search for the causes of behavior will be presented in later chapters—especially those of Part 2. The idea that *the causes of behavior can be learned* is the incentive behind much that enters into the work of behavioral scientists.

In the chapter immediately following, attention will be given to the methods that are used in scientific research in human behavior and development. The ways of thinking about behavior that have been presented in the present chapter should add to the student's readiness to appreciate the role of science in the development of knowledge of human growth and development. The persons who understand and accept the concepts that have been introduced in this chapter are those best prepared to grasp the significance of the findings of behavioral science and also of the methods involved in securing the findings.

CONCLUSION

The teacher who understands children thinks of their behavior as being caused rather than impulsive or capricious. Such a teacher sees a youngster's actions as derived from all his experiences, as modified by his purposes and his values, and as influenced especially by the image of what he sees himself becoming. In brief, this view of human behavior holds that "a child's actions can be understood if his relevant past experience is known, if his present situation is analyzed in terms of what it means to him, and if his desires and hopes for the future are taken into consideration" (*Helping Teachers Understand Children*, 1945) [2]. Teachers who hold to this view gain a perspective on human behavior in which the concepts and principles formulated and tested by the behavioral sciences will find a meaningful place.

Suggested Collateral Readings

Almy, Millie, *Child development*. New York: Holt, Rinehart and Winston, Inc., 1955. Pages 81–100.

Association for Supervision and Curriculum Development 1962 Yearbook, *Perceiving, behaving, becoming: A new focus on education*. Chapters 1 to 6 inclusive, and Chapters 9 and 14.

Bernard, H. W., *Human development in Western culture*, 2d ed. Boston: Allyn & Bacon, Inc., 1966. Chapter 3.

Cantril, H., *The "why" of man's experience*. New York: Crowell-Collier and Macmillan, Inc., 1950. Especially Chapters 2, 3, 4, and 6.

Dinkmeyer, D. C., *Child development: The emerging self*. Englewood Cliffs, N.J.: Prentice-Hall, Inc., 1965. Pages 10–23 and Chapter 2.

English, H. B., *Child psychology*. New York: Holt, Rinehart and Winston, Inc., 1951. Pages 15–31.

Eson, M. E., *Psychological foundations of education*. New York: Holt, Rinehart and Winston, Inc., 1964. Chapter 2.

Frankl, V., *Man's search for meaning*. New York: Washington Square Press, 1959.

Gardner, J. W., *Excellence: Can we be equal and excellent too?* Harper Colophon Books. New York: Harper & Row, Publishers, 1961.

———, *Self-renewal, the individual and the innovative society*. New York: Harper & Row, Publishers, 1963.

Gordon, I. J., *Human development: from birth through adolescence*. New York: Harper & Row, Publishers, 1692. Chapter 1.

Jersild, A. T., *Child psychology*, 5th ed. Englewood Cliffs, N.J.: Prentice-Hall, Inc., 1960. Chapter 2.

Lindgren, H. C., *Educational psychology in the classroom*, 2d ed. New York: John Wiley & Sons, Inc., 1962. Chapter 2.

Prescott, D. A., *The child in the educative process*. New York: McGraw-Hill, Inc., 1957. Chapters 2 and 10.

References

1. American Council on Education, 1945, *Helping teachers understand children*. Washington, D.C.: American Council on Education.

2. American Council on Education, 1945 (title above). Page 8.
3. Bettelheim, B., 1967, *The empty fortress*. New York: The Free Press. Page 15.
4. Gardner, J. W., 1964, *Self-renewal, the individual and the innovative society*. New York: Harper & Row, Publishers. Page 97.
5. ———, pages 102–103.
6. Jones, H. E., 1946, The educational psychology of persons. *J. educ. Psychol.*, **37**: 513.
7. Sinnott, E. W., 1950, *Cell and psyche*. Chapel Hill: The University of North Carolina Press. Pages 46–47.

CHAPTER 3

The Science of Psychology

Thoughtful reflection on the material already presented in this book will suggest that psychology is confronted with two major expectations. The very nature of its subject matter (its concern with the forces at work in human actions, for example) prompts us to look to it for principles and concepts that can be put to practical use. This is one expectation. The other is that the principles and concepts of psychology be trustworthy as well as practical—that they have in them the elements of truth.

Psychology, though still a relatively young discipline, has made definite progress in measuring up to both expectations. Obviously, how well it meets the first-mentioned expectation will largely depend upon its success with the second one. The focus of attention in this chapter will be on the kinds of conditions that make it possible for psychology to earn an increasing degree of trustworthiness.

Stated more definitely, the focus of attention will be on the *characteristics of psychology as a science*. Additionally, illustrations of psychology as a science will be given. Such attention complies with one of the principal objectives defined at the close of the first chapter. The statement was made that a major objective of the study of psychology by teachers is the development of *appreciation and understanding of research* in education. Construed broadly, the objective includes research into the growth and development of children and youth. For a person to appreciate and understand research in this area it is important that he be able to recognize the hallmarks of science.

As a science, psychology's job is to ask questions of Nature.[1] Its job, especially in educational psychology, is to ask questions about man and his behavior—not just any questions but such as have been carefully thought out in the light of well-defined problems. And the questions must be put to Nature in a clear and orderly way.

[1] This is a paraphrasing of a statement from Cronbach (1957, pp. 671–684) [7].

ESSENTIAL FEATURES OF PSYCHOLOGY AS A SCIENCE

There are definite features which characterize psychology as a science. These features are discernible in well-planned studies of human behavior and development. Among them are eight that are now to be described. Two of the eight will be considered as principal, or general, features. The other six are highly important essentials of the second main feature.[2]

Empirical Foundation

Psychology as a science is *empirical.* This means that as a science, psychology is based on factual investigation. The base does not consist of opinion, belief or consensus. Psychology as science does not rely on sheer argument as a means of establishing the truth about a given problem phenomenon. The psychologist engaged in experimentation or in systematically controlled observation (these are *empirical* procedures) hopes that what he does can be replicated by other researchers, thus to *test* not only the trustworthiness of his findings but also the soundness of his procedure.

Systematic Character

Psychology as a science is *systematic.* Its procedures are orderly, they are economical, and designed to minimize guesswork. Two writers, in commenting on the meaning of "systematic" as it pertains to psychology as a science remarked, "What is important in science is that observations 'make some sense' " (Morgan and King, 1966) [14]. Preceding the statement just quoted were comments to the effect that observations, essential as they are to science, cannot by themselves have much value. They may be accumulated without any guiding purpose, "piling up in a disorderly, meaningless array."

The orderly, meaningful way of attempting to get at the truth about problem phenomena can best be described by identifying what have already been referred to as "the highly important essentials" of systematic procedure.

Clear Statement of the Problem. An indispensable feature of psychology as a science is an accurate statement of the problem to be investigated. To define a research problem one must have good acquaintance

[2] The student who has access to Baller, ed., *Readings in the psychology of human growth and development* (New York: Holt, Rinehart and Winston, Inc., 1962), which was prepared as a companion piece to this textbook (1961 edition), will find in the researches there presented numerous illustrations of the essentials of the scientific method.

with the field in which the problem lies. Only as a person achieves a good grounding in a given field of knowledge can he expect to identify and define the kinds of problems that actually require investigation.

As was indicated in Chapter 1, the domain of psychology includes a number of "problem areas" (such as perception, motivation, and emotion). In each of these areas are innumerable puzzles whose solution awaits the wording of sharper, more penetrating questions than have yet been asked. Nature will not respond to hazy, superficial questioning.

One way of thinking about the puzzles of psychology is to think of them as representing *gaps* in existing knowledge about behavior. The researcher must, therefore, be capable of describing the general problem area (making use of the best available knowledge about it) and also of describing the nature of the gap he proposes to investigate. His ultimate aim is a sound explanation that not only closes the immediate gap in the particular puzzle he chooses to work on but also helps to round out an understanding of *a larger problem area*.

Use of Theory. The scientist makes use of theory as a means of achieving *provisional explanation* of the relationships among various facts and principles in a problem area under investigation. Theory is a conceptualization of the way these relationships bind a given body of knowledge together; it functions as a framework into which the facts and principles related to a given phenomenon can be fitted. The closely related functions of facts, principles and theory are well described in the following statement. After referring to one of the basic operations of psychology as that of organizing facts about human behavior into general useful principles, one writer says,

> To achieve scientific understanding, however, the scientist must go one step further and organize his principles into a logical framework which demonstrates in an orderly, consistent manner how the various observed facts and derived principles are related. Such a systematic statement of relationships is called a *theory*. The value of a theory is measured in terms of (1) its ability to explain the known facts and to show relationships among previously unconnected concepts and observations and (2) its usefulness in suggesting specific hypotheses that can be tested in further research. (Ruch, 1963) [16]

Not only does theory operate as a framework for facts and principles; it also provides a description of the hypothetical constructs needed to fill the recognized gaps in the over-all explanation of a given phenomenon. The expression "hypothetical constructs" refers to a planfully conceived *model* of something that a researcher knows about in a tentative way, by having observed certain of its functions or other characteristics. For example, the "something" which we call "motivation" cannot be observed as can the act of running, but it can be thought about and investigated advantageously by putting together in testable form some ideas regarding the manner in which various facts and principles are associated with it and with each other.

Varieties of "Explanation." Definitive as these features are, it would be a mistake for us to consider them separable. They are closely related operations which a person performs as he tries to "round out" a provisional explanation of a puzzling phenomenon.

Different people have different ways of achieving a rounded-out explanation of a problem phenomenon. A few illustrations may be helpful.

Appeal to authority is one way of "taking care of" a gap in knowledge. "That's what the *leaders* believe!" is a statement illustrating the appeal to authority. "What do you—an 'expert'—say about the cause of this?" is similarly an appeal to authority. A question is raised in a psychology class about what causes a certain kind of behavior in certain persons. After an exchange of ideas among the students someone declares, with an air of finality, "I have an uncle who has read more psychology than all of us put together and he believes . . . !" Well-read uncles, high-school principals, ministers, favorite college professors, syndicated feature writers in the daily paper, medicine men: these as authorities have had to carry quite a load of responsibility for filling some people's gaps in knowledge.

Another way of dealing with gaps in knowledge is to appeal to logic. Logic has its place—and a very important one—in straight thinking. But it is not one of the functions of logic to substitute for evidence. Nor is it a function of logic to *gloss over* a gap in knowledge. When someone declares "It stands to reason that this is true!" we are entitled to some skepticism—at least until he reveals the facts behind the reason. It "stood to reason" that the world was flat until, relatively unimpressed with his acquaintances' logic, Columbus set out to test what he believed to be some worthy guesses about the shape and action of the earth.

Magic has supplied many peoples' need to have their troublesome thoughts about a puzzling phenomenon put to rest. When a medicine man standing by a feverish tribesman performs certain gestures and incantations and the feverish one after a while recovers, this is enough to satisfy many of the medicine man's followers. The important thing was that, as they saw it, the magic worked.

The illustration just given may be carried a step farther to bring out an important difference between the points at which different people feel they have an acceptable explanation of a phenomenon. It is conceivable that for some of the medicine man's followers, the magic was enough; it "worked," and that satisfied their curiosity. But (as we can imagine) for the medicine man himself and certain of his followers the explanation had to go beyond the magic, per se. What caused the illness? What idea could they use to fill the otherwise troublesome void in their thinking? The answer: an evil spirit. Thus, "evil spirit" was the imaginary entity needed to "round out" this area of their knowledge.

What entity was injected by early New Englanders into their explanation of peculiar behaviors which we today would describe as hysterical symptoms? That is, *what entity served the purpose of filling the void* in their understanding of hysteria? "Demons" was the answer—with burning or hanging of the unfortunate victim the ultimate consequence of the "diagnosis." What, a century ago, caused "foolish" behavior in certain individuals: behaviors which we today would attribute to brain damage, traumatic experiences, and so forth? The sins of the parents, "innate perversity," "constitutional inadequacy": these and other entities helped fill the gaps in knowledge.

In an account that Brown and Ghiselli (1955) [5] give of man's attempts to bridge gaps in his explanations of various phenomena they speak of his use of "pixies." Pixies can't be seen; but pixies of one kind or another hold together the loose ends of pieces of knowledge.

The difference between the pixies of the naive person and the scientist is largely a matter of just how literal the concept is considered to be. The New Englander's "demon" was a pixie—and quite real. The "evil one" is very real—very literal—in the thinking of the illiterate tribesman. The science-oriented person, as we have already noted, thinks in terms of constructs (not pixies), principles, and postulates: explanations allowed to stand until they can be validated. Description, formulated in such terms, is the scientist's method for holding loose ends of knowledge together while he searches for the facts that will ultimately verify his theory.

A theory—to repeat—is a generalized idea about the relationships between various facts and principles where the actual relationships are not known. Proof of the soundness of the generalized idea will depend on how well it stands up as it is subjected to well-aimed questions. Some of the questions will be aimed at one part of the theory (at one of the "supports" that it stands on); other questions will be aimed at other parts. It is only the novice who will fire his questions, so to speak, without first determining where the questions will have the most effect—where they must be aimed to provide a real test of the supports on which the theory stands.

This way of defining theory suggests that it is one of the most *practical* as well as important devices employed by man—especially by men with truly inquiring minds. How better (how else, as a matter of fact), might a scientist begin his search for the explanation of some phenomenon than to deliberately, carefully work out a *provisional explanation* and then proceed to test it—or to test some aspect of it. Indeed, one of the requirements of a serviceable theory is that *it readily lends itself to testing.*

The value of theory in psychological research is, then, that it gives order and plan to our attempts to "firm up" our knowledge about man and his behavior. It provides the orderly scheme for conducting many separate, but well-related, researches into the problems of psychology.[3]

> . . . the ultimate source of the strength of science will not be found in its impressive products or in its powerful instruments. It will be found in the minds of the scientists, and in the system of discourse which scientists have developed in order to describe what they know and to perfect their understanding of what they have learned. It is these internal factors—the methods, procedures, and processes which scientists use to discover and to discuss the properties of the natural world—which have given science its great success.
>
> We shall refer to these processes and to the organization of science on which they depend as the *integrity of science.* (AAAS Committee on Science in the Promotion of Human Welfare, 1965) [1]

Employment of Hypotheses

Another essential among the methods of science is the hypothesis. In the preceding paragraphs we spoke of the function of well-aimed questions in the search for truth. Actually, in the procedures of science the principal questions which the researcher wants to ask are worded as propositions to be tested; they are worded as *hypotheses.* The hypothesis goes a step beyond a question. It is the investigator's best guess about what the answer to a given question will be. Having done his best to word the hypothesis clearly and definitely, the investigator sets about to test it to see if he has guessed correctly. As various hypotheses stand or fall, so accordingly will the supports stand, or fail to stand, under a theory.

Appropriate Research Method

A fourth feature of sound research is the selection of an appropriate method by which to secure the data that are needed for testing hypotheses. This involves a decision about whether the main question of the research is one which can best be answered by an *experiment* or, if not, by a method for testing the degree of a relationship (*correlation*) between two or more sets of data. Certain of the *research methods* employed in psychology will be described under the next main heading in this chapter. Some also will be mentioned and illustrated in some of the chapters that follow.

Appropriate Sampling Procedure

A basic question in research is the question of the satisfactoriness of the *sample* (of persons or traits, for example) on which determinations

[3] The student will find in the following quotation a helpful discussion of the kinds of thinking that scientists employ in their search for truth.

are to be made. How large must a sample be for it truly to represent the whole of which it is admittedly only a part—a part that is convenient to work with? And what else besides size must be taken into account in the selection of the sample?

An illustration may help here. How many people, how selected, must a researcher poll on a question of national interest before he may safely assume that the division of their answers will harmonize with the answers of *all* people of this country—were it possible to poll all the people? Five hundred persons might serve better for his purposes than five thousand—depending on how accurately they represented the individual differences within the total population. Does his sample conform to the proportions of persons of different ages, different sexes, different backgrounds, and so forth, that would be found in the entire population? Clearly, both the size of the sample and the accuracy with which the sample represents the whole population from which it was drawn are important to research, important to the conclusions one may reach on the basis of his findings.

Proper Implementation

Many research investigations in the behavioral sciences require the use of carefully prepared tests, inventories, or other data-gathering devices. Sometimes these tests and other devices are well known to teachers and frequently used by them. For example, an investigation may call for the measurement of the mental ability of individuals being studied.[4] Or it may make use of measures of achievement in such learning areas as language arts, mathematics, and science. Many studies necessitate the collection of data pertaining to interests, attitudes, beliefs, and the like. As stated, experienced teachers usually have some first-hand acquaintance with measuring devices of these kinds. There are many other instruments (the researcher's word for tests, inventories, and so on) that are employed in studies of human growth and behavior, and teachers should know something about most of them, even though they do not participate directly in their administration or the interpretation of their results. They include, for example, the projective techniques for measuring personality traits.[5] Some researches involve numerous physical measurements (such as height, weight, coordination, strength, blood pressure, blood content). When the reader reaches Chapter 9 of this book, he will find cited a number of researches that made use of a great many measures of physical-growth variables.

Regardless of the number of measuring instruments a research ne-

[4] See Chapter 10 for a discussion of the measurement of mental ability.

[5] Chapter 15 includes a brief description of projective techniques.

cessitates, the important question is how appropriate the instruments are for the purposes intended and how dependable will be the resulting data. Competent researchers give special attention to determining what are called the *validity* and *reliability* of measurements.

Validity. The term "validity" has reference to whether a test measures what it purports to measure. If, for example, a test is described as being designed for the measurement of pupil achievement in arithmetic, then it must measure achievement in arithmetic to be considered valid. Furthermore, it must specify what aspects of arithmetic it deals with and must have precisely the content required to evaluate achievement in these specific aspects.

The last sentence emphasizes a basic point where validity is concerned. "Validity is always *validity for the measurement of a particular variable;* there is no such thing as general validity" (English and English, 1958) [8]. A test is valid only in so far as it *actually* measures the particular thing it claims to measure. There is reason for stressing the word "actually." Let us consider again the test designed for evaluation of achievement in arithmetic. Probably this test requires the examinee to read the problems therein presented. But suppose an examinee is a poor reader; he may consume the major portion of the allotted time just trying to read the words used in the statement of the problems. What then, for this examinee, is the test? Is it really a test of what he knows about arithmetic, or a test of his ability to read? We certainly would not get an accurate rating of his proficiency in arithmetic from the obtained results.

Similarly, in a test constructed for the measurement of mental ability much care must be given to seeing that extraneous factors (those not inherently a part of mental ability) do not influence the performance of examinees. The unfortunate fact is that many, many individuals have been given mental tests which required reading ability much beyond their level. The result: misleading (and often damaging) inferences about these persons' true mental ability.

The point of the quotation from English and English may be further illustrated as follows. We may imagine a test being called *A Measure of Broad-Mindedness.* To say the least, this sounds like an ambitious undertaking for a test. Before we use the test, we would be wise to see how "broad mindedness" was defined by the test maker. What particular traits of people were presumed to be related to broad-mindedness? Do the various test items (the content of the test) have definite relationships to these traits? Or does the way the test was constructed suggest a kind of shotgun approach to a vaguely defined target, namely "broad-mindedness"? Shotgun approaches and vague targets have very dubious relationships to validity. The implication is not that broad-mindedness and other complex variables cannot be measured. It is rather that regardless of the complexity or simplicity of the thing to be measured, considerable pin-pointing of the aims of a test must be accomplished if the test is to have validity.

Reliability. A test is said to be reliable to the extent that it measures accurately whatever it is intended to measure. Realiability means that the test can be depended upon to give similar results when repeated use of it is made in similar situations. The question of reliability of a test is esentially one of the consistency with which the device performs. An exaggerated example of inconsistency (to help make the main idea clear) would be the results obtained by the use of an elastic tape measure in the calculation of distance. "How absurd!" would be the proper remark about the use of such a device. There are tests, however, that have considerable "elastic" in them—much too much to be useful.

There is always a question, where test reliability is concerned, of just how much consistency to expect in the test's performance. Suppose we were to determine a person's weight and took two measures separated by an interval of only two or three minutes. And suppose the two measures differed by two pounds. If such a difference were found to be wholly attributable to the way the scales operated we would have some uncomplimentary things to say about the scales. Although we would not expect to be quite this demanding of reliability in psychological measuring devices, we would, nevertheless, have reason, in numerous test situations, to anticipate considerable consistency in the results. This applies to measures of achievement in most school learning situations; it applies to measures of mental ability; it applies to most determinations of physical characteristics.

But we would be prepared to find certain kinds of variables much less inclined to remain stable—even for a relatively short period of time. A test that gives different reports of such a variable from one measurement to another may, therefore, still be performing in an acceptable manner. How much stability, for instance, would we expect in children's *professed desires* when indicated by their ranking of a number of listed statements? Would there be reason to be surprised if, even after a short interval of time, the respective listings were found to be considerably changed? The point is that we would be prepared to accept a lower index of reliability on the part of an instrument devised to measure traits known to be relatively changeable.

This is not the place to attempt an explanation of how test makers go about the determination of the reliability and validity of a test. It must suffice here simply to emphasize that the data gathered by a researcher can be rendered quite useless if the instruments employed by him are lacking in either of these characteristics: validity and reliability.

Accurate Data Appraisal

What is the significance of the data that are collected in a given research? Numerous difficulties may surround the answering of this question. An illustration of one such difficulty will help the reader understand the importance of the procedures that the scientist applies to this phase of research.

Let us suppose that we have found that the girls who are registered in the fifth grade in a certain school are, on the average, an inch taller than the boys. Does this warrant the conclusion that such a difference probably would be found in other schools of the city? How large a difference would we need to find, for how large a number of fifth-grade boys and girls, before we would be justified in generalizing from this one finding? We certainly would be hesitant to announce that fifth-grade girls in our city had been found to be taller than the boys, if the measured difference for our sample of fifth graders was, say, one-eighth of an inch. And we would place still less confidence in our findings if the number of youngsters were as few as six boys and six girls. It is easy to see that the very next measurement that might be made, on another such sample, might reverse the finding: the boys might average taller than the girls. So—to repeat the question—how large must the difference be, for how large a sample, before we can, with confidence, look upon our finding as representative of all fifth-graders in the city?

The problem of testing the significance of differences between sets of measurements such as those in the illustration above is one for which scientists have devised special techniques. Other special techniques have been developed for still other problems of data analysis. These various means of analyzing data are known collectively as *statistical methods.* By the use of statistical methods the scientist can test the significance of differences found between two or more sets of data. He can also express the degree of relationship between different sets of variables (see Chapter 4, especially, for a discussion of *correlation methods*). Few developments in science have contributed more to the improvement of the search for truth than statistics.

The student can have confidence that the researches that deserve to be cited in the psychology of human development have involved the use of rigorous methods of data analysis. As he becomes better acquainted with psychology as a science, he will begin to share with accredited behavioral scientists a deepening interest in and respect for statistical methods and other scientific methods of data analysis.

RESEARCH METHODS ESPECIALLY PRODUCTIVE OF KNOWLEDGE OF HUMAN DEVELOPMENT

There are numerous research methods that are used by psychologists and other behavioral scientists to add to the knowledge of man and his behaviors. They represent, respectively, different ways of asking questions of Nature (to use Cronbach's expression), although they have in common essential features of science. Understanding of how knowledge in the behavioral sciences is developed is of special importance to the reader of this book. It should be helpful now to examine some research methods that have been especially productive of these kinds of knowledge.

Experimentation

Frequently in research on human behavior it is important to determine the effect that a given circumstance has—or can have—on behavior. Experimentation is especially suitable to such a purpose. What constitutes an experiment? An illustration may best answer the question.

Suppose, for example, that a teacher wishes to determine the effects that some visits to selected civic institutions might have on student learning in a social studies course. Clearly it will be necessary to make sure that the knowledge the students demonstrate following the visit could not just as well be attributed to something other than their experiences during the visits. Several questions will help to indicate the steps that are necessary to insure dependable findings.

How can the teacher be sure that the students did not already know, *before* the visits, everything that they were able to report following these experiences? Obviously, there must be some measurement of the students' knowledge in these matters both before they engage in the special project and after it is concluded. And the measurements—the tests—must be equivalent. Nonequivalent tests before and after the visitations would produce invalid findings.

A second question is also important. How can the teacher know how much of the students' performance on the end test is to be attributed to learning experiences other than those derived from the visits? To answer this question he may employ a research tactic which is especially characteristic of experimentation. He may match two groups of students and then involve one of them (the *experimental group*) in the visitation experience, while holding the other group (*control group*) out of this experience.

Note that it was specified that these groups must be *matched*. What does this mean? What factors must actually be the same—or experimentally equalized—in both classes before the teacher can properly claim to have matched the classes? Doubtless, one would specify mental ability as such a factor. There would be much room for uncertainty as to what the teacher had established with the experiment if it happened that one of the classes included students of better learning aptitude than the other. And the researcher must know that the instruction in the two classes was the same *except* for the one experimental variable: the visits to civic institutions. The reader will be able to name other factors that would need to be controlled. There must be no loophole in the plan that would invite skepticism as to whether any measured differences in the accomplishment of the two groups at the close of the experiment might properly be attributed to the presumed effects of the project.

There very well may be, in the experiment described above, some characteristics of the two groups of students that cannot be equated. How, for instance, would one equate the influence of the teacher in the two classes? We might have the same teacher teach both classes. But could we be sure that his teaching methods in the control class would not be influenced by what he was doing with the experimental class? Fortunately for research, there are, in statistical methods, some ways of managing such difficulties. It would be out of place to try to describe them here, but the fact that they do exist is a boon to research—and something more to strengthen our faith in the methods of science.

This sketch of what an experiment consists of should help the student visualize the way in which many important questions pertaining to human behavior have been answered. As he ponders the research findings which are presented in later chapters, he will know that some were derived from experimentation; he will also recognize the experimental method as he reads certain articles in professional journals in psychology and education.[6]

Correlational Investigation

Many problems in psychology involve the determination of relationship or association between traits of individuals or groups. Such traits might be, for example, height, intelligence, social development, interest, attitude, and achievement. The primary purpose of correlational studies is to determine whether or not amounts of one characteristic are accompanied by proportionate amounts of a second characteristic when measurements of each are collected from the same sample of subjects.

[6] See, for example, the discussion in Chapter 6 of the experimentation by Hebb and his associates on the motivating effects of exteroceptive stimulation. For more understanding of the experiments referred to the student will benefit from study of the suggested collateral reading, Solomon, *et al.*, *Sensory Deprivation* [17], which is listed at the end of the chapter.

Answers to such questions as the following involve correlational techniques of research. To what extent are mental development and physical development related? Or at least to what extent does one appear to accompany the other? Is there a tendency for children who learn to walk early to have large vocabularies? Are social development and mental development significantly related? To what extent are personality traits related to youngsters' expressed self-esteem? Many hundreds of researches are aimed at answering these and similar questions—similar in the sense that the aim is to determine the amount of "co-relationship" between traits.

Emphasis in correlational studies is placed on the association between "variables" (the different factors involved) rather than the determination of cause and effect as in the case with experimentation. Thus, in interpreting the results of correlational studies it is important to recognize that the simple fact that two variables are related is not sufficient reason to conclude that one *causes* the other. For example, it has been found that in general students who obtain high marks in algebra also obtain high marks in physics. Although it may be conceivable that the cause of a high mark in physics *is* high achievement in algebra, the finding of a correlation cannot, alone, be considered as proof for such a conclusion. Only through the *control* of all other possible causative factors can such a conclusion be verified.

There are obviously some very exacting requirements that must be observed when correlational methods of research are employed. Correlational investigation has, nevertheless, made valuable contributions to the study of human growth and development. For an example of correlation method, the student may examine Table 4.4. in Chapter 4 and the related discussion.

Comparative Investigation

This method of research contains elements found in both experimentation and correlational investigation, as will become apparent from the following description.

The central focus of comparative investigation is upon the determination of relationships between membership in a group and some characteristic or trait under investigation.

For example, the question might be raised, how does the mental ability of delinquent children compare to that of their nondelinquent siblings? Or, are boys of a given age taller than girls of the same age? Or, how do the child-rearing practices of Samoan families compare with those of American families? Answers to these questions require that members of one group be compared with members of another group on the basis of the characteristic in question.

In both comparative and correlational investigations the researcher is attempting to determine the existence of a relationship. In correlational studies, however, the relationship is between characteristics or traits, as such, whereas in comparative investigations attention is fixed on the extent to which a particular characteristic or trait found in one group is also to be found in another group.

Both in the comparative method and in many experimentations it is *groups* that are being compared. However, there is one important difference between these two methods. In experimentation the investigator *deliberately introduces* an experimental variable into his procedure according to a prearranged plan, and then contrasts the groups concerned. In comparative investigation, on the other hand, no attempt is made to influence the characteristics of the groups involved. Rather the investigator simply compares the groups to ascertain similarities and differences between their respective members. In the comparative method, the researcher supposes that nature, or social interaction, or something else has introduced a *selective* (experimental) factor, causing people to sort themselves out according to different principles. By discovering differences, he hopes to infer what these selective (that is, experimental) factors are.

Clinical Case Study

Much may be learned about "people in general" by systematic study of individuals. One advantage of this method of study is that—fixed as the attention is on a single individual—it makes possible considerably "deeper" probing into human behavior than can generally be accomplished when groups of persons are being studied. Personal face-to-face situations are regular occurrences in psychological clinics, counseling rooms, and private offices of other professional persons who work with people and their problems. When professional persons arrange to organize their findings into a systematic, cumulative record of the growth, development, and behavior of individuals over a period of time, the result can lead to a significant advance in knowledge. Clinical psychologists, counseling psychologists, and school psychologists, as well as medical doctors, are in especially advantageous positions in this respect. Their studies must conform, nevertheless, to the essential features of scientific method, as earlier described, if they are to contribute substantially to basic knowledge.

This leads to the mention of a disadvantage that sometimes attaches to clinical studies. By and large the individuals who are seen by psychologists or other specialists in clinics and counseling rooms are persons with serious problems. In fact, the very word "clinical" suggests "bedside"—that is, illness. Great caution must be exercised, therefore, in the relating of clinical findings to generalized description and explanation of human behavior. With proper cautions in mind, however, researchers can find in the results of clinical case studies much that has potentially great value for extending our knowledge of man's behavior.

Systematic Biography

The statement in the first paragraph under "Clinical Case Study" would apply equally to a method we have chosen to call "Systematic Biography." A biography is a history of an individual's life written by another person. Obviously, for psychology to benefit from biography, the writing must be guided by sound knowledge of human growth and development and must be carefully controlled for objectivity of the observations being recorded. If these conditions are met and the recording of observations can be continued over a period of time, the result may comprise a wealth of penetrating insight not only into *moments* of development but into the *continuities* of development. The method may well be likened to time-lapse photography; as the researcher examines the instances of change as they merge progressively in the human creature he is, in a sense, watching a life develop much as the botanist may, through time-lapse photography, study the growth and "unfolding" of a plant.

The student will note that what we have called "systematic biography" differs from clinical case study in the fact that it is not limited to the observation of "problem" behavior. Actually, for the most part it is employed in the study of "normal" children. Furthermore, as a rule it includes a "built-in" plan for continuing observation—something which, for the most part, cannot be assured in clinical case study.

A good example of the use of systematic biography as a method of studying human development is the work of Piaget (for example, *The Child's Conception of the World,* 1951) [15]. To an important extent Piaget's concepts and penetrating insights into children's development derived from his meticulous observation of his own three children who constituted what one writer refers to as "unparalleled by the most ideal laboratory arrangements" (Maier, 1965) [13]. More about the methods of Piaget as well as his ideas and theories will be found in Chapters 10 and 11.

Another interesting example of systematic biography is contained in the publication, *Three Babies: Biographies of Cognitive Development* (Church, 1966) [6]. The life histories of three babies from birth to age two (age three in one case) were prepared from the recorded observations of the mothers who were "guided by a schedule, devised by the editor [Church], that sought to sensitize them to often-neglected forms of behavior without unduly narrowing their field of attention."

After considering the special features of the method just described and especially its possibilities for the development of *long-term* life histories, the student will find some common ground between it and the method next to be described.

Longitudinal Growth Study

During the last twenty-five years knowledge of human growth, development, and adjustment has been greatly increased by the results of studies quite aptly described as longitudinal. Their distinctive feature is that of continuous fact finding about the same *individuals* over an extended period of time. The student will appreciate the importance of this feature of *continuous study of persons as individuals* if he considers what makes a satisfactory answer to the question, "At what age do boys begin the adolescent growth spurt in height; and what sort of pattern does their growth in height follow for the next several years?"

One way to answer the question, or the two parts of it, respectively, is simply to generalize from data that show *averages* for boys' growth in height. We might, for example, in answering the second part of the question, find the average in height for ten-year-old boys, then do the same for eleven-year-old boys, twelve-year-old boys, and so on throughout the years under consideration. We may, in other words, simply "tie together" the various *averages* thus found and look upon the resulting diagram ("curve," it is called in the sciences)[7] as a description of the way boys' growth in height takes place. Many of the so-called "normal weight charts" have been constructed in such a manner.

Having found an average age for the beginning of the growth spurt and having determined what is *typical* of the adolescent growth pattern, a bothersome question remains. It is the question whether the growth of many boys—or any boy, for that matter—would actually conform to these generalized descriptions. The actual growth curves of boys, individually, might vary considerably from the schematized pattern based on averages, and many such variations might well be exactly "the way nature intended." In a later chapter (Chapter 9) it will be shown that a careful inspection of the growth curves for individual boys (boy A, then boy B, then boy C, and so forth, for a considerable number of boys) will show a variety of patterns of growth. Some will show early spurts followed by gradual deceleration over a given period of time; others will be the reverse of this; still others will have twice as many phases of acceleration and deceleration as most of the boys. The student will under-

[7] Investigations which result in a sequence of averages that show progression with age in the joining together of averages for different groups are commonly referred to as "cross-sectional" studies. How they differ from longitudinal studies is described in later chapters, especially Chapter 9.

stand, from the researches there presented, how important it is to our learning about human growth and development to know not only the limits within which variation is consistent with "good" growth, but also the variety of growth patterns that are altogether satisfactory for different individuals. This is knowledge of a kind that could come only from systematic, follow-up studies of individuals as individuals, where the facts about each individual contribute to a comprehensive idea of desirable growth differences as well as desirable growth similarities.

The importance of longitudinal study of human growth and development is well stated in the following quotation.

> One of the obvious reasons for continuous study of man's development is to discover classes of stable response systems and the developmental periods during which they become manifest. Is it possible to predict dependent or aggressive behavior in adulthood from the child's reactions with parents and peers? Does infant hyperactivity correlate with restlessness during the school years? These and similar questions require longitudinal observations of the developing child.
>
> A related and equally intriguing question concerns the emergence of derivative behaviors, that is, behaviors that bear a lawful relation to early childhood responses but that have been transformed in the course of development. . . .
>
> Adult behavior is a complicated code in which many responses bear a lawful relation to earlier behavior patterns. Insight into this code would provide important clues toward an understanding of human development and predictive power in forecasting adult reactions from childhood behavior. At present our knowledge of this cryptograph is meagre, and longitudinal information provides the opportunity to trace the connections between early and late forms of a class of responses. (Kagan and Moss, 1962) [12]

SPECIAL ATTENTION TO LONG-RANGE STUDIES

During the last four decades a number of studies have been conducted on a long-range, follow-up basis. Some of these are distinctly longitudinal in nature—they have systematically charted the course of the growth and development of groups of individuals *as individuals* over a considerable time span. Others, although not longitudinal in the strict sense of the term, have neverthless provided long-term contacts with the members of the subject group. The result has been an accumulation of data making possible various comparisons among members of the group and between the group and other population samples.

Increasingly in the years ahead the results of long-term human growth studies of both these kinds will influence the thinking and practices of teachers and other professional workers with children and youth.

A brief description of the objectives, plan, and scope of some actual studies and the kinds of data that come from them may help indicate their relevance to teacher education. Descriptions of them will have the further value of demonstrating the substantial nature of the foundations under many of the conclusions that are presented in later chapters.

Illustrative Longitudinal Studies

An illustration has already been given of a longitudinal study with special reference to physical growth. The method is equally suitable to the study of numerous other aspects of human growth and development. In fact, in a number of longitudinal researches, various aspects of human growth and development have been studied simultaneously. Such studies may involve, for example, not only different physical characteristics, but mental traits, emotional traits, and social traits. Frequently also, in such a wide-spectrum investigation, numerous surrounding conditions, such as those of the home, the school, and other agencies of the community, will be studied concurrently for evidences of the roles they play in the way traits develop.

A great value of multidimensional study is that it increases the validity of conclusions about the interrelationships which exist between the various aspects of growth. The steady increase during the past thirty years in the number of multidimensional, longitudinal studies of human growth and development from infancy (even from conception in certain researches) to old age, is one of the distinguishing and encouraging aspects of the forward march of the behavioral sciences.

Studies at the University of California (Berkeley). Three longitudinal studies at the University of California have now been in process more than a third of a century. Two of these, the Berkeley Growth Study and the Guidance Study, have developed research records for particular individuals from birth or early infancy. The other research—the Oakland Growth Study—began with a group of preadolescents. All told, nearly 500 individuals were involved in these studies, nearly two-thirds of whom are still included in the active files of the research staff (Jones, 1958) [11].

The first named of the studies (Berkeley Growth Study) enrolled a number of infants who were first observed during the neonatal period, then at monthly intervals throughout infancy, and semiannually and annually during their childhood and adolescence. They have been observed at longer intervals during adulthood. The data of this study relate especially to physical, motor, and mental development.

The Guidance Study began with a "sample" consisting of every third child born in Berkeley during a given period of eighteen months. Developmental records were kept on these individuals from the time they were twenty-one months old until their maturity. Factors involved in personality development were given central attention in this study.

The Oakland Study, initiated in 1932, has been conducted along two main lines of inquiry. One involved physical growth, physical abilities, and physiological functions; the other emphasized social behavior, patterns of emotional expression, attitudes, interests, and a number of other personality characteristics. At an average age of thirty-six years more than a hundred of these persons (about half the original group) were still actively identified with the study.

The student can imagine the wealth of important research findings that has accumulated during the past twenty-eight to thirty-two years from the extensive fact-finding operations of these three studies.

Longitudinal Studies of Child Health and Development (Harvard). Under the auspices of the Department of Maternal and Child Health at the Harvard School of Public Health a long-term study was instituted approximately thirty-five years ago. As the study drew to a close it had accumulated a rich fund of data derived from psychological, nutritional, anthropometric, and dental examinations. From the analyses of these kinds of data covering so long a time span in the life of particular individuals it is possible to arrive at better answers than we have had to many questions about what makes for physical fitness. It is significant that the study (actually numerous closely related studies) was from its beginning oriented to the importance of *progress,* that is, "growth and development" over a substantial time period (Stuart, 1939) [19].

Child Research Council Study (Denver). This study also spans more than a third of a century. A substantial percentage of the early enrollees in the project are still in the active files—some of them with records that reach back to their prenatal life. It is contemplated for this study that numerous individuals long enrolled in it will soon constitute the subjects for researches on adulthood and (eventually) senescence.

Changes in structure during growth, development, and adaptation; changing physiological functioning throughout life; and factors in personality development have constituted the principal areas of emphasis during this long-term inquiry.

The Fels Institute Researches. Another agency that has conducted wide-spectrum, long-term studies of individuals is the Fels Research Institute at Yellow Springs, Ohio, established in 1929. The following excerpts from a report of the Institute's work will serve to indicate its aims and methods.

The Institute's founders proposed to study human growth and development from the pre-natal period to maturity by the longitudinal method of research, using repeated measurements and observations of the same children over long periods of time. During the years since its inception, the Institute has expanded in the scope and in the direction of its research. . . . More than 300 children from Yellow Springs and neighboring communities have participated in the Fels program to date. Staff members in the fields of biochemistry, physical growth, physiology, and psychology now conduct experimental and cross-sectional research as well as longitudinal investigation. (Sontag, Baker and Nelson, 1958) [18]

We catch a glimpse of some of the research product of the Fels Institute in the following quotations from the same source.

Some problems in child development research can be approached only by the longitudinal method. One such problem is the study of individual differences in mental growth rate, or individual patterns of change in measured intelligence in children. The fact that significant changes in intelligence quotients (IQs) do occur among many children has been documented by data from nearly every research organization using longitudinal techniques. . . . The data on intelligence testing from Fels are unusually complete for this type of longitudinal record. We believe that our data on the extent and individual patterns of IQ change may contribute to the body of knowledge in the area of child development.

Our main interest, however, lies beyond the psychometric implications of the data on IQ change. For some time the director of the Institute has been interested in the relationship between IQ change and the personality structure of the child. He has watched the Fels children as they grew older and observed that shifts in relative mental ability over a period of years seemed to be associated with broader aspects of the children's individual patterns of adjustment in life. The development of personality patterns of adjustment in children with progressively increasing IQs appeared to be different from those of children with decreasing IQs.

Research of the Institute of Child Development and Welfare **(*University of Minnesota*):** A number of researches covering substantial periods of time have been conducted by this Institute. Especially notable among them is the Nobles County Study (Anderson, Harris, *et al.*, 1959) [2], discussed in Chapter 15. The study suggests the degree to which predictions can safely be made about individuals' adjustment over a period of time.

Because we wished to see how well ratings made by teachers would predict future adjustment of children, three rating forms were filled out by the teachers in 1950. These ratings concerned the child's responsibility, his personality traits, and his adjustment in the classroom or home room. Scores on these were combined to form the 1950 Teacher Index. . . .

In designing measures of outcomes in terms of later adjustment, the type of information that can be secured about a person's relation to the demands of life must be considered. There is first the record made by the person in school, community, and on the job, which is the most obvious sign of his success. Such information may be regarded as the objective aspect of the person's life and can be obtained from various records. Next, there are the person's own feelings about himself and his view of his relation to others. Does he feel happy and satisfied with his life? Does he think he gets along well? Such information may be regarded as more subjective evidence of the person's life adjustment and is obtained from the person himself. Last, there are the impressions made by the person upon other people. How is he seen by others who know him? Some who know him very well are likely to balance his traits and feelings against his objective record. Finally, an interview with the person himself secures information about his accomplishments and feelings. The psychologically trained interviewer may thus balance the objective and the subjective aspects of the process of adjustment. In our follow-up studies we attempted to secure information about the person for each aspect of his life, such as work, recreation, education, and family life, from each of the sources, that is, from the records, the person's own statement about himself, the impressions others had of him, and the judgment of skilled psychological interviewers with psychological training. (Anderson, *et al.* 1959, pp. 8–10) [2]

How better than through continuous observations of the same youngsters across a span of years might we expect to arrive at dependable conclusions regarding stability of personality characteristics? And how else might we expect to learn the conditions that influence change versus stability?

Genetic Studies of Genius. When, in 1960, the fifth volume [8] of the Genetic Studies of Genius was published, more than thirty-five years had elapsed since the beginning of Terman's investigation of a group of 1528 intellectually gifted individuals.

The purpose of the study was twofold. One objective was to determine what physical, mental, and personality traits characterized children of superior intelligence. The other was to learn by means of long-range follow-up how such individuals develop, what they are like when they grow up, and what factors have a bearing on their later achievements and adjustments.

The fact that five volumes of carefully analyzed data—published at intervals—have been required to tell the story of these persons' development from childhood and youth to adulthood expresses not only the magnitude of the research task, but also the sheer weight of evidence therein contained about intellectual giftedness and its development. Many fictions about the behavior and development of persons of high intellect have, because of this research, given way to dependable, factual conclusions.

Project Talent. During the school year 1959–1960 a long-range, wide-scale research into factors related to individuals' growth and development was launched. The study is known as Project Talent and is di-

[8] Terman and Oden, 1959 [20], *The gifted group at midlife.*

rected by a staff associated with the American Institute for Research of the University of Pittsburgh. Various advisory panels of representatives from many different educational and psychological agencies furnish advisory and consultative service to the project.

Especially relevant to the present discussion are these facts: (1) Project Talent involves a sample of nearly a half million high school students, scientifically selected to be representative of all high-school age youth in America; (2) the project has accumulated voluminous data about these individuals (their interests, aptitudes, achievement records, social backgrounds, and so on) and their schools and communities; (3) the project is expected to maintain contact with these half-million individuals for a period of twenty years. One can hope with the project's directors that so great a body of facts examined and reexamined over so long a time will lead to many important insights into human development—especially where different kinds of school experience are related thereto.[9]

Within six years of the launching of Project Talent, the thousands of items of information which had been gathered from the tests and the follow-up inquiries began to take form as highly important knowledge about America's young people. How many of the examinees finished high school? How many entered college? And of this latter group what appears to be the percentage of graduates from college? To what extent do students persist in an initially chosen curriculum? How do students who "migrate" from one selection of goals to another fare? These and many similar questions are, as indicated, requiring answers based on carefully designed research (Flanagan and Cooley, 1966) [10].

These are by no means all the important long-term research projects having to do with human growth and development. The purpose of describing them is, as we have said, to indicate the methodology and the kind of product that are associated with this type of research. The reader will find in later chapters mentions of at least a half dozen other long-term human growth studies.

Psychological Ecology

Another category of studies especially productive of growth and development data on children and youth is psychological ecology. It consists of studies of human behavior in the so-called natural habitat; more specifically, certain natural habitats deemed to be reasonably representative of American communities of normal complexity. How do children

[9] Descriptions of Project Talent and certain of its findings have been published in a number of reports. See, for example, Flanagan, J., *et al., The American high school student,* Pittsburgh: University of Pittsburgh, 1964; Flanagan, J. and W. Cooley, *Project Talent, One-year follow-up studies,* Pittsburgh: University of Pittsburgh, 1966.

and youth living in such a habitat acquire their attitudes, interests, values, and various other personality and character traits? What agencies most influence their styles of life? By what tactics can researchers gain accurate data with which to answer such questions? A brief description of one research will show something of the distinctiveness of this kind of inquiry into human behavior and development.[10]

Midwest U.S.A. and Yoredale

Midwest is a small town in the middle of the farm belt of the United States. Yoredale [4] is a place in England having various characteristics that are, for research, important for their comparability to Midwest. High on the list of objectives of the studies involving these places was the identifications of *situational* and *behavioral units* that could profitably be examined—that would furnish sound knowledge of the ways in which the life of children is influenced and shaped by their "natural" day-by-day experiences.

The principal researchers, Barker and Wright (1954) [3], have long emphasized the need in human behavior study of methods applicable to psychological ecology (from a Greek word meaning "home" or "homeland"). At their field station (Midwest is for them an actual and "natural" laboratory) they have attempted to discover the facts about the everyday behavior of Midwest's children and the nature of the circumstances that influence their lives. Voluminous and highly valuable data have been gathered both about the children and about their social-psychological surroundings.

Valuable as the data are, perhaps the most notable feature of the Midwest study and its English counterpart, Yoredale, is their contribution to methodology—specifically a methodology related to "the description and analysis of the naturally occurring behavior and the psychological living conditions of a community." With what behaviors or behavior episodes should a researcher attempt to deal in his study of children? Barker, Wright, and their staff soon learned in their study of Midwest that its 119 children engaged in about a hundred thousand episodes of behavior per day—over thirty-six million a year. How to systematize so great a quantity and variety of material was a major question. There was a similar problem regarding the number and variety of circumstances that entered the lives of these children during any given period of time as well as the number and variety of *objects* to which they reacted in a day, a week, or a month.

From the researchers' grappling with these questions came the

[10] For other studies that well illustrate research methodology useful in the assessment of the influence on children of factors in the life of the community see Havighurst and Taba in the Suggested Collateral Readings at the end of this chapter and also References 5, 18, 20, and 21 of Chapter 8.

methodology now in use. Fundamentally, it is based on what the Midwest research staff call *ecological units,* consisting of (1) systematically described behavior episodes, (2) behavior settings, and (3) behavior objects. These terms certainly are not self-defining and to make their meaning clear would necessitate more space than can here be given. The point of uppermost importance for our present interest is that the researchers in this study progressed from the initial reconnoitering stages in a research domain where few "landmarks" were available for their guidance, to the development of descriptions of the units to be studied, and finally to methods of analysis of these units—that is, of behavior episodes and behavior settings.

CONCLUSION

Thus, we can envision psychology as a science reaching out in numerous ways and in numerous directions as qualified researchers make determined efforts to close the gaps in the knowledge of man's development and behavior. We see also that the advance which psychology as a science makes is not haphazard; it is not the result of armchair "theorizing" or of investigations which have little, if any, grounding in the basic requirements of the scientific method. It is the result of the thorough preparation which interested, capable, persons have made in order that the right questions can be raised about man and the right methods used for arriving at the answers.

Suggested Collateral Readings

Anderson, J. E., *The psychology of development and personal adjustment.* New York: Holt, Rinehart and Winston, Inc., 1949. Pages 12–23.

Baller, W. R., ed., *Readings in the psychology of human growth and development.* New York: Holt, Rinehart and Winston, Inc., 1962. Section Three.

Barker, R. G., and H. F. Wright, *Midwest and its children.* New York: Harper & Row, Publishers, 1954. Preface and Chapter 1, especially.

Cole, L. E., *Human behavior: Psychology as a bio-social science.* New York: World Book Company, 1953. Chapter 1.

Dinkmeyer, D. C., *Child development: The emerging self.* Englewood Cliffs, N.J.: Prentice-Hall, Inc., 1965. Chapter 3.

Good, C. V., *Essentials of educational research.* New York: Appleton-Century-Crofts, 1966. Chapters 1 and 2.

Havighurst, R. J., and Hilda Taba, *Adolescent character and personality.* New York: John Wiley & Sons, Inc., 1949. Chapters 1, 2, and 3, and Part 5.

Hilgard, E. R., *Introduction to psychology,* 3d ed. New York: Harcourt Brace & World, Inc., 1962. Pages 9–23.

Johnson, R. C., and G. R. Medinnus, *Child psychology: Behavior and development.* New York: John Wiley & Sons, Inc., 1965. Chapter 1.

McDonald, F. J., *Educational psychology,* 2d ed. Belmont, Calif.: Wadsworth Publishing Co., 1965. Chapter 1.

Morgan, C. T., *Introduction to psychology,* 3d ed. New York: McGraw-Hill, Inc., 1966. Chapter 1.

References

1. AAAS Committee on Science in the Promotion of Human Welfare, 1965, The integrity of science. *American Scientist,* **53**, 1965. Page 173.
2. Anderson, J. E., D. B. Harris, Emmy Werner, and Elizabeth Gallistal, 1959, *A survey of children's adjustment over time.* Minneapolis: N.I.H. Project M690, Institute of Child Development and Welfare, University of Minnesota.
3. Barker, R. G., and H. F. Wright, 1954, *Midwest and its children.* New York: Harper & Row, Publishers.
4. ———, and Louise S. Barker, 1963, Social actions in the behavior streams of American and English children, in Barker, R. G., ed., *The stream of behavior.* New York: Appleton-Century-Crofts. Chapter 6.
5. Brown, C. W., and E. E. Ghiselli, 1955, *Scientific method in psychology.* New York: McGraw-Hill, Inc. Pages 50–54.
6. Church, J., 1966, *Three babies: Biographies of cognitive development.* New York: Random House. Page vii.
7. Cronbach, L. J., 1957, The two disciplines of scientific psychology. *The American Psychologist,* **12**: 671–684.
8. English, H. B., and Ava C. English, 1958, *A comprehensive dictionary of psychological terms.* New York: Longmans, Green & Co., Inc. (David McKay Company, Inc.)
9. Flanagan, J., *et al.,* 1964, *The American high school student.* Pittsburgh: The University of Pittsburgh.
10. ———, and W. Cooley, 1966, *Project Talent, One-year follow-up studies.* Pittsburgh: University of Pittsburgh.
11. Jones, H. E., 1958, Consistency and change in early maturity. *Vita Humana,* Vol. 1, No. 1.
12. Kagan, J., and H. A. Moss, 1962, *Birth to maturity: A study in psychological development.* New York: John Wiley & Sons, Inc. Page 2.
13. Maier, H., 1965, *Three theories of child development.* New York: Harper & Row, Publishers.
14. Morgan, C. T., and A. A. King, 1966, *Introduction to psychology,* 3d ed. New York: McGraw-Hill, Inc. Page 13.
15. Piaget, J., 1951, *The child's conception of the world.* New York: Harcourt, Brace & World, Inc.
16. Ruch, F. L., 1963, *Psychology and life,* 6th ed. Glenview, Ill.: Scott, Foresman and Company. Page 17.
17. Solomon, P., *et al.,* 1965, *Sensory deprivation.* Cambridge, Mass.: Harvard University Press.
18. Sontag, L. W., C. T. Baker, and Virginia L. Nelson, 1958, *Mental growth and personality development: a longitudinal study. Monogr. Soc. Res. Child Develpm.,* **23**, Serial No. 68, No. 2.
19. Stuart, H. C., 1939, *Studies from the center for research in child health and development* (School of Public Health, Harvard University), I. The Center, The Group under Observation, Sources of Information and Studies in Progress, *Monogr. Soc. Res. Child Develpm.,* **4**, No. 1.
20. Terman, L. M., and Melita H. Oden, 1959, *The gifted group at midlife,* Stanford: Stanford University Press.

The Bio-Social Foundations of Human Behavior

WHAT ARE THE "FOUNDATIONS of behavior"? These are influences within the individual himself and in his experience—especially his early experience—which give the basic structure to his behavior. A study of the foundations of behavior takes into account not only the basic causes of behavior but also the ways in which these causes operate interactively to produce the kinds of behavior patterns we find in different persons.

Genetic inheritance and prenatal experiences have profound influence on the characteristics of the individual. Authorities in the behavioral sciences are in steadily increasing agreement about the importance of these sometimes-overlooked phenomena. Chapter 4 is devoted to a summary of current knowledge about genetic inheritance.

In the course of growing up, every person develops a view of himself and his world which is peculiar and unique. Regardless of the reality or accuracy of these private world views, people behave in accordance with them. The influence of perception on behavior is explored in Chapter 5.

Motivation provides the "push" or "pull" behind behavior, and emotions provide the color, excitement, and much of the *raison d'être* of a person's life. Chapters 6 and 7 cover the topics of motivation and emotion.

Of all the external forces working on the individual, none is more potent than the culture that surrounds him from birth onward. The culture is not a garment which he puts on or takes off at will. The ways of the culture are internalized and interwoven with the individual's unfolding biological endowment in making him what he is. This is the theme of Chapter 8.

CHAPTER 4

Prenatal Origins of Behavior

When a cultural anthropologist sets out to learn the ways of a nation or a people, he uses many different techniques. He lives with the people, he talks with them, he observes their work and play. Sooner or later he discovers customs or habits which cannot be explained merely by looking at immediate activity. He finds that some of their behavior has causes which lie in the past, perhaps only partially remembered or understood.

The student of individual behavior is in somewhat the same position as the anthropologist. He looks at behavior and seeks causes in the context in which it occurs. Sooner or later he, too, encounters characteristics which can be understood only by examining the history of the individual.

We are accustomed to thinking of the biography of a person as an account that has its beginning at birth. We record the birth date in the family Bible or on a bronze tablet (depending on the social importance of our subject) and preserve as historical shrines the birthplaces of great men. For the individual, the "birthdate" of behavior is not at birth, but months earlier, for the infant at birth has already a history that will influence his behavior in all the years to come.

There are many crises in human life—being born, starting school, marrying. But the greatest crisis of all occurs at the moment when an egg is penetrated by a male sperm. This is really the beginning of life and of our history of a person.

Conception. Once every lunar month (about 28 days), usually midway between the menstrual periods, the mature female produces an ovum, or egg. It is thought that the two ovaries alternate in this monthly function. The egg is released from the ovary and is propelled by muscular contractions down the ovarian tube. Unless fertilization occurs, the egg completes its journey through the tube, enters the uterus, and is discharged during the menstrual flow which takes place in approximately two weeks. If, however, male semen is injected into the vaginal tract during this time, fertilization may occur. Viewed under the microscope the *sperm* cell resembles somewhat a tadpole and propels itself by lashing its whip-like tail. If a sperm cell succeeds in reaching the ovarian tube and in penetrating the wall of the ovum, fertilization takes place. It is at this moment that the existence of a future human being is determined and that life begins. The egg is now called a *zygote* and immediately begins to change, grow, and develop. Not only is life begun, but the sex of the developing organism is determined along with all its hereditary characteristics.

Gene-carrying chromosomes from both the father's and the mother's side of the family unite to determine traits. Some of these, such as eye color, are irrevocable. Others, such as bone structure, may be somewhat altered by environmental pressures. Let us examine in a general way the nature of inheritance.

WHAT IS INHERITED?

To what extent is behavior determined by inheritance? The answer to this question is an important one. Behavior that is the product of experience and the influence of environment may be changed and altered by new learning situations or by alterations in environment. Behavior that has its roots in the inherited characteristics of the individual, however, is not subject to the same degree of change and alteration as learned behavior. We say "the same degree," because as you will see, even inherited characteristics respond to environmental influences to some extent, both before and after birth.

Superstition and Popular Belief

Whenever we lack knowledge in an area which is important to us, we are prone to substitute superstition and imagination, or to make unsound generalizations based on inadequate samples or false analogies. Thus, prescientific man was likely to ascribe weather changes to the whims of some god or idol. Fertility of seeds or success in the hunt were thought to be determined by the phase of the moon or by some other natural phenomenon. With the development of science and technology and the advances in dissemination of knowledge most of these ancient superstitions have faded away. A surprising number of them survive, however, even among people of relatively good education.

Here are some everyday situations in which people have speculated about inheritance:

Bobby is eight and in the third grade. Twice he has been caught stealing from the desks of his classmates. His father is a ne'er-do-well who has been in frequent conflict with the law. Bobby's teacher sighs and says, "Well, there's just bad blood there and there isn't much we can do about it, I guess."

Jean is sixteen and has been outstanding in school musical productions since early grade school. She is now taking voice lessons and her teacher predicts a great career for her in music. Her mother says, "I just can't understand it. She can't have inherited any of her ability."

After months of eager anticipation, Connie reports sadly at school that her newly born brother has deformed hands—one hand is a "lobster-claw" type and the other has only two fingers. "My mother cries and cries because she says if she hadn't knitted so much before the baby was born, his hands would probably have been all right."

Nine-year-old Frank is cross-eyed and has very little vision in his left eye. "My father lost his left eye in the war and that's why mine is bad," says Frank.

Marcia is a problem in the sixth grade. She is thin, quarrelsome, her school work is poor, and she gets along with no one. Her teacher grew up in the community and was well acquainted with her parents. At the time of Marcia's conception, her father and mother were frequently quarreling and fighting. They separated before her birth, and her mother has worked as a waitress and scrubwoman to support herself and the child. The teacher is convinced that Marcia's nature would have been different if her parents had been happy and in love when she was conceived.

In every case above, of course, the supposition is false. How can we know the truth about inheritance? The answer lies in the science of *genetics.* It is not really very surprising that so much misinformation exists about inheritance, for genetics has been an active and productive science for only about fifty years, and each decade adds new and important evidence to the total already accumulated. Of course, all the answers are not yet known, but the basic facts are clear.

Some Inherited Characteristics

Because genetics is an exacting discipline or study by itself, any discussion in a general behavioral book like this is bound to be somewhat superficial and incomplete. However, it is safe to make general statements about inheritance of characteristics that are directly relevant to behavior. We inherit, first of all, a tendency toward a certain *structure.* That is:

1. A tendency to achieve a certain *body height.*
2. A tendency toward a general *"body type."* Body type is determined by the skeletal structure, the proportion of fat and muscle tissue, and the length of limbs.

3. *Sex.*

4. *Appearance.* Appearance is one of the most obvious and to the individual, at least, one of the most important areas of inheritance. Specifically, the child acquires genetically his skin and hair texture and color, eye shape and color, nose shape, ear structure, head shape—all the external, observable characteristics which make him unique in appearance.

5. *Internal structure.* The internal structure is governed by the size, proportions, and adequacy of the various organs and systems of the body. For example, the shape of the lens in the eye determines in part the accuracy and clarity of vision. The size of the heart and lungs relative to the rest of the body helps determine capacity for prolonged output of physical effort, as is demanded in many sports. The size and position of the girl's uterus helps determine her future capacity to conceive and bear children normally. In short, much of what we think of as capacity or ability begins with structures whose characteristics are determined at the moment of conception.

In addition to (and inextricably linked with) inherited *structure* is an inherited tendency to *function* in certain ways. Inherited functioning tendencies include:

1. *Neural responses.* The level of functioning of the nervous system is of great importance to behavior. As is pointed out in another part of this book, intelligence has several sources, but the basic element is the functioning of the cerebral cortex and entire nervous system. An individual may not reach his intellectual potential because of physical or environmental factors, but under no circumstances can he be any "brighter" than his nervous system allows him to be.

The functioning of the nervous system also predisposes the individual to react slowly or quickly to stimuli of all sorts.

2. *Sensory efficiency.* Keenness of vision, range of hearing, sensitivity of touch, ability to perceive odors, and similar attributes are basically inherited traits.

3. *Operation of the "vegetative system."* By "vegetative" we mean that part of the system which carries out basic life activities—the heart and circulatory system, the digestive system, the reproductive system, and so on. The efficiency of these systems is primarily genetically determined, as is their ability to function well under varying environmental conditions and their differing responses to body emergencies. Some evidence suggests that longevity or life expectancy is similarly determined, but this remains hypothesis rather than fact at present.

4. *The functioning of the endocrine system.* The endocrines are the glands of internal secretion. They are properly part of the vegetative system, but are deserving of special mention. Among the more important are the thyroids, which control the metabolic rate, the pituitary, which

seems to be the "growth-stimulator," the gonads or sex glands, which are concerned not only with the sex drive but with secondary sex characteristics, and the adrenals, which "stir-up" the organs in strong emotions. It is easy to see how the functioning of these glands helps determine the nature or temperament of an individual.

5. *Rate of physical growth.* The rate at which children progress through the growth cycle varies greatly from one child to another. There are many factors involved in determining this rate, but the basic one is inheritance.

6. *Predisposition to certain diseases.* Certain diseases—or, more often, a predisposition toward acquiring certain diseases—may be inherited. One does not inherit tuberculosis, for example, but some individuals seem more likely to succumb to exposure than others.

To summarize, the human being inherits a physical *structure* which is predisposed to *function* in certain ways.

Perhaps equally important is the question of what is *not* inherited. The reasons for looking for the answer to this question are about the same as those advanced for learning what is inherited. Behavior that is not a direct outgrowth of the biological inheritance of the individual may be more amenable to learning and to environmental pressures, and may therefore be more subject to change.

The child does not inherit *traits* as such. Eight-year-old thieving Bobby, mentioned previously, was not born with a predisposition toward law-breaking. He was unfortunate enough to be born into a family whose life-pattern made stealing a likely activity. Nor can we blame Marcia's quarrelsomeness on her inheritance. While temperament is partly the product of the functioning of the nervous, visceral, and endocrine systems, sociability and agreeableness develop in and from a social context.

Jean's outstanding skill in singing certainly reflects a structure predisposed to function well in vocal music, but she inherited not the actual *skill* or performing ability, but rather the *potentiality* for learning the skill.

In short, the child does not inherit specific traits or pieces of behavior, but rather differing capacities to learn them. Whether they develop and what form they take is dependent on his environment and his experiences.

HOW DO WE INHERIT?

Knowledge of inheritance began with the work of a monk named Gregor Mendel, who experimented with plant breeding in the early nineteenth century. Although his work was forgotten and unnoticed until the turn of the century, the basic rules of inheritance are now called Mendel's laws. The science of genetics has had tremendous expansion in the twentieth century; new techniques of study and new tools—the electron microscope, radiation treatment, electronic computers—have provided increasingly complex revelations of the mechanics of inheritance. The geneticist controls breeding and reproduction of molds, fruit flies, plants, and animals, and observes and records the traits of generations of human beings. From such studies come some answers to our question, "What has inheritance to do with behavior?"

Chromosomes

The carrier of genetic determination is the chromosome. Chromosomes, under a microscope, appear to be rod-like, sausage-shaped, or V-shaped bodies. The requisite number of these bodies in the normal human cell is forty-six. When the human sex cell (ovum, or egg, in the female and sperm cell in the male) reaches maturity at pubescence or later, the number of chromosomes is reduced by a process called *meiosis* to twenty-three in each cell. When mating occurs and a sperm cell penetrates the ovum, the two sets of chromosomes line up in appropriate pairs and the total number of forty-six is restored. All of these pairs are matched except for the twenty-third pair. If by chance a pair of like (called "X") chromosomes match up in this twenty-third set, the sex of the developing human being will be female; if they are unlike (*"X"* and *"Y"*), the child will be male. For some unknown reason, slightly more males than females are conceived. Incidentally, sex is determined by the male; so the rulers of ancient and modern times who put away wives who failed to give them sons were misplacing the blame.

Thus, in the *zygote,* or fertilized egg, two sets of twenty-three chromosomes have paired, half from the mother and half from the father. Whether a specific chromosome contributed by one of the parents—say, the father—came from *his* father or mother cannot readily be determined, and for all practical purposes can be said to be "chance-determined." In addition, which one of the millions of sperm cells present in one ejaculation will fertilize the ovum is due to "chance"—and only one sperm can do it; the others must be wasted. Thus, "chance" factors arising in meiosis and in fertilization are astronomical in number, and *which* of the ancestors' and parents' characteristics will be inherited is beyond present human ability to predict.

Occasionally, through some unfortunate bodily error, aberrations in chromosomes appear: two will become attached to each other, an abnormal combination of sex chromosomes will occur, or there will be a trisomy (triplet) of the small autosomal chromosome 21. In the latter case, where an extra chromosome appears, making 47 rather than the normal 46, mongolism (or Down's syndrome or Trisomy 21 Anomaly, as the condition is sometimes called) will result. A host of other abnormalities have been identified as the product of chromosomal or gene disorder.[1]

Genes

Chromosomes are not the actual determiners of traits. When they are studied microscopically, bands or markings appear, representing an entity called *genes,* which appear to be the actual determiners of traits. Each chromosome is made up of many genes; man has probably not less than 2000 nor more than 50,000. One authority estimates the actual number at 10,000 pairs for each individual (Stern, 1960) [22]. It was once supposed that each gene was the determiner of a specific characteristic, such as a straight nose or a deep-lobed ear. At present, it appears that there is no simple one-to-one relationship between genes and traits, that is, one gene may influence many characteristics or traits, or conversely, many genes may combine to determine one characteristic. Genes have been compared to catalysts, which precipitate changes in chemicals without being affected themselves.

Factors other than the assorting of chromosomes (and thus of genes) enter into the determination of traits. One of these is the dominant or recessive nature of some traits. In eye color, for example, brown is dominant over blue; and if one parent carries *only* brown and the other *only* blue determiners, their offspring will have brown eyes. Many people, however, carry both; and if two recessive blues happen to match up in the assorting process of meiosis and fertilization, the child would have blue eyes even though parents and all the immediate relatives have brown eyes. The knowledge of dominant and recessive traits is important because it explains how a structural or functional trait may appear in a child by inheritance and yet not be present in parents or ancestors within anyone's living memory. To appear in an individual, the recessive trait must, of course, be present in both parents, and the genes must pair up in the proper fashion.

Sex-linked Traits

Some characteristics are sex-linked; that is, one sex shows the characteristics while the other sex, not apparently affected, is the carrier. One such trait is color blindness. For example, the sons of a colorblind man and a normal woman do not inherit the defect, but the daughters may be carriers for the disorder to another generation of males—their

[1] For a good layman's discussion of this topic, see "Genetic syndromes in mental retardation," Chapter 4, pp. 93–123, in Robinson, H. B., and Nancy Robinson, *The mentally retarded child,* New York: McGraw-Hill, Inc., 1965.

sons. Another example is hemophilia, the "bleeder's disease," which rarely occurs in women but is transmitted by them to their sons (Stern, 1960) [22].

Mutation

Occasionally, in the reproductive cells of any living thing—plant, animal, or human being—a change occurs which causes the introduction of completely new traits in the next generation. Such changes are called *mutations.* Mutant plants and animals occasionally have characteristics that breeders can use to improve existing varieties. In human beings, unfortunately, mutations are almost always undesirable. Their causes are not clear, but it is known that they can be induced by atomic radiation.

Implications

We have considered briefly some of the basic concepts of genetics. We have touched upon the roles in inheritance played by meiosis, chromosomes, genes, sex-linked traits, and mutation. Now we must consider what some understanding—slight or profound—of inheritance has to do with understanding one child or a classroomful of children.

The first and most striking impression one gains from such knowledge is of an extremely complex process with "chance" operating at almost every stage. We put "chance" in quotation marks because this sorting out and matching process is probably mathematically lawful, but for the most part the lawfulness or orderliness is not clearly enough understood at the present time to be described in any way other than "chance."

The product of this complex process is an individual who is wholly unique, unlike any other person who ever lived. (Monozygotic or identical twins are exceptions to this, and will be discussed later). He is the product of a race, a culture, a family—but still he is biologically unique and in many ways is "a law unto himself." He cannot be treated or judged wholly in relation to his peers, his parents and ancestors, or even his brothers and sisters. It is this uniqueness—partly biological and partly cultural—which makes the human child so fascinating (and sometimes so frustrating!) a subject for study. But it is good for the teacher to remember this uniqueness and its biological sources when he ponders the many causes of his students' daily behaviors. This knowledge may be especially worthwhile if it helps to prevent the teacher or anyone else from having stereotyped ideas about the behavior or performance of a particular child because of what he knows about his parents, relatives, or siblings.

A second thought which suggests itself is that there must be something—some order, some predictability, some lawfulness—in this process *besides* chance. Fortunately, there is, or genetics would be only a description of chaos. To the teacher, it would seem that a basic question here would be, "Are children biologically more like their parents than they are like the general population?" and, "Are children more like their siblings than they are like other, unselected children?" The answer to both of these questions is of course "yes," but a qualified "yes."

The Distribution of Traits

We might ask ourselves at this point whether there is any order or system to the distribution of traits in the total population. Do tall peo-

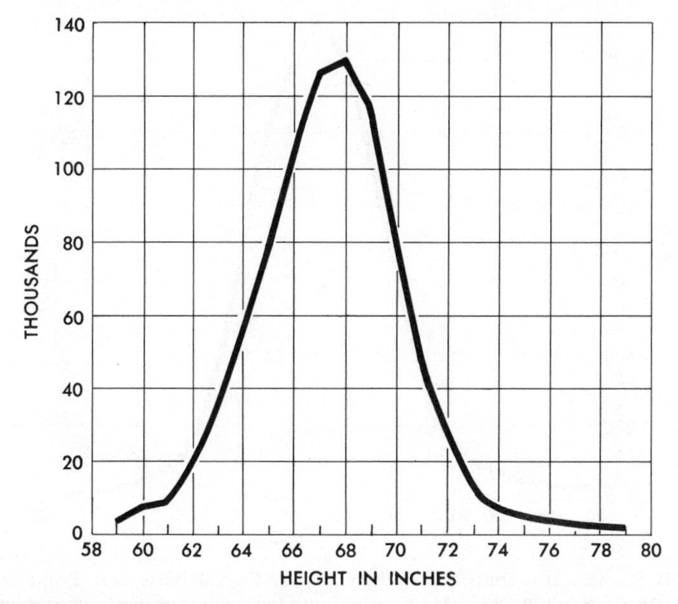

FIGURE 4.1 Distribution of height of American men drafted in World War I (864,445 cases). The lower end of the curve is curtailed because of rejection of men of very short stature. From Davenport, C. B., and A. G. Love, *Army anthropology* (*Medical Department of U.S. Army in the World War*, Vol. XV, *Statistics*, Part I). Washington: U.S. Government Printing Office, 1921.

ple outnumber short people? Are there more stupid people than bright people? In short, what pattern, if any, exists?

Let us examine a trait that can be observed readily and measured accurately—height. Our own observation tells us that there are a few very short people and a few very tall ones—few enough extreme cases so that we notice and comment on them. Most people, however, fall within a fairly narrow range—they are not far from "average." Figure 4.1 shows the distribution of height in American men drafted in World War I.

Note that the lower end of the curve is curtailed through rejection of men of very short stature. This type of curve, with few cases at either end and the mass near the middle is called the "normal" curve or sometimes the "bell-shaped" curve (see Figure 4.2).

If we measure any trait, psychological or physical, in a large enough segment of the population, we will get a distribution that resembles Figure 4.2 Perhaps the most relevant example would be of scores on an intelligence test. Figure 4.3 shows the distribution of scores on a psychological test for nearly 3000 children, aged two to eighteen.

A biological phenomenon that tends to keep traits normally dis-

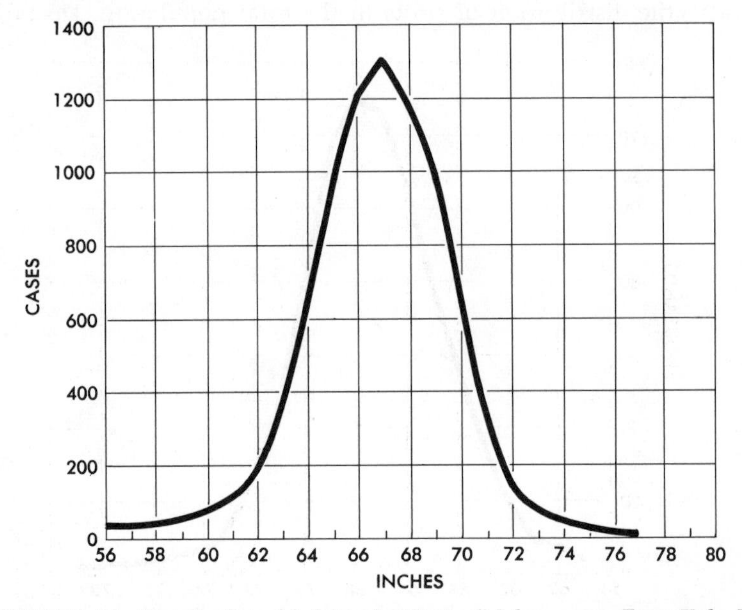

FIGURE 4.2 Distribution of height of 8585 English-born men. From Yule, B. U. and M. G. Kendall, *An introduction to the theory of statistics.* London: Charles Griffin & Co., Ltd., 1965.

tributed in the population is the law of filial regression. This concept was formulated by the great English mathematician, Sir Francis Galton, and is usually called "Galton's law." This law describes the tendency of quantitative or measurable characteristics in the offspring to regress or revert toward the average of the group to which the parents belong. For example, we would expect extremely tall parents to have children taller than average, but not as tall as themselves. Again, very bright parents would tend to have children brighter than average, but not as bright as themselves. Thus, the "normality" of the distribution is maintained generation after generation.

A logical question to ask at this point is, "Why are some children

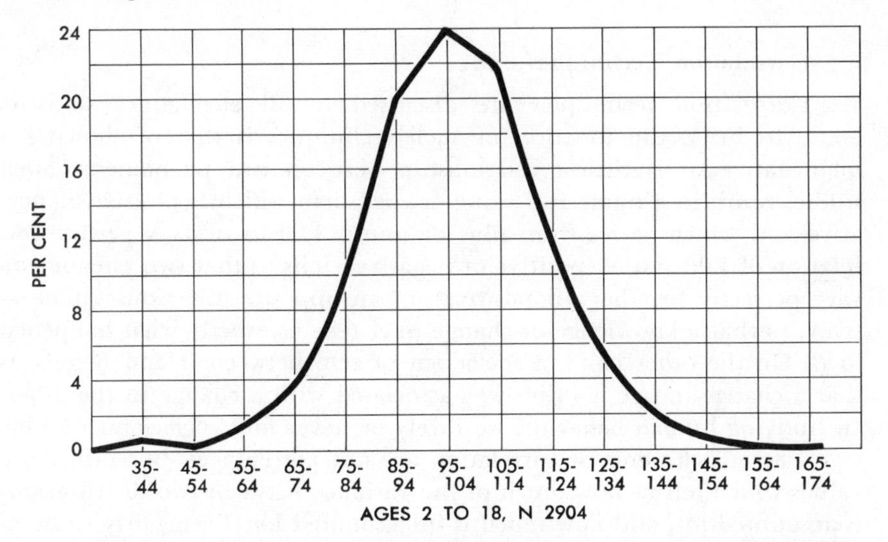

FIGURE 4.3 Distribution of composite L–M IQs of standardizaton group. From Terman, L. M., and Maud A. Merrill, *Measuring intelligence*. Boston: Houghton Mifflin Company, 1937. Used with permission.

nearer the mean or average than are their parents?" Galton answered this question in his "Law of Ancestral Inheritance." The explanation: the two parents between them contribute *on the average* one-half of each inherited characteristic, each of them contributing one-quarter of it. The four grandparents contribute between them one-quarter, or each of them one-sixteenth, and so forth, back through the entire family tree. This law, still accepted approximately as Galton formulated it, shows that the child's heritable traits really represent a combination of *all* his ancestors. Of course, he receives increasingly great amounts as his own parents are reached (Galton, 1889) [4].

With this explanation in mind, we may examine some actual studies of individual and family similarity.

STUDIES OF INHERITANCE

There are several ways of studying these familial resemblances, but the most common is probably the correlation study. As the term implies, the purpose of the correlation studies is to determine the extent of relationship between pairs of traits based upon the observation of groups of individuals. The pairing of the traits may involve parents with their children, siblings, and twins. Examples of the traits include intelligence, physical factors, personality characteristics, and the like.

Correlation Techniques

Correlation techniques are discussed in all elementary statistics texts. In brief, the function of such techniques is that of showing a quantitative or statistical relationship between two phenomena. Such studies result in a numerical value or coefficient which is positive or negative and which varies from plus or minus 1.00 to zero. A perfect correlation of 1.00 (either positive or negative) tells us that two phenomena vary perfectly together (if positive) or in opposite directions (if negative), so that a knowledge of change in *A* tells us exactly what happened to *B*. On the other hand, a coefficient of zero between *A* and *B* tells us that a change in one is in no way associated with a change in the other. In studying human behavior, we rarely or never find coefficients of 1.00.

These coefficients of correlation are not percentages, but rather are values which tell us how much of the variance between two distributions is accounted for, and how much is unaccounted for. Even fairly substantial correlation coefficients leave much variance unexplained. For example, we usually find a correlation coefficient of .50 between parents' and children's intelligence test scores. This means that 25 percent of the variance is accounted for by whatever it is that parents and children have in common, leaving 75 percent due to other factors—experience, environment, and so on. Table 4.1 shows the percentage of variance accounted for at different levels of the coefficient of correlation.[2]

When is a correlation coefficient large enough to be meaningful? Although we cannot go into detail here, it may be helpful to describe briefly the concept of *significance*. Whether a correlation coefficient is significant depends on whether, as inferred statistically from the data in a study, its difference from zero is greater than would be expected by chance. This difference is cited in terms of the probability (P), expressed as a number between 0.00 and 1.00, that a given result would have occurred by chance. In psychological studies we usually accept meaningful data in which $P = .05$ (results could be expected to occur by chance 1 in 20 times), or $P = .01$ (results could be expected to occur by chance only 1 in 100 times).

Family Resemblance

Exploring the nature of family resemblances is an intrinsically interesting activity to most of us. Certainly in your family or in the families of friends you have heard the tea-time comparisons: how Kermit is just the "spitting image" of Uncle Harry, how adolescent Sherry is just about as tall as her mother, how big-boned Davey is going to "carry a

[2] Wert, James E., Charles Neidt, and J. S. Ahmann, *Statistical methods in educational psychology*. New York: Appleton-Century-Crofts, 1954.

lot of weight" like his granddad. These comparisons, of course, are not valid, because they are usually the product of just "looking at" others, and they are clouded by emotions and attitudes.

The scientist has the same curiosity about family likenesses, but he has the tools and techniques for valid measures and comparisons. First, he chooses the subjects of his study. Sometimes they are a sample of the total population; that is, a representative portion of the whole. Sometimes they are a complete group, as all the brother and sister pairs in a given school. In still another case, he may match subjects from different locales on as many traits as possible. Whenever he has selected a group,

TABLE 4.1

Correlation Interpreted According to Variance

Coefficient of Correlation	Variance Accounted for by Correlation (%)
.10	1
.20	4
.30	9
.40	16
.50	25
.60	36
.70	49
.80	64
.90	81
1.00	100

he sets about measuring whatever it is that interests him. Instead of just observing, he uses proven measuring instruments: accurate rules and gauges for determining height or arm length, sphygmomanometers for blood-pressure checks, psychological tests which measure intelligence, attitudes, and the like. He also has at his command statistical tools for correcting for expected variations and errors in his measuring instruments. He can combine and compare and, in general, examine his data in ways that are meaningful and revealing. From such scientific studies we have considerable evidence on family similarities.

Studies of parent-child similarity are numerous, especially in the area of intelligence. After about age five, as noted earlier, a coefficient of about .50 is usually found; this is comfortably beyond a chance relationship (Anastasi, 1958) [1]. In one study of the similarities of height and weight of parents and their children, correlations as high as .60, .70, and higher were found. Tables 4.2 and 4.3 show these relationships for both sexes, at different ages. Discussing this and other studies, Bayley says:

TABLE 4.2
Correlations between Heights of Parents and Their Children

Age	*Boy*			*Girl*		
	N	Father (r)	Mother (r)	N	Father (r)	Mother (r)
Mo. 6	30	.25	.27	28	.42 [a]	.47 [b]
Yr. 1	28	.30	.31	28	.36	.67 [b]
5	23	.52 [a]	.30	24	.24	.70 [b]
10	23	.60 [b]	.37	24	.24	.72 [b]
15	21	.42	.71 [b]	20	.43	.68 [b]
18	21	.52 [a]	.44	19	.64 [a]	.52 [b]

[a] Significant at .05 level of confidence.
[b] Significant at .01 level of confidence.
Bayley, Nancy, 1954, Some increasing parent-child similarities during the growth of children. *J. educ. Psychol.* 45: 9.

TABLE 4.3
Correlations between Weights of Parents and Their Children

Age	*Boys*			*Girls*			
	N	Fathers (r)	Mothers (r)	N	Fathers (r)	N	Mothers (r)
Mo. 6	31	.33	.23	27	—.16	28	.23
Yr. 1	28	.19	.20	27	.12	28	.35
5	23	.34	.09	23	.37	24	.47 [a]
10	23	.31	—.01	23	.30	24	.74 [b]
15	21	.46 [a]	.15	19	.25	20	.88 [b]
18	21	.44	.13	18	.31	19	.43

[a] Significant at .05 level of confidence.
[b] Significant at .01 level of confidence.
Bayley, Nancy, 1954, Some increasing parent-child similarities during the growth of children. *J. educ. Psychol.* 45: 9.

From these data it does, however, seem reasonable to assume the existence of a hereditary core of parent-child similarities in both mental and physical characters, even though such similarities may not be evidence during the first year or so of the child's life. The similarities tend to increase as the children approach the mature status at which the characteristics were observed in their parents (Bayley, 1954) [2].

Marked similarities within families also exist for attitudes, conduct, vocational choices, socio-economic status, and occupational level, and for some personality characteristics and maladjustments (Roff, 1950) [18].

Sibling relationship shows a more variable picture. On intelligence, the range of coefficients is from as low as .30 to as high as .70, depending on the population, the similarity of environment, age, and other factors. Comparisons of personality traits show lower similarities, as they did in parent-child studies (Anastasi, 1958) [1]. It might be noted here that a great many psychologists would distrust the results of most existing personality tests and, thus, would question the meaningfulness of many personality studies. Measures of height relationship show a great similarity to those of intelligence. Table 4.4 shows height and intelligence correlation coefficients between identical and fraternal twins and between siblings.

TABLE 4.4
Correlation Values Measuring Resemblance in Standing Height and in Intelligence in Siblings, Fraternal Twins, and Identical Twins

Relationship	Correlation in Standing Height	Correlation in Intelligence Test Scores
Identical twins	.94	.90
Fraternal twins	.58	.70
Siblings	.50	.50

Adapted from Newman, H. H., F. N. Freeman, and K. J. Holzinger, 1937, *Twins: A study of heredity and environment.* Reprinted by permission of The University of Chicago Press.

Scores of correlation studies support our answer of "yes" to the question of whether siblings or parents and their children have greater similarity than chance would support. The size and nature of the correlation coefficients would make it safe for you to continue believing that people within families-in-general have similarities which set them apart from others. These studies, however, indicate that it is *not,* in the light of the evidence, scientifically sound for you to believe that Will is going to be "bright" because Dad and Sister Anna are top-flight scholars, or that Susie is going to be an excitable and emotional student in the sixth grade because her two older sisters were that way.

We must repeat, for emphasis, our warning: stereotyped or preconceived ideas about the behavior or performance of a particular child based on knowledge of his family may well be false and, thus, be potentially damaging.

Problem of Cause

Correlation studies, interesting and informative as they have been, are not good stopping places for research. The fact that two phenomena occur together does not prove that one causes the other. Similarity between related persons does not prove that the likenesses are genetically caused, for close relatives generally live together and, thus, share a somewhat similar environment. (We say "somewhat similar" environment because even within the family two siblings have a different environment because of age, sex, emotional relationship with like and opposite sex, parents, siblings, and others.) A study carried out some years ago on Louisiana school children by Sims illustrates this problem. The investigator located 203 pairs of siblings in the schools and found a nonrelated control child for each of the siblings. The controls were matched with the experimental subjects as carefully as possible for similarity of age, socio-economic status, and attendance at the same school. When all the children were given intelligence tests, it was found that the scores of the nonrelated pairs correlated .35, only slightly lower than between the siblings (Sims, 1931) [20].

This relatively high similarity of nonrelated pairs could be partially explained by the matching operation: children identified as alike in the above characteristics, especially that of socio-economic status, are certainly more alike than chance pairs could be expected to be.

To answer satisfactorily questions about causation, some other approaches are necessary. Perhaps only an experimental approach would give conclusive answers; but since this would involve complete control of human mating and pre- and postnatal environment, it is manifestly impossible. Some alternative methods, however, have been found which provide acceptable evidence. One of these approaches has been the study of animals, whose matings and environments are virtually completely controllable. Another interesting source of evidence comes from studies of foster children in adoptive homes. A third and in many ways most satisfactory method is the study of fraternal and identical twins. Let us examine some evidence from each of these sources.

Animal Studies

No one-to-one relationship exists between animal and human behavior, but animal studies are frequently suggestive of applications to human situations.

Animals are obviously superior to human beings in many ways for genetic investigations. Rats, guinea pigs, mice, and other animals are easily secured, their mating and other environmental circumstances can be controlled and their developmental periods are so short that many generations can be studied in what to human beings is a relatively short period of time.

One of the classical studies of inheritance in animals was a rat-breeding experiment by Tryon (1940) [24]. This investigator gave 142 unselected white rats a number of trials on a complex maze and then bred them on the basis of maze-running ability: fast learners were mated with other fast learners, while slow learners were mated with rats of intermediate ability for the first generation. For later generations, bright were bred with bright and dull with dull. Environment was held constant for the duration of the study. His original, unselected sample was distributed in a more or less normal fashion, but the last generation showed two distinct distribution of scores with almost no overlap. Selective breeding, in other words, had produced a strain which was extremely poor at learning this skill. While the terms "bright" and "dull" have been used in describing these animals, later studies suggest that such differences are specific rather than general (Munn, 1965) [15].

One must exercise care in making inferences about human inheritance from such studies; but when both heredity and environment can be controlled, the contribution of inheritance becomes apparent. In addition to the impossibility of controlling human heredity we can exert only partial environmental control over human subjects. Even with good controls we have the added problem of increased susceptibility to environment as we go up the genetic scale.

We may now turn to some studies in which the heredity of the subjects is uncontrolled, but in which environment is relatively constant. Subjects for such studies may be found in adoptive homes.

Foster Children

Foundlings or illegitimate children, about whose parentage little is usually known, are often placed in adoptive homes, where there also may or may not be biological children of the parents. Three major types of analysis, usually of intelligence, have been made:

1. Comparison of foster family and (where known) own family resemblances;
2. Relationship between foster child and level of foster home;
3. Study of change in IQ following placement in the home.

The major studies in this area show in general considerable similarity between the abilities of adopted children and their foster parents, but much less similarity than usually exists between parents and their true children. Such differences are usually attributed primarily to heredity, but Anastasi warns that the evidence should not be regarded uncritically. She expresses concern that the intrafamily relationships may not be strictly comparable in foster and own homes, that natal and prenatal factors might tend to increase the resemblance of children to own parents as contrasted with foster parents, and finally that foster and control groups may not in some cases have been truly comparable in cultural level (Anastasi, 1958) [1].

Twin Studies

The ideal situation for studying heredity would be to have subjects with identical inheritance but with different environmental experiences. Some twins provide us with just this kind of situation; as a result, they have been used as subjects of studies since the latter part of the nineteenth century. Twinning occurs in about one out of every eighty-eight births among whites and one of every seventy Negro births (Stern, 1960) [22]. There are two general types of twins: first, the dizygotic, or fraternal, which result when two ova, or eggs, are fertilized during the same period, and second, the monozygotic, or identical twins which result (from unknown causes) when a single zygote (fertilized ovum) divides into two identical parts and each develops into a separate person.

Dizygotic, or fraternal, twins may be like or opposite in sex and in general may have as much or as little resemblance to each other as any pair of siblings, since there are actually two separate and independent conceptions taking place. Because they share the womb and are born at about the same time, they have a more common environmental experience than other siblings. Monozygotic, or identical twins have, of course, identical inheritance since the zygote divides *after* the pairing-up of chromosomes and genes has taken place. They, too, have a similar prenatal environment. *Similar* prenatal environment for either kind of twin does not mean *identical* environment. Fraternal twins ordinarily have separate sacs or chorions, but identicals may have single or separate amnions and single or fused placentas. In fact, a given pair of monozygotic twins *may* have a prenatal environment which differs more than that of a given dizygotic pair (Sydow and Rinne, 1958) [23]. Despite these and other technical problems, studies of twins have provided us with some of the most impressive evidence on the relative effects of heredity and environment. The extensive literature of twin studies is well worth reading, but a look at even a few of the more significant studies is revealing.

Studies of intelligence have always been popular, and the typical differences found here are suggestive. The correlations of IQ scores between identical twins is close to .90, which is about the same as test-retest scores on the same person. Between fraternal twins the correlation is about .60, while the usual sibling relationship, as noted before, is on the order of .50 (Anastasi, 1958) [1].

Newman, Freeman, and Holzinger reported a number of comparisons on fifty pairs of identical twins reared together, fifty pairs of fraternal twins reared together, and nineteen pairs of identical twins reared apart. Correlations of height, weight and Binet IQ for fraternal twins ranged from .63 to .64 and for identical twins reared together from .88 to .93; for identical twins reared apart the correlations were .77 for IQ, .89 for weight, and .97 for height. The identicals were more alike whether reared together or apart than were the fraternals.

TABLE 4.5
Trait Correlations between Monozygotic Twins Reared Together and Apart, and Dizygotic Twins

Trait	MZ Twins Reared Together	MZ Twins Reared Apart	DZ Twins
Height	.94	.82	.44
Weight	.81	.37	.56
Intelligence	.76	.77	.51
Extraversion	.42	.61	.17
Neuroticism	.38	.53	.11

Adapted from Shields, J., 1962, *Monozygotic twins*. New York: Oxford University Press. Page 139.

In addition to the data shown in the table, Newman, Freeman, and Holzinger report other characteristics in which there was much greater consistency and similarity for the identicals than for the fraternals. Some of these characteristics were:

1. Physiology: blood pressure and heart rate;
2. Onset of menarche (first menstruations);
3. Longevity;
4. Capacity for and response to psychomotor activity, for example, sit-ups and jumping;
5. Pathological conditions: clubfoot, measles, diabetes, tuberculosis,

In a later evaluation of this and other evidence from similar studies it was found that the differences between identical twins reared apart were related to the relative quality of environment of each. Anastasi comments:

> The IQ differences . . . indicate the excess in favor of whichever twin received the better education. An examination of these IQ differences suggests

that, on the whole, they are not random differences such as might result from fortuitous factors, but rather tend to favor the better educated twin quite consistently (Anastasi, 1958) [1].

A recent English study generally supports the findings of the Newman, Freeman, and Holzinger research. Forty-four pairs of monozygotic twins brought up together were compared to an equal number reared apart, and a smaller number of dizygotic twins. Data on height-weight, intelligence, and some personality traits are set forth in Table 4.5. On all characteristics the monozygotic twins, whether brought up apart or together, showed sizable and significant correlations. There was little

TABLE 4.6

Concordance Rates in Monozygotic and Dizygotic Twins Summarized from Kallmann Studies

	Monozygotic Twins		*Dizygotic Twins*	
	N	%	N	%
Schizophrenia	268	86.2	685	14.5
Manic-depressive psychosis	23	95.7	52	26.3
Senile psychosis	33	42.8	75	8.0
Involutional psychosis	29	60.9	67	6.0
Homosexuality	40	100.0	45	11.5

Hurst, L. A., 1952, Research in genetics and psychiatry. New York State Psychiatric Institute: *Eugenical News,* 37: 86–89 [13].

difference between the reared-together and reared-apart groups, but the dizygotic pairs showed a much lower similarity (Shields, 1962) [19].

The power of inheritance extends beyond measured physical and mental performance to adjustment, at least adjustment as determined by diagnosed mental illness. Franz Kallmann of the New York State Psychiatric Institute has studied over 2500 pairs of twins of both kinds. Out of this large group he has isolated cases of behavioral disorders in monozygotic and dizygotic twins. When both of a pair have the disorder, they are said to be *concordant;* when it appears in only one of the pair, they are *discordant.* Table 4.6 shows the concordance of some disorders found by Kallmann in pairs of the two kinds of twins. Although the number of cases for all the disorders except schizophrenia is small, the differences between the types of twins is impressive indeed.

Evaluating the Research

Now we have examined some samples of research on the effects of inherited characteristics on various aspects of behavior. Is heredity the cause of behavior? Is environment the cause of behavior? Obviously, in the light of the evidence they are *both* causative. Once again, we must tell ourselves that the causes of behavior are multiple, complex, and interrelated. The forces of heredity endow the fertilized cell with developmental potentials in the form of structural and functional tendencies; some, such as color of eyes, cannot be altered or denied; some, such as growth rate of intelligence, may be retarded or modified somewhat by experiences; others, such as specific personality traits, may show little hereditary influence. We must think of heredity and environment not as inheritance *plus* experience, but as two interacting and interdependent forces which determine the characteristics of the organism at every stage of life. Tyler says:

> With the exception of a few simple physical characteristics, such as eye color, that depend upon genetic endowment alone, all human traits in which we are interested are produced through an interaction of heredity and environmental influences. . . . The most *usable* knowledge we can have with regard to any psychological characteristic is not the relative proportions of heredity and environment in its make-up, but how amenable it is to change, and under what circumstances we can expect changes to occur. One of the commonest misconceptions here is the idea that only the innate characteristics are fixed and unchangeable and that environmentally produced traits are modifiable at will. Neither part of the generalization is true. Hereditary tendencies can often be strikingly modified. Environmentally produced traits are often so firmly fixed that it is impossible to alter them. . . . We have come to realize that *all* traits, however they originate, are somehow built into the individual's nervous system. Since human beings show a considerable capacity for learning, most of these traits are subject to modification, but *both* heredity and previous experience set limits to its nature or amount. (Tyler, 1965) [25]

The Nature of Environment

The term environment is familiar to all of us, generally suggesting such things as socio-economic level of family, the kind of house lived in, or the quality of a community's schools. We will be examining these and other environmental factors in much of this book. But as we noted at the beginning of this chapter, "environment" begins at conception, not at birth; and the individual has a history at birth. Anastasi comments:

> The importance of the prenatal environment in determining the individual's development has been fully demonstrated. Variations in diet and nutrition, glandular secretions, and other physical conditions of the mother, for example, may exert a profound and lasting influence upon the development of the embryo. That the structural development of the organism is definitely influenced by early environmental factors is clearly indicated by a number of experimentally induced alterations in lower animals. (Anastasi, 1958) [1]

She cites studies in which a defective gene caused fruit flies to produce abnormal legs; the abnormality, however, will not appear under certain conditions of temperature. "Monsters" have been produced among fish by slowing down development at an early age through low temperatures, insufficient oxygen, or ultraviolet rays. Eye variations are produced in fish by altering the chemical composition of the water and the light. It should be noted, of course, that the prenatal environment is generally protective against the extremes of variation experimentally introduced to demonstrate the efficacy of environmental influences.

Since the prenatal months are obviously an important part of life, let us examine the typical course of development with an eye to factors which may affect later behavior.

PRENATAL DEVELOPMENT

The fertilization of the quiet ovum seems to endow it with something resembling energy and purpose. At any rate it suddenly becomes active, and in about three days it is moved by contractions down the ovarian tube to the uterus. The major activity of the newly fertilized cell at this time is cleavage—division into two cells, which in turn divide to become four, then eight, and on up to the immense number which is required to make up even the embryo's structure. (*Embryo* is the name given to the developing creature in the first two prenatal months.) On about the tenth day the developing mass of cells burrows its way into the blood-laden wall of the uterus. An irritation is apparently set up here, "clearing" an area on which the *placenta* develops. By the third week the placenta covers about a fifth of the area of the wall.

Words like "clearing," "burrows," "energy," and "purpose" come naturally to mind when describing the behavior of the newly fertilized egg. The terms are scientifically inaccurate, for the zygote is not a sentient, motivated being but a growing mass of cells with chemically controlled and directed characteristics. However unjustified scientifically, the words approximate the feelings of directness and efficiency which one perceives on studying the egg-becoming-embryo.

The placenta is a spongy mass of blood vessels attached, as we noted, to the uterine wall. The *umbilical cord* connects the placenta to the embryo, which by this time is enclosed in a fluid-filled, expanding envelope of tough tissue called the *amnion*. Here it will develop, protected from shocks and pressure until it is time to be born. The umbilicus is literally the lifeline of the growing organism; food and oxygen are transmitted from the mother's blood by the process of osmosis in the placenta to the child's blood through the umbilicus. Waste products are removed in the same (but reverse) fashion. You will note that there is no direct connection of blood or nerves or other tissue between the mother and her developing child. The recognition that they are separate helps us to abandon naive notions about the mother's thoughts or emotions "marking" the child, instilling interests, or attitudes, or modifying its disposition.

By the end of the first month the embryo is a small, soft creature about one-fourth of an inch long with bowed head, pointed tail, and nothing which could be called a face.

During the second month the embryo assumes more recognizable form and shape. In the beginning the greater part of the head is an expanding, bulbous brain. Below the brain, eyes bulge out from the side of the head, nasal pits appear and a wide mouth cavity develops accompanied on either side by gill-like slits. Inside the head the tongue and palate are formed. Within the body a cartilagineous structure forms; ossification later on will change this to the bones of the skeleton. The sexes are not distinct until the second month and even then the determination is difficult.

The second month of life closes with the stamp of human likeness implanted on the embryo. His face, although slightly grotesque, has a distinctly human character. Bones and muscles have given his body smooth contours as well as the ability to move. Sexual differences have arisen and the sex of the embryo can be determined. The internal organs are well laid down. During the remaining seven months, the chief changes will be largely growth and detailed development within each organ (Gilbert, 1938) [5].

Effect of Prenatal Environment

Development is a dynamic and on-going process which does not pause or hesitate for any cause short of death. The development of the embryo may be compared to construction of an automobile on a non-stoppable assembly line. A complete and perfect end-product depends on complete and perfect supply. Any failure of timing, of parts, any accidents or interruptions along the way would result in imperfect autos—one without doors, another without headlights, perhaps still another with a faulty engine. The embryo, like the auto, is developing "parts" of its structure and the mother is the "supplier." The analogy, like most, is imperfect, for the supply is not of parts but of nutrition, oxygen, and water; and development is growth and not assembly.

Recent research with animals as well as studies of human mothers has suggested the theory that many structural abnormalities are the product, not of bad inheritance, but of stress or insult to the developing embryo. Theodore Ingalls, of the Harvard School of Public Health, offers evidence that stress occuring during a specific phase of development will cause malformations or deformities of whatever part or parts of the structure are in a crucial phase at that time. Thus, insult in the first week will produce a "cyclops" or one-eyed monster. Damage in the second week will produce Siamese, or joined, twins. The third week sees the development of arm and leg "buds" and the formation of the tubes which will form the heart; stress at this time will produce heart and limb abnormalities. In the fourth week a variety of parts is developing, but the most common deficiency produced is an imperfectly formed or functioning trachea. In the fifth week the face is beginning to form; harelip (a divided upper lip), cataract, and other abnormalities of the outer layers of cells would be produced. A variety of malformations seem to be produced in the sixth week, especially if the mother suffers from the virus causing Rubella (German measles). In the seventh week cleft palate may result from damage, as well as microcephaly (abnormally small head). In the eighth week an arresting of or interfering with neural development seems to be a cause of mongoloid idiocy (now called Down's syndrome) [3] as well as a host of other difficulties (Ingalls, 1957) [14]. Whether or not further research supports the entire theory, there is adequate present evidence to prove that many abnormalities and malfunctions are products of the embryo's intrauterine development.

The terms "stress" and "insult" have been used in connection with the discussion of intrauterine damage. They refer to any circumstance which may interfere with optimum development of the embryo. Interference with the normal supply of oxygen in the mother's blood will have immediate and generally permanent ill effects. Nutritional deficiency in the mother naturally is passed on to the embryo in terms of an inadequate supply of the fuel for growth. This inadequacy may be qualitative as well as quantitative—lack of a specific vitamin or food element, a metabolic or digestive upset which interferes with the mother's manufacture of all necessary elements, an unwise choice of food during early pregnancy. Some viruses will be transmitted to the embryo through the placenta; one of the worst-known villains is the virus of Rubella. Drugs or anesthetic agents may also sometimes be transmitted with bad effect. Auto accidents, falls, and the like occasionally cause partial dislodgment of the placenta with a resulting shortage of food and oxygen. Indeed, the quality of the environment provided by the mother is influenced by her structure, bodily functioning, health, and personal habits, even her emotional status as it affects her metabolic and digestive processes. Harrell, Woodyard, and Gates studied the effect of mother's diet

[3] It should be noted that Rubella is only one of several hypothesized causes of mongolism or Down's syndrome. Various chromosomal abnormalities have been identified as a cause also.

on the intelligence of offspring. Twelve hundred pregnant women were given certain vitamins while the same number of controls received placebos (sugar pills). The nearly 1500 children resulting from these pregnancies were given intelligence tests at ages three and four. The children whose mothers had the enriched diet made higher scores which were statistically highly significant (Harrell *et al.*, 1955) [10].

Insult or stress in the first two months is, then, likely to produce gross abnormalities or malfunctions, while stress later is likely to have more of an effect on "quality" of development.

The Fetal Stage

After the end of the eighth week, the developing organism is called a *fetus*. Growth in size is not so rapid as it was in the embryonic stage. In the first two months growth was to 350 times original ovum size, while the rest of life sees an increase of about 35 times the size at the end of the embryonic period.

In the third and fourth month, the fetus grows six to eight inches in length, reaching about half of birth length. Proportions, as well as size, change. At two months the head is half the body; by three to five months it is a third; by birth, a fourth; and by maturity, only a tenth. The reason for the early large development of the head, of course, is the relatively large brain and central nervous system of the human being.

Research on discharged or operatively removed fetuses shows that by eight to nine weeks the nervous system and general structure is mature enough to produce flexion or movement in response to stimulation (Hooker, 1952) [11].

That it is not ready for life outside the womb does not mean that the early-stage fetus is just a fungus-like, parasitic blob, growing inside the host mother. It is dynamic and individual, already a being in its own right.

The fetus is developing as well as growing in size. In the third month the male develops sexually (although the testes do not descend into the scrotum until the seventh month), while the female sex organs wait until the fourth month to begin maturing. The tooth buds are laid down, vocal cords appear, and the digestive system (including kidneys) begins to function. In appearance the fetus is bony, dark red and wrinkled of skin, with closed eyes and plugged nostrils in a face covered with lanugo (colorless hair). He is not inhuman in appearance and by now has well-formed hands and feet (Gilbert, 1938) [6].

In the fifth month the body axis straightens and hair and nails appear. If aborted at five months, it will breathe, cry, and die. The lungs are too immature to function efficiently or long, but the principal difficulty lies in the immaturity of the brain and central nervous system;

there simply is not adequate control from the lower brain centers (Gilbert, 1938) [7]. Except for grasp, voice, and special sense responses, the fetus now has most of the reflexes of the newborn.

From fifteen weeks on, development is remarkable for rapidly increasing vigor. Not only are responses and reflexes present, but spontaneous movement begins and by the eighteenth to twentieth week can be felt by the mother. Before long movements will be so vigorous that they may be observed on the abdomen itself (Hooker, 1952) [12]. During the sixth month the eyelids open over completely formed eyes; the taste buds are present and developed; and the lungs mature enough so that they can function for a few hours at least.

By the seventh month there has been enough maturing of the nervous system to sustain the direct life-processes of breathing, swallowing, digestion of food, and the like. The seven-month baby is not pretty; it usually is about sixteen inches long with a weight of three pounds and is red-skinned, wrinkled, and old-looking. With modern hospital care, many if not most seven-month babies can survive birth (Gilbert, 1938) [8].

The last two months are spent in improving the "beauty" of the creature and in general maturing. During each month it gains about two pounds in weight and two inches in height. The fine body hair disappears, the nails grow, and the taste buds regress. By the end of the ninth month, it is usually lying head down and rump up with the back parallel to the mother's back and with bent legs and arms close to the chest.

PRENATAL FUNCTIONING AND POSTNATAL BEHAVIOR

Although speculation has been common, little sound research has been done on the relation between measured prenatal states and later behavior. The Fels Institute, however, has collected data on a limited number of subjects from prebirth to adolescence.

One measurable prenatal characteristic is quick fetal activity (arms and legs). This activity was studied in twenty-four males during the last two months of fetal life. The same group of males was studied in nursery school at age two and one-half years. The level of fetal activity was found to be negatively related to degree of aggression at that age, and positively related to social apprehension—shyness, fearfulness, and anxiety in groups, and so forth. This trait in early childhood in another group of subjects was found to be predictive of social apprehension at ages 22 to 25 years.

In another phase of this institute's work, fetal heart instability was found to be predictive of later heart instability at 14 to 18 years. Resting heart instability at 18 was found in turn to be statistically related to problems of dependency, achievement-striving, compulsive behavior, and anxiety over erotic activity (Sontag, 1963) [21].

Certainly, not too much should be made of these studies of a limited number of subjects, but the evidence is strongly suggestive of a continuing relationship between prenatal status and later measured personality traits. Research will continue in this area.

Birth

The foregoing content emphasizes the fact that behavior begins, not at birth, but at conception; birth is simply one incident (albeit a major one) in the life history of an individual.

About 280 days from the onset of the last menstrual period the fetus is likely to be discharged and become a neonate (the name which we give to the newborn during its first week or ten days). (Only 10 percent of children are born on this particular day, but about 75 percent are born within two weeks of this day.) Some time before birth rhythmic contractions begin in the mother's abdominal walls. These become very powerful just before birth. The amniotic bag ruptures, the fluid is discharged, and the fetus begins to be pushed out of the mother through the birth canal, along with the placenta, amnion, and other materials in the uterus. This is an arduous and hazardous experience, but the flexible and yielding nature of the structure adjusts itself to the canal and birth is usually accomplished safely. Occasionally, for medical reasons, the fetus is surgically removed through an incision made in the abdomen. This is called a Caesarian section, from the Roman law *Lex Caesarea* requiring the operation in certain cases.

Birth Damage

One of the great environmental hazards in life comes during the birth process. The human fetus is relatively large in comparison to the mother's size, and in comparison to other creatures has an extraordinarily large head. This proportion, of course, is due to the large and well-developed brain. Man's greatest advantage over other creatures is, at the time of birth, a great disadvantage. The rhythmic contractions of the uterine wall and the birth canal put considerable pressure on the fetus which is being passed. These contractions sometimes rupture blood vessels in the brain and cause actual structural damage to the brain. The tissue of the nervous system is peculiar in that damage is more or less permanent. Destroyed nerve tissue does not regenerate itself; and unless new, substitute pathways can be found in the brain or nervous system, sensation or function is permanently lost. Most common of the disorders following brain damage is cerebral palsy, which may take the form of partial paralysis, spasticity, or other malfunctions. Another source of danger is oxygen deprivation. The fetus, of course, secures its oxygen through osmosis from the mother; but as soon as the placenta is dislodged, the supply is cut off. Ordinarily, the fetus is discharged first and quickly begins to breathe and supply its own oxygen. Occasionally, however, something may alter or interfere with this process—the umbilicus may be entangled about the throat of the fetus, the placenta may be discharged first, respiration may not begin immediately—and the resulting oxygen lack may have as profound an effect on the brain as pressure damage.

The serious effects of anoxia were revealed in one study of 355 three-year-old children. Some had suffered anoxia at birth while others had experienced normal births. Abnormalities were present in 25 percent of the anoxic, but in less than seven percent of the normal-birth group. The anoxic were poorer in all cognitive functions, Stanford-Binet intelligence scores and especially in verbal concepts (Graham, 1962) [9].

The Neonate

Except to parents, neonates are not very prepossessing in appearance. The head is relatively large for the body, and it may be somewhat misshapen from the birth pressures. Legs and arms are spiderlike and are usually drawn up toward the potbellied trunk. The skin is usually a lobster red. The stereotype of the pink and white, plump and cute infant is gained from pictures or observation of two- or three-month old infants—not from neonates!

The first ten days are spent in shifting over the system from a parasitic existence to an independent one. As a result, the first week or two of life usually sees a weight loss. The neonate—and the young infant in general—spends most of his time sleeping, with an increased level of activity as the need for food increases. His movements are random and undirected except for the nipple-seeking activity of the head, mouth, and lips. He has no emotions per se but only generalized excitement stemming from internal causes—hunger and digestive processes.

The nervous system of the neonate functions on a very primitive level. As a result, he apparently responds only in a very general fashion to light, to noise, to temperature changes, and to other stimuli. "Response" is simply generalized body jerks, rather than specific or meaningful movements. The apparent great strength of grip (about 10 percent can be lifted by one hand) which is the pride of so many fathers is actually a symptom of a very immature nervous system and usually disappears in about six months (Pratt, 1954) [17].

AN END AND A BEGINNING

This then is our brief history of life to birth. What has our examination profited us? We have seen at work the forces that shape behavior through all the life span: inheritance providing the raw material and environment shaping and forming it. Birth simply provides a new, greater, and more varied opportunity for both to function. The design for growth and development is there in the neonate; and the physical, social world is waiting to channel or diffuse, to prod or hold back as experience may determine.

But we know that this newborn creature is not a *tabula rasa,* is no blank photographic plate waiting to be developed. It has already lived part of its life, and is already in part a product of its experiences.

Suggested Collateral Readings

Carmichael, L., The onset and early development of behavior, in L. Carmichael, *Manual of child psychology,* 2d ed. New York: John Wiley & Sons, Inc., 1954. Pages 60–187.

Davis, M. E., Ovulation and fertility, in M. Fishbein and R. J. R. Kennedy, *Modern marriage and family living.* New York: Oxford University Press, 1957. Pages 357–367.

Fuller, J. L., and W. R. Thompson, *Behavior genetics.* New York: John Wiley & Sons, Inc., 1960. Especially Chapters 2, 7, 8, 9, and 10.

Gilbert, M. S., *Biography of the unborn.* Baltimore: The Williams & Wilkins Company, 1938.

Montagu, A., *Human heredity,* 2d ed. Cleveland: The World Publishing Co., 1963.

Munn, N. L., *The evolution and growth of human behavior,* 2d ed. Boston: Houghton Mifflin Company, 1965. Chapters 2 and 6.

Penrose, L. S., *Outline of human genetics,* 2d ed. New York: John Wiley & Sons, Inc., 1963.

Sinnott, E. W., *Cell and psyche.* Chapel Hill: University of North Carolina, 1950.

References

1. Anastasi, Anne, 1958, *Differential psychology,* 3d ed. New York: Crowell-Collier and Macmillan, Inc. Page 64.
2. Bayley, Nancy, 1954, Some increasing parent-child similarities during the growth of children. *J. educ. Psychol.,* 45: 19.
3. Cole, L. E., 1953, *Human behavior.* Yonkers-on-Hudson, N.Y.: World Book Co. (New York: Harcourt, Brace & World, Inc.). Page 85. Adapted from Newman, H. H., F. N. Freeman, and K. J. Holzinger, *Twins: A study of heredity and environment.* University of Chicago, 1937.
4. Galton, F., 1889, *Natural inheritance.* New York: Crowell-Collier and Macmillan, Inc.
5. Gilbert, Margaret S., 1938, *Biography of the unborn.* Baltimore: The Williams & Wilkins Co. Page 51.

6. ———, page 65.
7. ———, page 76.
8. ———, page 89.
9. Graham, Frances K., 1962, Development three years after perinatal anoxia and other potentially damaging newborn experiences. *Psychol. Monogr.,* **76:** 1–53.
10. Harrell, Ruth F., Elda Woodyard, and A. I. Gates, 1955, *The effect of mother's diets on intelligence of offspring.* New York: Bureau of Publications, Teachers College, Columbia University.
11. Hooker, D., 1952, *The prenatal origin of behavior.* Lawrence: University of Kansas Press.
12. Hooker, page 71.
13. Hurst, L. A., 1952, Research in genetics and psychiatry. New York State Psychiatric Institute: *Eugen. News,* **37:** 86–89.
14. Ingalls, T. H., 1957, Congenital deformities. *Scientific American,* **197:** 109–116.
15. Munn, N. 1965, *The Evolution and growth of human behavior,* 2d ed. Boston: Houghton Mifflin Company.
16. Newman, H. H., F. N. Freeman, and K. J. Holzinger, 1937, *Twins: A study of heredity and environment.* Chicago: University of Chicago Press.
17. Pratt, C. C., 1954, "The neonate," in Carmichael, L., *et al., Manual of child psychology.* New York: John Wiley & Sons, Inc. Pages 215–291.
18. Roff, M., 1950, Intra-family resemblances in personality characteristics. *J. Psychol.,* **30:** 199–227.
19. Shields, J., 1962, *Monozygotic twins.* New York: Oxford University Press.
20. Sims, V. M., 1931, The influence of blood relationship and common environment on measured intelligence. *J. educ. Psychol.,* **22:** 56–65.
21. Sontag, L. W., 1963, Somatopsychics of personality and body function. *Vita Humana,* **6:** 1–10.
22. Stern, C., 1960, *Principles of human genetics,* 2d ed. San Francisco: W. H. Freeman and Company.
23. Sydow, von, G., and A. Rinne, 1958, Very unequal "identical" twins. *Acta Pediatrica,* **67:** 163–171.
24. Tryon, R. C., 1940, Genetic differences in maze learning ability in rats. *Yearbook of National Society for the Study of Education,* **39.**
25. Tyler, Leona E., 1965, *The psychology of human differences,* 3d ed. New York: Appleton-Century-Crofts. Abridged from pages 447–449. Copyright © 1965 by Meredith Publishing Company. Printed by permission of Appleton-Century-Crofts.

CHAPTER 5

Perception and Self-awareness

A baby who has reached his first birthday has already developed a considerable feeling of acquaintance with his world. It is a world inhabited by many objects which he has identified more or less to his satisfaction. But an increasing number of new things intrude upon his attention. This has especially been true for him during the past few months. When he is down on the floor, there is a bit of fuzz which he must inspect. He observes a hole in some furniture and feels compelled to probe it with his finger. An occasional object needs to be tasted before his curiosity about it is satisfied.

The world's boundaries become more and more extended as the baby grows and develops, and the objects that confront him multiply. Soon he is a toddler—instead of a baby who creeps, then crawls—and a whole new sphere for observation opens up to him. His determination to find the meaning in things will often delight his elders; sometimes it will alarm them. But follow what may, he must make the unfamiliar familiar . . . things must be identified!

Thus it is with every individual as he enters upon the lifelong process of "structuring" his world. This is inescapably a part of his life—*observing and identifying* objects and happenings.[1] This is *perception*. More formally stated, perception is an awareness, or a process of becoming aware, of objects or events—or characteristics—by means of sensory operations under the influence of *set* and/or prior experience (English and English, 1958) [10].

Perception is a highly complex process, which, as we shall see, in-

[1] The student will benefit by examining this sentence in the context of Chapter 11. Observation and identification are closely articulated with *differentiation* and *classification* which are central to thinking. Structuring and classification definitely have much in common.

volves considerably more than the fact that there are "things to see and eyes with which to see them." Some individuals quite obviously "see" more than others; some see if not more at least very differently; some see and enjoy where others in the selfsame surroundings are little impressed by what their senses report. Improved knowledge of this process is clearly a high-priority requirement for teachers if they are to deal successfully with children and youth. It is significant that during the last two decades perception has been accorded more space in research publications than any other problem of psychology—and properly so, as this chapter is intended to show.[2]

The comment just made regarding the heightened tempo of research on perception should not suggest that this phenomenon has only recently engaged the serious attention of students of human behavior. Actually, as several writers have shown, the study of perception has a long history. Solly and Murphy (1960) [31] have reported considerable interest, "among sensitive early observers of man's modes of contact with reality" dating before the time of Plato. Not all such observers were Greeks; the philosophers of India were also notably sensitive to the importance of perception.

Of significance to our present interest is not only the fact that the study of perception has a considerable history but that the history we are talking about rounded a corner, so to speak, when the idea began to dawn that man does not admit into his mind *miniatures* of reality. Stated differently, the study of perception gained momentum when students of the problem could understand that perception involves the assimilating, or reconstructing, of reality from disparate lights, sounds, pressures, tastes, and so forth.[3] With such realization, thinkers could begin to employ the empirical tactics of science. With this advancement in knowledge, the problem of perception was not left solely to speculation; it could be subjected to experimentation. But, to repeat a remark the authors have already made, "perception is an amazingly complex process"; after hundreds of years of study much remains obscure.

Some Major Questions about Perception

Inherent in the definition of perception, as given in the preceding section, are numerous questions. There are, for example, such questions as the role of sensations and the sense organs in an individual's observations of his surroundings; the manner in which meanings derive from

[2] For a comprehensive treatment of the many-sidedness of perception, see Dember, W. N., *The psychology of perception,* New York: Holt, Rinehart and Winston, Inc., 1960.

[3] For an interesting historical treatment, see Solly, C. M., and G. Murphy, *Development of the perceptual world,* New York: Basic Books, Inc., 1960, Chapter 1.

the individual's contacts, via his sense organs, with the objects around him; and the degree to which a person's present needs and past experiences influence his perceptions. These are questions that will be dealt with in the pages that follow.

Especially important—and difficult—is the problem of how the infant first "gets in touch" meaningfully with his world. How does he first discover relationships in the welter of sensory stimuli that bombard him and how does he from such a beginning develop the structure that becomes his own private world, never to be shared completely with other persons? Let us examine first of all these last-stated questions.

FIRST DEVELOPMENTS IN PERCEPTION

The year-old baby whose perceptual responses were briefly described at the beginning of this chapter had already become "proprietor" of a world of his own—a world in which there were for him, after so short a time, many familiar objects. In this brief span of twelve months he had acquired a perceptual scheme—or system of expectations—with which to deal with objects and the relationships among them. He had, in other words, become a relatively adept perceiver of the things of his world. But *how does an infant's perceiving get started,* and what sort of initial experiences does he have with his surroundings? This is a question for which conjecture must of necessity supply much of the answer in the absence of objective evidence: Neonates, and very young infants, cannot be interviewed about their perceptual experiences.

When we first lift the infant into our arms and carefully support his back and head he shows no signs of fixing his attention on anything around him. In fact, his eyes are not well coordinated; they move with a considerable degree of independence. At best—we must infer—his eyes simply catch the unassociated punctuations of brightness which light stimuli produce. There are for him, therefore, no surroundings of differentiable, meaningful objects.

But on the positive side we may infer that the neonate's eyes and ears are already equipped with the various, delicate "recording" parts on which stimuli make sensitive contacts, undifferentiated though they may be. He also has much of the necessary equipment to receive sensations of cold, of warmth, and of pain or pressure. The new baby does not lack the parts to be a receiver of "outside" stimuli.

We may infer, too, that the neonate's receiving "mechanisms" for stimuli from inside him are in similarly good working order. Warm milk trickling down from his mouth is satisfying to him; a well-filled stomach changes his behavior from crying and restlessness to peacefulness and sleepiness. Gas in his stomach or a cramp in his body tissues are among the kinds of inner distress that register forcefully if not meaningfully on his awareness.

During the first few days of his life the infant's experience would appear to consist of a series of disturbances of equilibrium. His comfortable stomach becomes uncomfortable; his warm, dry "nest" becomes damp and cold; his head gets into a bad position and his neck muscles hurt; bright lights flick on and not only startle him but hurt his eyes; loud, sudden noises break into his quietude. Sensations come and go but the circumstances that cause them have for him not the slightest relationship. Nevertheless, these sensations—his initiation into postnatal life—eventually occur in an order and under such circumstances that the first strands of meaning for the infant begin to be formed. From such beginnings, we must suppose, perception gets its start in an individual's life.

Initial Steps Toward Meaning

In the midst of the confusion of stimuli, the infant establishes contacts that bring gratification with them. For example, his mouth engages a nipple and the satisfaction that milk gives him is at least a beginning toward meaningful awareness. Stimuli arising from areas of his mouth and stomach may well be the first to register at the level of differentiable experience. In addition, among the earliest of his satisfactions are those he derives from rocking motions and his contacts with warm, soft objects. In some undetermined manner sensations such as these affect the neurophysiological structure that underlies the infant's perceptual capacities and the eventual result is meaningful awareness.

Early Differential Responses

By the end of the second week, the neonate can distinguish between cold and warm milk and between sour and sweet substances placed in his mouth. Sometime before the end of the third week infants generally are capable of avoidance reactions to such irritating stimuli as acetic acid and the smell of ammonia. It has been shown experimentally that infants will respond to sound within a few days after birth. Color discrimination becomes evident after the first half month of age; in general, it seems fairly well defined by about three months of age. Discrimination between saturated colors of green, yellow, red, and blue is evident among infants a year of age. They characteristically show a preferential response to red (Staples, 1932) [33].

The ability to fix objects in space and to respond differentially to distances depends considerably upon the convergance of the eyes in binocular vision. Such convergence is possible for infants near the end of the second month of age (Ling, 1942) [25]. It is not until much later, however, that the child in any very real sense "inhabits" space or localizes objects in space. These are steps in perceptual development which he can take only after he is able to locomote in space—when, at a year of age or thereabouts, he begins to crawl.

Are Any Perceptual Abilities Present from Birth? There is a question that quite naturally arises in connection with our thinking about the earlier phases of perceptual development. It is the question of whether any perceptual abilities are present from birth. Research in this area is quite limited but some important pioneering work has been reported. Following is a brief summary of one such research.

Gibson and Walk (1960) [14] investigated the idea that the ability to perceive depth is present in young humans and animals who have not had experience in "depth perception." For this purpose they developed some equipment which they called the "visual cliff." The equipment consists of a large section of glass supported by a tablelike structure. A thin board divides the glass into equal areas. Under one area a section of material is attached directly to the glass, thus giving the appearance of solidness and shallowness. Under the other area, the material is placed on the floor of the "table" some three or four feet beneath the surface of the glass. The visual effect is that of a cliff, since over the edge it appears three-dimensional; that is, it has "depth." The infants who were the subjects of the study refused to cross over the "deep side" when coaxed by their mothers, a fact which tends to support the conclusion of the investigators that the ability to perceive depth is probably present from birth. Other experiments with different species of animals, some only a few hours old, yielded similar results; that is, the refusal to cross over the "deep side" of the two-area equipment.

Differential Response to Persons. At what age can a baby distinguish a person from other objects in his surroundings? One answer is "probably not as soon as most fond relatives suppose." Buhler (1930) [5] reported that by the third month babies she observed were responding to grown persons by smiling. Gesell and Ilg indicated that at twelve weeks the baby "knows mother and recognizes her" (Gesell and Ilg, 1949) [13]. Spitz (1946) [32], attempting to learn whether infants could distinguish between the face of a person and the representations of facial expressions in various masks, concluded that infants seemed to make such differentiations between three months and six months of age. By the end of his first half year the baby may be expected to note characteristics that distinguish unfamiliar persons from those he has often seen. He is by that time capable of being frightened by an unfamiliar face or by a strange item of wearing apparel on an otherwise recognizable relative.

In general, person-awareness is not a sudden emergence in a baby's development. Gradually, from his experience of the things, for example, that his mother does to him (the satisfactions of being fed, warmed, fondled, rocked, sung to) there emerges for him a particular person-awareness. Also, with similar gradualness there begins to dawn the recognition that not all such perceptions add up to only one person. There are noticeable clues—stimulus differences—to distinguish the things people do to him: differences between the ways different people touch him or pick him up or rock him, the ways they speak to him, the ways they look at him. He has begun to "sense" some of these differences even before his eyes furnish him much help in the process. But, as indicated in the findings of Buhler and of Spitz, by the age of three or four months he is ready with the aid of his eyes to begin compounding various sensory stimuli into the awareness of differences among persons.

Discovery that Objects Are Enduring

The infant's discovery that there are enduring objects in his world is for him the beginning of perceptual order and stability. Through manipulation of various objects he becomes aware of certain of their differentiable features, and presently the fact dawns upon him that these objects with their identifiable characteristics appear and reappear in his experience. Thus, his perceptual world begins to be object-inhabited as well as person-inhabited.

Perception of Objects in Terms of Their Functioning

Various writers have called attention to the fact that for the baby an object *is* what the object can do and more especially for the very young baby what it can do to him. ". . . throughout infancy only those objects, and only those aspects of objects which have some behavioral meaning, some functional relevance, become differentiated for the baby" (Stone and Church, 1957) [34]. The writers just quoted speak of the persistence beyond babyhood of this tendency to perceive *action-objects* rather than things in themselves. They illustrate the point with the preschool child's definition, "a chair is to sit." We may speculate that even in adulthood there is considerable inclination to define a thing in terms of its action properties. Stripped of a few verbal refinements, the layman's definition of an atom might be, "It is to split." There is laid down in the beginning of the individual's awareness of the things of this world the element of function—of "what's it for?" and, especially, "what will it do to, or for, me?"

Objects are also responded to by the very young child in terms of what he can do to them. He begins to perceive them in this light when at about four months of age he grasps them and puts them in his mouth. At approximately seven months of age an object which he can get in his hands is likely to be something to bang against other objects; if the result is a not-too-loud noise, so much the better.

Of such are the beginnings of the individual's *expectations* about objects. Expectation becomes the core to perceiving—the controlling element in his observing and identifying of the things of his world.

ORIGINS OF PERCEPTUAL EXPECTANCY

An individual's expectations control his attention and determine what he will notice and respond to and the sort of response he will make. Out of his "living and learning" he develops his "system" of expectations. The more learning he has acquired—that is to say, the more he has been forced by his experiences to modify his responses—the more expanded and refined his system of expectations becomes.

To the infant a certain white object being proferred by someone leaning over his crib immediately arouses expectations. They are expectations of having his hunger satisfied. (More accurately, his expectations will thus be aroused if he does at that moment feel hungry. *Need,* as we shall soon see, enters into the situation.) Expectations give the set to the baby's behavior; they determine what will be in the focus of his attention. Other possible stimuli such as the white sleeve of a nurses' uniform or the soft tread of the mother's feet as she approaches the crib are at first not relevant to the baby's expectations. They quickly become so, however, if they regularly occur in association with the milk. They become cues that tell him what to expect, and his expectations give the *set* to his responses.

But cues can be deceiving. The baby will encounter surprises in his expectations. The white sleeve does not always mean that milk is about to be offered to him. Nor is the soft tread of feet to be relied upon as a sign that milk is present. In such moments there is learning—the learning that results from the need to differentiate between clues and then to reorganize their pattern. Perception involves a continuous process of cue refinement and reclassification—of guessing about cues and of correcting the guesses.

We shall return later in this chapter to the topic of guessing as an element in perception. Before we do this, we need to look into the role that is played in perception by the system of sense organs—the means by which the individual receives stimuli from his surroundings.

DEPENDENCE OF PERCEPTION ON THE SENSE ORGANS

A little girl once asked her mother, "Where would the world go if I did not have eyes to see it?" The question has two apparent implications. One is that the world would not have meaning except insofar as the little girl herself was there to give it meaning. The other is that there would be no world were there no eyes with which to see it.

If to some readers this child's question seems a little naïve, perhaps it is that they have not given much thought to what their world would be like if they lacked one or more of their sense organs. The importance of the role that is played by them is well expressed in the following quotation:

> Every student of psychology knows that his awareness of the world is completely dependent on the activity of his sense organs, although sometimes he does not realize that this is a startling fact and not a commonplace one. He tends to take for granted the familiar world which he sees before him, not realizing that in all its aspects and in every detail it is apprehended only because his sense organs are functioning, and that if these functions failed for any reason, so also would his awareness of the world. (Gibson, 1948) [15]

Quality of Behavior Related to Sense-organ Functioning

Tommy, a third-grader, performed in school like a dull boy. He stumbled through his reading and showed a growing dislike for it. Even his comments about the pictures in the reading books suggested that he was mentally dull. In many respects his responses were markedly different from those of his classmates.

Fortunately, Tommy had an unusually observant and well-informed teacher. She noticed signs of intelligence much above the level of the youngster's responses to reading. She observed his habit of squinting as he looked at various objects and she noted that he frequently kept one eye closed as he tried to look at something.

When an appointment was made for Tommy with an eye doctor, it was discovered that his fusion of visual stimuli was bad. Each eye got a separate image; when Tommy tried to use both eyes, the result was a blurred impression. When he used only one eye, he managed to avoid some of the blurring effect; but a different condition was present, namely, the lessening of his accuracy in judging distance and depth.

Corrective measures were taken by Tommy's doctor, and in time his eyes worked in perfect harmony and his visual images were fused. Objects took on a new appearance for him; it was then pleasurable for him to examine pictures and to study their details. Furthermore, it was gratifying to him to realize that what others reported seeing he too could see.

This being an actual case, it can here be stated that in a relatively short time Tommy became an excellent reader and one of the top students in his class. The world that Tommy had been perceiving was to a considerable extent the world of his faulty sight.[4]

Other sense organs play comparable roles in determining people's experiences and the kinds of world they know. Many children considered mentally dull have been found to be deaf or hard of hearing. Their world can greatly be changed when their hearing is improved.

Contrastingly, there are fortunate individuals who are highly gifted in their abilities to receive and to respond to the sound of their world. Because they hear sounds so well, they are able to reproduce them in music and in various other ways better than most people. There are, for example, those who have perfect pitch and, given the opportunity to make use of this gift in musical training, are that much more likely to perform well.

Similar importance attaches to the quality of other kinds of sensory data in people's awareness and interpretation of the objects and events around them. The quality of a person's experience is in large measure determined by the quality of the sensory components in his perceptions.

Sensory Precision and the Properties of Object

Our sense organs work with amazing precision. This applies even to some which we are most inclined to take for granted, such as those involved in the sense of touch.

Close to the surface of the skin lie many hundreds of tiny nerve endings which are sensitive to tactile (touch) stimuli. The precision with which they function is illustrated in a motorist's ability to identify objects beside him in the car seat without the slightest glance at them. Had he not remembered putting his sun glasses there he would, nevertheless, have identified them almost instantly by touching his fingers to them and noting their form and texture.

Texture and form are but two among the various physical properties we attribute to objects. Others are weight, density, position, brightness, and color. There are also in the chemical nature of some objects certain properties that give rise to sensations of odor and taste. Still other properties make sound possible.

By his experiences of the properties of objects, a person gains famil-

[4] During the half dozen years since the sketch about Tommy was written, he has graduated from college and has begun work on a medical degree. There should be no surprise about the fact that he hopes eventually to specialize in eye surgery. Both child and society are enriched by an observant and persevering teacher like the one described.

iarity with his world. Man, the most far-roving of all creatures, is additionally fortunate in having sense organs that are highly receptive to a wide range of stimuli thus providing him apparently limitless perspective on his world.

Interrelationship of Sense-organ Functioning. Another characteristic of the functioning of the sense organs, besides precision, is that of interrelatedness. For example, we are so accustomed to seeing objects at the same time that we touch them that we frequently make comments such as "It 'looks' soft" or "It 'looks' heavy." When we relate how something tastes we are more often than not actually giving our impressions of its odors and its consistency. "It 'tastes' sort of burned and sticky" we may complain—mentioning two qualities neither of which our gustatory (taste) sense is capable of reporting.

So simple an act as reaching for a doorknob illustrates the extent to which we rely on the interrelationship of sense-organ functioning. The distance is "measured off" both by the retinal images in the eyes and by the "feel" that goes with the extending of the parts of the arm, hand, and fingers.

The richness of our perceptions depends considerably upon this factor of coordinate functioning of the sense organs. What we see with our eyes alone is likely to be much less meaningful than what we "see," for example, when our fingers assist with the process. In the same moment and as part of the same act of awareness, our various sensory impressions of a given object may—and generally do—merge into a single perception.

Perception is, above all else, an orderly process. It is a process in which organization and pattern prevail over multitudinousness, variability, and incompleteness in the stimuli that register on the sense organs.

PATTERN IN THE PERCEPTUAL FIELD

There is an important theory which correlates with the idea that the perceiver is an active organizer of stimuli. It is that in every individual there exists the tendency to find structure, a pattern of relationships, in any given stimulus situation. The stimulus situation is often referred to by psychologists as the *perceptual field.* Within a perceptual field there may be said to be *figure* and *ground,* the former being that aspect of the stimulus situation which for the individual is predominant (seen in the sharpest relief) and the latter being the perceptual background, the less differentiated parts of the stimulus field.

When describing the way perception occurs, many psychologists make use of the term *Gestalt,* which means pattern, organization, or the configuration of wholes. A Gestaltist explanation of perception holds that a person does not perceive a thousand and one minutae as he observes the objects of his surroundings, but rather that he tends to see wholes—total configurations—in which certain features stand out relatively clearly against what for the moment is a contrasting, undifferentiated mass. In other words, individuals tend as perceivers to find structure in the fields of stimuli which they confront at any given moment.

Perceptual Patterning

The tendency to find pattern in a stimulus field is evident in one's reaction to such figures as are presented below.

Several principles have been suggested by Gestalt psychologists [5] to explain the perceptual phenomena illustrated in Figures 5.1 to 5.5.

Proximity. In Figure 5.1 the dots above A appear to be arranged in horizontal rows; those above *B* seem to be in vertical columns. The

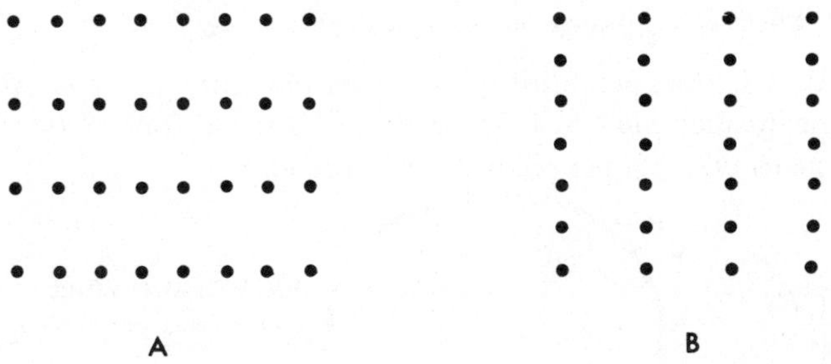

A B

FIGURE 5.1. Effect of proximity on perceptual patterning. After Hilgard, 1957 [17].

reason for these impressions is that the dots above *A* are in closer proximity in the *rows* than in the columns; the reverse of this is true in the dots above *B*.

Similarity. In Figure 5.2 proximity is not a controlling factor, but similarity now influences what we see. It is easier for us to perceive a pattern of horizontal rows than a pattern of vertical columns of alternating *m*'s and *n*'s.

Continuity. The compelling influence of continuity as a factor in perception will be apparent to the reader if he attempts to *see* either the organization *abefik* . . . or the organization *cdghjl* . . . as compared with the "natural" ones *acegij* . . . and *bdfhk* . . . in Figure 5.3. The

[5] See, for example, Beardslee and Wertheimer, *Readings in perception,* Selection 8, pages 115–135.

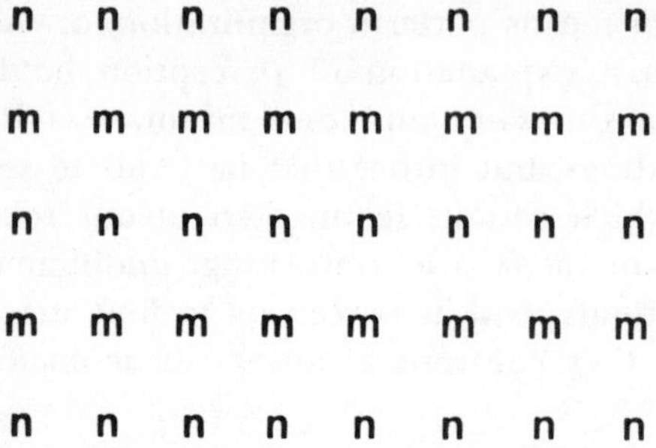

n n n n n n n n

m m m m m m m m

n n n n n n n n

m m m m m m m m

n n n n n n n n

FIGURE 5.2. Effect of similarity on perceptual patterning.

first two may not yield to his efforts to perceive them until he reproduces them separately with pencil and paper.

Closure. To look at Figure 5.4 is to see it as a circle. To concede

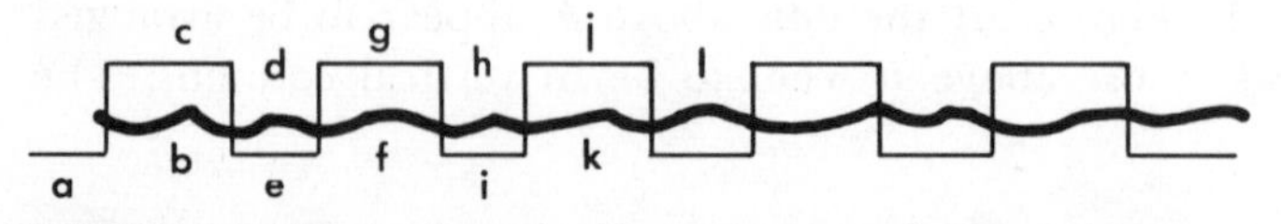

FIGURE 5.3. Effect of continuity on perceptual patterning.

to oneself that it does not quite close does not alter the over-all impression that the proper idea of it is "a circle." Indeed, one may experience a strong urge to take his pencil and fill in the gap.

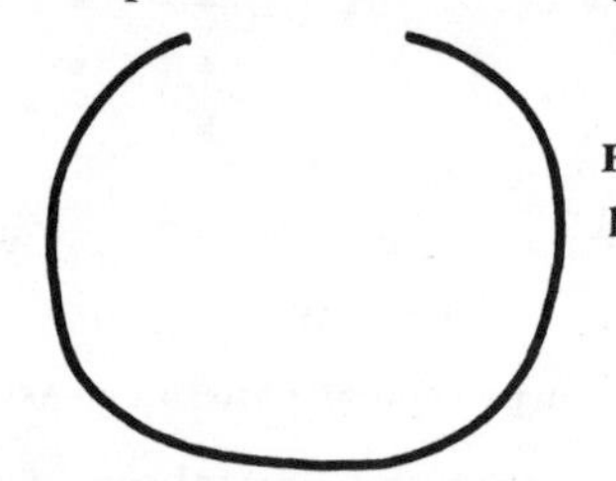

FIGURE 5.4. Effect of closure on perceptual patterning.

Anyone who would see Figure 5.5 as a formless scramble of black and white would indeed be an unusual perceiver. The effect of closure is

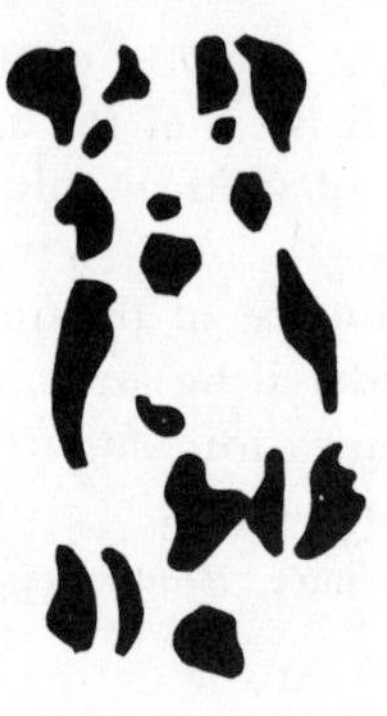

FIGURE 5.5. Illustration of closure. After Street, 1931 [35].

to achieve an organization and stability in the stimulus field which add up to a particular meaning that the perceiver's past experience dictates. Incidentally, how would someone who had never seen a dog be likely to respond to Figure 5.5?

THE PERCEIVER AS ACTIVE ORGANIZER

The attention given in this chapter to the importance of the functioning of the sense organs and to the nature of pattern in the stimulus field could lead to the erroneous idea that stimuli "make" perceptions—that stimuli in themselves determine the meanings that a person attaches to what he observes. Actually, regardless of the explanation we give of the existence of pattern in the stimulus field, stimuli in themselves have no direct power by which to bring about a person's perceptual responses. Impulses transmitted from the eyes to the brain do not themselves provide the representation of which the perceiving individual is aware.

This warning against a wrong interpretation of the manner in which perceptions are formed takes nothing away from the statement of our dependency on the functioning of our sense organs. Rather, it should prompt us to look even more closely into the process of perception and especially into the nature of being a perceiver. The fact is that a person is in no sense passive in his role as perceiver. The evidence of present-day research, as will be shown in a later part of this chapter, indicates that man perceives his environment in terms of his own individual habits of perceiving. What he "sees" in his surroundings may not fully agree with the objective "realities," but be that as it may, *he* invests his observations with their meanings. *He* is the active organizer of the features which the observed phenomena have *for him*.

Hallowell (1951) [16] states as follows the concept of perceiver as active organizer:

> . . . in the present state of our knowledge, we have departed a long way from the notion often held by the proverbial man in the street and, to some extent, by nineteenth-century psychophysics, that we literally see with our eyes and hear with our ears, the logical inference from this being that the world is mirrored in the perceiver. The myth of the passivity of the perceiver already has been disposed of.

Additional support for the concept of perceiver as active organizer is given by Cantril (1950) [6] in his exposition of the meaning of *transaction* as the term pertains to perception. He points out that each transaction of living calls upon many "capacities and aspects of man's nature which operate together" and adds, "each occasion of life can occur only through an environment; is imbued with some purpose; requires action of some kind, and the registration of the consequences of action." Cantril completes his point by noting that every action involves some awareness, which in turn "is determined by the assumptions brought to the occasion. All these processes are interdependent. No one process could function without the others."

Uniqueness of the Individual's Perceptions

That the perceiver is an active organizer of his perceptions is indicated by the fact of uniqueness in what each one perceives when two or more individuals observe the same object or event.

A large doll on display in a store window will be seen quite differently by a girl and a boy looking at it together. A rain cloud is likely to appear threatening to a picnicker. The same cloud may be viewed hopefully by a farmer whose corn needs moisture. An old dwelling much in need of repair may be looked upon by passers-by as a disreputable shack; to its occupants it is perceived as a comfortable place called "home."

In each of the instances just described perceptions involved more than can be accounted for by stimuli per se. The particularized meaning which each person found in what he observed points to the importance of the role of felt needs and past experiences in perception.

The central idea of the paragraphs immediately above is emphasized in a statement by Kilpatrick.

> Man never can know more of the external world than those aspects which are directly relevant to the carrying out of his purposes. Each man's perceptions are therefore his own, unique and personal; common perceptions become possible in so far as common experiences and common strivings are shared among individuals. This approach places perceiving squarely within the context of human striving, the "thing perceived" being inseparably a part of the "process of perceiving" and both reflecting "reality" only by virtue of the active participation of the perceiver in the full-bodied, ongoing process of living. (Kilpatrick, 1961) [23]

Experience as Part of the Perceptual Frame of Reference

A person tends to identify a given situation or object in terms of what is familiar to him. This tendency can be observed in many situations of importance to teachers. For example, there is the question which students everywhere seem prone to ask when they are given a new kind of situation to analyze, "What am I *supposed* to look for?" This is frequently the query of college students whose educational psychology course includes the observing of children in actual classroom situations. If they are left on their own initiative they see only what they are in the habit of seeing—what they expect to see. Significantly, they tend to see "bad" behaviors rather than good and even to infer on meager evidence the motives behind these behaviors. To see impartially, so to speak, and to record behavior *as it is* constitutes a formidable learning task.

The inclination to see only what is familiar can be a psychological hindrance to man's discoveries, inventions, and other creative accomplishments. The truly novel thing remains undetected because that which is so familiar overlays it and hides it. For creativity to be nurtured, individuals must be encouraged to practice the habit of anticipating an unfamiliar setting for a familiar thing or idea as well as unfamiliar things and ideas in familiar contexts. It is within the context of the familiar that discoveries are made and inventive ideas are born.

The quotation that follows not only illustrates the point being made but also helps relate the discussion of perception to the content of Chapter 11—especially to the sections on productive thinking. What follows is a considerably abridged reproduction of an article titled "Serendipity," written by the editor of a college *Newsletter*.

> Two teachers were walking beside a lake early one spring morning. One of them saw a flower and exclaimed with surprise: "A serendipity!" "No," replied the other, "it's a crocus." They were both right.
>
> Horace Walpole coined the word "serendipity" in 1754, basing it on a Persian fairy tale of the three princes of the Kingdom of Serendip. The legend held that when the princes of Serendip went on a journey something unexpected happened, and they found valuable things not sought for. A serendipity is a bonus that men and nature pay those who can see beyond their noses. . . .
>
> The discovery of penicillin by Fleming was a serendipity. Some plate cultures of staphylococci had become contaminated and the colonies of staphylococci around one colony had died. This was not an uncommon experience, but Fleming saw the unusual in the usual and discovered penicillin. . . .
>
> Roentgen's discovery of X-rays was a serendipity. He had been passing current through a tube and noticed a black line across the paper. The effect could only have been produced by the passage of light. However, no light could come from the tube because the shield which covered it was impervious to any light known. He investigated this chance happening and discovered the X-ray.
>
> How do you prepare yourself for serendipities? Obviously you must have rich experience in the field in which the serendipity appears. Beauty may well be in the eye of the beholder but there must also be preparation for seeing it. Lloyd Morgan said, "Saturate yourself through and through with your subject . . . and wait."
>
> There is some evidence to indicate that the so-called insight, the blinding flash ("sudden a thought came like a full-blown rose"), is already present in embryonic form. Something doesn't come out of nothing. What one needs, however, is a capacity for a novel rearrangement of his experiences, a willingness to twist and turn them around, to see them freshly.

Familiarity may breed contempt but it also breeds inattention. We have all failed to see something, a physical object right in front of us. Parents say to children who can't find an object, "If it were any closer, it would bite you." Poe used this inattention to the familiar in *The Purloined Letter*. The letter was "hidden" by putting it in full view. . . .

The story of serendipity is a parable. Few can experience the serendipities of great discovery, but there are special rewards to the disciplined person whose peripheral vision includes what others miss. We can learn to see relevance in the irrelevant, the unusual in the commonplace, the ounces of radium in tons of pitchblende. (Dale, 1966) [8]

Facilitating Role of Familiarity. Familiarity often plays a distinctly *facilitating* role in perception—in contrast to the inhibiting role which has been discussed. One writer, in emphasizing this circumstance, suggests that the lines of words on a printed page could be organized in several different patterns, but because of our years of experience with printed pages, we would organize them, regardless of the pattern, into letters and words. Also, had we spent as many years reading books upside down as we have with them in the conventional position, we might be expected to proceed undisturbed with the act of reading (Johnson, 1961) [19].

The doctor presses his stethoscope against a patient's chest and listens to the beat of the heart. His long experience in differentiating between various heartbeat patterns has prepared him to detect an irregularity deserving of his special attention. The irregularity, or unfamiliar beat, would not be likely to secure the attention of a person unskilled in this kind of examination.

We trust the automobile mechanic's ear rather than our own to locate the source of a malfunction in our car's performance. We engage the services of the horticulturist to examine our valued but somewhat "sick-looking" tree; he will tell us whether there is something actually worthy of special note about the tree's appearance. The reader will be able to think of other illustrations of the facilitating influence of familiarity.

EFFECT OF NEEDS, VALUES, INTERESTS, AND EXPECTANCY ON PERCEPTION

That a person's needs and values may affect his perceptions was mentioned earlier in this chapter. We shall now more closely examine the evidence supportive of this statement.

Influence of Needs.[6] Studies have been conducted which indicate

[6] See Chapter 6 for a definition of need.

that hunger tends to affect an individual's perceptions. In one study (McClelland and Atkinson, 1948) [26], 108 men applicants for naval submarine training were the subjects in an experiment to learn the influence of hunger on perception. A perception test was given to 44 of them one hour after eating, to 24 of them four hours after eating, and to 40 of them sixteen hours after eating. The question was whether any correlation would be found between length of food deprivation and increased interest in food as indicated in perceptual responses.

Each individual saw ambiguous stimuli projected on a screen. Actually, there were no pictures shown—the screens were either very dimly lighted or clouded with a smudge. The men were encouraged by such comments as "Three objects on the table"; "All the people in this picture are enjoying themselves"; "What are they doing?" to look for objects on the screens. In one comparison of results the one-hour subjects made 15 percent food responses, the four-hour subjects made 21 percent food responses, and the sixteen-hour group showed 23 percent food responses. The difference between the first and third of these responses was statistically significant.

Another part of the study required that the men estimate the size of objects "shown" in projected "pictures"—no actual picture being shown. To the question, "Here is an ashtray and a hamburger. What is the larger?" the men most hungry tended to "see" the food object as larger more often than those less hungry.

A phenomenon which has proven useful in the study of the influence of needs on perception is that of *resolution of binocular rivalry*. It will first be described as a method; then in the next paragraph it will be more directly related to the study of the influence of need on perception. Basically, the phenomenon consists of the tendency on the part of a perceiver to *fuse* structurally similar but discriminally different presentations of stimuli to the eyes, respectively. If such presentations are made the "targets," one on each side of a stereogram, and the exposure time is appropriately adjusted, the observer tends to get a fused image. Engel (1961) [9] employed the method in an investigation involving two differently posed faces. He reported that with few exceptions observers simply reported seeing a face; that is, *one* face. "Rarely," he stated, "is there any intimation that dissimilar figures are being viewed in combination."

In a study (Maehr, 1960) [27] based on the phenomenon of binocular resolution, several groups of college-age subjects viewed stereograms on one side of which food objects were shown, on the other various nonfood objects. As in Engel's work, the two pictures of the stereogram were so devised that the viewer tended to fuse them into one—that is, to see only one picture.[7] Neither side of the stereogram consistently dominated over the other for subjects who were on their regular eating schedules. But when the experimental subjects were deprived of food much beyond their regular eating times, there was a tendency for them more frequently to see the food-object picture. There was a particularly strong tendency [8] for this to occur when the slides were viewed at, or near, the customary eating time.

The extent to which an individual's deeply felt needs may influence his perceptions is illustrated in an excerpt from a term paper written by a college student. This student was reared in a home in which religious dogmatism played a prominent role. She had as a consequence suffered some personality disturbances from which she had recently recovered with the help of a psychiatrist.

In the same college class was a young man who also had grown up in a home in which religious beliefs and teachings were not to be questioned. Science was suspect in his home and continued to be so for him even in college.

> **I am fascinated with the contrast in Mr. A's needs and mine and the extent to which our needs influence our view of science. As I listened to him in class, I began to realize how desperately he needed his concepts of an indisputable religion and an all-knowing but easily angered God. Science for him is at cross-purposes with his concepts—it threatens his needs. . . . He sees only what he dares to see.**
>
> **In a different way this is true of me. For a long time I found science and religion to be quite incompatible. But now I *need* science. I experience no difficulty now in harmonizing science and religion. I now look at these matters with different eyes from what I formerly did. So, it is pretty hard under the circumstances for Mr. A and me to find a common frame of reference for our discussions in psychology. But at least I am learning how to be tolerant of other people's views on such matters!**

Values

Values are abstract concepts that serve the individual as criteria of what for him has worth or "rightness." What has worth, or rightness, or some other power of attraction for a person tends to fit into his "value scheme." Religious values, for example, weigh heavily in determining some people's behaviors; "power" is a major determining value for cer-

[7] Interspersed among the slides on which food-related objects appeared were slides that pictured a variety of other kinds of objects, thus disguising the fact that the effect of food deprivation was being investigated. Furthermore, the men who made up this subject group had previously been involved in several investigations—wholly unrelated to the one mentioned here—which also required that they delay or omit one or more meals.

[8] Significant beyond the .01 level.

tain persons; so also for some people is that which has esthetic or humanitarian implications.

Values, like needs, have been shown to have an effect on perceptions. For example, experimenters have shown that poor children tend to overestimate the size of coins more than children from economically privileged homes (Bruner and Goodman, 1947) [3].

In another experimental situation (Lambert, Solomon, and Watson, 1949) [24] nursery-school children were taught to turn a crank on a machine that would dispense a white poker chip which, when it was inserted into a slot, would automatically deliver a piece of candy. Control subjects were introduced to the same situation except that they got candy for "work," not for poker chips. After ten days of rewarded learning involving the poker chips, the experimental subjects increased their overestimation of the size of the poker chips by 13 percent as against a pretest overestimation of 5 or 6 percent on the part of both experimental and control subjects.[9]

Interests

Interest is a tendency on the part of the individual "to give selective attention to something" (English and English, 1958) [10]. It is a mental (or behavioral) *set* resulting from one's feeling that an object or circumstance makes a difference to oneself—that it "counts" and, therefore, should be attended to.

Has the reader ever been accompanied to a sports event by someone who had limited knowledge of the sport and little interest in it? Has he felt dismayed when, for example, just as the tying run was scored on an especially daring bit of strategy his companion exclaimed, "Oh, look at the way they spelled 'refreshments' in that ad on the fence!"

Interest is a prime determiner of people's perceptions. Slang phrases like the following have implications for perception's relationship to interest. "Mathematics I can 'see,' but that other course . . . !" or "I could just 'see' that gown before I even entered the store!" At every turn in a person's day-by-day experience *interests* dictate much of what his eyes, ears, and other sense organs will report to his consciousness.

Perceptual Expectancy

Running through this chapter has been a thread of continuity which relates closely to the idea of "perceptual expectancy." An earlier section was headed, "Origins of Perceptual Expectancy." The Maehr study which gave particular attention to *need* as an influencer of perception, pointed up, nevertheless, the role of expectation in perception.

[9] For a helpful discussion of another "side" to the values-perception relationship see Toch, H. H., and H. Cantril, "The learning of values: An experimental inquiry," in Kilpatrick, F. P., ed., *Explorations in transactional psychology,* Chapter 18 [36].

Considerable noteworthy research has been brought to bear on this phenomenon.

One group of researchers, sometimes identified as representing the "transactional school of thought," has presented considerable evidence to support the conclusion that there is implicit in perception an operation aptly called "best bet" (Kilpatrick, 1953) [21] or "provisional bet" (Ittelson, 1952) [18]. The *idea* is presented by Kilpatrick in the statement, "It is our conviction that the perceptual organization of the moment cannot be an absolute revelation of what *is*, but is instead a sort of 'best bet' based on past experience. . . . [It] is expressed in awareness as perceiving, and serves as a directive for further dealings with the environment."

To test the basic assumptions in the transactionalist position some very ingenious apparatuses are so constructed that they present stimuli that differ markedly in their physical properties but are identical at the receptor level. One such apparatus is the distorted room first constructed by Adelbert Ames (see Kilpatrick, 1952) [22].

The apparatus is actually a model of a crazily built room. (Ittelson, 1952) [18]. Its dimensions are those of a large packing case. The ceiling slopes up, the floor slopes down, and the back wall slopes away. The walls vary in sizes and shapes. But in spite of the peculiarities of the room, it has one main property: when seen from a particular point of view it looks like an ordinary rectangular room.

The particular point of view is obtained by having the observer look at the room from a fixed viewing position. Before doing this however, he is shown the room in detail. He is encouraged to become as thoroughly acquainted with it as possible and to learn all he can about it. He is then invited to sit at the fixed viewing position.

Familiar objects are introduced into the room and stationed opposite the observer. Identical teddy bears, for example, may be placed, respectively, near the corners of the room. Or different persons may appear simultaneously at two windows opposite the viewer. These are the so-called "target objects." One object seems larger than the other because of the distortions of the room—a room whose seemingly rectangular shape has imparted the impression of equal distances from the viewer to each object. Conflict arises between what the viewer sees and what he knows. The conflict gives rise to feelings of uncertainty and confusion. The facts about the room which the viewer has carefully gathered, only minutes earlier, now do not help him much as he tries to deal with the distortions that exist. When he is given a pointer and asked to touch a target spot on one of the walls he proceeds with a hit-and-miss effort that is hardly better than he could accomplish blindfolded.

Ames rigged the setting in such a way that the stimulus targets were different but yielded identical proximal stimuli (meaning that the stimuli are directly active on the body). It may be concluded that confronted with such a situation the perceiver's normal expectancies are operative. To preserve his perceptual "equilibrium," however, the perceiver *checks* what the stimuli "report" against those assumptions. Because the room is perceived as the kind usually experienced, the perceiver is fooled into perceiving normal objects within the room as distorted. Only with considerable practice (checking) can he achieve accuracy in placing the pointer, for example, on blocks of wood distributed about the room.

Another apparatus which Ames developed for these kinds of experiments, is the trapezoid window (Ames, 1951) [1]. This is a window that rotates, but which appears to oscillate because the shifts of perspective which occur with rotation do not conform with ("fit into") the perceiver's accustomed process of trial and check of assumptions. A stiff tube inserted through the lattice-type holes in the window will seem to bend at the ends and pass through the window. When the perceiver is informed that the tube is made of metal, he experiences the sensation of "seeing" it cut through the window. A viewer's reaction often contains an element of disturbed feeling, of anxiousness; he does not possess the stock of assumptions (experiential "traces") into which he can easily harmonize this, to him, bizarre information.[10]

SOCIAL INFLUENCE ON PERCEPTION [11]

Among the fundamental motivations behind an individual's behavior is the need he feels to be accepted and valued by others. Can this need influence a person's perceptions? An ingenious method of arriving at an answer was devised by Sherif and elaborated upon by others.

Sherif made experimental use of a phenomenon known as autokinetic imagery. The phenomenon involves the observing of a pinpoint of light in a darkened room. Most persons who look intently at such a pinpointed speck will report that it moves; hence, the term autokinetic—self-moving. Many people have had an experience with this phenomenon as they have gazed at a star in the sky at night. The shepherds of old were said to have amused themselves by speculating how much a given star would move while they stared at it. The distance which a star seems to move will vary with different observers. The same applies to the reporting of movement of a pinpoint of light in a darkened room.

[10] For discussion of influence of expectancies on perception see Ittelson, W. H., "The involuntary bet," in Baller, W. R., *Readings in the psychology of human growth and development*. New York: Holt, Rinehart and Winston, Inc., 1963.

[11] The question, "Does culture influence perception?" has lead to some informative and thought-provoking research especially on the part of anthropologists. Students will benefit from reading such a book as Segall, M. H., D. J. Campbell, and M. J. Herskovits, 1966, *The influence of culture on visual perception.* Indianapolis: The Bobbs-Merrill Company, Inc. [29].

Sherif's subjects made their judgments about the pinpoint of light under two different circumstances. First, each subject viewed the phenomenon alone and rendered a series of judgments strictly on his own. Under these conditions individuals "subjectively establish a range and a point within that range which is peculiar to the individual" (Sherif, 1935) [30]. Then the subjects as a group were exposed to the phenomenon. Working together in successive sessions under the latter circumstances the reports they gave tended to converge. The conclusion is that typically a person sets his own standard for judging the illusory movement when he is alone but later, in a group situation, adopts the group norms as a frame of reference.

In a study based on Sherif's method but with elementary-school children as subjects, Kaiser (1959) [20] reported the same trend toward convergence when judgments were made in a group situation. Furthermore, he found that judgments were influenced by the degree of friendship which existed between individuals. (He had previously made determinations about the friendship patterns existing among the children.)

It is important to our understanding of the significance of these studies to bear in mind that the subjects were reporting judgments about something which had no basis in fact at all. The dot of light did not move. The significant conclusions bearing on the study of perception are these:

1. Confronted with a perceptual situation for which there is not a familiar frame of reference (there was none at all in the autokinetic imagery experiment) the individual tends to furnish his own frame of reference. Some of Kaiser's subjects who were interrogated later about how they arrived at their estimates gave replies like, "I put one eye where it was when it started and the other eye where it moved."

2. Group—that is, social—influences affect the individual's perceptions. Individuals are more influenced in their perceptions by those of their friends than by those of individuals less close to them on a social distance scale. One's friends' frame of reference becomes to a significant extent the frame of reference for one's own perceptions.

PERCEPTUAL FACTORS IN THE DEVELOPMENT OF SELF-AWARENESSS [12]

To know an individual we must understand how he perceives himself as well as how he perceives his world. We must try to see him with

[12] The reader's attention is called to the fact that in the present chapter only the beginnings of self-awareness are discussed. There will be increasing emphasis upon the importance of self-perception as one chapter follows another. Finally, in Chapter 15, the development of the self-concept will be examined at considerable length.

his eyes, so to speak. It is logical and important that we consider as part of the study of perceptual development the question of the nature of self-awareness.

At what age does self-awareness begin for an individual? In what kinds of experiences does it have its beginning?

Initial Self-awareness

Many child psychologists think that the baby younger than a month of age simply makes no distinctions between the *not-me* and the *me*. Nor does he distinguish between the *outside-me* and the *inside-me*. However, by the time the baby begins to show signs of recognizing the presence of other persons he has at least developed a basis upon which to discover himself as a separate entity. As his vision reaches sufficient maturity so that he sees small objects, and as his motor coordinations become more sure, during the period from 16 to 28 weeks, his behavior begins to look more directed and purposeful. Whether or not he yet associates changes in the outer world (the disappearance and reappearance of his rattle, for example) with his own manipulations of it, is not certain. But it seems likely that out of many similar instances some sense of *me* and *not-me* may begin to arise.

It has been conjectured by one writer (Escalona, 1953) [11] that the infant's first "picture" of his own self is one in which whatever feels pleasurable is part of himself. Hence, his mother, being "nice," is a part of himself. In time, however, he is aware that she comes in contact with him and then separates from him, and this may well be a useful, though painful, exercise for him in learning the true extent of his own body.

Relevant to the problem of the child's developing sense of me versus not-me is the matter of de-subjectification of causality. By what sort of steps does the child manage eventually to grasp the idea of causality as something separable from his own actions? The problem is one that has received considerable attention from Piaget (1929) [28]. It was postulated by Piaget that the resolving of the sense of subjectification is the first of three processes which are foundational to the child's evolving perception of causality.

The de-subjectification step, according to Piaget, occurs with the child's developing awareness of *specific agents* (human or otherwise) that are *externally* existent. The second, and closely related process, is one of discrimination of events with reference to time accompanied by an emerging awareness that sheer contiguity in time is not an agent of causation. The third process consists of an accumulating stock of abstractions (concepts) of causation. Piaget holds that, in general, these several processes arrive at fruition by the time the child is approximately eight years old.

Discovery of One's Own Body

Just as the infant learns to identify objects through the varied contacts he has with them, so also does he come to identify certain things as being parts of himself. First of all, we may suppose, he is simply aware that his fingers and his hands are involved in some way with what happens to him—with what he "feels" when things make contact with him via his body parts. In other words, his first experiences of the parts of his body are similar to his first identifications of other objects: he is aware of their "doing" before he is aware of their "being" as distinguishable entities.

As the child begins the shift from passive to active relationship with his surroundings (at about four months of age) his behavior suggests dawning consciousness that some of the "things" that are performing in his presence are different from other objects. They stay with him rather than come and go; they respond to his impulse to manipulate them; they are his, that is, he possesses them. Presumably out of some such beginnings the child develops his initial sense of a *me* relationship with the parts of his body. Learning to discriminate between the *me* and the *not-me* is affected by the kind of care the baby receives—whether it is consistent and for him predictable or otherwise. The importance of this is indicated in the following observation.

> Other things being equal, those babies whose experience has a definite rhythm and sameness to it especially with respect to vital situations such as feeding and bathing may somewhat earlier and somewhat more easily acquire a sense of themselves as entities to whom things happen and who can make things happen. (Escalona, 1953) [11]

Within a period of eighteen months a child covers the distance from his first notice of the parts of his body to a quite definite sense of self. Three sentences will serve to outline this development.

1. At twelve weeks the baby regards his own hand.
2. At twenty-four weeks he smiles and vocalizes at his own mirror image.
3. At thirty months he is using the pronoun, I, with reference to himself.

This is indeed bare outline, for hundreds of experiences have served to sharpen the distinctions for him between the *not-me* and the *me* and to awaken in him a sense of the distinctively personal nature of being "I."

Social Factors in the Beginning of Self-awareness

Prominent among the experiences that awaken and foster the child's perception of self are those that involve social interaction. Accompanying his consciousness of the fact that meaning attaches to words is an awareness of the *value expressions* applied to him by other persons. From the comforting and pleasurable "darling baby," "mother's beautiful child," and the many variations on these, he comes sooner or later to hear some not so pleasant adjectives applied to his parts, to his actions, and to him—that is, to "me." At times his hands are called "pretty"; at other times they are slapped and called "bad" or "naughty." Doubtless, he experiences some confusion in his earlier involvements with things that are his but not of *him* and other things that are not only his but also of him. Dirty clothes and dirty face are both his—but with a difference, as he comes to learn.

Guilt by Association. Sometimes the baby's hands, face, and other parts seem to be especially praiseworthy. The reasons may not be very clear to him. At other times under circumstances no more significant to him, badness, dirtiness, or naughtiness is attributed to some part of him. How could anything be more confusing to the baby than his parent's threatening exclamations over certain of his toilet-related discoveries about himself. Whereas some parts of his body may be identified and classified by him as good or bad depending upon the circumstances, other parts (specifically the genitals), as he may presently be led to believe, are unvaryingly bad. Life becomes more complicated when he perceives that *he* is bad too if he associates with parts of himself that are bad. It is one thing to dissociate oneself from a pair of dirty pants and thus maintain one's essential cleanness and goodness; it is another thing to be disassociated from something that is a part of one's own body or, as the individual discovers in time, to escape sensations and feelings that originate in these parts. Ergo, to have the feelings is for some individuals tantamount to being a bad person.

A "Mirror" for Self-awareness

Other persons, as will be explained in some detail in Chapter 15, supply the "mirror" in which the child learns to see himself. They initiate him into the experience of developing a *self-image* that includes not only what he believes other persons' perceptions of him are, but also his own private "inward look."

If we humans did not *need* other persons—if we did not have in us so many learned needs involving other persons—we would view our world and ourselves very differently. This suggests that it is time now for us to examine the nature of the drives and motives that are—as here implied—so fundamental to a person's way of relating himself to his surroundings and to himself. This is the topic of the following chapter.

SUMMARY

The fact that our awareness of our world is completely dependent upon the functioning of our sense organs is not a commonplace fact. It is a fact of first-order importance to our understanding of human behavior. Much about the behavior of an individual may be attributed quite directly to the kinds of reports of his world that he gets from his eyes, ears, and other sense organs. Many differences in the actions and ideas of individuals may be traceable to differences in sense-organ functioning.

Another fact is that objects and events are not always seen the same by different individuals even when their sense organs are equally effective. People see things quite largely in accordance with their present needs and their past experiences. It is necessary for us, therefore, in our study of perception not only to know the functioning of the sense organs but to know also the facts about how awareness and meaning are influenced by what the individual wants and expects and the way he feels.

Human behavior is a very individual matter. Each person is an unique creature, whose responses to occurrences outside and inside him begin in early life to take on increasingly the characteristics of self-reference. At the center of his experience are his meanings; the makings of a changing but sustaining frame of reference that determines the way he perceives the succession of events around him and within him.

A major task of infancy and early childhood is that of learning to distinguish between self and not-self. And we would be missing much that is important about this task were we not to see beyond the child's efforts to make such distinctions. Actually he must not only differentiate; he must incorporate and integrate into the self of that moment what the new experience presents as more of self. Thus, the individual is engaged in a lifelong enterprise: the fashioning and refashioning of personal vantage positions from which better to know and understand himself as well as the affairs of the physical and social environments around him.

Suggested Collateral Readings

Cantril, H., *The "why" of man's experience.* New York: Crowell-Collier and Macmillan, Inc., 1950. Pages 65–78.

Combs, A. W., and D. Snygg, *Individual behavior,* revised ed. New York: Harper & Row, Publishers, 1959. Chapters 2 and 8.

Goodenough, Florence, and Leona E. Tyler, *Developmental psychology,* 3d ed. New York: Appleton-Century-Crofts, 1959. Chapter 14.

Hilgard, E. R., and R. C. Atkinson, *Introduction to psychology,* 4th ed. New York: Harcourt, Brace & World, Inc., 1967. Chapters 8 and 9.

Hallowell, A. I., "Cultural factors in the structuralization of perception," in Rohrer, J. R., and M. Sherif, *Social psychology at the crossroads.* New York: Harper & Row, Publishers, 1951. Pages 164–195.

Johnson, D. M., *Psychology: A problem-solving approach.* New York: Harper & Row, Publishers, 1961. Chapter 5.

Kendler, H. H., *Basic psychology*. New York: Appleton-Century-Crofts, 1963. Chapter 8.

Kilpatrick, F. P., ed., *Explorations in transactional psychology*. New York: New York University Press, 1961. Chapters 2–8, 12–21.

Krech, D., and R. S. Crutchfield, *Elements of psychology*. New York: Alfred A. Knopf, 1958. Part One.

Landreth, Catherine, *The psychology of early childhood*. New York: Alfred A. Knopf, 1958. Pages 241–270.

Morgan, C. T., and R. A. King, *Introduction to psychology*, 3d ed. New York: McGraw-Hill, Inc., 1966. Chapter 10.

Smith, K. U., and W. M. Smith, *The behavior of man: Introduction to psychology*. New York: Holt, Rinehart and Winston, Inc., 1958. Chapters 8 and 9.

Solly, C. M., and G. Murphy, *Development of the perceptual world*. New York: Basic Books, Inc., 1960. Chapters 1, 2, 6, 7, 8 and 9.

Solomon, P., *et al.*, ed., *Sensory deprivation*. Cambridge: Harvard University Press, 1965.

Stone, L. J., and J. Church, *Childhood and adolescence*. New York: Random House, Inc., 1957. Pages 84–91, 159–164.

References

1. Ames, A., Jr., 1951, Visual perception and the rotating trapezoid window. *Psychol. Monogr.*, **65:** No. 324.
2. Beardslee, D. E., and M. Wertheimer, 1958, *Readings in perception*. Princeton: D. Van Nostrand Co., Inc., Selection 8. Pages 115–135.
3. Bruner, J. S., and C. C. Goodman, 1947, Value and need as organizing factors in perception. *J. abnorm. soc. Psychol.*, **42:** 33–44.
4. Bruner, J. S., L. J. Postman and J. Rodrigues, 1951, Expectation and the perception of color. *Amer. J. Psychol.*, **64:** 216–227.
5. Buhler, Charlotte, 1930, *The first year of life*. New York: The John Day Company, Inc. Page 56.
6. Cantril, H., 1950, *The "why" of man's experience*. New York: Crowell-Collier and Macmillan, Inc. Page 50.
7. ———, page 59.
8. Dale, E., 1966, "Serendipity," *The Newsletter*. Columbus, Ohio: The School of Education, Ohio State University, Vol. XXXII, No. 1.
9. Engel, E., 1961, "Binocular methods in psychological research," in Kilpatrick, F. P., ed., *Explorations in transactional psychology*. New York: New York University Press. Pages 299–300.
10. English, H. B., and Ava C. English, 1958, *A Comprehensive dictionary of psychological and psychoanalytical terms*. New York: Longmans, Green & Co. (David McKay Co., Inc.).
11. Escalona, Sibylle, 1953, "Emotional development in the first year of life" in Senn, M., ed., *Problems of infancy and childhood*. New York: Josiah Macy Foundation. Page 25.
12. ———, page 26.
13. Gesell, A., and Frances L. Ilg, 1949, *Child development: The infant and*

child in the culture of today. New York: Harper & Row, Publishers. Page 343.

14. Gibson, Eleanor J., and R. D. Walk, 1960, "The Visual Cliff," *Scientific American,* **202:** 64–71.
15. Gibson, J. J., 1948, "Studying perceptual phenomena," in Andrews, T. G., ed., *Methods of psychology*. New York: John Wiley & Sons, Inc. Page 158.
16. Hallowell, A. I., 1951, "Cultural factors in the structuralization of perception," in Rohrer, J. R., and M. Sherif, *Social psychology at the crossroads.* New York: Harper & Row, Publishers. Page 165.
17. Hilgard, E. R., 1957, *Introduction to psychology,* 3d ed. New York: Harcourt, Brace & World, Inc. Page 195.
18. Ittelson, W. H., 1952, "The involuntary bet," *Vogue,* March 15; pages 76–77, 127, reproduced in Baller, W. R., ed., 1963, *Readings in the psychology of human growth and development.* New York: Holt, Rinehart and Winston, Inc. Pages 195–202.
19. Johnson, D. M., 1961, *Psychology: A problem-solving approach.* New York: Harper & Row, Publishers. Pages 140–144.
20. Kaiser, H. E., 1959, *The influence of group opinions and prestige factors on children's perceptions and judgments.* Unpublished doctoral thesis, University of Nebraska.
21. Kilpatrick, F. P., 1953, "Motivation, perception and action." Multilithed speech given at Panel on Human Relations and Morale, Research Development Board, Washington, D.C., March 6, 1953.
22. ———, ed., 1952, *Human behavior from a transactional viewpoint.* Hanover, N.H.: Institute for Assoc. Research.
23. ———, 1961, *Explorations in transactional psychology.* New York: New York University Press. Page 4.
24. Lambert, W., R. L. Solomon, and P. D. Watson, 1949, Reinforcement and extinction as factors in size estimation. *J. exper. Psychol.,* **39:** 637–641.
25. Ling, B. C., 1942, A genetic study of sustained visual fixation and associated behavior in the human infant from birth to six months. *J. genet. Psychol.* **61:** 227–277.
26. McClelland, D. C., and J. A. Atkinson, 1948, The projective expression of needs: I. The effect of different intensities of the hunger drive on perception. *J. Psychol.* **25:** 205–222.
27. Maehr, M., 1960, *The effect of food-deprivation in binocular conflict.* Unpublished doctoral thesis, University of Nebraska.
28. Piaget, J., 1930, *The child's conception of physical causality.* London: Kegan.
29. Segall, M. S., D. T. Campbell, and M. Herskovits, 1966, *The influence of culture on visual perception.* Indianapolis: The Bobbs-Merrill Company, Inc.
30. Sherif, M., 1935, A study of some social factors in perception. *Archives of Psychol.,* **27:** 26.
31. Solly, C. M., and G. Murphy, 1960, *Development of the perceptual world.* New York: Basic Books, Inc. Pages 4–5.
32. Spitz, R., 1946, The smiling response. *Genet. Psychol. Monogr.,* **34:** 57–125.

33. Staples, Ruth, 1932, The response of infants to color. *J. exper. Psychol.*, **15**: 119–141.
34. Stone, L. J., and J. Church, 1957, *Childhood and adolescence.* New York: Random House, Inc. Page 86.
35. Street, R. F., 1931, *A Gestalt completion test.* Teachers College Contributions to Education, No. 481.
36. Toch, H. H., and A. H. Hasdorf, 1961, in Kilpatrick, F. P., ed., *Explorations in transactional psychology.* New York: New York University Press. Pages 335–337.

CHAPTER 6

Human Drives and Motives

Helping youth to change and develop in ways that are personally satisfying and socially desirable requires sound knowledge of the "why" of behavior. The word "why" pertains to the operation of conditions that prompt and sustain the actions an individual engages in. WHY has reference to MOTIVATION. How well teachers understand motivation often makes the difference in the degree of effectiveness of their work with boys and girls and, indeed, with other associates.

TWO VIEWS OF MOTIVATION

To the question, "What is motivation?" there are two kinds of answers which derive from quite different ways of thinking about the meaning of the term. It is important, especially for teachers, that the distinction between the meanings be kept clear in the discussion that follows.

In the practical affairs of the classroom "motivation" often has reference to *something the teacher does* to get children to respond in certain ways. Inducements are offered by the teacher to his pupils as he tries to spark their interest and their efforts. As he makes use of various incentives the teacher may say, "I do this to 'motivate' learning." Clearly, "this" pertains quite directly to a teaching method. Good teachers employ many different methods of motivation suited to various phases of the guidance and instruction of their pupils. Rewards, punishments, and the ways in which teachers relate certain goals to the rewards are very much a part of motivation as thus defined.

The other meaning of motivation—an importantly different use of the term—has reference to *something going on within an individual.* This is the view to which the expression "basic drives and motives" relates in the more truly psychological sense. It is the view that emphasizes the word "felt" in the expression, *felt need.* To describe and explain these forces within the individual is distinctly a problem of psychology. We shall therefore, in this chapter, be dealing with motivation largely in the second sense.[1]

CHARACTERISTICS OF MOTIVATED BEHAVIOR

Motivation as a psychological concept (or "construct") has numerous important characteristics. Let us consider some of them by way of further introduction to the term.

Activation and Goal-governed Direction

Two aspects of motivations are especially distinctive. One is a "prompting" condition (activation) within the individual. The other is direction of behavior toward a goal ("goal-object") that will satisfy the prompting condition. Much behavior is not characterized by direction. Many body movements, for example, are simply reflexive. Some actions are vaguely conscious but largely random in nature. Motivated behavior, however, involves responses that occur in a sequence *governed by a relevant end result.*

Coping Behavior

Much of human behavior consists of episodes which merge one into another to form the stream of an individual's experience. To observe a given episode carefully is to see in it an element of goal-seeking characterized by various maneuvers and adaptations of behavior. These maneuvers and adaptations are directed at overcoming obstacles that interfere with goal attainment. What we are seeing is aptly termed *coping behavior.*

To cope with a situation is to strive purposefully toward the solution of a problem that it presents. The problem may be relatively simple or it may involve numerous complications and complexities.

There is the aspect of coping in the highly energized actions of the hungry baby. Another example would be a boy's hazardous climb into a tall tree to rescue a pet. Coping may also be seen in the strenuous effort of the college student to solve an abstract problem in one of his courses. Not to be lightly regarded as an illustration of coping behavior is what transpires as John, or Jim, or some other college male, tries for a date with an attractive coed.

[1] For a good distinction between two usages of the term "motivation" see Ryans (1942) [38]. See also McDonald (1965) [26].

Four illustrations do not go far toward indicating how much of life revolves around motivation-centered episodes. But they will help to show the wide range of behaviors in which *striving* is notably characteristic.

The illustrations will also serve to bring out another aspect of motivation: the fact that the goal-objects may be near or quite distant.

Motivation Often Involves Distant Goal-objects

Although in many situations the goal-object may be near at hand (as in the instance of the baby's milk) some may be far removed and at the end of a circuitous route. A date with a girl one has never dated before may be achieved only after a good deal of "thinking about it," cautious inquiry, rehearsing of what is to be said when one gets her on the phone, and some prepared-in-advance consolations in case she expresses her "regrets."

There are for most persons many goals that have the characteristic of distance and circuity of approach about them. College graduation is doubtless an example of one for some readers of this book. The job one wants as his permanent occupation is another. A high political office—to be attained only after long and arduous campaigning—is still another. The finding of a Dr. Livingstone in the jungles of a far-off land is no immediate nor easily approached goal for a Stanley.

Often the goal of motivation can be reached only after attaining intermediate, subsidiary goals along the way. A satisfactory grade in a college course is subsidiary to the goal of graduation. Graduation is an intermediate goal on the way to becoming a teacher.

Complexity of Motivation

In Chapter 2 considerable emphasis was placed on the fact that the causes of behavior are complex. This fact applies with special force to motivation. Different people seen doing the same thing may have various kinds of urges that "move" them, or attract them, into what they are doing. The fact of complexity in motivation is well presented in the following statement.

> Man is a purposive being who responds to challenges with his own counterthrust, who imagines goals which have to be brought into existence, who creates—at least in part—the very problems he struggles to solve. This process is like a long conversation between the individual and his milieu. Every stimulating word, every success and failure, every contact and opportunity enter into the shaping of the pattern which emerges. Sometimes it is a deepening thirst which grows out of real sensed lackings which becomes the dominant theme for a period of a man's life. Then his passion becomes an integrating core around which his thoughts, his choices, his rememberings, his actions are grouped. But

there are also lives in which a continual conflict between motives keeps morale at low ebb, and one motive neatly cancels another until there is no centered movement of the individual as a whole. (Cole and Bruce, 1958) [6]

CLARIFICATION OF TERMS AND IDEAS

Thus far motivation and certain of its aspects have been described in a very general way. It is time to examine more critically the meaning of some of the terms that have been used. What exactly is meant in psychology by such terms as *needs, drives, motives* and *goal-objects?* There are dozens of words in everyday usage that relate in one way or another to motivation. Besides those already mentioned, there are, for example, desire, want, aspiration, anxiety, urge, purpose. Of special interest at this moment are the ones chosen for principal use in this book. What connotations do they have that make them useful in a discussion of motivation?

Definition of Terms

Psychologists quite generally employ *motivation* as a generalized reference to the operation within the organism of invigoration and goal-seeking behavior. A useful statement, intended to provide what its author considered a "common sense" understanding of motivation is this, "The study of motivation has to do with the analysis of the various factors which incite and direct an individual's actions" (Atkinson, 1964) [1]. The author just mentioned then quotes from the editor of a well-established annual symposium on motivation who describes the problem as "how behavior gets started, is energized, is sustained, is directed, is stopped, and what kind of subjective reaction is present in the organism while all this is going on" (Jones, 1955) [17].

In the same general context with the statements just quoted is another that underscores the psychologist's focus of interest in the study of motivation which is, "to identify and to understand the effects of all the important *contemporaneous influences* [influences of the moment] which determine the direction of action, its vigor, and its persistence" (Atkinson, 1964) [2].

Perhaps it is quite apparent to the reader from what has been said that *motivation* is indeed an over-arching concept that includes a number of relatively particularized conditions. Additional terms are needed to denote the conditions encompassed by the all-inclusive one, "motivation." For the sake of precision in our thinking it becomes desirable to ponder the differences in shades of meaning that attach to various terms related to motivation. Possibly then the student can better understand why certain of them will be used in special ways in this chapter and in sections of later chapters. Possibly also, there will be better understanding of the fact that different writers make different choices of terms for what may appear to be the very same concepts.

Needs and Drives. The term "need" has been much employed in writings about motivation. With considerable consistency it has been intended by those who have employed it to refer to a condition of *lack*—of deficiency—in the organism. A creature may be lacking in food; it may be lacking in water; it may lack other kinds of requirements for satisfactory functioning (air, optimum temperature, a sense of being "in touch" with body-comforting objects). There would appear to be grounds for assuming some relationship between conditions of need, as thus described, and physiological *states* demanding of "satisfaction." Hunger is descriptive of such a state; so also is thirst. The *states* provide the incitement to action on the part of the organism. Another way of wording the idea just expressed is to say that the consequences of need add up to *drive*. The moisture need of a creature precipitates the thirst drive.

Although there is close association between needs and drives—as they are generally conceptualized—they do not articulate in a one-to-one relationship. For example, persons who have been without food for considerable periods of time have reported that their feelings of hunger tended to come and go in spite of the fact that the lack of food (need) continued. The illustration just given may remind the reader of the finding of Maehr (1960) [29] in his study of the influence of food deprivation on perception; the study was reported in Chapter 5. Proximity to the time when Maehr's subjects were in the habit of eating was more related to perception (the "seeing" of food-related objects) than the length of the interval that followed eating.

Perhaps enough has been said about need as it relates to the conceptualization of motivation; enough to indicate 1) that its most obvious value is the "rootage" it supplies for certain instances of *drive* (namely those involving physiological conditions of the organism) and 2) its limitations for helping us to understand a wide range of human behaviors that appear to have little, if any, relationship to conditions of deficit. Only as the word "need" takes on connotations quite beyond those which attach to "deprivation" does it do much to implement our thinking about the purposeful, choice-influenced, often highly individualized ranges of human experiencing.

The concept *drive* has already been accorded a place—a definition—in our thinking about motivation. We have noted that its meaning reaches beyond the attachments it has to need. The present authors prefer to restrict the use of the word "drive" to conditions that are preponderantly organic in nature. This usage would apply to such conditions as fatigue, sleepiness, thirst, hunger, and sex. There are also avoidance drives. Examples are: avoidance reactions to the prick of a pin; resistance to a condition of smothering; the urge to relieve accumulating waste products in the body.

Motives. Much use is made of the term "motive" both as it may be applied to certain behaviors having quite *basic* promptings and as it pertains to various experientially derived inclinations. In the first of these applications—to the basic promptings—it would include *activity, manipulation,* and *investigation.* Although these behaviors suggest physiological correlates, the correlates are not specific as in the case of thirst or hunger. The second kind of application of the term "motive" will be discussed in the section of this chapter which deals with *Social-Personal Motives.*

An advantage which the term "motive" has over other terms—such as need and drive—is an element of neutrality which attaches to it. The neutrality becomes evident when one is concerned with the "why" of behavior and tries to avoid the relatively arbitrary connotations of "push" versus "pull" ("attraction *toward*") with which so many words in the motivational context are fraught. The point may be clarified as the reader ponders whether it is "push forward" or "drawn toward" that is implied by such words as drive, anticipation, and wish. One writer pinpoints the problem by speaking of the difficulties of communicating one's notions about the nature of the "steering process" in motivation (Hall, 1961) [12].[2]

Goal-object. Behavioral scientists use the expression "goal-object" to designate that which the organism seeks or desires: something which "promises" the satisfying of a felt need, a wish, or a purpose. Milk would be such a goal-object for the hungry baby. Friendly responses from another child would be a goal-object for the youngster who is "hungry" for peer acceptance and companionship. A piece of money often becomes an intermediate goal-object for the person who sees in it the promise of some desired thing which it will buy—the ultimate goal-object. A mark of "A" in a school subject is a goal-object: it is attractive for the kinds of fulfillment it promises to bring to the student. Perhaps

[2] A very comprehensive and scholarly examination of the various major conceptualizations of motivation is contained in C. N. Cofer and M. H. Appley, *Motivation: Theory and research* [5], New York: John Wiley & Sons, Inc., 1965. The reader will find much in the book that will help him to understand the problems related to the employment of any given concept of motivation to a wide range of creature behaviors. Especially are the limitations of *deficit* concepts of motivation exposed. Certainly the reading of the book will quicken a reader's awareness of the complexity of the phenomenon of motivation. It will also show the enormous attention that behavioral scientists have given the phenomenon; over two thousand books and research articles are cited by Cofer and Appley.

beyond the mark of "A" is the prospect of seeing one's name on an honor roll and the further prospect of gaining the esteem of various highly regarded persons.

Causes and Motives

Occasionally, in a discussion of motivation there is a tendency to think of "motive" as being synonymous with "cause." The question, "Why did he do it?" is sometimes stated in such a way as to suggest that the explanation will consist of motive only.

Behavior is never that simple. Or, to state a proposition frequently emphasized in this book, the causes of behavior are multiple, complex, and interrelated. Motives are but part, though a very important part, of the total situation that gives rise to and direction to human actions. An adequate account of the "cause" of a particular behavior will include not only the factors of need, goal, and motive but also the relevant conditions of perception, thinking, and learning, as well as the nature of the environmental influences to which the individual is responding. In fact, behavioral causation, as just now described, might well be said to be what the entire Part Two of this book is about—inclusive of the present chapter.

Apropos the interrelationship of motivation factors and other factors in human behavior, is the following comment:

> Motivation theory is not synonymous with behavior theory. The motivations are only one class of determinants of behavior. While behavior is almost always motivated, it is also almost always biologically, culturally and situationally determined as well. (Maslow, 1943) [31]

Emphasis upon the Term "Basic"

In much of the discussion of motivation the word "basic" is coupled with the terms "needs" and "motives." This is significant; it calls for some explanation. In thus joining "basic" to "needs" and "motives" psychologists have hoped to force the issue as to what are the *prime movers* in the behavior of organisms. Exactly what conditions, in the case of man, are so tied into his essential welfare that not to have them satisfied would be to put his welfare in real jeopardy? This is the pertinent question. Or to put the question somewhat differently, how basic is *basic?*

The significance of the term *basic* as applied to human motivation begins to be evident when one answers the question, "Is food a 'basic' requirement?" and then tries to answer whether there are any psychological requirements that, unsatisfied, would put an individual's essential welfare in relatively comparable jeopardy. We need not—in fact, must not—consider physical well-being man's only kind of *essential wel-*

fare. Any hindrance to motives that threatens the stability of an individual's personality is a serious matter.

Perhaps these few comments about the term *basic* are enough to show what its function is in the discussion of motivation. Unless we keep its meaning and its implications clear we could end up with a list of basic motives that would include everything from food and water to refrigerators and swimming pools. Krech and Crutchfield deal with this in the following statement:

> Were we to allow for every finest shading and nuance of motives among all the different people on earth, we would find the number of separate human motives running well into the billions. But to bring some order into the picture, we must ignore the detailed differences and concentrate upon the common features. We must seek to find a limited set of groupings of motives that will encompass the behavior of most people.
>
> The best way to do this is to look for the most general aims of human behavior, whether in child or adult, in modern man or Hottentot. (Krech and Crutchfield, 1958) [20]

How then shall we go about the task of organizing the discussion of the *kinds* of human drives and motives? What categories will best serve this purpose and what drives and motives are so basic as to make appropriate their inclusion in the categories?

Different writers have organized in different ways their discussions of basic drives and motives.[3] A convenient and rather widely employed classification recognizes the essentially physiological basis of some drives and motives in contrast to the essentially social-psychological nature of certain others. This is the classification which will be used in this book, except that the expression *social-personal* will be substituted for social-psychological. (The latter term is often shortened by various writers to simply "psychological.")

PHYSIOLOGICAL DRIVES AND MOTIVES

As already suggested, there cannot be much argument about the *basic* character of certain physical needs. The authors will consider that enough has been said about food need, water need, and so forth, to suffice for the present purpose. A few comments may however be appropriate regarding the sex drive.

Although the urge to sex activity is physiological and organic, the pattern of an individual's sex behavior is to a considerable degree socially and psychologically determined. The selection of the sex *object*

[3] Compare, for example, Krech and Crutchfield (1958, page 279) [20], Dewey and Humber (1951, page 184) [7], and Hilgard (1957, pages 124–125 and 148–149) [15].

—the kind of person to whom one is attracted—is largely a matter of environmental influence. Cultural values and norms, the restrictiveness or permissiveness of the individual's guidance into sex knowledge and experience, the accessibility of a sex partner at a particular time and place: these and other environmental factors have much to do with the individual's expression of his sex urge.

Need for Better Understanding of Sex Drive. Perhaps nothing in our culture is more provocative of personal unhappiness than the practices surrounding the individual's experiences with sex drive. So deeply rooted in our culture and so vigorously supported by the various socializing agencies are taboos related to sex that they take hold of the individual early in life, producing in him as he grows up feelings of confusion, guilt, and anxiety.[4]

The following quoted statement was written to apply to more anxiety-developing situations than only those deriving from the individual's concern with his sex drive, but its pertinence to the present discussion is clear and its implications are important.

> One of the ironies of our culture (and other cultures, too, apparently) is that while anxiety is very prevalent we use our educational system to raise the evasion of anxiety to a high art. From such evidence as we have, we can prudently conclude that there probably is no school child, no college student or professor (or no reader of this book) who is not anxious to some degree. The human situation is such that there probably is no way to avoid anxiety. Anxiety thrives on the predicaments of human existence, but is not relieved by evasion. The academic program and the academic mind are geared to evasion when, in our educational program, we teach children to know about almost everything except about the intimate striving and conflicts which concern themselves. We evade anxiety (or seek to evade it) when we avoid the personal implication of knowledge and emphasize only the impersonal, objective facts. (Jersild, 1960) [16]

A person's experience of his drives and motives and his feelings and emotional experiences are inseparable—they derive from the same deeply flowing streams. There will be further discussion of this fact in another section of the present chapter.

Importance of Knowledge of Physiological Drives

What does the knowledge of physiological drives and motives have to do with the understanding of a person's conduct at any given mo-

[4] There is much evidence that sexual restrictions vary not only from one culture to another but from one subculture to another (Kinsey, Pomeroy, and Martin, 1948 [19]; Kardiner, 1954 [18]; and Mead, 1935 [34]). Teachers who venture to "influence" the thinking, feeling and overt behaviors of preadolescents and adolescents where matters pertaining to sex are concerned may well keep in mind that their own sexual experience may be limited indeed as compared with that of certain youngsters barely in their teens or younger.

ment? Such a practical question is likely to be asked in this kind of discussion. A few illustrations may help answer the question.

One can well imagine that parents who have sat through some evenings with Junior much past his usual bedtime will readily attest to the importance of unsatisfied states of the body's tissues. Often the crucial factor in such matters is the degree of recognition the adult has of the connection between Junior's difficult behavior and the reasonable demands of his body for rest.

Teachers may not often use the expression, "tension reduction," to refer to the purposes which the school's mid-morning recess serves; but they are well acquainted with the kinds of distressed behavior that are likely to result from failure to provide this period of relaxation. Recess is a time when pent-up energies may be redistributed and body tissues may be relieved of fatigue. Not the least important factor involved in such provision for physical needs is that of the rhythms—the behavior cycles—which are established in the organism. When these are neglected or infringed upon, the consequence is usually a condition of disturbance within the "offended" organism, accompanied by an outward show of "bad" behavior.

The mother who anxiously compares the progress of the meal on the stove with the approach of the dinner hour knows full well the force which physical requirements bring to bear upon behavior—especially when it is the behavior of the younger members of the family. The factor of rhythm enters into this situation as it does whenever tissue needs are involved. One twelve-year-old expressed the idea by explaining that meals must be on time, and "better still, they should always be a little ahead of time."

Relationship of Endocrine-gland Functioning to Physiological Drives. It is not the aim of the next several paragraphs to describe how the endocrine glands work—how they secrete certain substances (hormones) into the blood stream that on occasion greatly influence the tissue tensions of the organism. It is rather the purpose simply to note that the properties of these glands do have a powerful influence upon behavior. Disturbances in one's "internal environment" may have important repercussions in one's overt behavior—repercussions which someone may try to "treat" without adequate or sympathetic understanding. Surely the least that anyone can do—if his dealings with behavior are to be consistent with the role which such internal forces play—is to hold them in high regard and accord them a place of importance when hypotheses are being formed about a given behavior episode.

Do the occasional storms and stresses which loom up so threateningly in Junior's behavior originate, in part at least, in a disturbed internal environment? The wise teacher or parent will do well to give respectful consideration to that possibility. To "treat the storm" in this instance might be highly dubious procedure. To look for clues that certain basic physiological requirements are not being met would be much more intelligent.

SOCIAL-PERSONAL MOTIVES

The appropriateness of the term "basic" when applied to physical drives and motives is, presumably, quite apparent. But, as was earlier noted in this chapter, it may be less apparent that human beings also have psychological motives that are so basic and persistent as to constitute the essential forces in much that people do.

Safety Motives

It would be logical enough to deal with some aspects of *safety* under the heading of physiological needs. Indeed, there is an aspect of need for safety in the hunger drive, the thirst drive, and the individual's avoidance of pain and other noxious stimuli. But the motive pursues the individual into the social-personal aspects of his life; it is this aspect of it that we are now to consider.

Need for a Predictable and Orderly World. We have already noted the individual's need for definite rhythms and routines where certain of his physiological requirements are concerned (for example, the "need" to have meals on time). Predictability becomes a virtual imperative to the individual's satisfactory physiological "state of affairs." So it is in the realm of the individual's social-personal existence.

Children disclose a psychological safety motive in various ways. They recoil at what they interpret as unfairness, injustice, or inconsistency. They recoil because these kinds of treatment generate in them feelings of insecurity and apprehensiveness—apprehensiveness that their world has in it dangers too great for them to meet and overcome.

Children quite generally desire fairly well-defined boundaries for their own actions—especially where these involve interpersonal relationships. They may protest at the limitations which their elders impose on their behaviors. But their protests at being "regulated" have much less of basic anguish in them than the silent floundering that accompanies the absence of firm, predictable limits by which to chart the course of their conduct. Even those who are in their teens sometimes find it very supportive of their need for social-personal safety to be able to explain to their peers, "But this is what my 'folks' expect"—a statement that serves a dual purpose: it helps in maintaining familiar behavioral boundaries, and it functions as a face-saving device with one's peers.

Parental Reassurance. The safety motives of the child include the reassurance that comes from a parent whose own personality is secure in the area of ego (self) strength.

Little four-year-old Nancy's mother had died quite unexpectedly. Nancy, an only child, had been staying with her grandparents for most of a week while her mother—unknown to Nancy—fought a losing battle with a malignancy.

Some hours after the mother's death Nancy's father faced the moment when he must explain to his little girl what had happened. Several days later he told this story: "I dreaded this moment—I feared the shock that Nancy would experience. But now as I look back, I feel that there was an element of genuine relief and reassurance for Nancy in my grief-stricken explanation to her. I realize that certain things I had heard her saying like 'Mommy will soon do this,' and 'That is what my Mommy will soon tell me,' during her mother's absence were actually expressions of anxiety. She knew something was dreadfully wrong; her familiar surroundings were filled with threats she could not define. Sort of 'stunned' as she seemed when I made my explanation, I nevertheless believe that because I was not evasive . . . because I fully shared with her our common grief . . . her world was partly set straight again. In any case she soon appeared reconciled to bearing with me *our* loss."

Contrast Nancy's situation with that of the little first-grader whose mother deserted home one night never to return . . . leaving her with an unstable, unloving father whose principal concern was that his wife's leaving meant "a lot of inconvenience." This child's teacher reported, "She just sat at her desk most of the time staring blankly at the things in front of her." Here was a child caught in a situation where the numbness of terror makes normal responses quite impossible. It is the kind of situation which, with variations, lies behind considerable puzzling behavior with which teachers are confronted.

In speaking of the child's "need" for psychological safety in the home, Maslow (1943) [32] makes the following observation:

> The central role of the parents and the normal family setup are indisputable. Quarreling, physical assault, separation, divorce, or death within the family may be particularly terrifying. Also parental outbursts of rage or threats of punishment directed to the child, calling him names, speaking to him harshly, shaking him, handling him roughly, or actual physical punishment sometimes elicit such total panic and terror in the child that we must assume more is involved than the physical pain alone. While it is true that in some children this terror may represent also a fear of loss of parental love, it can also occur in completely rejected children, who seem to cling to the hating parents more for sheer safety and protection than because of hope of love.

Psychological Safety Needed Throughout Life. The individual's safety motivation is not limited to childhood and youth. It is discernible in the adult's fear of being ostracized. In primitive societies ostracism is feared no less than death. When we observe the lengths to which individuals will go in our society in order not to be "left out" or "made to go it alone," we could well believe that they, too, would find death not much less frightening. Dewey and Humber (1951) [7] document the adult's desire for security with the statement,

> In our quest for security we perform many unpleasant tasks, but prefer to do this rather than run the risk of loss of security as we define it in terms of houses, food, comfort, clothes, good health, social position, etc. The major part of the tax dollar is spent by the government in its efforts to provide security for its citizens; military expenditures, pensions for the old, the ill, the crippled, the blind, the deaf, and the unemployed are all expenditures for security.

The writers just quoted cite a study (Krout, 1934) [23] made among college students who had been asked to keep a week's record of their wishes. The record showed that the majority of the wishes could be classified under the heading of wishes for security.

Importance of Familiar Sensory Environment. The importance of having one's environment remain reasonably consistent has been mentioned in several places in this discussion of basic motives. There is an aspect of the matter, however, which calls for special consideration partly because of its recently demonstrated social-psychological significance and, furthermore, because psychology has important research evidence to bring to bear upon it.

What happens inside a grown man when, under some kinds of manipulation of his environment, he becomes a changed person—an individual whose character and personality have been altered? What makes brainwashing possible?

Psychology is not yet ready with the answers to all the questions of the kinds just asked. But, as already indicated, some facts derived from laboratory experimentation do have significant bearing on the phenomenon of personality change as seen in brainwashing. The work of Hebb and his associates at McGill University well illustrates the nature and importance of research findings.

The experimenters at McGill University secured the consent of college students to undergo a period of drastic isolation from the environment. The students were confined in a compartment in such a manner as to completely prevent visual perception, largely cut down auditory perception (to about a quarter of normal), and reduce tactual perceptions to about a tenth of the usual amount.

Some of the results of the experiment have been summarized by Hebb (1958) [14] in a report from which the following passages were taken:

The result, again in brief, was an acute disturbance of the normal personality. . . . There were great swings of motivation, which alternated between periods of apathy and an intense desire to get back to a normal environment. Any variation of sensory input was welcomed, but with this there was a lack of energy for problem solving; and, after leaving isolation, the subject found it difficult or impossible to get back to his normal work habits for about 24 hours. In addition, there were some handsome visual hallucinations, disturbances of perception of the self, impairment of intelligence test performance, changes in the EEG, and marked visual disturbances on first emerging from isolation.

With the possible exception of the effects of propaganda, the changes were reversible, disappearing in a day or so. For the problem of brainwashing we learned something of value, which should be as widely known as possible, since we do not know who will fall into Communist hands in the future and be subjected to this—appalling, indecent, choose your own adjective—this atrocious procedure; and knowing something about it may mitigate its effects.

Hebb mentions two valuable learnings that have relevance to brainwashing. First there is the fact that hallucinations are "normal" in such circumstances as the experiment provided and as presumably are used militarily in brainwashing. To know this and to know that the effects are reversible should be of help to a person made to submit to brainwashing. Second, impairment of critical thinking is a likely consequence of radical isolation from one's environment; knowing this a subject can better fortify himself against propaganda.

The reader will probably share some of Hebb's feelings as expressed in the following remarks:

It is hardly necessary to say that the experiment, taken as a whole, was very unsettling to us. Our subjects were of course free to walk out on the experiment at any time they chose (as soon as they felt they could give up the $20 a day pay!), but it would be very difficult for a man in fear of his life, with no choice in the matter and no termination in sight. It is one thing to hear that the Chinese are brainwashing their prisoners on the other side of the world; it is another to find, in your own laboratory, that merely taking away the usual sights, sounds, and bodily contacts from a healthy university student for a few days can shake him, right down to the base; can disturb his personal identity, so that he is aware of two bodies (one hallucinatory) and can not say which is his own, or perceives his personal self as a vague and ill-defined something separate from his body, looking down at where it is lying on the bed; and can disturb his capacity for critical judgment, making him eager to listen to and believe any sort of preposterous nonsense.

After considering the implications of this study, the student may ponder the reported abnormalities of behavior in persons who, for example, have been long-lost shipwreck survivors, persons long isolated in a snow-covered area, and the occasional person (usually a child) who has been rescued from an imprisonment in a dark attic. Some carefully conducted investigations of such circumstances as these by Lilly (1956) [24] and Boag (1952) [3] add confirmation to the idea that when man is subjected—either by accident or by deliberate prearrangement—to reduced exteroceptive stimulation, his personality is vulnerable and abnormal behaviors may be expected. There is a basic safety need involved in normal sensory contacts with one's environment.

The Love Motive

Early in life an apparent "need" [5] for body contact appears. It has been described variously as a physical need (the neglect of which may lead in the case of infants to a condition—marasmus—ending in death), as an emotional need (the need for "love") that must be satisfied if good intelligence and adjustment is to develop, and as a learned social motive. Some of its aspects are discussed in detail elsewhere in this book (Chapter 14).

Whatever its source, love is certainly a universal and powerful phenomenon in early behavior. Magazines or books showing animal mothers and their offspring provide numerous illustrations of the young nestled against the mother, as do pictures of primitive and preliterate mothers and children. Upon viewing a picture of a monkey mother with her baby clinging to her neck, one middle-class American mother was heard to remark, "There! That's *exactly* the way I feel. I get so tired of Baby hanging on me, clinging and crying! But I guess all babies are just that way." Apparently babies are, indeed, "that way," and it should be noted that in general we interfere with natural tendencies at some risk.

The desire (motive) to be loved must not be confused with the desire to be approved or accepted. The child in his relationships with his parents needs to feel esteemed—but he needs more than this. He needs to feel secure in the knowledge that whatever he may be and whatever he may do, his parents deeply love him.

Thus, much of an individual's day-by-day behavior may stem from the satisfaction or the dissatisfaction of the desire to be genuinely loved. When the teacher is hard pressed to understand the hostile actions of a particular pupil, he may well ask himself how much he knows about this youngster's experiences of convincing evidence that someone loves him. It may be that this behavior, which on its surface seems hard to understand, actually stems from a condition of prolonged neglect of this fundamental motive.

[5] The quotation marks around the word "need" are intended as a reminder of the ambiguity of the term. H. F. Harlow's widely read article, "The Nature of Love," [13] can profitably be examined not only for the insights which it gives into the origins and development of love but also for the way in which the topic is couched in the terminology of primary and secondary "reinforcers."

The Desire for Approval

The desire to gain and hold the esteem of one's fellows, friends, and family—to be praised, looked-up-to, or rewarded in some way—constitutes a powerful social motive. We do not have to look far for examples of it. A brief inventory of our own behaviors will probably suffice. The following situation will, however, show some of the ramifications of this basic need.

Ten-year-old Katherine has been working hard to sell some boxes of candy. She has been going from house to house in her neighborhood to make as many sales as possible. If we were to ask her why she is trying to sell so many boxes, she might explain that her goal is to sell more candy than anybody else in the club. Katherine wants to make a good showing; she hopes that her accomplishment will be outstanding.

To say that Katherine desires to be looked upon approvingly by her peers is correct enough. It is correct providing we do not underestimate the powerfulness of the underlying motive. For *Katherine needs approval.* She, like all other individuals, needs the experience of the evidence that she is a valued person. Katherine has learned in her relatively short period of living, how good it is to have the confirming evidence that her *self* (that which she calls "I") has worth. She has learned, also, what it does to her way of living to experience doubt about her worth; so she nurtures those relationships which confirm her worth. What Katherine is engaged in at this moment is but one of many endeavors which occupy her attention as she strives unceasingly to satisfy a basic motive: to be approved.

Much of the success of teachers whose pupils make important gains in scholarship and in personal conduct is due to their sensitiveness to the differences in the ways children go about satisfying the need for approval. Children from some social classes achieve status by a show of aggressiveness—even to the point of flouting the generally accepted code of conduct on the playground and in the classroom. Boys and girls from other social classes will, with greater consistency, expect to achieve status by exemplifying what their parents and friends call "good behavior."

Frequently a child is confronted with the dilemma of trying to satisfy different codes of behavior. That which he knows to be desired by the teacher may perhaps be out of harmony with his particular peer group. It is fortunate when a teacher can sense that such an impasse confronts a child and can find ways of helping him conform to the necessary regulations of the school without losing face with his peers.

The Desire for Independence

As the individual grows and develops in his powers of expression, his desire for independence increases. But being able to use an increase of independence is not a ready-made talent. The individual must learn how to be free—how to be independent. Thus, the natural inclination is to work at this phase of growing up. Much of human behavior is, therefore, an outward expression of the process of achieving and maintaining independence. Another view of Katherine may be helpful in this connection.

Katherine's mother, with good intention, raised a question on a certain chilly afternoon whether Katherine should go swimming with some little friends. Katherine, in a flare-up of emotion, burst into tears. With much feeling she exclaimed, "I hate my home; I don't like you anymore; I will go! I will go!"

What does such behavior mean? What should Katherine's mother have done? Katherine's mother did not do what some mothers would do. She did not treat the symptom behavior. She did not fight back at Katherine's show of hostility. She tried to think, in that moment when clear thinking was not easy, just what fundamental motivation in Katherine might be meeting interference—what need it was that required satisfaction.

As Katherine's mother later described the incident, she recalled her effort not to interpret Katherine's conduct as a genuine expression of hatred toward herself or as an indication of the importance of going swimming. She was able to recognize, in the disturbances of this moment, the outward signs of a child's reasonably normal effort in the direction of independence. Katherine's mother was able to see beyond the immediate, precipitating factors in this episode and to think in terms of fundamental needs.

The Desire to Know

To use the expressions "desire to know" or "urge to know" is to invite the feeling on someone's part that a sentence has not been completed. A reader may wish to ask, "To know what?" His question would miss the point—a basically important one—that sheer *urge to inquire into* may, for very sound reasons, be included among the fundamental personal-social motives. It is manifested in the persistent search which human creatures make for meaning in experience. It has reference to the insuppressible "what?", "where?", "how?", and "why?" that are characteristic of the young child, and generally less overtly, of the adult. Even the restriction implied in the words, "which *human* creatures make" may well be unwarranted. For those who have gone for a walk through the fields or the woods with a favorite dog the *urge to inquire into* may not seem to be a characteristic owned by man alone.

Some remarks of a youthful educator reflect something of the idea which has been advanced in the preceding paragraph. He had told of his boyhood distaste for much that took place in school. He had begged his grandfather, with whom he lived, to try to persuade the proper officials that there were good reasons why he should be permitted to leave school and get his "learning" from his grandfather. Whatever the persuasions were, the request was granted. Then there occurred "eight delightful years of adventure in communing with nature about her secrets" (a direct quotation). The account continued somewhat as follows.

How wonderful it was to discover *how* to look and *how* to see and *how* to feel as Grandfather and I followed the streams and tramped the hills together. How well I remember Grandfather's encouragement to "sharpen" my eyes and ears and other senses. To give special point to his admonition, he had me note how frequently Silver, our highly valued dog, would exercise alertness and curiosity in detecting clues that I overlooked. I am not trying to credit Silver with any "urge to know" motive but he did improve my tendencies toward, and my *satisfactions* in, being alert and curious. Grandfather's modest but thoughtfully selected library came, in time, to be the enjoyable "further version" of what I had learned to reach for—to try to decipher—as I pursued the *whats* and *whys* and *hows* of things with Grandfather and Silver.

Is it any great wonder that the person who told this story has become a highly regarded writer of books in science for use in schools? And should one be surprised at his concern about the paucity of common ground between youngsters' impulses to make inquiries and the opportunities the school provides for development of such inclinations? Closely related to the story is a discussion in Chapter 16: the part which is introduced as "the fifth condition" of *Good Psychological Climate*. Related also is the thought contained in the following lines.

When the myriad tasks of school
Are harmonized with the child's strong urge to know,
Then a breath of life prevails
O'er an oft-dull atmosphere,
And learning thrives.

Especially apropos the discussion of "urge to know" is a conclusion reached by Guilford (1965) [11]. He noted that from various sources among writers, "There is a growing recognition that in addition to the more obviously utilitarian motives, there is a unique source of drive for problem solving; a drive of an intellectual nature; a drive that appears to reach fulfillment merely through the mastery of problems." Guilford cites the inferences drawn by Rossman (1931) [37] from data pertaining to inventors that for many of them, to quote Guilford, "a dominant driving force was the thrill of surmounting difficulties or solving tough problems."

After observing certain similarities between "drive for gaining competence" (White, 1961) [39] and the term "self-actualization" as employed by Maslow (1943) [30] and Rogers (1962) [36], Guilford concludes:

From all this there comes, like a welcome breath of fresh air, a belief that children and others can be motivated by needs other than those of hunger, thirst, pain, and sex; that they can learn to know and to value the sweet taste of intellectual achievement.

Self-significance as a Motive

There is to a considerable extent a common denominator running through the motives that have been included in the social-personal category. It is the individual's learned requirement of an *abiding sense of self-significance and self-fulfillment*. In considerable measure the other social-psychological motives, though stemming from quite differentiable areas of experience, flow more or less directly into this common main current of motivation.

A basic fact is that the person whom the individual learns to call "I" cannot, for him, be otherwise than significant. His physical body may become impaired; his physical strength may ebb; and his best efforts may occasionally be overwhelmed by the tides of circumstance. But self-significance must be maintained. Like the buoy which the waves buffet and frequently wash over, the selfhood of the individual resists prolonged submergence.

The concept of a satisfying self-definition requires that there be both maintenance of significance and enhancement of it. The two terms, maintenance and enhancement, should be considered as two views of the one basic human urge. In the one view the individual is seen fending off that which he interprets as threatening to his satisfactory self-perception; in the other he is seen striving for that which "promises" to enhance his significance.[6]

An experience which nine-year-old Terry had illustrates the way in which self-perception determines the course of one's behavior.

Terry arrived home from school one noon in a state of considerable emotional distress. He hid his face in his hands and tried to hold back his tears as his mother attempted to find out what had happened that had so thoroughly upset him. Finally the explanation came pouring out along with a flood of tears.

Terry and his classmates had taken a spelling test during the class period just before the noon recess. And Terry had done something that definitely was out of character for him. In order to get a mark of 100 on his paper he had misrepresented his performance. Terry himself had written the mark on his paper; this was an occasion when the teacher had asked the children to make

[6] There is a most helpful discussion of this topic by Eiserer and Corey (1955) [9]. The distinction which is emphasized in the paragraph is related to the explanation contained in an earlier section of this chapter under "Two Views of Motivation" and for which there was a footnote reference to Ryans (1942) [38], and to McDonald (1965) [26].

use of a correct spelling list to grade their own papers. And Terry had given himself a perfect score in spite of the fact that he had misspelled one of the words. After he had marked the paper and before he could change the word, his teacher had come along to pick up the papers.

Why had Terry misrepresented his performance? The answer appears to have a direct relationship to the matter of self-perception. Much had been at stake for Terry in this test. He had, through considerable hard work, become a good speller and he was proud of the reputation he had gained, and especially of the esteem which this had earned for him in the eyes of his teacher. Getting all but one word right would ordinarily have been a satisfactory performance. But on this occasion, another circumstance had thrust itself into the situation to confront Terry with a dilemma. Clayton, who sat immediately behind Terry, had whispered as he finished marking his paper that he had gotten all the words correct. It was not simply that Clayton had correctly spelled all the words that upset Terry's composure; it was that Clayton's whispered remark carried a suggestion of challenge—a taunt, which Terry's pride resisted. In that moment when one aspect of Terry's self-image was being threatened, he countered with a protective action—an emergency measure for the sake of self-maintenance.

By the time Terry reached home and could pour out his anguish to his sympathetic mother he was aware of more than one bruise on the several aspects of his self-perception. Having missed a word in the spelling test was not then the most painful condition, nor was it the ill-advised response to Clayton's challenge. It was even more distressing that his teacher would no longer consider him "a really honest boy." And perhaps somewhat vaguely in Terry's mind at the moment was an awareness of a condition of imbalance in his concept of himself as a person. For the moment he had been thrown off his customary center of gravity. The fierceness with which he protested the unbearableness of his plight illustrates the dual processes of maintenance and enhancement of self-significance which was described above.

Self-actualization: A Basic Motivation

For a considerable number of psychologists, it seems very necessary in an adequate description of man's behavior to include the concept of "forward-going" orientation—of *ends* towards which the individual's personal growth and development are directed. The idea is that in the individual there is a basic tendency toward making actual that which is potential in him. The student will identify this idea with the interpretation that was given in Chapter 2 of the Boy Scout's sense of *becoming* an Eagle Scout. The idea is simply that *what a person can be he must be* (Maslow, 1943) [30].

To discuss self-actualization at any length in this chapter would result in considerable repetitiousness. The fundamental importance of the concept to an account of personality development has persuaded the present authors to give considerable space to it in Chapter 15—the full-scale discussion of personality development. The student is invited to join that part of Chapter 15 to this description of basic human motives.

THE CONCEPT OF HIERARCHY OF NEEDS

An emphasis on "higher-level" motivations is implied in the concept of self-actualization. The concept stresses the tendency in man to devote his attentions and his energies to concerns of an increasingly creative kind in keeping with the degree to which he is freed of the demands of his physiological drives. Furthermore, the idea holds that for most persons, most of the time (at least for such fortunate ones as ourselves) the basic physical requirements are *not* unsatisfied and are *not* demanding attention. They are, therefore, not the typical motivators in what individuals are seen doing.

Maslow, who is a leading proponent of the idea above expressed, proposes a hierarchy of "needs" arranged in order of prepotency. This means that the appearance of one need rests on the prior satisfaction of another. Maslow's list of needs arranged in their hierarchial order from the lowest to the highest is as follows:

1. Physiological needs, for example, to satisfy hunger, thirst.
2. Safety needs, for example, security and release from anxiety aroused by threats of various kinds.
3. Love needs, for example, love, affection, acceptance, and feeling of belonging in one's relationships with parents, teachers, friends, and other social groups.
4. Esteem needs: both self-esteem from mastery and confidence in one's worth, adequacy, and capacities, and esteem from social approval.
5. Need for self-actualization through creative self-expression in personal and social achievements; need to feel free to act (within the limits of general and social needs), to satisfy one's curiosity, and to understand one's world.

According to Maslow's theory, an individual's lower needs must be satisfied before higher ones can operate. However, it is not necessary that a lower need be completely satisfied before higher need systems can come into operation; they must be satisfied at a *particular level* before the next highest can emerge. Thus, loosely generalized, if only 10 percent of Need 1 is satisfied, Need 2 may not appear. If Need 1 is 20 percent satisfied, then Need 2 may appear.

How do the principles enunciated by Maslow apply to a school situation?

The reader will recall the pitiable situation of the little first-grader whose mother deserted home (the second illustration under "Parental Reassurance"). She was not a food-deprived child. She was not in any important way physically neglected. In these respects her situation illustrates a point made by Maslow: dire physical deprivations are not typical motivating conditions.

But this little girl could not have been more distracted from the planned activities of her classroom had she actually been starving for food. A basic requirement above the physical need level had laid siege to her thoughts and her feelings. Could she get interested in the creative things the teacher had other children doing? Sensing the child's emotional predicament as we do, the question seems almost foolish.

Here was a bright child. Few children in the school possessed more learning aptitude or more talent. Released from her feelings of loss of love and the accompanying anxieties about her psychological "safeties," this youngster could then have applied her attention, her energies, and her potentials of talent to the satisfying of motives which for her would have appeared at a high level in the "ladder" of human motivations.

Relatively free of persistent physical and/or psychological deprevations a child can—and will—manifest the desire to know, the desire to create, and the desire to share what he knows and what he creates. Experiences that build self-confidence and self-respect go far in helping a learner function effectively.

MEASUREMENT OF MOTIVES

A full and satisfactory explanation of human motivation will not be achieved by the development of theories alone—basically important as theories are to such an objective. Motivation will finally yield its well-hidden secrets (and there are many) only as theories can be fully tested. When "fully tested" is spelled out, it means well-designed researches implemented by adequate methods of measurement. The *scientific method* must be brought fully to bear on the problem of identifying motives, measuring their strength, determining how they are interrelated, and learning under what sorts of conditions they go into operation.

That the scientific method is being brought to bear on the problem of motivation is evident in various of the reports of research already mentioned in this chapter—and other researches described in Chapters 14 and 15 especially. But, were the student to talk with the most active and best qualified researchers in the area of motivation, he would find them in agreement that *measurement* (measurement instruments) has not caught up with theory.

Difficulties in Measurement of Motives

There are several major difficulties that surround the measurement of motives.

1. There is the fact, already emphasized, that motives are interoperative with numerous other causation factors in human behavior. How could we hope, for example, to measure an individual's desire for approval without knowing how he perceives his physical-social surroundings? The causes of behavior are complex and interrelated. This applies especially to motivation.

2. There is the fact that humans learn to hide their motives, to disguise them, and to suppress them. We need only ponder the extent to which this is true where sexual motives are concerned to sense the difficulties confronting measurement.

3. The causes of behavior are multiple—to repeat another axiom from Chapter 2. Behaviors that appear identical may derive from very different motivational patterns.

4. Knowledge that one's motives are being measured is itself a factor capable of altering the motivational scheme of things. What would have happened, for example, to Maehr's research results as reported in the preceding chapter had his subjects known that the need for food was a variable under investigation?

All of this means that the measurement of human motives has had to rely considerably on indirect and disguised methods. Some of these (the projective methods, especially) are described in Chapter 15. The student will be better prepared to understand the problems involved in measurement as applied to motivation when he reaches that chapter. What is said there regarding the measurement of personality applies quite directly to the assaying of human drives and motives.[7]

MOTIVATION AND LEARNING

The authors have already explained in several places that for a special reason they do not intend to devote much space in this book to the very important topic of learning. Briefly reiterated, the reason is that they would make *learning in the classroom* the content of an entire course which would be preceded by one for which the present textbook is written. The paragraphs that follow in this section are intended primarily to show that there is indeed a reason—a very important one—for thinking through the relationship between motivation as presented in this chapter and motivation as it pertains to teacher's endeavors to incite children's behaviors in ways conducive to desirable learning.

A major task of the teacher is to make effective use of the motives and goals of children in ways that will harmonize them with the acquisi-

[7] For extensive descriptions of the problems and methods involved in the measurement of motivation see, for example, Murray (1938) [35]; and McClelland, Atkinson, *et al.* (1953) [25].

tion of socially useful skills and knowledge as well as socially desirable attitudes and beliefs. One educational psychologist has emphasized the crucial tie between children's goals and the teacher's instructional effectiveness by stating, *"The goal is what the child is seeking; the incentive is what the teacher provides"* (McDonald, 1965) [26]. This statement may serve well to induce the reader to reflect upon the connections between his own personalized motives and goals and his acquisitions of new knowledge, new attitudes, new beliefs, and so on. As he does this he will sense the special relevance of McDonald's words, "invent motivational strategies" as they pertain to the tasks of the teacher. The student may also gain increased respect for such strategy concepts as 1) reinforcement through feelings of success, 2) encouragement of the impulse to do and to think in new ways, 3) elevating of levels of aspiration and 4) generating commitment to advantageously altered definitions of self. Such are some of the strategy concepts that constitute the bridge between the present discussion of motivation and the substance of textbooks written for courses that deal with learning in the classroom.

SUMMARY

Teachers have much to gain from the study of motivation. Never are they closer to the "why" of human behavior than when they are carefully considering the evidences regarding the satisfaction of a child's basic drives and motives. There is no part of psychology that is more suggestive of helpful insights into the actions of children and youth than the accumulated, scientific knowledge of human drives, and motives.

Lacking sound concepts about human motivation, a teacher is liable to make erroneous inferences about why a child does certain things. Motives do not come clearly labeled; it is easier for a teacher to see the "outer" environmental factors that appear to be associated with the child's conduct. Wrong kinds of dealing with the child follow from faulty interpretations of the forces that are hidden within his behavior.

Motivation, like most other aspects of human behavior must be, as far as possible, studied *in context*—that is, in the context of a particular "whole" individual functioning in a particular environment at a particular time. It is nearsighted practice to try to understand a person's motives without at the same time trying to see his world as he perceives it or to try to understand his motives apart from his past experiences, his thoughts, or his feelings.

Especially closely related are motives and feelings. Together, motivations, feelings, and emotions constitute the main current of the dynamics of human behavior. In this book the discussion of feelings and emotions follows, therefore, immediately after the study of motivation.

One final word: To raise our sights and to view mankind in the many and varied situations that obtain in today's world is to see that motivation as studied in the individual is, in a very real sense, a miniature of motivation as it pertains to whole societies of people. "The fundamental needs of the child are in truth the fundamental needs of society" (Frank, 1952) [10].

Suggested Collateral Readings

Atkinson, J. W., *An Introduction to motivation.* Princeton: D. Van Nostrand Company, Inc., 1964. Chapter 1.

Cole, L. E., and W. F. Bruce, *Educational psychology,* revised ed. Yonkers-on-Hudson, N.Y.: World Book Company (New York: Harcourt, Brace & World, Inc.) 1958. Chapter 6.

Cronbach, L. J., *Educational psychology,* 2d ed. New York: Harcourt, Brace & World, Inc., 1963. Pages 466–497.

Dinkmeyer, D. C., *Child development: The emerging self.* Englewood Cliffs, N.J.: Prentice-Hall, Inc., 1965. Chapter 10.

Eson, M. E., *Psychological foundations of education.* New York: Holt, Rinehart and Winston, Inc., 1964. Chapter 2.

Hall, J. F., *Psychology of motivation.* Philadelphia: J. B. Lippincott Company, 1961.

Hilgard, E. R., and R. C. Atkinson, *Introduction to psychology,* 4th ed. New York: Harcourt, Brace & World, Inc., 1967. Chapters 5 and 6.

Johnson, D. M., *Psychology: A problem-solving approach.* New York: Harper & Row, Publishers, 1961. Chapters 2 and 3.

Johnson, R. C., and G. R. Medinnus, *Child psychology: Behavior and development.* New York: John Wiley & Sons, Inc., 1965. Chapter 1.

McDonald, F. J., *Educational psychology,* 2d ed. Belmont, Calif.: Wadsworth Publishing Company, 1965. Chapter 4.

Maslow, A. H., *Some basic propositions of a growth and self-actualization psychology,* Chapter 4 in *Perceiving, behaving, becoming,* 1962 yearbook of the Association for Supervision and Curriculum Development. Washington, D.C., 1962.

Morgan, C. T., *Introduction to psychology,* 3d ed. New York: McGraw-Hill, Inc., 1966. Chapter 6.

McKeachie, W. J., and Charlotte L. Doyle, *Psychology.* Reading, Mass.: Addison-Wesley Publishing Company, Inc., 1966. Chapter 7.

Newcomb, T. M., *Social psychology.* New York: Holt, Rinehart and Winston, Inc., 1958. Chapters 3 and 4.

References

1. Atkinson, J. W., 1964, *An introduction to motivation.* Princeton: D. Van Nostrand Company, Inc. Page 1.
2. ———, page 2.
3. Boag, T. J., 1952, The white man in the Arctic: A preliminary study of the problems of adjustment, *Amer. J. Psychiat.* **109:** 444–449.
4. Bruner, J. S., 1960, *The process of education.* New York: Random House, Inc., Vintage Books. Pages 72–73.
5. Cofer, C. N., and M. H. Appley, 1965, *Motivation: Theory and research.* New York: John Wiley & Sons, Inc.

6. Cole, L. E., and W. F. Bruce, 1958, *Educational psychology.* Yonkers-on-Hudson, N.Y.: World Book Company (New York: Harcourt, Brace & World, Inc.). Page 227.
7. Dewey, R., and W. J. Humber, 1951, *The development of human behavior.* New York: Crowell-Collier and Macmillan, Inc. Page 184.
8. ———, page 184.
9. Eiserer, P. E., and S. M. Corey, 1955, *The Fifty-second Yearbook of the National Society for the Study of Education,* Part I, "Adapting the secondary school program to the needs of youth." Chicago: The University of Chicago Press (see especially pages 48–58).
10. Frank, L. K., 1952, *The fundamental needs of the child.* New York: The National Association for Mental Health.
11. Guilford, J. P., 1965, "Intellectual factors in productive thinking" in Aschner, Mary Jane, and C. E. Bish, eds., *Productive thinking in education.* Washington, D.C.: National Education Association. Pages 9–10.
12. Hall, J. F., 1961, *Psychology of motivation.* Philadelphia: J. B. Lippincott Company. Page 29.
13. Harlow, H. F., 1958, The nature of love. *The American Psychologist,* **13:** 673–685.
14. Hebb, D. O., 1958, The motivating effects of exteroceptive stimulation. *The American Psychologist,* **13:** 109–113.
15. Hilgard, E. R., 1957, *Introduction to psychology,* 2d ed. New York: Harcourt, Brace & World, Inc. Pages 124–125; 148–149.
16. Jersild, A. T., 1960, *Child psychology,* 5th ed. Englewood Cliffs, N.J.: Prentice-Hall, Inc. Page 275.
17. Jones, M. R., ed., 1955, *Nebraska symposium on motivation.* Lincoln: University of Nebraska Press.
18. Kardiner, A., 1954, *Sex and morality.* Indianapolis: The Bobbs-Merrill Company, Inc. Chapter 5.
19. Kinsey, A. C., W. B. Pomeroy, and C. E. Martin, 1948, *Sexual behavior in the human male.* Philadelphia: W. B. Saunders Company.
20. Krech, D., and R. S. Crutchfield, 1958, *Elements of psychology.* New York: Alfred A. Knopf. Page 272.
21. ———, page 278.
22. ———, page 279.
23. Krout, M. H., 1934, Wishes and behavior. *J. abnorm. soc. Psychol.* **29:** 253–268.
24. Lilly, J. C., 1956, Mental effects of reduction of ordinary levels of physical stimuli on intact, healthy persons. *Psychiatric Research Reports,* No. 5.
25. McClelland, D. C., J. W. Atkinson, R. A. Clark, and E. L. Lowell, 1953, *The achievement motive.* New York: Appleton-Century-Crofts.
26. McDonald, F. J., 1965, *Educational psychology,* 2d ed. Belmont, Calif.: Wadsworth Publishing Company. Page 151.
27. ———, page 114.
28. ———, pages 148, 155.
29. Maehr, M., 1960, *The effect of food-deprivation in binocular conflict.* Unpublished doctoral thesis, University of Nebraska.
30. Maslow, A. H., 1958, Emotional blocks to creativity. *Humanist,* **18:** 325–332.

31. ———, A. H., 1943, A theory of human motivation. *Psychol. Rev.,* **50**: 371.
32. ———.
33. ———.
34. Mead, Margaret, 1935, *Sex and temperament in three primitive societies.* New York: William Morrow & Company, Inc.
35. Murray, H. A., 1938, *Explorations in personality.* New York: Oxford University Press.
36. Rogers, C. R., 1962, "Toward a theory of creativity," in Parness, S. J., and J. P. Harding, eds. New York: Charles Scribner's Sons. Pages 64–72.
37. Rossman, J., 1931, *The psychology of the inventor.* Washington, D.C.: Inventors' Publishing Co.
38. Ryans, D. B., 1942, "Psychology of learning," Chapter VIII, *Forty-first Yearbook of the National Society for the Study of Education,* Part II. Chicago: University of Chicago Press.
39. White, R. W., 1961, Motivation reconsidered: The concept of competence. *Psychol. Rev.,* **66**: 297–333.

CHAPTER 7

Feelings and Emotions

Part of the answer to the question, "Why do people behave as they do?" must be that human beings are emotional, as well as rational, creatures. The previous chapter made it clear that the forces behind behavior are not all conscious or "intellectual." It is axiomatic that the younger the person, the more his behavior is dominated by emotions, and the less by reason. On the other hand, emotions become more complex and less obvious with increasing age. It seems apparent then that the teacher must be knowledgeable about this aspect of behavior and development.

The topic of emotions is of interest not only to the teacher and the behavioral scientist. Since the eighteenth century, physicians have been concerned with the influence of the emotional life upon physiological functioning. The diagnosis and treatment of physical conditions (ulcers, skin conditions, functional blindness, and so forth) associated with emotional reactions have since become the field of a medical specialty called psychosomatic medicine. It is estimated that over 50 percent of those seeking medical aid are experiencing emotionally induced illness (Schindler, 1955) [19]. Physiologists have also been much involved in the study of emotions. They have long sought the answer to such problems as the "center" of emotion in the body and the role of various glands during strong emotional experiences. Additionally, in the works of many novelists, poets, and playwrights, the description of various kinds of emotional behavior has occupied a prominent position.

Granting the importance of emotion, what does the teacher need to know about it? First, certainly, would be the *nature* of emotion: what are emotions, what do they do to or for the individual? Second perhaps in importance would be knowledge of the *origins* of emotion. To what extent are they inherited, to what extent learned? Why is there so much difference between individuals in their emotional behavior? A third concern of the teacher would have to do with the *development* of emotion and emotional responses. What can be expected at different ages with regard to states of fear, anger, or love?

It is the aim of this chapter to answer these and other related questions, in the light of the evidence of contemporary research.

THE NATURE OF EMOTION

The word "emotion" is derived from the Latin word *emovere* which means to "move," to "stir," or to "mix." Thus perhaps the simplest definition of the term would be "a stirred-up state of the body." This, however, is something of an oversimplification: one can stir up his system by eating too many green apples. In emotion, the system is stirred up in a particular way, with accompanying changes in subjective feelings, perception, motivation, and usually (although not always) in observable behavior. Let us examine this process in action.

Mary, a typical seven-year-old girl, is returning home from the grocery store after having purchased a loaf of bread for her mother. As she walks along the sidewalk, she is thinking about her recent birthday party, the outcome of an unfinished story she is reading in school, her new dress, and the surprise her father promised to bring her. In short, Mary is comfortable and happy. Her heart is beating normally; her stomach is digesting the cookie she ate just after school; her lungs are supplying only the necessary amount of oxygen; and minute amounts of blood sugar are being stored in her liver. Suddenly, however, she is confronted by a large dog, growling and snarling ferociously. Her immediate reaction is a "startle response"—an involuntary jerk of the large muscles—and the loaf of bread drops to the sidewalk as she gives a small shriek. Adrenalin (epinephrine) is released into her blood stream, which in turn causes the liver to release its supply of blood sugar. Blood pounds through her temples as her heart quickens its beat. Peristaltic action ceases in her stomach and her mouth starts to become dry. Her hair follicles tighten and the pupils of her eyes dilate. Her nostrils expand to accommodate the increased oxygen required by her lungs. Beads of sweat break out on her forehead.

Her first impulse is to run, but she cannot think clearly which way to go. Just as Mary is starting to cry, the man who owns the dog snaps a leash on its collar and leads it away. As Mary reaches down to pick up the loaf of bread, she is so weak her knees will hardly support her. She kneels beside it on the sidewalk sobbing deeply and shaking unsteadily. In a few minutes she has recovered her composure sufficiently to return home. She feels tired but relaxed; when she reaches home, she feels the need for more rest and for a trip to the bathroom.

How can the mere presence of an animal produce such devastating changes in a child's body? The answer to this question lies in the nature of the nervous system. First, the person must experience sensation—in Mary's case, it was a visual experience. Then the cerebrum—the remembering and reasoning part of the brain—must decide what emotion, if any, is called for. Mary's previous learning or experience determined that fear was appropriate to the situation. Then impulses were sent to other parts of the brain (principally the hypothalamus, the seat of emotional expression) and the autonomic nervous system set off the described changes.

Role of the Autonomic Nervous System

The autonomic nervous system contains two major divisions, the sympathetic and the parasympathetic. The two divisions of the autonomic nervous system have more or less opposing effects on the various internal organs. For example, the parasympathetic division slows the heart beat, facilitates peristaltic (digestive) action of the stomach, and increases the flow of saliva. The sympathetic division accelerates the heart, inhibits peristaltic action and salivary flow, constricts the blood vessels, and stimulates perspiration.

During periods of normal activity the two divisions are in balance, each having its effect on the particular organs and glands concerned. When an individual is experiencing strong emotion, however, the autonomic nervous system is thrown into a state of imbalance wherein the sympathetic division tends to dominate the effects of the parasympathetic division. Following an emotional disturbance the parasympathetic division gains control over the sympathetic division and for a time plays the dominant role. Gradually the two divisions regain their original balance and normal physiological functioning is restored.[1]

A Theory about Emotions

While there is more than one theory about the exact nature and function of this "stirring-up," probably the most reasonable and widely accepted is the "emergency" theory. It is hypothesized in this theory that man, like the lower animals, needs to mobilize all his physical resources to meet certain emergency occasions—he needs to be ready to "fight or run away." Reviewing the changes fear made in Mary's body, this conclusion seems sensible. Let us speculate about the "use" of each of the changes:

1. Adrenalin in the blood stream releases blood sugar from the liver. Blood sugar is the fuel for energy release by the muscles; it is like pumping a richer gasoline and air mixture into the carburetor of an automobile.

[1] For a detailed account of the physiological processes in emotion see Arnold (1954) [2].

2. The heart beat quickens and blood pressure increases, resulting in a faster supply of energy and withdrawal of wastes from the muscles.

3. Digestion slows down or ceases. This often-unpleasant reaction is designed to free a greater supply of blood for use by the muscles, as described above. Often in great emotion the bladder and bowel are involuntarily emptied also.

4. The eyes dilate. Dilation allows more light to enter the eye, presumably to improve vision in certain circumstances.

5. Respiration rate quickens. It is necessary for the lungs to make a faster exchange of oxygen for carbon dioxide in the faster-moving blood, so breathing must be both deeper and faster.

6. Perspiration increases. This makes possible faster cooling of the body, heated from its speeded metabolism or from exertion.

Measurement of Physiological Reactions during Emotion

It is not necessary to depend on subjective impressions to describe physiological changes during strong emotion. A variety of scientific devices can be used to make precise measurements of these changes. Among these methods, measures of skin resistance to electrical current have proven to be very useful in psychological investigations. Skin resistance provides a basis for measuring emotional reactions through the accumulation of perspiration. As perspiration accumulates, electrical resistance of the skin is lowered. This phenomenon is called the galvanic skin response (GSR). By using a voltmeter to reflect change in resistance to electrical conductance of the skin, the GSR can be measured. An instrument so constructed as to measure and record changes in skin resistance is called a galvanometer. The device is widely used in psychological research on emotions.

By combining the measurement of other physiological reactions, such as blood pressure, heart beat, and breathing rate, with the measurement of the GSR, relatively sensitive measures of the physiological accompaniments of emotion can be made. The combination of such measuring devices into one instrument is called the polygraph, or "lie detector."

Polygraphs have been used extensively in criminal investigations. Typical procedure involves obtaining measures of physiological reactions while a suspect is being questioned about some crime or related activity. Because most individuals are unable to control the internal reactions involved in emotion, unusual reactions to specific verbal statements may be identified. On the other hand, many individuals become so emotional during such questioning that polygraph readings are not valid. For this and other legal reasons, polygraph tests ordinarily are not recognized as conclusive evidence in court, but they do provide data to substantiate or refute hypotheses being explored in police work.

Overt Responses and Internal Reactions

Accompanying the internal reactions involved in emotion are the observable or overt responses made by an individual. Smiling, snarling, frowning, pouting, and crying all convey emotional experiences to others. Children early learn to perceive the emotion being depicted by others' gestures, facial expressions, and voices.

That gestures are not necessarily indicative of the internal reactions being experienced, however, is strongly suggested by the laboratory observations of infants. In an extensive study by Jones (1930) [12] the galvanic skin responses of infants were recorded while they were experiencing various emotions. The findings indicated that there was little relationship between overt movements depicting distress and the intensity of the internal reactions. Children who cried loudest frequently experienced the least amount of visceral change. Conversely, some children who showed the least overt responses were experiencing intense internal reactions. Among older children (Jones, 1935) [13] there was a closer relationship between overt response and internal reaction, but this was not sufficiently positive to infer one from the other. In fact, Jones indicated that with increasing age there are likely to be heightened visceral reactions with lessened overt response because of social influence.

Parents and teachers who do not recognize the implications of Jones' findings may easily make erroneous interpretations of children's behavior. As will be seen, children are quick to learn that some responses are far more likely than others to elicit preferential treatment from adults. Only after careful observation of a given child as he encounters different situations, it is possible to infer the intensity of his internal reactions as he experiences emotions.

The Uses of Emotion

Through many avenues of mass communication these days we are advised, "Control Your Emotions!" "Don't Let Emotion Make You Ill!" "Learn to Live with Your Emotions," and so on. One might gain the impression that the ideal state of human life would be one in which no emotions existed, or in which all emotions were inhibited or were kept rigidly under control. Not so! Emotion is as fundamental to life as eating or breathing.

Human beings have the same basic use for emotions that the lower animals have. There is the "emergency" function in fear or anger, which serves to mobilize the body's physical resources for "fight or flight," as described above. There also are the positive sexual and parental feelings of attraction, tenderness, and the like.

Beyond these rather utilitarian functions lies the subjective aspect of emotion. Life would be dull, colorless, and unpalatable indeed without emotional experience. Who would wish to live without the emotional experience of love and affection? Even fear may be pleasurable if kept under control—if not, why would anyone buy tickets for the roller-coaster or other "thrill-rides"?

Most people, consciously or unconsciously, use emotional expression to influence other people. A child's temper tantrum may gain favors or indulgence for him. The bully frowns and shakes his fist to frighten younger children. Mother smiles a welcome-home, father frowns when the ball goes in the rose garden, sister smiles coquettishly at the neighbor boy—each is using an expression of emotion to alter or affect the behavior of other persons.

Our attitudes and beliefs contain emotional components. In one study, emotionally appealing material was added to a rational article on crime. Three groups responded to a questionnaire after reading the prepared materials. Analysis of responses demonstrated that attitudes were significantly influenced by the emotional content: the degree of punitiveness expressed by respondents was related to their emotional arousal (Weiss, 1960) [22].

Emotions may also serve as motivators. People attempt to satisfy their desires and thus achieve pleasure; it will be recalled that both organic and learned motives may demand satisfaction. Fear generally has a negative effect, driving the person away from the feared object or situation. Anger on the other hand drives the person to attack.

It is apparent that emotion is a valuable attribute of human behavior. What undesirable or negative aspects of emotion are there?

Problems in Emotional Behavior

Because of the pervasive nature of the emotions, they are involved in nearly all behavior or adjustment problems. This aspect of emotion will be discussed later in this chapter and again in a more general way in the chapter on personality and adjustment.

At this point, however, the devastating effects on the body of strong emotion should be considered. Paramount among the implications of this for the teacher is recognition of the interference of emotional behavior with effective thought processes. The child who is emotionally disturbed cannot be expected to learn efficiently. If he has been in a verbal battle with his parents before coming to school, if he becomes severely angry or frustrated by an assignment, if he is threatened and is afraid of his teacher, or if he is humiliated by sarcasm, to cite but a few examples, very little if any learning will take place until homeostasis (balance) is restored within his physiological system.

The teacher and parent who understand the physiology of emotional behavior will recognize the desirability of periods of quiet or "cooling down" following intense excitement and emotion. Children cannot be expected to drop off to sleep when they are emotional. Likewise, a child cannot eat when his mouth is dry and his stomach ceases to function. Unfortunately, families will sometimes discuss unpleasant situations during mealtimes. Similarly, parents may unknowingly choose mealtimes to discipline their children for acts committed on occasions far removed from the dinner table. Obviously, these practices are psychologically undesirable.

In the case of Mary cited earlier, the circumstance provoking the emotion was quickly removed, and Mary's body readily adjusted itself to normal functioning. When the physiological accompaniments of strong emotions continue over a period of time, however, the individual becomes listless and physically exhausted. He has difficulty arising in the morning, he frequently loses weight, and he cannot think clearly. This condition was first recognized during World War I as "shell shock." During World War II it was called "combat fatigue" or "emotional exhaustion" and in medical terminology is referred to as "neurasthenia." When the body continues long in a state of marked imbalance, other unfortunate physical conditions may result. High blood pressure with ensuing heart damage or brain hemorrhage, and ulcers, are two common disorders linked to emotional upsets existing over a long period of time.

ORIGIN OF EMOTION

How do human beings come by their emotions? As is true of every other aspect of human behavior, learning and maturation both play a part. The infant is born with a capacity for certain rather limited emotional responses. With maturation, his capacity for both feeling and expressing increases markedly, giving rise to more varied and highly differentiated responses. At the same time, he has had the opportunity to learn appropriate (as well as inappropriate) responses to a great variety of stimuli.

Research Evidence on Early Emotions

The relative influence of inherent, as compared to learned, elements in emotion has been widely debated. Prior to World War I, it was commonly believed that emotional reactions to certain stimuli were inherited. It was held, for example, that a child was afraid of a snake or of the dark because of an inborn connection which began functioning when the child saw a snake for the first time or when he was placed in the dark for the first time. The list of such inherited fear stimuli became increasingly lengthy as new items were added to it.

Shortly after World War I, however, an American psychologist, John B. Watson, and his students began a series of observations upon newly born infants that vastly modified the concept of emotions and their origin (Watson, 1919) [21]. Watson postulated that there were three emotions experienced by the newborn infant: fear, rage, and love. He found that only two stimuli would result in the emotional reaction which he called fear—loss of support and sudden loud noises. He found that physical restraint elicited the response he called rage. Watson further postulated that all emotional reactions experienced throughout the life of the individual were outgrowths of these three primary emotions. Although Watson's original conclusions about the three primary emotions have been criticized and discredited in the light of additional findings, his work, nevertheless, resulted in the refutation of the heredity theory of emotions—an important first step toward understanding emotional behavior.

During the 1920s, psychologists undertook many investigations of the three emotional states which Watson postulated and the stimuli which would elicit these emotions. Many of the findings did not agree with Watson's contentions. It was found, for example, that several forms of intense stimulation would result in distress (rage) and that not all newborn infants displayed the startle response to loud noises and to being dropped (fear).

In 1927, Sherman conducted a study of the emotions of the newborn which cast serious doubt upon the existence of separate emotions at birth (Sherman, 1927) [20]. Sherman's subjects were two infants less than a week in age. He took motion pictures of them after being dropped, while hungry, and after being pricked with a needle. He then showed the films to nurses, medical students, and psychology students. When the pictures were viewed in original form, the observers showed considerable agreement as to the emotion being experienced. When Sherman cut the films and spliced them in such a fashion that the stimuli and the responses were interchanged at random, the observers were markedly inconsistent in their identification of the actual response.

Sherman's experiment was repeated with the babies and the observers in the same room. The babies were kept behind a screen, however, while they were stimulated. Again the judges were unable to identify the stimulus which had been used to excite them (dropping, restraint, pricking). In other words, the observers were unable to attach uniform labels to the emotion being experienced when they did not know the situation. Stated still differently, the labels assigned to the responses of the infants were based upon the situation as the observers perceived it rather than upon the responses made by the infants. Thus, Sherman demonstrated that emotional responses of the newborn are not as distinct as Watson had postulated.

On the basis of his findings, Sherman proposed a substitute explanation of the origin of emotions. He suggested that newborn infants experience two general kinds of emotion—pleasant and unpleasant—

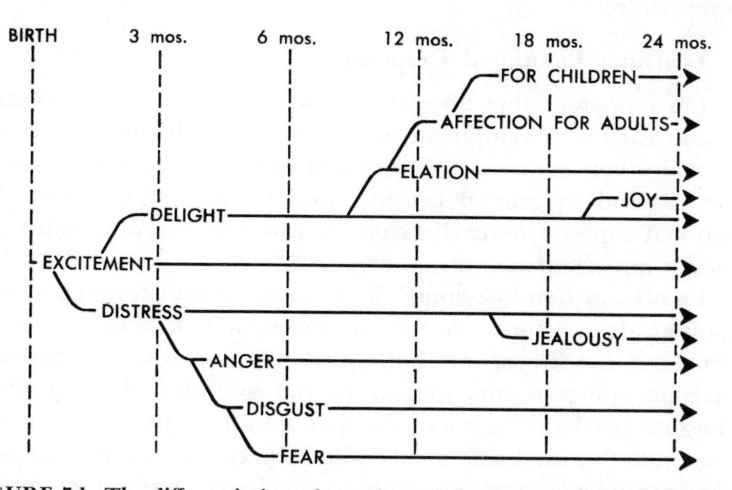

FIGURE 7.1. The differentiation of emotions. From Bridges, K. M. B., A genetic theory of the emotions, *J. genet. Psychol.,* 37: 514–527. By permission of the Journal Press.

and that they learn to make responses which result in pleasantness and to avoid responses which result in unpleasantness.

The modern concept of the origin and development of emotions was proposed by Bridges, who made extensive observations of newborn infants and nursery-school children after Sherman concluded the foregoing studies (Bridges, 1930) [4]. Bridges' concept of the differentiation of emotions is shown graphically in Figure 7.1. From this diagram it will be noted that the individual emotions derive from an undifferentiated "trunk" and that each new emotion is added to those which existed previously. Bridges proposes that the emotions of the newborn are best characterized by excitement or generalized excitement. At this stage of development the internal and external reactions are uncoordinated and individual emotional response is undistinguishable. As a result of a combination of maturation and experience, the child has by about three months of age developed a consistent pattern of response differentiated rather generally into two kinds of emotional experience—delight and distress. Relaxation, smiling, and cooing are indications of delight accompanying satisfying situations, whereas crying and muscular tension are indications of the distress accompanying unpleasant situations.

Distress has become differentiated into anger, disgust, and fear by the age of six months, while delight has become elation and affection by the age of one year. By two years the "trunk" has branched into several differentiated emotions. As age is accompanied by increased maturation and experience, the innumerable emotional responses which constitute the rich emotional life of older childhood and adulthood are added to the repertoire.

Learning Emotional Responses

It is apparent that after the early formation and differentiation of emotion further development occurs. Emotions become more and more specific in their expression, in the objects or situations to which they are attached, and in general become both broader and deeper. Although emotional capacity naturally changes with age, learning experiences are of major importance in this development.

Emotional Conditioning. The situations which result in emotional responses are not the same for all persons nor do they remain constant throughout the life of one individual. For example, the appearance of Policeman Jones results in fear to the motorist who has just driven through a red light, anger to the man to whom Jones gave a ticket yesterday, relief to the home owner who suspected that a burglar was in his basement, but pleasure and pride to the Jones family. Emotions become associated with a particular situation or stimulus through a process referred to as conditioning.

The process of conditioning was first studied about 1890 by the Russian physiologist, Ivan P. Pavlov. Pavlov conducted many laboratory experiments on conditioning and demonstrated several of its basic principles. "Classical" conditioning involves establishing an association between a specific response and some stimulus which was originally neutral. The procedure is well illustrated in the following original experiment conducted by Pavlov.

Pavlov noted that whenever meat was presented to a hungry dog, the animal would immediately salivate. He termed the meat the *unconditioned stimulus* and the salivation the *unconditioned response.* The word "unconditioned" used in this way means that the phenomena described are natural, or unlearned, stimuli or responses; meat is a natural inducement to salivation.

Pavlov then proceeded to present the meat to the dog immediately after sounding a bell in the dog's presence. After the bell and the meat were presented to the dog in this manner several times, the bell alone caused the dog to salivate. Pavlov referred to the bell as the *conditioned stimulus* and the salivation following the bell as the *conditioned response*. The experimenter also demonstrated that not only would a bell elicit the conditioned response, but a buzzer and other tone-producing instruments would also do so. This phenomenon he called *stimulus generalization*.

By extending the laboratory experiments on conditioning one step further, Pavlov demonstrated another important principle. He found that if he continued to present the conditioned stimulus (bell) without the unconditioned stimulus (meat) the conditioned response (salivation) would gradually disappear. This process, essentially the reverse of conditioning, Pavlov designated *extinction*. In other words, in this phase of his experimentation, he demonstrated that without reinforcement a conditioned response gradually declines in strength and disappears.

Another form of his phenomenon, called *operant conditioning*, has been much studied in recent years. In operant conditioning, the learner first makes a response to a problem situation, which response if reinforced is likely to be repeated. In a typical laboratory experiment, a hungry animal exploring a puzzle box by chance or design presses (that is to say, operates, hence "operant") a bar or trigger and is rewarded with a morsel of food. Soon he repeats the action and the ensuing food reward reinforces his tendency until the bar-pressing becomes a strong habit.

Conditioning is a major process in the association of emotions with certain situations or stimuli. Although Pavlov's original experiments on conditioning involved animals, many conditioning experiments have been conducted with human beings and have involved emotional responses as the unconditioned stimuli. Among these experiments, one conducted by Watson, whose work was cited earlier, is illustrative.

The subject for this experiment was Albert, an eleven-month-old boy. Before the experiment, Albert was not afraid of white furry animals. When a loud noise was sounded immediately preceding the presentation of a white rat, the procedure being repeated several times, Albert developed distinct fear reactions not only to the rat but to other furry white objects such as a rabbit and a white beard. When at a later time the objects which Albert had been conditioned to fear were presented while he was eating, reconditioning occurred. This phase of the experiment demonstrated that through reconditioning it was possible to replace the fear response with one of pleasure.

Thus, it can be seen that the processes of conditioning and stimulus generalization can account for the origin of many fears among children—depending on their experience with the stimulus. A child may fear *all* men in white coats because he associates them with pain resulting from hypodermic needles. Another child may fear all dogs because he was once knocked down by an overenthusiastic pet. Conversely, a child may associate his mother's smile with food and presents.

Children frequently learn to dislike a school subject such as arithmetic because of associations of humiliation or frustration. Fear of reciting, of teachers, and of examinations can also be included in this category. These and other examples serve to illustrate the important role which conditioning plays in emotions. The following account is from the clinical experience of the authors:

K. was referred to a psychological clinic for help. He was a vigorous, well-built man in his early twenties, pleasant in manner and appearance. His problem was illiteracy—not just inadequate reading skills, but a complete lack of ability to handle symbols, including numbers. He illustrated the extent of his problems by describing a situation in which he would meet an attractive girl who appeared to be interested in him. If she agreed to date him, he was incapable of recording or using her telephone number or street address.

Testing revealed that his intelligence was quite good, and he had had several years of formal schooling. His well-to-do family had sought help for him from many sources without avail. He had even been described as suffering from agraphia and alexia (brain malfunctions causing the inability to learn to read or write).

Psychological diagnosis brought forth an explanation. In early school years he had suffered from a glandular malfunction (now corrected) which had given rise to extreme obesity. In the little country school he attended, the teachers required children to stand up before the class (and thus the entire school) to read. His attempts were inevitably greeted with hoots and catcalls of "Fatty!", reinforced by the teacher's sarcasm. By means of conditioning the reading process was associated with the emotions of shame, humiliation, fear, and anger: small wonder that he rejected the whole reading process. Therapy and retraining in the clinic brought about some alleviation of his difficulty, but strongly conditioned responses are not easily changed.

It was much easier to deal with emotional problems of short duration than with severe problems like the one in the case above. Just as conditioning is of greatest importance in the origin of emotions, reconditioning and extinction are of great importance in overcoming emotional responses. Whenever some situation has become associated with an unpleasant reaction, the basic approach to overcoming the unpleasant reaction is that of substituting a pleasant reaction for it. The experience of Gary, a two-year-old boy, illustrates the process.

While on a family picnic, Gary was severely frightened by a motorcycle which overturned in the midst of the picnic dishes and food. Although at first his parents dismissed the incident, they became concerned several days later because Gary still showed extreme signs of fear of motorcycles.

To overcome this fear response to motorcycles, Gary's father located a machine in the neighborhood and took Gary to inspect it while it was parked. After several such trips, Gary's father had the owner of the motorcycle start it while he and Gary watched from a distance. Gradually the child was brought closer to the machine until his fear disappeared completely.

Certainly, not all fears arise or can be overcome so easily as the one just described. It should now be apparent, however, that emotional reactions to various stimuli are constantly undergoing revision as we gain new associations and have new experiences.

Models for Emotional Behavior. As illustrated above, much emotional behavior arises directly from the situation in which the child finds himself. Other emotional responses are the product of environmental forces, some intentional and others fortuitous.

Very early in life *imitation* begins to take place. It is not uncommon to observe a young child crying when he hears a brother or sister crying, even when he is unaware of the reason. Many parents of young children will have observed them looking quickly to one or both parents for cues in a tense situation, as when a thunderstorm breaks. If the parents laugh or seem unconcerned, the child may relax; but if the parents show distress, the child will quickly start crying and showing fear symptoms.

Later on, the child will learn more complex behavior patterns in the same fashion. "How do you act when you are angry—do you call names, withdraw silently, burst into tears? How much expression of love and affection is acceptable, and how can it be shown? What should you do when you are frightened?" Such questions are answered by example, not only by parents and family members but by the culture around the child. In one of many recent studies on aggression, nursery school children observed aggressive and nonaggressive adult models, who either behaved aggressively toward a large inflated toy, or passively assembled Tinker Toys. The children were subsequently mildly frustrated (to stimulate aggressive reactions) and released into a room containing a variety of toys. The children who had been exposed to aggressive models showed significantly more imitative physical and verbal aggression than did children exposed to nonaggressive models, or children in a control group who had not been exposed to the adult models at all (Bandura, Ross and Ross, 1961) [3].

Many cues as to emotional expression are explicit, rather than implicit. That is, direct *instruction,* advice, and indoctrination are used to structure behavior. When the young child becomes tearfully angry in church, his mother hurries him out and explains what being a "good boy" in church means. When the older child guffaws at the dinner table, father is likely to give him the alternative of being acceptably quiet or of leaving. And so it goes—parents, teachers, and even peers let the growing child know what is and is not acceptable in his emotional expression.

Individual Differences

Although we are more aware of observable differences among children in such characteristics as height and weight, there are, nevertheless, equally pronounced differences among children in such characteristics as the intensity of internal emotional reactions. Some children are relatively placid and "unmoved" in situations which bring forth intense reactions from other children. Emotional displays are a product of both environmental and hereditary factors. Emotional reaction involves sensitivity to external situations as well as sensitivity of the neurophysiological system.

The similarity of reactions involving the autonomic nervous system among persons of varying degrees of hereditary relationship has been studied by Jost and Sontag (1944) [14]. They observed children between the ages of six and twelve and obtained measurements of skin resistance, pulse pressure, salivation, respiration rate, vasomotor persistence time, autonomic balance, "Heart period," and volar conductance. The children included several pairs of identical twins and many pairs of brothers and sisters. A definite pattern of relationship was found between the physiological measurements and heredity. The measures for identical twins were most similar (correlations of .43 and .49), those for brothers and sisters were next most similar (correlations of .26 and .40), and those for unrelated children showed no relationship (correlations .26 and .16). The conclusion from this study was that individuals differ markedly in the intensity of their physiological reactions during emotion, and these reactions have a hereditary basis.

Thus, the child inherits a structure that is predisposed to function in a certain way or at a certain level. This gives him a *capacity* for certain kinds of emotional perception and expression. By indoctrination, imitation, instruction, and trial-and-error responses to situations, certain emotional responses, within the limits of his inherent capacity, are expressed and by the process of conditioning are learned and become truly a part of him.

An example of the uniqueness—and consistency of uniqueness—of individual emotional reactions may be reported from a longitudinal study of the Fels Institute. As we shall see, frustration is a basis for anger responses. In the Fels studies, *passivity* as a characteristic individual response to frustration was highly stable in boys and girls during the first ten years of life (Kagan and Moss, 1962) [15]. Early passivity in males was linked to nonaggressive, socially inhibited, dependent and conforming behavior during adolescence. As adults these same men had non-masculine interests and were highly dependent. Somewhat similar results were found for females (Kagan and Moss, 1962) [16]. It is interesting to note that the passive males showed a consistent autonomic reactivity; their passivity in childhood was associated with a minimal degree of spontaneous cardiac arrhythmia in adulthood (Kagan and Moss, 1962) [17].

Emotional reaction is closely related to personality; more extensive discussion of consistency of personality characteristics over time will be discussed in a later chapter.

DEVELOPMENT OF EMOTIONS AND EMOTIONAL RESPONSES [2]

In addition to an awareness of the nature and origin of emotions in general, the teacher should have a knowledge of the development of specific emotions—fear, anger, and love. Each of these will be considered in turn.

Fear

For the experienced speaker, the idea of giving a talk before an audience holds no fear. But for the novice, the very thought of appearing before an audience elicits internal reactions. The experienced ski jumper feels satisfaction and pleasure as he rockets down a steep jump and soars a hundred feet or more through the air, while the person who has never skied before clings timorously to the guard rail. The veteran window washer leans nonchalantly against his leather belt while hanging above a stream of traffic eighty floors below, while the office secretary hesitates to approach an open window closer than is required to water the plants. The herpetologist examines snakes with no more reaction than mild curiosity, while the adolescent school girl shrieks with terror at the very sight of one.

Likewise, as individuals grow older and more experienced, many fears which they once displayed are replaced by feelings of confidence and reactions of pleasure. The child who one year may be afraid to duck his head under water may two years later be diving from a ten-foot board. The four-year-old who covered his head during a thunderstorm last year may now shout with glee at thunderstorms. The two-year-old who was afraid of dogs may have an inseparable shaggy pal at age nine.

As we consider the individual differences among people with respect to what they fear as well as the variations within individuals at different stages of their development, it becomes apparent that there is a univer-

[2] For a summary and evaluation of research in emotional development, see Jersild (1954) [7].

sal perceptual condition in the stituation which provokes fear. That condition may be described as follows: *Fear arises according to the extent to which we perceive ourselves as being physically or mentally unable to cope with a situation.* Stated another way, fear arises when we perceive our progress toward our goals as being threatened, or when we envision ourselves as failing. Why is the previously mentioned novice speaker afraid? He "fears" ridicule by his audience. The girl is afraid that the snake might poison her. The child thinks the dog may bring him bodily harm. In other words, there is an underlying threat in all fear situations.

In some instances, such as that of the inexperienced skier, the fear may be justified by the actual circumstances, and the threat may be real. In other instances, such as that of fear of nonpoisonous snakes, the threat may be wholly unrealistic. To the individual involved, however, the reality or unreality of the threat is not the determining factor; rather it is his perception of the situation that accounts for the fear response.

Age Trends and Children's Fears. As a child gains new skills and new insights into his environment, the situations which result in fear vary accordingly. The graphs shown in Figure 7.2 summarize the findings of a study by Jersild and Holmes (1935) [10] of age trends and children's fears. From these graphs it will be noted that as childhood progresses, there is a decrease in fears relating to the concrete type of bodily injury and an increase in fears arising from imaginary stituations and from social situations. These graphs were based upon reports of parents and upon experimental situations in which children's behavior was actually observed. Part of this change is the product of the child's increasing ability to perceive the past and project himself into the future, and thus to imagine the misfortunes that might befall him. Many fears of a concrete nature persist, of course.

Through the school years, there is a striking discrepancy between the expressed fears of children, and the actual experience of misfortune they report. In one study (Jersild *et al.*, 1933) [11], school-age children were asked to describe the "worst happening" of their lives; 14 percent reported fear of animals while only 2 percent had been attacked, 19 percent expressed fear of ghosts, supernatural agents, and the like, without experience to confirm their fears. In contrast, far fewer mentioned actual bodily injuries and accidents among their "worst happenings," yet many had suffered from such misfortunes. Of interest to teachers are the findings of another study (Jersild, Goldman, and Loftus, 1941) [9]: over half of a group of 1124 children worried about "being left back in school," although in their particular school less than 1 percent was failed annually. Jersild, one of the authors of this study, comments:

In a situation such as this, the child's "fear" apparently gives an external reference to an internal or "intrapsychic" difficulty: even if there is every likelihood that he will "pass" according to the external standard imposed by the school, he still may regard himself as a failure according to internal standards, for his performance falls short of what he thinks he should be able to do. (Jersild, 1954) [8]

As children approach adolescence, there is a marked increase in fear of social situations. Such a condition is understandable when it is recalled that social interaction and social sensitivity characterize adolescence. It is natural to be threatened by imaginary failure in situations so important to this age level.

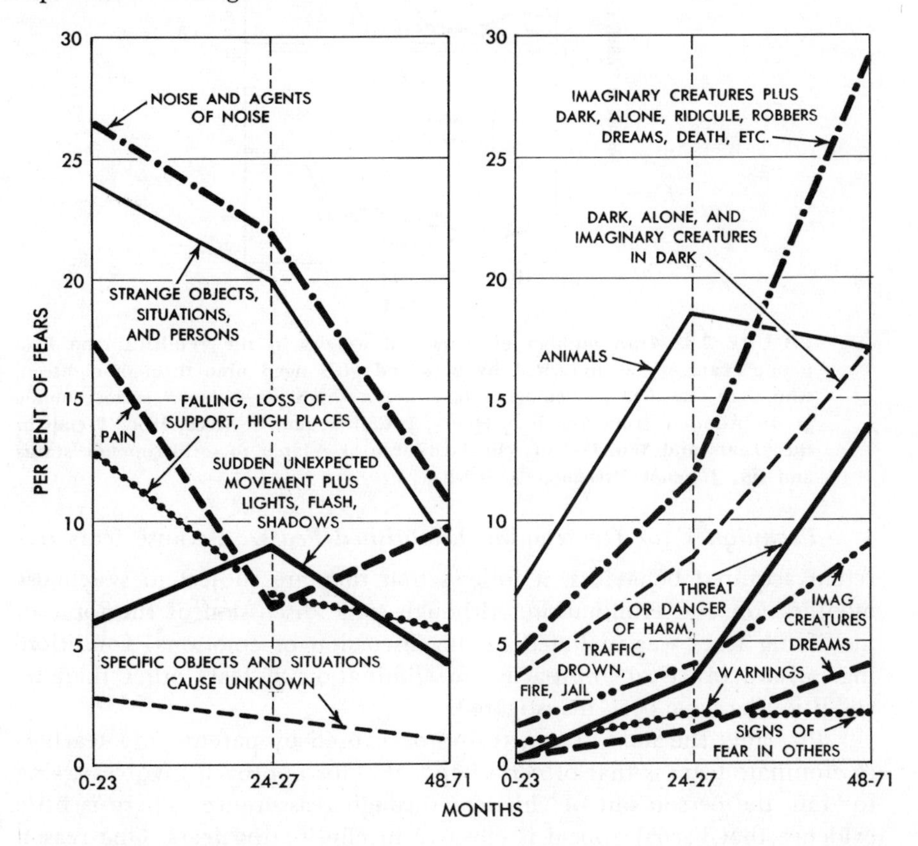

FIGURE 7.2. Relative frequency of various fear situations as described by parents and teachers. Drawn from 146 records of observations of children for periods of 21 days (31, 91, and 24 at the respective age levels), combined with occasional records of 117 additional children (27, 67, and 23 at the respective age levels). Adapted from Jersild, A. T., and Frances B. Holmes, Children's fears, *Child Develpm. Monogr.,* 54, 1935. By permission of the Bureau of Publications, Teachers College, Columbia University.

General social factors, as well as purely individual ones, may influence the development of fears and worries. For example, Angelino, Collins, and Mech (1956) [1] found different developmental patterns between ages nine and eighteen for several different fears and worries. The patterns for "Political and Economic" fears are shown in Figure 7.3.

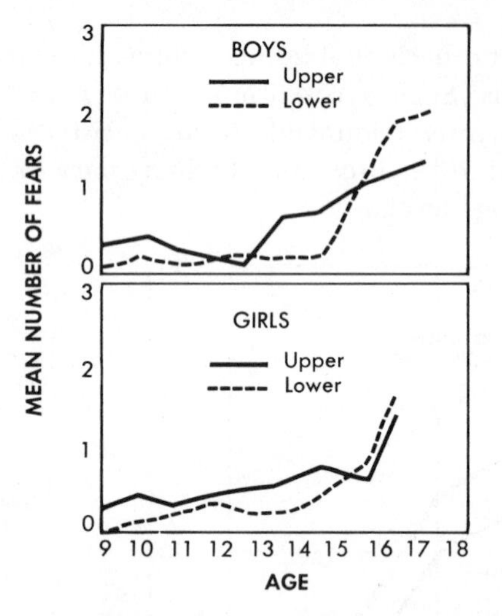

FIGURE 7.3. Mean number of fears and worries in the "Political and Economic" category as indicated by boys and girls aged nine through eighteen, who were classified as belonging to either a "high" or a "low" socioeconomic group. Adapted from Angelino, Henry, J. Collins, and E. Mech, 1956, Trends in the "Fears and Worries" of school children as related to socioeconomic status and age, *J. genet. Psychol.*, 89: 263–276.

Techniques for Overcoming Established Fears. Because fears represent acquired behaviors, it follows that they are subject to systematic modification and elimination. Although some discussion of the topic of modifying fears was included in the discussion of emotional conditioning, several practical approaches to elimination of fears other than reconditioning have been investigated.

Probably the most frequent approach used by parents and teachers to eliminate fears is that of *verbal appeal.* This approach involves trying to "talk the person out of" his fear through reassurance. There is little evidence that verbal appeal is effective in eliminating fears. One reason for its ineffectiveness is that verbal appeal is based upon abstract discussion rather than actual experience. Children, especially those with limited vocabularies, respond more readily to personal experiences than to verbal description.

Modifying fear through *disuse* or avoidance of the feared situation until new skills and understandings are acquired is an approach to dealing with the fears of children. Some fears, such as fear of fire or of knives, result from lack of understanding. In the method of disuse, however, it is assumed that the child will have some incidental learning experience which will provide understanding of the feared situation: this assumption is questionable. Disuse is appropriate for overcoming fear only when increased age is necessary for gaining physical strength or mental ability to cope with the feared situation.

Placing a fearful individual among others of his age group who show no fear is an effective method for dealing with some fears. This method is known as *social imitation*. This approach is similar to reconditioning in that a pleasant activity (socialization) becomes associated with the feared situation or object. In addition, the fearful individual may feel that he has a "reputation" to preserve in the group; also, he may gain self-confidence from the group.

A method of dealing with fear that has a long history of use in practical situations is that of *negative adaptation*. Negative adaptation involves repeating the feared stimulus so frequently that the individual learns to ignore it. For example, this technique has been used in breaking dogs of gun shyness. The gun-shy animal is taken to a shooting gallery or to some other place where a great deal of shooting is taking place and is kept there until it becomes accustomed to the sound of gun shots. Another use of negative adaptation is suggested by the cliché—"If you are afraid of the water, get someone to push you in." Obviously, negative adaptation is useful only when the original fear is mild and when there is reason to believe that increased understanding will result. Otherwise, the experience of being placed in the feared situation can be so traumatic as to make the fear even more pronounced.

To the extent that *distraction* does not cause dependency on other people in a feared situation, this approach may be helpful in overcoming some fears. When the distraction takes the form of concentrating on some skill, elements of reconditioning are present. In other words, if a skill is being performed in the feared situation, the individual may come to associate the feared situation with the satisfaction derived from his skilled performance. Persons who once feared social situations frequently report greatly diminished fear through participation in such activities as playing bridge and dancing. It is essential, however, if this approach is to be effective, that the skill be one from which the fearful individual derives satisfaction.

Of the various approaches available for overcoming established fears, the basic one is *reconditioning*. This approach permits a direct attack on the feared situation rather than an indirect attack as is the case with verbal appeal. The one restriction which must be recognized in reconditioning, however, is that care must be taken to avoid forming a reverse association to the desired one. For example, it is possible to recondition a child to fear candy. The probability of a reverse association being formed is lessened through using only highly satisfying situations for the reconditioning process.

Because fears involve actual and suspected inability to cope with situations, many fears which might otherwise arise can be prevented by giving the child as much realistic insight into new experiences as possible before they take place. In addition, underlying security and affection serve to prevent the development of many fears in childhood. Nevertheless, some fears will develop and consideration must be given to overcoming them.

Phobias. Phobias are persistent and irrational fears of specific objects or situations. Phobias are so deep-seated that the fearful person is ordinarily unaware of their origin. Usually, however, they may be traced to a traumatic experience during childhood. Among the more frequently encountered phobias are *claustrophobia,* fear of closed places, *acrophobia,* fear of high places, and *ochlophobia,* fear of crowds.

Knowledge of the treatment necessary for overcoming phobias is limited. The treatment of such conditions must be left to professional personnel. It is likely, however, that if reasonable care is exercised in preventing and overcoming fears in childhood, most phobias can be avoided.

Worry. Not all fears are related to specific or immediate conditions in a person's life. Whenever an individual continues to envision himself in threatening situations, the condition commonly known as "worry" results. To a limited extent, worry is a normal phenomenon and plays an important role in the lives of both children and adults. Everyone has some situations wth which he cannot cope and his concern about them is justified because realistic threats or danger are involved. For example, the salesman may worry about not meeting his quota. The mother of a two-year-old may worry about her child playing in the street. It is when worries persist or when no action is taken to relieve them that they become reactions which interfere with satisfactory emotional health. Normally, worries are dispelled by action. The salesman works to make his quota and his worries are over. The mother has a fence built and her concern is relieved. Thus, worry is a feeling of threat to progress toward goals.

Anxiety. Another term referring to non-specific or non-situational fear is "anxiety." This concept is important to almost any consideration of human adjustment or mental health. Anxiety may be defined in many ways but there is general agreement that it is a response to a threat to the self (or "ego," in psychoanalytic terms). The source of the threat may be—usually is—unknown to the anxious person.

There are two principal views of the source of anxiety, the psychoanalytic and the learning theory approach. Theorists of psychoanalytic persuasion see anxiety as stemming from the child's early fear of separation from parents, and later from conflicts betweeen his "instinctual" desires and the restrictions of society (Jersild, 1954) [8]. Learning theorists on the other hand believe that anxiety is generated by associations made in various stimulus situations such as those involving pain, unexpected or rapidly changing stimuli, and the like.

Whatever the source, anxiety gives rise to behavior aimed at reducing the distress it causes. We are all familiar with our own or others' reactions to mild anxiety—depression, moodiness, extrasensitivity to slights, and the like. More severe tension and anxiety may be expressed through aggressive reactions, or through defensive reactions like repression, daydreaming, or rationalization. Deep and long-continued anxiety may lead to psychoneurotic or psychotic behavior, requiring professional care and treatment.

Much anxiety is generated in children by school experiences, since these are a major aspect of early life. Inability to do acceptable classroom work, misbehavior in or out of class, rejection or conflict in relations with either peers or teachers—any or all of these may occur during the school years. Although anxiety is not easy to measure, some devices for the purpose have been constructed, making research possible on groups of children. Boys are found to have somewhat lower scores than girls—either because girls admit more anxiety, or because they are actually more anxious. In one study it was found that there was a low negative correlation (−.20) between anxiety generated by schoolwork, and IQ. This is reasonable, of course, because brighter children should have less reason for difficulty with schoolwork. Children with higher general anxiety tended, not surprisingly, to be more anxious over school tests. Boys with low anxiety fared better in school academic work than high-anxiety boys; the relationship did not hold for girls (Sarason, Davidson, Lighthall, Waite, and Ruebush, 1960) [18].

Anger

Just as was true of "fear" situations, so are there variations in the perceptions of situations provoking anger. Whereas one child willingly permits his toys to be taken away by someone else, another child physically attacks anyone who even hints that he will take the toys. One boy who is building a cart of wood endures extensive frustration in trying to fit pieces together, whereas another boy becomes angry immediately and smashes all pieces of wood within reach. One husband laughs at his wife's burned biscuits, while another stamps out of the house in a violent display of temper. These are but a few examples of the importance of perception in situations evoking anger.

Underlying anger in an individual is his perception of a block in his effort to reach a goal. A block perceived in this manner may be any of several types. For example, it may be a physical one as in the illustration of the boards not fitting together. It may be a personal one as in the case of a girl who becomes angry with herself because she failed an examination. Or the block may be a social one as in the case of a man who becomes angry as he reads about the treatment of a minority group of which he is a member.

In general, the tendency in anger situations is that of wanting to destroy the block which impedes progress toward goals and produces frustration. This tendency in anger-provoking situations is quite different from that in fear-provoking situations. In fear the tendency is to want to withdraw and avoid the threat.

Whether or not an individual perceives a situation as anger-provoking, that is, as containing a block, depends upon many factors operating singly or in combination. Among the most important factors affecting anger are the following: physical conditions of hunger and tiredness, previous success and failure experiences with similar situations, the importance of the goal involved, previous experience with the particular type of block encountered, boredom with some activity, and the anticipated effect of an anger display on others.

Age Trends and Children's Anger. In very young infants, the emotionalized response designated as "anger" usually results whenever there is interference with the child's activity. Pinning his arms to his sides, for example, will ordinarily produce screaming, face-flushing, and thrashing movements by the two-week-old child. By the age of six months, however, he has learned to direct his aggression toward the source of the blocking. Throughout the developmental period, anger displays go through a series of modifications—modifications involving the identification of the block, the expression of aggression, the final acceptance of the constraint or the selection of some path toward the goal which circumvents or removes the block.

Situations provoking anger during the first two years of life are almost exclusively associated with interference in the child's activity. Because personal care activities occupy such a large proportion of the young child's waking hours, situations involving eating, dressing, and toilet training elicit the majority of anger displays from young children (Goodenough, 1931) [5]. During the preschool years the aggression is usually directed toward the block, but it may be displaced toward other available objects or persons such as toys, peers, or siblings. Occasionally a preschool child will express aggression through thumbsucking or excessive eating, but the typical pattern is one of direct expression.

When the child learns to communicate with others, he encounters a new type of block as well as a new method of expressing aggression—verbal communication. That verbal communication embodies many new thwarting experiences for the child is well illustrated by the number of times in a day that the child hears his mother say, "Don't!" Likewise, as language is mastered, name-calling and similar blocks are experienced. The child soon learns that he can "respond in kind" and thus a new method of expressing aggression develops. Such expressions as, "Well, keep your old toy then!" "Sissy!" and the like are heard commonly among children in the lower elementary grades.

As adolescence approaches, the individual encounters an increasing number of social restraints from parents. Frequently adolescents perceive these restraints as interference with progress toward goals; as a result anger is generated. Adolescents as well as adults are likely to find situations involving social restraints especially trying. Conflicts between adolescents and parents can sometimes be resolved by a careful examination of the adolescent's goals. Occasionally, unrealistic goals will be revealed in this manner and extreme anger displays will be avoided.

Techniques for Dealing with Anger. It is inherent in the daily life of a small child that he will encounter blocking. His ability to manipulate objects, the necessity for protecting him from harm, the impossibility of his having all the possessions he wants, and his inability to understand reasons for interruptions contribute to blocking experiences. Likewise, in later childhood and in adolescence, blocking will be encountered. How, then, should we deal with anger realistically?

In general, when an angry individual perceives an object or a situation as blocking his reaching of some goal, internal tension is produced. This tension continues as long as the individual perceives the path toward the goal as being blocked. To deal with anger effectively requires that the individual perceive the situation in a new or different light. In short, his attention must be centered upon something else, at least momentarily, and then the blocked path must be reconsidered from a viewpoint not held previously. This is the basis for phrases such as "Count to ten before you strike" and "Sleep on it." It is assumed that the diversion in attention will permit a reevaluation of the original situation at a later time.

During infancy and early childhood when children are too young to communicate effectively, control of anger becomes primarily a matter of distraction. With older children it may be necessary to distract their attention momentarily and then discuss the anger-provoking situation after the diversion and after looking at the situation in a new light.

Love and Affection. The imperative need of the infant for love and affection is discussed elsewhere. The child who receives adequate love is ready to be a giver of affection as well as a recipient.

The first object of love is of course the mother (or mother-substitute). When a strong affectional relationship is established here, the child is ready to offer his affection to other members of the family present in the home—father, siblings, perhaps grandparents or other relatives. For a long time however, it is the mother who is the center of the child's life, and it is his relation to her that determines much of his later ability to love and trust others.

Once he is secure at home, he is ready to turn to others. Preschoolers develop momentarily strong friendships, but these may be severed quickly and new alliances made without distress. During the elementary-school years there is increasing friendship with peers. These relationships may be very close and arouse strong feelings. The trend in affectional ties is steadily away from the family and toward peers. This does not mean of course that love for mother or for family is lessened. It implies rather that the child feels secure enough, loving and being loved, to expand his horizons, to *stretch* his affections, so to speak, so as to include new and different persons.

From early until late childhood, there is an increasing tendency to establish close ties with like-sex peers. With pubescence comes an increasing interest in the opposite sex, followed by a period of "falling in love" with a succession of adolescent love-objects. This new interest in the opposite sex does not imply loss of affection for like-sex peers. On the contrary, these ties, like those with the individual's parents, become firmer. There is a parallel between the child's moving from the family to the peer group, and from the like-sex ties to opposite-sex ties: each movement implies that a previous stage has been negotiated successfully. Eventually, usually in the early twenties, a final selection of a mate is made and a home and new family are established.

Influence of Sexual Development. Although sexuality exists from earliest infancy, it does not usually manifest itself in peer relations much before pubescence. (Sex play with other children, viewing of the sex organs and the like occurs quite early but is regarded as a matter more of curiosity and self-satisfaction than of love or affection.) By pubescence, definite and powerful sex feelings occur and demand expression. The desire for sexual satisfaction, whether conscious or not, then enters into any boy-girl relationship, and the term "love" covers feelings and desires ranging from vague stirrings of liking and of tenderness, to explicit desires to exploit the other person as a sex partner. The implications of adolescent sex-social development are discussed in a later chapter.

SUMMARY

Since human beings are emotional as well as rational creatures, it is necessary to study the emotions to understand behavior. Emotions are defined as stirred-up states of the organism.

When a situation is perceived as calling for emotion, the autonomic nervous system triggers many functional changes which prepare the body for expression of emotion—that is, for action. In addition to putting the body on an emergency basis, emotions may be used to influence others, as well as to add color and enjoyment to life.

The capacity to feel and express emotion is inborn, but specific emotional responses are learned, in the same fashion that other responses are learned. Individual differences are the product of inherited structure and functional predisposition, interacting with learning experiences.

The developmental characteristics of fear, anger, and affection are discussed, and effective means of dealing with the first two are considered.

Suggested Collateral Readings

Breckenridge, M. E., and E. L. Vincent, *Child development,* 4th ed. Philadelphia: W. B. Saunders Company, 1960. Chapter 3.

Dunbar, Flanders, *Emotions and bodily changes,* 4th ed. New York: Columbia University Press, 1954.

English, H. B., Education of the emotions. *J. humanistic Psychol.,* 1961, **1:** 101–109.

Hurlock, Elizabeth B., *Child development.* New York: McGraw-Hill, Inc., 1964. Chapter 7.

Jersild, A. T., Emotional development, Chapter 14 in Carmichael, L., ed., *Manual of child psychology.* New York: John Wiley & Sons, Inc., 1954.

Morgan C. T., *Introduction to psychology.* New York: McGraw-Hill, Inc., 1961. Chapter 4.

Munn, N. L., *The evolution and growth of human behavior.* Boston: Houghton Mifflin Company, 1965. Chapter 14.

Prescott, D. A., Role of love in human development. *J. educ. Psychol.,* 1961, **19:** 4–12.

Ruebush, B. K., Anxiety, Chapter 11 in Stevenson, H. W., J. Kagan, and C. Spiker, eds. Chicago: National Society for the Study of Education, 1963.

References

1. Angelino, H., J. Dollins, and E. V. Mech, 1956, Trends in the "Fears and Worries" of school children as related to socioeconomic status and age. *J. genet. Psychol.,* **89:** 263–276.
2. Arnold, Magda B., 1954, Physiological differentiation in emotional states. *Psychol. Rev.,* **52:** 35–48.
3. Bandura, A., Dorothea Ross, and Sheila Ross, 1961, Transmission of aggression through imitation of aggressive models. *J. abnorm. soc. Psychol.,* LXIII, 575–582.
4. Bridges, Katharine M. B., 1930, A genetic theory of the emotions. *J. genet. Psychol.,* **37:** 514–527.
5. Goodenough, Florence L., 1931, The expression of the emotions in infancy. *Child Develpm.,* **2:** 96–101.
6. ———, 1939, Anger in young children. *Institute of Child Welfare Monograph,* No. 9.

7. Jersild, A.T., 1954, Emotional development, in Carmichael, L., *et al.*, *Manual of child psychology*. New York: John Wiley & Sons, Inc. Chapter 14.
8. ———, in Carmichael, *Manual,* page 868.
9. ———, B. Goldman, and J. J. Loftus, 1941, A comparative study of the worries of children in two school situations. *J. exper. Educ.,* **4**: 323–366.
10. ———, and Frances B. Holmes, 1935, Children's fears. *Child Develpm. Monogr.,* No. 20.
11. ———, Frances V. Markey, and Catherine L. Jersild, 1933, Children's fears, dreams, likes, dislikes, pleasant and unpleasant memories. *Child Develpm. Monogr.,* No. 12.
12. Jones, H. E., 1930, The galvanic skin reflex in infancy. *Child Develpm.,* **1**: 106–110.
13. ———, 1935, The galvanic skin reflex as related to overt emotional expression. *Amer. J. Psychol.,* **47**: 241–251.
14. Jost, H., and A. W. Sontag, 1944, The genetic factor in autonomic nervous system functions. *Psychosomatic Medicine,* **6**: 308–310.
15. Kagan, J., and H. A. Moss, 1962, *Birth to maturity*. New York: John Wiley & Sons, Inc. Page 52.
16. ———, page 276.
17. ———, page 81.
18. Sarason, S. B., K. S. Davidson, F. F. Lighthall, R. R. Waite, and B. K. Ruebush, 1960, *Anxiety in elementary school children*. New York: John Wiley & Sons, Inc.
19. Schindler, J. A., 1954, *How to live 365 days a year*. Englewood Cliffs, N.J.: Prentice-Hall, Inc. Pages 7–8.
20. Sherman, M., 1927, The differentiation of emotional responses in infants: I. Judgments of emotional responses from motion pictures and from actual observation. *J. comp. Psychol.,* **7**: 265–284.
21. Watson, J. B., 1919, *Psychology from the standpoint of a behaviorist*. Philadelphia: J. B. Lippincott Company.
22. Weiss, W., 1960, Emotional arousal and attitude change. *Psychol. Rep.,* **6**: 267–280.

CHAPTER 8

Social-cultural Basis of Behavior

The study of drives and motives and the closely related problems of feelings and emotions helps us to understand how human behavior is "set in motion" and how it is subject to changing intensities. Indispensable as such understandings are, they constitute only part of the full account of why people do what they do. There remains the equally important question of why people do the things they do *in the particular way they have of doing them.* To illustrate: the need for food is the reason why people eat, but this need does not explain the way they eat, nor their choice of things to eat. Some people like to eat eggs; others steadfastly, indeed religiously, avoid eating them. It is sufficient for some people simply to snatch their food from a common kettle and eat it without benefit of utensils or rituals; others would be horrified at such actions.

Thus it is with the behaviors that accompany the satisfying of the various human needs; they are often very different in different persons. More accurately, they are often very different in persons from different backgrounds. These backgrounds are the social groups—the different societies—of which the individuals are members.

Our purpose in this chapter will be to examine the nature of the behavior patterns that make for the contrasts—and conflicts—between persons from different social groups. The aim will be not only to find explanation for these different "styles of life," as they have quite aptly been named, but also to consider the implications of this knowledge for our better understanding, as teachers, of the persons we must work with in school.

THE SCHOOL AND CHILDREN'S STYLES OF LIFE

The problem of trying to understand the different styles of life of different people crops up in many places. Frequently it is in connection with the contrasting habits of thinking and doing of people who reside in different parts of the same city—parts that are not necessarily widely separated in terms of physical distance, but that are widely separated psychologically. Sometimes it is in connection with the strange customs of people from another part of the country or from a different—a "foreign"—country. Most often, however, for the teacher the problem is one which he confronts in the classroom or on the school playground.

Some of the Junior High pupils in Miss Johnson's English class are models of what their school wants in young people. There can be little doubt that their behavior is what the school values: They are seldom reproved by their teachers for what they do, they are frequently complimented for their actions and the ideas they express, and thier report cards are marked "Excellent" in citizenship.

But there are other children in Miss Johnson's class whose patterns of behavior are constantly at variance witl what the school approves and values. Tony, for example, seems to prefer copying the English papers of other pupils to preparing the assignments for himself. When he is reproached for his indifferent school work or his aversion to doing the lessons on his own he gives Miss Johnson further cause for disappointment by explaining that he does not like English, he does not like school, and he intends to quit as soon as possible. He does not hesitate to say in the presence of his teachers that he expects someday to make more money than "educated people" by working at his father's occupation; that his father manages to do all right on an eighth grade education. The stinger in Tony's remarks is his obvious disdain for much that the school stands for. His unyielding conviction that he knows a better way of life than that which the school proclaims is painful evidence to his teachers that they have lost a battle—a battle with a style of life that is much out of harmony with what they themselves believe in and what they try hard to get children to exhibit.

Tony's teachers are understanding persons. They recognize that Tony's attitudes toward school are not to be looked upon as a sign of contrariness. Furthermore, they know better than to think that his style of life is something inborn, something biologically inherited. They realize that his particular attitudes toward school, like the particular attitudes of other youngsters, are part of a larger, *learned pattern* of social behavior.

The disdain for school and for such niceties as doing his own assignments have been acquired by Tony from the same environmental mold as his food preferences, his "naughty" stories, and his threats to use his fists to settle even the most trivial playground dispute. Tony's teachers do understand the origins of the boy's behavior pattern and the strong hold which his particular social environment has on him. But, being the responsible teachers that they are, they keep trying to shape his attitudes and actions into a pattern which they believe to be better for him.

Tony, like all children everywhere, is living evidence of the strength of acquired behavior patterns that are characteristic of families and of larger circles of people and are portrayed in the ways of the individual members. To know the reasons why the Tonys, Manuels, Karls, Rose Maries, Mee Lees, and just plain Johns and Marys are as they are we must understand the nature of the influence that their environment—especially their social environment—has on them. To achieve our purpose of learning how individuals get their styles of life we must carefully investigate the dynamics of the situations that *shape and organize* the ways different groups and their individual members have of acting and thinking and feeling.

ON BECOMING A SOCIAL CREATURE

There is awaiting every new baby a surrounding that consists of more than physical things. It is an environment of ideas, feelings, and beliefs, and patterns of activities related thereto. This is the infant's human environment. It is a social-cultural environment that may consist of the ways of people who are illiterate, or of the ways of people who are well educated. In any case, as the days grow into months the ideas, feelings, and actions of the persons close to the child come to be in large measure his own; they will be almost as inescapable as the air he breathes.

Such is the nature of the relationship by which the persons who are close to the baby envelop him in a way of life—a "culture"—which he cannot but assimilate—and which, viewed differently, assimilates him. The shaping influence of society on the individual has been expressed as follows:

> The life history of the individual is first and foremost an accommodation to the patterns and standards traditionally handed down in his community. From the moment of his birth, the customs into which he is born shape his life experience and behavior. By the time he can talk, he is a little creature of his culture, and by the time he is grown and able to take part in its activities, its habits are his habits, its beliefs are his beliefs, its impossibilities are his impossibilities. Every child that is born into his group will share them with him, and no child born into one on the opposite side of the globe can ever achieve the thousandth part. (Benedict, 1934) [3]

After calling attention to the fact that on any given day in the United States some eleven and a half thousand babies are born (approximately four million a year) Alpenfels (1957) [1] says,

Like most immigrants to our country, these four million new citizens must learn in a very few years how to behave in the organized and accumulated heritage we call American culture. . . . The infant is nonsocial and "cultureless" at birth. Yet, he is already an individual. He is unique in his physical make-up, a bundle of almost infinite potentialities. The crisis of his birth is his first contact with the realities of culture that slowly shape him into a social human being.

Alpenfels then adds:

As the child grows, he will share the experiences of those close to him. He will take on the attitudes and behaviors of those whom he will learn to love. He will find no freedom from his culture anywhere in the world. It will mold his ideas and direct his actions, dominate his choice of life goals, and provide the stepping stones that lead to the fulfillment of the self.

The individual will find no freedom from his culture. It will dominate all that he thinks and all that he does. These statements express forcibly the role which the culture has in the development of an individual's style of life. But what precisely is the culture? Of what does it consist?

THE CONTEXT OF CULTURE

The answer to the question about the nature of culture may be constructed in part from various phrases in the quotations from Benedict and Alpenfels. Benedict spoke of "standards traditionally handed down in the community," of customs, habits, and beliefs. Alpenfels identified the culture with "organized and accumulated heritage."

Linton (1945) [12] calls the culture "a particular way of life characteristic of a society." A more expanded definition is one which presents the culture as the sum total of all thought and behavior that is handed down from generation to generation by *communicative interaction* rather than by genetic inheritance.[1]

Culture as Symbol System

It is a mistake to limit the idea of culture to the various artifacts which people in different societies have produced. By the same token it is a mistake to equate culture only with people's ideas, beliefs, wants, values, and so on. The crux of the definition above which contains the expression "communicative interaction" is the idea that through speech, gestures, art, writings, and the things that people make (their artifacts) there is expressed their ideas, beliefs, wants, values, and so forth. Spoken

[1] Davis, K., *Human society* [6], New York: Crowell-Collier and Macmillan, 1951, page 304; and Lee, A. M., ed., *Principles of sociology* [11], New York: Barnes & Noble, Inc., 1951, page 7.

expression, writing, art, and so on, *symbolize* a people's thought and behavior.

These symbols surround the individual as a member of a given society. They provide him with an interpretation of life as it is to be lived in his society. The symbols that operate in the closest association with his efforts to satisfy his own evolving needs are, by and large, those which most shape his style of life.

Can we now relate such ideas of the culture to an individual's life with his family and his community? Let us see if we can do this by taking a look at the home and neighborhood environment in which Tony lives. This is the Tony whose style of life concerned his teachers.

Culture and the Immediate Surroundings

Tony lives in a neighborhood that borders on the business section of his town, a place of eighty thousand people. Houses in his neighborhood are big but old; they were once the homes of well-to-do people before modern transportation and the desire for suburban life resulted in migration away from the center of town.

So situated, Tony's neighborhood is characterized in part by a particular pattern of sounds. There is a mixture of the noises of many vehicles, the steady hum of business and industry not far away, and the clamor of railway trains on tracks that bound the neighborhood on one side. There seems always to be the thumping and bumping that accompanies the loading of trucks at the warehouses only a few blocks from Tony's home. There are the shouts of children playing in the fenced-in backyards and other children playing in the streets. There are also the muffled sounds of voices in apartments which have been carved out of the former one-family houses, including the one in which Tony lives.

There is music too. It is not always that which the school prefers; it is seldom that which Tony has heard mentioned in connection with concerts. Sometimes it is a merry piece which is chanted by children at play; occasionally it is a lullaby which Tony's mother likes to sing at night in her native tongue. Often it is "popular music" which pours from juke boxes in cafes and taverns not far away.

Mingled with the sounds of Tony's neighborhood is the mixture of many smells. They emanate from the fuel oils and gases of trains, trucks, and cars. They come from the nondescript assortment of flowers and shrubs that adorn the rear lot-lines of the homes. Especially do they include the pungent aromas that drift from kitchen windows and signal the approaching meal times.

To the sounds and smells may be added the sights that make Tony's surroundings familiar to him. To him the houses do not look rundown; they look comfortable. The backyards and front yards do not look barren; they look as if they were intended to be used for such purposes as children and dogs have for them. In this respect the yards are in striking contrast with some that Tony knows about in other parts of town where lawns are to be looked at, not played on.

Some of the features that Tony likes about the outside of his house he also finds inside. Plainness and practicality are the rule. The furniture invites use and is obviously accustomed to it. The living room walls are hung with a few old paintings, but they also make room for a large family photograph and an oversized picture calendar. Since the living room is large, there is no problem of accommodating a somewhat battered piano which Tony's sister likes to play, and a TV set toward which most of the chairs face. Bookcases and books are conspicuous by their absence from Tony's home; there are, however, on a couple of living room "stands," some newspapers, several issues of a trade journal and a stack of comics.

Fused together in this way into Tony's experience are many impressions of the "good life" which derive from the world of his familiar sensations. Also fused into his experience is a developing pattern of ideas, attitudes, and values —the pattern about which his teachers were painfully conscious.

This, in brief, is the complex of vital experiences of the culture which Tony receives from the more proximate (close-up) situations of his family-neighborhood surroundings. They are the kinds of experiences that must be taken into account if we are to understand the Tony we see in school.

In summary, Tony's situation illustrates the following ideas of the culture and its working:

1. *Symbolization is evident everywhere in a person's social-physical environment.* We are quite prepared to find a people's "psychology" (ideas, beliefs, and so forth) revealed in speech, in art, and in the things that are written; we may be slower to recognize the "autobiography" of a people in the gadgets they make and use, in the kinds of dwellings they construct and occupy, and in the machines they have for doing their work. With the idea of symbolization in mind, we would not have difficulty in finding dozens of illustrations of the communication of the culture of a society to its members.

2. *Distinctive social-physical characteristics of a neighborhood play a part in determining an individual's pattern of behavior.*

Doubtless, it was apparent to the reader that in some respects the social-physical settings in which Tony was seen and the version of the culture which they supplied, differed from what one would expect to find in other parts of a town that size. Furthermore, while it was not indicated by the illustration, it might well be that in some important respects the culture of this town as a whole contrasts with the culture in other parts of the country.

Such local differences in culture have given rise to the use of the expression *subculture.* For the individual it is the subculture, or even more, the "sub-subculture," to which he is exposed during his formative years, that does most to set the behavior pattern of his life.

3. *The quality of the sensations an individual has of his surround-*

ings plays an important role in his experience of the culture. For example, there were for Tony the strident sounds and other characteristic sensations incident to living on the fringes of industry.

We need only in our imagination to contrast this setting with, for example, the peace and quiet of a ranch on a midwestern prairie, or a flat alongside of which a city's elevated trains run at frequent intervals, or a stately home on a suburban lake front, to sense the peculiar impact which distinctive sensations have in the shaping of an individual's style of life.

4. *The satisfaction of the individual's physical and psychological needs is basic to his acquisition of the culture.* We shall return to this theme later in this chapter.

5. *The interests and behavior preferences of a youngster's pals afford much of the social context in which he exercises his developing attitudes and values and thus crystallizes his style of life.* This topic will be discussed fully in Chapter 13; it will not, therefore, be elaborated upon in the present connection.

6. *The beliefs, values, wishes, fears, and so forth, of the individual's family enter his behavior pattern with special force*—being, as they are, intertwined with the meeting of his fundamental needs. The version of the culture conveyed to the child by his family usually harmonizes in general with that of the community as a whole but in certain important particulars may be different. But, different as this version may be, it is the one that reaches the individual first. Being *first,* where the culture is concerned, is of considerable psychological importance.

CULTURE IMPARTED IN "BEHAVIOR SETTINGS"

With our attention still fixed on the culture and the way it is communicated to the individual, let us consider the special manner in which the individual reacts in given situations.

In one of their reports on the life of "Midwest" (mentioned in Chapter 3), Wright and his associates (1951) [21] have described effectively the way in which behavior relates to what they have chosen to call "behavior settings." And they have shown the sizable place that the home occupies among the behavior settings.

A home in Midwest is seen by the people of the town, by the children, their parents and the others, as a place where particular kinds of behavior are appropriate. It is seen as a place where, for example, you put on almost anything but a hat, sit in a comfortable chair, and listen to the radio. A church in Midwest is otherwise perceived; it is seen as a place where you wear your best clothes, sit in a pew, and listen to a sermon. This home or that church is a stable and generally recognized center of activity in Midwest in which you commonly do some things, but not others. So are Clifford's Drug Store, the Courthouse Square, Hallowe'en, Thanksgiving, the 4-H Club, and the annual Pioneers' Picnic. All such stable activity centers of a community that are perceived by its people in general as appropriate for particular kinds of behavior, we call *behavior settings.* Two hundred and sixty-three of the behavior settings in Midwest are homes. . . . Behavior settings are by no means neutral scenes of action. They are the seats of social pressures and limiting physical properties and arrangements that impose in some degree certain kinds of psychological situations, with the net result that they tend to *require* certain kinds of behavior. . . .

What this adds up to is that Midwest's homes, as behavior settings, account for 67 percent of its children's waking hours. Parent educators do not have to be told that homes are of great importance in the lives of children. Here, though, is evidence as to how true this is for America's Midwests.

SOCIAL-CULTURAL INFLUENCE IN LARGER PERSPECTIVE

To be able fully to account for a person's style of life, we must see him in relation to the scheme of the larger society of which he is a member, as well as in closeup perspective. Considered in the larger view, the individual is seen to possess characteristics that are similar to those of many persons living in neighborhoods and communities other than his own and geographically removed by various distances from his own, but related thereto as parts of a more comprehensive whole—of a nation, in our case.

In this light, Tony would be seen to have numerous traits that are characteristic of the "American Way of Life"—traits that mark him as an American boy who would not be mistaken for a British boy or a boy from Madagascar or some other part of the world. Many features of Tony's behavior pattern could be traced directly or indirectly to the influence of the agencies that are at work in his larger social environment and convey to him the culture of the larger society of his city, state, and nation.

Although our main purpose in this chapter is to try to understand the *how* of social-cultural influence it is, nevertheless, very much to the point to ask *what* distinguishes the American way of life. What are the behaviors that the agencies of our culture are expected to develop in the members of our society?

FEATURES OF THE AMERICAN WAY OF LIFE

Enterprise (or enterprising) is a trait that many observers have placed high in their descriptions of the "typical American." Doubtless the trait has definite associations with the need—especially on the part of pioneering Americans—for venturesomeness, daring, and courage. As long as there are frontiers to challenge us, whether we see them as geographical, industrial, or otherwise, we are likely to value the enterpriser in our midst. The heroes of American history were strong in this trait. So, too, are our heroes of today—those of the "adult Westerns" as well as those in our most highly regarded literary novels.

Independence is a characteristic that the great majority of us in this country believe to be descriptive of us. Like enterprise, it has long been associated in this country with the spirit of the hardy pioneer and also the freedom-loving immigrant.

Humanitarianism has, especially in recent years, been a feature of our own self-view—and fairly consistently a feature ascribed to us by our friends in other countries. No people in all history have been more sensitive to appeals of various kinds on behalf of needy persons. We emphasize this human quality to our children by many illustrations of the virtue of kindness and generosity. Brutality in any form is obnoxious to our culture.

Cooperativeness has won a place in the American way of life by being so essential to the survival both of the individual and the group in our pioneering society. At the same time that we value the entrepreneur we applaud a good group effort. We tend to see enterprise and cooperativeness as mutually supportive behaviors which should be learned by every individual. "Someone must carry the ball and the others must clear the way for him" is a phrase for which American life has many applications.

Honesty is not only the best policy; it is required of all who measure up to the image Americans have of themselves. So energetically do we teachers strive to inculcate this trait that we sometimes defeat our purposes by failing to demonstrate another trait, trustfulness, which is a necessary ingredient of the learning situation in which honesty is developed. The point to be underscored, however, in the mention of honesty, is its definitiveness as a characteristic highly valued in Americans by Americans. One needs only to ponder the variety of ways in which we bank on other people's integrity in carrying on our way of life to realize the extent to which this trait has been assumed to be "built into" our style of life.

Other traits descriptive of the American pattern of life could be listed. Certainly in our culture there is emphasis upon the need to be God-fearing, loyal, clean (where will more soap be found than in our supermarkets?), and friendly. Our culture teaches and preaches law-abiding behaviors, respect for one's elders, and moral respectability. These are the kinds of behaviors most insistently and universally emphasized by the responsible culture-imparting agencies of our society. They are the good—the "ideal"—features of our social life.

To be realistic we must recognize that not all the forces at work in our society are governed by—or in harmony with—the ideals and values just described. There exist in our society selfishness as well as humanitarianism, ruthless individualism as well as cooperativeness and socially motivated enterprise, payola as well as honesty, and much crowd behavior where we would hope for responsible independence.

The mention of the seamy side of our pattern of life is not intended as a note of cynicism. Rather, it is a reminder that certain of the social-cultural forces that influence American boys and girls do not conform to the picture we teachers like best. To understand this fact is, as was stated, to be realistic; it is to be more alert to the problems a teacher faces in serving as an effective agent of the culture he values.

With this view of some of the features that characterize our culture we may now return to further consideration of *how* the culture works and specifically to the function of *agencies* in the socialization process.

The School as a Major Agency of the Culture

To call the school a culture-bearing agency seems platitudinous to say the least. But for any of us to say how it works in the accomplishment of that function is something else—something we may not have considered thoroughly.

Have we considered what it means to a child to learn the skills the school teaches him—what these skills mean in opening up to him the facts about the larger social-cultural world around him? Surely any naïve idea that reading is an end in itself disappears in a hurry when one thinks of its function in providing for the child's acquaintance with the larger world of ideas, beliefs, and values as well as the world's storehouses of factual knowledge.

Have we thought what it means to boys and girls to become acquainted through books and other media with great persons whom they may or may not ever meet face to face? No influence is greater in the life of the individual than the influence of persons who are for him significant persons. Is he to be introduced to persons who can furnish him ideas and aspirations beyond what some homes and some neighborhood acquaintances have to offer? Again: books, instructional films, class discussions, and other educational media can (and do) serve this function.

In the school many children and youths have their best (most learning-ful) opportunity to participate in the judging and applying of general moral principles, and especially in situations where there is real conflict of values. A learner's perspectives grow in moments of conflict if he can have wise guidance at such moments.

We could go on to examine other ways in which the school serves in a distinctive and important way to convey the culture, in large perspective, to the individual. But the purpose here is not to give a complete account of the school-culture relationship; it is rather to make certain that we do not minimize the role of the very agency for whose effectiveness we as teachers are to a major degree responsible.

Mass Media and the Culture

The mass media of communication provide many examples of the impression on the individual of the stamp of the larger society. What is the fad in wearing apparel? What does Hollywood recommend as the newest form of personal glamour? What should youth aspire to vocationally? How should youth regard their parents and other adults? What are the acceptable morals? What are the purposes that should most govern one's living? These and innumerable other aspects of the American way of life are channeled via the mass media to every remote crossroads of the country as well as to the centers of densest population. The advertising that induces skinny lads in the big cities to eat large quantities of cereals because they are claimed to be an important part of the diet of famous athletes also, for the same reasons, shapes the eating habits of scattered thousands of country boys. Similarly among girls and young women the body dimensions that are prescribed for Miss America are as well known on Main Street as on the Boardwalk.

Such is the functioning of agencies of the culture as seen in the larger perspective. These are the kinds of agencies which reach into Tony's life and the life of all youth to bring their individual styles of life into greater harmony with the style approved by the larger society.[2]

ON "BEING BROUGHT UP THAT WAY"

We have noted the part that different agencies play in bringing various behaviors to the individual's awareness and in providing him the opportunity to "practice" them and selectively to integrate certain of them into his own developing style of life. But this falls short of giving us the key to the explanation of how the behaviors which are "around" the individual get "into him" and become part of him.

Those Who Do the "Bringing-up"

After raising a series of questions about how the people of different societies came to have the behaviors characteristic of them (for example,

[2] A good presentation of the culture in an American community and the ways in which the culture influences the individual is given in West (1945) [20].

the Chinese dislike for milk and milk products and the willingness of the Japanese to die in a Banzai charge that seems senseless to us), Kluckhohn (1949) [10] proposes this answer:

> Not because different peoples have different instincts, not because they were destined by God or Fate to different habits, not because the weather is different in China and Japan and the United States. Sometimes shrewd common sense has an answer that is close to that of the anthropologist: "because they were brought up that way."

There are, as we have said, the *agencies* of society that provide the settings for the individual to learn the culture. There are also the *agents*—the "culture-bearers"—who teach "the way to behave." The concept that culture influences individuals *through* the culture-bearers is a valid one and very different from the notion that culture simply "acts on" individuals.

The Mother as Agent of the Culture. From birth onward the child learns new actions and develops new motives. His original drives become altered, and his acquired motives help direct his behavior. These are developments that begin while he is his mother's babe in arms. For example, the baby soon learns to anticipate his feedings, "not only for the food they bring but for the circumstances surrounding the food—the mother's talking, hugging, smiling, and so on" (Sears, *et al.*) [16]. The writers just quoted go on to say:

> In all this learning, the mother plays a central part, for she is the most common element in her child's experience. She it is who decides what behavior is changeworthy, and she it is who does the changing—or tries to. In so doing she must not only establish in her own mind what new behavior is to be added to the child's repertory of acts, but she must devise ways of training him. Not all her interactions with him are purposefully designed to this end, of course. Much that she does, day in and day out, is simply caretaking or enjoyment of him as another human being whom she loves. Sometimes, too, she reacts to him as an annoying person, and she hurts or frustrates him.

Here we have, in a manner of speaking, the social psychology and indeed the "personality psychology" of the cradle and the crib. The mother, wittingly or unwittingly, as she supplies her baby's needs surrounds the experience with a mixture of culturally approved behaviors. Much the same point is made in the statement, "Psychologically, it is a literal truth and no mere figure of speech to say that a child takes in attitudes and prejudices with his mother's milk" (Cole, 1953) [4]. And, one might add, the child takes in attitudes and beliefs with his mother's bedtime songs. In this manner a biological organism is developed into a social person by having fundamental desires channeled, satisfied, and adaptively changed.

The Family as Agent of the Culture. The close association between the individual's satisfaction of needs and his acquisition of culturally preferred behaviors extends beyond his mother and his cradle. Other relatives, as well as his mother, soon begin to be for him agents of the culture. How to behave in matters pertaining to feeding, elimination, rest and sleep, the impulse to cry or otherwise to vent strong feelings: these are learnings which occur in much the same need-culture context as has just been described. Thus, habit pattern upon habit pattern, the process of socialization takes place as the need-motivated child takes on the version of the culture that his family supplies.

Wider Range of Needs and Wider Circle of Culture's Agents. Gradually, as the child grows older and is able with increased maturity to do without the immediate presence of his mother, other persons become important to him; for, as he discovers, it *is* other persons who can give him what his ever-growing patterns of needs require and can also withhold what he needs or feels that he needs.

The child's relationships with other persons, especially those of his own age, become more and more socially involved. Of necessity he learns from his peers and others the roles required for being a socially acceptable person.

The Teacher as an Agent of the Culture. Just as the school is a highly important agency of the culture, so also is the teacher a highly effective *agent* of the culture. Every person who is professionally employed as a teacher, whether it be in the kindergarten, in the graduate college, or in a grade somewhere between, is in one way or another an influencer of individuals' beliefs, ideas, attitudes, and values. At many points the teacher's influence reinforces those of other agents and agencies; at some points his influence may be strongly at variance with other influences; in any case, if he *is* a teacher, other individuals are learning from him. The challenge he faces is that of helping his pupils not only better to interpret their culture and their society but to *want* to improve them and to learn how to do so.

Many Other Agents. We need only to think of the many agencies that touch more or less effectively the life of the individual to recognize that there are numerous other important culture-bearers. The preachers, priests, and rabbis in our society, and their counterparts as spiritual leaders in certain other societies, perform a major role in cultural influence. The personnel of youth-serving agencies outside the school and the church, the librarian, the officers of the law, and many persons having no formal connection with what we have been calling "agencies": all play a part in shaping the individual's style of life.

There is another feature of the culture which we must examine in this expanded context. It is the relationship of the individual's behaviors to the kinds of *positions* he occupies in his society.

RELATION OF BEHAVIORS TO SOCIAL POSITIONS

Every individual must learn the roles which his society expects of the positions which he occupies. There are numerous positions. Some relate to being male or being female. Some relate to age. Some relate to kinship. There are also positions in some societies which individuals may attain as a result of their own ingenuity and effort. But for every individual there is the task of learning the behaviors which his particular culture prescribes for different positions.

To understand the general concept of the learning of social roles it may be helpful to turn to a culture other than our own. Sometimes the facts about our behavior as human beings stand out in clearer relief when we can examine them against a relatively unfamiliar social backdrop.

The following example of how the individual must adapt his behavior to his place in society is taken from a description of Balinese life by Bateson and Mead (1942) [2].

> Each man's place in the social scheme of his village is known; the contribution which he must make to the work and ceremonial of the village and the share of the whole which he will receive back again are likewise defined. For failure to receive what is due him, he is fined even more heavily than for failure to give that which is due from him. Just as a man must accept his privileges as well as discharge his duties, so is he also the guardian of his own status and if, as may happen to a high caste, that status is affronted, he himself must perform a ceremony to restore it. Similarly, the elder of a village who may not come in contact with birth or death, must himself perform a costly ceremony, if someone enters his house fresh from contact with birth or death. And as order and status are maintained among men, so also, within the man, the head is the highest part of the body and not only must it be placed toward the gods, but a flower which has fallen to the ground may not be picked up and placed in the hair again. Younger brothers may not touch the head of an older brother, and nothing may be taken from above the head of one of higher status without much preliminary apology.

Bateson and Mead employed the term *status* in describing what they called "each man's place in the social scheme of his village." This place, or status, is usually defined not by some *one* fact or condition pertaining to the individual but by a pattern of interrelated conditions.

As an illustration of the effect of variable conditions on a person's status, let us consider the following. It is one thing to occupy the status accorded a person whose age is sixty-five. It is quite another thing to occupy a position reserved for a person who is age sixty-five and a woman rather than a man. It is a still different status situation that is defined when a sixty-five-year-old woman occupies the office of city mayor.

Status is the relative position occupied by a member of a group in a given social situation, which tends to define this member's rights and obligations with reference to those of other individuals who are in some way identified with the same situation.

Age and Status

Age is a circumstance around which societies arbitrarily organize and regulate behavior. The members of different societies have definite ideas about the appropriate behavior for persons of different ages. In our society there are regulations that pertain to the age when an individual is "old enough" to vote, to marry, or to drive an automobile. There are definite customs pertaining to such questions as who shall precede whom (the younger or older person) when individuals of different ages are being seated or being introduced in "polite company."

Chinese culture furnishes numerous examples of the privileges that attach to age—to seniority. For any member of a Chinese family to speak of the husband and father as "the old man" is to imply respect, even reverence.

In American society one of the earliest manifestations of a "pecking order" is the behaviors of children toward each other that are dependent upon age differences. Where is the person who has not in his childhood suffered from being discriminated against by older children who chose not to share their company with anyone a whole year or more younger? Where, on the other hand, is the person who has not discriminated against those who were younger? Putting those who are younger "in their place" is a widely practiced social convention.

Sex and Status

Many privileges, obligations, and expectations that are part of the individual's relationship to the group depend on the difference in sex. For example, positions and roles are differently defined in a situation that includes a solitary woman in a group of males than they would be in a group of males only.

In our society, we expect that little boys will want to play with toy machines and we expect little girls to want to play with dolls. We are dismayed if a small boy in our family insists on playing with dolls or if a small girl concentrates her attentions on a toy locomotive. We expect older boys to want to hunt and fish and to participate in the more vigorous sports. We expect older girls to be interested in domestic activities, in pretty dresses, in dancing, and in the care of babies.

Our ideas about what we can expect of males and females, respectively, extend upward in the age ladder. Who should take the initiative in arranging a social date, the young man or the young woman? Who should pay for the dinner at the restaurant, the young man or his date? Who is expected to take the initiative in a proposal of marriage? The answers to such questions are easy for us. The fact that the answers are easy further demonstrates the point that the behavior forms which a society assigns to its members on the basis of such an identification as sex do facilitate for all the task of getting along together.

Influence of Caste and Class on Behavior

There is to be found in many societies a complex pattern of expectations based on *kinship*—on family or blood relationships. References, for example, to "best families," the "blue bloods," "common people," and "white trash" are indicative of kinship-based status. In some social groups the idea persists that individuals have as their birthright a claim to distinction by virtue of being born to a particular, "superior" family. Conversely, other individuals are looked down upon regardless of their actual achievements and personal qualities simply because of "inferior" kinship.

Social Caste. Following along kinship lines is the social device known as "caste." In many parts of the world culture operates to subordinate certain groups of individuals in relation to other groups to the degree that the lower ones are rigidly barred from social intercourse with the higher ones. Such rigid separations occur in some societies without regard for color differences. This is true in India.[3] The outcast status of the "untouchables" is an instance. Caste also operates along lines that have reference to color differences. This fact is familiar enough to us, with our experience of American culture, not to require elaboration.

The point that is thoroughly relevant to the discussion in this chapter is that caste distinctions do carry with them the necessity on the part of individual human beings of "learning their place" in the society into which they are born and of learning the behaviors that their "place" requires. For an individual to be born to a family of a given caste is for him, regardless of his own innate personal qualities, to be caught up in restrictions on his behavior which he learns never to try to violate.

Social Class Influence. Social class separation has much less rigidity than caste. But it is, nevertheless, a powerful device in the privilege systems of various cultures, including our own. Social classes constitute a hierarchical scheme by which the people of a given society "sort" one

[3] There is much evidence, as indicated in numerous authoritative reports, that the caste system of India is yielding significantly to various pressures for change.

[4] For a full discussion of the social class structure, see Warner, *et al.*, 1948, [19]. See also Havighurst, R. J., P. H. Bowman, G. P. Liddle, C. V. Matthews, and J. V. Pierce, 1962, *Growing up in River City* [8], New York: John Wiley & Sons, Inc., pages 9–14 on *Social Structure.*

another and their behaviors and define their social statuses.[4] A social class is "a group of people who think of themselves as belonging to the same social level and who generally are willing to associate intimately with one another—to visit each other in their homes, to dine with one another, to have their families intermarry, and so on" (Havighurst and Taba, 1949) [9].

The concept of social class hierarchy is well illustrated by the authors just quoted in their sketch of the kinds of people who comprise the social classes of "Prairie City," an actual representative—but fictitiously named—place of about ten thousand population in the north-central part of the United States. In the description of Prairie City's social structure, there was included the *upper class* consisting of about 2 percent of the people of the town. They were known in their town as "the top crowd," "the aristocrats," "the four hundred." Included also was the *middle class* (professional men and their families, officials of industries, "better" businessmen); the *lower-middle class* (looked upon locally as the "average man" of Prairie City); the *upper-lower class* (the "poor but respectable" people, to quote the local citizenry); and *lower-lower class* who comprised "the bottom of the social heap"—placed there because of what their fellow citizens considered "non-respectability," which meant that they were thought of as being dirty, shiftless, dishonest, and of low morals.

Teachers' Interest in Pupils' Social Class Backgrounds. Out of such varied social backgrounds come the pupils whom we as teachers must help in their personal and social development. We have already met Tony and we observed the hold which his social class behavioral design had on him. He well represented the behavioral ways of the "upper-lower class" of his town.

The shaping influence of social class ideals and habits on Howard, who lived across town from Tony, was different. His family was "middle class." They were lower-middle class with a strong urge to "move upward." Howard would have had great difficulty in escaping the pressures of his family's urge "to succeed"—especially his mother's strong drive to see her children "make something of themselves."

In school Howard was known among his teachers as "a high achiever," meaning that he got the most out of his innate learning capacities where the school's academic assignments were concerned. Not that he was a bookworm or a social wallflower. On the contrary, he had many well-developed interests in sports and other school activities. He was president of his school's student council. In this latter respect he could be considered on the way to becoming much like the *upper*-middle class adult males of most urban places in America, who, in the words of Havighurst and Taba (in their description of social classes in Prairie City) tend to be "active community leaders," "members of the Rotary Club," and "members of the school board."

In contrast with the behavior patterns of the Howards and Tonys of our schools and their respective social class backgrounds is the situation of *Edward Dodge* whose status and social class were described by Davis and Dollard (1940) [5]:

Edward is a slim, strong boy of thirteen. He has brown skin with a coppery underglow, kinky hair and negroid features. His clothes seem to consist of odds and ends of apparel. . . . He is the only child of a hearty woman who has never been married to any man, though she has been common-law wife of two. . . .

[Edward] lived in a two-room "apartment" which is reached by walking down a long alley between two ramshackle houses. . . . There was no telephone, bathtub, running water or electric light in the house. There was a fenced-in toilet in the yard, and a tap for running water near it. Edward's mother, Mrs. Martin, paid $1.75 a week as rent for the two rooms, a lower-lower-class rental. . . . Edward slept with his mother in the one (double) bed. Where he slept when his stepfather was residing in the house was not indicated.

. . . His mother says Edward has been fighting all his life with other children in the neighborhood. She deplores this mildly, but seems to accept it as inevitable, as indeed it is, in the training of a lower-lower-class child. . . .

It must be clear that instead of talking about how high his grades are, what clubs he is secretary of, what possessions the family has, or what a high social mark he is aiming for, Edward filled the interviewing hours (with the research interviewer) with talk of conniving, fighting, violence and crime. His folkways are different from middle-class ways; they are the ways of the lower-lower-class and the only ones he knows. He is proud of being a leader along his own lines; instead of being president of Hi-Y, he is the best fighter in his gang. . . .

Does Edward have a secret itch to be up and doing? Does he not envy the better homes and softer ways of those above him in class position? Apparently he neither itches nor envies; he is fairly happy where he is, he is isolated from the prodding scorn of those above him, and he is held tight in the vise of his lower-lower-class folkways.

We have examined in brief the social biographies of three boys, Tony, Howard, and Edward. They are representative of the children who come into our classes in school and who willingly or reluctantly present themselves for our guidance and teaching. They, as well as others from their respective social classes and still others from higher social classes, share alike the fundamental human needs that were described in Chapter 6. But each has *learned* many needs and many ways of satisfying them that are importantly different, depending upon the social class which has provided his cultural nuturing.

Achieved Status

Much of what a society expects of an individual who is of a given age is, as already stated, quite arbitrarily determined. The individual cannot do much about it. The same is true with respect to sex difference. There are also strongly held social expectations that arbitrarily govern the behavior of individuals of given social castes, and other expectations that firmly regulate the life of individuals according to their social class. There are, however, positions in society's scheme which the individual may attain because of his own choice and his own capabilities. An example is that of the presidency of a group to which an individual is elected by his peers—his age-level associates. This might be the presidency of a high-school senior class or, for adults, the chairmanship of a luncheon club or of the board of directors of a bank.

Free as the individual's choice may be in allowing himself to be elected to an office, once he is the occupant of it his behavior is largely defined by the group concepts of the position and the roles associated therewith. The person who has been elected chairman of a board of directors will act toward other members of the organization in ways which, were they not practiced, would result in confusion. Similarly, much confusion would follow from the failure of a military officer to assume the role expected of his military rank. "A king who rules by divine right must nevertheless know something about the behavior required of a king" (Davis, 1951) [6].

The case of Hal, the town roustabout, who later became a trusted army officer, illustrates the effect upon an individual's behavior of the expectations that accompany a given role related to an achieved status position.

Hal at seventeen could have served as the "for instance" in a magazine article entitled "What's Wrong with Our Teen-Agers?" He was big, bright, cocky and bursting with vitality. He expended his energy in driving his family's cars too fast with too many carefree friends aboard, in creating havoc in his high school, and in sexual adventures with a variety of girls from all social levels. His well-to-do father, a prominent judge, bailed him out, bought off complainers, or used pressure when money failed. Hal had never had responsibility of any kind and was treated by adults with a mixture of condemnation and amusement.

Before Hal finished high school, the United States was involved in World War II and as soon as he was graduated he was drafted. Before long he was sent to the Armed Forces Officer Candidate School where, to everyone's surprise, he flourished. At nineteen, he was a tank platoon leader in Europe. While he still displayed his irrepressible high spirits, he was an able and conscientious officer. His men regarded him as a good officer and performed well under his command. He was decorated for bravery when he rescued under fire the wounded members of one of his tank crews.

Hal, as an Army officer, took upon himself a pattern of behaviors different from those which were part of being the town scamp. They were behaviors consistent with his new position. They were those which were *expected* of a person in this position—behaviors defined by status.

THE INDIVIDUAL AND SOCIETY'S CONCERN WITH BASIC PROBLEMS

As a person lives out his day-to-day experiences with his own culture, he is not likely to see his problems as being closely related to society's basic problems. Indeed, the idea of basic problems of societies—of all mankind, in fact—is pretty much an academic matter for most people. A perspective larger than any that has been illustrated thus far in this chapter is required to bring the basic problems of mankind into view. But a clear viewing of them, even though it be a short one, is relevant to our main purpose in this chapter.

Research on unfamiliar cultures and comparison of them with our own has given much needed breadth and depth to our understanding of human behaviors, especially of the relationships between behavior patterns and the concerns of societies for man's basic problems.[5] These problems as seen in the light of comparative studies of cultures are:

Health and staying alive	Rearing of children
Securing food	Socialization
Sex	Sickness
Reproduction	Death
Marriage	

To these may be added four which are no less a concern of society, but which in considerable measure derive their importance from their relationship to the first-named nine. They are:

Adjustment as a child
Adjustment as a youth
Adjustment as an adult
Adjustment as an elderly person

Every society prescribes ways of behaving which it considers appropriate for its members in their relation to these problems. Only in our imagination could we think of an individual being confronted with any of the kinds of problems mentioned above without benefit of a society's guidance. But simply to imagine such a circumstance is for us to appreciate something of the scope and complexity of the preparation which the individual receives from the various agencies of his society for meet-

[5] Margaret Mead (1956) [13] succinctly expresses the objective of the comparative study of cultures in speaking of ". . . the calculated use of primitive culture to throw light on contemporary problems."

ing these problems. How, for example (if we may do a bit of imagining), would an individual who had been completely deprived of any experience with the customary practices of a society proceed to rid himself or others of an illness? How would he proceed with the problem of improving his supply of food? How, under such circumstances, would people go about the rearing of their young?

Relevant to the answer is the fact that even for the most unenlightened people there is the question of causes behind their predicaments. What—or who—causes sickness? Or death? Or the dearth or abundance of food? The spirits? Or the gods? If it be the spirits or the gods then behaviors must be decreed—and learned by all members of the group—that will appease these supernatural forces. If germs, bacteria, natural elements, and so on are seen as the causes, then the behavior to be learned and the ways of inculcating these behaviors are different.

When we take a good look at the lists of basic problems do we recognize them as *our*—our society's—basic problems? Probably we do. So, let it be repeated: fundamentally, our problems (those underlying what we do and what other relatively privileged persons like ourselves do) are those of people everywhere. This is so because implicit in the problems is the fact that they derive from man's (*all* men's) basic urges: the urges to stay alive, to satisfy organic hungers, to feel safe, to find one's place in the scheme of things and adapt reasonably comfortably to it, and to get an explanation for the happenings in one's world.

EMPHASIS AGAIN ON THE ROLE OF THE SCHOOL

For us to recognize in this way the basic "sameness" in the problems of people everywhere puts us in a position to appreciate all the more a fact which this chapter is obliged to make explicit. It is a fact about *education* and the way men live their lives and the way they meet and deal with their basic problems. The fact is that education is a major instrumentality for gaining and disseminating enlightenment concerning people's problems—as problems are here defined. Futhermore, the *school* is a people's most efficient agency of education (let it be stressed that many agencies in various societies engage in *training* rather than education). Not only is the school the most efficient agency of education; it is also the most effective for raising the general level of a people's enlightenment.

Even though there is fundamental sameness in the problems of all peoples, there are highly noteworthy differences in the ways in which people face them and try to solve them—differences quite accurately attributable to the fact that people have, or do not have, schools and, if they do have schools, what kind they have.

Schools, Peer Influences, and Social Fidelity

There are two principles that relate in a very important way to the school's role as an agent to help individuals acquire satisfying social relationships and a sense of social fidelity. Both are principles that are easier for us, as teachers, to subscribe to verbally than to incorporate into our instructional practices.

One of the principles is that individuals learn from their own responses. In general: change in a person (that is, learning) occurs when *he* is the one who is engaged in expression rather than the recipient of another person's expression. Change in an individual occurs when *he* is talking, not when he is being talked to.

The other principle is that changes in a person's behavior are greatly facilitated by evidences of peer interest in what he is doing or saying. *Peer reaction counts!*

These principles hold both for the classroom and for numerous "co-curricular" activities; that is, the principles have much potency in the development of healthful social relationships and an awareness of social responsibilities whether the place of learning is the classroom or the school theatre or the playing field. The italicized statement numbered 5 on page 185 in the story about Tony may profitably be reexamined for its pertinence to our present concern. Also the student will find some discussion in the last chapter of this book (discussion of the *psychological climate* of the school) to be closely related to what is here being emphasized. Especially relevant is the emphasis upon youth's need to *achieve identity:* which for him is to be a person in his own right.

Being able to *achieve* identity involves the reaching of a developmental stage beyond the self-definition and social awarenesses that normally an individual has simply acquired (socially inherited) as part of his earlier growing up in a family and in a family-centered social environment. At the junior high school age, or thereabouts, a youth begins in earnest the pondering of what is *his* role, what is *his* position, and what are the social expectancies that apply to him. This is where the principles of learning by involvement and learning from experiences shared with peers take on the importance that has been emphasized in this section.[6]

[6] The reader will find a helpful discussion of the importance of youth's achievement of identity and the relevance of such achievement to *social fidelity* in R. J. Havighurst, "Unrealized potentials of adolescents," a chapter of *Re-assessing human potential, The Bulletin of the National Association of Secondary-School Principals.* Washington, D.C.: The National Association of Secondary-School Principals, Number 310, May 1966, pages 90–93. Havighurst's statements are especially important for

The Function of Rituals and Ceremonies

Before leaving the topic of a society's ways of meeting problems and helping its members to meet them we should take at least a brief look at the function of ceremonies. We should do this because they demonstrate in a special way how basically similar yet different are the methods used by different societies to inculcate the approved behavioral patterns.

Were we to be present at a marriage ceremony of the Hopi Indians of Arizona, we would see the bride and groom bow their heads together over a container of water in order that their hair could be entwined as it was being washed. Is there anything about this ceremony that requires more explanation than our familiar custom of exchanging wedding rings? If we listen closely to the pledge that is repeated while the ring is being proffered and accepted, it will be clear that this too, like the Hopi ceremony, is one of society's more or less elaborate ways of reinforcing something about the marriage—faithfulness to the marriage union and mutual love and helpfulness. The actual forms of these different rituals are relatively unimportant to our understanding of the ways of people; what the rituals stand for tells much about a people.

What is socially significant in the ceremony that attends the reaching of puberty by some youths of a given tribe? Is it not the nature of the individual's social responsibility that the group wishes to convey to its members? If after considering these ceremonial rites we could turn in our thinking to the high-school graduation exercises in any American community, we might find interesting parallels.

Why should we arrange an impressive graduation ceremony? Why not settle for simply posting the names of the graduates for them and other persons to see? Or why not save time and energy by simply handing out report cards showing so many years of schooling completed? No indeed! This would not do. We feel that we have something special to accomplish, which is the reinforcement of certain attitudes on the part of everyone concerned about youth's widening sphere of social responsibility. A youth is not—according to the commencement speaker—to rest on any laurels he may have earned; he must be willing to demonstrate his increased social usefulness. The commencement exercises, like ceremonies everywhere, are a part of a society's scheme for *institutionalizing* the behaviors of its members in problem areas of common concern.

Particularly noteworthy among ceremonies are those of different peoples relative to their protection from dangerous acts of other groups. There is, for example, the appeal to national loyalty and patriotism so strongly made in our Memorial Day and Fourth of July ceremonies.[7] In

their bearing upon the concern for education that can meet the needs of culturally disadvantaged youth and youth of high potential but low achievement.

[7] For a helpful discussion of ceremonies, see Warner (1953) [18].

this and in all other matters pertaining to basic social problems, the more or less elaborate ceremonies help the group's members contribute to group solidarity as well as to the achievement of individual peace of mind.

Ceremonial Reinforcement. The element of reinforcement of behavior by the appeal to feelings and emotions is in itself an interesting aspect of the ceremonies of different cultures. Of what use is the colorful headdress, the beating of drums, the eloquent speech? The aim in part is to inform. But information, *per se,* does not require color, noise, rhythmic motion, fervent oratory, or other such accompaniments. These accompaniments have the effect of reinforcing the attitudes and beliefs that a society considers important and more or less directly related to the significance of the event being celebrated. By the injection of emotional emphasis into the celebration of events a society bolsters the loyalties, the values, the common faiths that give strength to the social group. Events that are not celebrated by a combination of information-giving and emotional reinforcement soon lose their influence on the behavior of individuals.

RELATIONSHIP OF CULTURALLY APPROVED CHILD-REARING PRACTICES TO PERSONALITY

As a final problem in our study of the cultural bases of behavior let us examine the relationship between the child-rearing practices of different peoples and the basic features of personality associated therewith. Besides answering some questions about the relationship just mentioned, this discussion will provide something of a tie between the present chapter and Chapters 14 and 15, which deal respectively with the problems of child-family relationships and of personality development.

Several of the behavioral sciences have contributed to the development of an important theory regarding the formation of basic features of personality. The theory is that the basic personality characteristics of individuals in a given culture are to a considerable degree the product of the treatment which they receive from adults during their childhood. Particularly effective in personality formation—according to the theory—are the child-rearing practices employed by parents.[8]

Was the treatment which an individual received during his infancy and childhood loving and accepting? Was it free from harsh punishment? If so, certain resultant traits of a kindly nature would be expected to characterize his personality at maturity. Was his treatment by adults

[8] The impress of child-rearing practices upon personality will be discussed more fully in Chapters 13 and 14.

rejective and hostile? If so, unfriendliness and aggression would be the kinds of personality traits to be expected.[9]

The emphasis in this theory is upon *methods* of child rearing and the feelings that adults express by the methods they use. The theory does not, however, rule out the importance of a people's explicit goals of child rearing. Both method and goals are seen as contributory to the experience which the child has of the adult treatment of him. And this—the child's experience—is the crucial factor in his personality formation.

Thus, the fact that in our society humanitarian traits are valued and advocated does not furnish the full explanation for their presence in the pattern of personality of so many of our people. The explanation, which is suggested by the theory, is that not only do we value and advocate humanitarianism as a trait, but we also as a people so raise our children that they quite naturally grow up with humanitarian impulses. In other words, humanitarian actions are consistent with and dictated by their feelings.

Relationship between People's Views of Life and Their Treatments of Children

The theory being discussed has another important facet to it. It is the idea that a definite relationship exists between the view of life which adults have and the treatment which they accord children.

That a people's feeling of being in a hostile world may breed hostility in them toward their children is indicated in the description given by Margaret Mead (1935) [14] of the life of the Mundugumor of New Guinea. Their life as adults when Mead saw them was filled with impressions of being surrounded by hostile people. Their life was also characterized by open hostility on the part of fathers toward sons and on the part of mothers toward daughters.

Contrastingly, among the Arapesh people of New Guinea children were loved, protected, and highly valued. Indeed, the "growing" of children was thought by Arapesh parents to be the chief goal of life. All adults felt in these ways toward all children. If we accept the theory which was stated above, we will not be surprised to learn that the Arapesh are a peace-loving, nonhostile tribe whose world appears to them to be friendly and not to be peopled with dangerous enemies and threatening ghosts.

There is in these contrasting situations the clear suggestion that the

[9] Because this *is* a theory—and a relatively untested one at that—a person must be restrained in his suppositions about *what traits* of personality follow from a given pattern of adult-child relationships. The expectations which were stated in the discussion are simply illustrative of what might be hypothesized from the theory.

needs that adults feel most strongly are a determining influence in the kinds of treatment they give their children. To state the point a bit differently, a people's way of treating children is more than a response to their society's customs—it is also an expression of the deep demands of that people's personality. Newcomb (1950) [15] sums up the matter in the statement:

> In different cultures then, individual personalities are differently formed because of characteristic experiences through which most children go. Such childhood experiences vary between cultures but in many respects are similar within each culture. They are determined in part by the demands of the culture itself and in part by the personality needs of adults who already have been molded by the culture.

Concluding View of Culture and Personality

The idea that fundamental features of personality derive from the treatment accorded children by adults is one which calls for verification in research. It is an idea that promises much, however, for our ultimate insight into how the shaping influences of the culture and the needs of the individual converge and how out of the varieties of these convergencies of factors come the styles of life that we see and often want so much to understand. The great need for research into the relationships between personality formation and the child-training practices in various cultures is emphasized in the remark:

> If personality is partly a product of childhood experiences, then there seems some likelihood, too, that the forms of behavior which characterize a whole society may be partly explicable on the same basis. . . . Any process that can help to explain both the development of personality and the transmission of culture is important to the behavior sciences, for these two problems are the focal points for the study of man as a social organism. (Sears, *et al.*) [17]

SUMMARY

To understand the behavior patterns of individuals we must know the culture in which they have been brought up. The actions of the individual and his values, ideas, and beliefs are an inseparable extension of the culture of the society of which he is a part.

The individual's patterns of acting, thinking, and feeling are not something "born in him" through his gene-controlled inheritance, nor are they simply chosen by him as one might pick and choose from the shelves and racks of a clothing store. Neither are they imprinted on him directly by the culture. They are the result of the shaping influence of the particular kinds of experiences he has of a culture as conveyed by the lives of other persons, more especially of those persons with whom he interacts in the need-satisfying circumstances of his existence.

Not to understand the strong, deeply rooted connection between the individual's ways and the ways of his people—especially those closest to him—is to be poorly prepared to counsel and to teach the child or the youth; for our ways, as teachers, and the ways of our pupils will often be anything but similar. To give an indication to the youngster that we, as teachers, find his ways (his inevitable reflections of his culture) objectionable is to risk losing our chances of being his helpful mentor and his trusted confidant.

Comparing various cultures with our own is a desirable way of broadening and deepening our knowledge of the forces that operate in the behavior patterns of individuals and groups. Not the least of the benefits to be obtained by us from such a study is an awareness of the communality of the basic problems that face people everywhere and an understanding of how closely related the primary personality patterns of different peoples are to their particular interpretations of these problems and their conceptions of how to deal with them.

Suggested Collateral Readings

Britt, S. H., *Social psychology of modern life,* revised ed. New York: Holt, Rinehart and Winston, Inc., 1960. Chapters 4 and 5.

Cole, L. E., and W. F. Bruce, *Educational psychology,* revised ed. Yonkers-on-Hudson, N.Y.: World Book Company (New York: Harcourt, Brace & World, Inc.), 1958. Chapter I.

Davis, A., and J. Dollard, *Children of bondage: The personality development of Negro youth in the urban South.* Washington, D.C.: American Council on Education, 1940.

Dinkmeyer, D. C., *Child development: The emerging self.* Englewood Cliffs, N.J.: Prentice-Hall, Inc., 1965. Chapter 6.

Elkin, F., *The child and society: The process of socialization.* New York: Random House, Inc., 1960.

Havighurst, R. J., P. H. Bowman, G. P. Liddle, C. V. Matthews, and J. V. Pierce, *Growing up in River City.* New York: John Wiley & Sons, Inc., 1962.

———, and Hilda Taba, *Adolescent character and personality.* New York: John Wiley & Sons, Inc., 1949. Chapters 2–9.

Johnson, R. C., and G. R. Medinnus, *Child psychology.* New York: John Wiley & Sons, Inc., 1965. Chapters 7 and 13.

Kluckhohn, C., *Mirror for man.* New York: McGraw-Hill, Inc., 1949.

McDonald, F. J., *Educational psychology,* 2d ed. Belmont, Calif.: Wadsworth Publishing Company, 1965. Chapter 14.

Mead, Margaret, *New lives for old.* New York: Morrow & Company, Inc., 1956.

———, *The school in American culture.* Cambridge: Harvard University Press, 1951.

Morgan, C. T., *Introduction to psychology,* 3d ed. New York: McGraw-Hill, Inc., 1956. Chapter 12.

Newcomb, T. M., *Social psychology.* New York: Holt, Rinehart and Winston, Inc., 1950. Especially Chapters 1 and 12.

Waller, W., *The sociology of teaching.* New York: Science Editions of John Wiley & Sons, Inc., 1965. Especially Part Three.

Warner, W. L., *American life*. Chicago: University of Chicago Press, 1953. Chapter I.

References

1. Alpenfels, Ethel, 1957, Culture shapes self. *Childhood Educ.*, **7**: 94–96.
2. Bateson, G., and Margaret Mead, 1942, *Balinese character*. New York: Academy of Sciences, **2**: 7.
3. Benedict, Ruth, 1934, *Patterns of culture*. Boston: Houghton Mifflin Company.
4. Cole, L. E., 1953, *Human behavior*. Yonkers-on-Hudson, N.Y.: World Book Company (New York: Harcourt, Brace & World, Inc.). Page 187.
5. Davis, A., and J. Dollard, 1940, *Children of bondage: The personality development of Negro youth in the urban South*. Washington, D.C.: American Council on Education.
6. Davis, K., 1949, *Human society*. New York: Crowell-Collier and Macmillan, Inc. Pages 3–4, 115.
7. Havighurst, R. J., Unrealized potentials of adolescents, a chapter of *Reassessing human potential, The Bulletin of the National Association of Secondary School Principals*. Washington, D.C.: The National Association of Secondary School Principals, Number 310, May 1966. Pages 90–93.
8. ———, P. H. Bowman, G. P. Liddle, C. V. Matthews, and J. V. Pierce, *Growing up in River City*. New York: John Wiley & Sons, Inc. 1962. Pages 9–14.
9. ———, and Hilda Taba, 1949, *Adolescent character and personality*. New York: John Wiley & Sons, Inc. Page 16.
10. Kluckhohn, C., 1949, *Mirror for man*. New York: McGraw-Hill, Inc. Pages 17, 26.
11. Lee, A. M., ed., 1951, *Principles of sociology*. New York: Barnes & Noble, Inc. Page 7.
12. Linton, R., 1945, *The cultural background of personality*. New York: Appleton-Century-Crofts. Page 12.
13. Mead, Margaret, 1956, *New lives for old*. New York: William Morrow & Company, Inc. Page 10.
14. ———, 1935, *Sex and temperament*. New York: William Morrow & Company, Inc.
15. Newcomb, T. M., 1950, *Social psychology*. New York: Holt, Rinehart and Winston, Inc. Page 440.
16. Sears, R. R., Eleanor E. Maccoby, and H. Lewin, 1957, *Patterns of child rearing*. New York: Harper & Row, Publishers. Page 15.
17. *Op. cit.*, p. 4.
18. Warner, W. L., 1953, *American Life*. Chicago: The University of Chicago Press. Chapter 1.
19. Warner, W. L., Marcia L. Meeker, and K. Eells, 1948, *The measurement of social status*. Chicago: Science Research Associates.
20. West, J., 1945, *Plainville, U.S.A.* New York: Columbia University Press.
21. Wright, H. F., R. G. Barker, W. Koppe, Beverly Meyerson, and J. Nall, 1951, Children at home in Midwest. *Progressive Educ.*, **28**: 137–143.

Development and Adjustment

PART 3

WE EXAMINED IN PART 2 the general causes of behavior and attempted to answer some of the "why's." As long as we work with people, we continue to look for answers to the "why" questions, but there are also "what" questions. What can we expect by way of typical behavior at different stages of development? How can we tell when a child or adolescent is working his way through a growth stage in a satisfactory way? The teacher must have some working knowledge of growth as well as a generalized understanding of its causes.

Physical growth and motor competence are of the greatest importance to adjustment and behavior throughout the growing years; this aspect of development is the subject of Chapter 9. Performance in school and in society depends heavily on learning ability; the sources and development of general intelligence are matters of much relevance in this connection and are described in Chapter 10. The ways in which thinking or cognitive functions develop are of considerable current interest; this is especially true of the concept of creativity. Chapter 11 is devoted to these topics. Closely allied to thinking is communication, studied in Chapter 12. Social development—as distinct from the social cultural foundations of behavior—is the subject of the two succeeding chapters: Chapter 13 on peer social relationships, and Chapter 14 on family relationships.

CHAPTER 9

Physical Growth and Development

Why should the student of behavior concern himself with physical growth? The implications of motivation, emotions, social adjustment, and the like are readily discernible, but why should we add the study of physiology to our list of topics? The answer is, of course, that it is not merely physiology which demands our attention (although this is a valuable and fascinating study in its own right), but the whole process of growth and change, of physical structure and function and its effect on day-by-day behavior and adjustment. It might be said that physical growth is the analogy or model for psychological development.

Some ancient philosophers regarded mind and body as separate entities; this point of view is called *dualism*. Today the idea of separateness of mind and body is not seriously considered by many scientists. Medical authorities recognize that a sizable percentage—half or more—of patients visiting a physician's office are genuinely ill, but have emotional rather than organic causes for their ailments. Some individuals are mentally deficient, despite good inheritance and environment, because of chemical or endocrine imbalances. We have all seen children who fail to perform creditably because of physical fatigue, and others who fail because of emotional stress. On the other hand, we have seen happy, zestful learners in the classroom who are happy, zestful, and successful in part at least because their biological organisms are functioning well.

It is the body that acts, that expresses emotions, that performs tasks—in short, *behaves*. The human being functions as a whole organism, and it is not possible to look at any piece of behavior without considering the whole. The biologist La Barre (1954) [23] says: ". . . the general fact of culture ultimately rests upon biological traits of the species *Homo sapiens. Man's 'human nature' derives from the kind of body he has.*" For these reasons it is essential that anyone who works with people, especially with children and youth, understands the growing, changing human body.

Let us examine some accounts of children's behavior in which physical growth has had a clear and discernible influence on adjustment.

EACH GROWTH STAGE PRODUCES SOME CHARACTERISTIC BEHAVIOR

Until age ten, Susan had been a pleasant child, happy in her relations with her parents and popular with her schoolmates. Over a period of a few months she was with increasing frequency negativistic at home, refusing to do her household tasks, crying frequently, and spending much time alone in her room. She began to ignore or to pick quarrels with her former girl friends and seemed to be "out of step" with her peer society. Her parents and teacher were at a loss to explain her behavior and considered seeking professional help. About this time she menstruated for the first time, and began to fill out her slim frame with the first curves of adolescence. Her difficulties, of course, did not clear up dramatically or at once, but they did improve rather steadily with understanding help from the adults in her life.

Behavior has many causes and it is dangerous to oversimplify, but her parents and teacher should have been more alert to the symptoms of approaching *menarche* (period of first menstruation) and could have helped her more in the negativism that often accompanies approaching pubescence.

PHYSICAL GROWTH HAS AN EFFECT ON STATUS IN PEER SOCIETY

At age five, Jimmie was looking forward to kindergarten with eager anticipation. He was above average in ability and seemed ready to leave the protection of home to try his wings in the world of school. However, his physical growth was very slow and since he played with two younger siblings most of the time he was not prepared to take his place with larger, stronger children. He was weak and a half a head shorter than any other child in the class. After the first few days, he tried in every way to stay home—he cried, he had temper tantrums, he feigned illness. Investigation revealed that on the walk to and from school and on the playground away from the teacher he was the victim of teasing and of physical hazing from all the children. The more he cried the more he became the butt of teasing. His parents finally withdrew him for the year.

In the society of young children, physical size and strength are extremely important. Jimmie needed help in accepting his physical limitations—help he did not receive. He should have had more opportunity to play with older children, to learn to defend himself, to learn skills to help make up for his lack of size.

LEVEL OF MATURITY IS ONE OF THE DETERMINERS OF READINESS FOR LEARNING

Carl was a slow-developing child in the second semester of the first grade. He got along well with his age-mates but was a slow, below-average student. When reading instruction was introduced, Carl fell further behind and seemed to make almost no progress. The ability to translate symbols into words and then into ideas seemed to be completely beyond him and individual instruction did not help. His eyes had not matured enough so that he could perceive printed words easily, and his cerebral cortex was still not functioning on a high enough level to enable him to translate printed symbols into words and meaning. He was not promoted to second grade because of his reading failure and general immaturity. The next fall he appeared in general to be on a par with the other first-grade students and when he encountered reading training again he forged ahead steadily and made good progress.

Reading requires a certain level of sensory and neural maturity and until this stage is reached, training has little effect. Carl's slow rate of development did not prepare him for learning this skill until he was past seven.

PHYSICAL FUNCTIONING HELPS DETERMINE LIFE-STYLE

The cases discussed above all reveal problems of adjustment produced in part by physical status. We are far from being solely concerned with problems, however. A person's "life style"—his *joie de vivre,* his interests, his approach to people and situations—is in large part a product of his physical status, his available energy, and his general physiological functioning.

Lee at eight was bursting with energy. It was not uncommon to see him pedaling his bicycle around and around the block at top speed whooping and making roaring, motor-like noises, apparently from sheer exuberance. He was in the fore of any game on the playground and was a leader of his gang in most of their activities. He sailed through most classwork with ease, but his work often lacked in neatness and polish as he abandoned one task in favor of the next. His health and energy made his parents describe him sometimes as a kind of force of nature, like Niagara Falls or Old Faithful.

Children like Lee need help in channeling and directing their energy in constructive ways, but they can be a joy to watch and teach.

These brief examples suggest some of the relationships between physical growth and status on the one hand, and behavior patterns on the other. To deal effectively with children and adolescents, there are certain basic concepts and facts we need to know. What is the common pattern or form which growth takes? How do people differ in the way they grow and how does this affect them? What are the causes of growth? These are some of the questions we need to answer, or at least to examine in this chapter.

Terminology

Growth, development, maturation: these words are all terms one hears frequently in relation to changes of physical status. The words are often used interchangeably but distinctions should be made among them when a person is involved in systematic study pertaining to the phenomena which they denote. The reader is invited to refer to Chapter 1 for definitions of the two terms "growth" and "development." *Maturation* is often used much as is development but is more likely to refer to inherent body structures and the related functions than to skills or acquired characteristics. A concept frequently implicit in definitions of maturation gives emphasis to "changes that take place more or less inevitably in all normal members of the species so long as they are provided with an environment suitable to the species" (English and English, 1958) [6].

THE MEASUREMENT OF GROWTH

The influence of growth on behavior has been recognized for a long time and has been studied extensively. What are our sources of data about the physical organism? Thompson (1954) [45] says:

> The literature on the subject of physical growth is vast and widely scattered owing to a variety of scientific, professional, and business interests in the subject. Not only the anatomist, physical anthropologist, biometrist, and psychologist but also the obstetrician, pediatrist, dentist, educator, public-health doctor, actuarian, criminologist, and eugenicist are led to research in this field.

A review of the varied and extensive literature on growth is beyond the scope or purpose of this book. Instead, we will examine the major kinds of studies that have brought us to our present level of understanding.[1]

[1] For a discussion of measurement methods and problems, see Anderson (1954) [2], pages 10–18.

Cross-sectional Approach

Suppose you wished to determine the average length in centimeters of the "reach" or distance in the spread-out hand from the tip of the thumb to the tip of the little finger of children at each year of age from five to eighteen. The obvious way of getting such measurements would be to find a typical group of children at each of these ages (we call this "typical group" a *population sample*). Then you would measure the spread fingers of each child with an accurate rule, record the figures, and find the average for each age, the deviations from average, and so on. You would have carried out a cross-sectional or normative study. Much of our information about growth in general and growth of specific body parts or functions comes from just such studies. When results are analyzed in terms of chronological age or developmental level, we have two useful and important kinds of data: first, information on the growth process and second, *norms* or standards with which the performance of other children can be compared. If an adequate sample of children is used at each age, a scale becomes available for the evaluation of individual children.

To return to our example of finger-span measurement, suppose we actually measured a representative sample of children's hands at each age, and calculated the mean or average for, say, every six months of age from five to eighteen. We would then know the typical pattern of growth for the school-age period and the finger-span at each half-year of age. Practical application of such data might be made in determining how many keys on the piano or accordion could be spanned at any of these ages, and practice music or exercises could be written to fit. The finger span of an individual child aged nine might then be measured and this figure compared to the scale to determine his "finger-span age-status" or readiness for music at a particular level—which level of course might be quite different from his actual chronological age.

Most of the older studies of human development were cross-sectional studies, and most tables of norms have been derived from such research. If your family physician or school health official ever measured your height and weight and then reported that you were average or advanced or retarded in growth, he probably referred to a growth chart based on cross-sectional measures.

Herein lies the major deficiency of cross-sectional studies. Although they are of great value, they give only averages, in which individual variations disappear. Because children grow at different rates and reach similar developmental levels at different times, a cross-sectional study places together at the fifteen-year level many boys well past puberty and midway in adolescence and many other boys who are months away from puberty. For this reason, age norms based on cross-sectional studies are of more academic interest than of real help in understanding the phenomenon of growth and the ways of a particular child. Since the early 1930's the significant research in growth has been of a different nature.

Genetic, or Longitudinal, Approach

Let us return for a moment to our hypothetical growth study. Suppose that instead of measuring many children of different ages we measure the finger-span of one child at age six months, of the same child again at twelve months, again at eighteen months and so on up to eighteen years. We would have carried out a *genetic,* or *longitudinal,* type of study. Such studies are discussed in some detail in Chapter 3. This approach is particularly valaublе in learning about physical growth. In this connection Anderson (1954) [2] says:

> While means and standard deviations can be obtained at each age level, as in the cross-section study, the longitudinal study, in addition, permits: (1) an analysis of the development and growth of each individual child; (2) a study of growth increments, both for the individual and the group; and (3) an analysis in detail of the interrelations between growth processes, both maturational and experimental, because all data have been obtained on the same children.

In other words, the uniqueness of growth of each child is not only recognized but becomes the major theme of the research. Thus in our finger-span study we would know what the averages were at each age, but in addition we could distinguish patterns of individuality in development. We could identify the slow and rapid developers and compare their rates of growth to other specific or complex characteristics. We might, for example, study the differential effects of sex, of race or ethnic background, of diet or exercises, and the like. We might examine the rate of finger growth in relation to speed of response or to ultimate finger span. It is apparent that the possibilities for examining individual physical growth in relation to complex aspects of behavior are great in longitudinal studies.

THE PATTERNS OF GROWTH

As defined earlier, growth implies a change in size, a "getting bigger." From the moment of conception, growth is progressing toward a definite maturity. This progress is continuous, but the growing organism does not develop at a steady or regular rate. Instead, we find that growth has a cyclic nature and it is from the study of these cycles that we identify the patterns of growth. The recognition of these patterns and of the roles they play in behavior and adjustment is essential to our understanding of growing children.

Major Growth Periods

When the data from cross-sectional measures of skeletal or body-as-a-whole growth are plotted for the first twenty years of life, three major development periods are apparent. These are illustrated in Figure 9.1.

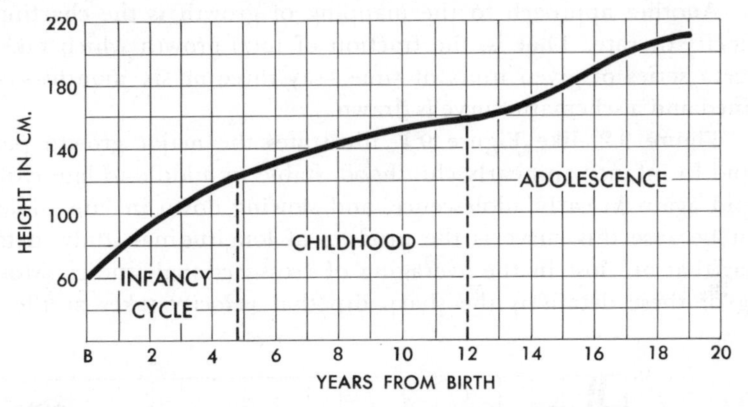

FIGURE 9.1. The three cycles of growth in height. Adapted from Scammon, R. E., The first seriatim study of human growth, *American Journal of Physical Anthropology*, 10: 329, 1927.

First period: Infancy and Early Childhood. The average baby weighs about seven and one-half pounds at birth and is about twenty inches in length. Early growth is so rapid that by the end of the first year weight will have trebled and height will have increased by half. Growth continues to be rapid through early childhood (up to about age six) but is slowed down somewhat from the tremendous gains of the first year. These years of rapid growth are also years of rapid development of the skills of walking, talking, and learning the basic "ways of the world."

Second period: Middle and Late Childhood. The years from six to pubescence are relatively stable in growth—that is, growth is continuing toward maturity, but the gain per unit of time is not so great or so noticeable as in the early period. In this period of stable growth, the child concentrates on mastering physical, social, emotional, and intellectual skills appropriate to his age.

Third period: Puberty and Adolescence. It is not possible to give any precise age for puberty because of the great variation in individuals, as will be seen later in this chapter. In boys, the testes increase in size at the beginning of this period, while in girls ovarian development is more gradual. The second postnatal period of rapid growth takes place at the beginning of this period, and then growth begins to slow down in the middle of adolescence, terminating in skeletal maturity in the late teens or early twenties. The flowering of both physical and intellectual capabilities takes place in these years.

Velocity of Growth

Another approach to the mapping of growth is the charting of its velocity or rate. That is, the fraction of total growth which takes place over a series of given units of time—say three or six months—is determined and a schematic curve is drawn.

Figure 9.2, like Figure 9.1, illustrates the major growth periods—rapid in infancy and early childhood, stable in middle to late childhood, rapid again in early adolescence, and slowing down in late adolescence. But because this curve is the product of longitudinal study, details appear that are lost in the averaging of cross-sectional studies. Most striking of these details is the sharp dip that velocity takes at the end of

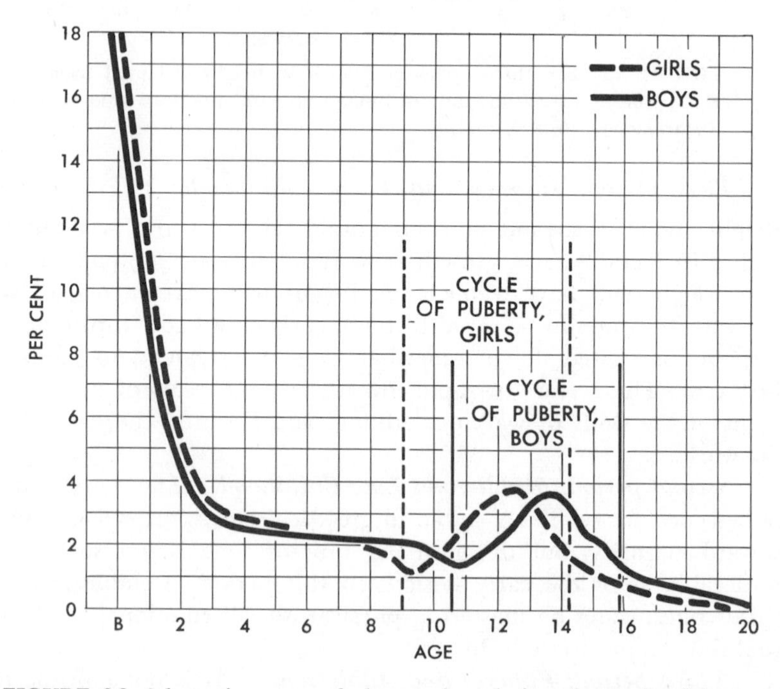

FIGURE 9.2. Schematic curves of changes in velocity of growth of boys and girls from birth to age twenty. From Ahrens, M. R., *et al. Physiological aspects of child growth and development,* Division of Child Development and Teacher Personnel, Commission on Teacher Education, American Council on Education, 1941.

childhood. This is the signal that pubescence is at hand and that a period of rapid growth will soon be under way.

A consideration of the research data discussed above yields a general principle of growth: *There is a common growth pattern through which all human beings pass.*

To this must be appended a second generalization, as important as—or even more important than—the first: *Each person has potentially his own unique and proper growth pattern.*

Are not these two generalizations antithetical? How can there be a universal growth curve and also a curve unique to each person? The reconciling of these different statements demands a consideration of individual differences of rate, sex, body type, and many other characteristics. How do these individual differences operate, and how do they affect the behavior of the child or adolescent? The questions and their answers are important. Discussing the question of individual uniqueness, Williams (1946) [52] comments:

> The people who make up society are certainly not all alike, and any attempt to deal with them as if they were is foredoomed to failure. Obviously the world which we inhabit would be wholly different from what it is if every individual were an exact replica of every other individual. . . . Once we know what the differences are, and how human beings may be classified with respect to them, the individual problems which will confront us will be essentially like that of fitting a human population with shoes. . . . Our attempted social adjustments, however, are often so crude that they might be compared to furnishing an entire army with *average-sized* shoes. For purposes of calculating the amount of leather required to put shoes on an army it would be valuable to know the average size of the soldiers' feet, but this information would be of no value in ordering the sizes to be made. An average-sized shoe would fit very few individuals.

In describing the standard human growth curve, we have in effect been examining the "average size" of growth. Because the "average size" actually does not fit more than part of the child population, it is necessary that we see the nature of the individual differences.

UNIQUENESS OF THE INDIVIDUAL

In what way is the individual different from others? We would not be facetious or unrealistic if we replied "In every way."

> The ways in which human beings exhibit marked individuality are literally so numerous as to be overwhelming. . . . Individuals differ from each other even in the minutest details of anatomy and body chemistry and physics: finger and toe prints; microscopic texture of hair; hair pattern on the body; ridges

and "moons" on the finger and toe nails; thickness of skin, its color, its tendency to blister; distribution of nerve endings on the surface of the body; size and shape of ears, of ear canals, of semicircular canals; length of fingers, character of brain waves (tiny electrical impulses given off by the brain); exact number of muscles in the body; heart action; strength of blood vessels; blood groups; rate of clotting of blood—and so on almost *ad infinitum.* (Williams, 1953) [53]

Even if it were possible, there would be little point in examining *all* the dimensions of uniqueness. Instead, we will discuss some of the more obvious and striking differences of individual uniqueness of growth, and will emphasize those differences which have the most direct effect on behavior.

Differences between Sexes in Rates of Growth

Anyone who has attended a school, church, or social function at which grades or other groups of age-matched boys and girls appeared will have noticed the relative immaturity of the boys when compared to the girls. By junior high school age the differences are truly striking. Girls enter the period of acceleration in growth at about nine years of age—about two years earlier than boys (Tuddenham and Snyder, 1954) [46]. They reach the maximum phase of growth at about 12.5 years, while boys do not reach their peak rate until 14.8 years. Figure 9.3 from Shuttleworth (1939) [38] illustrates this difference.

This disparity in relative physical maturity between the sexes is present from birth onward. Because differences in rate are greater *within* each sex than *between* sexes, we are likely to pay little attention to them in a group of children in the lower grades in school. By the time fifth or sixth grade is reached, however, some of the girls begin forging ahead in growth and by junior high school age the differences, as noted above, are striking. The teacher of this age group is likely to have in the same class many girls who have reached the menarche, whose breast and general bodily development identifies them as budding young women, together with a majority of boys who are still children physiologically. In a seventh- or eighth-grade class one might expect to find seven out of ten girls as compared to three out of ten boys already in the puberal cycle. But this also means that at least three of the ten boys will be more advanced than a similar number of girls (Ahrens *et al.,* 1941) [1]. The girls on the average are likely to be a little taller than the boys between the ages of eleven and thirteen. Since development is global and involves much more than height and weight, puberty brings with it changes in hormone balance that elicit new motives, interests, and general patterns of behavior. Any adult who has been a sponsor or chaperone at a junior high school party (or who remembers his own experi-

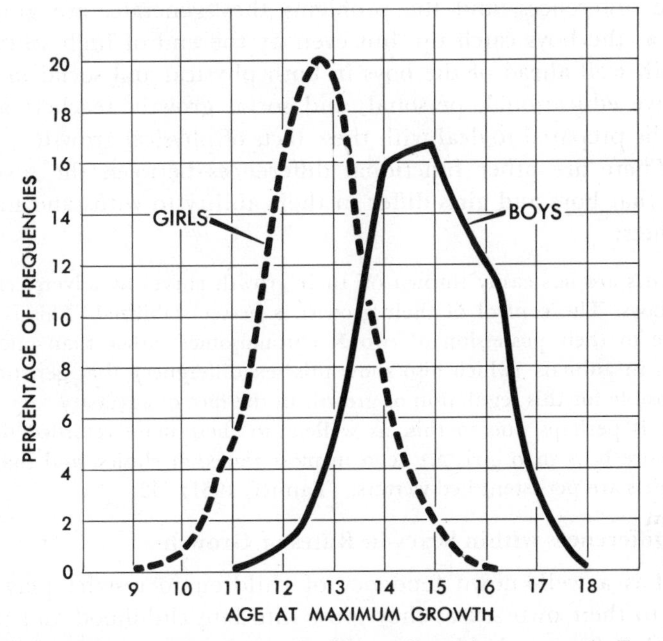

FIGURE 9.3. Ages at which boys and girls reach maximum growth. From Shuttleworth, F., The physical and mental growth of girls and boys age six to nineteen in relation to age at maximum growth, *Monographs of the Society for Research in Child Development,* 4: 9, 1939. With permission of the Society for Research in Child Development.

ences clearly) can recall a number of boys huddled together in a defensive cluster, stubbornly resisting the entreaties of the more mature girls to dance or in some fashion to socialize. From a newspaper column dispensing advice to teenagers comes a problem which, while probably a little unusual, is suggestive in this context:

I am fifteen years old and am going with a fourteen year old girl. She is cute and dresses well.

She comes from a nice family. In fact she is tops except for one thing—she is always trying to wrestle with me!

She is the only girl in a family of three boys and she has always played with them just as if she were a boy. My problem is this: It is very embarrassing to have her grab me in a hold and to find I can't break it.

Sometimes this happens in front of other kids and you should hear them tease me. I've told her several times to cut it out, but she thinks it is very funny.

At dances and movies she is very refined, but when we're just hanging around—what a muscle girl she is! I am getting sick and tired of her making me look silly.[2]

2 "Teen-age Mail," *Des Moines Register* (1956), March 23, page 18.

These differences, and the problems they generate, are gradually lessened as the boys catch up, but even by the end of high school the girls are still well ahead of the boys in both physical and social maturity. For effective educational, personal, and social growth, teachers and schools must be prepared to deal with these facts of physical growth.

There are other functional differences between the sexes. Tanner notes that boys and girls differ in their ability to withstand malnutrition or illness:

> Girls are less easily thrown off their growth curves by adverse circumstances than boys. The control of their growth is better stabilized. This is believed to be due to their possession of two X chromosomes rather than one, since it is known in animals (which also show this sex difference) that genetic factors are responsible for this regulation of growth in the face of adversity.
>
> It is perhaps due to this, as well as to their more retarded development, that more boys than girls are seen in most remedial clinics, and that more boys than girls are persistent bed-wetters. (Tanner, 1961) [42]

Differences within Sexes in Rates of Growth

It is a well-known tendency of children to restrict play more and more to their own sex as they grow into late childhood and pubescence. It is therefore probable that differences in growth rate (and thus secondarily at least in size) *within* each sex have a greater effect on behavior than *between-sex* differences. Table 9.1 shows the median height for children of each sex through the school years, and the height at the third and ninety-seventh percentiles at each of those ages. At age fourteen for example, boys range over twelve inches in height; girls at ages eleven to thirteen range over ten inches. Then there is an additional 6 percent of extreme cases at each age not reported here. One can hardly speak of children at these ages as "peers" on any but an age basis! Two boys of the same age standing side by side may look like a heavyweight and a flyweight.

In our society, "conforming" is a dominant way of life. In the society of children and especially of adolescents, "conforming" is about the *only* way of life. The child whose growth is markedly different from that of the norm is likely to have some special problems and possibly some special rewards.

Because of the pressures to be like others, the adolescent constantly compares himself to them. He is likely to view with alarm any differences that he perceives. In the course of growing up, he develops a concept of his own body; the "satisfyingness" of this concept is determined largely by the group he uses for comparison. He uses not only his peers as the criteria for "normality" but also popular figures in his world—entertainers, athletes, and the like. His growth may be adequate and normal for his particular inheritance and growth pattern, but significant deviation from his criterion group—primarily his peers—is likely to cause him to view his own body as inadequate or, in some cases, equally erroneously, as superior.

Some examples may serve to point up psychological effects of growth rate. Figure 9.4 shows the incremental growth of two individuals in puberty: one is an early maturer and the other is a late maturer. These

TABLE 9.1
Height Percentile Table

	Height in Inches					
	Boys			*Girls*		
Age	Third %ile	Fiftieth %ile	Ninety-seventh %ile	Third %ile	Fiftieth %ile	Ninety-seventh %ile
5	40¼	43¼	46½	40	43	46¾
6	42¾	46¼	49¾	42½	45½	49½
7	45	49	52½	45	48	52
8	47	51¼	55¼	47	50½	54
9	49	53¼	57¼	48¾	52¼	56½
10	50¾	55¼	59¼	50¼	54½	58¾
11	52¼	56¾	60¾	52	57	62
12	54½	59	63¾	54¼	59¾	64¾
13	56	61	66¾	56½	61¾	66¼
14	57½	64	69¾	58¼	62¾	67¼
15	59¾	66	71½	59	63½	67½
16	61½	67¾	73	59½	64	67¾
17	62½	68½	73½	59½	64	67¾
18	62¾	68¾	74	59½	64	67¾

Adapted from Watson, E. H., and G. H. Lowrey, 1962, *Growth and development of children.* Chicago: Year Book Medical Publishers, Inc. Pages 72–73.

individual curves are superimposed on a schematic "normal" curve.

For girls there are some special problems involved in early maturity. The girl who is first in her class or peer group to reach pubescence may begin her period of rapid growth as early as age eight. She is very likely then to be not only the biggest girl in her group, but also bigger than any of the boys. Our society cherishes in girl-children daintiness, slimness, and femininity. The Amazonian proportions of the early maturer, her strident adolescent voice, broadened hips, and budding breasts are honorable badges of nearing womanhood, but she may wish the process had been delayed a bit. Her wishes may well be echoed by her parents and teachers. Her size alone makes her conspicuous and out of place in

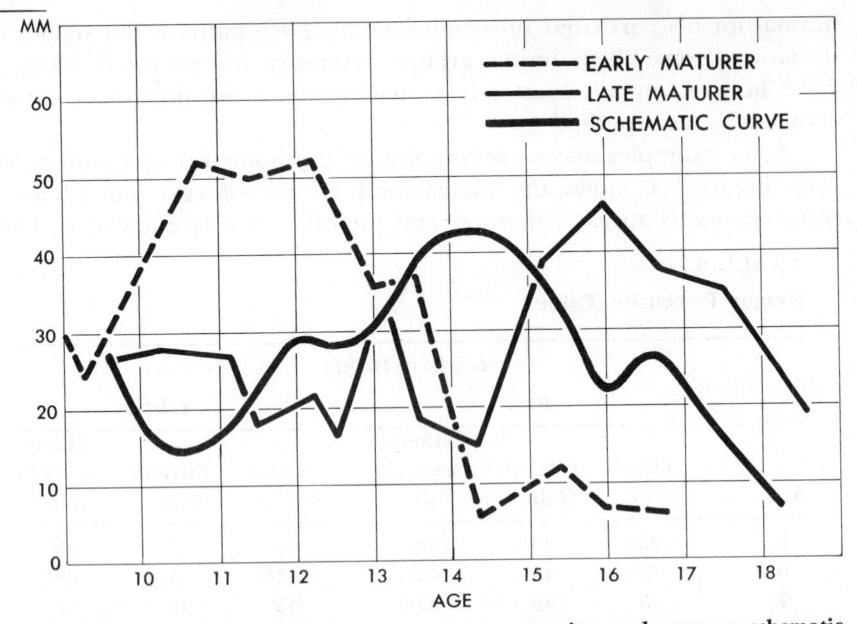

FIGURE 9.4. Two individual growth curves, superimposed upon a schematic curve, showing the velocity of growth during the puberal cycle. From Ahrens, M. R., *et al. Physiological aspects of child growth and development,* Division of Child Development and Teacher Personnel, Commission on Teacher Education, American Council on Education, 1941. (Schematic curve adapted from Stolz, H. R., and Stolz, Lois M., *Somatic development of adolescent boys,* New York, Macmillan, 1951.)

many playground and school activities. Menstruation disturbs her physical functioning periodically (irregularity is the rule rather than the exception for the pubescent period) and entails the problem of explaining why some of her regular activities may have to be curtailed. Many of her age-mates may be ignorant of the whole process and thus may further embarrass her.

The pubescent girl develops new drives and interests and may reject (as well as be rejected by) her former girl friends. The boys of her age are usually shying away from girls in general and will especially avoid one so far from them in maturity. Her physiological peers are years older and if she is unable to make satisfying contacts with older girls and boys she may be isolated indeed—primarily because of her rapid rate of growth.

Her slow-growing age-mate avoids these problems, but if her development is markedly retarded she too may suffer emotionally and socially. The last girl in the group to mature cannot share fully the interests and activities of her adolescent age-mates and her lack of bodily development may cause her to be overlooked or noticed for her differentness rather than for her desirable traits.

In a study of a group of California school girls, late-maturing girls were found to be lively, exuberant and expressive, but were also judged higher on traits of sociability and prominence. Late-maturers were much more likely than the average girls to be mentioned in the high school paper while early maturers were much less likely to be so noticed. The correlation between ratio of skeletal to chronological age and rank order of mention was —.42 (Everett, 1943) [8].

It would be naïve of course to suppose that late maturing is advantageous for all girls at all times and at all places. For example, Jones and Mussen (1958) [19] studied the problem in a sample of early- and late-maturing California females. Although differences between the two groups were slight, early-maturing girls, contrary to expectation, had more favorable self-concepts than the late-maturing. It is apparent that complex psychological and cultural factors as well as maturational status contribute to the development of any individual.

The boy is in a situation different from that of the girl. Our culture in general, and that of children and adolescents in particular, glorifies big, strong, brawny, athletic males. The bigger, faster-growing boy discovers his advantage early in life and his whole behavior pattern is affected by it, as is the behavior of the smaller, slower grower.

A study by Jones and Bayley (1950) [18] is suggestive here. Using skeletal age as their criterion of maturity, they studied two groups of boys at opposite ends of the developmental range. The fast growers were, of course, larger; at age eleven they found that *all* the late-maturing boys were shorter than the mean of the early-maturing group. The boys were studied in small, like-sex free-play situations. The early-maturing boys were rated as superior in physical attractiveness, and they tended to be more "masculine" than the late-maturers, markedly so at ages fifteen and sixteen. In behavior they were less "expressive"—that is, they were quieter and given less to aimless and exuberant activity. In this study, they were not found to differ in leadership, prestige, popularity or in sex interest. The authors summarized their behavioral findings by suggesting that the fast-maturers are accepted and treated as mature by peers and adults and thus have less need to strive for status. Here is behavior and personality again in large part determined by growth rate.

However, other data revealed that some discrimination did exist within the peer culture in high school: over half the early-maturers demonstrated outstanding athletic performance or were elected to important offices while the late-maturers provided only one athlete and one officer. Four of the twelve boys receiving the highest number of mentions in the school paper came from the early-maturers while none of the late-maturers were mentioned. In the school studied, five of the nine boys never mentioned in the three-year period were late-maturers, while only one early-maturer was omitted (Jones, 1958) [17].

The boys of Jones and Bayley's study were later, at age thirty-three, followed up to determine the long-term effects of rate of maturing upon personality. The physical differences earlier present had tended to disappear in adulthood. Some favorable personality characteristics still appeared more frequently in the early than the late maturing, and there was some evidence of better vocational adjustment among the early-maturing group. The differences were not great between the two groups as they entered their thirties, but it seems that there is some long-term psychological advantage accruing to early-maturing boys (Jones, 1957) [16].

Studies of the self-concepts of early- and late-maturing boys and girls have been made, employing projective tests to get at these self-views. Late-maturing adolescents of both sexes are characterized by less adequate self-concepts, slightly poorer parent-child relationships, and by some evidence of stronger dependency needs. The differences in many ways were not great, however, especially between the early- and late-maturing girls (Jones and Mussen, 1958) [19]; (Mussen and Jones, 1957) [30].

One should not, of course, conclude from this discussion that average growth poses no problems or that rapid or slow growth precipitates any stereotyped kind of behavior. It does suggest, however, that the teacher must concern himself with the growth pattern of each child if he is going to make any serious attempt to understand and help the child. Tanner comments, ". . . there are no social steps by which we can significantly reduce the range of individual differences in speed of physical maturation. It, therefore, behooves us to fit our educational system, in theory and in practice, to these biological facts" (Tanner, 1961) [43].

HELPING CHILDREN WITH GROWTH PROBLEMS

Probably every child at some time or other has some concern about his physical self—his growth, his strength, his attractiveness. What can the teacher do to aid him? Because problems are unique, each child at times needs individual help, but some general possibilities suggest themselves. The teacher can help him in the following ways.

1. *Knowledge about his own physical functioning.* Parents and teachers worry about giving their children the "facts of life." Certainly it is important for children to know about the structure and function of the reproductive apparatus, but too frequently they are quite as ig-

norant about the rest of the body. They need to know what to expect of their own physiology in its present state and its future changes.

2. *Knowledge about differences in growth rates.* A distressing number of children worry unnecessarily about being abnormal. They need to know at every age about the range of normal differences in growth, and they need help in accepting (emotionally as well as intellectually) the idea that they may be quite different from average and still be normal; they sometimes need assurance that just about everyone reaches maturity eventually!

3. *Regular medical checkups.* These serve the major purpose of detecting physical problems and may serve a second purpose of reassuring the child that he is in a desirable physical condition.

4. *Opportunity to contact physical peers.* Children sorted out by age are not sorted out by level of physical maturity. Playground recreation, hobby activities, and the like should be planned so that there may be frequent contacts between children of a variety of ages. Thus they may at least part of the time find others on their own maturational level.

5. *Individual attention.* Parents, teachers, and professional workers must cooperate in working with children with special physical or growth problems.

RECORDING GROWTH: THE WETZEL GRID AND IOWA GROWTH CHART

In past years it was the practice in many schools to check each child's height and weight against a table of norms based on cross-sectional averages recorded by age. Thus a child who deviated very far from average was in danger of being labeled too fat, too thin, too something, without regard to his rate of growth or his body type. Norman Wetzel developed a grid for the evaluation of growth based on the longitudinal growth records of many children. On the grid, body-type is accounted for by the use of "channels," and level of growth and chronological age are separately considered (Wetzel, 1941) [48].

An example of the grid is shown in Figure 9.5. On the left are columns for recording height, weight, and age. Next is the grid itself, with superimposed channels. These physique channels are given clinical labels:

A_4	Obese
A_3, A_2	Stocky
A_1, M, B_1	Good
B_2	Fair
B_3	Borderline
B_4	Poor

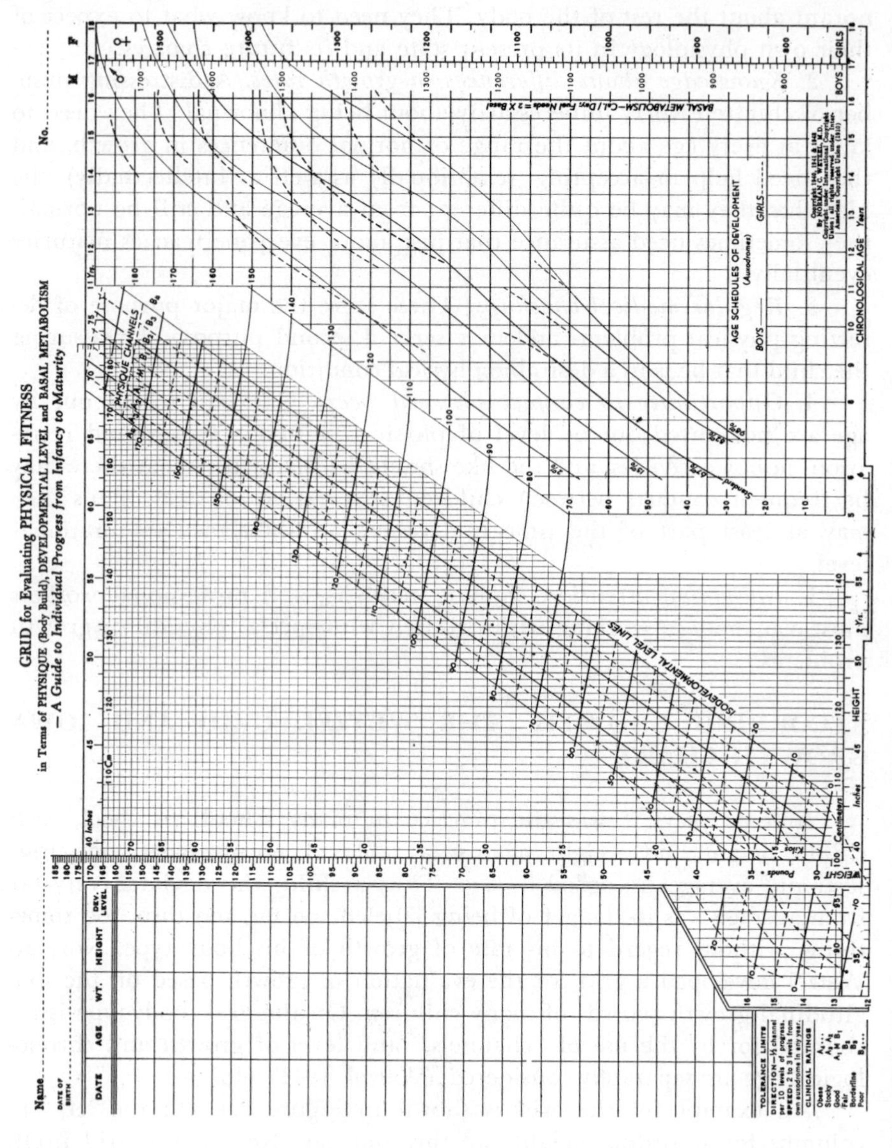
GRID for Evaluating PHYSICAL FITNESS
in Terms of PHYSIQUE (Body Build), DEVELOPMENTAL LEVEL and BASAL METABOLISM
— A Guide to Individual Progress from Infancy to Maturity —
PHYSIQUE CHANNELS
ISODEVELOPMENTAL LEVEL LINES
AGE SCHEDULES OF DEVELOPMENT
CHRONOLOGICAL AGE
HEIGHT
WEIGHT
DATE
AGE
WT.
DEV. LEVEL
CLINICAL RATINGS

You will note that *only* height and weight, not age, are considered here. Cutting across the channels are "isodevelopmental lines" numbered by tens, from zero to 180; these are in effect levels of progress toward maturity. To the right is the age schedule of development (auxodromes), in which the developmental stage is compared to chronological age for each sex. At the right edge of the form, figures are provided which make possible the calculation of the caloric needs of a given child.

Of greatest interest to us is the tendency of the normal, healthy child to stay in one channel throughout his developing years. He may be of a slim build (B_3) or a stocky build (A_3), but if he is healthy and he stays in his channel his growth is normal for him. If he deviates more than one-half channel per ten levels of growth, it can be assumed that something is wrong—just what, of course, the grid does not tell us. But we do have a warning that the child need professional attention to determine whether there is a problem, and if there is what should be done about it.

Another instrument designed especially to meet the needs of schools for meaningful developmental records is the Iowa Growth Chart (Meredith, 1949) [28]. It is made up in the form of a four-page booklet for each child, with two pages of instructions and separate pages for recording the growth of a boy or a girl.[3] The chart has a separate division for height and weight. Unlike the Wetzel Grid, all growth data are recorded in terms of the chronological age of the child: one of the curves is termed age-height, the other is age-weight.

Norms are based on thousands of longitudinal measurements of Iowa City school children (Jackson *et al.,* 1945) [15]. The height and weight curves each have six divisions. For height, the group from the first to tenth percentile is described as Short, from tenth to thirtieth as Moderately Short, from thirtieth to seventieth as Average, from seventieth to ninetieth as Moderately Tall, and from ninetieth to ninety-ninth as Tall. Similar evaluations are made of weight from Light to Heavy.

It should be noted that these or any other growth-charting devices are based on norms gathered several years earlier and thus some caution must be exercised in evaluation. The general acceleration of physical development in our society has been commented on elsewhere.

[3] The Chart may be secured from the American Medical Association, 535 North Dearborn Street, Chicago, Illinois, or from the National Education Association, 1201 Sixteenth Street, N.W., Washington, D. C.

FIGURE 9.5. The Wetzel Grid for evaluating physical fitness. This sample grid has been filled out, showing the erratic growth and recovery of an institutionalized child. Copyright by Norman C. Wetzel. Used with permission of Newspaper Enterprise Association, Cleveland, Ohio.

GROWTH WITHIN THE BODY

We have been considering growth in general and growth differences between individuals. To have a clear picture of what is going on in the development of a child, we must also be aware of the nature of changes *within* the body.

The body does not grow as a whole and in all directions at once. Each part must be considered separately (Thompson, 1954) [45].

Changes in Proportion

Perhaps most apparent to the casual observer is the change from infancy to maturity in the relative size of the head, trunk, and limbs. The *head* is relatively more mature than the rest of the body at birth and therefore larger. Between birth and maturity the head height doubles, while total stature increases about three and one-half times. By age six, the *trunk* is twice as long and wide as it was at birth. From six to ado-

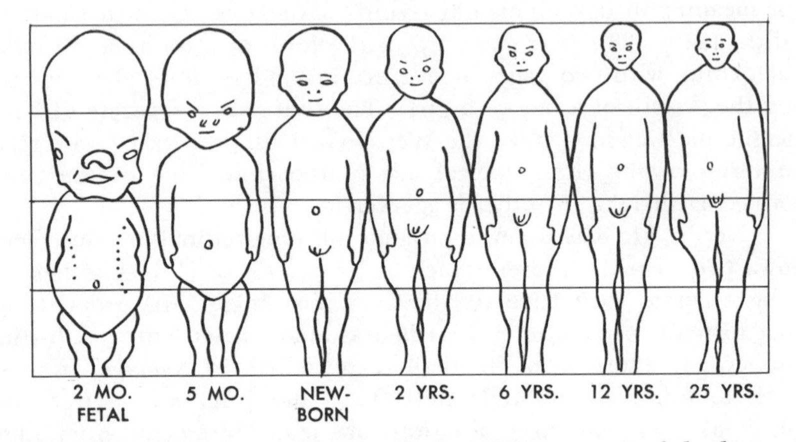

FIGURE 9.6. Changes in body proportions at different stages of development. Used by permission from *Morris' Human anatomy,* edited by B. Anson. Copyright 1953, © 1966 by McGraw-Hill, Inc.

lescence the increase in body length is about 50 percent; by maturity, then, the birth dimensions are approximately trebled. The greatest growth occurs in the *limbs,* especially in the legs. By adolescence the legs are four times as long as at birth, and by maturity, five times as long (Hurlock, 1956) [13]. The change in body proportions illustrates one of the basic laws of growth, *the law of developmental direction:* growth proceeds in a *cephalocaudal* (literally, head-to-tail) direction. As we shall see, motor control follows this line of growth. Figure 9.6 illustrates the change in proportions with age.

One of the results of this change in proportions is a shifting of the center of gravity, which is a determiner of both posture and body balance. In the newborn, the center is near the xiphoid (the lower point of the breastbone) and throughout early childhood it remains near the umbilicus. By five or six years it is below the umbilicus and by thirteen is below the crest of the ilium (lowest division of the small intestine). This lowering of the center, combined with improved muscle coordination and strength, leads to steady improvement in ability to maintain balance, and affects the characteristic changes in posture that occur during the developing years (Watson and Lowrey, 1951) [47].

Growth of Various Systems

If we cut a figurative slice out of the life of a person at any age, an examination of the "cut" would show many systems at various levels of development. If we examined the systems of a six-year-old we might find:

1. Skeletal system at about 45 percent of mature level.
2. Neural system at about 90 percent of mature level.
3. Lymphoid system at 100 percent of mature level. (By age twelve it will achieve almost 200 percent of normal mature level, then decline to 100 percent level by age twenty.)
4. Genital system at only about 10 percent of mature level.

Figure 9.7 shows these varied rates of growth and describes the components of each system.

Although imbalance in growth rates inharmonious functioning in the structure of an individual child may occur (and we should be on the lookout for symptoms of such difficulty), it would be erroneous to assume that this is a frequent or expected occurrence. Unity and integration are characteristic of all biological development. The developing organism does not reach biological integration in the process of growth; it maintains an originally present integration at increasingly higher and more complex levels of development (Wheeler, 1937) [49].

FACTORS AFFECTING OR ACCOMPANYING GROWTH

The causes of growth, like the causes of behavior in general, are varied and complex. Basically, of course, growth is the product of the internal forces of maturation, acting under the press of the external environment. But this generalization raises questions: "What causes maturation?" and "What does the environment do to growth?" Let us examine some of the evidence here.

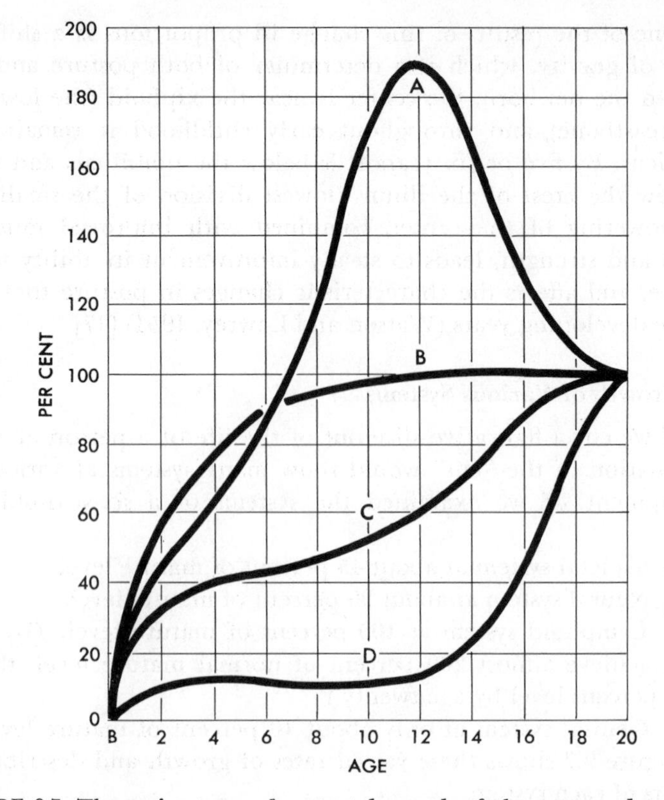

FIGURE 9.7. The major types of postnatal growth of the parts and organs of the body. *A, lymphoid type*—thymus, lymph-nodes, intestinal lymphoid masses. *B, neural type*—brain and its parts, dura, spinal cord, optic apparatus, many head dimensions. *C, general type*—body as a whole, external dimensions (except head and neck), respiratory and digestive organs, kidneys, aorta and pulmonary trunks, spleen, musculature as a whole, skeleton as a whole, blood volume. *D, genital type*—testes, ovary, epididymus, uterine tube, prostate, prostatic urethra, seminal vesicles. The several curves are drawn to a common scale by computing their values at successive ages of their total postnatal increments, to twenty years. From Harris, J. A., *The measurement of man*, Minneapolis, University of Minnesota Press, 1930, page 193. Used with permission.

Inheritance

The effect of inheritance on behavior was discussed at length in Chapter 3. You will recall that we inherit, first, a tendency toward a certain structure: that is, we inherit a tendency to achieve a certain height and weight, a general body type, and our sex. Second, we inherit a tendency toward certain levels of functioning, including a rate of physical growth and maturation. The correlation of height and weight between identical twins was found to be about .95, between fraternal twins about

.60, and between siblings .50. Between parents and children, correlations in the .60s and .70s were found. It is obvious that we must consider a child's growth in the context of his familial inheritance.

Race

Racial differences in body proportions as well as rate of growth have long been observed. North and South European stock (Scandinavian and Italian, for example) may differ as much as four years in rate of maturation, with the latter more accelerated. Members of the yellow race tend toward shortness of stature and Italians tend to be shorter than Anglo-Saxons (Shuttleworth, 1938) [37]. Comparisons of white and Negro babies during the first years of life revealed that the developmental level achieved by the Negro babies was about 80 percent that of the white babies (McGraw, 1931) [26]. In comparing children of various races in Hawaii, it was found that children of North European stock had the greatest stature at each age, followed in order by Hawaiian, South European, Chinese, and Japanese (Shuttleworth, 1949) [39].

Some of these early studies of race and growth were naïve in ignoring socio-economic status. However, even taking this into account, differences still exist, but not to as great an extent. In research on Negro and white infants in which adequate controls were exercised, it was found that lower developmental trends for Negro infants did not appear until the third half-year, and then the difference was slight (Pasamanick, 1946) [34]. In one recent extensive medical research project, nearly 900 matched pairs of American-born and native-born children of Japanese parents were studied. The American-born (California) children were found to be taller, heavier, and more advanced in development than had been supposed. At every age included in the study (six to nineteen years) the American-born Japanese boys exceeded in average stature the boys of Japan by an amount greater than the increase which has taken place in the average stature of the boys of Japan since the beginning of the present century. The differences among females was similar to that of the males. However, despite the great gains made by the American-born children of both sexes, they still lagged somewhat behind a white American control group (Greulich, 1958) [11].

Thus it is apparent that in our evaluation of a child's growth, we must consider him in relation to his racial and ethnic group, but we must not overlook the effect of his particular home environment.

Nutrition

The necessity of providing good nutrition for optimum growth is obvious, but the degree to which nutrition in combination with other factors can influence growth is startling. Anyone who has visited old houses preserved with original furnishings from Revolutionary times may have noted the low chairs and tables, short beds, and other evidences of a people short in stature. The average height of college men of Old American stock increased nearly three inches between 1830 and 1930. The Harvard men of the 1930s averaged one and three-quarter inches taller than their fathers. The same changes have been noted in other ethnic groups (Bowles, 1932) [4]. Measurements of draftees in the two World Wars showed similar changes. In the first half of this century, age of menarche dropped from above fourteen years of age to below thirteen.

Medical and other factors of course influence these figures, but better nutrition is undoubtedly the major cause. However, a study is reported on German orphanage children in which growth in the first half-year of the experiment was compared to the second half, in which a 20 percent increase in food ration was given. At the time of the second half, unfortunately, a new and exceedingly stern matron was assigned to the institution; she scolded the children at mealtime. The result was a greater gain during the first half than during the supplemented, except for seven favorites who gained more than average all the time, and especially more during the second half of the study (Widdowson, 1951) [50]. Surveys of children's growth in twelve European and Asian nations showed a universal retardation of development during the years of World War II. The effect of wartime emotional stress on these children was thought to be another retarding factor, but its effects were inseparable from nutrition, for the areas of greatest food scarcity were also areas in which conditions favoring emotional upset were at a maximum (Markowitz, 1955) [24].

Poor nutrition as a cause of growth failure may occur isolated from other environmental circumstances, but generally it is only one aspect of the social, economic, and emotional environment of the child.

Social and Emotional Status

Considerable evidence has been accumulated on the relationship between growth and the child's socioeconomic class. Rate of development is more rapid and height and weight are greater in children from middle and upper classes. This relationship has been particularly clear in countries such as England, where social classes have been typically somewhat more clearly stratified than in the United States. Diet has been shown to be one of the determining, class-linked factors (Berry and Corwin, 1954) [3].

When no physical causes have been found in studying growth phenomena, investigators have probed into family histories and found that growth lag (or occasionally, growth lead) resulted more frequently than chance would explain when children were subjected to emotional stress. "Emotional stress" of course is peculiar to each individual, but various stressful situations have been identified, such as the death of a parent, institutionalization of a sibling, entrance of father into military service, conflict with a hostile teacher, divorce of parents, and the like. The degree and duration of growth lag approximates that of the stress situation (Fried and Mayer, 1948) [9].

Intelligence

It has generally been reported in the research literature that bright children tend to grow faster than the average and dull and tend to be larger at each level of maturity. As early as 1926, Terman found clear relationships between intelligence and onset of walking, talking, and the like (Terman, 1926) [44]. The basic cause of this relationship has been attributed to the general constitutional developmental rate, but other factors have been considered also.

Brighter children tend to come from better homes where good health care, affection, and nutrition encourage growth. Indirect causes may be involved—the fast grower walks earlier, expands his horizons faster, and therefore has more intelligence-stimulating contacts, which in turn stimulate more development. With the widespread improvement in living standards at every economic level in our society such differences may be reduced or disappear. In a Wisconsin study of the relationships among physical, mental, achievement and personality measures of children of low, average, and high intelligence, no significant relationships were found between the physical growth measures and IQ or achievement (Klausmeier, Feldhusen, Check, 1959) [20]. At any rate, there is no justification for judging an individual child's ability by his size.

We have mentioned above some of the conditions affecting or accompanying growth. Many others—climate, season, endocrine functioning, body type, and so on—have not been considered. The complexity and interdependence of the factors mentioned should make us cautious about jumping to conclusions in our consideration of the growth of one child or of a roomful. This brief summary should instead alert us to the variety of forces acting on the child, and encourage us to develop as constructive an atmosphere for him as is within our capabilities.

GROWTH OF PHYSICAL CAPACITIES

As we have seen, the relative size of the child or adolescent, and his rate of growth, is of major concern to him. Of equal or greater importance to him is what he can and cannot do with his body. With this in mind, let us survey the growth of his motor and sensory capacities.

Motor Development

General growth and motor development are highly related—in fact, motor growth can be said to be one aspect of general physical growth. The direction of motor growth (actually, of neural control) is like that of total growth—cephalocaudal or head-to-tail in direction. Thus, the infant lifts his head before his trunk, sits upright before he stands, and controls his arms fairly well before he walks. The direction of motor growth is also *proximodistal*—from the center of the body outward. Thus, the infant can grasp an object with both arms before he can hold it in his hands and he can use his hands together to grasp a ball before his fingers can grasp a pellet. Early motor development is almost entirely a product of maturation. A number of co-twin control studies have shown that attempts to train an infant or young child in a basic skill (stair-climbing, for example) are of no value until the child has reached an appropriate level of maturity (McGraw, 1935) [27].

By the time he starts school, the child has learned most of the basic motor skills of walking, running, jumping, throwing, and so on. He actually learns few *new* skills in the elementary years, but rather spends his time practicing, improving, and combining the ones he already possesses (Millard, 1958) [29]. It is nearly impossible to overestimate the importance of motor abilities to the child. He gains independence and amusement from them in his preschool years. The emphasis on drawing, painting, shopwork, writing, and making numbers means that his school adjustment is dependent on his skills. Because most of the child's social contacts are made through play, and because childhood play is largely motor play, it is easy to see how his social status and adjustment depend on these same skills. The child who lacks the skills important to his group —ball-throwing, skating, bicycle-riding—is in for a bad time socially. This is especially true for boys. There is evidence that the resulting maladjustment and withdrawal may persist into adulthood (Hurlock, 1956) [13]. Havighurst (1953) [12] describes the situation.

> To an increasing extent, a child's conception of himself is tied up with the skills he has. It is as though his acceptance of himself comes in part from his ability to master different forms of the world outside himself. . . . As a child becomes a part of an activity group . . . he contributes certain skills, certain knowledge. He has an opportunity to test his skills against those of his peers. He adds to his conception of himself as his peers react to his skills.

Motor skills in general and athletic skills in particular continue to improve through adolescence. Sex differences are not important until

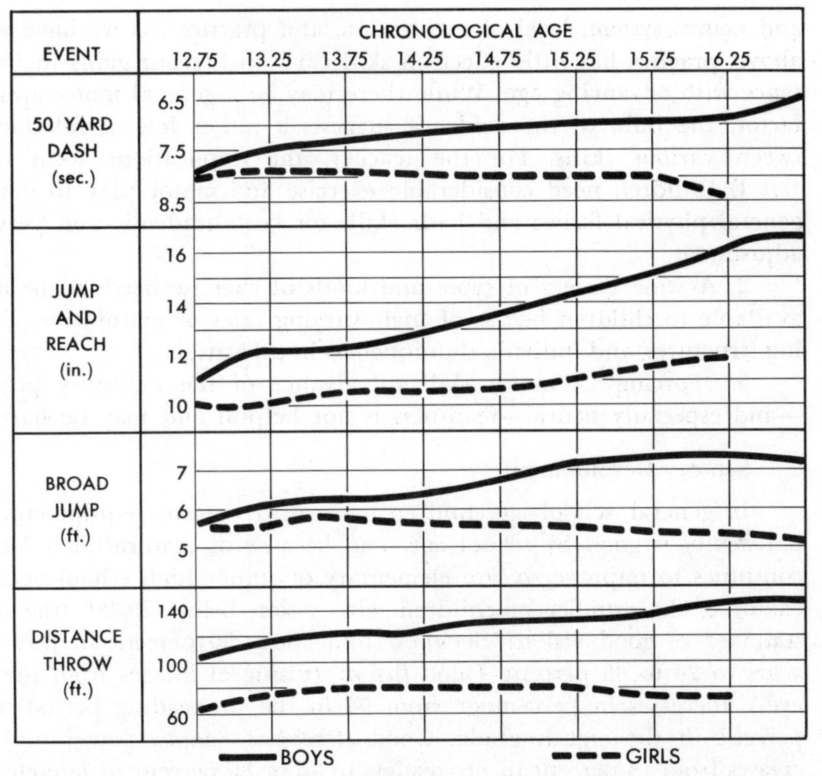

FIGURE 9.8. Increase in athletic skills during adolescence. From Espenschade, A., Motor performance in adolescence, *Monographs of the Society for Research in Child Development*, 5:49–53, 1940. Used with permission of the Society for Research in Child Development.

about age thirteen, when boys begin to pull ahead of the girls. One should avoid ascribing all these differences to the structure and function of the sexes. During adolescence, motor and athletic skills are prestigeful for boys but not for girls—except in some specific communities (for example, in small midwestern towns where interschool girl's basketball is popular) or in special interest groups (golf, tennis). Thus, motivation may have a powerful effect on level of skill.

The alleged awkwardness of the adolescent is either not a fact, or is at any rate not caused by poor coordination. In fact, coordination continues to improve steadily through adolescence without any dips or regressions in the curve (Espenschade, 1940) [8]. Kuhlen suggests that the *apparent* awkwardness of the adolescent is a social phenomenon—that is, the teenager is unsure of himself and others, is embarrassed easily, and thus appears clumsy and poorly coordinated (Kuhlen, 1952) [22].

Motor skills are the product of many factors—inherited physique and neural system, level of maturation, and practice. As we have noted above, practice has little effect on skill early in life but gains in importance with advancing age. While there may be a general motor-aptitude factor, the bulk of the evidence suggests a rather low correlation between various skills. For the teacher, the implications seem clear:

1. Children need considerable exercise and motor play to develop general physical fitness and basic skills for both academic and personal adjustment.

2. A wide variety of types and kinds of exercise needs to be made available to children becase of their varying rates of maturation, differing structures, and individual uniqueness in capacities.

3. "Forcing" a motor skill in advance of the necessary physical —and especially neural—readiness is not helpful and may be harmful.

Sensory Development

In general, school-age children have superb sensory equipment. Visual acuity is good by school age, and because of maturational factors, continues to improve to late elementary or junior high school age. For example, the number of children with vision below 20–20 (the usual standard of good vision) declines from about 50 percent in preschool years to 20 to 35 percent. Good *fusion* (fusing of images from the two eyes) increases in percentage from 54 in the pre-reading period to 80 percent in the eighth grade. Good *stereopsis* (depth perception) increases from 18 percent in pre-readers to 75 or 80 percent in late elementary years (Park and Burri, 1943) [33]. The evidence on the effect of minor aberrations of vision on reading and other academic skills is complex and contradictory, so we must assume at present that there is little direct effect.

Hearing, like vision, is relatively good in the school-beginner. Like vision, it improves during childhood years and reaches a peak of acuity around age thirteen (Williams, 1932) [51]. The other senses develop at a similar rate.

Hearing and visual deficiencies present a real and significant hazard to learning and good adjustment. The extent of deficiencies is considerable. Screening programs among public school children have demonstrated an incidence of 3 percent to 6 percent for mild to moderate hearing loss (McCabe, 1963) [25]. Incidence figures released by the National Society for the Prevention of Blindness show approximately one seriously visually handicapped child for every 500 pupils (Myers, 1961) [31]. Other estimates suggest that as many as one out of four school-age children need some eye care (Gibbons and McCaslin, 1962) [10]. These problems and their treatments are too complex and extensive to discuss in a general text of this kind. Excellent material is available in specialized volumes. (See, for example, Cruickshank, 1958 [5].)

GROWTH AND LEARNING

Most of our discussion has emphasized the personal-social aspects of growth. The place of maturation in readiness for learning is well known and must not be overlooked. In a discussion of attempts to teach a skill before adequate maturation has been achieved (in this case toilet-training), Tanner comments, "It may indeed be reprehensible and in some cases it is certainly savage, but at all events it is foolish" (Tanner, 1961, page 125) [44]. Studies documenting other aspects of growth influences on learning range from correlation studies to prediction of mental stature based on height-weight growth patterns.

In one representative longitudinal study (Nally, 1955) [32] it was found that the percentage of total height development was an excellent predictor of beginning of reading. (We should note that prediction was based not on absolute height, but on percentage of individual growth completed; in this study reading began at 72 percent of total height growth for boys, 76 percent for girls.) Little relationship was found between percent of development in height and chronological age at which reading began.

In the Wisconsin studies mentioned earlier, children's height, weight, carpal age, and number of permanent teeth were unrelated to achievement, but strength of grip was positively related to achievement. Again, chronological age showed no relationship to children's school performance (Klausmeier, Feldhusen and Check, 1959) [20]. Chronological age is probably one of the least useful predictors of behavior we can use.

Although the predictive value of physical growth data for school achievement is not clear, it is apparent that any aspect of academic achievement is a function of the total psychological state of the child. We should no more ignore the child's physical state than his intellectual state.

THE ROLE OF PHYSICAL GROWTH

At the beginning of the chapter we raised the question "Why should the student of behavior concern himself with physical growth?" It should be apparent by now that the student of behavior cannot afford *not* to study physical growth. The child's rate of development and his size, shape, appearance, and strength help to determine the psychological situation in which he finds himself. His perception of himself and the reception accorded him by others is a product in large part of his physical status, and his readiness to learn is to a considerable degree a product of his maturity. To return to the beginning of this chapter, "The human being functions as a whole organism, and it is not possible to look at any piece of behavior without considering the whole." A very important part of the whole is physical growth.

Suggested Collateral Readings

Breckenridge, Marian E., and E. Lee Vincent, *Child development.* Philadelphia: W. B. Saunders Company, 1960. Chapters 7 and 8.

Charles, D. C., *Psychology of the child in the classroom.* New York: Crowell-Collier and Macmillan, Inc., 1964. Chapter 2.

Cole, L. E., and W. F. Bruce, *Educational psychology,* revised ed. New York: Harcourt, Brace & World, Inc., 1958. Chapters 2 and 3.

Eichorn, Dorothy H., "Biological correlates of behavior," in Stevenson, H. W., J. Kagan, and C. Spiker, eds., *Child psychology,* Part I, N.S.S.E. Yearbook. Chicago: University of Chicago Press, 1963. Pages 4–61.

Garrison, K. C., *Growth and development,* 2d ed. New York: Longmans, Green & Co., Inc. (David McKay Company, Inc.) , 1959. Chapter 5.

Jones, H., *Motor performance and growth.* Berkeley: University of California Press, 1949.

Lee, J. M., and Doris M. Lee, *The child and his development.* New York: Appleton-Century-Crofts, 1958. Chapter 3.

McCandless, B. R., *Children and adolescents.* New York: Holt, Rinehart and Winston, Inc., 1961. Chapter 9.

Meyer, W. J., *Developmental psychology.* New York: Center for Applied Research in Education, Inc., 1964. Chapter II.

Munn, N. L., *The evolution and growth of human behavior.* Boston: Houghton Mifflin Company, 1965. Chapters 9 and 10.

Mussen, P. H., *The psychological development of the child.* Englewood Cliffs, N.J.: Prentice-Hall, Inc., 1963. Chapter 3.

Pressey, S. L., and R. G. Kuhlen, *Psychological development through the life span.* New York: Harper & Row, Publishers, 1957. Chapter 2.

Pressey, S. L., F. P. Robinson, and J. E. Horrocks, *Psychology in education.* New York: Harper & Row, Publishers, 1959. Chapter 2.

Stolz, H. R., and Lois M. Stolz, *Somatic development of adolescent boys.* New York: Crowell-Collier and Macmillan, Inc., 1951. Especially Chapter 18.

Tanner, J. M., *Education and physical growth.* London: University of London Press, 1961.

References

1. Ahrens, M., W. R. Baller, Z. S. Henderson, and H. E. Wright, 1941, *Physiological aspects of child growth and development.* Division on Child Development and Teacher Personnel, Commission on Teacher Education, American Council on Education.
2. Anderson, J. E., 1954, "Methods of child psychology," in Carmichael, L., *et al., Manual of child psychology.* New York: John Wiley & Sons, Inc. Page 7.
3. Berry, W. T. C., and P. J. Corwin, 1954, Conditions associated with the growth of boys, 1950–1951. *British Medical Journal,* 1: 847–851.

4. Bowles, G. T., 1932, *New types of old Americans at Harvard and at eastern women's colleges.* Cambridge: Harvard University Press.
5. Cruikshank, W. M., ed., 1958, *Psychology of exceptional children and youth.* Englewood Cliffs, N.J.: Prentice-Hall, Inc. Chapters 7, 8, 9.
6. English, H., and Ava C. English, 1958, *A comprehensive dictionary of psychological and psychoanalytical terms.* Page 308.
7. Espenschade, Anne, 1940, Motor performance in adolescence. *Monogr. Soc. Res. Child Develpm.,* 5, Number 2.
8. Everett, Evalyn G., 1943, *Behavioral characteristics of early- and late-maturing girls.* Unpublished Master's Thesis, University of California.
9. Fried, R., and M. F. Mayer, 1948, Socio-emotional factors accounting for the growth failure in children living in an institution *J. Pediat.,* **33**: 444–456.
10. Gibbons, Helen, and M. F. McCaslin, 1962, Prevention of blindness—the contributions of medical, social and statistical research. *Education of the Blind,* II, pages 116–120.
11. Greulich, W. W., 1958, Growth of children of the same race under different environmental conditions. *Science,* **127**: 515–516.
12. Havighurst, R. J., 1953, *Human development and education.* New York: Longmans Green & Co., Inc. By permission of David McKay Company, Inc.
13. Hurlock, Elizabeth B., 1956, *Child development.* New York: McGraw-Hill, Inc. Pages 116–119.
14. ———, page 139.
15. Jackson, R. L. and Helen G. Kelly, 1945, Growth charts for usé in pediatric practice. *J. Pediat.,* **27**.
16. Jones, Mary C., 1957, The later careers of boys who were early- or late-maturing. *Child Develpm.,* **28**: 113–128.
17. ———, 1958, A study of socialization patterns at the high-school level. *J. genet. Psychol.,* **XC**: 87–111.
18. ———, and Nancy Bayley, 1950, Physical maturing among boys as related to behavior. *J. educ. Psychol.,* **41**: 129–148.
19. ———, and P. H. Mussen, 1958, Self-conceptions, motivations, and interpersonal attitudes of early- and late-maturing girls. *Child Develpm.,* **29**: 492–501.
20. Klausmeier, H. J., J. Feldhusen, and J. Check, 1959, *An analysis of learning efficiency in arithmetic of mentally retarded children in comparison with children of average and high intelligence: Research report to the United States Office of Education.* Madison: School of Education, University of Wisconsin.
21. Kodlin, D., and D. J. Thompson, 1958. An appraisal of the longitudinal approach to studies in growth and development. *Monogr. Soc. Res. Child Develpm.,* **23**: 15–20.
22. Kuhlen, R. G., 1952, *The psychology of adolescent development.* New York: Harper & Row, Publishers.
23. La Barre, W., 1954, *The human animal.* Chicago: The University of Chicago Press.
24. Markowitz, S. D., 1955, Retardation in growth of children in Europe and Asia during World War II. *Human Biology,* **27**: 258–273.

25. McCabe, B. F., 1963, The etiology of deafness. *Volta Review,* **65**: 471–477.
26. McGraw, Myrtle B., 1931, A comparative study of a group of Southern white and Negro infants. *Genet. Psychol. Monogr.,* **10**: 1–50.
27. ———, 1935, *Growth: A study of Johnny and Jimmy.* New York: Appleton-Century-Crofts.
28. Meredith, H. V., 1949, A "Physical Growth Record" for use in elementary and high school. *American Journal of Public Health,* **39**: Part 2.
29. Millard, C. V., 1958, *Child growth and development,* revised ed. Boston: D. C. Heath and Company. Page 104.
30. Mussen, P. H., and Mary C. Jones, 1957, Self-conceptions, motivations, and inter-personal attitudes of late- and early-maturing boys. *Child Develpm.,* **28**: 243–256.
31. Myers, R. S., 1961, Program needs of visually handicapped children in Oregon. *Sight Saving Review,* **31**: 35–40.
32. Nally, T. P. F., 1955, The relationship between achieved growth in height and the beginning of growth in reading. *J. educ. Res.,* **49**: 153–154.
33. Park, G. E., and Clara Burri, 1943, Eye maturation and reading difficulty. *J. educ. Psychol.,* **34**: 535–546.
34. Pasamanick, B., 1946, A comparative study of the behavioral development of Negro infants. *J. genet. Psychol.,* **69**: 3–44.
35. Scammon, R. E., 1927, The first seriatim study of human growth. *American Journal of Physical Anthropology,* **10**: 329.
36. Schaeffer, J. P., ed., 1953, *Morris' Human Anatomy,* 2d ed. New York: McGraw-Hill, Inc.
37. Shuttleworth, F., 1938, The adolescent period: A graphic and pictorial atlas. *Monogr. Soc. Res. Child Develpm.,* **3**: No. 3.
38. ———, 1939, The physical and mental growth of girls and boys age six to nineteen in relation to age at maximum growth. *Monogr. Soc. Res. Child Develpm.,* **4**: 9.
39. ———, 1949, The adolescent period: A graphic and pictorial atlas. *Monogr. Soc. Res. Child Develpm.,* **14**: No. 1.
40. Strang, Ruth, 1957, *The adolescent views himself.* New York: McGraw-Hill, Inc.
41. Tanner, J. M., 1961, *Education and physical growth.* London: University of London Press.
42. Tanner.
43. ———, page 121.
44. Terman, L. M., 1926, *Genetic studies of genius,* Vol. II. Stanford: Stanford University Press.
45. Thompson, Helen, 1954, "Physical growth," in Carmichael, L., *et al., Manual of child psychology.* New York: John Wiley & Sons, Inc. Page 293.
46. Tuddenham, R. D., and Margaret M. Snyder, 1954, *Physical growth of California boys and girls from birth to eighteen years.* Berkeley: University of California Press. Page 199.
47. Watson, E. A., and G. H. Lowrey, 1951, *Growth and development of children.* Chicago: Year Book Medical Publishers, Inc. Page 74.
48. Wetzel, N. C., 1941, Physical fitness in terms of physique, development and

basal metabolism. *Journal of the American Medical Association,* **116:** 1187–1195.

49. Wheeler, R. H., 1937, "The problem of integration," in Hopkins L. T., ed., *Integration: Its meaning and application.* New York: Appleton-Century-Crofts. Chapter 3.
50. Widdowson, E. M., 1951, Mental contentment and physical growth. *Lancet,* **1:** 1316–1318.
51. Williams, H. M., 1932, Audiometric test for young children. *Child Develpm.,* **2:** 237–241.
52. Williams, R. J., 1946, *The human frontier.* New York: Harcourt, Brace & World, Inc.
53. ———, 1953, *Free and unequal.* Austin: University of Texas Press. Page 17.

CHAPTER 10

Development of Mental Ability

Although interest in human abilities is probably as old as civilization, scientific study of the topic is primarily a twentieth century phenomenon. Until fairly recently, performance in school has been the criterion of ability, and most research has been concerned with measurement of individual differences and prediction of performance.

The first intelligence test was developed shortly after the turn of the century; the first major American individual test and the first group or "paper-and-pencil" test were developed during the World War I period. Testing of all sorts proliferated in the 1920s, preparing the way for intensive cross-sectional and longitudinal research and for predictive studies in later decades. Tests were developed for a variety of subjects and situations, and were refined through use of new statistical techniques.

But there has been growing dissatisfaction with these traditional approaches to the investigation of abilities. For one thing, the predictive efficiency of the IQ has not been as great as once was hoped. Correlations between IQ and academic success or failure of about +.40 to +.50 are about as high as are found in most studies, and these figures mean that only 16 percent to 25 percent of the variance can be attributed to what is being measured. Campbell comments, in reference to a major longitudinal study, "One very disconcerting finding was the demonstration that there has been no progress in accuracy of grade point prediction since 1936. . . . It is disturbing to note that at the University of Minnesota, . . . it has not been possible to increase even slightly the accuracy of student selection procedures" (Campbell, 1965) [13].

More serious than inadequacies in predictive efficiency has been the neglect of research into the *nature* of abilities. How does thinking go on? How do the child and the adolescent develop intelligent thought? What is the nature or structure of cognitive functions in the human being? What are the sources of original or creative thought? (The last three of the questions are central to the discussion in Chapter 11.)

Fortunately, the neglect of these areas is being corrected through stimulation from Jean Piaget and the "Geneva School" in Europe and from many researchers in major American universities. Theoretical formulations, supported by observational and experimental evidence, have been accumulating. Many persons feel that the new approaches to study of human abilities constitute the most exciting research ventures going on in psychology and education today.

The fact that the research in traditional views of intelligence has reached something of a plateau does not, of course, reduce the value of that which has been done in the past. In the present chapter we will review the evidence accumulated in the past half century on the nature and development of human abilities. Then in Chapter 11 we will consider some of the new concepts in the studies of abilities.

Importance of Knowledge of Mental Development

The mental ability of the individual determines much of his life experience. In many places a child's mental age, rather than his chronological age, is considered the criterion for his entrance to school. Many decisions about his educational experience will be made on the basis of his level of ability. If he desires to enter college, his level of intellectual functioning may be one of the determinants of his admission; the same situation may obtain when he applies for a job. If he enters military service, he will be accepted or rejected for certain kinds of specialized training partially on the basis of mental ability.

What is intelligence, that it is so vital to human beings? How is it measured or evaluated? How is ability distributed in the population? What are the determinants of intelligence, and how stable is it after it is acquired or developed? How does it grow and change through the years? These are questions to be considered in this chapter.

THE NATURE OF INTELLIGENCE

By "intelligence" we usually mean a person's ability to learn, to adapt, to solve new problems. It is not an entity of itself, but simply a way of behaving. In our culture, and especially in our schools, a person is likely to be regarded as "intelligent" if he has good verbal and conceptual abilities and is able to reason and solve abstract problems. A youngster may be strong, able to run swiftly, and may possess a highly developed sense of smell, and still be "unintelligent" by the standards of our culture. (Although, as we shall see, favorable traits tend to be correlated in the same person.) In a primitve hunting culture such a boy might be highly admired for his abilities. We might say that intelligent behavior in our culture on the other hand is the kind of behavior which makes a child successful in school work. In other words, intelligence is culturally defined.

How is this ability structured or organized? There are three major theories, each giving rise to some particular measuring technique and each with its proponents. Let us examine each one briefly.

Global Theory

One point of view holds that intelligence is a global or unitary phenomenon. Thus a person is assumed to have a generalized ability to solve all kinds of problems, to respond to stimuli, to acquire skills and knowledge, to reason and so on. This point of view results in general tests yielding a single score—the familiar IQ (intelligence quotient) or a scaled score of some sort. Through the years since the inception of intelligence testing, this theory has probably had more followers than any other. If this theory were to be accepted without reservation, it could be assumed that two children of the same mental age and intelligence quotient would function alike qualitatively as well as quantitatively. They do not necessarily function alike, however, as any teacher knows. A pair of eight-year-old boys with identical IQ's may be quite different in their ability to handle some intellectual task, say mathematical computation. More important than our common-sense observation is the evidence of statistical analyses of test results; they give us further reason to doubt the validity of this theory.

Factor Theory

Analyses of test scores by means of a mathematical technique called factor analysis has led many persons to believe that the mind is made up of several almost totally unrelated functions. These "factors" as they are called are thought to function in relation to each other in a patterned way, but no general or global ability is hypothesized. The number of factors deduced from the mathematical analyses ranges from as few as two to more than thirty in one contemporary study. Perhaps the best-known factor test is Thurstone's *Primary Mental Abilities Tests.*[1] In one form this test gives scores for Verbal Meaning, Number, Reasoning, Spatial, and Word-Fluency abilities. Unfortunately, the factor tests have not been particularly useful in predicting intellectual achievement and thus are probably of more theoretical than practical significance at the present time.

[1] Published by Science Research Associates, Chicago, Illinois.

General-Plus-Special-Abilities Theory

A third theory, first proposed by Sir Francis Galton nearly a hundred years ago, hypothesizes the presence of both general and special abilities in the same person. Both statistical and neurological data have been marshalled to support this idea and have been quite convincing. Burt (1958) [10] comments as follows:

> However, what is far more important from the practical standpoint of educational guidance is this: in nearly every factorial study of cognitive ability, the general factor commonly accounts for quite 50 percent of the variance (rather more in the case of the young child, rather less with older age groups) while each of the minor factors accounts for only 10 percent or less. . . . For purposes of prediction—forecasting what this or that individual child is likely to do in school or in after-life—the general factor is by far the most important, though admittedly not our only, guide.

Thus, because it does the best job of predicting general academic success, the prevailing practice is to use one of the standard intelligence tests yielding a single score, or perhaps a verbal and a performance ability score. The psychologist or teacher working with children will keep in mind, however, that two children with the same intelligence score have about the same *general* ability, but may differ somewhat in their aptitude for learning in some *specific* areas. Although we recognize the existence of the general-plus-special abilities, we do not at present have any very satisfactory tests for spelling out this pattern in the individual case.

MEASURING ABILITY

How can abilities be measured, and how can learning performance be forecast? Detailed or intensive answers to these questions will not be undertaken at this point, but it seems desirable to examine the theories behind ability testing and to discuss some of the general types of tests used with school-age children.

The idea of ability testing dates back to shortly before the turn of the century. The first practical intelligence test was devised by Alfred Binet and his associates in 1905. Binet had been asked by French school officials to devise some means of identifying children who would be unable to perform satisfactorily in the regular school curriculum. After a number of false starts, he hit upon the idea of asking children of each age questions about material to which they had almost certainly been exposed—questions dealing with home, community, and school experiences. He reasoned that the greater the number of correct answers given by the child, the greater would be his ability to *acquire* new learning. His judgment proved sound and the resulting test was successful for its purpose.

Mental Age. Test items were tried out on groups of children and were arranged in ascending order of difficulty; some items could thus be passed by average children six years and older; other items by seven-year-old children and older, and so on. This relationship between age and test performance gave rise to the concept of mental age which Binet introduced in 1908.

When a child succeeded on the items which had generally been passed by six-year-olds in the standardizing group, that child was assigned a mental age of six, regardless of his chronological age. This concept was a boon to teachers, for children with the same mental age are more likely to perform similarly in the classroom than are children who have only chronological age in common.

Intelligence Quotient. A logical next step was to consider mental age (MA) in relation to chronological age (CA). William Stern, a German psychologist, first suggested this in 1912, but the concept was not used widely until Terman adopted it for use with the 1916 Stanford-Binet scale. This ratio between MA and CA became known as the intelligence quotient, or IQ. It is found simply by the formula $MA/CA \times 100 = IQ$. Thus, for a child who has a chronological age of eight, and who demonstrates a mental age of ten on a test: $10/8 \times 100 = 125$ IQ; or for a child whose chronological age is twelve and whose mental age is 10: $10/12 \times 100 = 83$ IQ. The term IQ then is simply a convenient way of expressing *rate* of intellectual development: the rate of intellectual development for the first child described above is 20 percent faster than average, for the second child it is 17 percent slower than average.

It should be noted here that the term IQ applied to older adolescents or adults is somewhat misleading, for mental growth is no longer continuing at an appreciable rate. Artificial ways of computing the score are used, but many tests used with grownups yield a standard score of some sort—such as a percentile score—instead of an IQ. The same technique may, of course, be used with children also.

Types of Tests

Individual Tests. The test devised by Binet was given in an individual interview, and the better clinical instruments are still "individual" tests. The Stanford-Binet, developed in this country by Terman in 1916 and revised in 1937, has been perhaps the most widely used test of this sort (Terman and Merrill, 1937) [41]. It has been revised again, and the 1960 edition (Terman, 1960) [42] is now available, but has not entirely supplanted the older versions.

The test can be administered to children with a mental age as low as two, and its useful range extends up to adults with superior mental ability. The whole scale contains 142 tests, covering both verbal and nonverbal concepts. The rating derived is that of a global or general score.

Another clinical instrument developed originally for use with adults but now revised downward to include children is the series of Wechsler tests (Wechsler, 1955, 1958) [44, 43]. They differ from the Binet in several ways, but primarily in their organization: three scores are elicited, a Verbal IQ, a Performance IQ, and a Full Scale IQ which is a composite of the first two. Many clinicians feel that the nonverbal score is highly useful; the fact remains that a verbal score (such as the Wechsler Verbal IQ or the Stanford-Binet) is the best predictor of academic success.

Specialized individual tests are also available to the clinician for use in situations where traditional instruments are inadequate. Such situations might arise in work with blind, deaf, or otherwise handicapped children, in cases of environmental deprivation, with children from non-English speaking homes, and the like. Tests for infants are also available and, although somewhat unreliable at very early ages, are used to estimate rate of sensorimotor development as a guide to probable later ability.

The above tests and others like them are all clinical instruments and are useful only in the hands of well-trained and experienced psychological testers. They cannot be used by untrained teachers or other laymen.

Group Tests. As just noted, individual instruments are intensive and require considerable time for administration, since the clinician can test only about one person an hour. When the United States was preparing to enter World War I, it seemed desirable to have a test which could be given to a group of persons. Accordingly, a number of psychologists were commissioned with the task of devising such a test. The *Army Alpha* test was developed in 1916 and proved very useful for ranking draftees by ability level. Later, the *Army Beta* test was added for men who were illiterate or who had little language facility. After the war, these and other group tests (sometimes called "paper-and-pencil" tests) were adopted by schools and by industry and business. Today there are many group tests of ability for general evaluation as well as for specific purposes.

How good are the paper-and-pencil tests, compared to the clinical interview type? For the great majority of persons, they do a quite adequate job of giving an estimate of general intellectual ability. For atypical cases—poor readers, handicapped children, and the like—an individual test is desirable. A clinical evaluation is also recommended when a group test score is inconsistent with other evidence, for example, when school marks are much higher or lower than intelligence score, or when tests reults may have a profound effect on the child's life, as in placement in an adoptive home or commitment to an institution for the mentally deficient.

Evaluation of Intelligence Tests

Most schools use intelligence tests at regular intervals throughout the students' academic careers. How valuable are these tests, and what is really learned from them? In general, the test scores suggest the level at which a student can be expected to achieve. For example, a recent study of several hundred children was reported in which intelligence was tested at grade one and achievement measured in grade three. Standardized group tests were used on both occasions. Between IQ and general achievement a correlation of .50 was obtained, between IQ and reading achievement a correlation of .44 and between IQ and arithmetic achievement a correlation of .45 (Edwards and Kirby, 1964) [18]. A pupil whose work is significantly below that predicted can probably benefit from further evaluation and individual help. Knowledge of ability is invaluable in guidance and counseling, especially in the areas of educational and vocational planning. Some schools find intelligence level a useful consideration in assigning students to sections of certain classes.

On the other hand, there are many things they will not do. Nothing is learned about a child's drive or motivation from an intelligence test. His personality, his interests, his special aptitudes are not revealed in his score. If he is extremely bright or dull, the test may not give a true picture of his potentialities. Furthermore, the test does not reveal *why* he earned the score he did—it simply reveals his level of functioning at the time of the test.

These latter comments are not criticisms of intelligence tests: they simply are warnings that the test are designed for a specific job: the prediction of academic success. They are useful for other predictions only insofar as academic aptitude is a factor in them. For example, an intelligence test will not tell a teacher or counselor whether a boy should enter the study of law; it *will* tell him, however, whether he has the necessary ability to do college work, and work beyond the baccalaureate degree. To evaluate other aspects of behavior it is necessary to use other instruments or techniques.

At least one major public school system—New York City—abandoned group intelligence testing in 1964, substituting group achievement (knowledge and skill) testing for the ability measurement. The reasons behind this move are too complex to go into here, and the action has been both supported and condemned. (See Hughson, 1964, and Yourman, 1964, for pro and con discussion [27]). Most schools, however, feel the benefits of intelligence testing far outweigh any hazards.

DISTRIBUTION OF ABILITY

Mental ability or intelligence, like all human traits, has a normal distribution within the total population. That is, a few persons are extremely bright and a few are extremely dull. A somewhat greater proportion is moderately bright or moderately dull. The great majority is average—neither very bright nor very dull. A graphic representation of the intelligence test scores of a sample of the total population is shown in Figure 4.3, Chapter 4.

What are the characteristics of people at these different levels of ability? How far are they likely to be able to go in school and what kinds of jobs can they handle as adults? Since intelligence testing was initiated more than forty years ago, considerable evidence has been amassed in answer to these questions. In examining this evidence it should be borne in mind that these are *generalizations,* valid for population but not necessarily completely applicable to an individual with a particular intelligence score. The proportion of the population at each ability level is an estimate based on one sample, and may vary slightly from one test sampling to another.

IQ 140 and Higher: Very Superior

This group, comprising less than 1 percent of the population, has sometimes been designated erroneously as the "genius" group. The title is erroneous because the true genius must have some special, creative abilities in addition to high general ability. Although not properly designated geniuses, they are extraordinary people.

What are they like? The layman's conception of the very bright youngster is likely to be that of an undersized, bespectacled, withdrawn, and peculiar child. One even hears parents say, "I'd rather have my child healthy and happy than too bright." Is there any truth in these allegations?

Fortunately, we do not have to speculate about the answer. In the early 1920s, Lewis Terman and his staff began studying over 1500 children with IQ's above 140. The studies have continued to the present, and the data are reported in five volumes (Terman) [40]. Their characteristics as children are as follows:

1. They were slightly better physical specimens than average. This finding was consistent and unanimous in the medical examinations, the health histories, and the anthropometric examinations.

2. They were accelerated in grade placement about 14 percent of age, but achievement tests revealed 44 percent acceleration. The achievement quotients were not equally high in all school subjects, but were best in reading, language, science, arts, and arithmetical reasoning. They were above average in *all* achievement areas, however, and were no more uneven than average children.

3. They had a great variety of interests, generally accelerated two or three years beyond age.

4. They were above average on character measures of all sorts.

Another stereotype is that of the person brilliant in youth but "burned out" by maturity. Most of the Terman group has been available for continued study up to the present—a period of forty-five years. To what extent have these brilliant children fulfilled their early promise? This is how they appear in middle age:

1. Their death rate has been much lower than that of the population average.

2. Mental illness and suicide have occurred less frequently than in the general population.

3. Their divorce rate has been lower than the average of their native state of California.

4. Ninety percent of the group entered college; of these, over 90 percent graduated—about forty times the rate for the general population when they were of college age. They were highly successful as a group in college, both intellectually and socially.

5. Their earnings have been well above the general population despite the fact that many are members of the relatively poorly paid profession of teaching. At age thirty their average income was twice the national average.

6. Although no true genius has appeared among them, they have been many times as productive and creative as would have been a similar group chosen from the general population. By 1950, 800 males had published 1400 technical articles, 67 books, 200 short stories and plays, and many other unclassified creative works. (Women were not included in the report on productivity and creativity because so many of them were housewives.)

The answer to our question, "What are they like?" is that they are superior human beings: superior physically, intellectually, socially, and emotionally. It must be noted, of course, that problems arise even among the very able. Because of emotional or environmental difficulties, not all these subjects fared well in school or went on to higher education. In other studies it has been found that some children in the very high reaches of intelligence—180 IQ and above—may have problems of social adjustment and communication with their duller age-mates.

There is good evidence that the very able children are overlooked in the classroom more frequently than any other group. Because of lack of stimulation, many do not achieve particularly well or go on to train for the high-level work of which they are capable. Identifying, stimulating, and guiding these extremely bright youngsters is an important part of every teacher's task. Besides, what could be more satisfying than having a part in the development of these extraordinary children? (Gallagher, 1964) [20]

IQ 120–139: Superior

This group comprises about 10 percent of the population, but has an influence far out of proportion to its size. It might be called the "college graduate" group, for it is the population segment out of which the great majority of successful college students is drawn. The more able and studious in this group make up the bulk of scholars in graduate colleges. (Reference is, of course, made here to *numbers;* a greater *proportion* of the 140 IQ group is in graduate school, but they comprise a smaller total *number.*) Thus, it is evident that the greatest number of successful scientists, professional men and women, technical authorities, scholars, and the like come from the "superior" group.

Like the "Very Superior," not all members of this group are successful, not all are motivated to make use of their abilities—or are even aware that they have high learning capacities. With the present demand for able, highly trained people in research jobs and industry, it is up to the schools to make greater efforts to hold these students and encourage higher educational achievement.

IQ 110–119: High Average

In this category is included about 15 percent of the population. Educationally, persons of this level of ability are likely to succeed moderately well in high school and many will go on to college at the present time. Although they are below the average [2] of ability of graduates of

[2] In discussing "college average" one must ask "What college?", for there are top-flight institutions where the IQ of the average student will be in the neighborhood of 140, and there are other institutions where the intellectual demands would not

most good colleges and universities, some will graduate from curricula which are not too demanding. They are likely to be employed in business and technical occupations which do not demand too much abstract ability.

IQ 90–109: Average

About half—40 percent to 50 percent of the population—falls in this classification. It is the group about whom Lincoln is reputed to have said "God must have loved the common man, or he wouldn't have made so many of him." In every way they are "typical": educationally, they are likely to complete high school or less (Berenert, 1958) [7]; vocationally, they are likely to work at skilled or technical jobs which do not require education beyond high school. Very few can succeed in college work. Although some may enroll, it is undesirable to encourage them, for they lack the necessary abstract and verbal abilities to succeed in higher education. Except for occupations requiring college training, the person of average ability may fare very well in business, industry, agriculture, and the like.

IQ 80–89: Low Average

From this point downward, the picture is less bright. This low-average group, about 15 percent of the population, is likely to struggle along through grade school, if no special provision is made for them. In junior high school they are likely to encounter considerable difficulty, for they will be generally poor readers and low in mathematical competence. What happens to them after they reach legal school-leaving age depends on environmental circumstances. Lower-class adolescents of this ability are very likely to drop out of school and loaf or enter the labor market as soon as the law allows. If the school has only an academic or college preparatory program, those who remain will be likely to fail and be dropped if the school's standards are high. If the school practices regular promotion and has only the academic channel, these youngsters are likely to learn little but will drift along serving as a nuisance and a drag on the more able students. If, however, the school system offers appropriate technical and vocational training along with general education courses at their level, both society and the student will profit from their continued presence in school. Vocationally, they will work at unskilled or semi-skilled tasks in business, industry, and agriculture which do not require too much "book learning." They may become, with appropriate schooling, very worthwhile and productive citizens.

---

challenge the average high-school junior. In this text, "college average" refers to students in the great majority of institutions of higher learning whose curricula and standards are acceptable to one of the major college accrediting groups.

IQ Below 80: The Low Intelligence Population [3]

Sixty to 79 IQ is on the borderline of mental deficiency, and persons with scores below 60 IQ are almost inevitably deficient. About 10 percent of the population scores below 80 IQ on tests, with about 1 percent or less in the group below 60. Although small, this portion of the population has serious problems.

It was the custom a few years ago (and still is, in some quarters) to describe as mentally deficient anyone whose score fell below a certain level—usually 70 IQ. It has become increasingly apparent, however, that mental deficiency is a *clinical* concept and not just a statistical one. The most widely accepted definition today is probably that presented by the American Association on Mental Deficiency in their manual on terminology and classification in mental deficiency:

> Mental retardation refers to subaverage general intellectual functioning which originates during the developmental period and is associated with impairment in adaptive behavior. (Heber, 1961) [24]

Thus, one individual with an IQ of 70 may be less "deficient" in his behavior than another of 80 IQ. It is necessary to evaluate the whole person in his environmental setting to make the diagnosis of mental deficiency.

The teacher or other layman is properly not so much concerned with technical definitions or labels as he is with practical matters. He wants to know what kind, and how much, schooling is appropriate for a specific child, what kind of work the child should be trained for, and so on.

Intellectually retarded children are usually divided into two distinct groups for educational purposes. One group, the mentally handicapped, is described as *educable* and the other group, the mentally deficient, as the *trainable*.[4] The determination of the appropriate group is a problem for a clinical psychologist with special training and competence in the area of mental retardation.

The mentally handicapped or educable are those children who are too retarded to be handled in the regular classroom, but who can acquire academic skills at a level that will be useful to them in the outside world. With proper help and training, their chances of becoming self-sufficient and independent are very good. Usually they attend special schools or special classrooms in regular schools.

[3] A comprehensive evaluation of the whole field of mental deficiency may be found in Robinson and Robinson (1965) [36].

[4] For a general discussion of educating children of poor ability see Kirk (1962) [30].

The mentally deficient or trainable group is too retarded to profit from education in the academic skills. They usually require institutionalization and can profit only from training in self-care and in simple tasks.

The teacher will ask himself, "What lies ahead for children of low intelligence? Can any of them live normal lives? Are they worth the educational effort they demand?"

Perhaps the best answer to these questions is to examine the lives of a group of children of low abilities. Baller, Charles, and Miller have followed the careers of such a group in somewhat the same fashion that Terman followed the careers of the gifted (Baller, Charles, Miller, 1967) [2].

The subjects of this study were 206 persons who, as children, had IQ's below 70, had failed to make normal progress in school, and had been placed in an "opportunity room" in the schools of their Midwestern community. In their twenties, their forties, and their middle fifties they were found to be getting along much better than might have been expected. Their social adjustment at the time of the most recent study was generally quite good:

1. Less than 6 percent were institutionalized.
2. About half were married and living with the spouse.
3. About 80 percent were "usually employed," with 60 percent to 70 percent fully self-supporting.

On the other hand, they differed from the general population in some ways not so favorable: they had difficulty in getting and keeping spouses, some needed public support to survive, about 6 percent had civil law violations (not of a very serious nature, however) and their level of social involvement in the community was low.

A summary statement from an earlier report on the group is still appropriate:

> The great variation in the present abilities and achievements of the subjects should dispel any notion that persons who give evidence of low ability in childhood develop and perform according to a rigid stereotype. . . . Psychologists, educators and parents may gain encouragement in the knowledge that many children whose test scores and academic performance suggest mental deficiency develop into self-sufficient and desirable citizens as adults. (Charles, 1953) [15]

THE ORIGINS OF ABILITY

How do people come by their abilities? Are they "born with them" or do they acquire them from their social environments? These questions have been widely debated, but in the past two or three decades some rather solid evidence has been accumulated. This evidence makes it clear that capacity to learn is inherited but that intellectual performance at any given time is influenced markedly by environment and by individual functioning. Let us examine the evidence which supports these generalizations.

Inheritance of Ability

Inheritance has been discussed in an earlier chapter (see Chapter 4), in which it was pointed out that the closer the genetic relationship between two persons (monozygotic twins, dizygotic twins, siblings, and so on), the greater the similarity of measured traits. Burt studied the effect of genetic relationship and environmental similarities on tested intelligence (Burt, 1958) [11]. The correlations range downward in stairstep fashion from the high 90s for identical twins reared together, to the 20s for unrelated children reared together. The data are set forth in Table 10.1.

TABLE 10.1
Correlations between Mental Assessments

	Group Intelligence Tests	Individual Intelligence Tests
Identical twins reared together	.944	.921
Identical twins reared apart	.771	.843
Nonidentical twins reared together	.542	.526
Siblings reared together	.515	.491
Siblings reared apart	.441	.463
Unrelated children reared together	.281	.252

Adapted from Burt, C., 1958, The inheritance of mental ability. *The American Psychologist*, 13: 6.

The reasons for the high degree of similarity between closely related persons are readily understandable. The structure primarily responsible for what we term intelligence is the brain and central nervous system. This structure, together with its tendency to function at a certain level, is inherited in the same fashion that other structures are inherited.

But what of environment? What part does it play? Burt comments as follows:

> Environment appears to influence the test results chiefly in three ways: (a) the cultural amenities of the home and the educational opportunities provided by the school can undoubtedly affect a child's performance in intelligence tests of the ordinary type, since so often they demand an acquired facility with ab-

stract and verbal modes of expression; (b) quite apart from what the child may learn, the constant presence of an intellectual background may stimulate (or seem to stimulate) his latent powers by inculcating a keener motivation, a stronger interest in intellectual things, and a habit of accurate, speedy and diligent work; (c) in a few rare cases illness or malnutrition during the prenatal or early postnatal stages may, almost from the very start, permanently impair the development of the child's central nervous system. (Burt, 1958) [12]

Studies of Environment

Because of the obvious implications for education, interaction between environment and measured ability has been studied intensively both in the United States and in Europe. Some representative studies will outline the relationship and may suggest the nature of a propitious environment for optimum mental growth.

Family and Social Class. It is apparent from the data in Table 10.1 that children reared together are more alike than children reared apart. Examining data from the California Growth Studies, Bayley found that the correlations between tested intelligence and "mid-parent education level" rose from .40 at age three to above .60 by age eighteen, thus suggesting greater likeness with continued association (Bayley, 1954) [6]. In another examination of the California data, it was found that the parent-child correlation was observable and statistically significant for girls by three years but not until five for boys, probably because of sex differences in rate of development (Honzik, 1963) [25]. These findings are consistent with those demonstrated in numerous studies reported from the 1920s to the present.

There is considerable homogeneity of ability within social classes. Tests of several thousand children have revealed correlations as high as .43 between social status (parental occupation, education, housing, dwelling area, and so on) and certain intelligence tests. The social-class effect is most marked on tests with a high verbal symbolic content (Eels, 1959 [19]. A range of about 20 IQ points has been found between the averages of children from highest to lowest social class in various studies in the public schools.

It may be argued, of course, that these family and class similarities are simply the product of genetic forces. The genetic factor is undoubtedly a large one, but the Burt and Bayley studies mentioned above show increasing similarities between children and their family-social milieu with increasing contact—that is, with greater similarity in age, education, and association.

Effect of Deprivation. Another way of evaluating environmental influences is to examine groups of persons who have lived in deprived or underprivileged environments. Such studies usually show not only lower-than-average test scores for the population of the study, but a steady *decline* in median score with age. An early study of this sort was an investigation of children of gypsies and of canal-boat operators in England. The families of these children were mostly illiterate and were constantly on the move, thus permitting little or no formal education. A marked negative correlation was found between age and ability (Gordon, 1923) [22]. In the United States, a similar study was made of eastern Kentucky mountain children. There the median IQ dropped steadily from 84 at seven years to 60 at 15 years (Asher, 1935) [1].

The high interest generated in recent years in effects of cultural deprivation has led to many new studies. One example is an investigation of 543 children who were stratified by race, grade level, and social class. Intelligence was tested in the first grade and in the fifth grade. No significant differences between IQ in the two grades were found, but highly significant differences were found between Negro-white test performance and between social class levels (Deutsch and Brown, 1964) [17].

It should be noted that the question of racial, religious, or ethnic influence on intelligence, apart from social class and experiential deprivation, is extremely complex; it is related to motivation, cultural expectation, and other forces which are difficult to control or even to discern in research. Generalization is not possible at this point. Each child in the school must be studied as an individual and not as a representative of a particular group.[5]

Poor homes and neighborhood deprive children physically, socially, emotionally, and intellectually. The content of many tests, especially the increasing verbal emphasis, make them less and less appropriate for deprived children as they moved into the upper grades and beyond.

Children in Foster Homes. Another group of subjects readily available for studies of environmental influence has been that of foster children. In these studies, the natural (that is, biological) mother's intelligence is usually known or is estimated from her academic record or accomplishments. The intelligence of the foster parents is also measured or estimated. If after some period of time in the foster home, the child's intelligence resembles that of the foster parents more than that of the natural mother, it is assumed that that the environment is responsible. In numerous studies of this kind, the children have generally shown a greater resemblance to the foster parents than to the natural mother. From one long-range study of this kind, the authors offer the following conclusion:

> The intellectual level of the children has remained consistently higher than would have been predicted from the intellectual, educational or socio-economic

[5] For a review of social influence on intelligence, see Gordon (1964) [21].

level of the parents, and is equal to or surpasses the mental level of own children in environments similar to those which have been provided by foster parents. (Skodak and Skeels, 1949) [38] [6]

The results of such studies must be interpreted with some caution, because of problems of validity of mothers' test scores, lack of evidence on fathers' ability, selective placement (that is, matching foster parent and child), and other technical problems. The fact remains, however, that results of these studies have tended to support the idea that environmental stimulation is of major importance in determining level of intellectual functioning.

Effect of Environmental Change. In most studies of the influence of foster homes on environment, placement was made in infancy before any very reliable tests could be made. There is, however, some evidence on the *age* in which environment has the greatest effect. Case studies were examined for 100 children who had been in good foster homes for four years. Their ages at placement ranged from three to fourteen years and their IQ's ranged from 70 to 130. It was found that placement before age six resulted in average IQ increases of more than six points, while later placement resulted in very small to nonsignificant gains. The amount of gain or change decreased steadily with age (Reymert and Hinton, 1940) [37].

A study that has much significance for the understanding of mental development has been reported by Skeels (1966) [37]. Thirteen individuals constituted an experimental group who during infancy and early childhood were placed in an institution for the mentally retarded. Provision was made for them to receive special attention from mother-surrogates. These latter were female inmates selected for qualities of responsibility and other attributes favorable to providing considerable mother-substitute care for the children—care that Skeels described as having considerable developmental stimulation and intensity of relationship.

A contrast group of twelve children whose intelligence was initially higher than that of the experimental group was also included in the study. These children were not afforded the attention that was given those in the experimental group; their experience was that of a relatively nonstimulating orphanage environment.

During a period of two years the experimental children demonstrated significant gains in rate of mental growth; the opposite was true of the children in the contrast group: progressive mental retardation characterized them. An average gain of 28.5 IQ points was made by the

[6] It should be noted that, in the study above, there is a very strong correlational resemblance of the children to the true mothers despite the statistically significant difference between them and their children.

children of experimental group; an average loss of 26.2 IQ points was recorded for the contrast group.

A follow-up study was conducted two and a half years beyond the termination date of the original study. Eleven children from the experimental group had been placed in adoptive homes and these had maintained and even increased their earlier gains. Two children of the experimental group had not been placed in adoptive homes; they had declined in rate of intellectual growth. During approximately the same period of time the children of the contrast group continued to show marked mental retardation.

When a period of years had intervened, Skeels conducted another follow-up study which resulted in information about all of the individuals of both the experimental and the contrast groups. Significantly, the two groups had continued their divergent courses of development (of competence) into adulthood. The thirteen individuals of the experimental group were, without exception, self-supporting; none was a ward of any institution. Of the individuals in the contrast group, one had died during adolescence without having left an institution for the mentally retarded; four individuals were wards of institutions: one in a mental hospital, the others in institutions for the mentally retarded.

The difference in educational accomplishments of members of the two groups was especially noteworthy. The median grade level completed by the members of the experimental group was the twelfth grade; for the contrast group it was less than the third grade. Similarly marked differences were found with respect to the occupational levels attained by the members of the two groups respectively. For the experimental group the occupations ranged from professional and business to domestic service (the domestic service employment was reported for two females who had not married but had, as already indicated, continued, in adulthood, to be self-supporting). Four members of the contrast group were institutionalized and unemployed. With only one exception, those who did have employment were, in Skeels' words, "hewers of wood and drawers of water."

Other important differences were noted in the adult comparisons (for example, important differences in numbers of persons married and in the number of offspring). Clearly, from the standpoint of the kinds of life the members of the groups lived—what life may mean to them as individuals—the findings of the study command the most respectful attention. Also there is much social significance in the findings. These are summed up by Skeels (1966, page 55) [37] as follows:

> The cost to the state for the contrast group, for whom intervention was essentially limited to custodial care, was approximately five times that of the cost for the experimental group. It seems safe to predict that for at least four of the

cases in the contrast group costs to the state will continue at a rate in excess of $200 per month each for another 20 to 40 years.

Effect of Bodily Functioning

As was noted earlier, there is some relationship between intelligence and physical functioning. This relationship does not necessarily mean that physical health is a *causal* factor in the development of abilities. (In fact the reverse may be true: more intelligent persons take better care of themselves and their children thus effecting a better level of health.) There are, however, some physical conditions which do affect intelligence. One of these is malfunction of the thyroid gland. If the thyroid—the "governor," so to speak, of body metabolism—is missing or malfunctioning at birth or fails in its function in early life, all body activities will be affected. If the thyroid undersecretes to a critical degree, the child will become slow and lethargic and suffer some growth failure. If he does not receive medical help (thyroxin may be administered to supplement the hormone lack) or if his system does not respond to such therapy, he will become a *cretin*. "Cretin" is the French word for imbecile, and this is a fairly accurate description of severe cretinism. Although appropriate medical therapy produces some improvement in most cases, only about a fourth of afflicted children achieve normal ability. Other abnormal physical conditions may lead to other kinds of deficiency.

Although health and physical status are not generally important factors in the development of intelligence, it may be seen that even with good inheritance and good environment, abnormal development may occur when the physical system malfunctions.

STABILITY OF INTELLIGENCE

It is important to know whether one can expect approximately the same level of performance from a person year after year, or whether ability level is highly variable through time. Obviously, long-term educational and vocational plans cannot be made if the ability of a child is likely to change markedly. On the other hand, if a child earns a low score on an intelligence test in early life, some hope for improvement would provide motivation for him, as well as for his parents and teachers.

The question of reliability or consistency of test scores cannot be described in a simple positive or negative statement. Of course, intelligence tends more toward stability than toward instability. But how strong is this tendency, and what are the circumstances that lead to greater and less reliability (that is, consistency)?

Age

One of the most influential factors in test-score consistency is the age at which ability is tested. Test scores obtained in early infancy—indeed, during the first two years of life—are of limited value in prediction of later abilities.

The reason for this is the nature of the capacities tested. In early life, only alertness and responsiveness, sensorimotor functions, and the like may be tested. By school age, we are primarily interested in, and are able to test, symbolic functions. The relation between early sensorimotor behavior and later verbal and conceptual skills is so low as to cause great unreliability of early test scores. In fact, one of the major authorities in this area (Bayley, 1955) [4] says:

> Whenever careful statistics have been applied to comparisons of repeated test scores of infants and very young children the correlations between tests separated by a year or two are low. It is now well established that we cannot predict later intelligence from the scores on tests made in infancy.

There is, however, a minority report—one piece of evidence gathered on more than 100 children tested early in life, placed in adoptive homes, and retested some years later. Instead of being tagged with specific IQ's, these children were placed in one of five categories ranging from "Superior" to "Mental Defective." At the time of retest, correlations of .56 to .82 were found between original tests and the later evaluations. Table 10.2 shows the correlations by age at original test. There was no deviation from the original category in half the cases, and only 5 of the 102 deviated more than one category. In no case was more than a two-category deviation found (MacRae, 1955) [31]. Although evidence and opinions differ, it is apparent that ability testing in the early months of life is relatively less reliable (that is, less consistent) than later testing.

From about school age onward, test results become generally more consistent. Some children show steady trends upward or downward, while others show marked test-to-test change. Some evidence from longitudinal studies will suggest the extent of such change. For one group of children tested regularly from infancy to early maturity, correlations between tests changed from .49 between the 18–24-month and 42–54-month scores, to .87 between the 5–7 year and 14–16 year scores, to .96 for the three-year period for 14–16 and 17–18 (Bayley, 1949) [3].

When children of the original standardizing population of the Stanford-Binet tests were retested after twenty-five years (original test

TABLE 10.2
Test-Retest Correlations by Age

Age at Infant Test	N	r
0–11 months	40	.56
12–33	41	.55
24–35	21	.82

All correlations are significant at the .01 level.
MacRae, J. M., 1955. Retests of children given mental tests as infants. *J. genet. Psychol.,* 87: 115.

given at ages 2½–5) their retest scores correlated .59 with the original. However, when scores earned in adolescence were compared with those obtained in maturity, the correlation rose to .85, indicating a much higher consistency (Bradway and Robinson, 1961) [9].

Variability in Individuals

These school-age test-retest correlations show good consistency or predictability. This means that the teacher can feel some confidence that test scores two or three years old will be close to the present level in most cases. Why not, then, give every child an intelligence test when he enters school, stamp the score on his record, and waste no more time or money on further testing? Another longitudinal study reveals the undesirability of such a procedure. The correlation between scores earned at age six and those earned at eighteen in this study was .62, which is a fairly high relationship. Individual changes, however, were considerable in some cases. Nearly 10 percent of the children changed 30 IQ points or more; 30 percent changed 20 or more points; and 60 percent changed 15 points or more (Table 10.3) Honzik, Macfarlane, and Allen, 1948) [26]. Changes of this magnitude are significant and have important implications for long-range planning and counseling.

The causes of these individual variations may be genetic, situational, or both. Some children inherit a tendency toward atypical intellectual growth patterns, just as they may be inclined genetically toward atypical physical growth patterns. Marked changes in cultural environment can be influential in score change as we have shown earlier. Some children may slow down in intellectual growth as they reach the ceiling, so to speak, of their family's and subculture's intellectual milieu. Others may be involved in emotionally stressful situations over a period of time (or adjust to such situations) and speed up or slow down accordingly. Glandular malfunctions may occur, and illness may affect good functioning (Wiener, Rider, and Oppel, 1963) [45].

TABLE 10.3
IQ Changes between 6 and 18 Years

Amount of Change (IQ points)	Percent of Group Changing (N = 222)
≥ [a] 50	0.5
≥ 30	9
≥ 20	37
≥ 15	59
≥ 10	85
≤ 9	15

[a] ≥ = "equals or more than"; ≤ = "equals or less than."

Honzik, M. P., J. W. Macfarlane, and L. Allen, 1948, The stability of mental test performance between two and eighteen years. *J. exper. Educ.*, 17: 309–324.

Unless a traumatic event occurs, such as brain damage from an accident, the changes do not occur abruptly.

Although each child has his own individual pattern of progress, the patterns are not completely random. After the period of infancy there is a strong underlying consistency or constancy. Some children forge ahead and maintain relatively advanced positions after 5 or 6 years of age. Others grow slowly and lag behind. There is some shifting of position, but the changes are gradual over rather long intervals of time. Within such intervals we can expect to obtain fairly constant Standard Scores (IQ's). (Bayley, 1955) [5]

Some psychologists feel that the nature and distribution of items in intelligence tests—the uneven concentration of easy and difficult tasks —may contribute to some of the irregularity of scores from one test period to the next (Pinneau, 1961) [34].

The implications for the evaluation of intelligence in the school seem clear. Ability should be measured fairly frequently, perhaps every two years in the lower grades of school, and a test more than three or four years old should be regarded as quite tentative until middle to late adolescence is reached. Reliance in later school years on test scores obtained in the lower grades will lead in many cases to erroneous guidance.

PERSONALITY AND INTELLECTUAL CHANGE

Consistent increase or decrease in measured ability through the developing years has been related to personality. Investigators at the Fels

Research Institute studied 35 children making the greatest gain during the 6- to 10-year age period, and the 35 showing the greatest decrease out of a subject population of 140. Personal characteristics of each of these subject groups were examined. Boys were found to be twice as likely to gain as girls, who were more likely to show an IQ decrease. The qualities of independence, aggressiveness, problem-solving concern, anticipation, and competitiveness all appeared to be related to IQ improvement. The authors describe these traits in total as making up the "achievement motive" (Sontag, Baker, and Nelson, 1958) [39].

Children's early relations with parents, especially the mother, appear to be of prime importance in the development of such characteristics. Girls especially are likely to gain in measured intelligence if their mothers display acceleratory, critical maternal behavior during the pre- and early-school years. Furthermore, girls who reject the traditional sex role have higher IQ's than other girls (Kagan and Freeman, 1963) [28]. The relation between maternal behavior and boys' abilities is less pronounced, perhaps because of different identification tendencies of the sexes. From whatever source, concern with intellectual mastery and achievement is quite stable. In another Fels study mentioned, concern with intellectual mastery at age 10 to 14 was significantly highly correlated with similar concern measured in adulthood (Kagan and Moss, 1962) [29].

Change in intelligence from adolescence to middle age has been related to coping and defense mechanisms in one report from the Oakland Growth Study. Middle-aged adults whose measured intelligence had increased since adolescence were found to have engaged in successful coping behavior in their life experiences, while a decline in IQ was found in subjects who had developed defense mechanisms instead of more positive ways of dealing with life. As in the Fels studies of children, males were more likely to have increased in ability than females (Haan, 1963) [23].

The studies cited above, and others like them, make it clear that even in the abstract, human beings cannot be considered as "disembodied intellects."

THE GROWTH OF INTELLIGENCE

The curve of intellectual growth bears some general similarity to the curve of physical growth up to adolescence. Development is very rapid in infancy through early childhood. The rate slows down somewhat in middle to late childhood and continues at a less accelerated pace (unlike physical growth) into adolescence. It has been estimated that from conception to age four, the human being develops 50 percent of his adult intelligence, from ages four to eight he develops 30 percent more, and from 8 to maturity the remaining 20 percent (Bloom, 1964) [8]. In middle or late adolescence the rate of growth slows down markedly. Until recently it was thought that intelligence reached a peak at this time and began a slow but steady decline. Longitudinal studies in recent years offer contrary evidence: it now appears that ability continues to develop well into maturity. In a thirty-year study mentioned earlier, retarded subjects were found to have improved markedly in tested intelligence and general performancy by middle age (Baller, Charles, Miller, 1967) [2]. College students tested before age twenty and retested about thirty years later had made significant gains, and a decade later in their sixties, were found to be maintaining their improved scores. A similar thirty-year improvement in college graduates was found in another sample (Campbell, 1965) [14]. "Average" (approximately 100 IQ) children were retested in their thirties in still another study; although they showed a wide range of retest scores, the mean was higher than the original level (Charles and James, 1964) [16]. In one of the longest-term studies in the literature, Owens reported significant increases in intelligence test performance in men first tested as college students in 1919, and then retested in their fifties and sixties (Owens, 1953 [34]; 1966 [35]).

The studies cited above demonstrate that many, if not most, persons continue to grow in intellectual capacity into maturity. This finding has important implications for education. The school should not be too ready to give up on a youngster whose performance is poor in early adolescence. Although marked changes are unlikely to occur after this time, slow but steady development may bring the student to a more promising level by late adolescence or maturity. Especially in view of the extremely rapid scientific and technological advances of our time, post-adolescent education must expand.

Although there is a general curve of intellectual growth, each child has his own unique pattern. This uniqueness is demonstrated in test-to-test variations in performance (as discussed earlier) which through time form the individual pattern. Thus, the children in a given classroom will differ among themselves not only in the *level* of ability which they have reached, but in the *rate* at which they are developing. Figure 10.1 shows the actual patterns of intellectual development of five boys from the California Growth Study, from birth to age twenty-five years.

Test scores and growth curves, valuable as they are, cannot give us any real feeling or appreciation of the dynamic and striving nature of the child's developing abilities. Thinking or cognitive behavior is very complex, much of it is private, and it is not easily perceived by the

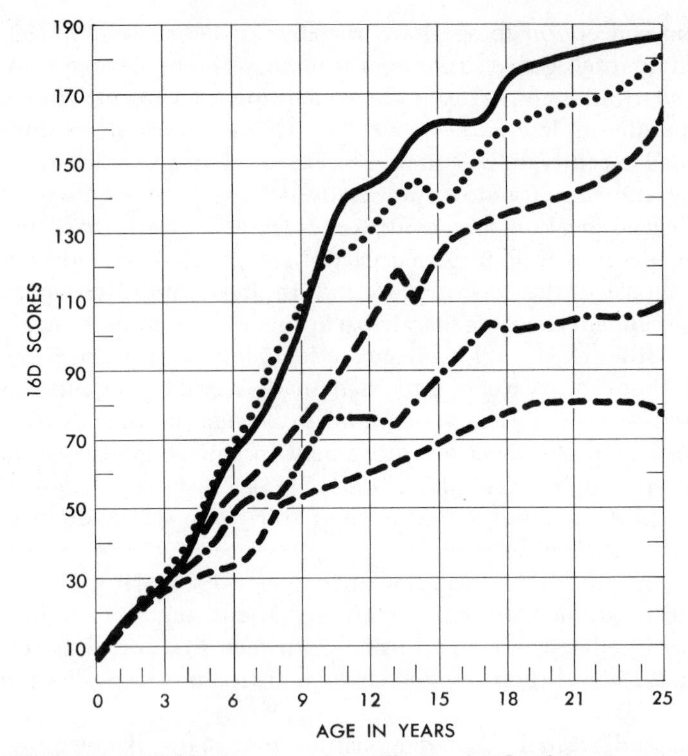

FIGURE 10.1. Individual curves of intelligence for five boys, from one month to twenty-five years of age, from the Berkeley Growth Study. From Bayley, Nancy, On the growth of intelligence, *The American Psychologist,* 10:814. Used with permission of the American Psychological Association.

casual viewer. It is, however, in just this area that the most exciting insights into human abilities have been made in the past few years. We turn our attention to cognition in the next chapter, and also consider special abilities and creativity.

Within-group Differences

From birth to old age, the spread or range of intelligence test scores increases for any group. Neonates and infants are for the most part fairly similar in their intellectual functioning. Kindergartners obviously vary in capacity, but all save the very extremes of high and low can be handled quite comfortably in a single group. Through childhood, the differences increase. By the middle grades, the range of abilities is so great that many schools find it expedient to divide classes into more than one section, stratified by ability. By junior high school, differences are even more apparent, and in senior high school the range of abilities has increased to the point where it becomes extremely difficult to satisfy the intellectual needs of all the students in a mixed, unstratified classroom. Figures 10.1 and 10.2 illustrate the increasing range of abilities.

Studies such as those on which the figures are based usually refer only to *quantitative* changes in intelligence. *Qualitative* changes in learning occur also. Intellectual interests vary more with increasing age. Motivation and satisfaction with school become more complex and variable. The effect of social class, family, and intellectual milieu becomes more pervasive as children become adolescents and young adults. Factor-analytic theory suggests that the structure of intelligence becomes more

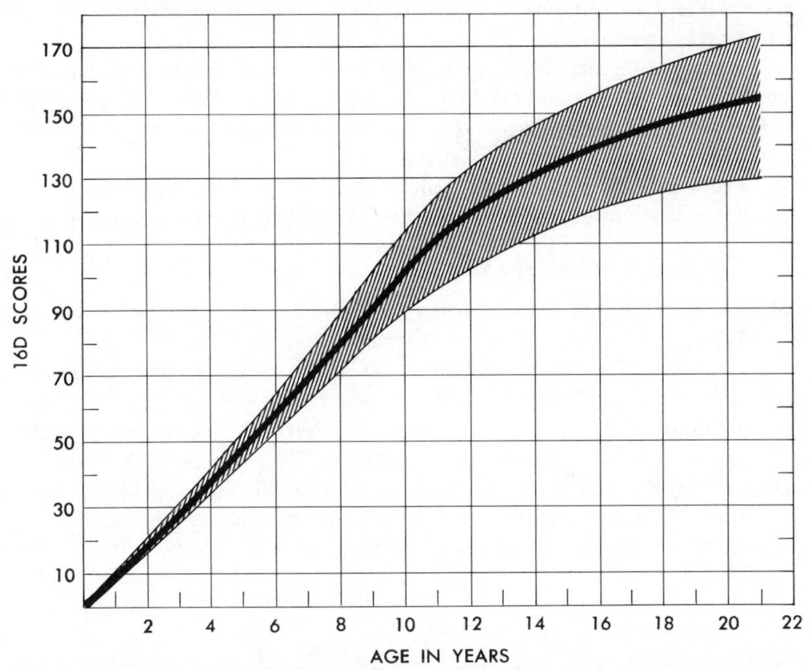

FIGURE 10.2. Curves of means and S.D.'s of intelligence, from birth to twenty-one years of age, from the Berkeley Growth Study. From Bayley, Nancy, On the growth of intelligence, *The American Psychologist,* 10:811. Used with permission of the American Psychological Association.

diversified and unique in the individual with increasing age. In short, the school in general and the teacher in particular have to make more and more individual adjustments as the child goes up the age and grade ladder. More channels and avenues for learning must be provided and more ways for the individual to realize his full capacities. This is difficult; it can be done only imperfectly, and it is expensive. It should be apparent, however, from the research cited here and elsewhere that no one-channel, lockstep type of educational program can satisfy the needs of more than a small percentage of learners, particularly from the upper grades through high school.

SUMMARY

Intelligence is ability to learn, to adapt, and to solve problems: it is defined by the culture in which it occurs. There are three major theories of intelligence: global, factor, and general-plus-special-factor. Of these the third seems to be best supported by evidence; the large general factor is the easiest to test and is the best predictor of academic success. Individual and group intelligence tests attempt to compare persons of like age on problems to which they have had equal exposure.

Intelligence, like all human characteristics, is normally distributed in the population, and individual behavior varies at the different levels. Individual ability is the product of the interaction of inheritance, physical and cultural environment, and bodily functioning.

From infancy onward the ability level becomes gradually more stable, but some persons experience considerable variability in intelligence through time.

Suggested Collateral Readings

Bloom, B. A., *Stability and change in human characteristics*. New York: John Wiley & Sons, Inc., 1964. Chapter 3.

Dinkmeyer, D. C., *Child development: The emerging self*. Englewood Cliffs, N.J.: Prentice-Hall, Inc., 1965. Chapter 8.

Goodenough, Florence L., and Leona E. Tyler, *Developmental psychology*, 3d ed. New York: Appleton-Century-Crofts, 1959. Chapter 15.

Hilgard, E. R., and R. C. Atkinson, *Introduction to psychology*, 4th ed. New York: Harcourt, Brace & World, Inc., 1967. Chapter 16.

Munn, N. L., *The evolution and growth of human behavior*. Boston: Houghton Mifflin Company, 1965. Chapter 13.

References

1. Asher, E. U., 1935, The inadequacy of current intelligence tests for testing Kentucky Mountain children. *J. genet. Psychol.*, **46:** 480–486.
2. Baller, W. R., D. C. Charles, and E. L. Miller, 1967, Mid-life attainment of the mentally retarded: A longitudinal study. *Genet. Psychol. Monogr.*, **75:** (2) 235–329.
3. Bayley, Nancy, 1949, Consistency and variability in the growth of intelligence from birth to eighteen years. *J. genet. Psychol.*, **75:** 165–196.
4. ———, 1955, On the growth of intelligence. *American Psychologist*, **10:** 806.
5. ———, 814–815.
6. ———, 1954, Some increasing parent-child similarities during the growth of children. *J. educ. Psychol.*, **45:** 1–21.
7. Berenert, Eleanor H., 1958, *America's Children*. New York: John Wiley & Sons, Inc. Page 57.

8. Bloom, B. A., 1964, *Stability and change in human characteristics.* New York: John Wiley & Sons, Inc. Page 68.
9. Bradway, Katherine, and Nancy Robinson, 1961, Significant I. Q. changes in twenty-five years. *J. educ. Psychol.,* **52**: 74–79.
10. Burt, C., 1958, The inheritance of mental ability. *The American Psychologist,* **13**: 5.
11. ———, 6.
12. ———, 9.
13. Campbell, D. P., personal communication.
14. Campbell, D. P., 1965, A cross-sectional and longitudinal study of scholastic abilities over twenty-five years. *J. counsel. Psychol.,* **12**: 55–61.
15. Charles, D. C., 1953, Ability and accomplishment of persons earlier judged mentally deficient. *Genet. Psychol. Monogr.,* **47**: 67.
16. ———, and Suzanne James, 1964, Stability of average intelligence. *J. genet. Psychol.,* **105**: 105–111.
17. Deutsch, M., and B. Brown, 1964, Social influences in Negro-white intelligence differences. *J. soc. Issues,* **20**: 24–35.
18. Edwards, A. J., and Elsie M. Kirby, 1964, Predictive efficiency of intelligence test scores: Intelligence quotients obtained in grade one and achievement test scores obtained in grade three. *Educ. psychol. Meas.,* **24**: 941–946.
19. Eels, K., *et al.* 1959, *Intelligence and cultural differences.* Chicago: University of Chicago Press. Pages 22–28.
20. Gallagher, J. J., 1964, *Teaching the gifted child.* Boston: Allyn & Bacon, Inc.
21. Gordon, E. W., 1964, Characteristics of socially disadvantaged children. *Rev. Educ. Res.,* **30**: 377–388.
22. Gordon, H., 1923, Mental and scholastic tests among retarded children: An inquiry into the effects of schooling on the various tests. *Education Pamphlets,* Board of Education, London.
23. Haan, Norma, 1963, Proposed model of ego functioning: coping and defense mechanisms in relationship to I. Q. change. *Psychol. Monogr.,* **77**: 1–21.
24. Heber, R. F., 1959, A manual on terminology and classification in mental retardation. *American Journal of Mental Deficiency,* **64**: Monogram Supplement (revised 1961).
25. Honzik, Marjorie, 1963, A sex difference in the age of onset of the parent-child resemblance in intelligence. *J. educ. Psychol.,* **54**: 231–237.
26. ———, Jean W. Macfarlane, and L. Allen, 1948, The stability of mental test performance between two and eighteen years. *J. exper. Educ.,* **17**: 309–324.
27. Hughson, A., 1964, The case for intelligence testing; Yourman, J., The case against group I. Q. testing. *Phi Delta Kappan,* **67**: 106–108; 108–110.
28. Kagan, J., and Marion Freeman, 1963, Relation of childhood intelligence, maternal behaviors and social class to behavior during adolescence. *Child Develpm.,* **34**: 899–911.
29. ———, and H. A. Moss, *Birth to maturity: A study in psychological development.* New York: John Wiley & Sons, Inc. Pages 129–136.

30. Kirk, S., 1962, *Educating exceptional children*. Boston: Houghton Mifflin Company. Chapters 3, 4, 5.
31. MacRae, J. M., 1955, Retests of children given mental tests as infants. *J. genet. Psychol.,* **87:** 1955.
32. Owens, W. A., 1953, Age and mental abilities. *Genet. Psychol. Monogr.,* **48.**
33. ———, 1966, Age and mental abilities: a second adult follow-up, *J. educ. psychol.,* **57:** 311–325.
34. Pinneau, S., 1961, *Changes in intelligence quotient infancy to maturity.* Boston: Houghton Mifflin Company. Page 113.
35. Reymert, M. L., and R. T. Hinton, 1940, The effect of change to a relatively superior environment upon the IQ's of one hundred children. *39th Yearbook, National Society for the Study of Education,* Part II.
36. Robinson, H. B., and Nancy M. Robinson, 1965, *The mentally retarded child.* New York: McGraw-Hill, Inc.
37. Skeels, H. M., 1966, Adult status of children with contrasting early life styles. *Monogr. Soc. Res. Child Develpm.* Chicago: The University of Chicago Press, Society for Research in Child Development.
38. Skodak, Marie, and H. M. Skeels, 1949, A final follow-up study of one hundred adopted children. *J. genet. Psychol.,* **75:** 85–125.
39. Sontag, L. W., C. T. Baker, and Virginia L. Nelson, 1958, Mental growth and personality development: A longitudinal study. *Monogr. Soc. Res. Child Develpm.,* **23:** No. 2.
40. Terman, L. M., *Genetic Studies of Genius,* Volume I (1925), Volume II (1926), Volume III (1930), Volume IV (1947), with Melita Oden, Volume V (1959) with Melita Oden. Stanford: Stanford University Press.
41. Terman, L. M., and Maud A. Merrill, 1937, *Measuring intelligence.* Boston: Houghton Mifflin Company.
42. Terman, L. M. 1960, *The Stanford-Binet intelligence scale.* Boston: Houghton Mifflin Company.
43. Wechsler, D., 1958, *Measurement and appraisal of adult intelligence,* 4th ed. Baltimore: The Williams & Wilkins Company.
44. Wechsler, D., 1955, *Wais manual.* New York: Psychological Corporation.
45. Wiener, G., R. Rider, and W. Oppel, 1963, Some correlates of I. Q. change in children. *Child Develpm.,* **34:** 61–67.

CHAPTER 11

Development of Thinking

A sizeable part of an individual's experience consists of dealing with objects and relationships that are not at the moment physically present. This involves a process of representation which we commonly refer to as thinking. The purpose of this chapter is to inquire into the nature of thinking and its development.

MEDIA OF THINKING

Thinking was just referred to as process of representation. As such it can be understood in either of two ways: in terms of the *medium* employed or in terms of *objectives* (Bruner, 1966) [9]. After specifying what the media are, perhaps the distinction between medium and objective can be clarified by an illustration, which will also serve to show how closely interrelated media and objectives are. The media of thinking are 1) images; 2) doing, that is, an involvement of muscle activity; 3) language; and 4) concepts.

Illustration of Medium and Objective

When one person asks another for directions to help him find an address in a city, it is likely that the latter person will respond by giving a "word map" for the purpose. The person who gives the directions is not, at the moment, actually looking at the various "landmarks" (traffic signals, street signs, service stations, and so on) which in step-by-step fashion he mentions. He is employing the media of imagery (his own and that of the listener) plus words. He employs these media to serve the objective of guiding an action without being physically engaged in it. To guide action in this way—that is, by representation—is economical of time and energy. An alternative would be for the helping person to get into his own car and lead the way to the address. In commenting on *objective* of representation, Bruner suggests that there is the question of what things "are represented *for*" (1966, page 7) [9]. He then states in the same context, "an utterance can be, in effect, a recipe or prescription or a step-by-step account to guide some action."

With this much of introduction to ideas relating to the process of thinking, we may proceed to examine more closely what we have called media or what are some times termed the "tools" of thinking.

Imagery

A definition of images is that they are mental representations of things and happenings which at the moment are not physically activating any sensations. A dictionary definition of the term image is, "A mental copy of something not present to the senses" (English and English, 1958) [14]. As was indicated in the illustration about how one person may direct another to a particular street address, "seeing" something which is not physically present serves important functions in practical situations. Imagery also serves to enchance many experiences that are at the moment quite removed from present reality. The reader may, by looking away from this page, *imagine* the sights and sounds and other sensations of a picnic in the park, a fishing trip, or a stroll along Fashion Avenue. A person's imagery may lead considerably beyond sheer "daydreaming"; he may proceed to reconstruct (reinterpret) reality by allowing his images to guide him in the painting of a picture, the writing of a sonnet, the designing of a "new creation" in evening gowns or in some other image-inspired departure from the world of objects as they are.

It is relevant to the discussion of imagery to note the closeness to imagery of the means of representation which was referred to as "muscle activity." For example, a person is likely to involve, at least incipiently, some of his muscles when he imagines himself catching a fish, or driving a car down a winding road.

Muscle Activity

A considerable part of the reality with which a person deals is represented in the form of implicit muscle movements. We manage, with appropriate adjustments, to make our way around in our home, in a college library, or in other surroundings of physical things with minimal explicit attention to the sensory contacts we have with them. We can reach and find a doorknob in the dark. We develop a set of implicit muscle representations for the "movements-within-movements" that constitute the skills of driving a car, of swinging a golf club, of using table utensils, and so forth. Stored as implicit muscle "impressions" are cue-producing signals that can set off a chain of conscious events in the thinking process. If the reader will for a moment consider the operation of tying a shoelace he will appreciate a statement Bruner makes about the act.

There is a fair amount of sensorimotor feedback involved in carrying out the act in question, yet what is crucial is that such a representation is executed in the medium of action. (1966, page 6) [9]

Language

Language is a medium of thinking. Clearly it serves us much of the time in the absence of the things being represented by it. Without engaging at length in a discussion of language (it is the subject of the next chapter), let us simply note that if the individual did not possess the capability of *symbolizing* his encounters with objects and relationships, he would indeed be bogged down in a stimulus-response predicament. He would be reacting only (and incessantly!) to the immediately sensory bombardments of the objects and events in his surroundings. Fortunately, as we shall see from later discussion in this chapter, the individual develops the capabilities of coding the objects and relationships of his experience; that is, he learns from others, or devises for himself, some representations of things. Coding is part of the individual's repertoire of ways of *managing* (taking in, classifying, storing, and reactivating) the "pieces and aspects" of experience.

Perhaps it is evident to the student from so little explanation as has now been given that *thinking* and *language* are closely interrelated. Indeed the closeness of their interrelationship has induced many writers to discuss them in an undivided context (for example: Piaget, J., 1955, *Language and thought of the child* [42]).

Concepts

Especially important to the process of thinking is the individual's ability to conceptualize (meaning to abstract and generalize) his perceptual encounters with the objects and happenings of his experience. The acquisition of the ability to generalize from particulars of experience enables the individual to cope with increasingly wider ranges of the data of experience—the bits and pieces of information, so to speak. In the domains of the physical sciences for example, such concepts as "mass," "energy," "velocity," and "molecular attraction" are essential to understanding and the communication of understanding. In psychology we employ such concepts as "motives," "feelings" and "intelligence"—to name only a few.

A somewhat inelegant but nevertheless fairly accurate statement of the functioning of concepts was supplied by an imaginative student who was a lover of dogs. His statement was, "It is the *doggishness* of dogs that helps me know more than just *a* dog, and *a* dog, and *a* dog." *Doggishness* is a concept—an abstraction of something dogs have in common; something effectively classificatory of dogs in general.

KINDS OF THINKING

In order better to understand the discussion in the sections that follow in this chapter, let us consider briefly what may be called varieties, or kinds, of thinking. Is a person *thinking* when he is "simply meditating," as he may call it, "about the pleasures of life"? Is a person thinking when his train of ideas carries him beyond the boundaries of reality to explore a make believe world of fantasy? What about reasoning and problem solving? Are all of these ways of behaving properly known as thinking? The answer in each instance is an affirmative one. All of these ways of behaving comprise an area of highly important psychological study—an area that quite recently has received markedly increased attention. The increased attention has been spurred by a growing awareness among psychologists of the need for better knowledge of the *development of thinking.* With this much of introduction to the phenomenon of thinking, we shall now proceed to the important questions of how thinking develops, and especially how *productive thinking* develops. We shall also examine some implications that the study of thinking has for the teacher-learner relationship.

DIFFERENCES BETWEEN PRODUCT AND PROCESS OF THINKING

As we have commented earlier, the traditional view of intelligence has been useful in psychological and educational work. It has, however, failed in recent years to add much to our understanding of what goes on in the individual child in thinking and problem solving. The mental test, in the words of Russell, "is concerned primarily with the result or product of thinking rather than the process itself" (Russell, 1956a) [45].

Concern with the "process itself" is not altogether new. Every observant parent and teacher will have been impressed by the complex and varied ways in which children come to both accurate and inaccurate solutions to problems and to explanations of phenomena observed. The change in thought processes from one state to another in early life is impressive, as is the difference between two children of similar age and IQ. Until the late nineteenth century, studies of thought processes, or "cognition" as the process is usually called today, were primarily the province of philosophy. The new science of psychology entered the field at that time with both speculative and empirical approaches, especially in relation to learning in school and laboratory.

The rapid development of intelligence testing in this country around World War I tended to divert psychologists from their early concern with process rather than product. Not all research work ceased, of course. Studies were made of thinking as a product of association, thinking in relation to perception, inductive-deductive thinking, problem-solving, critical thinking, and creative thinking. But the efforts were scattered, individual and to a large extent, unrelated.

During this period, a man outside the American empirical tradition was occupying himself with exactly that approach which was neglected in the United States—the systematic study of how children's thinking develops. The man was Jean Piaget. Because he has had so much influence on contemporary developmental psychology, a statement about him and his methods of study is in order. Men—and their ideas—are best understood if one has some knowledge of the circumstances which produced them.

Jean Piaget

Piaget was born in 1896, and at this writing, is still working actively in his native Switzerland. He was educated as a zoologist, published his first paper at ten years of age, and had twenty publications in print by age twenty-one. Although mollusks were his main objects of study, he read extensively in philosophy, religion, biology, sociology, and psychology. After gaining his doctorate in 1918, his interests shifted from zoology to psychology, and he improved his acquaintance with the major researchers in Europe. For his future work, the most significant of these experiences took place in the laboratory of Simon, Binet's colleague in intelligence test development, at the Sorbonne in Paris. There he undertook the standardization of the American Burt's reasoning tests on Parisian child subjects. He was fascinated, not so much with the psychometric and normative aspects of the tests, but with the *processes* by which the child achieves his answers—especially the erroneous ones. By adapting the clinical, psychiatric technique he had learned working in a Parisian clinic, he studied the children's thought processes through searching questions, following the child's ideas wherever they led and probing in depth for understanding of what was going on (Flavel, 1962) [15].

Back in Switzerland during the period 1921 to 1925, Piaget wrote five books which expressed his ideas on the development of language, judgment and reasoning, moral judgment, and the like. These were really first drafts to be followed by years of more intensive study of a psychological, philosophical nature.

The early works were translated and were read with some interest by American psychologists but were soon neglected and forgotten by most psychologists in this country. American psychology was trying to establish itself as a science and was emphasizing objectivity, measurement and control; Piaget's descriptive, philosophical and speculative consideration of the thought processes of a handful of children (including his own offspring) were simply not regarded as relevant to "modern" psychology. Furthermore, little more of his work was translated.

Because of the before-mentioned dissatisfaction with current methods of study, and through the advocacy of a few prominent American psychologists, there has been since the late 1950s something of a Piaget "revival," and a growing international interest in cognition, concept formation, and the like. Piaget's original ideas have been modified and expanded, his theories and hypotheses have been and are being subjected to controlled study in the American fashion, and many theorists are using his insights as the bases for further hypothesizing and research.

Let us examine now the principal developmental formulations of Piaget and the "Geneva School," as he and his co-workers are sometimes labeled. Later, some of the current research stimulated by this group can be considered.

PIAGET'S VIEW OF INTELLECTUAL DEVELOPMENT

Attempting to summarize this work is difficult and hazardous: by 1962, Piaget personally had published 25 books and over 160 articles, some nearly of book size. Much of the work is not yet translated and Piaget, to an important degree, has modified various of his views over the years. Thus an early, translated article may not reflect the view of a current but unavailable publication. Furthermore, his approach to psychological work is unorthodox by American standards, and his writing is difficult and obscure (Flavell, 1962) [16]; but a basic and useful outline seems possible at this point. Perhaps the best summary has been made by one of his principal co-workers, Bärbel Inhelder (1962) [26].

Piaget sees the development of understanding or knowledge in the infant as the result of a process of elaboration based on the child's own activity. He sees two types of activity in the early months of life: in one type objects are only a support—ordering, counting, bringing together, disassociating; in the other type, physical exploration of objects yields knowledge of their colors, form, weight, and so on.

Animism

Before proceeding to the main body of Piaget's work, we should consider *animism,* because the idea is central to Piaget's view of developing intellectual capabilities. Animism is the attribution of life, or even of human characteristics, to nonhuman objects. In Western culture, animism pervades fairy tales and children's stories—"The Gingerbread Man," for example. In primitive cultures, animism abounds; the willful malevolence seen in storms, in thunder and lightning, might be cited. And what automobile driver has not been half-convinced that the refusal of his car to start when he is in a hurry some cold morning is conscious, willful, and malevolent?

The child is seen as successively attributing life to activity in general, to movements, to spontaneous movement, and finally to plants and animals only. He assumes that life exists in objects as he attributes consciousness to them. The end result, especially in early life, is a kind of magical explanation of cause.

There are three phases in the progression from magical causation to objectivism. First is in dissociation: confusing the real and subjective, the external and internal. Second is introjection: projecting his own feelings onto the object in question (for example, the thunder roars because it is angry). Third is interpretation: the child makes a social interpretation of events; objectivity replaces his earlier egocentrism (Russell, 1956b) [46].

It might be noted that there is a great range in the degree to which even adults escape magic, animism, and egocentricity in their reactions to experience.

Criteria for Stages

Piaget, like many who study or work with children and adolescents, describes development in terms of quite definite stages. His criteria for stages:

1. In each stage there is a period of genesis or formation, and a period of attainment.
2. While one structure is reaching a level of attainment, another is in its beginning or genesis.
3. The order of states is constant: one inevitably follows another.
4. Each structure as it develops becomes an inherent part of succeeding structures.

In the discussion of stages following, the three stages will first be named and described briefly as they are seen by the Geneva School. Then each stage will be illustrated, and relevant research and critical discussion will be introduced.

The Stages of Cognitive Development

Stage I: Sensory-motor. This stage occupies approximately the first year and a half of life, from birth until the time language is appearing.

During this time the child is "exploring" his immediate spatial surroundings visually, aurally, and tactually. He begins with reflexive mechanisms and proceeds to a system of movements and displacements. During this period the child establishes relations between objects and his own body, and comes to recognize the permanence of objects. Six substages make up this major stage.

Stage II: Concrete Thinking Operations. During the early part of this period, the child's activity consists primarily of symbolic play: imitating and representing what others do. Of course, much of his energy goes into language development. The second stage lasts until the eleventh or twelfth year. An "operation" is defined here as an action which can be internalized and which is reversible. From five to seven, there is a preoperational substage during which there is much elaboration of mental operations, made possible by the development of language and symbolic processes. The child must reconstruct at a level of representational thought all that was developed on a sensory-motor level earlier. Around age seven a "thought structure" is formed; it must operate on objects, not on verbally expressed hypotheses, but operations of classification, ordering, construction of the idea of number, spatial and temporal operations, and all the fundamental operations of elementary logic of classes and relations, of elementary mathematics, of elementary geometry and even of elementary physics may be realized.

By age eleven or twelve the system of concrete operations has reached equilibration, and the basis for formal thinking operations has been established.

Stage III: Formal Thinking Operations. Beginning about eleven or twelve, formal thinking operations develop, and by fourteen or fifteen years of age, a stable system of thought is formed. The adolescent is capable of forming hypotheses and deducing possible consequences from them. Thought can be expressed in linguistic forms containing propositions and logical constructions. Experiments are carried out in a mature way, and proofs are provided (Inhelder, 1962) [26].

Illustration and Research: Stage I. Early infant behaviors are primarily internally-stimulated, reflex-like activities: sucking, swallowing, crying. The infant quickly learns to modify these, especially in relation to the external objects to which they are related: the neonate will suck anything when hungry but he soon learns to reject fingers and blankets in favor of the nipple; when he is satisfied, the sucking reflex may generalize, however, to all sorts of objects. Similar discrimination and generalization occurs with his other responses. By eight to ten months, an unfamiliar object given to the infant may be thrown down, picked up, squeezed, scratched, patted, swung about; in short, his entire repertoire of movements will be exercised on the object. From these trials comes knowledge and understanding of the world of things. Piaget describes a habit of his own infants in making standardized responses to specific objects. For example, a toy above the crib was habitually batted with the hand, producing a swinging motion in the suspended toy. Later, a glimpse of the same toy would elicit a brief handwave, still later, an even briefer opening and closing of the hand. It is Piaget's contention that such responses are part of the object's "meaning" to the child (Wallach, 1963a) [57].

It is an easy step from this view to the development of hypotheses about the importance of very early experience:

> . . . the more new things an infant has seen and the more new things he has heard, the more new things he is interested in seeing and hearing; and the more variation in reality he has coped with, the greater is his capacity for coping. . . . This hypothesis provides a pretty explanation for the effects of early experience on later capacity. (Hunt, 1961) [25]

By the eighth or ninth month, the child has advanced considerably in his intellectual capacity. By this time he begins to develop means-end behaviors. For example, he learns to use a stick or rattle as a tool, as an extension of his hand, to touch or secure something otherwise out of reach. Another example of his improved conceptualization of objects is his ability to remember an object: until this age, an object like a rattle presented to his vision but suddenly snatched from sight will be promptly forgotten. Between the third quarter of the first and the middle of the second year, he will be able to remember and search for objects, even in somewhat complicated games (Piaget, 1952 [38], 1953 [40].

For Stage I and the early years of Stage II (about three or four), there is little formal research to report; reliance must be placed on the observations and speculations of Piaget and his Geneva collaborators. Obviously, there is a need for supporting studies.

Illustration and Research: Stage II. While many of Piaget's notions (like Freud's) have not lent themselves well to controlled research, his speculations about the development of "conservation" in Stage II have provided a rich source of testable hypotheses. "Conservation" may be defined as ". . . the understanding that no change has occurred regarding one or more aspects of an object or a relationship, despite change in other perceivable features" (Wallach, 1963b) [58]. These studies reveal how different the world of the child is from that of the adult—how dependent he is on momentary changes in perceptual impressions.

Conservation of quantity or amount. The basic approach to studying this concept is to show the child two identical balls of clay. Then one of the balls is rolled into a sausage shape, is patted flat, cut into pieces or otherwise distorted. With each distortion, the child is asked if the two balls are still the same. A variation on this approach is to use a glass container of colored liquid, which is then transferred (in the presence of the child) to a tall thin glass, a low flat pan, two small glasses and so on. Discontinuous stimuli like beads and marbles have also been used.

The child progresses from an intuitive stage (the studies usually begin about age five), where he seldom grasps the abstractions necessary to understand conservation of substance, to a transitional stage (about age seven to eight), where he vacillates between an answer which indicates conservation and one which does not, to a final phase around age ten to eleven, where he masters the concept and is even able logically to reverse the process (Piaget and Inhelder, 1941) [37]. These observations have been subjected to several systematic replications. Carpenter (1955) [10], Elkind (1961) [13], and Lovell and Ogilvie (1960) [29] have all confirmed the succession of stages reported by Piaget. However, the ages at which specific stages are reached and the stability of conservation at different ages have not been agreed upon.

Conservation of weight. This is more difficult for the child to master than the concept of volume, and thus Piaget identifies its appearance a couple of years later than that of volume. For the study of this concept, children were again shown identical balls of clay. One ball was cut up or deformed and the children were asked if the pieces totaled the same weight as the original. From this and similar approaches, Piaget concluded that there were three stages in the development of the concept: first, denial of the conservation of weight; second, admission of it sometimes during a transition stage; and finally, agreement to it with firm conviction. Conservation of weight is attained when the child is about nine to ten years old.

Lovell and Ogilvie (1961a) [30] in their studies of the developing concept of conservation of weight confirmed, in general, the findings of Piaget and Inhelder both with regard to the stages and the later age of attainment. They used clay balls of different size, with the smaller weighted with lead; the children were queried about the weight of the larger when it was deformed.

Conservation of area. Piaget, Inhelder and Szeminska (1960) [41] studied the child's concept of area by providing two identical green cardboard squares as "fields" for the children to observe. First two model cows—one to each field—and then increasing numbers of model houses were placed on the fields. On one field the objects were close together and on the other widely spread. The subjects were asked as more objects were added, "Do both cows now have the same amount of grass to eat?" The children saw the areas as equal when there were no objects, and unequal when one had a house and the other none. At age five to six, they denied equality after the first pair of houses had been put in. Between six and seven they agreed when up to twelve pairs were used, but disagreed when more were added, with a greater cluttering of the visual field. Past seven they generally regarded both as equal when as many as fifteen or twenty houses were added; their attainment of reversibility made it possible for them to carry out in their minds steps necessary to solve the problem.

Lovell, Healey, and Rowland (1962) [32] replicated the study and found a developmental sequence somewhat similar to that found by Piaget, but most children either denied conservation of area as soon as two houses were placed in each field, or grasped the concept immediately. Age was not a good indicator of performance: some five- to six-year-olds grasped the idea at once, while some older children did not. Other studies have also yielded results that conflict with Piaget (Wallace, 1965a) [56]. The topic requires more study.

Conservation of volume. From the same Piaget, Inhelder, and Szeminska (1960) [41] book referred to above, some generalizations about volume comprehension may be made.

1. Below age six to six and a half there is no understanding of the concept.
2. Between seven and eight or nine, there is increasing understanding that shape of an object may be altered without changing its volume.
3. By about eleven or twelve years children attain understanding of volume as the function of length, breadth, and height.

In general, followup research studies have confirmed this basic sequence (Lunzer, 1960 [33]; Lovell and Ogilvie, 1961a [31]). Many studies have delved into more subtle aspects of the concept, and it is proving a fertile area for research.

Concept of length. Piaget, Inhelder, and Szeminska (1960) [41] experimented with five-millimeter straight sticks, laid on a table parallel to each other and with ends aligned. The sticks were judged equal by the children who were subjects of the study. One stick was moved forward a centimeter or two. Children aged four or five said the forward stick was longer. Apparently at this age, children cannot consider both front and back edges at the same time. When the sticks were realigned, they again appeared equal to the children. By age six to seven years of age, both ends of the stick can be considered at once and there is no problem in handling the concept. Lovell, Healey, and Rowland (1962) [32] have replicated the study with similar results.

Other concepts. The concepts mentioned briefly above are only a few which have been studied. The Geneva group has investigated space, time, velocity, horizontality, classification, and seriation, as well as causality and logical thinking.

As has been true of the topics discussed in this chapter, each concept considered by Piaget and his followers has been further investigated by other researchers. A vast literature is accumulating which we cannot begin to review here. But before proceeding to the description of concepts in the upper years of childhood, the concept of number should be discussed, because of its importance in our culture.

Concept of number. As is true with other concepts, Piaget finds a number of stages in the development of number concept. There are three major ones. First, by about age six, when most children have an interest in numbers and have learned to count, Piaget feels they have only a vague, perceptually determined notion of what numbers are really about. He calls this the stage of "global comparison." It is followed by an "intuitive" stage during which the child begins to realize that numbers are really attributes of objects or sets of objects and are invariant even though the perceptual field is transformed. The third period is independent of perceptual transformation and is the "concrete operations" stage (Piaget, 1952) [39]. Several research studies have followed Piaget's reports, some confirming and some conflicting with the Geneva view. The most painstaking work has been that of Hood (1952) [24]. Using Piagetian experiments, he studied a large number of children, who were also given intelligence tests.

Hood found that prenumber concepts advanced with age to about seven, under-fives having little appreciation and sevens generally having full understanding. During the period from five to seven no assumptions about an individual child should be made. It was during mental age six to eight that most of the change took place.

Illustration and Research: Stage III. Much of the research illustrating development during the third period stems from problem-solving studies carried out by the Geneva group on children aged seven, to those in mid-adolescence.

A typical problem, described by Wallach (1963c) [59], is one in which the subject is presented with four numbered bottles and a smaller fifth one with a dropper; the latter is labeled *g*. Two other glasses, appearing the same but containing different combinations of the chemicals 1 through 4, are shown the child. The experimenter puts a few drops of *g* in each of the latter two glasses; the contents of one turn yellow, the other does not. The child is asked to reproduce the yellow color. The child is observed, and sometimes queried, during his attempts to solve the problem.

From ages seven to eleven, children combine *g* with the contents of flasks 1 to 4, one at a time, but not until the upper range of the age group are they likely to combine contents of two of the flasks at a time. From twelve on, children tend to work systematically trying each of the flasks singly, and then trying each possible combination. Older children thus appear to be more oriented toward structuring hypotheses, and then testing them systematically (Inhelder and Piaget, 1958) [27].

THE PLACE OF "STAGES" IN DEVELOPMENT

Many questions come to mind in studying Piaget's descriptions of stages of development. Has the existence of definite stages been documented by other researchers? This question has been partially answered in the research material discussed above: in general, stages similar to Piaget's have been found, but not with complete consistency of course.

The stages *do* seem to exist, but what is their source: are they the product of maturation alone, learning alone, or some combination of the two? How reliable are the chronological ages at which the various stages reportedly appear? Evidence bearing on these questions will be discussed below.

Sources and Stability of Stages

One explanation for consistency of intellectual development by stages would be the existence of some maturing physiological structure underlying the thought processes. The brain and central nervous system is just such a structure of course. The physiologist Tanner offers this explanation:

> In short, there is plenty of evidence that in the brain functions appear when structures mature, and not before. There is no reason to suppose that the truth of this generalization suddenly ceases at age 2, or 3, or 13. On the contrary there seems every reason to suppose that the higher intellectual abilities of the brain also appear only when maturation of certain structures is complete. . . .
>
> The stages of mental functioning described by Piaget and Inhelder and the emergence of mental abilities . . . have all the characteristics of developing brain or bodily structures. . . . The stages follow in a sequence which may be advanced or delayed as a whole but not altered, just as in a wrist bone or a cortical primary area. . . . There seems every reason to suppose that Piaget's successive stages depend on progressive maturation or at least organization of the cortex. (Tanner, 1961) [50]

Tanner goes on to comment on the relationship between neural development and experience in the formation of new stages of thought:

Environmental stimulation may or may not be necessary to create the required cell assemblies. For the cognitive stages to emerge brain maturation is probably necessary, but not, of course, sufficient. Without at least some degree of social stimulus the latent abilities may never be exercised. (Tanner, 1961) [50]

Tanner's statement is consistent with what we know about many other aspects of human development. As Tanner comments, it is not clear at this time just what effect, if any, environmental stimulation has on the rate of neural development; in general the latter seems to be primarily a matter of genetic determination. Regardless of this, however, the effect of stimulation on the development of stages is of great interest, both theoretically and practically. Can the appearance of a stage be speeded up by appropriate instruction? Can a given stage be bypassed, or shortened? What effect have different instructional techniques on the development of thinking? Research is under way on all these and other similar questions. No definitive answers are yet available, but the following research suggests some trends.

Several investigators have attempted to accelerate concept formation by giving a child specific experiences in a laboratory situation. Jan Smedslund (1961a) [47] was able to instill the concept of conservation of weight in children who, prior to the experience, were not conservers. However, in a subsequent experiment, Smedslund (1961b) [48] showed that those who had learned the concept "artificially" quickly relinquished it when confronted with evidence at variance with what they had learned. Other children who had acquired the concept "naturally" resisted the experimenter's attempts to extinguish (that is, to eliminate) the conservation response. These findings reinforced Smedslund's position that instructional experience alone will not lead to stable concepts. However, Wholwill in a number of studies (1959 [63], 1960 [64], 1962 [65]) has shown that training can help the child attain conservation of number and weight. Wallace has also presented evidence which suggests that number concepts can be acquired prior to the age levels designated by Piaget (Wallace, 1965b) [56].

Such researches are being studied with great interest by educators. It is to be hoped that, as the data become clearer and more agreement is reached, changes will be made in curricula and teaching methods, in harmony with the new understanding of the child. In the past few years, many curricular innovations have been aimed at the acceleration of learning in school without much regard for the child's cognitive development.[1]

[1] In 1964, conferences were held at Cornell University and at the University of California, Berkeley, to consider curriculum and cognitive development. For a discussion of problems and approaches, see Ripple, R. E., and V. Rockcastle, eds., *Piaget rediscovered, A report of the conference on cognitive studies and curriculum development,* March 1964, Ithaca, N.Y.: Cornell University, School of Education.

Age Relation to Stage

We have commented elsewhere in this volume that individual differences are so great that chronological age is not a very useful index to any characteristic of the child. Piaget and almost everyone else working in this area specify chronological age levels for the various stages. Is cognitive development an exception to our generalization about the lack of usefulness of chronological age?

The question has had little research attention. In a British study of development of number concept, Hood (1962) [24], mentioned earlier, gave each of his 125 subjects an individual intelligence test. He found that "mental stature," as he termed it, seemed to be of prime importance, rather than chronological age. He suggested that chronological age grouping conceals the same diversity in cognitive functions as it does in mental age development.

One approach to this problem of chronological age and stage would be to examine two groups of subjects with the same mental age, but with differing chronological ages, and thus with different amounts of natural experience. Keasey and Charles (1967) [28] studied groups of normal and retarded subjects, matched on mental age but differing by more than eleven years in chronological age. Achievement of the concept of conservation of substance or amount was evaluated. The two groups reached a satisfactory level of understanding at about the same mental age; correlation between mental age and understanding was .70. The additional eleven years of experience of the older, but duller, subjects was of little help in developing the concept of conservation of substance.

Thus it appears that the stages are "natural," that is, tied to neural maturation. What kinds of learning experiences will encourage optimum development, and how and at what time these experiences should be offered remain unclear and a major concern of current and future research.

PRODUCTIVE THINKING

While psychologists and workers from some allied fields have been engaged in the examination and explanation of cognitive development, much of their attention has been devoted to two particularly important operations. These are problem solving and creative thinking. Although we separate them in this chapter for convenience in discussion, they are closely allied and overlapping. Guilford comments that as he considers the two operations at relatively close range, "it is even more clear that [they] are made of the same cloth . . ." (Guilford, 1965) [20].

Problem Solving

How does an individual proceed when he confronts a circumstance whose meaning is not evident, whose explanation defies his initial efforts at apprehension? What ensues when the individual becomes aware that one event does not relate to another event in the way he first assumed to be true?

Different writers have given answers to the question just stated. Some have answered by listing *stages* through which the individual proceeds as he thinks his way through a problem. Rossman (1931) [44] who studied more than 700 productive inventors arrived at a listing of seven stages:

1. Observation of a need or difficulty
2. Analysis of the need
3. Survey of all available information
4. Formulation of objective solutions
5. Critical analysis of the solutions
6. The birth of a new invention—the idea proper
7. Experimentation to test out the idea

There are other lists, such as John Dewey's familiar five steps: 1) recognition of the problem, 2) analysis of the problem, 3) suggestions of possible solutions, 4) testing of consequences, and 5) judgment of the selected solution (Dewey, 1933) [11]. All the lists include approximately the same basic operations. Perhaps the most crucial is the first item: the awareness that there is indeed a problem, a need, or a difficulty to be resolved. Once the individual is clearly aware that he confronts a problem, he may take the other steps as listed.

Although the various descriptive lists are helpful in considering problem solving, we need more searching and analytical evaluations of the process. One recent attempt at such an analysis has been made by J. P. Guilford. Because his attempt to illuminate the problem-solving operation is based on his own structure-of-intellect model, it is necessary to describe this model before proceeding.

Guilford's Model

Guilford has proposed a theoretical model of the "structure of intellect," based on his research in the nature of primary mental abilities. Through factor analysis of large numbers of intelligence test items, he has identified (out of a possible 120) approximately 50 different primary mental abilities. He classifies these primary mental abilities according to a) the *contents* or type of information dealt with, b) the *operations* performed on the information, and c) the *products* resulting from the processing of the information (Guilford, 1959) [23]. Because the entire model is difficult to describe or discuss briefly, we will consider only the operations aspect here.

Guildford categorizes mental operations as cognition, memory, divergent production, convergent production, and evaluation. Let us examine each of these briefly:

A. *Cognitive factors.* These abilities have to do with the discovery, recognition, or comprehension of information. Six main types of products are distinguished in terms of the kind of thing known: units (single items of "think" character), classes, relations (connections between units), organized systems, transformations (changes or redefinitions), and implications.

B. *Memory factors.* Rather than being a unitary ability, as might be inferred from traditional IQ tests, memory exists in at least eight separate factors, according to Guilford. These eight abilities include visual and auditory memory, memory span and memory for ideas (these four referring to substance or content), rote and meaningful memory (association), memory for spatial order and for temporal order (systems).

C. *Divergent-production factors.* This has to do with production of a diversity of answers in situations where more than one answer may be acceptable. Information is a kind of "springboard" to many possible responses. It may be subdivided into units, classes, relations, systems, transformations, and implications, like *A* above.

D. *Convergent-thinking factors.* This has to do with the production of "right" answers, determined by the information given. It is common in the classroom, where the teacher wants a specific correct answer. It may be subdivided like the abilities above.

E. *Evaluation.* Evaluation has to do with determining whether information or conclusions are correct, suitable, acceptable, or good. It has not been well explored as yet (Wilson, 1965) [62].

Guilford's Transfer Theory of Productive Thinking

Guilford feels that productive thinking is well defined in terms of factors in the areas of divergent production and convergent production (Guilford, 1965) [21]. Let us examine briefly some aspects of his theory:

A. *Role of information.* Once a problem has been sensed, and action——that is, solution-seeking—decided upon, Guilford feels that information becomes of primary importance. Information may be offered by the immediate environment or recalled or retrieved from memory storage. The retrieved information is likely not to be in exactly the same form or is not recalled in the same context in which it was learned or committed to storage. The generation of ideas by recall from storage is likely to be by way of transfer, because information is retrieved by a new cue in connection with which it had not been learned. The theory of productive thinking proposed is therefore given the label "transfer theory."

B. *Idea-generating phase.* Guilford concerns himself with four characteristics of thought in this phase: fluency, flexibility, insight, and evaluation.

1. *Fluency.* Factor analysis reveals three kinds of fluency: ideational, associational and expressional. These fluencies represent efficiency in calling out of memory stored items of information to fulfill certain specifications. A fluent thinker can run through logical possibilities or alternatives quickly. Guilford notes that although persons with good memories are often disparaged today, there is considerable importance in having good retention as well as retrieval abilities.

2. *Flexibility.* Flexibility is the opposite of rigidity in thinking. One type of flexibility is in production of classes and the other in production of transformations. In seeking items from storage one examinee will roam about from one subclass to another, while another person will try to exhaust each class before shifting to a new one. A thinker who roams widely, when the information called for may be in a number of classes, has a greater probability of coming up with the needed idea. Abilities in the category of divergent production have been called "adaptive flexibility"; those in the category of convergent production have been called "redefinition abilities."

3. *Insight.* Sudden transformations observed in solving problems are sometimes described as "insights." Guilford disagrees with the psychologists who downgrade insight by describing it as simply a matter of past experience. He points out that although past experience helps, there is always something new, something added in insight.

The significant step in creating is often in the form of a system of some kind. A few experiments have been done in the study of the production of systems, but not much is really known about what happens.

4. *Evaluation.* Two important concepts from the structure-of-intellect model enter into verification of a possible solution to a problem. One is the elaborative abilities of the divergent-production category. The thinker, having adopted his general scheme, proceeds to give flesh and skin to the skeleton by adding detailed information. The other important aspect is that of evaluation. The structure-of-intellect model provides for a whole set of evaluative abilities, abilities pertaining to sensing what is proper and what is not.

Guilford concludes by pointing out that although productive and creative thinking depends most upon divergent-thinking abilities and abilities to effect transformations of information, with abilities of fluency, flexibility, elaboration, and redefinition playing significant roles, we see that, "any or all kinds of abilities represented in the structure of intellect can play their useful roles, directly or indirectly" (Guilford, 1965) [22].

Bruner's Work in Cognitive Growth and Learning

Jerome Bruner's theories of cognitive functioning and development have been highly stimulating—stimulating in the sense of producing testable hypotheses which have resulted in rewarding research and in giving promise of application in education and child rearing. Much of Bruner's work has to do with the nature of learning and the structuring of efficient learning experiences. Because a consideration of learning and instruction *per se* is beyond the scope of this book, we will consider primarily his cognitive theories and research.

Cognitive development. Bruner's principal concern in intellectual development is with what he calls "techniques": "We move, perceive, and think in a fashion that depends on techniques rather than upon wired-in arrangements in our nervous system" (Bruner, 1964) [6]. It follows that development from infancy to the mature level is shaped by technological advances in the use of the mind, and depends on the mastery of techniques, which are transmitted by the culture in which the person is developing.

These techniques used by developing persons in representing the recurrent features of environment—the models of the world—are action, imagery, and language. A second matter of concern is integration: the way in which acts are organized into higher-order ensembles, in which larger and larger units of information are used in solving problems. Let us examine the modes of representation.

Modes of Representation. Representation of the environment is more than "mere memory," according to Bruner. He postulates three modes of representation. The first mode is enactive representation, that is, the representing of past events through suitable motor responses. Experiences like riding a bicycle "get represented" in our muscles. A second mode is iconic representation, the summarizing of events by selective organization of percepts and images, and by the structures of the perceptual field and their transformed images, which stand for events in the way a photograph stands for an object. The third mode, of course, is that of a symbol system—words or numbers.

The child proceeds through these modes of representation in somewhat the same fashion that he proceeds through Piaget's stages. We have discussed the part of muscle activity on meaning earlier in this chapter; it is necessary and important, but limited. Little is known about the growth of iconic representation, or about the circumstances affecting it in early life. Symbolic representation is the most complex and also the subject of much research. Bruner and his associates have carried out a number of studies on the transition from the image to word representation.

From these studies, it is apparent that from ages four to twelve or so, language plays a larger and larger role as an implement of knowing. Translating experiences into words (or other symbols, such as numbers) makes it possible for the child to achieve remote reference, transformation, and combination. These capabilities expand his intellectual performance capacity tremendously.

Integration. Integration of intellectual activity is also accomplished primarily through the medium of language, for language releases the child from immediacy. Productive combinatorial operations in the absence of what is represented become possible (Bruner, 1964) [5].

Improving Thinking. Bruner is not much concerned with capacities or aptitudes. He points out, "What is significant about the growth of mind in the child is to what degree it depends not upon capacity but upon the unlocking of capacity by techniques that come from exposure to the specialized environment of a culture" (Bruner, 1964) [7].

What experiences might encourage development of effective techniques of problem solving and thinking in general? Operations studied by Bruner and his associates may be described under the general headings of *organization* and *manipulation*.

Bruner suggests that if we are to make use of past learning, we must organize it in such a way that it is not bound to the situation in which the learning occurred. Because we can deal with only about seven independent items of information at once, we must get our facts into some kind of coherent order, or they are useless to our thinking and problem solving. Masses of information are unmanageable, and must be condensed and recoded (Bruner, 1959) [2].

This manipulating is done by the person in line with his existing cognitive structure, that is, by extension or combination of previously formed groupings. Thus, presented with an assortment of objects, children will group them according to what they see as common attributes; the grouping scheme or cognitive style will vary from child to child in relation to past experience and personal qualities.

The techniques or strategies are individual and are produced by earlier experience and other uncontrolled factors: Is there any possibility, then, of helping a child develop effective strategies? Bruner's answer to this question is yes, and he suggests that the answer lies in the student's learning experiences: emphasis on *discovery* in learning, as opposed to the acquisition of information, helps the child to "learn the varieties of problem solving, of transferring information for better use, helps him go about the very task of learning." (Bruner, 1962) [3]. His hypothesis has been that the more children practice the "heuristics of discovery," the more likely they will be to generalize what they have into a style of problem solving or inquiry that serves for any task they encounter (Bruner, 1962) [4].

IMPORTANCE OF CLASSIFICATION AND GENERALIZATION

Whatever specific abilities are used in thinking, it is apparent, as we pointed out early in this chapter, that the process of classification is of major importance. It is central to concept formation; it makes generalization possible; it is involved in problem solving and other productive thinking. From the moment that the individual as infant becomes capable of the simplest kinds of differentiation in his encounters with things and happenings, he is embarked upon a lifelong task of arranging and rearranging many of them; of classifying and reclassifying them. His grasp of relationships among things, the relationships among happenings, and the relationships between things and happenings is the *leverage operation* by which he makes sense, and gains understanding, of his world.

An operation whose importance in discussions of thinking cannot be overemphasized is *re*classification. What an individual does in his efforts to code events and organize relationships is facilitated by what other persons do for him. They supply words to help him with his naming of things and events; they acquaint him with many ready-made "guides" to thinking (formula, principles, and so forth) ; they indoctrinate him with ideas and concepts. To repeat, such kinds of assistance considerably expedite his coding and categorizing of experience. There is, however, another side to the matter: Along with the benefits that the learner receives from the formulations that he thus acquires are many habits of thinking that are restrictive to his own efforts at free involvement in problem solving and other kinds of productive thinking.

An emphasis on discovery, as Bruner suggests, and an absence of rigidity in the demands of the classroom should help reduce stereotyped and constricted thinking in problem solving and productive thinking.[2]

[2] The following publications are noteworthy examples of the present lively concern with instruction and curriculum which are in keeping with the newer insights into productive thinking: Ausubel, D. P., 1961, *Learning by discovery: Rationale and mystique* [1], Urbana: Bureau of Educational Research, University of Illinois; Bruner, J. S., 1960, *The process of education* [8], Cambridge: Harvard University Press; Gallagher, J. J., 1964, *Teaching the gifted child* [17], Boston: Allyn and Bacon, Inc.; Goodlad, J. I., 1966, *The changing school curriculum* [19], New York: The Fund for the Advancement of Education; Suchman, J. R., 1961, "Inquiry Training: Building skills for autonomous discovery" [49], *Merrill-Palmer Quarterly,* **7:** 171–180; Taylor, C. W., 1962, "Effects of instructional media on creativity: a look at possible positive and negative effects" [51], *Educational Leadership,* **19:** 453–458.

CREATIVITY

In spite of conditions of life in a crowded, conforming, technologically oriented society (or perhaps because of them), individual creativity has become a matter of great concern in recent years. There is fear that our social and educational system is structured in such a fashion that it will produce a satisfactory supply of competent persons, but will fail to produce the seers, the thinkers, the artists, the inventors that we need to realize our collective ambitions. Then too, there is concern that personal happiness and fulfillment is handicapped by lack of self-realization, spontaneity and originality. The response to these concerns has been a flood of books, conferences, and papers on the topic of creativity. At this point there is much speculation, some evidence, but few conclusions. Let us examine the general nature of the problem and consider some of the speculation and evidence.

The Nature of Creativity

There are about as many definitions of creativity as there are people interested in it. Rather than quoting a number of writers on the subject of creativity, we shall define the concept operationally. Creativity may be defined (in terms preferred by some researchers) as high scoring on tests of original thinking. Or it may be defined as production of work evaluated as creative by competent judges. Let us examine each of these approaches.

Tests of Creativity. A variety of methods has been used to assess creativity in children: drawings, inkblots, paintings, observation of play and working behavior, verbal originality, and the like. Among the more extensive attempts to measure creativity is that of Torrance of the University of Florida. The early efforts of Torrance and his group consisted of adapting some tasks developed by Guilford—unusual uses, impossibilities, consequences, problem situations, improvements, and common problems—to the identification of originality. New tasks, both verbal and non-verbal, have been tried out continuously. To suggest the diversity of tasks, the following examples may be cited: Ask and Guess, "Just Suppose," Incomplete Figures, Picture Construction, and Sounds and Images.

The validation of tests, especially measures of such amorphous concepts as creativity, is always difficult. Torrance has used two principal approaches to validation. First, he has identified high and low groups on his tests, and then determined whether they can be differentiated on other behavior that can be regarded as creative, for example high production of ideas in a small group problem-solving session. Second, he has identified criterion groups on some behavior regarded as creative—being nominated by a teacher as a "high-creative"—and has then tested these children to determine whether they score high on his tests. On the basis of these procedures, he feels that his test batteries are valid, that they are truly identifying children who are creative. Unfortunately, there has not been enough time for longitudinal, predictive studies. If children who earn high scores on the Torrance types of tests do indeed grow up to be producers of original work, educational research and planning can move forward rapidly in the area.

The devices referred to above have been used primarily as research instruments; Torrance has made them available freely to other workers —he reports that at least 400 individuals and agencies have had his permission to work with them (Torrance, 1965) [53]. They are now available in published form.[3]

Original Productivity. Another approach to the study of creative persons is to avoid the problems of test validation by studying people who have already demonstrated by their productive lives that they are creative. Certain individuals readily come to mind—Michaelangelo, Einstein, Mozart; but retrospective research has many inherent defects. Work with contemporary creative persons is more rewarding. D. T. MacKinnon at the Institute of Personality Assessment and Research at the University of California studied forty architects nominated by their peers (other American architects) as highly creative workers. These selected architects were tested and evaluated and then compared to competent, but non-creative, fellow architects. Some results of that study will be discussed shortly (MacKinnon, 1962) [34].

The study of persons who have demonstrated creativity in their lives is usually limited to adults, because children ordinarily lack the technical competence to produce work of recognized quality. In one study, however, art work produced by children aged three to eighteen was judged by artists and art educators, with separate evaluations for competence and for creativity. The judges separated the two concepts with no indication of difficulty and with high agreement. Comparisons of these high-creative and low-creative children will be discussed later (Trowbridge and Charles, 1966) [55].

Creativity and Academic Predictors

Can the same predictors used for academic evaluation be used in predicting creativity; that is, are creative persons simply brighter, more academically apt, than their less creative peers? In general, the evidence

[3] From Personnel Press Inc., 20 Nassau Street, Princeton, N.J.

points to an almost complete lack of relationship between general mental ability and creativity.

School grades have little validity in prediction of creative behavior; the public school demands conformity, not originality. The gifted child is not infrequently in the same situation as a sixteen-year-old boy who apologized to a psychologist (while the latter was working with him) for not becoming a high achiever. "I've read all of Freud and Shakespeare this year," he explained, "and lots besides, and I'm so busy educating myself that I just don't have time to get more than B's in my school work" (Drews, 1963) [12]. Undergraduate college grades have a correlation of almost zero with later research productivity in science. Obviously, to be a creative chemist, one must be bright enough to acquire the basic knowledge and skills of the field, but acquisition of knowledge does not guarantee incubation and insight (Taylor, 1962) [51].

Using a high-level intelligence test, MacKinnon found a correlation of −.08 for architects on the intelligence-creativity variables, and a −.07 for research scientists. The same lack of relationship exists between measured intelligence and on-the-job achievement, especially in science. The further up one goes, the less the validity of the traditional tests. MacKinnon discovered in one of his studies that an inventor with the greatest number of patents in the research group had a score of six on a test on which Air Force captains average 60, architects 113, and research scientists 118. (These are not IQ's!) MacKinnon points out that the inventor was obviously, "not so dumb as his score of six would suggest," but the incident does tell us something of the lack of value of traditional tests for predicting non-academic behavior (MacKinnon, 1965) [36].

A number of investigators of traditional IQ tests and creativity tests reveal rather low correlations between the two types of instruments. These low correlations, however, do not provide any assurance that quite different things are being measured because the devices have different labels. After an extensive review of creativity and intelligence measures, Wallach and Kogan (1965) [61] pointed out that although IQ-Creativity correlations are low, correlations between various creativity instruments are equally low. They concluded from their investigation that these (creativity) instruments measure nothing in common that is distinct from general intelligence.

The authors cited above felt that failure of the tests to measure anything other than a "potpourri of abilities" was due to a lack of understanding of the creative act, which in their view contains two elements: first, the production of association content that is abundant and unique, and second, a playful, permissive attitude toward the task on the part of the associator. Their attempt to evaluate creativity in children is described elsewhere in this chapter.

Personality of Creative Persons

There is a kind of stock comic figure in our society, the "mad genius." Are creative persons really "different" in their personalities, in the way they behave? Research shows that they are indeed different, but not in the sense of abnormality or maladjustment. Let us look at evidence from a variety of studies.

Studies of Creative Adults. Again, MacKinnon's studies of architects provide us with interesting data. From the personality assessment we learn that these creative men first of all valued themselves highly: they saw themselves as inventive, independent, individualistic, and enthusiastic. The less-creative control subjects saw themselves instead as virtuous and of high character. The creative men scored high on femininity in one test. This does not refer to sexuality, but rather to the personality traits of openness to experience, and artistic sensitivity, which are usually seen as more feminine than masculine in our society. They tended to be dominant in human relationships, not sociable (this asocial trait has been found in many studies), sharpwitted, demanding, and self-centered. They were free from inhibitions, not concerned with the impression they made on others, strongly motivated, but not where conforming behavior was expected.

These creative adults reflected on their childhood experiences. They recalled that their parents showed high respect for their children, gave them freedom and expected them to do what was right. They recalled a lack of closeness to parents—not rejection, but an absence of dependence. (This lack of dependence brings to mind the high-achieving, intelligence-improving children described in the immediately preceding chapter.) Their families were different from most, having more interest in culture and artistic values and teaching their children ethics rather than religion (MacKinnon, 1962) [34].

Studies of Creative Children. Test-identified creative children resemble the adults described above in many ways. They are independent and self-absorbed, and so may seem less sociable or friendly than other children. They are often so interested in their own ideas and efforts that they may be indifferent scholars, with little concern for order or studiousness, especially when work of a routine nature is demanded. Because of their own quick mental responses and ofttimes unique humor and playfulness, they may be overcritical of their peers—sometimes of their teachers—which serves further to isolate them.

Torrance speaks of the "psychological estrangement" of creative children. Behaviors like those above lead to severe pressures from peer groups; Torrance states that he has never failed to find evidence of the operation of such pressures in any group he has studied. He reports that in the early grades in the Minnesota studies, such children receive many times the number of nominations that are received by average or highly intelligent but uncreative children for "thinking of the most ideas for being naughty." With this kind of reputation established, both the children and the teacher are likely to see all the ideas of such youngsters as silly or naughty (Torrance, 1965) [53].

Getzels and Jackson (1962) [18] in a widely cited study of adolescents found similar traits in the creative individual: openness and unconventionality.

In a study mentioned earlier, the four most creative and four least creative art students in each of five age groups from three to eighteen were studied individually; parents, classroom teachers, and art teachers of the subjects were interviewed also. The high-creatives, compared to the low-creatives, were found to be:

1. Less conforming in every way. Such behavior sometimes creates classroom problems. For example, a personality description is offered of one ten-year-old boy in the study:

> David liked his own ideas, being very independent in his actions and thoughts, with little concern for what others did or thought. In things he cared about he set very high standards for himself. David seemed to see himself as an individual, was self-confident, liked himself, felt very much someone in particular, and was completely at ease and comfortable, being motivated from within. In school he was constantly looking for a new approach to everything, some different, original way of doing each thing, sometimes to the extent of missing the main point the teacher was making. At home, in school and in art class, David frequently chose to be alone; the teacher even called him "a loner." Whereas his independent actions caused him little trouble at home, relatively little with his peers, and hardly at all at the art school, he frequently met with unpleasantness at school because of insisting on his own approach. Examples given by the teacher which caused David unhappiness of this kind were (1) an insistence on trying out a new kind of alphabet in reading class, trying to write and read with it, and (2) responding to a remark by the teacher that the principal didn't like something he was doing by saying "So what?" David seemed to the interviewer to be a delightfully curious, frank, honest youngster. (Trowbridge, 1964) [54]

2. More generally creative in areas outside art, in their everyday lives.

3. More stable emotionally. This has not been the case in all studies.

4. More self-motivated. They were inclined to set their own stan-

dards, establish independent work habits, and work to please themselves. One little girl expressed her feeling by commenting, "When I have to do things because other people want me to, I just get all scrunched up inside. So I hurry up and get it done, and then when I can go back to doing what I want to do, I feel better all over.'"

5. More solitary. They were likely to spend their free time alone, reading, working, daydreaming. They belonged to fewer organized groups than the low-creative and were likely to spend most of their time in an individual, self-originated activity, such as art or music (Trowbridge and Charles, 1966) [55].

Wallach and Kogan (1965) [61] studied creativity, intelligence, and general school behavior in 151 fifth-grade children. They compared various combinations of high and low intelligence and high and low creativity and summarized their findings by reporting:

1. Children with high creativity and high intelligence exercise within themselves both control and freedom, exhibit both adult and childlike kinds of behavior.
2. Children with high creativity and low intelligence are in angry conflict with themselves and the school environment. They are beset by feelings of unworthiness and inadequacy.
3. Children with low creativity and high intelligence are "addicted" to school achievement and do very well at it.
4. Children with low creativity and low intelligence are bewildered and defensive. They engage in maneuvers ranging from intensive social activity to passivity or psychosomatic symptoms.

Development of Creativity

We should begin this section by saying that creatvity has been studied formally too short a time to allow for the collection of much longitudinal data. Therefore, only reports of various cross-sectional studies can be used as evidence.

Most of the data come from Torrance's studies. A generalized developmental curve of creative thinking ability may be seen in Figure 11.1 The first peak is shown between four and five years of age. At five there is a slight drop, then there is a steady rise to the fourth grade where a sharp drop is shown. There is then a rise to the seventh grade, where a drop is once more seen. Following this there is a steady rise until the end of school, followed by a slight drop.

The reasons for these variations are not at all clear. Torrance attributes the drop at fourth grade to conformity pressures from peers. However, the fourth-grade drop is coincident with the shift in testing from oral to written questions, and writing responses is likely to restrict versatility. Also, as noted above, the data are cross-sectional, that is, they are

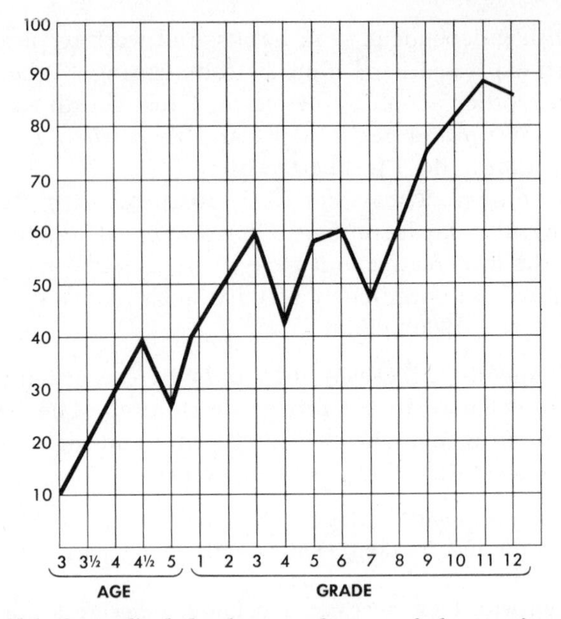

FIGURE 11.1. Generalized developmental curve of the creative thinking abilities. From Torrance, E. P., *Constructive behavior: Stress, personality, and mental health.* Belmont, Calif. Wadsworth, 1965. Page 102. By permission.

composed of test scores of different children at different ages, rather than of periodic tests of the same children over time. There is simply too little data available yet to generalize comfortably about the development of creativity.

It must be emphasized that we are discussing scores on tests, not creative productivity *per se*. This comes much later, in the twenties and thirties for most phenomena.

Implications for Education

As has been stated, evidence regarding the role of education in the development of creativity is still somewhat sparse. Until more is known about the phenomenon itself, definite prescriptions for educational practices are not on very firm ground. The evidence to date does warrant, however, some general comments:

1. Because creativity seems not to be closely related to either general intelligence or to school achievement, teachers should not overlook those youngsters who show little promise or performance in the academic area. Obviously, they should not be overlooked anyhow, but the teacher should remember that they are as likely—and as unlikely, of course—to exhibit creativity as their brighter, higher-achieving peers.

2. Because not all creative children are lovable, likeable, sociable

and group-minded, a teacher needs to offer some of these children at least some additional leeway in "being themselves" in the classroom. MacKinnon says ". . . I continue to think that one of the best methods for nurturing creativity is to de-emphasize group participation, with its demands for conformity, and to provide maximum opportunity for the able student to work out his own interests" (MacKinnon, 1965) [36].

3. The teacher should look for and encourage unique approaches to problems and ideas. If we don't know how to develop originality, at least we should not discourage it when it appears.

4. Teachers should make use of *indirect* approaches to creativity through student-teacher relationships. Present evidence leaves considerable room for skepticism that direct, formal methods of instruction will succeed in the development of creativity.

5. Intellectual "fun" should be encouraged—play with words, objects, ideas. The teacher should not be concerned too exclusively with competence.

6. Diversity should be encouraged.

7. Teachers should persist in the view that the mainspring of creativity is, as Rogers (1959) [43] puts it, the individual's *"tendency to actualize himself, to become his potentialities."*

SUMMARY

After several decades of neglect on the part of psychologists, especially in this country, *thinking* has quite recently been accorded serious and very active attention. Interest has been directed to better "description" of thinking and to researches into the development of thinking—particularly the thinking of children. Especially spotlighted in the studies of thinking is the question of the nature of productive thinking and how productive thinking is to be nurtured.

A most important challenge to teachers is contained in the fact just noted: the fact that psychologists have committed their abilities to the task of learning how productive thinking is brought about. There is apparent today considerable desire among psychologists in collaborating with teachers and other educators in an effort to discover how things to be learned can best be organized and presented in order that there may be a development of habits of inquiry, involvement in discovery and inventiveness, creativity, and other forms of productive thinking.

Suggested Collateral Readings

Almy, Millie, *Young children's thinking, studies of some aspects of Piaget's theory*. New York: Columbia University Teachers College Press, 1966.

Andersen, H., ed., *Creativity and its cultivation*. New York: Harper & Row, Publishers, 1959.

Anderson, R. C., and D. P. Ausubel, eds., *Readings in the psychology of cognition*. New York: Holt, Rinehart and Winston, Inc., 1965.

Aschner, Mary Jane and C. E. Bish, eds., *Productive thinking in education*. Washington, D.C.: National Education Association, 1965.

Berlyne, D. E., *Structure and direction in thinking*. New York: John Wiley & Sons, Inc., 1965. Final chapter.

Bruner, J., Jacqueline Goodnow, and G. Austin, *A study of thinking*. New York: John Wiley & Sons, Inc., 1962.

Flavell, J. H., *The developmental psychology of Jean Piaget*. Princeton: D. Van Nostrand, Inc., 1963.

Hilgard, E. R., *Introduction to psychology*, 3d ed. New York: Harcourt, Brace & World, Inc., 1962. Chapter 11.

Hunt, J. McV., *Intelligence and experience*. New York: The Ronald Press Company. 1961. Especially chapters 5, 6, 7.

Kneller, G. F., *The art and science of creativity*. New York: Holt, Rinehart and Winston, Inc., 1965.

Morgan, C. T., and R. A. King, *Introduction to psychology*, 3rd ed. New York: McGraw-Hill Book, Inc., 1966.

Ripple, R. E., and V. Rockcastle, eds., *Piaget rediscovered, A report of the conferences on cognitive studies and curriculum development*. Ithaca, N.Y.: Cornell University, School of Education, 1964.

Russell, D. H., *Children's thinking*. Boston: Ginn & Company, 1956.

Torrance, E. P., *Constructive behavior: Stress, personality and mental health*. Belmont, Calif.: Wadsworth Publishing Company, 1965. Pages 315–317.

Wallach, M., and Kogan, N., *Modes of thinking in young children*. New York: Holt, Rinehart and Winston, Inc., 1965.

References

1. Ausubel, D. P., 1961, *Learning by discovery: Rationale and mystique*. Urbana: Bureau of Educational Research, University of Illinois.
2. Bruner, J. S., 1959, Learning and thinking. *Harvard Educational Review*, **29:** 184–192.
3. ———, 1962, *On knowing*. Cambridge: Harvard University Press. Page 87.
4. ———, page 94.
5. ———, 1964, The course of cognitive growth. *American Psychologist*, **19:** 1–15.
6. ———, 2.
7. ———, 14.
8. ———, 1960, *The process of education*. Cambridge: Harvard University Press.
9. ———, Rose R. Olver, and Patricia M. Greenfield, 1966, *Studies in cognitive growth*. New York: John Wiley & Sons, Inc. Pages 6 and 8.
10. Carpenter, T. E., 1955, A pilot study for a quantitative investigation of Jean Piaget's original work on concept formation. *Educational Review*, **7:** 142–149.
11. Dewey, J., 1933, *How we think*. Boston: D. C. Heath and Company.

12. Drews, Elizabeth, 1963, The four faces of able adolescents. *Saturday Review,* January 19, 1963. Page 70.
13. Elkind, D., 1961, Children's discovery of the conservation of mass, weight, and volume: Piaget replication study—II. *J. genet. Psychol.,* **98:** 219–227.
14. English, H. B., and Ava C. English, *A comprehensive dictionary of psychological and psychoanalytical terms.* New York: Longmans, Green & Co., Inc. (David McKay Company, Inc.). Page 251.
15. Flavell, J. H., 1962, Historical and bibliographical note. Chapter 2 in *Thought in the young child. Monogr. Soc. Res. Child Develpm.,* **27:** 5–18.
16. ———, 15–16.
17. Gallagher, J. J., 1964, *Teaching the gifted child.* Boston: Allyn and Bacon, Inc.
18. Getzels, J. W., and P. W. Jackson, 1962, *Creativity and intelligence. New* York: John Wiley & Sons, Inc.
19. Goodlad, J. I., 1966, *The changing school curriculum.* New York: The Fund for the Advancement of Education.
20. Guilford, J. P., 1965, "Intellectual factors in productive thinking," Chapter 1 in Aschner, Mary Jane, and C. E. Bish, eds., *Productive thinking in education.* Washington, D.C.: The National Education Association. Page 9.
21. ———, pages 5–20.
22. ———, page 18.
23. ———, 1959, Three faces of intellect. *American Psychologist,* **14:** 469–479.
24. Hood, H. B., 1962, An experimental study of Piaget's theory of the development of number in children. *Brit. J. Psychol.,* **53:** 273–286.
25. Hunt, J. McV., 1961, *Intelligence and experience.* New York: The Ronald Press Company. Pages 262–263.
26. Inhelder, Bärbel, 1962, Some aspects of Piaget's genetic approach to cognition. Chapter 3 in *Thought in the young child. Monogr. Soc. Res. Child Develpm.* Pages 24–28.
27. ———, and Piaget, J., 1958, *The growth of logical thinking from childhood to adolescence.* New York: Basic Books, Inc.
28. Keasey, Carol T., and D. C. Charles, 1967, Conservation of substance in normal and mentally retarded children. *J. genet. Psychol.,* **111:** 271–279.
29. Lovell, K., and E. Ogilvie, 1960, A study of the conservation of substance in the junior school child. *Brit. J. Psychol.,* **30:** 109–118.
30. ———, and E. Ogilvie, 1961a, A study of the conservation of weight in the junior school child. *Brit. J. educ. Psychol.,* **31:** 138–144.
31. ———, and E. Ogilvie, 1961b, The growth of the concept of volume in junior school children. *J. Child Psychol. Psychiat.,* **2:** 118–126.
32. ———, D. Healey, and A. D. Rowland, The growth of some geometrical concepts. *Child Develpm.,* **33:** 751–767.
33. Lunzer, E. A., 1960, Some points of Piagetian theory in the light of experimental criticism. *J. Child Psychol. Psychiat.,* **1:** 191–202.
34. MacKinnon, D. T., 1962, The nature and nurture of creative talent. *American Psychologist,* **17:** 484–495.
35. ———, 1965, "Personality correlates of creativity." Chapter 8 in Ascher and Bish, *Productive thinking in education.* Page 161.

36. ———, page 165.
37. Piaget, J., and Bärbel Inhelder, 1941, *Le developpement des quantités chez l'enfant.* Neuchatel: Delachaux and Niestle.
38. ———, 1952a, *The child's conception of number.* London: Routledge & Kegan Paul, Ltd.
39. ———, 1952b, *The origins of intelligence in children.* New York: International Universities Press, Inc.
40. ———, 1953, *The construction of reality in the child.* New York: Basic Books, Inc.
41. ———, Bärbel Inhelder, and A. Szminska, 1960, *The child's conception of geometry.* London: Routledge & Kegan Paul, Ltd.
42. ———, 1955, *Language and thought of the child.* New York: Meridian Books, Inc.
43. Rogers, C., 1959, "Toward a theory of creativity," in Anderson, H. H., ed., *Creativity and its cultivation.* New York: Harper & Row, Publishers. Page 72. Page 72.
44. Rossman, J., 1931, *The psychology of the inventor.* Washington, D.C.: Inventors Publishing Company.
45. Russell, D. H., 1956a, *Children's thinking.* Boston: Ginn & Company. Page 32.
46. ———, 1956b, pages 158–160.
47. Smedslund, J., 1961a, The acquisition of conservation of substance and weight in children: external reinforcement of conservation of weight and of the operations of addition and subtraction. *Scandinavian J. Psychol.,* **2:** 71–84.
48. ———, 1961b, The acquisition of conservation of substance and weight in children: extinction of conservation of weight acquired "normally" and by means of empirical controls on a balance. *Scandinavian J. Psychol.,* **2:** 85–87.
49. Suchman, J. R., 1961, Inquiry training: building skills for autonomous discovery. *Merrill-Palmer Quarterly,* **7:** 171–180.
50. Tanner, J. M., 1961, *Education and physical growth.* London: University of London Press. Pages 84–85.
51. Taylor, C. W., 1962, Effects of instructional media on creativity: A look at possible positive and negative effects. *Educational Leadership,* **19:** 453–458.
52. ———, 1962, Who are the exceptionally creative? *Exceptional Children,* **28:** 421–432.
53. Torrance, E. P., 1965, "The measurement of creative behavior in children," Chapter 7 in Aschner, Mary Jane, and C. E. Bish, eds., *Productive thinking in education.* Washington, D.C.: The National Education Association.
54. Trowbridge, Norma T., 1964, *Creativity in children in art classes,* Ph.D. Thesis. Ames, Iowa: Iowa State University. Page 49.
55. ———, and D. C. Charles, 1966, Creativity in art students. *J. genet. Psychol.,* **109:** 281–289.
56. Wallace, J. B., 1965, *Concept growth and the education of the child.* The Mere, Upton Park, Slough, Bucks, England: National Foundation for Educational Research. Pages 101–107.

57. Wallach, M. A., 1963a, Research on children's thinking, Chapter VI in *Child Psychology,* Sixty-second Yearbook of the National Society for the Study of Education, Chicago. Pages 238–240.
58. ———, 1963b, page 246.
59. ———, 1963c, pages 60–78.
60. ———, 1963d, pages 264–267.
61. ———, and N. Kogan, 1965, A new look at the creativity-intelligence distinction. *J. Personality,* **33:** 348–369.
62. Wilson, R., 1965, The structure of the intellect, in Aschner, Mary Jane, and C. E. Bish, eds., *Productive thinking in education.* Washington, D.C.: The National Education Association. Pages 21–32.
63. Wohlwill, J. F., 1959, Un essai d'apprentissage dans de domaine de la conservation du nombre. *Études d'épistémologie génétique,* **9:** 125–135.
64. ———, 1960, A study of the development of the number concept by scalogram analysis. *J. genet. Psychol.,* **96:** 348–377.
65. ———, and R. C. Lowe, 1962, Experimental analysis of the development of conservation of number. *Child Develpm.,* **33:** 153–167.

CHAPTER 12

Communication and Behavior

Communication is a major aspect of human behavior. Except for the physical closeness of a parent and infant or of two adults in love, people probably get "closer" psychologically to each other through language than they do in any other way. In his efforts to study and understand children the teacher must therefore be continually alert to their attempts—both spoken and unspoken—to communicate. Speech, says Baldridge (1949) [2]:

> . . . is a kind of behavior which helps to form the world of the child; to transform him from an egocentric to a social being; to make assumptions for him; to set up conventions to guide and control him; to inform him; to instill in him thoughts, feelings and attitudes; to make him feel secure and insecure—all these effects and many more may be brought about in the child through the use of words.

Language and speech, of course, come to mind first as a means of communication, but people communicate also by gesture (the umpire's arm-movement which says "You're out!"), by posture and facial expression (the sagging shoulders and drooping mouth of sorrow), as well as by written word and by art. In this chapter we will be primarily concerned with speech, with the "internal speech" that is part of thought, and to a lesser extent with written speech—the printed word.

Awareness of language is, of course, not new for any adult; from infancy he has had daily language interchanges with all sorts of persons. He has learned consciously or unconsciously to make judgments about people, to respond or not respond to them; in general, to interact with them, partly on the basis of inferences made from their use of words. The teacher, in his efforts to understand behavior, makes maximum use of this rich experiential background. It is the purpose of this chapter to structure and to examine some of the psychological aspects of language behavior that will help him to sharpen his observations and make use of his experience and knowledge.

What are these "psychological aspects of language behavior"? First, the teacher should know something about normal speech development. How do children acquire speech and what are the factors that produce individual differences? What kinds of problems arise in development? Second, he needs to know something about the relationship between social behavior and language. What effects does speech have on self-perception, relations with other people, and general personal adjustment? Finally, he needs to have some idea of the influence of children's language characteristics on school adjustment. How does word manipulation affect reasoning, problem solving, and learning in general? What are some of the special problems of reading and writing?

The Nature of Language [1]

Before development of language in the child is discussed, we should comment briefly on what it is that is being developed. One definition is:

> A language is a socially institutionalized sign system. It is the result of centuries of gradual development and change at the hands of many generations of speakers, but at any one point of history it exists as a set of patterns of behavior learned and exploited in varying degrees by each member of the community in which it is used. (Carroll, 1964) [7]

To paraphrase, we emphasize that language is a kind of *behavior,* it is *learned,* it is intimately related to a *social group,* and *individuals vary* in their use of it.

Language is extraordinarily complex, and thus research is difficult and complex. Most research on language by psychologists has been quantitative and normative, that is, descriptive of acquisition and growth of speech in children. In recent years the behavioral science called "descriptive linguistics" has been flourishing. This discipline has concerned itself with the description and study of languages as sign systems.

> The most important contribution that modern linguistics has brought to child language studies is its conception of what a language is. A language is a system that can be described internally in terms of the two primary parts or levels—the phonological (sound system) and the grammatical. A complete description of a language would include an account of all possible phonological sequences and also a set of rules by which we can predict all the possible sentences in that language. (Ervin and Miller, 1963) [11]

[1] The discussion in this section depends largely on Chapter 7, "Language and cognition," in Carroll, J., *Language and thought* [7], Englewood Cliffs, N.J.: Prentice-Hall, Inc., 1964.

Finally, language can be analyzed as a "content system," or system of meanings; this has traditionally been the province of philosophy.

Much of this chapter will be devoted to the traditional research on speech development, because such knowledge is important to the teacher. Descriptive and content-oriented data will be referred to also, where appropriate.

ACQUISITION AND DEVELOPMENT OF SPEECH

Speech illustrates, perhaps more clearly than any other characteristic, the complete interdependence of maturation and learning. The motor apparatus for producing speech—diaphragm, vocal cords, tongue, lips, and auxiliary parts—is present at birth and is functioning after a fashion within a few weeks, but until the areas of the brain concerned with language and symbols and with control of speech motor functions are at an appropriate level of maturity, no amount of stimulating, teaching, or urging will elicit anything but gibberish from the infant. At the same time, lack of the environmental stimulation of hearing others speak and engaging in vocal play (as in the case of a child born deaf) will result in a lack of intelligible speech.

For further illustration of the neural basis for speech, reference may be made to numerous animal studies, all of which demonstrate failure to develop true speech, even in creatures with brains as advanced and complex as those of the chimpanzee and other primates. The term *true* speech is used because the word-sounds made by parrots and other "talking birds" are simply conditioned responses.[2]

With this interrelationship in mind, let us examine the normal developmental pattern of language acquisition.

Early Communication

In the development of speech, there are four classes or types of responses to be mastered. The first of these are the distinctive, basic sounds called *phonemes,* which include vowels and consonants. Second are *morphemes,* the smallest meaningful combinations of sounds in a language, like "ma" or "pa." Third are *morphological rules,* the rules by which sequences of sounds or phonemes are combined to form, construct or alter words, as "s" is added to "boy" to form the plural. Finally, there are *syntactic rules,* the patterns or arrangements of words into sentences or phrases (Berko and Brown, 1960) [3].

There is no completely adequate or generally accepted theory to explain *how* a child acquires these language responses. Some form of con-

[2] For a discussion of animal language, see Munn, N., 1965, *The evolution and growth of human behavior,* Boston: Houghton Mifflin Company. Pages 377–402.

ditioning is usually hypothesized; this theory explains the child's understanding of others' language, but does not account for his ability to produce meaningful words himself. Mowrer's "autism" theory is regarded as more adequate by many students of language. Mowrer (1960) [26] compares the child's learning to talk to that of pet talking birds. The pet birds are eager for the master to appear, and sounds associated with the master become associated with comfort. The child in the same fashion finds comfort in the mother's presence, for a host of reasons, and thus associates certain sounds with her presence and the accompanying comfort. The child, like the pet, makes remembered sounds in the master's/mother's absence, thus calling up the good feeling associated with the comforter's person. Mowrer comments, "Words are reproduced if and only if they are first made to sound good in the context of affectionate care and attention" (Mowrer, 1958) [25].

The infant undoubtedly communicates first by crying. Early crying is simply a product of the infant's bodily discomfort and thus is no more communication than is a belch. Before three months, however (well before three months in some infants), he has learned that he can get relief from physical distress—or even from loneliness—by crying, and thus he begins to use his voice to influence others. In addition to crying, he has a repertoire of sounds in early infancy: grunts, belches, coughs, sneezes, sighs, whines, and the like, followed in a few weeks by cooing.

Gradually the number of sounds increases, and from about the third month on, the vocal play known as *babbling* emerges. Babbling consists of vowel and consonant combinations repeated over and over—"ma-ma-ma," "bu-bu-bu," and so on. These sounds may be made just for the fun of it, or they may be made in an attempt to reconstitute the pleasing affective situation generated by the mother's presence, as postulated by Mowrer. They do serve to give the infant practice with various sound combinations which he will need later in making words.

Along with his growing command of the sound-producing apparatus the infant has a growing awareness of the communication attempts of other people. He probably perceives the emotions and general intent of communication long before words themselves have any meaning. Anyone who has raised a pet cat or dog will have observed the animal reacting to his master's posture, tone of voice, and mien without regard to the actual *content* of the speech; so it is with the infant.

When the infant has gained some voluntary control of his speech apparatus and has grasped the *idea* of sounds as communication, he is ready to talk. This state of readiness is usually reached somewhere around the twelfth month, but with considerable earlier and later deviation in some infants. When the necessary readiness has been achieved, stimulation and learning experiences become essential.

The child's "first word" is usually a parrot-like conditioned response, rather than a true, meaningful word. Suppose for instance that a nine-months-old infant's mother is playing with him after his nap. He babbles, "ma-ma-ma," she mimics him, "ma-ma," he delightedly responds, "ma-ma," and thus happens on a pair of syllables meaningful to her. She is likely at this point to exhibit pleasure, to fondle and praise him—in general to reward the response and increase the likelihood of its being repeated. She may rush to the telephone to tell daddy the news about Junior's first word; her joy, while harmless, is ill-founded. Until he associates the words with his mother, he has not really used "mama" as a word. In a variety of ways, of course, the association is soon made, as are associations with other persons, objects and sounds. Thus both the affective or emotional atmosphere the child lives in, and the learning stimulation he receives, contribute to the development of true language.

After the child acquires his first few words, he seems to gain fairly rapidly some insight into the meaning and usefulness of language in general. Then the early trickle of words becomes a stream and the stream becomes a torrent. By the age of two he has 200 or more words, and by school age, several thousand. His early words are likely to be nouns, but there is usually a sprinkling of verbs, adjectives, and adverbs, with pronouns coming along later.

Adding new words to the vocabulary is only a part of the process. Much (in the average child, probably *most*) of early speech is unintelligible to the listener, especially one unfamiliar with the child. For instance the mother, who is usually in pretty constant contact with the child, is likely to understand more of his speech than does the father. With increasing maturity and experience there is a gradual but steady decline in unintelligible speech. Ervin and Miller (1963b) [12] note:

> By the fourth year, the child's phonological system closely approximates the model, and the remaining deviations are usually corrected by the time the child enters school. Occasionally, earlier substitution patterns persist, and the child is usually described as having speech problems.

We will discuss some of these problems later in the chapter.

Later Development

After speech is well established, the most obvious aspect of development is the growth of vocabulary. A more rapid acceleration in word-acquisition occurs after the child enters school, for here he is taught new words, he learns to read, and in general broadens his intellectual horizons. In the later years of grade school, he may have a vocabulary of scores of thousand of words. Estimates of the absolute size of children's vocabularies vary so much that they are not particularly meaningful. The rapid increase in size is consistent, however.

In language development, as in physical development, growth implies more than change in size; it implies also changes in function. Perhaps most important is a steadily increasing improvement and deepening of understanding. The child learns more precise meanings for words he has been using for some time, and thus he uses them more accurately. He perceives the connotation, the flavor, the subtleties of both old and new terms. He learns the various (and variously difficult) meanings of words with multiple definitions—words like "strike" and "run." His word-knowledge grows in *depth* as well as *breadth*. The vocabulary items used in most intelligence tests reveal both of these changes. In the Stanford-Binet Intelligence Test, for example, the first word is one familiar to all ages: "orange." Later in the test we find words which are more abstract and thus more difficult: "priceless" for instance. Yet even for a simple, concrete word such as "orange," differences appear with age. Terman and Merrill (1937) [33] comment:

> Then, too, there are characteristic differences in quality of responses for older and younger subjects even on the simpler words. Thus the adult gives a response which classifies a common object, but also isolates it by excluding other objects which do not belong to the class. Both a six-year-old and a sixteen-year-old know the meaning of orange—"it is round and has seeds" or "it is a citrus fruit"—but their thinking is characteristically different.

Acquisition of Grammar

As we pointed out in the beginning of this section, there is more to learning language than acquiring a vocabulary: the morphological and syntactic rules must be learned also. Children display no evidence of grammar in the early stages of word acquisition, yet by four years they have acquired the fundamentals. This mastery is described by Ervin and Miller (1963c) [13] as "one of the most complicated intellectual achievements of children." *How* they acquire grammar has been the topic of considerable research in recent years. Imitation probably plays a part, and some comprehension of adult rules also may account for some more skill. But neither is sufficient to explain all the grammatical skill preschoolers develop. It seems possible that children build, by analogy, a system of classes and rules to guide their grammar, but how they go about this is not at all clear. Brown and Belugi (1964) [5] comment, "It looks as if this last process (introduction of the latent structure) will put a serious strain on any learning theory thus far conceived by psychology." But the child does acquire a functional grammar, and begins building sentences early. The first (usually two-word) sentence ordinarily occurs at about a year and a half. The number of words included in the sentences shows an increase throughout the developing years, even though college age. This growth in length of sentences is of a cyclical nature, showing a sharp upturn during adolescence.

From birth to maturity then, there is a continual improvement in every aspect of communication. To summarize:

1. Almost complete speech intelligibility is achieved by most children before starting school.
2. Vocabulary grows steadily in both quantity and quality up to maturity.
3. Understanding deepens along with vocabulary growth.
4. Sentences become longer and the structure becomes more complicated. This phase of development shows a rapid increase at adolescence.

Although not always as obvious or as dramatic as physical growth differences, variability in language development is great from one child to another, and the causes of these differences are numerous. Because of the importance of language in the child's life, it is worth the teacher's while to examine these differences and their causes.

CAUSES OF INDIVIDUAL VARIABILITY

The interrelationship of maturation and learning has been discussed briefly earlier in this chapter. Both of these factors appear in varying degrees in the following causes, but maturation is perhaps primarily involved in the "personal factors," while learning is paramount in "motivation" and "environmental factors."

Motivation

The desire to communicate in some fashion seems to appear in all animals, including the human infant. However, it is the *result,* rather than the process, of communication that interests the infant. Thus if cries, screams, and gestures are adequate to get the results he wants, cries, screams, and gestures will be his mode of communication. For the same reason, the child whose needs are always anticipated—who is fed before he is really hungry, who is changed before he is uncomfortable, who always has before him an attractive choice of toys—will have less need for communication of any kind than the child who suffers a little normal neglect by a busy mother. One possible result of this lack of motivating circumstances is a delay in the onset of speech and a limited vocabulary in childhood and adolescence. If baby talk or a bizarre speech pattern is understood and accepted by parents and playmates, there will be no reason to improve or develop better speech. On the other hand, failure to be understood will spur him to greater effort.

In later childhood and adolescence, the peer group is a powerful determiner of standards. These standards may be higher or lower than his own. The possessor of an extensive vocabulary, who is able to express himself concisely and accurately, may actually repress his admirable verbal skills if his peer-reference group disapproves of them, and may take on the vernacular speech and sloppy articulation of that group—so long as it remains his reference group.

The teacher should be aware that motivation may serve to retard, accelerate, or modify language at any age; its greatest effect occurs in early years, but these early years see the development of basic speech proficiency.

Personal Factors

Sex. A single sentence may be cited to summarize the evidence on sex differences: "One of the most consistent findings to emerge from the mass of data accumulated on language development in American white children seems to be a slight difference in favor of girls in nearly all aspects of language that have been studied" (McCarthy, 1954) [22].

Girls show their superiority in the earlier age of onset of speech, which may be attributed in part at least to their generally faster developmental rate (see Chapter 9). Faster physical development results in earlier myelinization of the neural speech pathways, and thus earlier activation of the speech-producing apparatus. Girls' speech is comprehensible earlier and they have fewer defects. Girls use sentences earlier than boys, and age for age, they use longer sentences. Their vocabularies are consistently larger. In school, they write longer papers, they read earlier and better, and have fewer reading problems. Finally, the proverbial claim that females are more talkative than males seems to be born out by the evidence. Most of the differences seem to increase with age.

In addition to their intrinsic interest, the facts of feminine verbal superiority are worthy of consideration because they have some application to school situations. We can expect girls as a group to be consistently superior to boys in school tasks which emphasize language. Because our schools are strongly oriented toward verbal types of subjects, boys as a group labor at somewhat of a disadvantage, and may need more help and more stimulation than girls. It must be remembered of course that within-group sex differences are likely to be greater than the differences between the means of the sex groups. Thus in a given class, *any* boy may exceed *any* girl. The mean is likely still to be higher for girls.

Race and Ethnic Background. Race and *ethnic* (referring to a group of culturally related people) background, unlike sex, does not appear to have much if any influence on early language development. Studies of Negro and white infants in the United States have shown no differences when groups were matched properly. Comparative studies of language development in European, Asian, and other children have demonstrated the similarity of rate and type of development the world over. Studies of later language development are meager, but the findings are uniformly negative. We must apparently look to factors other than these to explain differences between individuals in our culture. This comment on ethnic influence on language concerns only *ability* and *performance.* The ethnic factor has a great influence on the *form* of the language utterance.

Health. Good general health has about the same relationship to early language development that it has to other kinds of growth. In the first two years of life, severe or prolonged illness is likely to delay the onset of speech, or to cause regression from a level of speech proficiency already established. Illness in middle and later childhood may have less predictable effects on language growth. On the one hand, the child who is immobilized or at least cut off from his contacts with other children may lose some incentive for speech, as well as some environmental stimulation; thus his development may suffer. On the other hand, he may be driven by his isolation from children to a greater degree of association with adults, to a great amount of reading if he is old enough, and in general to more verbal and less physical activities; thus he may forge ahead of his peers in language growth. The effect of deafness and other defects will be discussed later.

Intelligence. Intelligence is probably the most important single factor in language development. It is perhaps unfortunate but certainly true that our concept of intelligence is tied up with the tests we have developed and have used so widely to measure ability. As the student will recall from an earlier discussion our tests in turn have been developed to meet the needs of the schools to make predictions of academic success. Therefore when we say that intellectual development and language development are very highly related, we are really saying that language is a major factor in school success. This is useful knowledge, but knowledge which describes rather than explains. Does the high relationship indicate that basic mental development is largely linguistic development, or simply that the criteria of intelligence in our culture—tests and school grades—happen to be highly verbal? The answer to this question has simply not been determined as yet. Whatever the answer, the fact of a close relationship remains.

Parents and relatives of babies who talk early are usually sure they have an extraordinarily bright child, while the families of late talkers may be somewhat concerned about the child's intelligence. As is often the case with popular belief, there is some scientific justification for relating early or late development of speech to intelligence. However, there is not enough to support the sweeping generalizations and individual applications often made by the layman. Bright children *do* talk earlier: Terman's gifted children (IQ 140 and above) talked on the average four months earlier than the norm. However, there were some in this group who did not talk until two, two and a half, and three years of age (Terman, 1925) [32]. Feeble-minded children usually talk many months later than average, and never talk early. In later childhood and in maturity most mentally deficient children have abnormal speech, and the lower the intelligence, the poorer the speech. Because there are so many causes for speech retardation or language incompetence, we must not be hasty in judging any individual child.

Intelligence measures are in general so dependent upon language that we have had indifferent success in devising tests for the prelinguistic growth period which will predict later intellectual levels. In later years of childhood and adolescence on the other hand, vocabulary is usually the best *single* measure of intelligence.

Linguistic ability is not all of intelligence by any means, but it is undeniably a very large part.

Environmental Factors

Socio-economic Status. Parents' occupational and social level has a direct relationship to all phases of language development. Children of middle- and upper-class homes talk earlier, form sentences earlier, and use more mature sentence structure than their lower-class age-mates. At every age during the school years, the higher-class children have a vocabulary advantage. Their articulation and general speech performance is better. Although the data are sometimes contradictory, these differences seem to increase with age.

Some of these differences are probably due to intelligence, because there is a fairly high relationship between ability and social or occupational status. Much of the difference is probably due to the relationships within the family, and to the general quality and quantity of experience. These influences will be examined in the following discussion.

Family Relationships. In addition to the factor of intelligence, the consistent relationship between socio-economic status and language development is probably due primarily to different family-life patterns at various levels. Although lacking in some respects, an interesting study by Milner (1951) [24] suggests that children of high language ability came from homes where:

1. Families usually had breakfast together;
2. Families engaged in two-way conversation before school, after school, and at supper, with the children participating in the conversation;

3. Children received much overt affection from significant adults in the home.

The experience of the low-verbal group was opposite: meals not eaten together, little conversation, and little overt affection.

Children in disadvantaged families generally suffer from language deficiency, and thus from inadequate intellectual development and poor achievement. This language deficiency stems from a general lack of vocal stimulation in infancy, a lack of verbal contact with adults, the limited nature of mature cognitive experience and emotional restrictions on conceptual-verbal skills (Raph, 1966) [29].

Irwin (1960) [15] demonstrated experimentally how a change in the home environment could modify this lack. Infants from lower socio-economic levels were visited regularly in their homes, where tape recordings were made of their vocalizations. Parents of some of the infants were provided with story books, which they were encouraged to read to the children; they were also asked to show children the pictures and to discuss them. Parents of a control group of children were given no supplementary material or instruction. At the end of the experimental period, there were highly significant differences in favor of the stimulated children in number of phonemes used.

More than quantitative differences exist between the language competence of disadvantaged and more fortunate children. Hess and Shipman (1965) [14] compared behavior of Negro mothers and children of various social classes, and communication between them in experimental situations. Cognitive styles on tests given separately to the mothers and to the children showed less abstraction and more simple relational responses by lower-class subjects and a difference in the direction of impulsiveness for the latter. Communication was generally more successful for the middle-class families.

The age of the persons with whom the child associates most has an effect on his development: in brief, the greater his association with adults, the better his language. Here again, the social-class-linked family situation is apparent: middle- and upper-class children spend more time with their parents and with other adults than do lower-class children.

In the same context, the size of the family (the number of children) and the position of the child in the family are influential factors. The only child has a very clear and consistent advantage. Some of this advantage can be attributed to intelligence (there is an inverse relationship between family size and the intelligence of its members) but the superiority of the only child is out of proportion to what would be expected on the basis of his age, sex, mentality, and socio-economic status. Children who associate with older children are somewhat above the average in language growth, while those associating with younger children are below average.

From the standpoint of linguistic development, being born a twin is unfortunate. Every study of twins shows retardation and inadequate language proficiency. There is of course no suggestion of structural or functional deficiency; the cause is simply the peculiar social situation of constant companionship with a person at the same level of development. Triplets appear to be more retarded than twins. One of the frequent linguistic concomitants of being a twin is the development of *jargon,* a private language or communication system which may be so satisfying to the pair that one or both may be unwilling to make the effort to learn English—or whatever tongue is spoken in the home. Fortunately, some of the retardation disappears when the twins enter school and enlarge their social world. This reversal is especially apparent in middle- and upper-class children. It is probable, however, that there is some permanent effect from this slow start.

Institutionalization. Life in an institution seems to have a depressing effect on every kind of development. Thus we find that infants and young children who spend their early lives in orphanages, hospitals, or other group homes are retarded in all aspects of language development. Significant differences in prespeech sounds between institution children and those in homes have been noted as early as two months, and the differences increase throughout infancy. The onset of speech is delayed in the institution children, and they have smaller vocabularies and generally poorer language skills throughout childhood. The cause seems to be simply the monotonous and nonstimulating atmosphere.

That such effects are partially reversible has been shown in institutional educational programs which emphasize the understanding and use of language symbols. In one study, the children given such training surpassed a control group at a statistically significant level on nearly all language measures considered. Sentence length and vocabulary changes were most noticeable. Their intelligence test scores also rose, although no direct coaching on test items was given (Dawe, 1942) [10]. A number of studies make it clear that such training has its greatest effect in preschool years.

General Experience. As the foregoing discussion would suggest, the general quantity and quality of experience is of the greatest importance in language development. Travel seems to have a markedly stimulating effect on vocabulary. In these days when so many American families travel a great deal—not only on vacation but in the course of frequent changes of jobs and homes—we can expect to see an improvement in the general language level and a widening gulf between children with restricted environments and those with stimulating experiences.

The general increase in public communication and entertainment facilities (television, radio, movies, books, and papers) would augur general improvement also. In one study, college students possessed significantly better vocabularies and verbal skills than did their parents in their own college days a generation earlier (Jensen, 1951) [16].

PROBLEMS OF DEVELOPMENT

As anyone can infer from his own experience and observation, speech adequacy is a significant factor in good social and academic adjustment. Unfortunately, this adequacy is far from universal. Van Riper (1963) [34] reports that about 6 percent of the total population has some variety of speech defect. Four percent of the total population has an articulation disorder. Seven of every thousand persons are stutterers, five of every thousand have a voice disorder, five have delayed speech, two have speech disorders due to brain injuries, and one in a thousand has a cleft-palate speech defect. The diagnosis and treatment of speech problems is a job for the professional speech therapist, but an examination of some of the major causes of defect should give the teacher some clues to good and poor practice in the classroom and home. The development of adequate speech is in line with general educational objectives, and failures in development may lead to educational and emotional maladjustment. Thus the school and ultimately the teacher have responsibility.

Etiology of Defects [3]

The following conditions are frequent causes of speech and general language deficiences:

Poor Speech Models. Because speech is acquired largely by imitation, it is obvious that many errors in articulation are simply imitations of what the child hears from parents, companions, or—regrettably—teachers. Twin jargon, mentioned earlier, is a kind of horrible example of the bad influence of a poor model.

Poor Teaching Methods. Understimulation in the home may delay the appearance of speech. This situation is especially common in lower-class homes. Overstimulation may have an adverse effect of another kind. "Pushing" the child toward speech too difficult for his level of maturity may make him overly conscious of his speech. One prominent speech therapist and psychologist (Johnson, 1956) [19] feels that the in-

[3] For a general discussion of the causes of speech deficiencies see Van Riper, C., 1963, *Speech correction* [23], Englewood Cliffs, N.J.: Prentice-Hall, Inc.

sistence of anxious, striving parents and teachers on speech precision beyond the capabilities of the immature child is a major cause of stuttering. All young children stutter when their thoughts outrace their speech capacity, or when they are excited. Adolescents and adults too are likely to suffer from blocks or repetitions in a stress situation. Making an issue of such errors is likely to arouse emotions and build habits which lead to permanent defects.

Poor Teaching of Oral Reading and Phonics. Oral reading in the early grades is used in order that the teacher can get some idea of the child's proficiency. If the student's reading is inadequate and the other children (or the teacher) ridicule him, both speech and reading problems may ensue. The teaching of phonics is not, as some have claimed, a cure-all for language or reading problems, but ignorance of the structure of words leads to errors in spelling, pronunciation, and understanding.

Bilinguality. The waves of immigration early in the century and the G.I. brides of World War II and the following Occupation have brought a stream of non-English speaking people to our shores. As a result, we have had scores of thousands of families in which the parents spoke different languages and in which the children have been of necessity bilingual. The problems of learning two languages at once in early childhood have been widely investigated. Numerous studies agree that children in bilingual homes are retarded in every phrase of language development, frequently to the point of being unable to start school at the normal age. The problems of learning two words for everything and two sets of grammar and syntax cause inferiority in size of vocabulary, length of sentence, construction, and articulation. Bilinguals are of course not uniform in kind: different ethnic backgrounds and different environments make individual prediction impossible. Bilinguals are no longer handicapped by high school and college age, but whether this is the result of learning or of selection is unknown (Darcy, 1963) [9].

Mental Deficiency. As noted earlier, this condition almost always causes general linguistic handicap.

Partial or Total Deafness. The totally deaf can learn to talk, but the learning process is slow and laborious. The story of Helen Keller and her teacher, Anne Sullivan, is widely known. Not so widely known is the plight of the partially deaf. When a part of the total range of sound normally heard by human ears is screened out by deafness the sounds are not heard as they were produced. If the hearing deficiency is in the sound range of the human voice, the words used by the child *as he has heard them* will be inaccurate.

Emotional Disturbances. This topic will be discussed later in the chapter.

Physical Factors. Among these causes are anatomical anomalies, accidents and injuries to the brain or speech mechanism, endocrine disturbances, malnutrition, and biochemical deficiency.

Aiding Optimum Development

The school and the teacher have no control over many of the factors that influence good language growth, especially in the critical preschool years. Intelligence, physical status, level of home, and similar personal and environmental characteristics are more influential than educational programs. This does not mean, however, that the teacher is powerless to affect language growth and competence. Knowledge of the influential factors in language development—both benign and maleficent—should help him to create an atmosphere in which optimum growth is possible. What does such an atmosphere include? Let us summarize the material presented thus far in the chapter.

Motivation. It is true that verbal ability is already highly rewarded in our schools. This is appropriate for reasons we have discussed. The teacher's problem is in motivating the poor language students who in effect are punished daily for their linguistic inadequacy by poor grades and criticism from the teacher. Many of these children come from homes where any upward deviation in vocabulary or expressiveness is regarded as "showing off" and is punished. Boys in general need more stimulation than girls. In dealing with language the junior high and secondary school teacher must walk a fine line between pedantry, which will be ridiculed and (properly) rejected, and acceptance of the standards of the mass, which will be the surrender of an educational obligation. It is the solving of such problems that makes teaching an art and not a science.

Experience. This is the teacher's most potent educational device. The child needs an opportunity to express himself verbally, to report, discuss, argue—and listen. The use of communication devices—television, radio, phonograph, tape recorder, or movie—that bring the world to the classroom provides a partial substitute for the experience families may fail to provide at home. Considerable reading, both required and voluntary, is important at every stage up through high school, as is the frequent use of written and oral reports.

An Accepting Atmosphere. Because emotional tension is associated with many language problems, the elementary teacher especially should avoid fear- or anxiety-producing situations associated with speech. This does not mean an uncritical atmosphere in which errors are accepted without correction, for this leaves the child without standards. Fear and ridicule, however, are poor stimulators in the classroom—or elsewhere, for that matter.

In addition, the school shares with the home the responsibility for physical checkups and referrals, health education, conservation of sense organs and functions, and remedial work where it is needed.

LANGUAGE AND SOCIAL BEHAVIOR

Thus far, our discussion of language has been confined to a description of its growth, a description similar to that given earlier of organic growth. Knowledge of the structural development of language in the child—the origin, increase in vocabulary and sentence length, harmful and beneficial environmental circumstances, and the like—is necessary and useful to the teacher. This knowledge does not by itself, however, give a clue to the real importance of language in behavior. It is in its social functions that we find the study of communication most rewarding.

The earliest speech of the child is primarily *egocentric,* that is, speech engaged in for its own sake, or out of pleasure in the company of whoever is around. Piaget has emphasized that this early speech is not really conversation, because the child is not involved in reciprocal discussion with exchange of views; the major cause of this egocentricity is the child's intellectual limitations, inability to analyze his own thought processes and evaluate conclusions. *Socialized speech* develops as the child becomes able—and willing—to exchange ideas, to order or request something, to ask questions and to answer questions (Piaget and Inhelder, 1958) [28]. At an early age, the child's language is often, especially to an unfamiliar adult, a confusing blend of egocentric and socialized speech.

Communication is by definition a social process; it is a reciprocal reaching out toward other people. Whatever understanding one human being has of another is largely the product of how well he reaches the other in his attempts to share his experiences, his ideas, and his emotions. Communication is thus a two-way process with a constant reversing of roles, the roles of *communicator* (the one who gives the message) and *communicant* (the one who receives the message). The communicator provides the stimulus, the communicant becomes a communicator, the stimulator instead of the receiver. This situation, of course, is not unique or peculiar to the communication process. In any social context the person is at once a social stimulus, affecting other people, and a responder to the social presence of others. This interaction between two persons, or a person and a group, is the basis of all social behavior.

The importance of this interaction cannot be emphasized too strongly. The student or teacher who perceives communication as a "putting out" process only will, in a very real sense, be talking only to himself. "Talking at" rather than "talking with" is fatal to understanding.

Because the communication process is so important a part of social behavior, an examination of some of its aspects would seem desirable in our attempts to bring about increased understanding of behavior in general.

Communication and Understanding

First, a distinction must be made between the words which a speaker uses and the real message he means to convey. For a great variety of reasons, people fail to say what they mean. Young children especially are troubled by inadequate vocabularies and language control. Older children and adolescents too may find it impossible to locate the precise words they need to convey their meaning. At any age conventions of etiquette, local custom, or the mores of a particular group may force a person to rely on hackneyed phrases or stereotyped generalizations for much of his communication. Take for instance the phrase, "That's a pretty dress," used by a male at different ages:

Age	*Hearer*	*What He Means to Say (Latent Intent)*
Three	**Mother**	**I like you. You make me feel secure and comfortable when you're around. I like having you where I can see you.**
Seven	**Seven-year-old girl**	**I like you and I think you're pretty. I'd like to play with you after school but if I did the gang would call me a sissy. I want you to know I like you, but I can't just say so, or you'd make fun of me too. I wonder if you like me?**
Fourteen	**Teacher**	**A little flattery may help my English grade. I heard you tell another teacher that I was a cute boy. As a matter of fact you're pretty nice looking even if you are almost as old as my mother. Girls and women are sort of exciting and I like being able to look at you all I want in class. I wonder if you noticed that I have to shave sometimes.**
Sixteen	**Fifteen-year-old girl**	**I'd like to know you better—how can I get you interested in me? Maybe I could ask you to a movie —if you don't give me a cold shoulder now, I'll work up the courage in a couple of days. I wonder what it would be like to kiss you.**

Almost any communication involves more than reaches the ear. For achievement of real understanding, both speaker and hearer need to be aware of the *intent* of the communicator; his *manifest* (outward or apparent) intent as well as his *latent* (and basic) intent. The communicator himself may be unaware of his real intent, some of which may be below the threshold of consciousness. It is unfortunately true, for example, that many nagging, scolding parents and teachers are really rejecting their children under the guise of controlling their behavior. The teacher needs to question himself continuously about the real intent of his own and his students' verbalizations.

Second, to understand any communication, it is necessary to *perceive* both or all members of the interchange with reality and clarity. What are some determinants of realistic perception? What are some important factors, some clues to look for?

One is the "set" of speaker and hearer. By "set" is meant selectivity of attention, or readiness to respond to some stimuli rather than to others. For example, the child interested in his play may be quite unaware of the call to lunch, but later when he is hungry the slam of the oven door may mean "cookies!" and bring him on the run. What in turn determines "set"?

Perhaps the best answer is self-interest. People of any age respond most readily to what is important in their lives. A review of Chapter 5, "Needs and Motives Underlying Behavior," will point up some of the significant needs at various stages of development. The teacher of any age group will succeed in his efforts to communicate to the degree that he is aware of the needs, and thus the "set" of his students.

He must also be conscious of the experience of the communicant. As we have seen, children from homes where there is much verbal interchange within the family are linguistically more apt than others. It is reasonable to assume that the child who listens and is listened to in the home will have a set that gives him more accurate perception of himself and others, at least in the area of communication. Not only quantity and quality of experience, but content of experience is important. A discussion of the mathematical calculation of velocity will be perceived more readily by the speed-conscious adolescent boy if it is couched in terms of an automobile performance than if it is presented as an abstract concept. The teacher must not only consider past experience of his communicants, but for most effective present and future communication he must provide them with new experiences in line with the objectives of his area of learning.

Another circumstance affecting perception is the emotional state of both parties to the communication. The fifteen-year-old girl whose dress was praised by an older boy may, if she is interested in boys in general and the speaker in particular, interpret his remark as he intended she should—as an expression of personal liking and interest. Or, if she is uninterested, she may take him literally and suppose he meant nothing more than he said.

Attitudes, which are both emotional and ideational in form, help to structure perception of all kinds.

The small town of———was troubled by its teenagers. Despite many complaints of delinquency, the principal difficulty seemed to be noisy behavior at night—cars racing through the streets with mufflers cut out, tires screaming in fast turns, horns honking, boys and girls shouting. The town council proposed a curfew of ten o'clock on weeknights and eleven on weekends. The high school students were up in arms at this proposed suppression: they snake-danced in the streets, proposed a school strike and in general threatened the peace of the community. A school administrator wisely proposed that a committee of student leaders be selected to consider the problem. This was done democratically and after deliberation the committee proposed a voluntary curfew, which, although more liberal than the town council's, was still a curfew. It was accepted with relatively little complaint, and was fairly effective in correcting the situation.

In the above account, it was the attitude of the teenagers toward the group suggesting the control which was the major factor in structuring the perception of the curfew as acceptable or unacceptable. A number of studies in which statements are fictitiously attributed to popular and unpopular public figures have shown that understanding and misunderstanding, as well as acceptance or rejection, are frequently determined by the attitude toward the communicator rather than by the content of the message itself (Lewis, 1941) [20].

Third, in getting meaning out of any communication, the context in which it occurs must be considered. A fourteen-year-old girl who cries, "I hate you!" to her parents when she is denied permission to attend a party is usually only expressing anger and frustration. The same words spoken in serious, calm, and thoughtful discussion of her feelings about her parents would have quite a different connotation. The teacher who says with a laugh "Bill, you are a clumsy oaf!" to Bill as he drops the football in a casual playground game is communicating something quite different than is the grim-visaged cafeteria supervisor who uses the same words when Bill spills a bowl of soup. Children (and sometimes adults) do not always stop to consider the context in reacting to words. It is the communicator's responsibility then to make sure in some way that the intent of the message is clear. Otherwise misunderstanding may develop and problems will ensue.

Language and Culture

The influence of culture on behavior in general has been discussed in Chapter 8. There are, however, some special applications to language which are worthy of emphasis.

Almost all persons live in groups, and most individuals are members of several groups. In the course of group living, customs, standards, and norms are developed. These norms serve to set the group to some extent apart from other groups, to identify it, and to give the members a feeling of belonging—and outsiders a feeling of not belonging. Language is one of the kinds of behavior which reflects group norms or standards. The English language, for example is the norm in the United States, Great Britain, and other countries influenced by England.

People are members not only of large groups such as nations, but also of regional, occupational, educational, socio-economic, age, sex, neighborhood, and other groups. To some extent, each of these memberships helps to structure the language of the person. Take the case of a particular individual named John Jones. Even a brief sample of his speech reveals some clues to his status as:

1. A male
2. An American
3. A New Englander, specifically one hailing from Maine
4. A man of early maturity, probably in his mid-twenties
5. A man of better-than-average formal or informal education, probably a college graduate
6. A member of the middle class

His inflection and grammatical usage alone will reveal these characteristics, and further analysis of his speech will tell more about him. The child in school reveals as much about himself by his language as does our fictitious John Jones mentioned above. He may reveal more, because he is not, at least in his early years, sophisticated enough to try to disguise his origins. Thirteen-year-old Bobby may demonstrate daily that his family and neighborhood culture is lower-class and uneducated. Because most teachers are like Jones, middle-class and college-educated, children like Bobby are under considerable pressure in our schools. The English they learn at home is "wrong" in the school, while the middle-class language pressed upon them is just as "wrong" in their homes.

A nine-year-old boy of a lower-class home was frequently scolded for using vulgar and profane language on the playground. Finally after some really horrendous epithets, he was soundly paddled by the stern principal. When she asked him if he were going to talk that way again, he replied tearfully "Yer G——— d——— right I'm not!"

Speech patterns are not easily altered.

The teacher has, of course, an obligation to bring up the language level of his students: this is one of the school's functions. He must recognize, however, that the cultural background is a primary factor in the development of the child's language usage, and that no one is easily or happily separated from his culture. This awareness may not make the teacher's task easier, but it should help him deal with the problems more intelligently and less emotionally.

One culture group influencing every child is his peer group, or more accurately, peer groups. The peer culture is strong at every age, but probably reaches its height of power in the adolescent years, when the teenager is struggling to find a place for himself in his own society. Conformity is the price of belongingness, and this is demonstrated in language usage as clearly as it is in dress and social behavior. If the peer group rejects good English usage, no amount of exhortation by teachers will bring about good usage. Fortunately, groups change with age, individuals drift from one group to another, and by maturity the adolescent is likely to identify with a group appropriate to his abilities and background.

One phase of peer group language behavior is the use of slang, which may alternately amuse, mystify, and distress adults. Some slang is colorful, lively, and picturesque; some is crude, vulgar, and scatological or sexual in implication. An esoteric slang vocabulary frequently develops in minority groups or strong in-groups of any kind—G.I.'s in wartime or jazz musicians, for example. Adolescent peer groups borrow freely from such groups and also develop their own terms. The slang of a particular group gives the members a feeling of belongingness and thus of security, and does no real harm although occasionally objectionable terms are used; these are often borrowed without a real understanding of their implications.

Most teachers wisely ignore slang, at least outside the classroom. Occasionally an ambitious teacher wages a campaign against it; he is doomed to failure. Sometimes, too, a teacher, especially a young one, will try to join an adolescent group verbally and use their slang; he too is doomed to failure, for slang is somewhat ludicrous outside the group and it changes faster than he can learn it. Yesterday's slang is more to be scorned than the clothing fashions of a decade ago.

COMMUNICATION AND ADJUSTMENT

One of the significant differences between man and lower animals is the ability to verbalize. When the child develops a vocabulary and verbal facility, he frees himself from the limitations of nonverbal logic. The advantages inherent in this are tremendous. He learns to carry out both public and private manipulations with words, which produces results impossible to achieve by dealing directly with objects themselves. There are, in addition to the advantages, some problems inherent in this operation. As Johnson says, ". . . man seems to be the only creature who can talk himself into difficulties that would not otherwise exist" (Johnson, 1946) [17]. What kinds of problems does the gift of words engender?

Language and Conformity

One of the penalties of being a verbal—and thus a social—creature is loss of some individuality of attitudes and some privacy. In order to communicate, the child must speak as others speak. In acquiring understandable sounds (words) he also acquires ready-made attitudes, beliefs, and values. What he acquires in association with others he carries over to his private life, somewhat modified by his own needs, and developmentally, by his own experiences. Every individual who learns to talk thus achieves a certain amount of socialization and gives up a certain amount of individual uniqueness.

Because socialization is so dependent on language, it is important that the person's perception of the language he uses be close to that of others.

> Sharing one's responses and attitudes overtly with other persons is the most effective way of bringing them into line with those of the prevailing cultural patterns. Reactions which for any reason are left uncommunicated and unshared with others are likely to play a leading part in behavior pathology because they lack this controlling influence. . . . The child or adolescent, if he has learned to seek his chief satisfactions in the asocial techniques of passive observation and covert fantasy, is certainly in graver danger of misusing these techniques later on than the ones whose predominantly overt, shared satisfactions follow the design of his culture, and include the reciprocal behavior of his fellow human beings. In popular terminology, we say that the former's attitudes do not correspond to "reality," by which we mean that they are not oriented adequately to the field of shared social operations. (Cameron, 1947) [6]

It seems apparent that this kind of conformity is a prerequisite to good adjustment. The school can aid development here by providing adequate language instruction at every level and by encouraging individual students to share their ideas, attitudes, and feelings. This is especially important in the early years of life.

Language as Symptom of Emotional Problems

Because speech is a function of the whole person, it is not surprising that clinical behavior syndromes are frequently discovered among persons manifesting various types of language disorders. The clinical literature is too complex and extensive to review here (McCarthy, 1954) [21], but some general observations may be of value.

As noted earlier in the chapter, emotional disturbance is one of the causes of speech problems. One pediatrician, experienced in treating speech-defective children, describes four major categories of emotion-linked problems (Allen, 1947) [1]. After eliminating the physically handicapped and mentally deficient, he identifies these types:

1. Delay in learning to speak. This is often present in a "protest child" who has rejected food in infancy and who has always been difficult.
2. Babylike speech in the older child. This is a frequent result of overprotection.
3. Variations in speech function due to being deprived of emotional dependence.
4. Stuttering, in which an emotion is mismanaged by being throttled down.

These difficulties are all symptoms of inadequate emotional development or status.

Among older children and adults, language problems other than speech deficiencies appear. Johnson describes three of these aberrations as high verbal output, low verbal output, and linguistic rigidity (Johnson, 1946) [18].

The people in the high verbal output group talk nervously and incessantly to conceal truth, to avoid silence, or to attempt to reach a state of certainty about everything. This technique reflects basic insecurity and anxiety; truth, silence, and uncertainty are feared because the individual feels unable to cope with his world.

People who talk very little may also be struggling with insecurity. They are, in general, Johnson feels, more demoralized and convinced of their inferiority than the first group. Silence for them is a kind of protection against revelation of their unworthiness. Neither quietness nor talkativeness should be construed *by itself* as suggesting maladjustment. Only in the context of total behavior should such judgments be made, and then with caution.

Rigidity of various sorts is a frequent concomitant of personality maladjustment. Verbal rigidity may take the form of *content* rigidity—the range and variability of conversational topics; of *formal* rigidity; monotony of sentence structure, style, word usage, and mannerisms; or of *evaluational* rigidity—persistence of verbally expressed beliefs, attitudes and values. Such verbal behavior may range from a boring personality characteristic to a near-psychotic state.

Another characteristic of linguistic individuality is the verb-adjective ratio. This is a kind of "activity quotient," determined by dividing the total number of verbs in a speech sample by the total number of adjectives. The higher the ratio, the more "active" the speech.

This ratio has been used as a measure of personality characteristics, especially of emotional stability. School children who are rated by their teachers as being unstable tend to use more verbs in their speech and to have higher ratios. This higher ratio is also noted in chronically anxious patients in psychotherapy (Boder, 1940) [4].

It is in the psychosis schizophrenia that maladjustment is most dramatically revealed in language. Schizophrenia is not a single clearcut disease with specific symptoms, but many different psychotic states which have in common a loss of contact with reality. Many schizophrenics are typified by emotional "flatness," confusion of sense and nonsense in language, lack of self-criticism, and confusion in the abstracting process. They may use meaningful words but do not make sense because the words are unrelated to a central topic or, frequently, to each other. This speech pattern is sometimes described as "word-salad." In some cases the psychotic person coins new words or combines parts of words into "neologisms" which sound impressive but are meaningless. Other schizophrenic children may be entirely mute. Church (1961) [8] describes these children as never having been able to use language to come to grips with reality.

It is a long way from delayed or babyish speech to schizophrenic "word-salad," but both may be recognized as symptoms of general behavioral maladjustment. It is obvious that diagnosis and treatment of language malfunctions should be referred to well-trained professionals, and should not be undertaken by amateurs—that is, by classroom teachers. The teacher has, however, an important function in creating conditions in which good language skills will flourish, and in referring to experts children with problems.

LANGUAGE IN THINKING AND LEARNING [4]

Language may facilitate thinking, by making it more complex, effective, and accurate. When a child learns a new word in a meaningful way, he acquires the concept that underlies the word. As he uses the word (and thus the concept), over- or under-generalization will be corrected by experience, thus rendering the concept more accurate and precise.

The child learns not only words, as we have pointed out, but the linguistic forms larger and smaller than words. These linguistic forms symbolize concepts of classes of experience themselves, and are combined in a lawful way. By means of grammatical constructions, it is possible to

[4] A useful review and discussion of concept attainment may be found in Sigel, I. E., "The attainment of concepts," in Hoffman, M. L., and L. W. Hoffman, 1964, *Review of child development,* Vol. 1. New York: Russell Sage Foundation. Pages 209–248.

learn, remember and manipulate more complex concepts than would otherwise be possible. Some examples might be: "the boy's hat," "herbivorous mammals," and "preoccupation with litigation."

The process of reasoning consists largely of formulating steps in an inferential process in terms of language. It is difficult to gather evidence on the effectiveness of language in the operation; nevertheless, the content of reasoning processes can frequently be stated only in verbal terms.

In problem solving, the learning of a concept verbally ("middle-sized" for example) may be highly related to the child's performance on a task which otherwise might depend largely on trial and error. Language also helps in various tasks where perceived impressions have to be "stored" and remembered.

Can language ever inhibit or misguide thinking? This would seem to be the case when verbal labels are deceptive; the phenomenon has been demonstrated both in everyday observation and in experimental studies. Verbal labels are not useful either, when they fail to refer to a well-learned class of experiences: attempts to teach people to recognize visual patterns by assigning nonsense labels to them have not been successful.

Written Language

In our society, reading is a communication skill which is very nearly as important to the individual as his speech. It is a high-level, symbolic, psychomotor skill like speech; the symbols are seen rather than heard, written rather than spoken. In complexity, it is one stage beyond speech and develops from the base of language comprehension acquired in learning verbal communication.

Because reading is a high-level skill, it is not learned by all children readily or with ease. But no difficulties should be regarded by the school as too great to overcome, in order that all children might learn. The penalties for illiteracy in our society are extensive in their emotional, social, and even economic consequences. The illiterate person lives in a sense on the fringes of society; he is a stranger in a strange land, whose customs and truths are never fully revealed to him.

Who can learn to read? Almost everyone. There are particular, individual problems, but most difficulties, even low intelligence, are not a bar to literacy. The present authors have seen mentally deficient children in institutions reading mail from home, and have read letters written by persons with intelligence so low as to preclude much formal schooling of a traditional nature.

Reading Is a Complex Skill. First, visual processes must be mature enough to enable the reader to see the letters with ease. Second, an understanding of the functions of words must be present, as well as an adequate vocabulary. Third, the relationship between printed symbols and word-concepts must be developed: this is a rather high-level intellectual operation. Finally, of course, experiences must occur which will result in meaningful combining of these operations.

There is a maturational limit below which this complex operation is impossible. The point at which it becomes possible—when "readiness" exists—varies for each child, because learning to read is a function of the child's total development (Olson, 1940) [27]. For most children this age is reached at about six and one-half years, but it may occur much earlier or later. As noted earlier, girls reach a state of readiness earlier than boys, and retain their advantage.

Once the basic skill has been achieved, reading vocabulary increases at a very rapid rate. It is difficult to estimate the total vocabulary, but some attempts have been made. In one study, recognition vocabulary grew from an average of 23,700 words in grade one to 80,000 in grade twelve (Smith, 1941) [31]. This is, not surprisingly, higher than the estimates of childrens' oral vocabularies.

A number of studies indicate that reading difficulties often accompany emotional problems in childhood, either as cause or as symptom. McCarthy has identified two reading disability syndromes: one, the aggressive predelinquent type with severely rejecting parents, and the other the shy, submissive, withdrawing child with severely overprotective parents (McCarthy, 1961) [21].

Because it results from the interaction of so many factors, reading skill varies a great deal among individuals at every age level, and problems in this area are numerous. There is no single cause of reading difficulty, as some popular writers would have the public believe, nor is there a single cure. The diagnosis and treatment of reading deficiency calls for the services of experts who are acquainted with the total development of individual children as well as with the techniques of learning (Robinson, 1952) [3].

Learning to write naturally occurs later than learning to read; for most children, some skill is attained by age eight. Writing requires the same readiness as does reading, plus considerable finger coordination. Improvement with maturity and practice is shown by the greater length of sentences (see Figure 12.1) and by a gradual reduction of errors.

SUMMARY

Communication is a major aspect of human behavior. From the time an infant learns that he can affect others by his cries, he works steadily to develop his communication skills. Learning and maturation interact to effect this improvement which appears in the form of increased intelligibility, deeper understanding, and improved vocabulary and sentence structure.

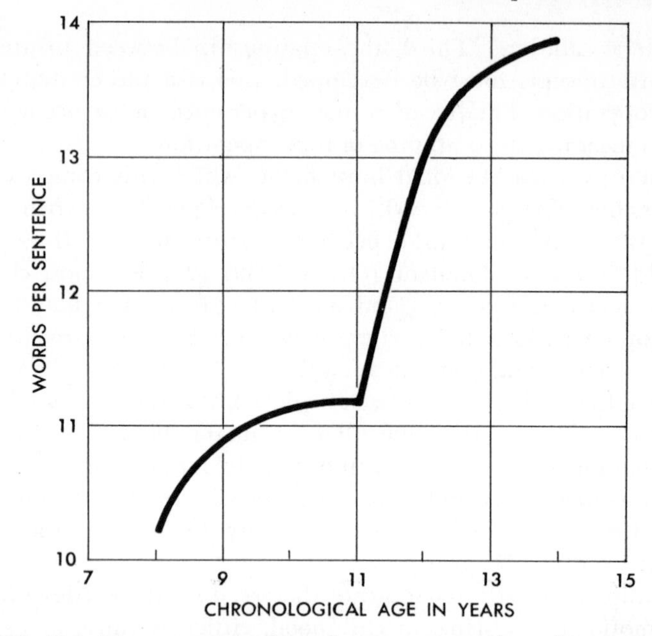

FIGURE 12.1. Mean number of words per sentence in written composition. From Millard [24], C. V., *Child growth and development* (rev. ed.). Boston-D. C. Heath and Company, 1958.

Motivation and personal and environmental factors cause great individual differences in performance. These differences appear not only in academic learning but in social behavior and personal adjustment.

Suggested Collateral Readings

Brown, R., *Words and things*. New York: The Free Press, 1958.

Church, J., *Language and the discovery of reality*. New York: Random House, Inc., 1961.

Lewis, M. M., *How children learn to speak*. New York: Basic Books, Inc., 1959.

Piaget, J., *The language and thought of the child*. New York: Humanities Press, Inc., 1952.

Smith, D. E. P., and Patricia M. Carrigan, *The nature of reading disability*. New York: Harcourt, Brace & World, Inc., 1959.

Weir, Ruth H., *Language in the crib*. The Hague: Mouton and Co., 1962.

Whorf, B. L., *Language, thought and reality*. New York: John Wiley & Sons, Inc., 1956.

References

1. Allen, I. M., 1947, Defect of the speech functions in childhood. *New Zealand Medical Journal,* **46:** 297–307.
2. Baldridge, M., 1949, Three decades of language study. *Childhood Education,* **26:** 117.

3. Berko, J. and R. Brown, 1960, Psycholinguistic research methods, in Mussen, P., ed., *Handbook of research methods in child development.* New York: John Wiley & Sons, Inc.
4. Boder, D. P., 1940, The adjective-verb quotient: A contribution to the psychology of language. *Psychological Record,* **3:** 309–343.
5. Brown, R., and Ursula Belugi, Three processes in the child's acquisitions of syntax, in Lenneberg, E. H., ed., *New directions in the study of language.* Cambridge: The Massachusetts Institute of Technology Press. Page 161.
6. Cameron, N., 1947, *The psychology of behavior disorders.* Boston: Houghton Mifflin Company. Pages 86–87.
7. Carroll, J., 1964, *Language and thought.* Englewood Cliffs, N.J.: Prentice-Hall, Inc. Page 8.
8. Church, J., 1961, *Language and the discovery of reality.* New York: Random House, Inc.
9. Darcy, Natalie T., 1963, Bilingualism and the measurement of intelligence, review of a decade of research. *J. genet. Psychol.,* **103:** 259–282.
10. Dawe, H. B., 1942, A study of the effect of an educational program upon language development and related mental functions in young children. *J. exper. Educ.,* **II:** 200–209.
11. Ervin, Susan M., and W. R. Miller, 1963, Language development, Chapter III in Stevenson, H. W., ed., *Child psychology.* Chicago: National Society for the Study of Education. Page 108.
12. ———, 1963b, page 116.
13. ———, 1963c, page 116.
14. Hess, R. D. and V. Shipman, 1965, Early experience and the socialization of cognitive modes in children. *Child Develpm.,* **36:** 869–886.
15. Irwin, O. C., 1960, Infant speech: effect of systematic reading of stories. *J. Speech Hear. Res.,* **3:** 187–190.
16. Jensen, Bonnie E., 1951, Parent-child resemblances in eight intellectual functions. Unpublished Master's Thesis, Iowa State University.
17. Johnson, W., 1946, *People in quandries.* New York: Harper & Row, Publishers. Page 268.
18. ———, pages 244–467.
19. ———, 1956, *Your most enchanted listener.* New York: Harper & Row, Publishers. Pages 189–190.
20. Lewis, Helen B., 1941, Studies in the principles of judgments and attitudes: III. The organization of prestige suggestion. *J. soc. Psychol.,* **14:** 229–256.
21. McCarthy, Dorothea, 1961, Affective aspects of language learning, in *Newsletter, Division of Developmental Psychology.* Washington, D.C.: American Psychological Association. Page 8.
22. ———, 1954, "Language development in children," in Carmichael, L., ed., *Manual of child psychology.* New York: John Wiley & Sons, Inc. Pages 492–630.
23. Millard, C. V., 1958, *Child growth and development.* Boston: D. C. Heath and Company. Chapter 7.
24. Milner, E., 1951, A study of the relationships between reading readiness in grade one school children and patterns of parent-child interaction. *Child Develpm.,* **22:** 95–112.

25. Mowrer, O. H., 1958, Hearing and speaking: an analysis of language learning. *J. Speech Hear. Dis.,* **23:** 143–151.
26. ———, 1960, *Learning theory and symbolic processes.* New York: John Wiley & Sons, Inc.
27. Olson, W. C., 1940, Reading as a function of total growth of the child. *Supplement to Educational Monographs,* **51:** 175–179.
28. Piaget, J. and Barbel Inhelder, 1958, *The growth of logical thinking from childhood to adolescence.* New York: Basic Books, Inc.
29. Raph, Jane B., 1966, Language development in socially disadvantaged children. *Rev. Educ. Rsch.,* **35:** 396.
30. Robinson, Helen, 1952, Fundamental principles for helping retarded readers. *Education,* **52:** 596–599.
31. Smith, M. K., 1941, Measurement of the size of general English vocabulary through the elementary grades and high school. *Genet. Psychol. Monogr.* **24:** 311–345.
32. Terman, L. M., 1925, *Genetic studies of genius, I.* Stanford: Stanford University Press.
33. ———, and Maud A. Merrill, 1937, *Measuring intelligence.* Boston: Houghton Mifflin Company. Pages 302–303.
34. Van Riper, C., 1963, *Speech correction,* 4th ed. Englewood Cliffs, N.J.: Prentice-Hall, Inc. Page 36.

CHAPTER 13

Development of Peer Relationships

From the time a child begins to venture away from the protection of home and mother, one of the most insistent problems facing him is that of getting along with his peers. It is a problem which demands at least a partial solution every time he encounters another child. It cannot be evaded or long postponed.

If the problems of peer adjustment are great, so are the rewards. Parental or other adult love and protection, although essential to sound development, does not offer the same kinds of satisfactions as do good relations with peers. Both are of paramount importance and neither is a substitute for the other. Acceptance, friendship, status—these come to mean more and more to the developing child until by adolescence the desire for them will have become a major need.

More than personal satisfaction is involved. Even from preschool age a youngster's concept of himself, his personal worth, and his place in society are strongly influenced by the attitudes his peers express toward him. His values, morals, and beliefs reflect the standards of his peer group. He cannot, in short, enter happily and effectively into the society of adults without first having been a member in good standing of the society of children and then of adolescents.

Learning to get along with peers is one of life's important "developmental tasks." What is a "developmental task"? Havighurst defines it as a task that arises at or about a certain period in the life of the individual, successful achievement of which leads to his happiness and to success with later tasks, while failure leads to unhappiness in the individual, disapproval by the society, and difficulty with later tasks.

The child moves out from the family circle into the world of his age-mates at the beginning of middle childhood. This is a move from a situation in which the child gets emotional security by his close relations with his mother and

> other family members into a new world where he must make a place for himself among a group of age-mates or "peers," all more or less competing for the attention of one "mother person" or "father person"—the teacher or adult supervisor. The child must learn to get more and more satisfaction from his social life with age-mates.
>
> The process of learning to get along with age-mates is really the process of learning a "social personality" or acquiring social stimulus value. The child learns ways of approaching strangers, shy or bold, stand-offish or friendly. He learns how to treat friends. He learns what it means to "play fair" in games. Once he has learned these social habits, he tends to continue them throughout life. Consequently, the nine- or ten-year old shows what he will be like, socially, at fifty. (Havighurst, 1952) [14]

A number of questions about the mastery of this task will suggest themselves to the teacher who is daily an observer and sometimes (whether willing or not) a participant in peer group activities. What techniques does the child use in acquiring social skill with peers? How does the home situation and early experience in general influence his relations with age-mates? What can be expected by way of social behavior from preschoolers, elementary children, children-becoming-adolescents-becoming-adults in junior high and high school? What effects are exerted on social behavior by personal characteristics? Finally, what can—or should—the school do to help? It is the purpose of this chapter to examine some answers to these and related questions.

STUDYING SOCIAL BEHAVIOR

Social behavior may be viewed or classified in a variety of ways. One useful approach to understanding the social functions of a particular child is to examine the following three aspects of his behavior.

1. The effect of his presence or behavior on other people—his characteristics as a *social stimulus;*
2. The way he reacts to the presence and social behavior of other people—his characteristics as a *responding organism;*
3. The *interaction* of these two sets of variables.

It is possible to make some progress toward understanding 1 and 2 above simply by observing the child in various situations. To gain any insight into 3, however, somewhat more sophisticated techniques are required.

Sociometry

"Sociometry" is a generic term for any device used to measure dynamic social interaction. The first sociometric tests were devised by J. L.

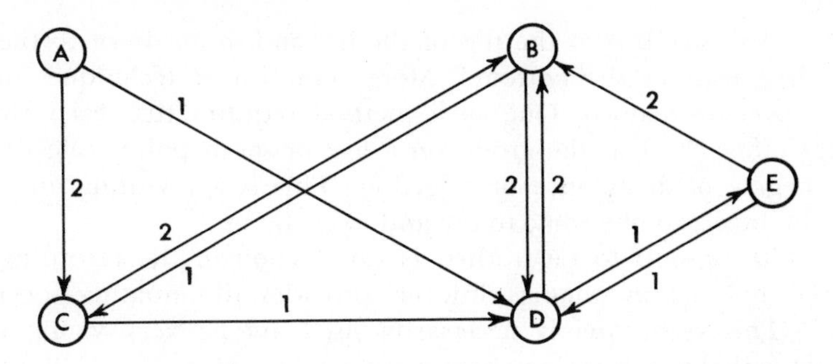

FIGURE 13.1. A sociogram. In this situation *D* is highly chosen, while *A* is chosen by no one. (The first and second choices are indicated by the numbers *1* and *2* respectively.)

Moreno (1934) [29]. In general, children (or adults for that matter) in a group situation are asked to make choices among the group members. These choices are then analyzed by techniques which reveal the group structure and the interaction within the group. To illustrate, in one study of leadership in an elementary school, the following directions were used:

You are seated now according to directions your teacher has given you. The neighbor who sits beside you is not chosen by you. You are now given the opportunity to choose the boy or girl whom you would like to have sit on either side of you. Write down whom you would like best; then, whom you would like second best. Look around and make up your mind. Remember that next term your friends you choose may sit beside you. (Jennings, 1950) [22]

From these choices a sociogram, or chart, can be constructed showing the choices as in Figure 13.1; then a tabulation of the number of choices received by each individual can provide an index of his status in the group—his sociometric status.

In the years since it was developed, a great number of variations on the original technique have evolved, literally hundreds of studies have been made with these devices, and a journal with the name *Sociometry* has been founded.

Other Approaches

One variation of the original technique is to ask each respondent for negative choices—for children with whom he would *not* want to associate. Although this yields useful information, it may crystalize existing antipathies among children and thus have an undesirable effect on behavior.

Various kinds of rating scales are used. Some are simple ranking devices, for example, "Rank the members of your Scout troop, placing the person you like best at the top of the list and so on down to the person you like least at the bottom." More complicated techniques of rating have been developed. One such method requires that each child rate every other child in the group on a five or seven point scale describing the degree of acceptance or rejection. This is a revealing and reliable system, but is cumbersome to use and to evaluate.

If the group to be studied is small enough, the recording of observed interaction among children provides illuminating social-choice data. This technique is necessarily used among very young children whose verbal responses may be untrustworthy.

The "Guess Who" technique is often used to study children's impressions of each other. A number of descriptive statements are used, for example, "This person never wants to wait for his turn," and children are asked to "guess" which child in his group is being described. Used in conjunction with sociometric devices it provides revealing descriptions of individual children, plus evaluation of admired and disliked traits.

Evaluation of Social Maturity

Although social maturity is a little difficult to define, it is clear that behavior patterns change with maturation and experience, and that some ways of behaving and some skills are characteristic of certain ages.

Needing a scale to evaluate the social accomplishments of mentally retarded children, Edgar Doll developed the Vineland Social Maturity Scale (Doll, 1946) [11]. This instrument consists of a series of rating scales arranged in a developmental sequence, grouped according to the ages at which certain behavior patterns typically appear in most children.

In use, a competent observer rates the child's behavior on a series of items like those in Figure 13.2. Then the child's "social age" is computed in much the same fashion that his "mental age" is computed on a Binet-type intelligence test. That is, his performance on each item is compared to that of a normative population of selected children of different ages. His "S. A." describes his social performance in terms of an age-group which he is most like. Although the scale was developed originally for use with mentally deficient populations, it has been widely applied to normal populations in research studies, and to individual children in clinical studies.

Social measurement has not reached the level of intellectual measurement, nor is it likely to. However, techniques developed in the last thirty years, such as those above, have provided us with a considerable body of data which can help us to gain insight into the growth and development of social relations, into the dynamics of interpersonal relationships, and into some techniques for helping children in their adjustment.

Now let us examine some of the accumulated evidence.

Age Level	Behavior
0–1	"Crows," laughs
3–4	Buttons coat or dress
6–7	Goes to bed unassisted
9–10	Goes about town freely
12–15	Plays difficut games
18–20	Has a job or continues schooling

FIGURE 13.2. Selections from the Vineland Social Maturity Scale. From Doll, E. A., *Vineland Social Maturity Scale*. Minneapolis: Educational Test Bureau, 1936. Used with permission.

PREPARATION FOR LIFE WITH PEERS

Some of the characteristics of social behavior have been discussed earlier, in Chapter 8. Early socialization comes primarily from the family. For most children, social horizons soon broaden. As soon as possible after the child learns to walk, he begins to get around the neighborhood under his own power. His education in the larger world begins at this point, and persons other than family members begin to contribute to his socialization.

> The moment he steps out of his home unaccompanied, the child loses his status as a privileged and protected individual, and becomes merely one more individual in the neighborhood. The patterns of friendliness, aggression, and defense he now encounters are different, and less predictable for him than the ones in which he was reared. Other children are apt to be casual and unconcerned about him, or surprisingly hostile and critical. Differences that arise are usually settled directly between the contestants without adult intervention or, if adults do mix into a squabble, it is often only to aid their own child. Friendly adults treat a neighborhood child more objectively than his parents do, more like a person, less approvingly but less critically, and with quite different emphases. (Cameron, 1947) [7]

The kind and quality of adjustment the child makes to the society of his peers and others is determined to a considerable extent by the preparation he gets at home. Family structure, functioning, and influence will be discussed in some detail in Chapter 14, "Child-Family Relationships," but the home's influence on development of peer relations should be examined here. Research on child-rearing practices and on children's social adjustment in nursery school reveals some common types of home atmospheres and accompanying behavior patterns. The term "atmosphere" in such research refers to ways in which observers perceive parents interacting with their children in terms of warmth, possessiveness, severity, interference, and the like. Three of these "atmospheres" are called *democratic, indulgent,* and *authoritarian* (Baldwin, 1949) [2]. Accounts of the school experiences of children from these different types of homes may help to reveal some of the relationships.

Margaret is the younger of two children in a *democratic* type of home. Her parents have always spent a considerable amount of time with her and her brother. The children play freely through the house in a noisy, boisterous, and carefree manner. They are seldom punished and there are frequent displays of affection among the family members. Margaret enjoys nursery school. She did not appear to miss her mother when school began, and she entered at once into the activities of the group. With the other children she is active and socially outgoing, sometimes friendly and sometimes hostile and aggressive. Her bossing is usually successful and if not, she quickly takes a new task. Her home experiences have encouraged her to engage in activities demanding originality, intellectual curiosity, and constructiveness. The workers in the school feel that in time, she, like her brother before her, will learn to control her nonconforming and aggressive ways and will maintain a favorable status in the group.

Kevin is the only child of a couple in their middle thirties. Both parents are highly intelligent college graduates whose main interests are in artistic and intellectual pursuits. Kevin has had the best of physical and medical care and has been supplied with carefully chosen "educational" toys, books, and activities. His parents love him but rarely fondle or play with him and in general maintain a rather detached attitude toward him. His play activities are somewhat restrained in the carefully kept home. He has been impressed with the necessity of keeping himself clean, picking up his toys, being polite, obedient, and in general "grown up." Discipline is strict in the home, for Kevin's parents disapprove of children who are dirty, noisy, rude, and disobedient.

Kevin has been amenable to his parents' ways and maintains the same kind of behavior in nursery school that he does at home. He conforms to the requests of teachers, is quiet, well behaved, and nonresistant. He gets along reasonably well with the group, but tends to be dominated much of the time by freer and less restrained children such as Margaret. His work and play is lacking in originality and fancifulness. Kevin is a "good boy," obedient and pleasant, but too passive and incurious to learn from and enjoy his peer group as much as he should. He is a product of an *authoritarian* type of home atmosphere.

Mark resembles Kevin in his lack of aggressiveness. Instead of conforming and being agreeable, however, he is often sullen and resentful, and gets along with neither his nursery-school peers nor his teachers. He is one of three children of a relatively young couple who operate a successful appliance business

together. Neither parent has much education and both came from lower-class homes. When his mother brought him to the school, he cried, clung to her, and refused to join the group for some time. Investigation by the school staff revealed that his home is of the *indulgent* type. At three and a half, he is still fed by his mother most of the time when she is not working, or by her younger sister who lives in the house and babysits for her keep. His diet is poor because he eats only what pleases him and he fills up on candy, cake, and soft drinks between meals. He is taken on weekly toy-buying expeditions, which elicit little pleasure from him. His father says, "I know Mark is spoiled but I had it so tough when I was a kid that I want mine to have it easy." His wife agrees with him. Mark is physically fearful, sulky, and withdrawn when he is with the group, and is showing little progress or improvement.

Home atmospheres exist in many other "dimensions" besides those illustrated above. There are, for example, authoritarian-indulgent, authoritarian-rejectant, and the like. Home atmospheres, like individual personalities, are much too varied to fit a handful of labels. In addition, one would have to be extremely naïve to suppose that any one factor is *the* determiner of behavior. We can conclude, nevertheless, that home atmosphere has much to do with early social adjustment.

The time of the child's emergence into the world of peers is also influential in his adjustment. By reason of geographical isolation, physical incapacity, or parental intent, many children are delayed in making their early contacts with other children. They are likely then to be inferior in social techniques and skills to other children their own age who had an earlier start.

If the social patterns developed in early childhood ended or were altered readily by school age, the problems would not be so important. Such is not the case, however. Social patterns tend to persist, and the child who gets off to a bad start acquires a reputation which will follow him from class to class and he will continue to make a poor social adjustment unless he is given help (Hurlock, 1955) [21]. The proper function of the home is described by Cameron:

> If a child is to get the most out of his social operations in the wider community, he must above all have a secure and dependable home base, one that he can leave without anxiety, one he can return to confidently for supplies, repairs and reassurance. The protection of home is necessarily limited in scope . . . therefore, every child is bound to suffer rebukes, belittling, discrimination, mishandling, and downright defeat from time to time at the hands of his associates. If, however, he can be sure of his home, if life there provides emotional security and support when he needs them, a child can learn to weather frustration and correction at home and by using the same general techniques that he acquired there. (Cameron, 1947) [8]

PEER RELATIONS IN CHILDHOOD[1]

If the child's physical neighborhood and home situation permit, he will be somewhat experienced in dealing with his peers by his third or fourth year. If not, he will be forced into their company by the demands of school at age five or six. Gradually, the peer group increases in importance and the family influence diminishes. Let us examine the typical changes in behavior through the developing years, recognizing as always that what is typical may not be true for a specific child.

Early Childhood

We have already discussed the "moving outward" from the home in the early life of the child. What does the child do when he gets away from adults and spends his time with his peers? Ask him, and he will say, "I play." The child's play in his principal source of social experience in early life, and free play is particularly valuable to him because he can make social contacts without the controls and structuring of the home or school. Before age two his play is likely to be solitary, even if there are other children in the same room or close by. This is called *parallel play,* since no interaction is taking place. After two, the child may take time out from his own play to watch others or may even attempts to capture from another child a toy which interests him.

From three and four years there is an increase in social play. Toys are shared—although the sharer may make his toy contribution involuntarily: fights are frequent but brief at this age and are usually over playthings. As verbal skills and practice in taking turns increases, the fights decrease in number.

The child's first playmates are likely to be provided by his immediate neighborhood and will be accepted by him without much regard for sex, race, or other characteristics. By age four or so, however, he is beginning to show much more definite selectivity in choices. Sex, age, race, intelligence, and other factors begin to weigh in his preferences. Because of his limited mobility he may have to accept whatever children the neighborhood offers, or do without companionship. The desire for playmates is so great that many lonely children resort to imaginary playmates where none exist.

Carl was an only child whose home was in a neighborhood of older couples without children at home. He rarely had an opportunity to play with other

[1] A good discussion and review of the literature on this topic may be found in Campbell, J. D., "Peer relations in childhood," in Hoffman, M. L., and L. W. Hoffman, 1964, *Review of child development research,* Volume 1. New York: Russell Sage Foundation. Pages 289–322.

children. At three and a half, he invented a pair of imaginary playmates, whom he called "Big Pal" and "Little Pal." They accompanied him everywhere, participated in all his play, and even went to bed with him. After some months he reached the point where he refused to eat unless two extra places were set for his friends. His distraught mother, fearing that something was seriously wrong with him, sought professional help. She learned that his behavior was common to young children and was advised to find real playmates for him. She enrolled him in a nursery school, and the imaginary friends gradually diminished in importance in his life and eventually disappeared.

If the child is reasonably fortunate in his home atmosphere and opportunities for companionship, he will be experienced in cooperative play by the time he starts school. He will have lost some of his self-centeredness, will be able to share and to take turns, and will still stand up for his rights and be a leader part of the time.

Middle and Later Childhood

Whether well or poorly prepared by early experience, the school-age child channels an increasing amount of effort and attention into relations with his peers. There are strong forces at work here, some external and some internal. The external forces are the pressures of the playground and the classroom which force him to conform to the standards and ways of the group. Whether he wishes to or not, he *must* take his turn, he *must* suppress his wishes part of the time in favor of some other child, he *must* dovetail his own activities into those of others.

More important than environmental pressures in molding social behavior are internal forces or motives. The child soon learns that a substantial part of his enjoyment of life depends on his relations with his peers and his status in the group. Thus he is not only forced but actively *desires* to be accepted by the group, and eagerly molds his behavior to fit his perception of what will please his peers.

The result of this combination of forces and experiences is the existence of a very effective learning situation: a strong motive, daily practice, and a fairly clear system of reward or reinforcement (acceptance) or its lack (punishment or nonacceptance). It is not at all surprising, therefore, to find that the peer group plays a growing part in the life of the child, and gradually supplants much of the influence of parents, teachers, and other adults.

It is imperative that success in this "task" be achieved in the early school years. Psychologists have learned that there is an optimum period of life for learning most skills, and that delay leads almost surely to inferior achievement. Millions of children have committed to memory the lines:

> There is a tide in the affairs of men
> Which, taken at the flood, leads on to fortune;
> Omitted, all the voyage of their life
> Is bound in shallows and in miseries.[2]

The "floodtide" for social learning occurs early in life.

Peer Groups

The "peer group" has been described as an "aggregation of people of approximately the same age who *feel* and *act* together" (Havighurst, 1953) [15]. It is, of course, first of all a play group which furnishes companions for games and sports—companions who, unlike adults, are of approximately equal skill and strength and who provide a fair test of each child's capacities.

It is more than a play group, however. It is the *reference* group which determines many of his standards. (The term "reference group" is used by social scientists to denote a group to which an individual looks for rules or norms of behavior.) As he gets well into middle childhood, the peer group vies with his parents and teachers in many contexts as the arbiter of right and wrong, good and bad, acceptable and unacceptable. He does not, of course, suddenly abandon all that he has been taught at home and in the classroom. He simply has another perspective when he examines a situation—the perspective of his own society. Thus, the question of whether or not the boy should wear a cap to school, or the girl a skirt and blouse instead of a dress, is likely to be viewed as it may affect standing in the group. "What will the kids say?" "What will the other kids wear?" are questions which they ask themselves in addition to "What does mother (teacher) want me to do?" If they never asked these questions, or acted on them, they would never grow up socially and emotionally. After all, when their father buys a hat, is he not likely to ask himself, "What are the other fellows at the office wearing?" in addition to, "Is it warm and comfortable?"

There is both gain and loss in this socialization. The child must give up a little of his individuality to be acceptable socially. He must, some part of the time at least, curb demonstrations of superior development or abilities, and must attempt to raise some of his characteristics to fit those of the group. The loss of some individual uniqueness is perhaps regrettable, but there is no alternative in our society.

Partly as a result of group pressures and partly as a result of maturation, there is general improvement of social behavior in the early grades of school. In his association with adults the child who was brash, boisterous, and noisy at six has become more responsible and more trac-

[2] Shakespeare, *Julius Caesar,* Act IV, Scene 2.

table socially by age eight or so. Within his own group, his early experiments in integrative behavior have either been successful so that he is acceptable, or have failed and have left him still struggling for recognition and acceptance.

The Gang

By third or fourth grade the large and changing play groups of children will have coalesced into a number of groups with fairly consistent membership. Each of these groups is likely to be referred to by the members themselves as "the gang." This is not to be confused with the delinquent gang of adolescents, but is rather a group of boys or girls who regularly play together. It is the specific, rather than the general peer group for the children who make up its membership. It may be small in number with only three or four members, but is likely to be larger, simply because the larger group provides more members for playing games and doing things.

The existence of the gang is most apparent to adults in the play activities of children. Boys play various sorts of ball games, go exploring, build shacks or airplanes or boats—and occasionally engage in pure mischief directed against adults or rival groups. Girls are more likely to spend their play time in passive activities—talking and gossiping, playing with dolls, listening to phonograph records, going to movies and the like. The girls' groups tend generally to be smaller than the boys', perhaps because they engage less in game activity requiring teams.

In the years of later childhood, adult-supervised groups become important to many children, especially those of the middle class. Boy and Girl Scouts, Campfire Girls, and similar organizations provide some of the satisfactions of spontaneous gangs (except for exclusiveness) together with constructive activities and adult guidance.

Friendship and Popularity

One of the needs of the child seems to be that of forming warm, personal ties with someone outside of his family, someone in his peer group. Next to affectionate relations with parents the experience of close friendship with other children is probably of primary importance in developing the capacity for love and affection in adulthood.

On what basis are friends sought and chosen? In the early years, propinquity or availability is the principal factor. By later childhood there is more freedom and mobility, and real choices can be made. Through all the grade-school years, children tend to choose their friends primarily from their own sex group. Friends tend to be somewhat alike in many ways. They resemble each other in social class, ability, physical status, and other observable traits. More important are the similarities of a psychological nature such as the tendency toward similar social perception and like interests (Davitz, 1955) [10].

Choosing another child for a friend does not guarantee that he will reciprocate. Sociometric studies frequently reveal these one-way choices; one child will seek the company of another, associate with him as much as possible and call him "friend" while the chosen child will be bored, indifferent, or even hostile to his admirer. Studies of friendships suggest that children seek others who would seem to satisfy some psychological need; and if satisfaction occurs, the friendship is likely to continue. When needs change, choices will change also (Thompson, 1952) [39]. Because of stabilization of personality and interests, there is a steady decrease in the variety or number of friends with age (Figure 13.3) (Horrocks and Buker, 1951) [20].

Because of the individual and personal nature of psychological needs, any listing of individual traits leading to acceptance or rejection is likely to be somewhat misleading. However, in sociometric studies published over the years, certain characteristics or traits appeal regularly in association with highly chosen children. Some of these traits are: cheerfulness, cooperativeness, friendliness, kindness, honesty, generosity, even-temperedness, and good sportsmanship (Austin and Thompson, 1948) [1].

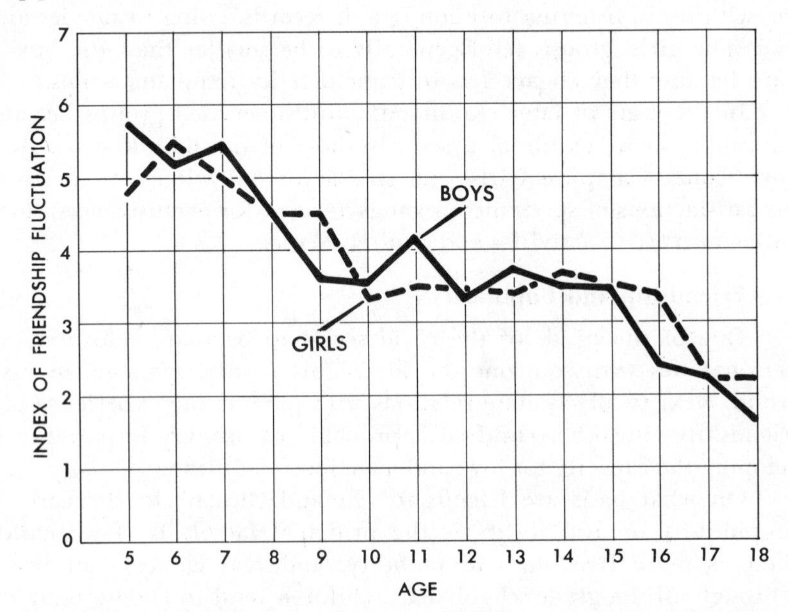

FIGURE 13.3. Relationship between chronological age and friendship fluctuation for an urban sample of 585 boys and 647 girls. From Horrocks, J. E., and Mae E. Buker, A study of the friendship fluctuations of preadolescence, *J. genet. Psychol.* 78: 139, 1951. Used with permission of The Journal Press.

A simple cause-and-effect relationship cannot, of course, be inferred from the existence of such lists. The causes of behavior, as noted before, are multiple, complex, and interrelated. Popularity may stem in part from the pleasant traits listed above, but is it not also true that it is relatively easy to be cheerful, cooperative, friendly, kind, honest, generous, even-tempered and sportsmanlike if one is liked admired, and highly chosen? Here again we see the effect of *interaction* between the child as social stimulus and the child as a social response organism. Popularity and acceptance by peers are qualities which develop through time, and thus tend to be cumulative. The child who has satisfying early play-group experiences gains skills and techniques which help him make new friends and gain further experience. The unfortunate child who, because of personal characteristics, home environment, or other factors does not learn to get along with peers in early childhood is likely to suffer from progressive rejection. The vicious circle leads from early play-group failures to further isolation which results in failure of normal social development and greater social rejection. It is apparent that such a child needs early and continuing help to avoid this cumulative social failure.

Longitudinal sociometric studies give evidence of the constancy of social acceptability with increase in age. In one study, socially acceptable children were distinguished from those socially unacceptable from the second to the fifth grade. The similarity of "acceptance" scores of the same children was high from grade to grade: from second to third, the correlation was .84, from third to fourth it was .77, and from fourth to fifth it was .67. For these particular children the magnitude of the correlations was nearly as great as that for intelligence test scores from grade to grade (Bonney, 1943) [4].

Although acceptability remains fairly constant, the characteristics which determine it change somewhat with age. At each stage of development the peer group values a particular pattern of personality and behavior, and the more closely a child approximates this "model" the more likely he is to be popular, or at least accepted.

For example, in one study, highly esteemed first-grade boys were "real boys"—good at games, daring, good sports, not bashful. By third grade the traits of fairness and leadership were valued, while by fifth grade the chosen boys needed to be good looking, not bashful, and "real boys." First-grade girls who were highly chosen were those who were quiet, not quarrelsome nor bossy, who in general acted like "little ladies." By fifth grade acting like a lady had little social value: at this age good looks, good sportsmanship, friendliness, tidiness, and the like were at the top of the list (Tuddenham, 1952) [41].

At first glance it may seem contradictory to say that popularity or acceptance is relatively constant, while admired traits change steadily. What actually happens, of course, is that the highly chosen children adapt readily to changes in themselves, their peers, and their environment, and thus maintain their positions over a period of time.

Leadership

Leadership is a phenomenon distinct from popularity. Leaders tend to be popular, but not all popular children are leaders. Who are leaders then, and what are they like? Two separate theories have been posed to answer this question: First, the leader is a dynamic and dominant person who bends others to his will, and second, the leader is a person who is particularly sensitive to the needs of others and who helps them achieve their goals. The evidence gathered by social psychologists and other researchers would suggest that there is a strong element of truth in each theory, and that leadership in a specific situation is really the product of interaction between a particular kind of person and a particular group situation. In late childhood, leaders have been found to be somewhat above average in most desirable traits, such as intelligence, scholastic achievement, physical size, and skill, and in personality traits such as dependability, responsibility, and the like. The situation has been summarized in these words:

> The average person who occupies a position of leadership exceeds the average member of his group to some degree in the following respects: sociability, initiative, persistence, knowing how to get things done, self-confidence, alertness to and insight into situations, cooperativeness, popularity, adaptability and verbal facility. (Stogdill, 1948) [36]

Although experience and status or prestige achieved as a leader in one context has some carryover to a new situation, it should be noted that as the situation changes, so does the leadership. For example, the child who is usually the organizer and director of play and games may become a humble follower in the classroom situation or in a special interest area such as music, where he may have little skill.

One consistent characteristic of leaders is their social perceptiveness, their awareness of the desires and needs of others. This quality outweighs any other personality trait or facet (Bell and Hall, 1954) [3].

PEER RELATIONS IN ADOLESCENCE

Before discussing adolescent social behavior, two facts should be considered. One is that the social aspects of adolescence are in large part the product of a specific culture, and that generalization to other cultures or sub-cultures is not safe. Although certain basic phenomena—such as the rapid rise of the sex drive—are universal, little else is constant from one culture to another. The second and related fact is that most of our evidence on adolescent social behavior is derived from studies of middle-class, school-attending teen-agers. Although this is the group of major concern to secondary teachers, it by no means represents the total adolescent population. About 90 percent of children between the ages of fourteen and seventeen are in some kind of school. Compulsory attendance laws keep most of the younger members of this group in school, but attrition increases rapidly after legal school-leaving age, which is fifteen or sixteen in many states. Of every 100 children who enter the fifth grade, 67 will graduate from high school (Statistical Abstract of the U.S., 1965) [33].

This out-of-school group rarely appears in research reports other than those dealing with delinquency. With these reservations in mind, let us examine some aspects of adolescent peer relations.

Although the fact of adolescence is basically physical, its significance in our culture is primarily social. As noted earlier, allegiance is gradually transferred from home and parents in early childhood to agemates and the outside world in adolescence. The process is natural and necessary in our society. It is, however, resented or feared by many parents and other adults as they see themselves losing their influence with adolescents, especially as this influence is supplanted by the immature standards of the peer group.

Why does the adolescent cling so fiercely to his peer culture? The answer lies in our contemporary society. In many primitive groups some kind of test or ceremony marks formal entry into the society of adults. In the earlier agrarian phase of our national development young men and women could marry and set up their own homes about as soon as they were physically ready. In our modern, complex industrial society the point at which a young person is ready to be completely independent is much less clear. In the dominant middle class, especially, a long period of training and of at least economic dependence is necessary in preparation for successful and productive maturity.

The adolescent today then really has little choice. His maturing body tells him that he is no longer a child, as a result he rejects his childish, dependent relationship to the adult world. But his parents and teachers refuse to accept him as their equal because of his inexperience. Thus, rejecting childhood and being rejected by adult society, he can find acceptance, status, and social satisfaction only among his peers, who share his condition. Without his peer group as a reference, his life has little focus, stability, or meaning.

General Social Change

Adolescence sees both constriction and expansion of social relations. Social *expansion* occurs as the greater freedom and mobility of these years make possible acquaintance with a new and more varied group of persons of both sexes. Social *constriction* occurs as the teenager becomes more finicky and selective in his choice of companions.

Instead of being tied to the closeknit gang of childhood, the adolescent has a greater number of social contacts of varying degrees of intimacy. He is first of all a member of what has been called a "set"—in effect, the total population from which he finds it possible (or desirable) to choose friends and associates. The set may be made up of adolescents of similar characteristics: the politicians, the brains, the wolves. Or it may be formed of youngsters with similar future plans, as those who are aiming for college. Another group might be those who have been rejected and who draw together in their distress. Interest may be a factor. Social class is a powerful selection criterion in this developmental stage (Stone and Church, 1957) [37].

The principal social group is the "crowd." It is larger than the gang and by later adolescence is likely to include members of both sexes. The earlier gang supplied members for play and games. The crowd supplies members for social activities—and in our contemporary society just about everything the adolescent does is social: going to movies, dancing, watching athletic contests, even studying and eating.

Within the crowd there are likely to be several "cliques"—groups of three or four especially close friends. In early adolescence these cliques are usually composed of one sex, but later on they frequently include both sexes, sometimes two or three dating couples.

Some of these groups are formalized into clubs, fraternities, or sororities. More often they are not. Formal or informal, the closeknit group has a positive function in giving the adolescent emotional satisfaction which comes from "belonging," in giving him a group of peers of like status and interests on which to practice his social and ideational skills, and a standard by which to measure his own behavior and accomplishments.

The group gains its character not only by including certain persons, but also by excluding others. To the members, one of the real values of the clique is its exclusiveness. To be a member of the "in-group" provides the satisfaction of viewing all those others in the "out-group" as less desirable; thus, the self-esteem of the members is enhanced. This is a cruel business, but it is the way of youth.

A study of 800 adolescents in one community revealed (by means of factor analyses of activity reports) the existence of a number of very nearly discrete social groups, based on role, socio-economic status, and preferred activity. Some of the major groupings were

1. A group, largely lower-class and of lower ability, emancipated from home and assuming adult roles;
2. A higher socio-economic group of high moral code and conformity to home and school ways;
3. A nonemancipated home-, school-, and community-centered group;
4. A group whose ways derived mostly from very low socio-economic status.

There were ten groups in all, each reflecting a way of life deriving from shared background and interests (Phelps and Horrocks, 1958) [31].

> A good deal of the misery and heartache of youngsters during the school life arises out of this fact of exclusion. Their infinite longing for acceptance, and their inability to rely wholly on themselves, make approval in the form of admission to a group the indispensable ingredient of happiness. To be left out, to be disregarded or passed over, is misery indeed . . . let the reader beware before taking the amused view that these are the quaint customs of adolescents only. They are the "quaint customs" of the adult world, too. What else is the country club, the club of any sort, but an adult expression of a tendency first seen in adolescence? (Farnham, 1952) [12]

Friendship, Status, and Popularity

Friendships become more intense and more stable in adolescence (see Figure 13.3). In the early part of this period friends are usually of like sex; some very deep relationships of this kind continue into late adolescence and indeed into adulthood. By middle to late adolescence friendships with the opposite sex have developed, and especially in the late years very intense attachments are common. However, when the adolescent speaks of friendship, and especially of a "best friend," he is almost sure to be referring to a member of like sex. The social distance between the sexes is still generally too great to allow the easy camaraderie and personal (as distinct from physical) intimacy possible between members of like sex. As one teenaged girl commented, "It is taken for granted that your best friends are of your own sex—boys have boys and girls have girls for best friends. . . . You *can't* tell everything—all your troubles—to a boy the way you can to a best friend. Boys *can't* be best friends" (Kuhlen, 1952) [27].

Friendships are no longer made solely on the basis of individual likes and dislikes; the friend must not only be congenial to the person making the choice but must also be acceptable to members of his crowd. This is true to some extent of relationships between the sexes, but is especially true of like-sex friends. Thus, friends generally have high similarity of ideals, interest and values (Thompson and Nishimura, 1952) [40].

The relationship between best friends is frequently very intimate. They seem inseparable, unable to function without each other, and they spend every available moment together. Their interdependence is exhibited by their need for constant communication. When they are separated by circumstances, they have almost immediate recourse to the telephone to continue their examination of what (to the adult) seems trivial and unworthy of consideration. Apparently they feel secure only when they have some kind of contact with each other.

The search for popularity and security leads the adolescent to experiment, to broaden his social horizons, and to form attachments with a variety of persons. This experimenting is especially apparent in the early stages of interest in the opposite sex.

Some of these attachments—probably the majority—are healthy and beneficial to both parties. Occasionally, however, a particular adolescent will come deeply involved in a relationship with someone of like or opposite sex which may disturb his parents and teachers. These unwise attachments (if indeed they are as unwise as the concerned adults feel) are the product of many forces. One, of course, is the poor judgment of the young adolescent, who has relatively little practice in choosing and evaluating his own companions. Another cause lies in his search for security. Being accepted by an exciting, glittering, sensational companion may give promise of status and acceptance by the previously cold group. Insecure and unhappy adolescents are most likely to lose their orientation and values in such situations. Marynia Farnham, a psychiatrist specializing in work with adolescents, cites the following case:

> This was true of Josie, a youngster in her very early teens who was the despair of her parents because of her incorrigible determination to associate with youngsters considerably older than herself and of very unsavory reputation. Her parents regarded her as unmanageable. And it was a fact that no matter what they said or did Josie continued to pursue her own course. . . . She was beginning to develop a great deal of interest in what boys thought of her, and was susceptible to almost any kind of influence. . . . The difficulty was that this youngster could be counted upon to follow the request of any boy who paid her the slightest attention. This was a situation obviously made for trouble. The young boys who were not themselves too well established, promptly began to take advantage of her easy compliance. The rest of the story can be easily imagined. (Farnham, 1952) [13]

Fortunately, Josie was given professional treatment. It was apparent that she felt unloved and unworthy, and was eager to do anything to get love and attention. Most adolescents do not require psychiatric attention, but from the foregoing account it becomes clear that some attachments are the products of the needs of the individual, rather than of the attractive characteristics of the sought-after partner.

What characteristics make for social acceptance? Obviously, popular and highly accepted youngsters are high in desirable traits and the rejects are low in these traits. To examine these differences, an intensive study was made of the social characteristics of 122 students in a California high school (Jones, 1953) [23]. The high and low groups were identified by a rating system, and were then compared on eleven variables. The significant findings were as follows:

1. *Skeletal age.* Chronological age was not a factor, but skeletal age was relatively advanced for high-mention boys and low-mention girls. (It has been pointed out earlier in the text that early maturity is an advantage for boys and a disadvantage for girls.)

2. *Behavior ratings.* Boys and girls in the high-mention group were described as more buoyant, poised, and as having prestige. The high-mention girls were more expressive, but there was no difference in this characteristic between the boys' groups. Both boys and girls in the prominent group were mentioned by adults as making a good impression on the basis of appearance and grooming.

3. *Reputation ratings.* Not surprisingly, the high group was judged on a sociometric test to be well above average on all prestige traits—popularity, friendliness, humor.

4. *Drive ratings.* Both sexes in the high group were found to have relatively high drive characteristics, but these were significant only for boys on the need for recognition and for control.

5. *Intelligence.* Differences in intelligence were not significant between the high and low groups.

6. *Physical abilities.* As in intelligence, no significant differences were found between groups for either sex.

7. *Socio-economic status.* The influence of this factor was slight.

Numerous studies of qualities making for popularity have been reported. There is much commonality in these reports, but differences do appear between them. The reason that there is no universal list of popular traits is that qualities are valued differently within various groups. Physical skill, for instance, was not a differentiating factor in the superior, urban high school described above. In a small rural school it might well have had a more powerful effect. The same could be true for social status, intelligence, and other factors.

Leadership

The characteristics of leaders in adolescence are highly similar to those of leaders in childhood as described earlier in this chapter. Leaders are popular, but not all popular adolescents are leaders. Leaders tend to be superior on most measured traits; one newly important characteristic is personal attractiveness. Leaders in adolescence need to be nice looking, well groomed, and must wear attractive and acceptable clothing (Stogdill, 1948) [36]. Although leaders in primary, elementary, and intermediate grades are not different from their followers in adjustment, leaders at the secondary level have been found to be significantly better in personal adjustment than their followers (Marks, 1957) [28].

Teenagers in one school characterized their own high-school leaders in slang terms. Girl leaders were described as "big wheels": they were seen as attractive, as style setters, and were found to have higher interests in science than nonleaders. Boy leaders were described as having "good-guy" qualities: they had high social interests, were popular, accepting of others and were prominent in athletics (Terrell and Shreffler, 1958) [38].

SEX-SOCIAL DEVELOPMENT

Although sexual motivation is basically glandular in origin, it is so molded and structured by cultural taboos and customs that it must be considered largely as a social phenomenon. Both of these forces—physiology and culture—begin to influence behavior early in life.

Early Development

The child takes an early interest in his body, and in the course of play discovers that he can produce pleasurable sensations by stimulating the erogenous zones of his body. Thus, marked sex responses occur very early and tend to continue throughout development. He also exhibits interest in the differences between his own body and those of other children and adults. Some—perhaps most—children engage in a certain amount of sex play throughout childhood. Some of this play is simply exploration, but in other children it seems to be truly sensual in nature. However, masturbation is the principal sexual outlet through all the developing years (Kinsey *et al.*, 1948 and 1953) [24, 25].

The sexuality of childhood is generally ignored in our culture. Cultural pressures are great, however, on children in the area of "acting like a boy" or "acting like a girl." These pressures result in what Havighurst describes as the developmental task of "learning an appropriate masculine or feminine sex role" (Havighurst, 1953) [16].

There is little if any physiological reason for different behavior between males and females until late childhood. Our culture, however, insists that boys and girls behave differently, learn different "sex roles."

These sex roles are learned in a multitude of ways. Boys and girls are treated differently by their families, are given different clothing to wear and different toys to play with.

Teachers and playmates further reinforce the child's concept of appropriate behavior in later childhood. Often there are local (subculture) versions of permissible behavior.

Jill grew up in the suburb of a city noted for its big-league ball team. There was an almost continuous pickup ball game going on in a neighborhood lot, with players of both sexes and all ages, ranging from toddlers to their fathers. A child, to be accepted, had to play ball and play reasonably well. Jill was as skilled as most boys her age, and was among the first to be chosen in games or other social situations.

When Jill was eight, her family moved to a distant small town. When she tried to participate in the ball games, she was rebuffed by the players—all boys —and was ridiculed by the girls. The teacher supervising the playground told her that playing ball was for boys, and that girls should be more ladylike.

Jill had a miserable first year in her new community, trying to adjust to a new concept of appropriate feminine behavior.

On the whole, girls probably have a somewhat easier time of learning their sex role than do boys. For one thing, less aggressive, daring, venturesome behavior is ordinarily expected of girls. In addition, the girl has a greater variety of models than does the young boy. In much of our urban and suburban society, the boy has few contacts with men until he is nearly in adolescence. He is raised by his mother; his father may go to work before the boy gets up and return after he is in bed at night, and may frequently be busy or absent on weekends; the boy's elementary teachers are usually women; even his Sunday School and Cub Scout leaders are female.

In much of modern middle-class society, male and female roles overlap to a confusing degree. Both parents may be employed, they may share the housework, either mother or father may paint or make repairs about the house, either may be the disciplinarian or the affection-giver. It is small wonder that insecurity about the sex role exists in many children.

Despite the difficulties, the task must be accomplished. Satisfactory relations with the same sex are impossible if the child fails to act out the appropriate sex role, and later heterosexual adjustment will be even more seriously handicapped. Much more is implied, of course, than just "acting out." There must be an internal feeling of security, acceptance, and satisfaction in being a boy or a girl. Most children, of course, accomplish this without undue strain, but teachers should recognize the existence and difficulty of the task among their charges.

Dating

Dating behavior, which starts in most groups around the age of pubescence, serves several needs. Obviously, dating provides opportunities for some sexual stimulation and satisfaction. This "satisfaction" does not necessarily include organic sexual release (although this may occur). The satisfaction provided is more likely to be in the nature of shared social experience, emotional acceptance, and "valuing" by a member of the opposite sex, plus generalized sexual pleasure such as is found in body contact in dancing.

More is involved than sex, of course. From pubescence to maturity, social activities center increasingly around small, bisexual groups. Parents become less and less acceptable as escorts, and even a like-sex chum is not regarded as a desirable companion on all occasions. Thus, a date is a social convenience, or on occasion a social necessity.

In addition, being invited or accepted as a dating partner is evidence of acceptable personal qualities—evidence that the teenager in our society wants and needs deeply. It offers at least limited proof of popularity, of acceptability, of possession of those traits valued in the society of young persons. An avid interest in dating may thus occur in a youngster (more likely in a girl than in a boy) who is too immature physically to have much interest in the opposite sex.

In early adolescence, boys' and girls' cliques tend to join forces on occasion; within this mixed-sex group some couples pair off while some boys and girls remain unattached. Thus, social experience is gained within the supporting framework of a familiar group. This early group dating tends to occur at about thirteen or fourteen, and because of earlier maturation, the girls tend to be the aggressors. The boys, although more interested than they appear to be, are often shy and ill at ease with the girls. As confidence is gained, the large groups are replaced by two- or three-couple associations, and by middle to late adolescence much dating is done by the couple alone.

In recent years, the pattern has been changing somewhat. For one thing, dating starts earlier. The most striking change is the high incidence of "going steady" at a very early age. Some years ago "going steady" was a late and serious phase of dating, and was frequently the last step before engagement and marriage. In many communities today youngsters begin to "go steady" almost as soon as they date at all. Emotional involvement is not a necessary part of the arrangement; in many cases (perhaps a majority in the early teens) it is simply a matter of convenience and social security—a partner is always available for social affairs. These steady arrangements may be dissolved and replaced by others many times during the dating years—a sort of serial monogamy in dating (Herman, 1955) [19].

Adolescent Sexual Behavior

Although sound data on individual sexual behavior are hard to come by for obvious reasons, a sizable number of studies have been made. Perhaps the best known of these are the Kinsey studies. Although these reports have been widely criticized, especially for poor sampling procedures, the findings are suggestive and the reports are generally consistent with other similar studies and with reports of individual clinicians (Kinsey *et al.*, 1948 and 1953) [24, 25].

Masturbation, of course, is the principal outlet for both sexes; 92 percent of boys reported the practice and 40 percent of girls. More than a third of boys reported one or more homosexual experiences; we will have more to say about this later.

Despite moral, religious, and legal strictures, a high proportion of adolescents engage in premarital intercourse. When the naturally strong biological urges are combined with social stimulation (such as the Hollywood image of "love"), steady and solitary dating with one person, and an automobile to remove the couple from adult supervision, the results are inevitable.

Obviously, many teenagers come through these experiences unscathed emotionally and with little behavioral effect. Any counselor or youth worker knows, however, of many who are not so fortunate. Guilt and anxiety are inevitable when mores and laws are flouted. A pattern of behavior once established is difficult to change. Reputations, too, are hard to live down. Sympathetic aid and understanding are needed more than censure and condemnation.

One of the practical problems arising from illicit sex relations is pregnancy.

The rate of illegitimacy has been rising for many years. In 1940, the rate of illegitimate births per thousand live births was 7.1. By 1963, the figure was 22.5, more than triple the earlier report. Births to unmarried mothers under fifteen numbered about 2000 in 1940; 5400 were reported in 1963. For the fifteen- to nineteen-year group the total went from 40,500 in 1940 to 101,800 in 1963 (Statistical Abstract of the U.S., 1965) [34].

High School Marriage

High school marriage is a phenomenon allied with but in part separate from the pregnancy problem. In a survey of high schools in one Western state it was found that 90 percent had one or more marriages during the year. Ten times as many girls as boys were married in these schools. (Teenage girls rather typically marry a man who is older, poorly educated, and who has already left school.) In the schools surveyed, 2.4

percent of the sophomores were married, 4.0 percent of the juniors and 5.7 percent of the seniors (Christiansen, 1958) [9]. In 1960, the number of married high school students in the United States was over a hundred thousand; by 1964 the total was nearly twice that (Statistical Abstracts of the U. S., 1965) [35].

In a study in a Midwestern state, it was learned that nearly 40 percent of the high-school brides were pregnant at the time of marriage, and it was assumed that fear of pregnancy or guilt over relations was a factor in many others (Burchinal, 1959) [5].

Although there are many factors—socio-economic, emotional, environmental—in these early marriages, there is one consistent and striking difference between the married (whether pregnant or not) and the unmarried. Girls who marry in high school begin to date and go steady earlier, have a greater number of steady boy friends, and report themselves in love with a greater number of steadies than do the unmarried girls (Burchinal, 1959) [6].

It is not the writers' purpose simply to view with alarm, although some aspects of adolescent sexual behavior are alarming. It is rather to point out that learning a sex role, getting along with the like and the opposite sex, dating, and making a satisfactory adjustment to sexuality is a serious business and one of consuming importance to the adolescent. It is also, in many cases, too difficult a problem for him to handle without help from home, school, and community.

Homosexuality

Homosexuality is probably a disturbing topic to most individuals. Why should it be considered in a book devoted primarily to the development of normal persons? The answer is that in the course of normal development many children have erotic experiences with like-sex playmates, and some of these children unfortunately settle on homosexual activity as their preferred outlet.

We know that a great many children, prior to or early in adolescence, engage in genital play with like-sex companions. In addition to the exploratory experiences of childhood, about 37 percent of boys and 10 percent of girls are reported to have one or more homosexual experiences during adolescence (Kinsey *et al.,* 1948 and 1953) [26]. Any experience common to so many persons (even assuming a considerable amount of inaccuracy in reporting) cannot be ignored or treated as a rare variant of normal behavior.

Whether the origin of the behavior is due to hereditary influences, unsatisfactory relations with the like- or opposite-sex parent, early traumatic experience, or some combination of these and other causes is not clear at present. Neither is there any explicit, agreed-upon treatment.

What are the implications of these facts for the teacher? First, he must recognize that from one to three or four out of every ten adolescents have had some homosexual experience. Second, the great majority of these youngsters seem to escape any serious or long-lasting effects. Third, some adolescents (an increasing number, according to some authorities, are developing homosexual behavior as a way of life. This latter group needs help and needs it immediately, for homosexuality, like most aberrant behavior, is more likely to be responsive to treatment in its early stages. Finally, it must be said that this is a problem which for treatment must be referred to medically trained specialists.

THE TEACHER AND PEER ADJUSTMENT

It is apparent that getting along with peers is learned in a variety of ways and is influenced by many factors. The school is only one factor, but a major one. What can the teacher do to aid social growth? For the elementary teacher, Havighurst suggests:

> School is the place where most children work out the task of learning to get along with age-mates. Whether the teacher pays any attention to it or not, the child's chief concern is with this task. Often the key to understanding a child's difficulties with his school subjects, or to understanding a discipline problem in class, is given by a knowledge of his difficulties in achieving this particular developmental task.
>
> The skillful teacher studies and understands the peer culture of her school and community. She uses sociometric devices to learn the social structure of her particular class. She learns both to cooperate with the peer group in some of its activities, and to direct and control it at places where it may do harm to individual children. (Havighurst, 1953) [17]

Havighurst suggests that among adolescents, lower-class boys and girls are forgotten and neglected, and that the school has an obligation to help them.

> School and college people might as well get used to the idea that their institutions are laboratories for the learning of social skills. Becoming used to it, they might do some things to raise the level of accomplishment of this task, and to help some of the backward boys and girls. . . .
>
> The successful achievement of this task is especially important for lower-class boys and girls who want to rise in the social scale. . . . If the school aims to help . . . it must offer them opportunities to learn social skills.
>
> The secondary school and college should work largely through informal, nonacademic activities, such as clubs, parties, student government, athletics, music, arts.

He further suggests informal instruction in dancing, party behavior, entertaining, and planning parties. It is recommended that boys and girls of similar tastes and interests should be thrown together for the social activities of the school. Because girls mature faster than boys, it is necessary to break up the previously rigid grade separation to allow each sex to find partners or companions of similar developmental level (Havighurst, 1953) [18].

SUMMARY

Learning to get along with peers is one of life's important "developmental tasks"; social habits learned in childhood structure the behavior of the adult.

The atmosphere of the child's home prepares him well or poorly to get along with peers. The peer group gradually replaces the family as the reference group and as a source of acceptance and emotional support. Friendship and popularity within the peer group are determined by the interaction of the child's characteristics with the characteristics of the members of the group. The same is true of leadership, although leaders do tend to be somewhat superior to their followers in many ways.

The adolescent peer group is particularly important because this age group has rejected childish dependence but has not yet been granted equality by the adults. Thus, the peers offer status, acceptance, and social satisfaction not available elsewhere.

For healthy social development, it is necessary for the boy or girl to learn the appropriate sex role. Dating begins around pubescence, and soon becomes the major social activity. Adolescents need help in learning to control their sex-social activities.

The teacher and the school have a major role in promoting and guiding healthy social development.

Suggested Collateral Readings

Bernard, Jessie, Teen-age culture, an overview. *Annals Amer. Acad. Pol. Soc. Sci.,* **338:** 1–12, 1961.

Coleman, J. S., *The adolescent society.* New York: The Free Press, 1961.

Gronlund, Norman, *Sociometry in the classroom.* New York: Harper & Row, Publishers, 1959.

Havighurst, R. J., *Developmental tasks and education,* 2d ed. New York: Longmans, Green & Co., Inc. (David McKay Company, Inc.), 1952. Pages 17, 18, 33–37.

———, *Human development and education.* New York: Longmans, Green & Co., Inc. (David McKay Company, Inc.), 1953. Chapters 5 and 9.

Hurlock, Elizabeth B., *Child development,* 4th ed. New York: McGraw-Hill, Inc., 1964. Chapters 8 and 9.

Mussen, P. H., J. J. Conger, and J. Kagan, *Child development and personality.* New York: Harper & Row, Publishers, 1963. Chapters 11 and 15.

Pitts, Jesse, The Family and peer groups, in Bell, N. W., and E. F. Vogel, eds., *A modern introduction to the family.* New York: The Free Press, 1960. Pages 266–286.

References

1. Austin, M. C., and G. G. Thompson, 1948, Children's friendships: A study of the bases on which children select and reject their best friends. *J. educ. Psychol.,* **39**: 101–116.
2. Baldwin, A. L., 1949, The effect of home environment on nursery-school behavior. *Child Developmt.,* **20**: 49–51.
3. Bell, G. B., and H. E. Hall, 1954, The relationship between leadership and empathy. *J. abnorm. soc. Psychol.,* **49**: 156–157.
4. Bonney, M. E., 1943, The constancy of sociometric scores and their relationship to teacher judgments of social success, to personality self-ratings. *Sociometry,* **6**: 409–424.
5. Burchinal, L., 1959, Adolescent role-deprivation and high school marriage. *Marriage and Family Living,* **21**: 378–384.
6. ———, 1959, Comparisons of factors related to adjustment in pregnancy-provoked and non-pregnancy-provoked youthful marriages. *Midwest Sociologist,* **21**: 92–96.
7. Cameron, N., 1947, *The psychology of behavior disorders.* Boston: Houghton Mifflin Company. Page 41.
8. ———, pages 41–42.
9. Christiansen, H. T., 1958, Why all these young marriages? *National Parent-Teacher,* **52**: 4.
10. Davitz, J. R., 1955, Social perception and sociometric choice of children. *J. abnorm. soc. Psychol.,* **50**: 173–176.
11. Doll, E. A., 1946, *The Vineland Social Maturity Scale.* Minneapolis: Educational Test Bureau.
12. Farnham, Marynia F., 1952, *The adolescent.* New York: Harper & Row, Publishers. Pages 88–89.
13. ———, pages 94–95.
14. Havighurst, R. J., 1952, *Developmental tasks and education.* New York: Longmans Green & Co., Inc. (David McKay Company, Inc.). Pages 17–18.
15. ———, 1953, *Human development and education.* New York: Longmans, Green & Co., Inc. (David McKay Company, Inc.)
16. ———, page 18.
17. ———, page 19.
18. ———, pages 36–37.
19. Herman, R. D., 1955, The "going steady" complex: A reexamination. *Marriage and Family Living,* **17**: 36–40.
20. Horrocks, J. E., and M. E. Buker, 1951, A study of friendship fluctuations of preadolescents. *J. genet. Psychol.,* **78**: 131–144.
21. Hurlock, Elizabeth, 1955, *Child development.* New York: McGraw-Hill, Inc. Page 263.
22. Jennings, Helen H., 1950, *Leadership and isolation, a study of personality in interpersonal relations.* New York: Longmans, Green & Co., Inc. (David McKay Company, Inc.). Pages 10–11.
23. Jones, Mary C., 1953, A study of socialization patterns at the high school level. *J. genet. Psychol.,* **93**: 87–111.

24. Kinsey, A. C., *et al.,* 1948, *Sexual behavior in the human male.* Philadelphia: W. B. Saunders Company.
25. ———, 1953, *Sexual behavior in the human female.* Philadelphia: W. B. Saunders Company.
26. ———, *Sexual behavior in the human male,* page 624; *Sexual behavior in the human female,* page 452.
27. Kuhlen, R. G., 1952, *The psychology of adolescent development.* New York: Harper & Row, Publishers. Page 198.
28. Marks, J. B., 1957, Interests and leadership among adolescents. *J. genet. Psychol.,* **91**: 163–172.
29. Moreno, J. L., 1934, *Who shall survive?* Washington, D.C.: Nervous and Mental Diseases Publishing Company.
30. Oetinger, Katherine B., Report to National Conference on Social Welfare, *Des Moines Register,* June 16, 1959, page 10.
31. Phelps, H. R., and J. E. Horrocks, 1958, Factors influencing informal groups of adolescents. *Child Develpm.,* **29**: 69–86.
32. U. S. Department of Health, Education, and Welfare, Office of Education, 1957, *Progress of public education in the United States.* Washington, D.C.: U. S. Government Printing Office. Pages 5–9.
33. Bureau of Census, Department of Commerce, 1965, *Statistical abstract of the United States.* Washington, D. C. Pages 110–111.
34. ———, page 51.
35. ———, page 129.
36. Stogdill, R. M., 1948, Personal factors associated with leadership: A survey of the literature. *J. Psychol.,* **25**: 35–71.
37. Stone, J. L., and J. Church, 1957, *Childhood and adolescence.* New York: Random House, Inc. Pages 285–286.
38. Terrell, G., Jr., and J. Shreffler, 1958, Development study of leadership. *J. educ. Res.,* **52**: 69–72.
39. Thompson, G. G., 1952, *Child pyschology.* Boston: Houghton Mifflin Company. Page 468.
40. Thompson, W. R., and R. Nishimura, 1952, Some determinants of friendship. *J. Personality,* **20**: 305–313.
41. Tuddenham, R. D., 1952, Studies in reputation: I. Sex and grade differences in school children's evaluation of their peers; II. The diagnosis of social adjustment. *Psychol. Monogr.,* **333**.

CHAPTER 14

Child-Family Relationships

Reference has been made to the great variety of influences and conditions that contribute to behavior at any given time. The importance of parents as an influence on children's behavior may be inferred from the frequency of their mention in preceding chapters. It is the purpose of this chapter to answer some questions about the nature of parental influence and of child-family interaction.

Specifically, how do experiences in the months of infancy affect later behavior—or *do* experiences during this period influence behavior at all? What emotional and affectional climates seem most beneficial (or troublesome) in childhood? In adolescence? What are some common sources of conflict between children and parents. How does the presence of siblings affect development?

AFFECTIONAL NEEDS IN INFANCY

We have discussed the generally accepted theory of the origin of mother-child ties: in brief, the infant's physiological needs are satisfied by the mother and she becomes a symbol for need-reduction of any type. This learned need then generalizes to the presence of many different people. Although widely accepted, this theory leaves some behavior unexplained.

> It is entirely reasonable to believe that the mother through association with food may become a secondary-reinforcing agent, but this is an inadequate mechanism to account for the persistence of the infant-maternal ties. There is a spate of researches on the formation of secondary reinforcers to hunger and thirst reduction. There can be no question that almost any external stimulus can become a secondary reinforcer if properly associated with tissue-need reduction, but the fact remains that . . . such derived drives suffer relatively rapid experimental extinction. Contrariwise, human affection does not extinguish when the mother ceases to have intimate association with the drives in

question. Instead, the affectional ties to the mother show a lifelong, unrelenting persistence and, even more surprising, widely expanding generality. (Harlow, 1958) [24]

Many psychoanalysts attempt to explain the mother-infant relationship by positing a theory of the infant's *inherent* need for suckling at the breast or for being loved and fondled.

Unfortunately, the human neonate does not make a very satisfactory research subject because of his inadequate motor capacities, and because humane considerations prohibit treatment that might have ill effects. Thus, the various theories have remained theories only, each with some evidence in support, but none firmly enough grounded to eliminate the others.

Harlow has resolved many of these difficulties by using infant macaque monkeys as subjects for research. These small animals bear resemblances to human infants in most basic responses relating to affection, including nursing, contact, clinging, visual and auditory exploration, and the like.

Infant monkeys were first separated from their natural mothers immediately after birth: some were returned to their natural mothers; others were turned over to "wire mothers"—electrically warmed wire figures; a third group was given to "cloth mothers"—warm terry-cloth-covered wire forms. Some of the wire mothers and some of the cloth mothers had built-in nipples with a milk supply, while others did not, so that these infants had to be fed by laboratory attendants. Thus, attachment to a mother-figure as a function of hunger-satisfaction could be studied.

The results supported the hypothesis that contact comfort was the important variable rather than hunger reduction in the infant's attachment to mother. The wire mothers were biologically adequate but psychologically inept. The infant monkeys developed a strong sense of security from the presence of their cloth mothers (Harlow and Zimmerman, 1959) [26]. However, in other ways, they were no different from the infants reared in a barren cage. They became socially and sexually aberrant; they did not involve themselves in normal social play with peers, and with few exceptions did not display sexual and mating behavior, even when paired with normal monkeys of opposite sex (Harlow and Harlow, 1962) [25].

Let us turn now from monkeys to human infants, and their mothering needs.

Maternal Deprivation

A variety of physical, intellectual, and emotional disorders has been attributed to infantile maternal deprivation. Most of the reports of these disorders have been made by psychiatrists or by psychiatrically oriented child specialists.

In the influenza outbreak during World War I, thousands of young parents died, leaving infants who were necessarily placed in hastily organized institutions. Many of these infants died without apparent physical cause. The cause of death was attributed to a lack of fondling and loving, and was termed "marasmus." A sizable body of literature has appeared in the ensuing years setting forth in detail accounts of various ill effects of mothering deficiency. Bowlby 1952 [15] summarized the alleged effects: backwardness in talking, drop in IQ, poor locomotor balance, retarded physical growth, shallowness of emotional response, aggressiveness and distractibility, impairment of the capacity for abstract thinking, and inadequate capacity as a parent and neglect of children.

> . . . It is sufficient to say that what is believed to be essential for mental health is that the infant and young child should experience a warm, intimate, and continuous relationship with his mother (or permanent mother-substitute) in which both find satisfaction and enjoyment. Given this relationship, the emotions of anxiety and guilt, which in excess characterize mental ill-health, will develop in a moderate and organized way. When this happens, the child's characteristic and contradictory demands, on the one hand for unlimited love from his parents, and on the other for revenge upon them when he feels that they do not love him enough, will likewise remain of moderate strength and become amenable to the control of his gradually developing personality. It is this complex, rich, and rewarding relationship with the mother in early years, varied in countless ways by relations with the father and with siblings, that child psychiatrists and many others now believe to underlie the development of character and mental health. . . . Thus, a child is deprived even though living at home if his mother (or permanent mother-substitute) is unable to give him the loving care small children need. . . . Complete deprivation . . . has even more far-reaching effects on character development and may entirely cripple the capacity to make relationships. (Bowlby, 1952) [16]

Institutional care is usually regarded as the "worst and common" (O'Connor, 1956) [40] form of deprivation, but neglect may, as Bowlby suggests, occur in the home with the mother present.

Bowlby's rather grim conclusions have not gone unchallenged; there have been many reassessments (Ainsworth *et al.*, 1962 [1]; Casler, 1961 [21]; Yarrow, 1961 [57]), but consensus has not been reached on the meaning of the available evidence. A widely held view was expressed by O'Connor:

> Thus, whatever may be thought of the conclusion reached by Bowlby, it is considered on the basis of a re-examination of the evidence he presents that the hypothesis that children separated from their mothers suffer permanent damage must be considered as still a hypothesis. (O'Connor, 1956) [41]

Perhaps most crucial is the question of the permanence of any ill effects of infant-mother separation. Here again, the authorities are divided; one group regards the damage as irreparable; the other sees the probability of later recovery. If the ill effects are irreparable, then the parent or foster parent, the clinician or the teacher is faced with a situation in which caretaking rather than therapy or education is the appropriate treatment. If the effects are reparable, the child neglected in infancy may be regarded as simply one more child who has some specific behavioral problems and who will require specialized treatment.

We might note here briefly a later aspect of Harlow's studies of monkeys. In experimentally varied conditions, several groups of motherless infant monkeys were reared in close association—cages, play area, large play room—with one another. These young monkeys appeared at last report to be developing normally, at least in regard to infant-infant relations and in sexual relations. Harlow feels it is possible that optimal interaction with peers may compensate for maternal lack (Harlow, 1962) [25].

But to return to the "human condition":

> If it can be shown that major structuring of personality takes place after the first year or year and a half, clearly the contribution of infant experience in general and of those disciplines in particular to subsequent personality formation has been exaggerated by some therapists. We believe that this is the case. . . . The picture, however, is not entirely clear, and the honest investigator must confess that apparently discordant facts are faced at every stage of the inquiry. These facts must be reconciled, and not ignored, before any solution of the problem can receive general acceptance. (Orlansky, 1949) [43]

In the face of conflicting evidence and opinion, what useful inferences can be made by the layman, teacher or parent? It would seem that some such conclusions as the following would be justified:

1. The neonate and older infant have a need for body contact, fondling, and mothering that assumes the proportions of a major drive. The cause may be an inherited need, a learned one, or some combination of the two.

2. Thwarting the satisfaction of this need is undesirable and has deleterious effects on the infant in several aspects of development and adjustment.

3. These deleterious effects may be permanent, may be reparable, or may have some permanent and some temporary effects. Until such time as the accumulated evidence may prove otherwise, teachers should probably continue to act as if the effects of unfortunate early experiences could be ameliorated by proper care and training. After all, is not an attitude of guarded optimism part of the successful teacher's approach to problems?

Maternal Influence

It is to be hoped that most children are not deprived of the mother's presence in infancy, or later. But there is more to the relationship than presence or absence. Maternal behavior is a powerful force in the development of personality and behavior in general. For this reason, the child-mother relationship has been widely studied.

One of the more intensive longitudinal studies has been carried on at the Fels Institute. Some variables studies from infancy to maturity have been maternal protection, restrictiveness, hostility, acceleration, and the stability of these variables over time. Considerable differences have been found, both in treatment and in results, for boys and for girls.

The four maternal behaviors named above were not highly predictive of adult dependency, especially for men, and were poorer predictors of adult passive or dependent behavior than the child's own behavior between ages six to ten or ten to fourteen. Protection was a better predictor of passivity for boys, while restriction was better for girls. The authors note that mothers' protective reactions depend somewhat on the child's requests for nurturance: a very passive or dependent child will elicit more protection than a more independent one.

One of the most interesting findings was what the authors termed the "sleeper effect": the fact that maternal behavior during the first three years was more highly associated with child and adult behavior than similar treatment during ages three to six and six to ten (Kagan and Moss, 1962) [30].

In a report from the California Growth Study (Schaefer and Bayley, 1963) [47] other aspects of mother-child relations are examined, from infancy to adolescence. As in the Fels study, somewhat different results were reported for boys and for girls. For boys, significant correlations were reported between maternal love and sons' behavior to twelve years, but not later. For girls, on the contrary, maternal behaviors were unrelated to behavior from ten months to twelve years, but intercorrelations were found at adolescence. Unlike the Fels study, behavior in the first two years was generally unrelated to later behavior.

Differences in variables measured, populations studied, and evaluation techniques make generalization about *specific* influences of mother on child very difficult.

FAMILY PATTERNS AND PERSONALITY DEVELOPMENT

Although the mother is certainly the dominant influence on the child, especially in her child's infancy, it is only a matter of months before the entire family begins to exert molding influences on the child's developing personality. The human infant is so immature that years pass before he can survive without the care and protection of his parents; thus, it is inevitable that most of his early learning experiences are family centered. Anthropologists have identified many forms of family structures, each with its resulting "central tendency of personality." The family pattern of our society is labeled the "nuclear structure"—essentially the mother, father, and their children.

Because of the close and exclusive nature of the relationships in the nuclear family, emotional relationships between parents and children are exceptionally intense. This pattern of life has a number of typical results (Shaffer and Shoben, 1956) [49]:

1. Strong and intimate affective (emotional) relationships are produced.
2. Individualistic responsibility is enhanced and a sense of personal distinctiveness develops.
3. A sense of wrongdoing is created, and guilt and anxiety about behavior may exist even in the absence of others. This happens because the child's failure to live up to the models presented by the parents is often punished by real or threatened withdrawal of love.

The fact that our culture has a common family type does not imply, of course, that families are alike. Anyone who has had normal contact with many families will have observed different ways of accomplishing family tasks and will have perceived different atmospheres in the homes. It is accurate to say that every family is unique; however, studies of family relations reveal some general patterns of parental behavior.

Dimensions of Parental Behavior

Numerous studies have been conducted on family structure, attitudes, customs, and so forth. One of the most significant of these was a survey of 124 homes in which patterns of parental behavior were described, using the *Fels Parent Behavior Rating Scales* for the collection of data (Baldwin *et al.*, 1945) [3].

The *scales* were thirty separate rating devices designed to reveal the presence or degree of certain traits or characteristics of parents thought to be important in child adjustment. Parents (principally mothers) were observed in action with their children at home and were judged or evaluated on the scales by trained raters. Most of the homes were above population-average in social, educational, and economic levels.

When the data were analyzed, three major patterns revealed themselves: democracy in the home, acceptance of the child, and indulgence. It was further found that various combinations of these patterns existed in the different homes, as well as varying high or low positions on each.

A study of the most frequent combinations appearing in the homes of the study revealed three major categories or patterns which were labeled "rejectant," "acceptant," and "casual."

Rejectant Homes. About one-quarter of the homes were characterized as rejectant. In these homes there was little affection shown toward children; hostility and disapproval were expressed instead. These attitudes lead the parents to be generally autocratic in their dealings with their children rather than democratic or solicitous. Even within this classification, treatment ranged from nonchalant (ignoring) to dominant (hostile). The expression of rejection may take the form of neglect, separation, denial of advantages or privileges, punishment, threats, humiliation, and so on.

An abbreviated report of a case from the above study will serve to illustrate rejectant behavior.

Betty McKane: Active Rejectance

Mrs. McKane is fundamentally a selfish, ego-centric woman who evaluates events and people in terms of the extent to which they contribute to her own satisfaction. . . . When Betty was six months old, Mrs. McKane remarked: "I hate to sit and hold her . . . I don't care to hold babies . . . for some reason or other I never did."

. . . For Mrs. McKane the model child is the quiet, unobtrusive one. She attains this goal in two ways—by imposing on the child rigid standards of behavior which become habitual, and by meeting immediate situations with arbitrary commands. Throughout, there is a note of suspicion, as if the mother believed that her whole disciplinary policy would collapse unless constantly reinforced by fresh and more virulent commands. The measures taken to insure obedience (severe tone, harsh words, sarcasm, etc.) are as caustic as those many parents use as punishment after the fact.

If Betty eats an ice cream cone, her mother says: "I suppose you're going to spill that down the front of your dress." If Betty is sent upstairs to take a bath, Mrs. McKane says: "I suppose you're going to leave those dirty clothes all over the floor when you're through." If Betty starts out the door, she says: "I suppose you're going to leave the screen open and let every fly in town into this house." Always it is taken for granted that Betty, left to her own volition, will do something that is irritating to the mother or contrary to the accepted standards of the home.

. . . Second only to the severity of the atmosphere is the consistency of policy. "Nonsense" that may draw down severe punishment one time may on another occasion be laughed off, depending on Mrs. McKane's mood; she indulges in rough joking horseplay with the children when *she's* feeling good; but when the mood passes, she flares up with sudden anger and clamps down on the girls with heavy-handed parental authority.

. . . In reaction to this vigorous and constricting policy Betty has steadily become withdrawn, shy, and stubbornly resistant, in a passive fashion, to adult authority. At school her decorous and superficially docile behavior cannot be criticized, but in any situation which demands a response she retreats into an almost inaudible, "I don't know." Her bewildered, discouraged teacher says: "I just can't get at her—nothing seems to reach her." (Baldwin *et al.*, 1945) [4]

As is always the case, an individual child's response to a particular treatment cannot be predicted with accuracy. There have been many studies of rejected children, and some behavior trends do appear. In general, such children try in every way to gain affection. Failing in this, they engage in attention-getting behavior—hyperactivity, loud and boistrous shouting, striving for superiority on the playground or classroom, naughtiness, and even neurotic disturbances of body function or health. Seriously neglected or harshly treated children may even develop unstable or psychopathic tendencies.

Although parental attitudes of rejection must be condemned, it is important to recognize that some children react constructively to deprivation. They sometimes learn to amuse themselves, to satisfy their own wants, and to make satisfactory substitute social and emotional ties outside the home (Symonds, 1949) [53]. A wise teacher may capitalize on these possibilities.

Acceptant Homes. Another quarter of the homes in the study were labeled "acceptant," and although taking a variety of forms, they provide a much pleasanter picture than the rejectant group. Some were indulgent without being democratic, others were democratic without being indulgent, still others were democratic and indulgent.

In differing degrees and with different forms of expression, acceptant parents use sincerity and common sense in dealing with their children: they identify with them so they may understand their thoughts and feelings, they express their love and affection—as well as their impatience and displeasure—they take an interest in their children's pleasures and activities, they exercise firm, quiet, and consistent control over the children's behavior, they provide an orderly but not oppressive environment in which the children may develop optimally. Although few homes will be consistently and ideally acceptant, descriptions of children from such homes reveal the beneficial effect of this atmosphere; these secure children have desirable character qualities, they are friendly, enthusiastic, realistic, emotionally stable and in general well-adjusted, *good* children (Symonds, 1949) [54].

A description of a real, rather than an idealized, family situation illustrates the application of some of these principles.

Leonard Rampion: Warm Democratic

The Rampion household represents a rather happy combination of those factors judged by the authors to be productive of a "good environment" for a child. The parents themselves are well-adjusted, vital, outgoing; they enjoy children as such, and their own children as individuals. . . . The child occupies his proportionate place in the household, is a full member of the family group, and is neither catered to nor ignored.

Mrs. Rampion herself is a healthy "farm-woman" type of person, sturdily built, stable, kindly and good-humored. . . . Liberal in her political philosophy, she is a genuinely democratic person in the home and in the community.

The maturity Mrs. Rampion exhibits in her personal life is also displayed, naturally enough, in her behavior toward the children. Respecting them as individuals, she makes a conscious and conscientious effort to maintain an emotional distance, a detachment giving objectivity to her appraisal of them. An incident which reveals her imperturbability in the area of sex behavior is equally illustrative of her ability in general to see the children's behavior in perspective. "There is some possibility that Leonard masturbates, although Mrs. R. does not know definitely. He likes to stick out his penis and run around the house. Bobby is disgusted with the performance; Carol and Bud think it funny. Leonard also likes to rub himself on a toy horse which the children play on. 'He's very sexy,' Mrs. R. remarked. She had no emotional reaction to it, seemed casual and straightforward about the situation. It is definitely not a problem in her mind."

Her philosophy of non-intervention is further illustrated by the following incident: "The three children were playing well together. Once Carol got too near a ladder the boys were balancing. Mrs. R. called out the window for Leonard to watch her. She remarked that she hated to do it, and only resorted to warnings when she could forsee serious injury." If anything, the parents are too loathe to intervene.

. . . "A situation has recently arisen in the Rampion family which is significant in that it shows the technique of settling difficulties among members of the family. While Bobby was combing his hair upstairs, Leonard 'dibbsed' on the wishbones from two chickens. Bobby was furious when he found what L. had done, said that it was unfair because one could never dibbs on more than his share, that he never had done it, etc. As a matter of fact, Bobby had done it more than any of the others. The two argued about it far into the night. Both Mr. and Mrs. R. kept out of the argument, hoping, however, that Leonard would stick to his guns and that Bobby's fallacy in argument would be brought out by him. The night of my visit Bob had called a family council to settle the question, said that he would abide by the council's decision. Mrs. R. said that she was going to bring up the fact that Bobby was the prize dibbser unless the other children mentioned it first."

. . . The warm tone so evident in all the family's relationships characterize their attitudes toward one another. Without a great deal of fondling or other symbols of affection the parents convey to the children their deep devotion.

. . . Leonard is, at present, making an excellent social adjustment, although his development in the past has illustrated some of the difficulties peculiar to such a closely knit and satisfying family structure. On the one hand his home background has been so encompassing in its satisfactions that Leonard found the outside world, by comparison, somewhat dull and uninteresting. His social adjustment during the preschool years was marked by shyness and withdrawal. At the same time Leonard has suffered from his failure to meet the high standards of the Rampion household. He had been the most irresponsible and lazy of the children and, as a consequence, has been subject to tremendous pressures, not from the parents as much as from his siblings. As a result, he has suffered from rather severe feelings of inferiority which have only been alleviated by his quite remarkable popularity in school . . . his talents for leadership and organization have blossomed until, at present, he is making a good adjustment. (Baldwin *et al.*, 1945) [5]

Casual Homes. About half the homes of the study fell into the "casual" pattern, not so much because they fit a clear third pattern, but because they did not fit the rejectant or acceptant patterns. In general, parents in these homes had no clear philosophy of child-raising but worked out their problems as they went along. This group was further divided into casual autocratic and casual indulgent subgroups. Because of the variety of home atmospheres, no generalizations can be made about resulting behavior in the children; each home produces its own pattern of results.

One casual home is described in the following case from the study.

Evelyn Roberts: Casual Indulgence

Mrs. Roberts takes the . . . course of giving in to Evelyn and indulging her whims unless her behavior is too extreme or the reasons why she must be denied very powerful. . . . Mrs. Roberts has no explicit philosophy of child care or parental policy to guide her, beyond a statement made to one visitor that her mother had always kept her in her place and that she intended to be a friend to *her* children.

. . . Both Mr. and Mrs. Roberts are mature, well-adjusted individuals. Their relationship with each other is congenial and psychologically healthy; in relation to Evelyn they show a wholesome emotional detachment, quite free of neurotic dependency or demands. If anything, they fail to recognize Evelyn's dependency on them.

. . . Authority in the Roberts family is lodged in the parents. Mrs. Roberts may make a request of Evelyn; but if she is ignored, she finds it easier to carry out the errand herself than push Evelyn to do it. Often when she is trying to rebuke Evelyn for something she has done, Evelyn succeeds in diverting her mother's attention, making her laugh or arousing her sympathy in one way or another. "That Evelyn, she's a caution," Mrs. R. will remark with rueful amusement.

. . . During the visit Mrs. Roberts made very few requests, and those in a humorous voice, and was not particularly annoyed when the requests were disregarded. Evelyn was very eager to run errands for her, but was more hesitant to pick up the toys. Most of the time the request was disregarded by Evelyn and forgotten by Mrs. Roberts. As usual, there was an atmosphere of perfect understanding between them.

Evelyn's latest and most amusing misbehavior is to let the cows and pigs out of the gate, then watch her mother chase them down the road. Finally Mrs. R. discovered that it was Evelyn who was unlatching the gate and punished her. She told about it in Evelyn's hearing, however, and laughed. Such punishment as it meted out is sporadic and inconsistent, depending largely on Mrs. R's mood and Evelyn's ability to wriggle out of the situation.

. . . Mrs. Roberts rather consistently overhelps Evelyn, not from any conscious policy of babying but because she doesn't have a clear idea of what the child's capacities and abilities are, what she may justifiably be expected to do and what she is incapable of. For the same reason, she shelters Evelyn somewhat from dangers in the environment. . . . Evelyn is definitely the baby of the family has had very little demanded of her and is played with somewhat like a toy in my estimation. She is coddled and laughed at and indulged, both by the family and by the hired hands.

. . . Mrs. R. will let Evelyn do something she feels is wrong just because Evelyn is getting so much fun out of it and it isn't worth while to frustrate her. There are boundaries, of course, as to how much she will sacrifice her own convenience to Evelyn's pleasure, but the very mildness and placidity of her disposition make these limits rather wide. On the other hand if she thinks Evelyn's own safety and health are involved she may go to some lengths to impose her judgment—e.g., when Evelyn was an infant and fought against taking the bottle there is an instance of Mrs. Roberts' slapping her, and then, when she opened her mouth in protest, stuffing the bottle in.

. . . Evelyn's reaction to the inconsistencies of the home has been to develop striking conflicts of her own. She is a tremendously shy child outside the home situation and, at the same time, outstandingly aggressive. During the nursery school periods she would frequently complete a four-week session without having spoken a word to adult or child; her only technique for establishing contact with the other children seemed to be violence or a timid hanging around the periphery of the group. So destructive was she that the other children christened her "that ole bear" and assigned her the role of the villain in their imaginative play. This preschool behavior, continued on into grade school, makes her relationship to other children precarious and seriously complicates her school adjustment. (Baldwin *et al.*, 1945) [6]

The foregoing patterns and case-studies can by no means be considered to be "the" family structures. After the above studies had been completed, Roff (1949) [47] attempted to improve the definition of the basic variables involved by means of a factor analysis of the intercorrelations found. He extracted seven factors; five of these referred to parent-child relationships and two to characteristics of parents without reference to the child. The five referring to parent-child relations were named: I—"concern for child," II—"democratic guidance," III—"permissiveness," IV—"parent-child harmony," and VII—"non-readiness of suggestion." Although some rearrangements and alterations were made, the factor analysis in general validated the earlier "syndrome" or pattern analysis. Other students of family life have evolved their own research techniques and in turn, their own patterns.

Although the specific pattern names and details may vary from study to study, some general impressions may be summarized:

1. Children from cold, unloving homes tend to be aggressive, to have a variety of adjustment and behavior problems, and to be especially resistant to adults. In school, they are frequently problem children, misbehaving and hard to reach.

2. Children from warm, loving homes, where recognition and acceptance as individuals and careful guidance predominate, tend to be outgoing, active in home and school affairs, friendly and individualistic. These are the children who are most likely to satisfy the classroom teacher, to be "good" students in the best and broadest sense of the word.

3. Children whose wants are satisfied indiscriminately, who dominate their parents, who do have the experience of consistent guidance and discipline, do not as a group fare very well outside the home. In school they tend to be shy, withdrawn, inactive, unpopular with other children, and in general, unsuccessful.

Parental Problems

In an earlier chapter it was shown that the family was the primary socializing or acculturating agency. The relationship of family patterns to personality and adjustment has been discussed above. Parents, and especially parents of the middle class, have been made aware of the vital part their actions play in their children's development. They are bombarded by advice from "experts" writing in newspapers, magazines, and books and addressing them on television. As a result, a great many parents are anxious about their ways of handling their children. Their anxiety most frequently has to do with specific behaviors rather than with general principles. Child-rearing authorities have answered their questions over the years, but for reasons of inadequate evidence, incorrect inferences, popular but unsupported theories and the like, these answers have been in and out of fashion in the same way as long and short skirts for women or tight or loose suit jackets for men.

To illustrate these cycles and fashions in child rearing, successive issues of the U. S. Children's Bureau *Infant Care* have been analyzed from 1914 to the 1950s (Wolfenstein, 1953) [56]. The topics under consideration were those about which parents seem to have the greatest anxiety: masturbation, thumb sucking, weaning, bowel training, and bladder training.

The changes are shown in Table 14.1. Thumb-sucking, for example, was regarded very seriously in 1914 and thus was to be prevented at all costs—elbows were to be held rigid by means of cardboard wrappers or the fingers were to be painted with some bitter substance. Severity decreased during 1921–1929, remained constant until 1938, and continued to decline to the present. In general the contemporary, rather relaxed approach to all these problems has been increasingly popular since the 1930s.

TABLE 14.1
Trends in Recommended Infant Care, 1914–1951

Severity in Handling of	1914 to 1921	1921 to 1929	1929 to 1938	1938 to 1942–45	1942–45 to 1951
Masturbation	decreases	decreases	constant	decreases	constant
Thumb-sucking	constant	decreases	constant	decreases	decreases
Weaning	increases	increases	constant	decreases	constant
Bowel training	increases	increases	decreases	decreases	decreases
Bladder training	increases	decreases	decreases	decreases	decreases

Wolfenstein, Martha, 1953, Trends in infant care. *Amer. J. Orthopsychiat.*, 23: 129. Copyright, the American Orthopsychiatric Association, Inc., reproduced by permission.

What is *the* proper way to raise children? Obviously, it is not possible to make detailed prescriptions for parents to follow. This is so only in part because of lack of evidence; it is so primarily because child-rearing practices are influenced by parent-child relations, which are in turn influenced by the fact that parents and children are involved in a unique family context. Although formulas are not possible, some general clues as to what is important and unimportant may be inferred from some contemporary research findings.

One group of researchers (Sears *et al.*, 1957) [48] studied nearly 400 mother-child combinations in an attempt to determine what effect various methods or practices had on behavior and adjustment. Some of the findings on various practices are as follows:

1. *Breast feeding.* There was no evidence of different characteristics in breast-fed and bottle-fed children. The warmth exhibited by the mother was a factor in adjustment and traits, however.

2. *Toilet-training practices.* The techniques used and age at which they were instituted had no relation to bed-wetting, as is often supposed. The warmth of the mother (as opposed to coldness and severity) again had an effect.

3. *Sex practices.* A wide variety of behavior was observed here. General clinical evidence indicates that sexual repression in childhood is related to later guilt and anxiety feelings.

4. *Aggression.* Punishment, which is often satisfying to the parent,

stifled aggression in the children observed, but led to increased hostility. Permissiveness increased aggression in the children, but aggression led to retaliation by siblings and playmates. Punishment tells the child what *not* to do, but not what *to* do.

The *warmth* of the mother, rather than any specific practice, was by far the most pervasive factor in the study. When the mother lacked warmth, a host of problems appeared: feeding difficulties, bed-wetting, high aggression, emotional upset in toilet training, and slowness of conscience development.

Punishment was seen not so much as harmful, but as ineffectual in eliminating the behavior at which it was directed. Permissiveness had no effect on dependent or independent behavior. As noted above, it tended to foster aggression. Children reared in permissive homes did show low incidence of feeding and bed-wetting problems.

CHILDREN AND FATHERS

Most of the foregoing discussion concerns child-*mother* relationships. It is true that mothers in our culture are closer to their children than fathers. In part because of the necessity of physical care of the children, mothers are likely to be present in the home more and have more contact with children. Research indicates that children in general are more favorably disposed toward their maternal parents (Harris and Tseng, 1957) [27]. Figure 14.1 illustrates these attitudinal differences for both boys and girls. But how about children and *fathers?*

Despite the impression given by cartoons, television family skits, and popular fiction, the father is still an important (and in many families an authoritative) figure. While the mother is in hourly, intimate contact with the children—especially the very young—her ways of dealing with them reflect her husband's attitudes in many ways. Thus, the research on mother-child relationships really includes both parents.

The father serves as the model of maleness for boys and girls both, giving them an ideal (good, bad, or indifferent) of what a man should be like. It is especially important for older boys and adolescents to be able to identify with the father. In a comparison between boys who identified with fathers and those who did not (Payne and Mussen, 1956) [44] it was found that strong identification led to seeing not only father but *both* parents as rewarding and affectionate persons. The boys with high father identification were more masculine in their attitudes and behavior than the low-identification group; they were calmer, friendlier, and got on better with their peers.

Another approach to evaluating the father's influence on children is

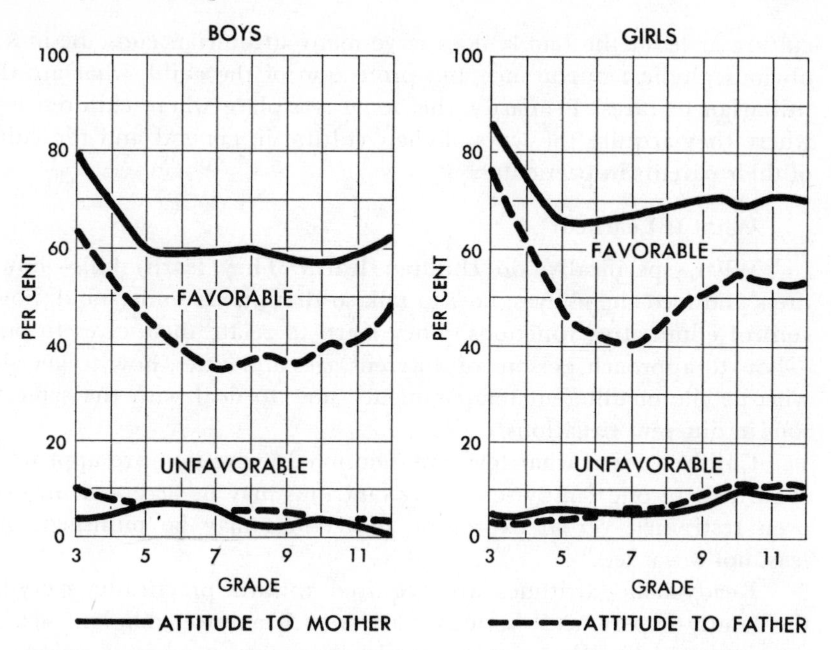

FIGURE 14.1. Attitudes of boys and of girls toward their parents at different ages. From Harris, D. B., and S. C. Tseng, Children's attitudes toward peers and parents as revealed by sentence completions. *Child Develpm.*, 28:401–411, 1957. Used with permission of the Society for Research in Child Development.

to study homes where the father is absent. Stolz (1954) [52] found that children whose fathers were away from home on wartime military service generally had more problems and poorer adjustment than children in homes where the father was present. They had a greater number of feeding problems, were less independent, had poorer relations with their age-mates, and showed more signs of anxiety. Boys were more seriously affected than girls. Stolz found in addition that the father's return to the home affected the regimen and adjustment of his children more than his absence. The sudden entrance of an adult male into a two- or three-year-old's life may be more unsettling than father deprivation in the first place.

LEARNING FROM PARENTS

The emotional climate of the home, discussed above, is not the only important aspect of family living. If one were to ask parents and children the purpose of living in family groups, he would probably receive a variety of responses emphasizing utility rather than emotion. And in our culture at least, the family does serve many utilitarian ends. Besides the obvious physical nurturance and protection of the child, what are these utiliarian features? Primarily, the home is a place where children learn, where they acquire the ways of their culture in general and the culture of their parents in particular.

What Is Learned?

What, specifically, do children learn? They learn skills—how to dress and feed themselves, how to talk so that others understand, how to control eliminative functions. They learn to relate themselves to others —how to approach persons of different ages and sexes, how to get along with people of different temperaments, how to deal with the same persons in different situations.

Children learn what forms of emotional expression are approved or rewarded: in one family screaming tantrums may be accepted; in others even restrained verbal expression of feelings may be punished, or at least not rewarded.

Ready-made attitudes are acquired toward practically everything the family experiences—serious matters such as race, religion, sex, and politics, as well as less significant phenomena such as food, colors, and music. This learning is of major importance because when a person holds particular attitudes he is by definition predisposed to act consistently with them. For example, if a child acquires at home a negative attitude toward "cultural" subjects such as music or art, it is most unlikely that he will exhibit much interest or enthusiasm in studying them. Although attitudes are made up in part of ideas or notions, they also include large emotional components, which of course have powerful effects on behavior.

Numerous studies exist which reveal the similarity of child-parent attitudes at different ages. In early life, the child mirrors most of his parents' attitudes. As he grows in knowledge and independence, he modifies many of these attitudes in the direction of those of his peer group, or of his own individual experience. In general, those attitudes with the least emotional content are modified most readily.

One of the authors has made a practice of asking large classes of undergraduates to indicate how many have the same general religious beliefs as their parents. Nearly every hand in the auditorium goes up. Then he asks how many hold the same political beliefs as their parents. A majority—perhaps two-thirds—of the hands rise. Finally, he asks how many enjoy the same light or popular music as their parents. Only a scattered few hands rise. The more important (emotion-arousing) attitudes are learned early and well and are highly resistant to change. Children acquire ideals, values, and goals from the family; not merely external forms of religious practice or verbalized attitudes, but deep feelings about the value of individual human life and the responsibility of one person for another.

How Intrafamily Learning Is Implemented

Consciously and unconsciously, families structure attitudes, beliefs, and actions in a variety of ways. Let us look briefly at some of them.

Indoctrination. Indoctrination is a familiar device: "Jane, quit slumping!" "George, we don't play with our food!" "Don't drink from that fountain, it's been used by the dirty people in this part of town." As a stimulating or motivating device, indoctrination is not very effective if the child has strong motives to behave in a way which is different from that recommended; that is, if his thirst is greater than his fear of the "dirty people" he may well ignore his mother's warning. Nevertheless, he absorbs an impression of certain undesirable people along with his water, and when he is less thirsty or more thoroughly indoctrinated, he may well pass up both the fountain and the "dirty people."

Imitation or Social Modeling. Much of a child's behavior originates in his interaction with family members. Even in the absence of direct teaching, he is likely to acquire ways of reaction and behaving by simply borrowing ready-made bits of behavior from parents, especially from the like-sex parent. This modeling of behavior has been studied extensively by Bandura. He describes behavior acquired in this fashion as response learning in which complex novel patterns are developed solely by observing the performances of social models, often without opportunity to perform the models' behavior in the experience setting, and without immediate reinforcement (Bandura, 1962) [7]. In a representative study, Bandura and Huston (1961) [8] found that children tended to imitate certain aspects of an experimenter's behavior even when those aspects were irrelevant to the task of the experiment. This imitation was stronger when the adult had been warm and rewarding in earlier interaction with the child than in the case of an aloof and cold adult. Aggressive behavior was imitated regardless of previous nurturance or non-nurturance, however. Aggression seems a behavior easily acquired in this fashion. Bandura and Walters (1963) [12] found that fathers of aggressive grade-school boys were more aggressively punitive than fathers of withdrawn boys. The former boys in general were found also to have adopted dissocial values to a greater extent than withdrawn boys. Boys, it might be noted, are more likely than girls to imitate such behaviors, especially from male models.

Social Reinforcement. Whatever the source of a bit of behavior, it will be retained in the child's repertoire only if it is rewarded or reinforced; that is, when behavior results in some conscious or unconscious feeling of satisfaction, it is likely to be repeated under similar circumstances in the future. Therefore, reinforcing or nonreinforcing responses on the part of parents are most important in structuring the child's behavior.

Why is it then not possible to condition a child to behave exactly as one desires? There are many reasons, but one of the major ones is that it is not easy to determine what will be reinforcing or nonreinforcing. Suppose, for example, that a father sees his seven-year-old boy kicking the family puppy. He reacts quickly, scolds the boy, and spanks him. The next day he sees the youngster repeat the act. How can this occur, when the father has *not* provided reward or reinforcement, but has instead provided punishment or negative reinforcement? We can only speculate:

1. Perhaps the boy needs attention so much that spanking (a kind of very personal attention!) is actually satisfying.
2. Perhaps the boy's need to express (or project) some bottled-up hostility is so great that the satisfaction in the release which comes with kicking outweighs the unpleasantness of spanking.
3. Perhaps his peer group approves of boys who dare to disobey their parents to a degree eliciting physical punishment. Peer approval may be more to be desired than parental approval.

The list could be extended almost indefinitely. Behavior is not simple, nor are its causes always obvious in the visible situation. Still, it is apparent that very many of the behavior patterns of children are developed and maintained primarily because of parental reinforcement.

Stimulus Selection. Parents select the kinds of stimuli to which the child will be exposed, and thus to some extent delimit the kinds of responses which can be made. The number and kind of toys, the number and quality of books, magazines, newspapers, radio and television programs, travel experiences, church attendance—these and other stimuli influence the developing child.

Development is an irreversible process, and once a child has had an experience, or has *failed* to have that experience, he can never be quite the same person again. And these parent-provided stimuli have a cumulative and profound influence on the intelligence, character, attitudes, and general behavior of children.

Illustration of Family Learning

For illustration of how families influence their children, let us turn to the behavior we call "aggression." This topic has been the subject of intensive research in the last decade or so.

Sears, Maccoby, and Levin (1957) [48], in their study of child-rearing practices at the Laboratory of Human Development at Harvard, used a standardized interview technique with mothers of five-year-old children. Every mother reported coping with some form of aggression, and the researchers concluded that conditions of living breed aggressive behavior. Two important themes in the control of children's aggression were noted: first, non-permissiveness (the tendency of parents to believe that aggression toward parents is wrong) prevents such outbursts or stops them when they occur. The other important theme was related to punishment, which, they found, has complex effects. For one thing, physical punishment particularly is an aggressive act on the part of the parent toward the child. Thus the parent is actually providing a model for aggression when he is trying to teach the child not to be aggressive, and the child may learn more from this model of successful aggression than from the pain of the punishment. The Sears Group's findings indicate that if the mother does not permit aggression toward her, but handles this in a non-punitive way, the child will not be aggressive. If the mother is tolerant in her attitude towards aggression or if she administers severe punishment, the child is more prone to angry, excessive outbursts. During the doll play sessions the children whose mothers were nonpermissive differed little from those whose mothers were permissive in fantasy aggression. However, children whose mothers punished them severely demonstrated significantly more fantasy aggression.

Bandura and Walters (1959) [9] reported an extensive study of child training and family factors that contribute to the development of antisocial aggressive behavior in adolescent boys. They attempted to use the methodology and framework used by Sears, Maccoby, and Levin with an older group. The population for their study consisted of fifty-two adolescent boys and their parents; twenty-six boys had histories of aggressive antisocial behavior and twenty-six had not but in other ways were comparable. The fifty-two boys, aged fourteen to seventeen, were all of average to above average intelligence and came from legally intact families, that is, families not broken by separation, divorce, or death of a parent. The parents were steadily employed and did not live in deteriorated or high-delinquent areas. Location of the study was a large urban area. The boys were matched by age and father's occupation. Three-fourths of the fathers held minor white collar jobs or skilled laboring jobs. Father, mother, and boy were interviewed separately by an interviewer of their own sex. In addition, the boys were given a projective test designed to assess their attitudes toward socially deviant behavior. The interviews were rated by trained raters on a rating scale.

Bandura and Walters hypothesized that "aggression was a manifestation of a learned motive developed over a period of years, first in interaction with the child's parents and with other authority figures who may in some respects be regarded as parent-surrogates" (Bandura and Walters, 1959) [10] and that the conditions for the development and establishment of aggressive patterns are to be found in the parents' techniques of handling the child, both in early years and in current situations.

They found these characteristics typical of the aggressive boys:

> . . . they expressed aggression in a much more direct and uninhibited manner, particularly outside the home. . . . They felt somewhat rejected by both parents, but retained a good deal of affection and respect for their mothers. In contrast, they were critical and resentful of their fathers, with whom they showed only limited identification. They were markedly distrustful; they feared and avoided situations in which they might have become emotionally dependent on others. Their sexual behavior was likely to be less inhibited than that of the average adolescent, and they tended to confound sex and aggression. Aggressive and sexual behavior aroused in them fewer guilt feelings than they did in the control boys and, in general, their impulses were more likely to be controlled by fear than by guilt. They were, in many respects, like small children whose impulses are held in check by external, rather than by internal, restraints. Their behavior, moreover, was apparently self-defeating because it alienated them from the affection of which they already felt deprived and brought them under the more direct control of the authority figures whom they distrusted and resented. (Bandura and Walters, 1959) [11]

In identifying factors in the child training process that could be conductive to socialization defects, Bandura and Walters found that early dependency behavior was subtly discouraged by the mother; the boys had rejecting, punitive, disparaging fathers; they experienced few behavioral limits, which were poorly defined and inconsistently enforced. The mothers were lax and inconsistent; fathers punished their children severely; fathers may have encouraged children's aggressiveness by their own belligerent, combative attitude.

SOCIAL INFLUENCES ON FAMILY LIFE

The influence of society on behavior has been discussed in an earlier chapter. The family is the basic social unit: it reflects the society in which it functions—it is a "culture bearer," and the collective families of a particular society in turn influence the nature of that society. Thus, in the earlier comment, "The actions of the individual . . . are an inseparable extension of the culture of the society of which he is a part," the word "family" might have been substituted for the word "society." The statement, although somewhat more restricted, would have remained valid.

Because the child's family is, for him, so large a part of society, it would seem desirable for his teachers and others to recognize some of the ways in which the general culture influences and structures the specific (that is, the family) culture.

Influence of Class

In interviews with over 300 mothers of upper-middle and upper-lower class, researchers found a number of differences in child-rearing practices (Maccoby *et al.*, 1955) [37].

1. *Toilet training.* The lower-class mothers were more severe and used more punishment in the training process.

2. *Sex-training.* Again, the lower-class mothers were more severe in training. They viewed masturbation and other sex play with much more emotion than their middle-class opposites, and were less likely to perceive sexuality in their children.

3. *Aggression.* The middle-class mothers permitted their children to direct more aggression toward them than did lower class.

4. *Punishment.* In the lower class, physical punishment, ridicule, and deprivation of privilege were likely to be used as punishment instead of reason and withdrawal of love.

5. *Affection.* Middle-class parents were found to be consistently more demonstrative and affectionate with their children and each other and to be more permissive even when age, education, and ethnic origin were held constant.

Child-rearing practices do not remain constant. As noted earlier in this chapter, the recommendations of experts have changed markedly since World War I. An analysis of studies of actual practices in different social classes shows marked changes over the years (Bronfenbrenner, 1958) [18]. In infant care, the practices of mothers have tended to follow the recommendations of the U. S. Children's Bureau bulletins; this has been especially true of those who have had ready access to these bulletins or similar materials—the middle class. All classes have become more flexible in infant feeding and weaning. From about 1930 to the end of World War II, working-class mothers were uniformly more permissive in these practices than were other classes. Since World War II, however, the situation has been reversed and it is the middle-class mothers who are more permissive.

In child (as distinct from infant) training, middle-class mothers have become much more permissive toward the child's expressed needs and wishes. Though more tolerant of his desires, the middle-class parent has higher expectations for the child in his home and especially in the school. Over the entire twenty-five-year period, middle-class parents have consistently been more acceptant and equalitarian. The working-class parent is interested in maintaining order and discipline while the middle class encourages freer expression of affection and exhibits greater tolerance of the child's impulses and desires. It is the feeling of those reviewing the data that the gap between the classes is steadily narrowing.

Father's Occupation. In a study of several hundred adolescents, Bronfenbrenner (1958) [19] found the expected class differences: the higher-class, better-educated parents were more equalitarian, more expressive of interest in the child, less punitive, protective and indulgent, and had children who were more responsible, competitive, imaginative, and accepted by their peers. In addition to studying social class differences, the investigator employed a two-dimensional system of classification based on the father's education and type of occupation. Within each educational group (grammar school through graduate work) cases were dichotomized "on the basis of occupational orientation or the degree to which the father's job involved evaluation of the quality of a concrete product of his own work or the work of others, the evaluation being based on his own specialized knowledge and skill" (Bronfenbrenner, 1958) [20]. Thus, skilled workers, artists, scientists, and the like were classified as "quality-oriented," while unskilled laborers, clerks, salesmen, and similar workers were classified as relatively "non-quality-oriented."

Using this "quality" criterion, the researcher found a number of differences *within* the four educational groups: parents classified as "quality-oriented" were likely to spend more time with their children, to make higher achievement demands, and to be more reserved in the expression of affection. In contrast, "non-quality-oriented" families were less demanding, warmer, and showed a higher degree of parental role differentiation. Although these are preliminary results, they should make us cautious of glib generalizations based on too-simple classification systems.

National Differences

Study of national or ethnic child-rearing practices and resulting trait differences offer further evidence on the effect of family training on behavior. To explore this material would be manifestly impossible in a text of this sort. However, a study of the comparative development of one trait—independence—in American and Swiss children will serve as illustration.

Swiss parents, like most Europeans, tend to be more autocratic than American and to keep their children "young" and dependent longer. The study referred to below is rather loose by American standards, and included a limited number of cases. The results may be suggestive, however.

1. American children are emancipated from their parents sooner than the Swiss.

2. At every age they (American children) are less subjugated to parents and to adults in general.

3. This independence from adults makes them more dependent on their peers for social and emotional support.

4. American children enjoy a greater degree of freedom of thought than the Swiss, and achieve independence of judgment earlier.

5. As a result of this independence and freedom, American children develop more autonomous, though less complex, consciences (Boehm, 1957) [14].

PARENT-CHILD CONFLICTS

From the discussion in the chapter thus far it might be inferred that children become just what their families try, consciously and unconsciously, to make them. Such is not the case, of course. Each child has his own unique structure, function, needs, desires, emotions, and the like; some of the time he is thus bound to be in conflict with his family.

From infancy to adolescence, relations between child and parent may gradually worsen. As the child grows in experience, skill, and general competence, he feels less need for his parents and is less willing to be "bossed" by them. The parents in turn find the child less attractive and appealing as he gets older. Parents of nine-year-olds, as compared to parents of three-year-olds, have been found to be less warm, less indulgent, less affectionate, more restrictive in their discipline, more punitive for misbehavior and less intellectually stimulating (Baldwin, 1945) [2]. By late childhood and adolescence, the atmosphere of many homes is tense and conflicts are frequent, mostly over requests and orders issued by the parents.

One piece of advice on child-rearing sometimes offered young parents is "love 'em and leave 'em alone." This has its appeal, but is not likely to be practiced by many couples. Why is it so difficult for parents to "love 'em and leave 'em alone"? In the first place, of course, it is obviously impossible to leave a child very much alone in our complex society. He must not only be fed, clothed, sheltered, and loved, but must be taught, guided, and led in order to survive and succeed.

It is in the effort to help the child "succeed" that many conflicts are born. Succeed at what, for what purpose, to satisfy whose needs? Parent and child, and to a greater extent, parent and adolescent, may have very different views of "succeeding." To the parent of the toddler, dry pants and bed are evidence of successful growing up: the youngster may feel complete indifference about staying dry. Learning to read is likely to be viewed by the parent as an essential skill: to a particular six-year-old it may seem, for a time, irrelevant to his life. To the older child and teenager so many of the expectations and demands of parents (and teachers for that matter) may seem meaningless or nonrewarding: being neat and punctual, getting good grades, having the "right" friends, spending spare time in "worthwhile" pursuits, planning for what seems the far-distant future.

Another source of difficulty lies in the difference of perception by the parent and child. The parent with his years of living cannot but view the world differently from his inexperienced child. Then there is the matter of perceiving the child himself: the parent may or may not see his offspring as the person he really is. The homely child may be perceived as attractive, or the situation may be reversed. The clever, scheming, persuasive child may be seen as simple, easygoing, and undemanding. The personable and agreeable youngster of limited intelligence may be seen as brighter than he really is. The greater the lack of correspondence between reality and the parent's perception of the child, the greater likelihood there will be of inappropriate treatment by the parent.

Some errors of perception, or of treatment, may result from the parent's projection of his own needs, ambitions, or fears onto the child. Every teacher knows the inept boy whose father demands athletic achievement, the shy introverted girl whose mother pushes her toward the role of social butterfly, the intellectual parent who demands achievement impossible in his average-ability offspring.

Parents and the Adolescent

It is in adolescence that the major conflicts occur with parents. The adolescent wants desperately the freedom of adulthood, but he needs some of the protection and guidance due children. Even though he may recognize his need, he is likely to resent what he considers parental interference in his affairs. Why is this? The sociologist, Kingsley Davis, suggests some causes (Davis, 1953) [23]:

The rate of social change in our culture complicates the problem: the adolescent quite literally is growing up in a different world than his parents, even if they are relatively young.

Physiological differences are a factor: the parental generation is declining while the adolescent is just reaching his full power.

Adults, because of their greater experience, are more realistic than adolescents.

Parental authority is temporary, and the adolescent sees it waning as he matures.

The family and the peer group have conflicting norms, and thus conflicting loyalties are set up, with the peer group winning most of the time.

Although conflicts increase for both boys and girls, it is the latter who seem to experience the greater amount of friction with parents. The reasons for this difference are not obvious, but are probably due to the relative amount of control exerted in our culture on girls', as compared to boys', behavior. Any topic may precipitate conflict—clothing, chores, dates, friends, school achievement, use of time, money, automobiles, the telephone, but problems related to discipline and social control occur most frequently (Punke, 1943) [45].

Parents (as well as teachers) would do well to look for the causes underlying conflicts. Although understanding will not eliminate disagreement, there is reassuring evidence of improvement of family relations when adolescents perceive their parents as understanding of them and their needs (Briggs and Schulz, 1955) [17].

By late adolescence, fortunately, most teen-agers and their parents have worked out compromises and emerge from the period on a new, more grownup level of greater mutual respect and affection.[2]

VARYING FAMILY CONDITIONS

When we speak of a "family" we are likely to be thinking of a father who is a wage-earner, a mother who is present in the home, and two or three children. Although this is the typical American family, variations from this pattern are so numerous that they can hardly be thought of as atypical.

Working Mothers

In early, rural America, the husband and wife formed an economic partnership. With the development of an urban culture, the status of the wife changed from that of a partner in the family farm operation to that of a housekeeper. Increasingly in the last half-century, however, the wife has contributed to the family income by working outside the home as well as in it. In 1890, 4.6 percent of married women were employed outside the home, in 1940 the figure was 16.8 percent, and in 1950, 26.8 percent (Ogburn and Nimkoff, 1955) [42]. In the years between 1948 and 1958, the number of mothers in the work force increased by 80 percent and in proportion by almost 50 percent, to a total of seven and a half million by 1960. The majority had children of school age only, but

[2] An excellent essay on the topic of parent-adolescent difficulties may be found in Farnham, Marynia, 1952, *The adolescent.* New York: Harper & Row, Publishers.

almost four million had children of preschool age. Another way of describing the situation is to say that the work force included 30 percent of all mothers, 20 percent of those with preschool children, and 41 percent of those had children of school age (Herzog, 1960) [29]. Since the date of the latter report, the proportion of working mothers has probably increased.

What is the effect on children of the mother's employment? The evidence is sparse, but some differences do exist between working and nonworking mothers. Professional women emphasize discipline and independence more than nonworking: they have more rules and expect more from their children. The nonprofessional mothers emphasize the protective, empathic, and understanding functions of motherhood: they believe the child should enjoy himself while he is young (Von Mering, 1955) [55].

In a summary of late research, Nye and Hoffman (1963) [39] report little evidence of influence of mother's employment *per se* on children's welfare. There is more consistent evidence, however, on the deleterious effects of maternal employment on husband-wife relations.

Broken Homes

Divorce, desertion, death, military duty—all these remove one of the marriage partners from the home and leave any children without the care of one parent, usually the father. Because it is a product of the characteristics or the behavior of the partners, unlike death or military duty, divorce has been the subject of considerable study.

Divorce has been a prominent feature of twentieth century American life. The divorce rate increased from less than two per 1000 married females after the Civil War, to four by 1900, eight by 1920, and nearly fifteen in the mid-1940s; the rate seems to have stabilized around nine or ten by the mid-1960s (*Statistical Abstract of the United States,* 1965 [51]. The number of desertions (sometimes termed the "poor man's divorce") is difficult to determine for obvious reasons, but it is probably as frequent or more frequent than divorce. The average divorce, separation, or desertion case involves at least one child. Thus, as many as four out of ten American children come from broken homes.

What is the effect of these home disruptions on children? As was noted earlier, children in homes with missing fathers had more problems than children in father-present homes. In another study, adolescents from broken homes showed many personality maladjustments (Havighurst, 1952) [28]. Children in homes broken by divorce have been found to have no more problems of adjustment than those from homes broken by other causes. Disunited, unhappy homes with both parents present are in many ways quite as bad for the children as the broken homes; in some ways they are worse because there is no possibility of a happy remarriage for the parent (Nye, 1957) [38].

Adoption

Because children are highly desired by most couples in our society, most unattached children are legally adopted or are placed in foster homes, especially if they become available for placement at an early age. How do these "acquired" children fare, as compared to natural children (those born to the parents)?

The evidence is not extensive, but it points consistently toward one conclusion: adopted children are not significantly different from natural children in any way. They show as much evidence of receiving love and security; they have no more delinquent or problem behavior; their general adjustment is as good. There are certainly individual exceptions; but in general, the teacher dealing with adopted children in the classroom need not expect them to exhibit behaviors different from the other children as a result of their parental status.

SIBLING RELATIONSHIPS

The child interacts in the home not only with parents, but in most cases with siblings. What effect this interaction has on him depends on his position in the family, his age at the time of birth of other children, and his relationships with his parents.

Jealousy

If a child is an infant when a sibling is born, he will have too little perception of the situation to be jealous. If, however, he is old enough to recognize that he is sharing his mother's affection—or, more concretely, her attention—with someone new, he is almost sure to be jealous. This is perfectly normal and leads often to aggressive and hostile behavior directed toward the newborn. If the child is too insecure emotionally to express his anger and fear openly, he may regress into earlier habits of bed-wetting, thumb-sucking, and the like. With proper preparation and intelligent management, the jealousy is not likely to be severe or serious (Levy, 1937) [36].

Although damaging rivalries can ordinarily be controlled, a certain amount of conflict is to be expected among siblings. Squabbling is universal in early childhood, but there are some balancing satisfactions. The experience of living in a group and having easy access to playmates is rewarding to most children.

The attitudes parents demonstrate and their ways of handling problems have much to do with sibling relationships. Holding a brother or a sister up as a model, insisting that a child take a younger sibling along when he leaves home, showing favoritism or treating unlike siblings alike are all resented and occasion hostility between a child and his parents as well as between siblings. Table 14.2 shows the incidence of such complaints as reported by children in one study.

TABLE 14.2
Mother-Child Conflicts over Siblings

Item	Boys (%)	Girls (%)
"Holds my brother or sister up to me as a model"	66.9	75.8
"Insists I take my brother or sister wherever I go"	50.5	82.3
"Shows favoritism to my brother or sister"	30.6	44.4
"Makes me go to bed at the same time as younger brothers or sisters"	30.6	45.1

Block, Virginia L., 1937, Conflicts of adolescents with their mothers. *J. abnorm. soc. Psychol.*, 32: 193–206.

Ordinal Position

The ordinal position of the child (first-born, second-born, and so forth) undoubtedly has an influence on his behavior. The only child, for example, has greater contact with adults and less with other children than the member of a large family. There is some tendency for him to be overprotected, simply because there is more of everything for him—parent's time, money, attention, and so on. It would also seem reasonable to assume that the child in the larger family would have more opportunity to learn social give-and-take and to acquire skills in dealing with people. There is, however, little evidence of the alleged deleterious effect of "onlyness" on behavior.

The evidence of the effect of ordinal position in the large family is conflicting. It has been reported, for example, that the first-born of a family has a greater chance of acquiring emotional problems, shyness, and withdrawal tendencies, that the youngest tends to be more ambitious, outgoing, and competitive than his older siblings, and that the middle children lie between these extremes (Cobb, 1943) [22]. In one study of girls only, first-born children were found to be somewhat more anxious in a laboratory stress situation, to exhibit greater emotional change or fluctuation, and to be less confident about self-ratings of emotion (Ring, Lipinsky, and Braginsky, 1965) [46]. Generalizations fail to be very enlightening about a specific family. Does the first-born have certain traits regardless of sex? Does the age spread between first and second, second and third, and so on affect relationships? Does the total number of siblings have any influence on the behavior of the youngest or oldest? Obviously the variety of family structures is almost infinite, making generalizations extremely hazardous.

Perhaps the most intensive examination of sibling relationships has been that of Koch, who studied 384 five- and six-year-old children in two-child families. Taking into account the sex, ordinal position and age difference of the siblings, she studied sibling effect on attitude toward peers, interaction with playmates, emotional attitudes, "sissiness" and "tomboyishness," and work attitudes. Even in so restricted a group as hers, rarely was there any simple effect of sex, age, or ordinal position of siblings. Having a sibling unquestionably affected children's behavior, but she states, "Most of the significant relations in our data appear in interactions. This would warn against sweeping generalizations about the effect of birth-order, sib's sex, sex of child or age differences between sibs" (Koch, 1956) [31, 32, 33, 34, 35].

The thoughtful teacher will view the family as one of the important causes of a child's behavior, but will be wary of oversimplifying and of making too easy generalizations about so complex a phenomenon.

SUMMARY

One of the major sources of behavioral structuring is the family. The infant needs not only physical care from his parents, but also love, expressed affection, and sensory stimulation.

The personality of the child is rather clearly influenced by the emotional atmosphere of the home and the pattern of family interaction. Some divergent patterns have been studied and their effect on behavior explored.

The home is the earliest source of learning experience, and continues to be the major one through childhood and early adolescence.

The segment of society to which a child belongs also has a powerful effect on him, both within and outside his home.

In the close family relationship of our society, conflicts are inevitable and increase with the age of the children.

Broken homes, working mothers, number and age of siblings have an effect on developing personality and behavior.

Suggested Collateral Readings

Barker, R. G., and H. F. Wright, *Midwest and its children.* New York: Harper & Row, Publishers, 1951.

Bowlby, J., *Maternal care and child health.* Geneva: World Health Organization, 1951.

Breckenridge, M. E., and E. Lee Vincent, *Child development,* 4th ed. Philadelphia: W. B. Saunders Company, 1960. Chapter 5.

Brody, Sylvia, *Patterns of mothering: Maternal influence during infancy.* New York: International Universities Press, Inc., 1956.

Frankiel, Rita V., *A review of research on parent influences on child personality.* New York: Family Service Association of America, 1959.

Glidewell, J. C., ed., *Parental attitudes and child behavior.* Springfield, Ill.: Charles C Thomas, Publisher, 1961.

Martin, W. E., and Celia B. Stendler, *Child behavior and development,* revised ed. New York: Harcourt, Brace & World, Inc., 1959. Chapter 10.

Miller, D. R., and G. E. Swanson, *The changing American parents.* New York: John Wiley & Sons, Inc., 1958.

Olson, W. C., *Child development,* 2d ed. Boston: D. C. Heath and Company, 1959. Chapter 9.

Sears, R. R., Eleanor E. Maccoby, and H. Levin, *Patterns of child raising.* New York: Harper & Row, Publishers, 1957. Pages 442–488.

Smart, Mollie, and R. Smart, *An introduction to family relationships.* Philadelphia: W. B. Saunders Company, 1953. Pages 137–181.

Thompson, G. G., *Child psychology.* Boston: Houghton Mifflin Company, 1952. Pages 502–524, 542–546.

Winch, R F., *The modern family.* New York: Holt, Rinehart and Winston, Inc., 1952. Pages 182–258.

References

1. Ainsworth. Mary D., R. G. Andry, R. G. Harlow, S. Lebovici, Margaret Mead, D. G. Prugh, and Barbara Wooton, 1962, *Deprivation of maternal care: A reassessment of its effects.* Geneva: World Health Organization.
2. Baldwin, A. L., 1945, Differences in parent behavior toward three- and nine-year-old children. *J. Pers.,* **15:** 143–165.
3. ———, Joan Kalhorn, and Fay H. Breese, 1945, Patterns of parent behavior. *Psychol. Monogr.* **58.**
4. ———, pages 22–24.
5. ———, pages 31–33.
6. ———, pages 49–51.
7. Bandura, A., 1962, Social learning through imitation, in Jones, M. R., ed., *Nebraska Symposium on Motivation.* Lincoln: University of Nebraska Press. Pages 216–217.
8. ———, and A. C. Huston, 1961 Identification as a process of incidental learning, *J. abnorm. soc. Psychol.,* **63:** 311–318.
9. ———, and Walters, R. H., 1959, *Adolescent aggression.* New York: The Ronald Press Company.
10. ———, page 29.
11. ———, pages 312–313.
12. ———, 1963, *The social learning of deviant behavior: A behavioristic approach.* New York: Holt, Rinehart and Winston, Inc.
13. Block, Virginia L., 1937, Conflicts of adolescents with their mothers. *J. abnorm. soc. Psychol.,* **32:** 193–206.
14. Boehm, Lenore, 1957, The development of independence: A comparative study. *Child Develpm.,* **28:** 92.

15. Bowlby, J., 1952, Maternal care and mental health. *W.H.O. Monograph Series.* Pages 16–155.
16. ———, Chapter V.
17. Briggs, V., and L. R. Schulz, 1955, Parental response to concepts of parent-adolescent relationships. *Child Develpm.,* **26**: 279–284.
18. Bronfenbrenner, U., 1958, Socialization and social class through time and space, in Maccoby, Eleanor E., T. Newcomb, and E. Hartley, eds., *Readings in social psychology.* New York: Holt, Rinehart and Winston, Inc. Pages 400–425.
19. ———, 1958, Family structure and development. *Newsletter, Division on Developmental Psychology.* New York: American Psychological Association.
20. ———, page 2.
21. Casler, L., 1961, Maternal deprivation: A critical review of the literature, *Monogr. Soc. Res. Child Develpm.* **26**: 1–64.
22. Cobb, E. A., 1943, Family press variables. *Monogr. Soc. Res. Child Develpm.,* **8**: 327–361.
23. Davis, K., 1953, 'The sociology of parent-youth conflicts,' in Winch, R. F., and R. McGinnes, eds., *Marriage and the family.* New York: Holt, Rinehart and Winston, Inc.
24. Harlow, H. F., 1958, The nature of love. *The American Psychologist,* **13**: 673–674.
25. Harlow, H. F., and Margaret K. Harlow, 1962, Social deprivation in monkeys. *Scientific American,* **34**: 136–146.
26. ———, and R. R. Zimmermann, 1959, Affectional responses in the infant monkey. *Science,* **130**: 421–432.
27. Harris, D. B., and S. C. Tseng, 1957, Children's attitudes toward peers and parents as revealed by sentence completions. *Child Develpm.,* **28**: 401–411.
28. Havighurst, R. J., 1952, Social class and personality structure. *Sociology and Social Research,* **36**: 355–363.
29. Herzog, Elizabeth, 1960, *Children of working mothers.* Washington, D.C.: U.S. Department of Health, Education and Welfare, Superintendent of Documents. Pages 3–5.
30. Kagan, J., and H. A. Moss, 1962, *Birth to maturity.* New York: John Wiley & Sons, Inc. Pages 204–228.
31. Koch, Helen L., 1956, Children's work attitudes and sibling characteristics. *Child Develpm.,* **27**: 310.
32. ———, 1956, Some emotional attitudes of the young child in relation to characteristics of his sibling. *Child Develpm.,* **27**: 393–426.
33. ———, 1957, The relation in young children between characteristics of their playmates and certain attributes of their siblings. *Child Develpm.,* **28**: 175–202.
34. ———, 1956, Sissiness and tomboyishness in relation to sibling characteristics. *J. genet. Psychol.,* **88**: 231–244.
35. ———, 1956, Attitudes of young children toward their peers as related to certain characteristics of their siblings. *Psychol. Monogr.,* **70**.
36. Levy, D. M., 1937, Studies in sibling rivalry. *Research Monographs of the American Orthopsychiatric Association,* No. 2.

37. Maccoby, Eleanor E., *et al.,* 1955, Methods of child-rearing in two social classes, in Coladarci, A. P., ed., *Educational psychology: A book of readings.* New York: Holt, Rinehart and Winston, Inc.
38. Nye, F. I., 1957, Child adjustment in broken and in unhappy unbroken homes. *Marriage and family living.* **19:** 356–361.
39. Nye, F. I., and Lois W. Hoffman, 1963, *The employed mother in America.* Skokie, Ill.: Rand McNally & Company.
40. O'Connor, N., 1956, The evidence for the permanently disturbing effects of mother-child separation. *Acta Psychologica,* **12:** 174.
41. ———, page 175.
42. Ogburn, W. F., and M. F. Nimkoff, 1955, *Technology and the changing family.* Boston: Houghton Mifflin Company. Page 145.
43. Orlansky, H., 1949, Infant care and personality. *Psychol. Bull.,* **46:** 28.
44. Payne, D. E., and P. H. Mussen, 1956, Parent-child relations and father identification among adolescent boys. *J. abnorm. soc. Psychol.,* **52:** 358–362.
45. Punke, H. H., 1943, High school youth and family quarrels. *School and Society,* **58:** 507–511.
46. Ring, K., C. E. Lipinski, and Dorothea Graginsky, 1965, The relationship of birth order to self-evaluation, anxiety reduction, and susceptibility to emotional contagion. *Psychol. Monogr.,* **79:** 23.
47. Roff, M., 1949, A factorial study of the Fels Parent Behavior Scales. *Child Develpm.,* **20:** 29–45.
48. Schaefer, E. S., and Nancy Bayley, 1963, Maternal behavior, child behavior and their intercorrelations from infancy through adolescence, *Monogr. Soc. Res. Child Develpm.,* **28:** No. 3, Whole No. 87, pages 1–127.
49. Sears, R. R., Eleanor E. Maccoby, and H. Levin, 1957, *Patterns of child rearing.* New York: Harper & Row, Publishers.
50. Shaffer, L. F., and E. J. Shoben, 1956, *The psychology of adjustment.* Boston: Houghton Mifflin Company. Pages 432–433.
51. *Statistical Abstracts of the United States,* 1965, Washington, D.C.: Bureau of Census, Department of Commerce. Page 62.
52. Stolz, Lois M., *et al.,* 1954, *Father relations of war-born children.* Stanford: Stanford University Press.
53. Symonds, P. M., 1949, *The Dynamics of parent-child relationships.* New York: Bureau of Publications, Teachers College, Columbia University. Page 38.
54. ———, pages 110–126.
55. Von Mering, F. H., 1955, Professional and nonprofessional women as mothers. *J. soc. Psychol.,* **42:** 21–34.
56. Wolfenstein, Martha, 1953, Trends in infant care. *Amer. J. Orthopsychiat.,* **23:** 120–129.
57. Yarrow, L. J., Maternal deprivation: Toward an empirical and conceptual reevaluation. *Psychol. Bull.,* **58:** 459–490.

Personality and the School's Role in Its Development

PART 4

THE MAJOR CONCEPTS of the psychology of human development have been discussed area by area and age by age in the preceding sections of this book. To be useful to the teacher, these concepts must be related to each other, and in such relationship they must disclose their relevance to the teacher's dealings with persons and especially those who are pupils in the classroom. Part IV is designed to assist the student in integrating his ideas into a meaningful whole.

Personality is a unifying concept in psychology. In Chapter 15 an attempt is made to show how individuals develop unique personality patterns from their inborn characteristics and their experiences. Considerable attention is given to the relationship of self-identity and personality development. The emphasis upon the individual's striving for self-definition and significance is a projection of the central theme of the book.

Chapter 16 gives some practical answers to the question, "What do I do with my knowledge of human behavior and development?" There is no magic formula for understanding one's self or others; there is no bag of tricks to be used in helping young people develop the potentialities they possess. Nevertheless, teachers do achieve effectiveness as they integrate the principles of psychology with their developing insight and acceptance of individual human beings. Thus in the final chapter, the psychological "climate" of the school is discussed, evidence of the changes in teachers' perceptions of their role in the school is presented, and finally the idea is emphasized that enjoyment can—and should—characterize the teacher's relationships with children and youth.

CHAPTER 15

Personality and the Self-concept

An individual's personality is a summation of all his qualities and capabilities as a person; it is the "form" in which these are joined and correlated into the totality of his life. It includes the individual's motives, his ways of perceiving, his feelings, his thinking, his expressing of himself, and his relating of himself to other persons. It incorporates physical and mental traits and abilities. It includes weaknesses as well as strengths. Virtually everything, therefore, that has been discussed in the preceeding chapters of this book relates in one way or another to personality development.

Especially important to our understanding of personality is what we may consider the personal "center of gravity": The individual's conception of himself. The title of this chapter implies that there is a relationship between personality and self-concept. The principal objective of much that will be found in the sections that follow is to examine this relationship and especially the inseparability of personality development and self-concept development.

THE MEANING OF PERSONALITY

The term "personality" derives from the Latin word *persona,* which means a mask worn by an actor while he is speaking and performing his parts in a play. The actor thus disguised by the mask becomes known through his actions and his speech. This concept harmonizes with that which many psychologists have of the nature of personality. A person's behavior makes his personality known: What he thinks, feels, says, and what he does in various situations, all contribute to the revealing of his personality.

Definitions of Personality

There are differences in the terms used by various writers in their definitions of personality. Close scrutiny of the definitions, however, will disclose considerable agreement regarding the inclusion in the definition of certain key ideas. Specifically, there is emphasis in most definitions upon the ideas of unity and organization, uniqueness, continuity and stability (within which, desirably, there will be the flexibility that makes for openness to experience—an essential to learning and healthy self-development). The idea expressed in the parenthesis carries over to a discussion later in this chapter. It is discussion that points up the importance for self-development of the capability to *change* and to *actualize potentialities* at the same time that one sustains a sense of being *essentially oneself.*

An often-quoted definition of personality calls it the "dynamic organization within the individual of those psycho-physical systems that determine his unique adjustment to his environment" (Allport, 1937) [1]. Jersild (1960) [26] speaks of personality as "the sum total of an individual's properties as a distinct and unique human being." McDonald (1959) [32] defines personality as "the unique, integrated and organized system of all the behavior of an individual." Hilgard (1957) [25] has defined personality as "the individual characteristics and ways of behavior which, in their organization and patterning, account for an individual's unique adjustment to his total environment."

In a statement that contains much that is thought-provoking about *the nature of personality* (without giving a closely worded definition of personality) Sandford (1962) [44] notes that the highly developed personality is characterized both by complexity and by wholeness. Sandford finds in the highly developed personality such differentiation of perceiving, thinking, feeling, and willing that the individual is "uniquely responsive to multitudinous aspects of his natural, social, and cultural environments; the largeness of his world is matched by the diversity of his interrelated sensibilities and capacities; he has breadth of understanding, subtlety of appreciation, and freedom of judgment and action." In his statement, which gives strong emphasis to complexity and diversity, Sandford balances such emphasis by underscoring the *organization* of "different parts and processes of the person" as well as the individual's capability of "acting as a unit."

Outer and Inner Aspects of Personality

There are two different views of personality that are open, respectively, to (1) persons other than the one whose personality is under consideration at the moment and (2) the individual himself. Both of these views have validity and importance in the study of personality.

On the one hand, psychology has benefited from objective, systematic descriptions of human characteristics that differ and are measurable. Such characteristics include those that are physical and often strikingly different from person to person. They also include demonstrable talents and abilities, various mannerisms, habits of conduct, and observable qualities of temperament and disposition. Countless physical and psychological measures have been devised for the purpose of assessing these kinds of characteristics. Certain theories of personality are based largely on the kinds of data that are procurable in the form of measurable, outer dimensions of human behavior.

The inner aspects of personality consist of "an individual's drives, the total system of ideas and attitudes that constitute his awareness of himself, and the unrecognized or unconscious tendencies that have an important bearing on his feelings, thoughts, and actions" (Jersild, 1960) [27]. In recent years psychologists have focused a great deal of attention on these inner phases of personality. Much effort has been expended in the development of methods for probing the "deeper" recesses of human behavior and especially methods for inducing the individual to *project* his inner life in responses that can be evaluated. The so-called projective techniques (described later in this chapter) were developed for this latter purpose.

At the expense of being repetitious let it be reemphasized that to understand personality we must keep the two aspects, above-mentioned, closely associated in our thinking. They are inseparably joined in what a person is. He *is* that unique combination of all the characteristics that are outwardly evident, and he *is* at the same time all that is concealed in his inner and relatively private experience. What the individual sees of his own outer manifestations and what he believes other persons see and think about them has much to do with the way his inner person develops. Similarly, these inner aspects influence to an important degree the pattern of the outer characteristics of his personality.

However we choose, therefore, to define personality, the *wholeness of the organism* must not be lost sight of. That is to say, probably the surest thing about the individual is that he is one individual, and however we "divide him up" for purposes of study we must realize that he is not simply an arrangement of parts but rather a unit which, unfortunately, we are sometimes forced to view one part at a time.

Furthermore, personality is not just the organism separate from the environment but the organism as it interacts with the environment. Thus the organism's "wholeness" implies a perceived and structured environment which is continually modifying the organism and which in turn is modified by the organism. What we learned from the study of perception is especially relevant to the relationship herein being described. To understand a person—that is, to understand his personality

—we must know both how he perceives himself and how he perceives his world. And, more to the point, we must bear in mind how inseparable the two views are.

What "Personality" Does Not Mean

A usage of the term "personality" that is unscientific and confusing to clear discussion is that of indicating by it certain traits considered to be especially desirable. Occasionally someone, wanting to pay a compliment, will say "He has 'personality.' " Or, in the case of a quiet, shy person, the remark may be, "He has very little personality." The objection to such usage is well expressed in the statement:

> To the scientist . . . *everyone* has personality—no matter how good or bad, how entertaining, or how dull, how attractive or unattractive he may be. If social or moral values are to be attached to a particular personality, the scientist would much prefer to use a qualifying adjective, as when it is said, "he has an engaging personality" or "he has a weak, personality." The term *personality* should, then, be reserved for any general or total view of that which makes a person distinctive or a "person." (Anderson, 1949) [3]

FACTORS THAT PATTERN PERSONALITY DEVELOPMENT

There is one idea pertaining to personality that is today quite generally accepted by psychologists. It is that the characteristics and behaviors which contribute to personality development are at once the product of the individual's organic nature *and* of his socialization. Or, to state the idea a bit differently, it is that the individual's biological origins and his socialization are interrelated conditions which operate together in the patterning of characteristics and propensities into what we think of as personality. But, to begin the inquiry into the factors that contribute to personality patterning, let us examine the role that heredity plays.

Innate Differences in Personality Development

How much of what we identify with the personality pattern of the individual is already present at birth? How enduring are the characteristics of the individual that are identifiable in his infancy? Such questions are clearly relevant to our understanding of personality development.

Observation of newborn babies shows that there are certain predispositions to development which are evident even then. One does not need to be very scientific in his observations where several newborn babies are together—as in the infants' room of a hospital—to note certain striking differences between them. Some lie quietly while others are extremely active. Some react almost violently to the slightest stimulus while others remain motionless or even sluggish. Some cry loudly, others simply whimper, and still others scarcely make any noise at all. Although pediatricians and psychologists would be very hesitant to predict later "life styles" on the basis of such early behaviors, there are, nevertheless, quite obvious differences among individuals at the time of birth.

In a study of the personality manifestations of twenty-five babies during their first twenty-four months, Shirley (1933) [46] concluded that numerous differentiable characteristics were present at birth. Included among these characteristics were, for example, irritability, tone and timbre of crying, and motility. She made the further observation that certain personality manifestations tended to remain quite unchanging as the babies' ages increased. The more irritable, for instance, tended to remain more irritable, although there was modification in this trait as well as in other traits over a period of time.

This statement from Shirley's report is especially pertinent to the present discussion:

> The early appearance, pervasive nature, and relative stability and permanence of traits, their consistent pattern and their harmony with familial traits all point to a hereditary basis. Developmental changes in the frequency with which each trait is manifested support the maturation hypothesis.

Fifteen of the individuals in Shirley's investigation were studied some fifteen years later by Neilon (1948) [40], who asked a group of judges to try, independently, to match personality sketches that were prepared for the subjects at babyhood and at seventeen years of age. The success of the judges in their matching efforts led Neilon to conclude that personality manifestations remain with the individual with remarkable consistency. The continuing similarity of behaviors speaks for the role that nature plays in personality development.

Relationship of Ability Endowments to Personality

There can be little doubt that an individual's endowment of abilities will influence personality development. The boy, for example, who has inherited a strong and well-proportioned body may, because of these characteristics and because he also possesses better than ordinary coordination, turn out to be a capable athlete. Certainly the fact that he is a good performer in athletic events will have its bearing on the way he relates himself to other persons, and they in turn to him. These kinds of factors in the long run play a sizable part in shaping the pattern of personality. Or, more accurately, they are the kinds of factors which, *interacting with various social influences,* determine the individual's personality pattern.

Similarly, the individual who has special talent in music or unusual ability to interpret colors and forms in painting is likely to be influenced by them in his total personal development. So also will innate differences in intelligence play important roles in the kinds of relationships which individuals have with others and thus will influence the patterning of their personalities.

Relationship of Inherent Physical Differences to Personality

Individuals differ in body build and they also show striking dissimilarities in facial features and such other features as coloring of the skin and the hair. Are characteristics of physique, facial features, hair color, and so on correlated with personality traits?

Psychologists do not now put much credence in the notion that body build and personality are inevitably correlated (although there has been and continues to be considerable testing of this hypothesis). Not many psychologists would hold to the notion, for example, that simply because an individual is of "rotund" build he will be good natured and of easygoing disposition.

But there are, nevertheless, some possibilities of relationship between physical traits and traits of personality. Often in various cultures certain behaviors are *expected* of individuals who possess this or that physical feature or body characteristic. The individual who possesses the trait learns to live up to the expectation—that is, to adjust to the expectation. In this way, the very tall person, or the fat person, or the person with red hair and freckles learns the behaviors his culture associates with such traits and tends to adopt the role expected of him.

A Biological View of Personality

Beyond the relatively limited view afforded by the immediately preceding section of relationship of some physical features to personality there is a considerable range of factors best referred to as *biological* that warrant attention in the present discussion. Especially relevant and noteworthy are the morphological variations that are to be found within what the specialists in the field recognize as "the normal range." Some conception of the variety of relevant variations and their implications for the understanding of personality differences may be gained from the following excerpts drawn from a presentation by Williams (1960) [52] to the Berkeley Conference on Personality Development in Childhood.

> It makes no difference where we look, whether at the skeletal system, the digestive tract, the muscular system, the circulatory system, the respiratory system, the endocrine system, the nervous system, or even at the microscopic ana-

tomy of the blood, we find tremendous morphological variations within the so-called normal range.

For example, normal stomachs vary greatly in shape, and about six-fold in size. Transverse colons vary widely in the positions at which they cross over in the abdomen; pelvic colon patterns vary widely. Arising from the aortic arch are two, three, four, and sometimes five and six branch arteries; the aorta itself varies greatly in size and hearts differ morphologically and physiologically so that their pumping capacities in healthy young men vary widely. The size of arteries and the branching patterns are such that in each individual the various tissues and organs are supplied with blood unequally well, resulting in a distinctive pattern of blood supply for each.

Morphological differences in the respiratory systems of normal people are basic to the fact that each person exhibits a distinctive breathing pattern as shown in the spirograms of different individuals made under comparable conditions.

Each endocrine gland is subject to wide variations among "normal" individuals. Thyroid glands vary in weight about six-fold (Grollman, 1947) [19], and the protein-bound iodine of the blood which measures the hormonal output varies to about the same degree (Williams, 1956) [53]. Parathyroid glands also vary about six-fold in total weight in so-called "normal" individuals, and the number of lobes vary from 2 to 12 (Grollman, 1947b) [20]. The most prevalent number of lobes is 4, but some anatomists estimate that not over fifty percent of the population have this number. The number of islets of Langerhans, which are responsible for insulin production, vary over a ten-fold range in diabetes-free individuals (Pincus & Thimann, 1948) [41]. The thickness of the adrenal cortex where the critical adrenal hormones arise, is said to vary from 0.5 mm to 5 mm (ten-fold) (Goldzieher, 1939) [18]

Consider the fact (I do regard it a fact and not a theory) that every individual person is endowed with a distinctive gastro-intestinal tract, a distinctive circulatory system, a distinctive nervous system, and a morphologically distinctive brain; furthermore that the differences involved in this distinctiveness are never trifling and often are enormous. Can it be that this fact is inconsequential, in relation to the problem of personality differences?

I am willing to take the position that this fact is of the *utmost* importance. The material in the area of anatomy alone is sufficient to convince anyone who comes upon the problem with an open mind, that here is an obvious frontier which should yield many insights.

Complexity of Factors

The foregoing discussion of the contribution of biological and inherent traits to personality was separated from the discussion of environment only as a matter of convenience. Even while a person is trying to talk about heredity's part in personality development, his remarks inevitably touch on the related role being played by environment. To a considerable extent environment—especially the social environment—tends to perpetuate certain behavior "styles," many of which are *learned* and molded into habits.

The simple fact is that a given inheritable trait or combination of traits may have a very different influence in the ultimate shaping of an individual's personality if the trait or combination of traits occurs in one kind of environmental surroundings rather than another. For example, the personality of a youngster with limited intelligence may be quite different if he happens to be a member of a family that is considerate and wise in their rearing of him. The same individual brought up in an unwise and unsympathetic family would be likely to develop into a considerably different kind of person. In similar manner a child who is frail in physique may be affected in one way if he is the son of nonathetically inclined parents and in another if he is the son of sports enthusiasts.

The point of these illustrations is that no sound basis exists for predicting the pattern of an individual's personality directly from the kind of abilities and physical traits which he may possess. These abilities and traits unquestionably have a bearing upon what the person is to be, but the actual development cannot be anticipated except in the light of the particular environment that surrounds him.

The important question for teachers and other persons who deal with children and youth in their formative years is the question: *How durable are personality characteristics* in the face of the kinds of influences which various environments bring to bear upon them? How *adjustable* is personality?

However much we talk of school as a place where children wrestle with their *immediate* problems, to a considerable extent it is a place where the *future* is of major concern. Will the "bad" boy in the back row outgrow his badness? Will the happy, cooperative, well-adjusted boy in the next row remain so outstanding, or is he just going through a fortunate phase at the moment? These are some of the questions that teachers ask themselves.

CONSISTENCY OF PERSONALITY

That problems are encountered in defining, measuring, and predicting personality has been made clear in this chapter. But with all the problems, scientists have had some success in research explorations of personality. Some of this research is highly important in responding to questions of great importance to teachers and others who deal with children and young people. To repeat questions already asked: "How predictable and consistent are personality characteristics? How adjustable is personality?" Longitudinal studies provide us with the best available data bearing on these questions. Major, on-going studies will be discussed below, but first some aspects of the research problems should be considered.

Some major concerns have been discussed by Yarrow (1964) [54]: First, what type of continuity is to be considered—that of specific, overt traits, or that of behaviors dynamically related to the entire personality pattern? For instance, *dependence* in an infant is quite different in implication than is the same trait in an adolescent. Second, what kinds of variables should be studied—physiological-psychological traits like energy level, or social characteristics like dominance? Third, how consistent is the environment of the subject? For example, does the parental love and affection for an infant change as the child develops, and new infants enter the family? Finally, at what ages should personality be studied; over what time span can consistency be looked for or expected? Because research projects vary widely in the way they deal with these variables, broad generalizations about consistency are hard to come by. But let us now examine some of the data.

LONGITUDINAL STUDIES

Berkeley Growth Study. Subjects of the Berkeley Growth Study were fifty-four selected cases of Berkeley children born in 1928 and studied regularly to the present, along with their mothers in the early years. The mothers of the boys of this study showed more stability of loving, compared to hostile behavior and less stability in control factors, than did mothers of girls. Boys exhibited more persistent correlations with these early maternal behaviors as they grew older.

On specific variables over time, there was found understandably a "confusing array of changing patterns." Some consistent reaction-tendencies were found, however; the most stable of these was the dimension of active and extroverted, versus inactive and introverted. Girls were more stable in this behavior from the first year of life through adolescence than were boys. Boys were more stable for task-oriented behavior, and as one would expect, the girls showed adolescent disruption of stable childhood patterns earlier than boys, and an earlier return to consistency with their childhood patterns (Bayley, 1964) [6].

The Guidance Study. This is another of the University of California longitudinal studies. Subjects were studied systematically from early life until age eighteen on such variables as developmental X rays, bodybuild measures, mental tests, projective tests, and the like; personal interviews and interviews of parents, teachers, classmates, and others were carried out. At age thirty a core group of these measures was again taken, and subjects and their spouses were interviewed.

It was observed that interage correlations were a function of time span and age level for physical and mental measures, with correlations between physical measures far greater than between mental measures in early years. Most other personality and behavior variables did not approach mental and physical variables in interage correlation. The correlations were often higher for an age span straddling a period of marked change, like adolescence, than for adjacent age levels. For example, for girls higher similarities were found for some traits between nine and fourteen than between eleven and twelve years.

The highest consistency of variables over a long time span (two to sixteen years) related to styles of behaviors: reactive-expressive or reactive-inhibitive (note the similarity to the Berkeley study consistencies in active-extroverted, inactive-introverted characteristics).

The researchers were impressed by the subjects' capacity, from babyhood to maturity, not only to survive and cope with all sorts of internal and external stimulation, stresses, and perplexities, but to flourish—to enjoy, explore and to seek new stimulation. Many of the most mature, well-integrated, competent, self-accepting, and clear-valued adults in the study came from the ranks of adolescents who had been chronic rebels, who had been socially inept, unhappy, hostile, dependent, or otherwise seriously maladjusted. These individuals who had changed so radically attributed much of their effective maturity to the experience and insights they gained working their way through their difficult adjustment problems. On the other hand, a number of subjects who had easy and comfortable childhood lives and who had academic and athletic success, social acceptance, and popularity in adolescence had become, "brittle, discontented and puzzled adults whose high potentialities had not been realized. . . ." Of course many adults in the study fulfilled the theoretical expectations and predictions made from early life study by the researchers.

From the unpredictability of social adjustment in so many adult lives, the researchers inferred that much of personality theory based on pathological samples is not useful for prediction for the larger number of persons (Macfarlane, 1964) [34].

Menninger Foundation Study. The subjects of this study were sixty working class and business-professional class children in Topeka, Kansas. They were not studied continuously, but rather at critical life periods: infancy, preschool, latency (middle childhood), and pre-puberty. The focus of the study was on processes contributing to continuity and to change.

Over half the children changed markedly in one or another aspect of functioning. Children showing most continuity had greater developmental balance and less vulnerability when they were infants. A major factor in the continuity exhibited by these children was the relatively homogeneous environment in which they were growing up, one which was stable and free from trauma, and congenial to the child's natural style of development (Murphy, 1964) [39].

Fels Institute Study. The Fels researchers studied the relationship between the adult (aged twenty to twenty-nine) and the childhood status of more than seventy subjects. Longitudinal study was made of the first fourteen years of the subjects' lives, and a followup study was made at maturity. Most of the variables dealt with the areas of achievement, passivity and dependency, aggressive behavior and maternal treatment of the child.

For males, childhood aggression was a good predictor of adult aggression; this relationship was not stable for females. Childhood passive-dependent status for girls was predictive of similar status for adult females. Both sexes were stable on achievement behavior, as was noted in our chapter on intelligence.

A major finding of the study was that maternal behavior during the child's birth to three-year age period was more predictive of child and adult ratings, than were later maternal behaviors (Moss and Kagan, 1964) [37].

Other Studies [1]

Stott (1957) [27] studied the behavior of over 100 youngsters for approximately twelve years. The first observations of them were made while they were in nursery school; later they were observed in recreational activities of clubs to which they belonged. The traits to which Stott gave special attention were those measurable on a scale of "ascendance-submission." One conclusion reached by Stott was that "persistence of pattern was far more frequent than change." Changes that occurred in the youngsters were in most instances temporary; the tendency was for conduct to return to the earlier patterns. In later years there was still evident in some of the children certain characteristics that they had exhibited in the nursery school in spite of the fact that teachers and others had tried hard to change them.

> Many aspects of each child's personality did change in the sense of becoming more mature, and marked changes in overall social behavior occurred. But even with these changes in capacity to function and modifications of patterns of functioning, the fundamental qualities of his person and of his functioning remained to give him uniqueness and individuality among his play peers. (Stott, 1957) [48]

One of the most intensive studies of continuity and adjustment of behavior was made in a longitudinal study of the children of a Minne-

[1] In addition to the studies reported immediately below, see the mention of the Shirley study under the section on *Innate Differences in Personality Development.*

sota county, from 1950 to 1957 (Anderson *et al.*, 1959) [5]. The subjects of this study were between nine and seventeen years of age and were followed up five to seven years after the beginning of the study. Original adjustment was evaluated by means of several personality and adjustment inventories, in addition to teachers' ratings. Later adjustment measures consisted of interviews, evaluation of community reputations, and self-ratings.

These children in general showed considerable age-related improvement in areas such as work habits, family attitudes, and responsibility. The authors note that ". . . if these measures are valid, the overall picture with respect to age across a normal population of children is one of progress toward maturity and adjustment, with at least the suggestion that maturity can, in some degree, be distinguished from adjustment."

Prediction of individual adjustment was, as might be expected, less successful than that for groups. Groups of well-adjusted and poorly adjusted persons were separated quite definitely, however, on many of the prediction devices. The prediction of outstanding adjustment was more successful than that of inadequate or poor adjustment.

In a comprehensive review of literature on adjustment over time, Lewis (1965) [30] considered the continuity hypothesis, that is, the idea that emotionally disturbed children will become emotionally disturbed adults. He found the evidence indicated that adult mental patients often had problems in childhood. However, the reverse statement—that children with adjustment problems frequently grow up to be mentally disturbed—could not be made. Lewis says, in summary, "that some disturbed children will grow up to be disturbed adults is undoubtedly true, but many others will grow up to be ordinary adults with no more than their share of problems" (Lewis, 1965b) [31].

In a research aimed primarily at the emergence of intellectual achievement motives, Sontag (1963) [47] observed some personality characteristics that *do,* under certain circumstances, tend to persist. After noting that the period from six to ten years of age is highly important for the crystallization of a desire for task mastery and intellectual competency, Sontag reported that high levels of achievement behavior at that age are markedly correlated with achievement behavior in adulthood.

PARENTAL INFLUENCES ON PERSONALITY

The personality of the individual has its beginning in the experiences of infancy. There are, as was explained in the preceding chapter, the effects of infant-mother relationships on the early shaping of behaviors. These effects "enter" personality via the satisfying of the baby's basic need for body contact, cuddling, and so on (the "mother love" need). There is also in the early phases of personality development the influence of the mother's attitudes and beliefs imparted to her baby as she attends his needs. This relationship was referred to in Chapter 8 as the "personality psychology" of the cradle and the crib. A quotation used in that connection might well be paraphrased to read: the infant not only takes in attitudes and prejudices with his mother's milk but also many feelings and motives, all of which enter into the pattern of his personality. The subtle influencing of personality by factors in the infant-mother relationship is admirably expressed in the following quotation:

> Some babies find the world a warm, comforting place where their cries are met with a ready response, where they are fed when hungry, cuddled and rocked, and treated with gentleness and love. They react to this treatment by becoming alert, pleasant, and responsive little persons. Other babies, treated more mechanically, develop quite a different set of reactions toward the world. Infants who are kept on a rigid feeding schedule, held as little as possible, and provided with plenty of opportunity to "cry it out" when they are not actually hungry or physically uncomfortable, may respond in several ways. Some learn that they can expect little satisfaction from their outer environment and turn to their own bodies for pleasure. This is one explanation for behavior such as thumbsucking, masturbation, rocking, headbanging, and various other stereotyped, repetitive movements.
>
> Other infants learn that they have to yell to get any satisfaction out of the world. Later they may use temper tantrums and aggressive behavior as a means of controlling the persons around them. Still others find no way at all to gain control over their environment, so they withdraw from it. In infancy such children may lie passively in their beds, refusing to be stimulated, showing little animation, and even refusing to eat. They may become good babies, quiet babies—in some cases so quiet that they just shrivel up and waste away.
>
> These responses are not intellectualized; they are preverbal behavior patterns which become deeply imbedded in the child's feelings. This makes it extremely difficult later to change these original reactions through an intellectual or reasoned approach. (Kaplan, 1959) [29]

Interpersonal Aspect of Child-Parent Relationships

In our efforts to understand the way the parent's personality influences the personality development of the child we must take into account the factor of *interaction* between the two—between the parent's personality and the developing traits of the child. Important as maternal "warmth" is, for example, it does not operate on a one-way current, so to speak, in its influencing of a child's personality.

Especially relevant to the present discussion is a refutation by Bet telheim (1967) [8] of the notion that early infancy is a period in life (the only such period) when the human creature "neither wishes nor needs to do anything on his own." Bettelheim remarks, "We as adults know how helpless the infant really is, but the infant does not know it." Under the heading, The World of the Newborn, Bettelheim expresses his conviction that the infant is very much an active participant in some matters of great importance to him. Notable is his sucking activity—an activity in which it may be said that the infant is not so much a creature being suckled as a creature actively engaged in sucking. The notion that the infant does nothing is one that "his own mother does not usually share" (Bettelheim, 1967 p. 14).

What is the special relevance of the remarks just quoted? Simply this: there are *two* active (and interacting) individuals in a relationship that is filled with the ingredients of deepest satisfaction and *personality nurturing* as well as those that could lead to mutual disappointment and disillusionment.[2] In short, whether it be an infant or an older child, his own active, assertive nature and the character related thereto, as well as those of the mother, determine what the *actual* relationship will be. To reiterate the main point, it is out of this relationship that much of the "style" of an individual's personality may begin to be determined. Is the baby inclined to be responsive or quite unresponsive, cuddly or not so cuddly, happy or fretful? Such behavioral inclinations tend to elicit, respectively, different reactions on the part of the mother toward her baby (Coleman *et al.,* 1953) [12]. Hence, in spite of what may be the essential structure of the mother's personality, the flow of influencing responses from her to her child is in part governed by characteristics already resident in the child's behavior patterns.

A Further Note on Rearing Practices

What has just been said regarding the interplay of reactions between a mother and her child may also be applied to *rearing practices* as they bear upon the child's personality development. Although there seems to be much reason to believe that rearing practices have important influences on a child's personality, we may surmise that it is not the practice *per se* that accounts for this or that behavior manifestation in the child but rather a constellation of factors inclusive of the practice. The effects, for example, of breast feeding or bottle feeding cannot be judged in isolation from the mother's feelings toward her baby, her fondling of her baby, the baby's own inherent traits, and so on.

[2] The student who is able to follow up these brief quotations from Bettelheim by more extended reading from the reference will find in the exposition concerning the origins and treatment of autism some provocative ideas for understanding other children and youth besides those clinically classified as autistic.

Similarly, the consequences of relatively rigid schedules for the baby's feeding and sleeping and of insistence upon early toilet training seem not to be safely predictable apart from the total of the infant's experience with his human and physical environment. The following comment is very much to the point:

Thus, to ask the question—What is the effect of breast feeding upon the personality development?—is to ask the wrong, unanswerable question. Rather we should ask: What is the effect of breast feeding as performed by a particular mother in a particular way as perceived by a particular child under particular circumstances, with regard to both time and space? (Martin, 1957) [35]

Special Attention to Dependence-Independence.[3] There are some half dozen trait-patterns of personality that have received quite rigorous research attention. Among them could be mentioned dominance-submissiveness, sociability-social isolation, aggression behaviors, anxiety, and dependence-independence. It is not intended in this place to discuss all of these kinds of personality characteristics. Most of them have been dealt with in other parts of this book, especially in the immediately preceding chapter. It is the intention, however, to examine the nature of one of them, namely, dependence-independence, and to do this for the purpose of further illustrating the close tie between variables of personality and some aspects of parental influence (and other adult influence).

Quite understandably, the presence of pronounced dependency behaviors in the "life style" of persons who are beyond the early childhood years would invite some concern among people in general and would also become a matter for the attention of researchers. Anything so obviously damaging to personal effectiveness and maturity of personality as prolonged dependence upon other persons warrants serious study. Parenthetically, let it be noted that researchers have tried to identify not only the conditions that produce habits of dependence but also those that relate to the development of independence.

As stated earlier, we recognize a considerable degree of dependence to be a natural state of the human infant. During infancy the human creature is, of necessity, dependent upon the mother. She becomes identified with the satisfaction of the baby's essential biological requirements, and in this context of experience there is soon developed on the part of the infant a reenforcement of emotional dependence on her

[3] There are few concerns of American psychologists that have received more attention during the past fifteen years than the dependence-independence variable in personality development. It is noteworthy that the reference list at the end of the chapter, "Independence-Dependence" by W. W. Hartup in H. W. Stevenson, ed., *Child Development, The Sixty-Second Yearbook of the National Society for the Study of Education* [22], contains 56 titles, from a total of 62, that date 1953 or later.

(Heathers 1955) [23]. Out of what kinds of circumstances does the individual develop independence as he grows from early infancy into childhood, adolescence, and adulthood? Quite clearly, the generalized answer is that independence derives from maturation and learning. But how much does such a statement really tell us?

When preschool children have been studied over a period of time changes have been observed both in the mode of dependence and in the object of dependence. In general, the studies indicate that there is a shift with age (from approximately age two to age four) from *affection-seeking* to *approval-seeking*. The observers' records in a study of preschoolers conducted by Heathers (1955) [24] showed that dependency on teachers was significantly more pronounced in a group of two-year-olds, while four-year-olds exhibited dependency on peers. The study also indicated a noteworthy shift with age in *ways* of showing dependency. The older children manifested much less of clinging behavior and direct affection-seeking.

A generalized conclusion from studies of dependence-independence in very young children is that *with maturity* there is a tendency on the part of children to shift away from clinging, and other forms of close attachment, toward approval-seeking behaviors. But is there more to the explanation? Could it be that movement away from clinging, seeking help, seeking proximity, and the like is pretty generally encouraged by the child's elders and initiated with quite general regularity by mothers? The answer appears to be an affirmative one, provided that we do not hastily generalize beyond the data of researches conducted in the United States. We would appear to be at least a step closer to understanding dependence-independence by taking stock of the fact that with maturity there is the tendency to shift away from clinging and other forms of close attachment to the mother, or mother surrogates, toward approval-seeking behaviors. Incidentally, it appears quite relevant to the present discussion to note the presence and the *naturalness* of this sort of *shift* in the behaviors of the rhesus monkeys studied by Harlow (1958) [21]. Where the *opportunity* was provided for them to do so, they manifested in the course of time an unmistakable satisfaction in "making the acquaintance" of other monkeys of their own age and in being involved in "peer associations" with them. (The quotation marks have been inserted by the present writers.)

The inclination to venture away from clinging and other forms of comfort and security-assurance is quite generally encouraged by the child's elders as a socially approved behavior.[4] But *what* specific behav-

[4] Caution should accompany the generalizing of this statement beyond data from researches conducted in the United States. There is evidence that in the cultures of some peoples (even in some Western cultures) child-rearing practices do not encourage independent behaviors in young children.

iors are we talking about when we say independence is encouraged? And in what ways is encouragement given? How is it received? The first of the questions may be answered by analyzing the concept of independence into such components as initiative, adventuresomeness, persistence toward goals even in the face of formidable obstacles, carrying tasks to completion, and assuming responsibility for getting jobs done by oneself (Beller, 1955) [7].

What about the questions of how encouragement of independence behavior is given and how it is received? One way of trying to answer a question is to ask still other questions. Possibly such a method can help in this instance.

1. Are the child's first steps away from dependence and toward independence empathically [5] and skillfully *paced?* Precipitous involvement of a youngster in radically new experiences may shake his confidence and produce an inclination to retreat into the securities of dependence. In this connection, who has not seen the "back-firing" of behavior that can follow from a parent's arrangement of a "party" for a small child which occasion involves the inviting of a half dozen or more children of approximately the same age? Little Junior is overwhelmed by it all; he is afraid and ill at ease. He may slip away and, to his mother's dismay, leave his "guests" in their own company. Worst of all, he is not about to be drawn again into any such experience at some early date. How much better it would have been had Junior been allowed first to try out the requisite skills in the company of just *one* guest! An individual must learn to stand before he tries to walk; figure-skating comes after the mastering of many intermediate skills.

2. Does the parent (more especially the mother) genuinely *accept* the child's detachments from dependence? Another way of asking the question is to speculate that in a good many instances the mother is the one who cannot give up the close dependence relationship. In such an instance it is not a case of a clinging child but a clinging mother.

3. Is the young adventurer into independence *helped to enjoy* his adventuring? Does he receive reinforcement (for example, genuine praise) for having assumed initiative, or for having carried quite independently to a conclusion what for him was a difficult task?

4. Is the child helped to discover the intrinsic rewards in the tasks which he undertakes? The transition from the need for approval (as reward) to the satisfaction derived from sheer doing and achieving is not to be accomplished simply by being told, in effect, to "plunge in and see how you like it."

5. Does the child's adventuring into independence carry with it a developing sense of personal worth—a sense of being a part of some-

[5] Empathy is used here as in the quote, "I *see* as you see yourself": the act of trying vicariously to experience with another person what he is experiencing.

thing useful and significant? It is out of such a perception of one's actions that the individual gradually acquires a basis for self-trust and (to use a forceful psychological expression) genuine ego-strength.[6]

The inference from the answers that appear best to fit the questions just asked is that independence, as something that *can* emerge out of considerable dependence, doesn't "just happen." It is a characteristic of personality that depends on adequate nurturing—especially in the early stages when a mother's wisdom about handling her child's needs and her own needs for safety and trust enter so importantly into this domain of experience. What has just been said regarding the development of independence may be applied in much the same way to the development of other such characteristics as were mentioned at the beginning of this section.

Personality (to repeat) gets it start in the cradle and the patterning process continues for many months on terms more or less unwittingly communicated by the family. The child gets the initial indoctrinations in role behaviors from the family. There are role behaviors suitable to the boy; there are others for girls. There are roles appropriate to being eldest boy or eldest girl. There are roles that are required because one was born to a particular family having a particular social status and living in a particular locality. The family communicates to the young child in a variety of ways what roles his culture prescribes.

RELATION OF ROLE BEHAVIORS TO PERSONALITY DEVELOPMENT

Throughout life role playing inculcates new response patterns that keep personality constantly shifting and adjusting. This we noted in the discussion of the essential harmony between adaptation of behaviors and the basic personality features (Chapter 8). Hal's case was cited for illustration. The child gradually works out some of the answers to the question, "Who am I?" as he engages in the role behaviors that comprise much of his experience with his peers and others.

> Through social experience he has to learn whether he is brave or cowardly, handsome or homely, quickwitted or deliberate, likeable or surly, leader or follower, prophet or clown. In childhood the process often works in a fairly open fashion: children are not backward in calling each other names and classifying each other's behavior. Later the judgements of others are more apt to be inferred, but they still operate to retouch in various ways the picture one has of

[6] The student who can pursue these ideas into the reading of Chapter 2 (this especially) of Erik H. Erikson's *Identity and the life cycle* (1959) [13] will, the authors believe, be much rewarded.

himself. Thus even the concept of self, central and integrative in personality, cannot be formulated without reference to social interaction and membership in groups. (White, 1952) [51]

Learning the answers to "Who am I?" is a major developmental task. There is much of striving about it and often some moments of bewilderment. The problems which a youngster may encounter as he plays out various roles sometimes force him into behaviors that on the surface appear quite illogical. Only an understanding and observant adult will see the essential continuity in the kinds of behavior which the following situation illustrates.

Bobby, a seventh grader, had volunteered to help gain student support for improved safety practices in his school. He agreed to appear before several home-room groups to explain safety rules and to encourage his schoolmates to observe the rules. His appeal was earnest and well delivered; the teachers and principal of the school warmly praised him for his help. Bobby—we may assume—found satisfaction in his perceptions of himself as a serious advocate of law and order.

Not many days later Bobby, of all persons, became involved in a series of minor disturbances. He would rush toward the exits at recess time and jostle his classmates in the process; he precipitated a few fights on the playgrounds; he emitted loud, startling shrieks in the corridors for no apparent reason.

A teacher with lesser understanding than Bobby's might well have seen little connection between the earlier, "good citizen" role in which Bobby had so admirably performed and this later development. She might, in fact, have looked upon these later manifestations as "the true Bobby" and have discounted the genuineness of his appeal to his schoolmates on behalf of safety regulations. Indeed, she might have tried to *treat* these later behaviors instead of pondering the possible causes of them.

Through skillful, friendly conferences with Bobby, his teacher was able to gain some understanding of these apparently reversed patterns of behavior. She was able to find an explanation which even Bobby could not very accurately have given to himself.

Bobby's teacher saw that the role the youngster had played in the safety campaign had not gotten the response he had expected from his peers. While they had shown respect for him and for the "cause" he represented, they had somehow left much to be desired by him in the way of approval. He sensed an inclination on their part to *cast* him in a more serious role, as more of a conformist to adult standards, than he was ready to accept. His change of behaviors represented, therefore, in his teacher's opinion, a hasty, impromptu, attempt to avoid being "typed" by his associates as something he was not ready to be.

By following through along these lines of interpretation, Bobby's teacher helped the youngster to find ways of relating himself to his peers and also to his teachers that were acceptable to all concerned. More specifically, she helped him to find some less conspicuous ways of expressing his sense of responsibility

—behaviors that would not seem in Bobby's thinking to be discordant with another, equally attractive image which Bobby had of himself, namely, that of an exuberant, fun-loving boy (not man).

The illustration shows how an individual as he enacts different roles learns the responses that express the conception that he has of himself and what he is striving to be. What we saw Bobby doing—his effort to accommodate to certain role requirements—is the sort of thing that is happening much of the time in every person's experience though not always with such dramatic overtones. Personality develops as an individual grows into new behavioral parts which fit comfortably into what he feels he is and what he views himself as becoming.

There is the additional fact that as the individual adopts certain behaviors expressive of the roles he plays, his associates learn to anticipate and depend on these behaviors. "A boy who jokes and jollies his friends soon finds that his companions expect jokes from him. If he tries to meet their expectancy, in time he will become the funny man of the group. Another boy who gets things done because he is more persistent may find himself thrust into leadership" (Anderson, 1949) [4].

Thus, through his experiences with role behaviors not only does the individual learn what to expect of himself; others learn what to expect of him. The learning of role behaviors and the functioning of *social expectancies* operate together in the shaping of the individual's style of life. They involve him in the lifelong task of trying to clarify and understand the different "me's" of the individual:

1. The me that I see;
2. The me that others see;
3. The me that I think others see;
4. The me that I think others think I see;
5. The me I'd like to be.

The problem is that of reconciling these different views of himself and establishing a self-concept that is satisfying to him.

THE SELF-REFERENCE IN PERSONALITY

From the very beginning of this book there has been a sustained emphasis upon the importance to the individual of his interpretation of the place *he* occupies not only in what happens around him but in what happens to him and *within him*. The study of growth and development as it is conceived of in this book should be—first and last—an attempt not only to know growth and development but to understand as best one can the individual's experience with *his* growth and development. Much of the remainder of this chapter will be devoted to the individual's efforts to know himself and to gain and maintain significance. This means giving attention to the *inner aspect of personality*—the private world of the individual.

Development of the Self-concept

The word *structure* was used in Chapter 5 to describe an aspect of the individual's perception of his surroundings. The word was used as a verb. It meant that the individual *organizes* perceptually that which he attends to in his environment. We may now apply this same idea to the individual's self-experiences. He may be said to "construct" the self that he is.

What is involved in this process of self-structuralization? How is the "structure" kept intact?

From Self-awareness to the Self-concept. The dawn of self-awareness was briefly described in Chapter 5; it was clearly implicit in the remarks quoted from Bettelheim on page 25. Let us try to pick up the thread of that discussion and then trace the developments that lead to the individual's enduring self-concept.

It was explained in the discussion of perception and self-awareness that the child has not lived long before he has become engaged in the task of interpreting the world around him and, more importantly, his own relationship with it. His experience soon begins to thrust upon him an awareness that he is a creature separate and apart from other objects and creatures. Besides the kinds of experiences that help him distinguish between "me" and "not me," he makes other discoveries that foster self-perception. These include learning that he has a name (something which in time he will cherish and defend, or perhaps covertly hate), learning that certain things belong to him but that they must be distinguished from things that belong to others, and learning that he is held responsible for his own behavior. The fact that he is being treated by other people as a "unit" tends to hasten his perception of himself as a unit.

The "Social Mirror" for Self-perception

As was suggested in the discussion of role learning, other persons supply the "mirror" in which the individual learns to see himself. Out of their responses to him he constructs his self-image. This is a process that is accentuated and hastened as the child becomes increasingly involved with other children. Youngsters' uninhibited remarks about facial features, other body characteristics, manner of speech, items of clothing, and so on provide a perceptual screen on which a child gets much of the imagery out of which to construct his self-concept. Thus, from what others say or seem to him to be saying about him, what others do or seem to be doing to show that he is valued or not valued—from such interpersonal relationships the individual develops the picture he has of himself. Something that we may call *experience of the evidence* that he is loved and admired by his parents and favorably regarded by his peers contributes to a picture he gets of himself as a desirable person. On the other hand, experiences of being rejected and neglected by his parents, of being indifferently regarded by his peers, or of being overlooked, often criticized—or even ridiculed—by his teacher, lead to a self-picture with which the individual finds it hard to live.

SELF-ACTUALIZATION

Strong within every person is the urge to give expression to what he believes are his strengths—to make actual that which he senses within himself as potentially significant assets. Fromm (1947) [14] in his *Man for Himself* declares, "Man's main task in life is to give birth to himself, to become what he potentially is." Fortunate are those boys and girls whose teacher subscribes to this idea of what youngsters are *really* working at. Not always do their efforts appear to make sense; but when one of us finds it hard to discern any indication of striving for personal growth on the part of another individual, he might ask himself the sobering question, "Have my own strivings for significance always been readily apparent to the people around me and appreciated by them?"

"Becoming" and the Importance of Self-renewal

Personality development is not to be described as one would describe the *building* of a house. For one thing, houses take no hand in their own construction. The same applies to the growth of a plant and even to the "growing up" of one's favorite animal. Man is the only creature that *does* take a hand in determining what he is to become.

It is in the nature of human development for the individual not to wait until a particular goal of development is reached before he visualizes still more that *needs to be actualized.* Every stage in his personality growth brings up new potentialities to a level where they "prompt" the need for *their* fulfillment.

Prescott (1957) [43] in describing the factors that operate in the development of the self, remarks, "I do not believe that purposiveness and creativeness can be eliminated from the human personality, because the tendency toward greater differentiation seems to be a law of nature. It occurs in the growth and development of the body, and it seems equally characteristic of mental functions and the development of the meanings that underlie selfhood."

Cantril (1950) [10] makes a similar observation in the comment, "It is the capacity man has to sense added value in his experience that accounts for his ceaseless striving, his search for a direction to his activities, for his characteristic unwillingness to have things remain as they are."

It follows from such points as have just been made that what the individual sees himself becoming, in a very real sense he already is. The reader will recall the situation of the Eagle Scout candidate described in Chapter 2. He still had some of the requirements to meet before he would have earned the rank of Eagle Scout. But what he visualized himself as becoming was even then very much a part of him. In his self-awareness he could not have been, after the formal recognition, any more an Eagle Scout than he was at the moment.

So it is also with another youngster's view of his *becoming* an engineer, or another's picture of himself as a chemist-in-the-making, or a girl's dream of becoming a great actress. This is the emergent aspect of personality. This is part of the work and the excitement of the inner life of the individual that often is at best only faintly glimpsed by anyone else.

Self-renewal. It is one thing for us to accept the idea that there is indeed an urge within the individual to actualize what are potentially his unique powers. It would seem to be adding something of value to this concept to speak of the capability of *self-renewal*. Gardner (1963a) [15] has written with force about the prospects for something more than survival of our society (or any society). He emphasizes the difference between the maturing of a person, an organization, or a society and the *how* of the maturing. He states, "A society whose maturing consists simply of acquiring more firmly established ways of doing things is headed for the graveyard—even if it learns to do these things with greater and greater skill." Then he adds, in italics, *"In the ever-renewing society what matures is a system of framework within which continuous innovation, renewal and rebirth can occur."* It is clear from the context out of which the italicized statement was drawn and from later passages in the book that Gardner's hope for self-renewal as a distinctive characteristic of a society is, in no small measure, pivoted on the widespread occurence of self-renewal in *individuals*. Two passages from another part of Gardner's book not only support this conclusion but also help relate the idea of self-renewal to the theme of *search for meaning* which the present authors have tried to make central to this chapter. Gardner says, "Storybook happiness involves a bland idleness; the truer conception involves seeking and purposeful effort. . . . True happiness involves the full use of one's powers and talents." Gardner goes on to state that real happiness cannot be separated from a "striving toward" meaningful goals; it does not necessarily depend upon the attainment of the goals.

Accordingly, goals for the individual who is caught up in the satisfactions of striving simply recede before him (Gardner, 1963b) [16].

The Self-process Includes More than Self-"concepts"

The accent on the striving and the urges involved in self-actualization lead to the mentioning of another aspect of *self*. In one's *self*-experience there is more than self-ideas; there is more than *concepts* of self. Feelings, values, and aspirations enter in also.

There is operative, therefore, in the individual's striving for self-significance and goal attainment, all the dynamics that were discussed in the chapter on basic drives and motives and the chapter on feelings and emotions. The individual in his self-processes *needs* to feel secure, loved, and accepted. He needs evidence that his values are respectfully regarded and that his cherished purposes are viewed as significant. There flows through these kinds of inner experience many deep currents of feeling, emotion, and, sometimes, anxiety. We cannot, therefore, complete the account of personality development without some examination of the ways in which individuals provide for the protection of the self-concept.

Maintenance and Enhancement of "Self"

An individual *works* at the task of maintaining and enhancing his self-concept. He learns a variety of behaviors which, though they may not always make sense to other people, are part of a *protective system* within which he can sustain in his own eyes his self-significance. It is a protective system behind which to maneuver when "self" is threatened.

There is an intriguing interpretation which Plant (1950) [42] gives of the individual's resources for matching his personality strength against the constantly shifting pressures of his environment (especially his social environment). He speaks of an *envelope* which, figuratively, surrounds and gives protection to the personality. Plant describes the *envelope* as a sort of "osmotic membrane . . . a property of that part of the personality which is in touch with the environment. . . ." This "membrane" makes it possible for the individual to see only what he can afford to see, to hear only what he can afford to hear, and "at the level of outgo" to respond only with that which will invite no more environmental repercussion (no more pressure) than his personality can withstand.

ADJUSTMENT AS SELF-PROTECTION

The term "adjustment" has had wide usage in relation to personality development. The term implies that all human beings have needs which cannot be satisfied immediately, or in some cases, ever. The resulting deprivation may lead to frustration and thence to a heightening of tension or anxiety which must be reduced or handled in some fashion.

Frustration

If all of a person's needs were gratified, that is, if all of his goals were reached immediately, there would be no need to "adjust." The need-tensions would be discharged when the goal was achieved, and there would be no energy to channel into "adjustment mechanisms." But throughout life frustration is inevitable and much of a person's energy is spent in trying to resolve frustration.

Perhaps the most obvious kind of frustration is a barrier placed in the path of the goal drive by something in the *environment*. Even with the best of care, an infant will often be cold or wet or hungry. As a child, he may be denied ice cream when he wants it or may be stuffed into a snowsuit when he doesn't want to be. Later as a child, he may be forced to sit in a classroom when he wishes to go fishing. When he can go fishing, the fish won't bite. The girl he admires may not return his affection, or his boss may refuse him a raise. And so it goes throughout life.

Not all frustration is produced by the environment. Much of it, and, from adolescence on, perhaps most is produced *within* the person. The infant may be enraged by his inability to reach a toy, or to walk without falling. The schoolboy may find he is unable to hit the ball which is pitched to him. The teenage girl may see herself as less attractive than her "competitors."

These feelings of frustration are in large part due to the standard a person sets for himself—sometimes called the "level of aspiration." The schoolboy's inability to hit the ball is not, for him, a failure unless he *expects* to hit it, or feels he *should* be able to hit it. The ball may have been thrown, for example, to a six-year-old by the high-school's star pitcher. Most boys have had the experience of trying to build an airplane or a boat much too complex for their skill or tools or materials, and then have felt a sense of dejection upon the failure that was foreordained. Probably most girls have attempted a sewing or cooking project too advanced for them. We do not fail except by our own definition. And as may be inferred from the above examples, our expectation may be realistic or unrealistic, but the effect is the same in either case—frustration due to failure to achieve a goal.

Frustration may also occur as a product of motive conflict. A person may, for example, have two concurrent goals that seem equally attractive. A child must choose between cherry and apple pie. A girl must decide which of two dance invitations to accept. The young man must decide which of two job offers to accept.

In another circumstance, the desired goal may be accompanied by some threatening circumstance. The high school boy may wish to earn extra date money by working all week end, but he fears that his girl friend may start dating someone else while he works. Or a desirable job for an adult may be in a part of the world which has an unhealthful climate.

Frustration, either from within or from without (or combinations of both), is a part of daily life from birth to death. Frustration produces heightened emotional responses and serves as a motivating force. It is motivating in the sense that when a person is under the stress of frustration, he usually tries to do something to relieve the situation. What he does may solve the problem and reduce or eliminate his tension, or his action may prolong or actually worsen the stress.

The great majority of frustrating situations in the life of a normal person are resolved fairly quickly and with no particularly harmful effects. The person may find ways of overcoming the obstacle to his need-satisfaction: the child described earlier may, for instance, succeed in getting his ice cream cone by crying. In some cases, a substitute goal may be achieved to replace the unattainable one. Frequently, the goal must be abandoned entirely. Whenever there are failures to solve problems satisfactorily, certain rather common reactions are likely to occur. These reactions are called *mechanisms of adjustment*.

MECHANISMS OF ADJUSTMENT

The kinds of reactions described above are attempts at dealing with increased tension and anxiety. Through a process of trial-and-error, or perhaps by imitation of someone else's behavior, a child tries out a particular way of behaving. It may be healthy or unhealthy, efficient or inefficient. If this action is reinforced or rewarded, it will be "stored up" to be used again in a tension state. In the course of growing up, people develop habitual patterns of response in this fashion. What are some typical ways of responding to stress?

Aggressive Reactions

A very common response is to attack the offending person or object. Who has not kicked a footstool he has just fallen over? It is natural for the child to lash out at whoever or whatever gets in his way. If the three-year-old kicks his father in the shins when he is told it is bedtime, and then is allowed to stay up another half hour, he is likely to use overt aggression in future frustration experiences.

The trouble with aggressive responses is that they lead to retaliation from others and thus to more frustration and hostility—"I ups to him and he ups to me" behavior. Thus, as they mature, most people learn not to make overt aggressive responses, even though such responses seem satisfying at the moment.

Displacement. Sometimes when it is inexpedient for an individual to display aggression in a specific situation, the hostility will be *displaced,* that is, transferred to a "safe" person or object.

Miss M. is usually agreeable and well liked by staff and students in her school, but on one particular day her sixth-grade classroom was in a state of continual pandemonium. In the morning she shook one boy and sent two others to the hall. In the afternoon her caustic criticism reduced three girls to tears. What occasioned this change from her usual pleasant behavior? The fact was that Miss M. had been dating the attractive bachelor principal. On the evening before her difficult day, she had broken up with him because it was apparent that his interest was in amusement, not marriage. But he was still her boss, and thus she was forced to express her hostility by displacement, instead of by direct approach.

The objects of displaced hostility are likely to be those persons or objects that are convenient and cannot fight back effectively. The child may kick a pet or quarrel with a younger sibling or even an adult—parent or teacher—whose affection and responsibilities precludes damaging retaliation. Adults are likely to choose family members—mate or child—or inferiors outside the home. Teachers like Miss M. above not uncommonly "pick on" their students. Sometimes when no other suitable object presents itself, minority groups may become the "scapegoats," as the Jews were in Germany in the 1930s and early 1940s.

Defensive Reactions

Because aggressive responses so often lead to further difficulty, human beings learn early to defend the self in other ways against the effects of frustration. Defensive reactions include a great variety of behaviors that are normal; some, if not all, may be found in any person's repertoire. The greatest danger in defensive reactions is, of course, the possibility that a person will concentrate an excessive amount of energy on defending his ego, rather than on attacking his problems and solving them.

Suppression and Repression. Suppression is the *conscious* act of trying to forget something unpleasant. Probably everyone is aware of attempting to forget a failed examination, some foolish or unworthy behavior, or a narrow escape in swimming or motoring. If not overdone, such attempts have some value in helping a person maintain his self-esteem and may enable him to concentrate on positive or constructive kinds of behavior. They are damaging if they result in evasion or denial of responsibility, and if they prevent learning from experience.

Repression is the *unconscious* stifling of thoughts, wishes, memories, or ideas that may seem threatening or damaging to the ego or that in general are likely to produce anxiety. It is really the basic mechanism of defense and thus may act on any threat to emotional security in the present or past experience of the individual. Repression is usually highly selective, operating to control conscious awareness of a particular act or fear or motive. It may in some circumstances become generalized in the condition known as *amnesia,* in which the sense of personal identity may be lost along with knowledge of family, home, and the like. It is not unusual for children who have been witnesses to violence such as murder or rape to repress the memory of the entire happening or period of time.

Shutting such knowledge or awareness out of the conscious mind does not, of course, eliminate it. It is still present, affecting the general anxiety level; it is ready to appear in disguised or indirect forms.

Compensation. Every person has areas of greater and lesser competence; it is normal to emphasize the most effective areas of competence. In addition, there may be an unconscious attempt to make up for real or fancied deficiencies. An unattractive high-school girl might try to become a leader in every exclusively feminine group in the school as compensation for her failure with boys. Her adjustment, while not entirely adequate, could be described as essentially healthy. If, however, she tried to cultivate popularity with boys by encouraging sexual intimacies, her compensatory behavior would obviously be unhealthy. This example illustrates the point that most adjustment mechanisms have a real, if limited, usefulness but may be damaging to the individual if used excessively or injudiciously. When the compensatory device is misused as in the illustration, it is called *overcompensation.*

One should, of course, not jump to the conclusion that anyone who is striving to make the most of a particular trait or characteristic is necessarily compensating for a failure in some other area of life. High achievers in any area tend to be average or better in other capacities, also.

Daydreaming. This phenomenon needs no definition: the reader may have been utilizing such an escape or defense mechanism within the last hour or perhaps earlier in the day during a dull class or in a period of relaxation. Daydreaming or reverie starts very early in life and is the constant companion of most people. It is relaxing, helps make boredom endurable, and enables an individual to gain—vicariously and temporarily—status, achievement, or satisfaction otherwise unobtainable.

The content of reveries varies with the age, sex, and individual needs of the dreamer. Achievement of some kind—physical, vocational, sexual—is probably the most frequent topic by late adolescence and maturity (Shaffer and Shoben, 1965) [41]. A reversal of the "success-story" dream is that of the martyr or "suffering-hero" fantasy which children often engage in—especially children recently punished; this is a reverie in which the hero sees himself as unjustly punished and then as the object of pity or remorse.

Samuel Clemens ("Mark Twain") must have had some such boyhood dream in mind when he allowed the supposedly drowned Tom Sawyer and his companions to attend their own funeral service. How many youngsters have had fancies such as this, but how few have experienced the reality!

> **The clergyman drew such pictures of the graces, the winning ways, and the rare promise of the lost lads that every soul there, thinking that he recognized these pictures, felt a pang in remembering that he had persistently seen only faults and flaws in the poor boys. The minister related many a touching incident in the lives of the departed, too, which illustrated their sweet, generous natures; and the people could easily see, now, how noble and beautiful those episodes were, and remembered with grief that at the time they occurred they had seemed rank rascalities, well deserving of the cowhide. The congregation became more and more moved, as the pathetic tale went on, till at last the whole company broke down and joined the weeping mourners in a chorus of anguished sobs, the preacher himself giving way to his feelings, and crying in the pulpit. (Clemens, 1910) 11**

Daydreaming is normal and may be constructive: certainly many aspirations are born during daydreams, and plans or schemes may be developed that bear fruit in real life. The practice is unhealthy when the dreams become so much pleasanter than reality that the dreamer ceases to grapple with real-life problems and thus fails to solve them.

Rationalization. Another mechanism is rationalization: finding false or half-true explanations for behavior, which enable a person to preserve the fiction—for himself at least—that his actions have been blameless. This is another universal phenomenon: how many of us have blamed bent fenders on "the idiot in the other car" or have failed tests because of "the trivial and ambiguous questions asked by the professor"? Rationalization is a protective device which insulates people somewhat from the ego-damaging effects of their own stupidity or carelessness.

The process begins very early—as witness the three-year-old, newly exposed to Sunday School, who was asked for an explanation of a broken cookie jar: "I guess the Devil just got in me and made me do it, mama." By adolescence it reaches full flower: "I mustn't study too much and miss out on any social or sport activities in high school—after all, learning to get along with people is more important than learning from books." Or in college: "The social contacts I make here are more important than grades." Or still later in life: "I must be careful not to strain my heart, so I won't mow the lawn" (or shovel the snow, or wash the car).

Although rationalization is almost universal, it is potentially damaging to good personality development. The danger lies in the individual's fooling himself with his exaggerations, excuses, and lies. If he really can accept the idea that his failures, errors, or misbehaviors are not his own fault and responsibility, he is most unlikely to do anything constructive to improve himself or his situation. Self-deceit is fatal to good adjustment. Although it is reasonable for parents and teachers to allow youngsters some face-saving rationalization, it is most unwise to encourage the practice by rewarding or condoning it.

Two familiar versions of rationalization are the "sour-grapes" and "sweet-lemon" devices. In the former, a desired goal is lost but explained away by asserting that it wasn't really worthwhile: "The girl who stood me up wasn't good enough for me anyhow." In the sweet-lemon approach, the person explains the desirability of even the most miserable circumstances. Perhaps the greatest practitioner of this art (except possibly childhood's Pollyanna) was Candide's teacher, Dr. Pangloss. At one point in Voltaire's satire, the pair had suffered unspeakable indignities and were at the moment victims of tempest, volcano, and earthquake in Portugal. Pangloss explained the desirability of their situation, however:

> "For," said he, "all this is for the best; for if there is a volcano at Lisbon, it cannot be anywhere else; for it is impossible that things should not be where they are; for all is well." Thus he continually illustrated his proposition that "This is the best of all possible worlds." (Voltaire) [50]

Some Other Mechanisms

There are other mechanisms than those described above which do not fall readily into a specific category. These are used almost universally by normal, healthy persons.

Denial. Failing to recognize that a situation exists results from unconscious repression of awareness or understanding. The protective nature of such a device is obvious: a situation that does not exist for the person produces no problems and requires no adjustment. A very simple example might be that of the child who "can't hear" his mother calling him home for a nap, or who "doesn't know" that it is long past the time he was required to be home. Another example, familiar to the teacher and guidance worker, is that of the student with low abilities and failing grades who insists he is going to college and is going to train for a profession requiring high academic achievement. Occasionally there may be a tragic example of denial, as when a parent refuses to admit the death of a child and goes on acting as if all were well. This indicates the degree to which the mechanisms of denial may function in mental illness.

Reaction-formation. In reaction-formation, the person's conscious behavior is opposite to his true, but unconscious, desires. Thus the sexually frustrated person may wage a vigorous campaign for improvement of others' sex behavior. An extraordinarily solicitous mother may actually resent or hate the child on whom she lavishes so much care. This kind of behavior reflects the guilt and anxiety-feelings of the individual but is usually not very effective in reducing tension.

Reaction-formation is often clearly exhibited in sibling relationships. The older sibling is advised continually that he must love baby brother or sister, and he *does* love the baby, perhaps to the extent of being lonely when the younger child is absent. But he also has forbidden feelings of hatred and jealousy toward the interloper. As a result, it is easy for his pats to become blows, his kisses to become bites, and his hugs to become dangerously tight. His hostility is imperfectly masked by excessive displays of affection which, if observed closely, may readily show his true feelings.

Identification. Identification is another mechanism that is normal and practically universal but that may cause problems. Identification is the next step beyond imitation. The five-year-old boy wearing his father's work cap and carrying his lunch bucket is not only imitating his father, for the moment he *is* his father in his own mind. Later on, he may identify with a cowboy star or a ball player or a famous racing driver. From each of these trials he will acquire some mannerisms and experiences that will contribute to his total personality development.

It is when an inadequate person gets his life satisfactions vicariously that identification becomes harmful. The child who grows up in the shadow of a successful and dominating older sibling or parent needs help in developing his own personality and in learning to value himself.

To the teacher, perhaps the most familiar and painful kind of identification is that of a parent who lives through his or her child. Too frequently such a parent will try to achieve through the child's life what he desired and failed to gain in his own. It may be a father's desire for athletic fame or a mother's yearning for social success, or any one of a dozen other wishes that lead a parent into identification, without regard to the child's own needs, capacities, and characteristics. Much damage can be done in this fashion.

Projection. This is the mechanism by which human beings attribute to others their own traits, or by which blame is placed outside the self. The girl who is wildly jealous of her "steady" in many cases is repressing her own desires for new adventures and projecting them on her boy friend. Thus, it is often the skinflint who accuses others of penuriousness and the loafer who maintains that his fellow employees are lazy. Projection is often utilized in rationalizing failure or misbehavior. The device is learned at an early age.

Little Kevin was being toilet-trained by his mother, with indifferent success. The family owned a puppy who was also incontinent, so Kevin learned quickly to point to any puddle on the floor, saying "Doggie!" This occasionally saved him from censure, rightly or wrongly. On a visit to his grandparents' home for a few days he was taken to task by his grandmother for a puddle. There being no dog in the household, he looked thoughtful and said, "Grandpa?"

Such incidents are relatively harmless and amusing; but if continued or relied upon, they tend to lessen a sense of personal responsibility and reduce attempts to adjust to life. Although practically universal, projection may result in some very unpleasant and unhealthy situations.

The mechanisms described above are not the only devices that people use to deal with frustration. They include, however, most of those employed by normal people in everyday life. Not all persons, obviously, are normal or well adjusted. It is not within the scope of this discussion, however, to attempt a description of markedly aberrant behaviors—of the mechanisms involved in them.

This brings us, finally, to a question that has become more and more pressing as teachers and other professional workers try to improve their insights into personality. The question is, "Can personality be satisfactorily appraised?" And more importantly, are there methods for examining the inner aspects of personality?

THE ASSESSMENT OF PERSONALITY AND SELF-ADJUSTMENT

The appraising of personality and of self-adjustment is something almost everybody engages in whether he possesses any training for it or not. How could it be otherwise? We all must "size up" the persons we are to work with, to employ, to teach, and to trust with our most guarded secrets. We need dependable appraisals in order to know how to get along with another person—to know what to *expect* of him.

There are other reasons for wanting accurate assessments of personality. As employer, teacher, or parent, we may wish to help an employee, a pupil, or one of our own children, with what we consider a personality problem—a "difficulty of adjustment," as we are likely to call it.

Probably for many people the most compelling reason for wanting to fathom personality is the wish for better insight into their own personality. Where is the person who has not "taken" some kind of "personality test"? Who among us can resist filling out the kind of "examination" that frequently appears in some popular magazine?

A stubborn fact confronts us, however, in our efforts to "test" personality. It is a fact which should now be quite evident to the reader—not only from what he has learned in this chapter but from his study (in preceding chapters) of inborn traits, human motives, perceptions, emotions, and the pressures exerted by the culture.

The fact is that the psycho-physical systems that determine a person's adjustment (to borrow from Allport's definition of personality) are neither simple nor open to easy inspection. The expression "deeper forces" is often used by specialists in personality assessment and therapy to indicate the complexities of motivations and other factors that must be probed if an individual's personality structure is to be accurately interpreted.

Does this imply that teachers had better give up the whole idea of trying to investigate the personality of the youngsters they teach? Not at all! Indeed, the main reason for this chapter—for all the chapters—is to encourage teachers to become more competent as investigators of human behavior and more insightful into personality. We simply must know the limits of our qualifications for doing these things; we must use the kinds of methods that are appropriate to our level of training. We should know when and how to seek out the specialist to secure help with personality difficulties that we are not qualified to diagnose or to treat.

Values of Systematic Observation

One thing every teacher can do to improve his ability to assess personality is to learn to be a better observer of behavior, a more systematic observer. He can make a determined effort to practice the ways of thinking about behavior that were mentioned in Chapter 2. Especially, in this connection, he can learn not to make snap judgments and not to draw hasty inferences about behavior. He can learn to "let behavior tell its *own* story"—which sometimes has considerable reference to the inner aspect of personality.

These are, in fact, the kinds of rules which even the specialist must be guided by if his observations are to help in his assessment of personality. He must rely on what behavior "tells." For this, systematic observation is a prime prerequisite.

Actually, in certain respects the teacher is, of all persons, in the most strategic position to make good use of behavior observation. Few parents see more children in more kinds of personality-revealing situations than the observant teacher. Certainly the teacher is in a position to get more views of certain children's "life styles" than these same youngster's doctors.

One of the most helpful things that a teacher can offer in the case of the extremely troubled youngster are his observations judiciously shared with the child's parents. Sometimes there is real significance for the specialist in what a parent is able to reveal to him in "something the teacher has observed." Or, in a functioning team work arrangement, the teacher's observations shared with the nurse, the school physician, the school psychologist, and others may have value greater than any other data.

Paper-and-pencil Techniques for Personality Assessment

Dozens of so-called "tests" have been devised for the purpose of getting at some aspect or other of personality. Many of these are the kind referred to as paper-and-pencil tests. An examinee taking such a test marks his responses to a variety of printed statements or questions. His answers are then compared with those of some norm group deemed to contain in it individuals whose personality traits ranged over a certain spectrum, or spectra, depending upon how many characteristics the test purports to measure.

There would be little point in an elaborate description here of paper-and-pencil devices for personality measurement. For one thing, a sizable percentage of such devices are of dubious value even in the hands of competent examiners. In general, what a teacher might learn from the use of such instruments he would have learned, more accurately, from the systematic observation advocated above.

There are some measures of personality traits that employ the paper-and-pencil approach and that *are* reasonably valid. They are few in number. When they are used, they should, in general, be given under the direction of a qualified examiner and be interpreted by him. Again (if the right kind of teamwork obtains among teachers and the other professional personnel of the school), the teacher should be in a position to get from the specialist such findings as can properly be shared and can be of use to him—the teacher.

Projective Techniques

Many of a person's motives and needs are hidden from view—even from the person himself. This is part of the "stubborn fact" already mentioned. One thing seems certain about the chances of having them revealed: if they are revealed, this is likely to occur only in some indirect manner. In other words, there is the possibility of their being unwittingly reflected in the behaviors (the speech, writing, drawing) of an individual, who, as he supposes, is simply describing something that an examiner has set before him. The individual, the examinee, is encouraged to put (project) himself into the situation being presented.

Illustrative of this kind of technique is one called the Thematic Apperception Test (TAT). It consists of a series of pictures in each of which one or more human figures are engaged in, or confronted with, a situation that different examinees will interpret differently. That is, the situations presented in the pictures are not highly structured; they are —to use the professional jargon—ambiguous situations. Each examinee finds in a picture *the meanings that he puts into it.*

Presumably an individual will put into his interpretation of a picture what he *needs* to put in—what his own drives and motives would require in the situation *as he sees* the situation. The examiner's role is to encourage the examinee to try to tell the real drama which the picture suggests, thus leading the examinee not only to project his feelings into the situation but also to *identify* with the human figure, or some one of the figures, being described.

Some of the pictures of the TAT are standardized for use with children and older youngsters; there are some for adults only. Various picture-type projective tests are more exclusively for use with children.

Some clinical psychologists and psychiatrists make considerable use of standardized doll-play situations for essentially the same purpose as that described for the TAT. Children, after being introduced to the miniature dolls, blocks, and other items that constitute the test, will be asked by the examiner if he may be excused from the room. He invites the child to play with the miniature objects while he is away. Then, by watching from behind a one-way screen, the examiner observes the situations the child creates with the objects and notes especially how the miniature human figures fare. Some figures may be designated by the child as a father, a mother, a brother, a policeman, the child himself, and so on. The child's conversation as he brings about imaginary interpersonal relationships and drama-filled experiences is, presumably, indicative of happenings in his own life—especially of the inner side of his personality.

The Rorschach Ink-Blot Test is perhaps the best known of all the projective techniques. Briefly, it consists of a series of cards (plates), on each of which is the sort of blot that might be expected to result if some ink were dropped on the center of a piece of paper and then the paper were folded down the middle. Different cards have on them differently shaped configurations of black and white (with some there is color, too).

What does an examinee "see" when, one at a time, he views the ink-blot cards? The inference is, as in the case of the TAT, that he sees what he projects—that he thus indirectly and unwittingly reveals conditions operative in his personality that otherwise would not be discernible to the clinician.

Let it be emphasized again that such instruments as the projective techniques are for the use of properly qualified psychologists and psychiatrists. But, teachers ought to know that there are such devices, that rightly administered and interpreted they often do point the way toward finding some deeply hidden difficulty in personality, and that the very fact such instruments have been devised and are being used is indicative of the imaginative and determined efforts psychologists are making to find adequate means for exploring the deeper recesses of personality. As more is learned about the structure and *the structuring* of personality the more there will be of sound knowledge upon which teachers can develop their understanding of children and youth.

MAIN IMPLICATIONS OF THE EMPHASIS UPON SELF-UNDERSTANDING

In this chapter considerable emphasis has been given to the idea that wholesome personality development is, at center, a matter of healthy self-attitudes. This requires the ability to "know thyself" and to accept thyself.

There is no greater service that a teacher can give than to help a child achieve self-understanding and self-acceptance. How well we as teachers measure up in this respect is a question that we shall look into in the next chapter. But one thing should now be clear: there is no substitute for sound knowledge about how personality develops and how individuals get their self-images—no substitute if the teacher is to try to understand children as individuals.

Another point of emphasis that seems in place here is that teachers must understand themselves if they are to gain sound understanding of children and a psychologically healthy relationship with them. And—fortunately—as teachers improve their knowledge of how children grow and how their personality develops, they greatly enhance their chances of self-understanding. The two tend to go together.

A statement by Jersild (1960) [28] serves well to underscore the significance for teachers that there is in real understanding of self-concept development: ". . . human beings from an early age have a greater capacity for taking a thoughtful and realistic view of the affairs of their inner lives than we have commonly assumed in our psychological theories and our educational practices." Jersild then adds, "Each child is deeply immersed in the psychological issues that influence his way of life. Each, in his way, is a psychologist."

SUMMARY

Personality is psychology's most ambitious construct. The way one explains personality tends to sum up his psychology of human behavior and development. In the present chapter the discussion of personality development has held close to the dynamic, inner-governing aspects of behavior. *"The pattern of life of every individual is a living out of his self-image; it is his road map for living"* (Anderson, 1952) [2].

This view of personality centers on the individual's striving for self-significance. It is a view which calls attention not only to the factors of stability and continuity in personality—inclusive of the defense mechanisms—but also to the uniquely human factor of *desire for improvement.* This is man's most distinguishing characteristic—*his urge to become* that which he feels he is potentially —the urge to self-actualization.

Such a view of personality and self-concept development cannot but make a difference to the teacher as he tries to understand his role in the improvement of the lives of boys and girls. He should, from this point of vantage, see himself not as reformer or rebuilder of persons, but rather as a skillful arranger of experiences favorable to youngsters' strivings for self-actualization.

What implications do these ways of thinking about personality and of the teacher's role in the development of mature personalities have relative to the psychological climate of the classroom? How does what we have been discussing relate to the quality of teacher-pupil relationships and the part the school plays in the producing of emotionally secure, self-accepting human beings? Such are the kinds of questions that we must try to answer in the next—the final—chapter of this book.

Suggested Collateral Readings

Allport, G. W., *Personality: A psychological interpretation.* New York: Holt, Rinehart and Winston, Inc., 1937.

Anderson, J. E., *The psychology of development and personal adjustment.* New York: Holt, Rinehart and Winston, Inc. 1949. Chapter 16.

Breckenridge, Marian E., and E. Lee Vincent, *Child development: Physical and psychological growth through adolescence,* 5th ed. Philadelphia: W. B. Saunders Company, 1965. Chapters 12, 13, and 14.

Dinkmeyer, D. C., *Child development: The emerging self.* Englewood Cliffs, N.J.: Prentice-Hall, Inc., 1965. Chapter 11.

Gardner, J. W., *Self-renewal: The individual and the innovative society.* New York: Harper & Row, Publishers, 1963. Chapter 10.

Hilgard, E. R., and R. C. Atkinson, *Introduction to psychology.* 4th ed. New York: Harcourt, Brace & World, Inc., 1967. Chapters 18 and 19.

Jersild, A. T., *Child psychology,* 5th ed. Englewood Cliffs, N.J.: Prentice-Hall, Inc., 1960. Chapters 6 and 20.

Johnson, R. C. and R. G. Medimus, *Child psychology: Behavior and development.* New York: John Wiley & Sons, Inc., 1965. Chapter 15.

Klausmeier, H. J., and W. Goodwin, *Learning and human abilities,* 2d ed. New York: Harper & Row, Publishers, 1966. Chapter 11.

Linton, R., *The cultural background of personality.* New York: Appleton-Century-Crofts, 1945. Pages 125–146.

Morgan, C. T., *Introduction to psychology,* 2d ed. New York: McGraw-Hill, Inc. 1961. Part 2.

Murphy, G., *Personality: A bio-social approach to origins and structure.* New York: Harper & Row, Publishers, 1947.

Sears, Pauline S., and Vivian S. Sherman, *In pursuit of self-esteem.* Belmont, Calif.: Wadsworth Publishing Company, 1964.

Strang, Ruth, *The adolescent views himself.* New York: McGraw-Hill, Inc., 1957. Chapter 3.

Symonds, P. M., *The ego and the self.* New York: Appleton-Century-Crofts, 1951.

References

1. Allport, G. W., 1937, *Personality: A psychological interpretation.* New York: Holt, Rinehart and Winston, Inc.
2. Anderson, Camille M., 1952, The self-image. *Mental Hygiene,* **36**: 227–244.
3. Anderson, J. E., 1949, *The psychology of development and personal adjustment.* New York: Holt, Rinehart and Winston, Inc. Page 399.
4. ———, page 417.
5. Anderson, J. E., D. B. Harris, Emmy Werner, and Elizabeth Gallistel, 1959, *A Survey of children's adjustment over time: A report to the people of Nobles County.* Minneapolis: Institute of Child Development and Welfare, University of Minnesota.
6. Bayley, Nancy, 1964, Consistency of maternal and child behaviors in the Berkeley Growth Study. *Vita Humana,* **7**: 73–95.
7. Beller, E. K., 1955, Dependence and independence in young children. *J. genet. Psychol.,* **87**: 25–35.
8. Bettelheim, B., 1967, *The empty fortress.* New York: The Free Press. Page 15.
9. Burks, Barbara S., 1942, A study of twins reared apart under different types of family relationships, in McNemar, Q., and M. A. Merrill, eds., *Studies in personality.* New York: McGraw-Hill, Inc.
10. Cantril, H., 1950, *The "why" of man's experience.* New York: Crowell-Collier and Macmillan, Inc. Page 28.
11. Clemens, S. ("Mark Twain"), 1910, *The adventures of Tom Sawyer.* New York: Harper & Row, Publishers.
12. Coleman, R. W., E. Kris, and S. Provence, 1953, A study of variations of early parental attitudes, in *The psychoanalytic study of the child.* New York: International Univeristies Press, Inc., **8**: 20–47.

13. Erikson, E. H., 1959, *Identity and the life cycle. Psychological Issues,* Vol. 1, No. 1, Monograph 1. New York: International Universities Press, Inc.
14. Fromm, E., 1947, *Man for himself*. New York: Holt, Rinehart and Winston, Inc.
15. Gardner, J. W., 1963, *Self-renewal: The individual and the innovative society*. New York: Harper & Row, Publishers. Page 5.
16. ———, pages 97–98.
17. Gesell, A., and Helen Thompson, 1941, Twins T and C from infancy to adolescence: A biogenetic study of individual differences by the method of co-twin control. *Genet. Psychol. Monogr.,* **24**: 3–111.
18. Goldzieher, M. A., 1939, *The endocrine glands*. New York: Appleton-Century-Crofts. Page 589.
19. Grollman, A., 1947, *Essentials of endocrinology,* 2d ed. Philadelphia: J. B. Lippincott Company. Page 155.
20. ———, 1947b, page 247.
21. Harlow, H. F., 1958, The nature of love. *The Amer. Psychol.,* **13**: 673–685.
22. Hartup, W. W., 1963, "Independence-dependence," Chapter VIII in Stevenson, W. W., ed. *Child development, the Sixty-second Yearbook of the National Society for the Study of Education*. Chicago: The National Society for the Study of Education.
23. Heathers, G., 1955, Acquiring dependence and independence: A theoretical orientation. *J. genet. Psychol.,* **87**: 277–291.
24. ———, 1955, Emotional dependence and independence in nursery school play. *Child Develpm.,* **24**: 169–179.
25. Hilgard, E. R., 1957, *Introduction to psychology,* 2d ed. New York: Harcourt, Brace & World, Inc. Page 472.
26. Jersild, A. T., 1960, *Child psychology,* 5th ed. Englewood Cliffs, N. J.: Prentice-Hall, Inc. Page 440.
27. ———, page 441.
28. ———, pages 455–456.
29. Kaplan, L., 1959, *Mental health and human relations in education*. New York: Harper & Row, Publishers. Page 116.
30. Lewis, W. W., 1965, Continuity and intervention in emotional disturbance: A review. *Exceptional Children,* **31**: 465–475.
31. ———, page 472.
32. McDonald, F. J., 1959, *Educational psychology*. Belmont, Calif.: Wadsworth Publishing Company. Page 6.
33. McKinnon, Kathern M., 1942, Consistency and change in behavior manifestations. *Child Develpm. Monogr.,* **30**.
34. MacFarlane, Jean W., 1964, Perspectives on personality and change from the guidance study. *Vita Humana,* **7**: 115–126.
35. Martin, W. E., 1957, Effects of early training on personality. *Marriage and family living,* **19**: 39–45.
36. Morris, D. P., E. Soroker, and G. Buruss, 1954, Follow-up studies of shy, withdrawn children: I. Evaluation of labor adjustment. *Amer. J. Orthopsychiat.,* **24**: 743–754.
37. Moss, Howard A., and J. Kagan, 1964, Report on personality and change from the Fels longitudinal study. *Vita Humana,* **7**: 127–138.

38. Murphy, G., 1947, *Personality: A biosocial approach to origins and structure.* New York: Harper & Row, Publishers. Page 86.
39. Murphy, Lois B., 1964, Factors in continuity and change in the development of adaptational style in children. *Vita Humana,* **7**: 96–114.
40. Neilon, Patricia, 1948, Shirley's babies after fifteen years. *Pedagogical Seminary and J. genet. Psychol.,* **73**: 175–186.
41. Pincus, G., and K. V. Thimann, eds., 1948, *The hormones.* New York: Academic Press, Inc. Vol. 1, page 303.
42. Plant, J. S., 1950, *The envelope: A study of the impact of the world upon the child.* New York: The Commonwealth Fund.
43. Prescott, D. A., 1957, *The child in the educative process.* New York: McGraw-Hill, Inc.
44. Sandford, N., 1962, Implications of Personality Studies for Curriculum and Personnel Planning, in R. L. Sutherland, W. H. Holtzman, E. A. Koile, and B. K. Smith, eds., *Personality factors on the college campus.* Austin, Texas: The Hogg Foundation for Mental Health, The University of Texas. Page 3.
45. Shaffer, L. F., and E. J. Shoben, Jr., 1956, *The psychology of adjustment.* Boston: Houghton Mifflin Company.
46. Shirley, Mary M., 1933, *The first two years: Personality manifestations.* Minneapolis: University of Minnesota Press.
47. Sontag, L. W., 1963, The emergence of intellectual achievement motives. *Amer. J. Orthopsychiat.,* **43**: 532–535.
48. Stott, L. H., 1957, Persisting effects of early family experiences upon personality development. *Merrill-Palmer School Quarterly* **3**: 145–159.
49. ———, page 158.
50. Voltaire, *Candide.* New York: Hartsdale House, 1930.
51. White, R. W., 1952, *Lives in progress, a study of the natural growth of personality.* New York: Holt, Rinehart and Winston, Inc. Pages 121–122.
52. Williams, R. J., 1960, May 5, *A presentation to the Berkeley Conference on personality development in childhood.* Berkeley, California: University of California, unpublished address.
53. ———, 1956, *Biochemical individuality.* New York: John Wiley & Sons, Inc. Page 53.
54. Yarrow, L. J., 1964, Personality consistency and change: An overview of some conceptual and methodological issues. *Vita Humana,* **7**: 67–72.

CHAPTER 16

Psychology of Teacher-Pupil Relationships

The title of this chapter might well have been "The Psychological Climate of the School." The expression refers to the feelings, the purposes, and the sense of accomplishment of the pupils and their teachers. It includes the interest and enthusiasm, or lack of these, with which pupils and their teachers enter into learning situations. Important to it is the nature of the discipline—interpreted in the broadest sense—that obtains in the classroom and on the playground.

A school's psychological climate derives largely from the quality of the interpersonal relationships among pupils, teachers, and all other persons more or less directly involved in the life of the school. It is a climate influenced in many important ways by the kinds of ideas teachers and school administrators have about the psychology of human growth and development. Especially is it influenced by the kinds of *self-definition* pupils and teachers have of themselves. The reader will recognize the special emphasis as one that is closely associated with the central theme of the book. Within this emphasis are incorporated numerous of the concepts that help us answer the "So what?" of the topics of the psychology of human behavior and development. They are concepts whose practical importance should begin to be discernible as we progress through this final chapter.

CONDITIONS OF GOOD PSYCHOLOGICAL CLIMATE

There are at least eight distinguishable conditions that are prerequisities to a favorable psychological climate in the school. The discussion of some of the eight will tend to interrelate closely with the material in certain later sections of the chapter.[1]

[1] Parts of the discussion of "climate" are reproduced from Baller, W. R., 1956, "Conditions that influence the psychological climate of the school," in *School and*

The First Condition: *Evidence that one is a valued person.* This applies to teachers and pupils alike; if teachers have the conviction that they are valued, the chances are greatly enhanced that pupils will make a similar discovery about themselves. When teachers were asked in a certain elementary school, "What one factor means most to your feelings of satisfaction with teaching?" the most frequent answer was, "Having a principal who knows how to make me feel like a valued person." [2] Grady, the principal of that school, was such a person. In appearance, he was a modern version of Abraham Lincoln. In manner he was friendly, sincere, and always eager to hear another person's interests, problems, and successes.

Someone asked Grady, "What makes your school such a friendly place? . . . The teachers here seem to be unusually cheerful and the children appear without exception to be happy." To this Grady had a ready reply. School, he said, should be a place where everyone can discover the satisfaction not only of being valued but also of making others feel valued. There was, he believed, no more important experience for anyone than the *experience of the evidence that* one is a valued and worthy person.

There is a striking contrast between Grady's school and another not far distant from it. In this other, the principal believes that he has some teachers of real quality, some of fair quality, and some whose ways, skills, and opinions he finds it difficult to approve. Quite unconsciously perhaps, he ignores the opinions of the less valued teachers, especially in teachers' meetings; he avoids placing them on committees; he prefers the personal company of a select few of his associates. So the rejected teachers have separated into little cliques in which they share confidences about the ways in which their feelings have been hurt or the ways in which cold water is thrown on their ideas. They hope soon to find other jobs. They do not feel valued as Grady's teachers do.

These illustrations emphasize especially the influence which a principal's concepts of human dynamics have on the life of a school. Doubtless certain of the readers of this book will someday be school principals or supervisors. The moral of the discussion as it pertains to them should be clear.

College [2], published by Arizona State University. They have been adapted to the present discussion with the expressed consent of the publisher of *School and College.*

[2] The importance of this trait in the principal as it bears upon the morale of the school is attested to in various studies. See, for example: National Education Association, *The Elementary School Principalship, Today and Tomorrow,* 27th Yearbook of the Department of Elementary School Principals, Washington, D.C., September, 1948; and the Bronxville Public School, *A Message from the Board of Education,* Bronxville, N.Y., June 5, 1953. See also Yeager, W. A., 1954, *Administration and the teacher,* New York: Harper & Row, Publishers, pages 235–238.

The kinds of relationships which hold between principal and teachers also pervade the realm of teacher-pupil relations and in turn the relatively private domain of the pupils.

The Second Condition: *Commitment to tasks that are meaningful and significant.* Teachers' meetings that deal with trivia, pupil assignments that amount to dull busywork, tasks that require capabilities which the teacher or pupil does not at the moment possess: these are illustrative of experiences that are ruinous to morale. To be engaged in a worthwhile undertaking is to find significance in oneself, and this is essential to good psychological climate.

A quotation from Gardner (1961) [7] is apropos: *"The best-kept secret in America today is that people would rather work hard for something they believe in than enjoy a pampered idleness."* What may be said of people in general may be stated with additional emphasis as it pertains to youngsters in school—a fact that many people find quite difficult to believe.

The Third Condition: *The right to judge and to know the worth of the product of one's efforts.* It is a "bad climate" that gives the teacher a feeling of uncertainty about the satisfactoriness of the outcomes of his instruction. And by the same token, children and youth need the experience of assessing the worth of their accomplishments against criteria that have meaning and importance to them.

Youth have great potential for realistic self-appraisal. There are not many places in the total scheme of the school where we as teachers have more to achieve—more to improve—that in our evaluative methods. Suffice it to state that we often confuse and dishearten boys and girls when we show distrust of *their* judgments about their potentialities; when intentionally or unintentionally we snare them in examinations where their performances are interpreted as showing how wrong they are. Why can't we make *more* of our classroom tests a means for coursework clarification—for learning—rather than devices to serve our "built in" need for *classification* of learners?

The Fourth Condition: *Evidence that one is expected to have freedom and to use it constructively.* An atmosphere of freedom and confidence is one in which there is an absence of useless tension. Basic to this condition is a disposition on the part of the principal to judge *with* the teacher, not *for* him, the quality of freedom and control in his classroom. One teacher said, "My pupils and I dread a visit from the principal. I wish that when he comes he would stay longer. Then he would get the feel of the purpose and healthy motivation that underlie the apparent confusion that he sometimes finds in my room." The pupil has the same need for reassurance from his teacher that the teacher has in turn from the principal.

Classrooms are places in which to develop self-reliance and self-confidence. The psychological climate for the development of healthy personalities is not provided by a classroom that breeds a feeling of uneasiness and a fear of making mistakes. It is a classroom whose "ways" are in harmony with a position that is forcefully stated in The Yearbook, *Perceiving, Behaving, Becoming* (1962) [1]. Somewhat abridged the statement of the position reads:

> The right to make choices, which is central to becoming, implies also the right to make mistakes. Learning conditions which do not permit mistakes limit the child's freedom and his willingness to make his own choices. The very process of becoming involves the challenge of new experiences, of trying the unknown, and necessarily must result in mistakes. When children, teachers and administrators accept errors as a natural part of the learning process, growth is facilitated.

The Fifth Condition: *A contagious learning situation.* This condition is one that depends in part upon the belief that productive learning is a "reaching out" on the part of children rather than a passive conformity that they have imparted to them by the methods of the teacher and the "packages of knowledge" prepared in the form of curriculum.

Every course taught in a school finds its justification first of all in the contribution it makes to the child's urge *to know* (as this need was described in Chapter 6) and to reach out for meaning. One of the characteristics of the truly effective teacher is that he has mastered ways of being alert to what each individual student is "trying to tell": he learns to "see with" each pupil in the adventures of learning (Murphy, 1966) [17]. In remarks about youthful learners' "great craving to understand and make sense of the world." Murphy goes on to say ". . . The most relevant question is, *do we* find what they are curious about, and do we feed that flame?" (Murphy had previously referred to "curiosities which are burning so intensely and fiercely. . . .") Several paragraphs beyond these remarks and with a change in figure of speech, Murphy asks, ". . . Have we arranged for a two-way traffic in the great tunnel between the rich cultural tradition that we want to impart to the youngster and the craving for life which he brings to it?"

Certain ideas that received special emphasis in Chapter 11 and Chapter 15 bear directly on the points made in the paragraph above. In the chapters just mentioned, considerable attention was given to an assumption held by a sizable number of educators and behavioral scientists today. It is the assumption of an *active* and *creative* mind that engages the content and the methods of instruction by which the experiences of the classroom are presented. Viewed from the vantage point of this assumption, *learning* can be seen as "a transaction between the content and the learner" (Taba, 1962) [24].

The transaction just mentioned is one that can be greatly enhanced by a psychological climate characterized by contagious enthusiasm.[3] Who is the good teacher? Is he the one who finds his own organization of knowledge being "dutifully reproduced" by his pupils? Or is he the one whose pupils *catch* from him a zest for inquiry, and find themselves joining him in an adventure which has a chance of resulting in their own organizing of knowledge? Is he the teacher who helps pupils to understand and accept with satisfaction the idea—the *fact*—that meaningful goals always tend to move on ahead as one journeys toward them? Is he the teacher whose guiding ideas could be represented in such terms as "fully functioning and self-actualizing," "toward openness of experience," "trust of one's own experiencing," and "living as a process"? (*Perceiving, Behaving, Becoming,* 1962) [1]

The crux of the relationship between student and classroom experiences that the authors have tried to spell out under *The Fifth Condition* was poignantly expressed by a poorly clad and physically frail little ninth-grader named Rosie. As the principal of Rosie's school went to his office one evening at dusk some two weeks before classes were to open in September, he recognized, about fifty feet away, the silhouette of Rosie, who was sitting on a bench in front of the school. "Well, Rosie—imagine finding you here!" was Mr. A's friendly greeting. "And, may I ask what brings you here?" To which Rosie replied, "It's what school means to me. I just can't wait 'til it begins . . . so . . . I have to come here close to it and think about all it tries to tell me." After a few matters were attended to in his office, Mr. A. with his arm around Rosie, walked her to her home, nearly a dozen blocks away in a "shabby" part of town. As they strolled along, Rosie and Mr. A. told each other about life and about how a wonderful place called SCHOOL "talked" to them about *learning.*

One of the interesting features about today's schools is the number and variety of in-service learning situations in which teachers engage. Encouraging indeed is the extent to which principals and teachers work in these situations together. "How can our understanding of children be improved?" This and many similar questions are being examined earnestly and cooperatively by principals, supervisors, and teachers—often in in-service child-study classes.[4] The spirit of the venture seems

[3] A very intriguing phrase was employed by Bruner (1965, page 78) [4] in telling of some "inspired" teaching that was demonstrated by two of his acquaintances. Bruner's phrase: "Both of them practiced the *canny art of intellectual temptation.*"

[4] See for example: Commission on Teacher Education (Staff on Child Development and Teacher Personnel), 1945, *Helping teachers understand children,* Washing-

generally to carry over into the classroom and to affect the ways of the children.

The Sixth Condition: *Meaningful membership*. In Chapter 8, attention was given to the importance of what Havighurst called *social fidelity*. Havighurst stressed the importance of this aspect of youth's development as it complements the characteristic of self-esteem and as the two characteristics relate to an individual's achievement of *identity* "as a person in his own right." There is much in the literature (as was shown in Chapter 13) pertaining to the functions of peer relationships which, for one thing, express the strong urge of the individual to "belong." This need is especially operative during adolescence.

The success of a particular high school in channeling the *urge to belong* into an effective *esprit de corps* is noteworthy and relevant. A little more than a dozen years ago the youth of this school could hardly have cared less about the participation of any of its members in such activities as music, dramatics, athletics or debate and, least of all, demonstrations of academic accomplishment. Through some highly imaginative and skillful planning by the principal and his staff (with much well-timed involvement in planning on the part of key members of the student body) the students of this school now identify with it as something *central,* an expression—or projection—of themselves. Today the attainment of distinction by a class, a team, or any individual member of the student body, adds, in the thinking of the students, to *their* school's stature and to the stature of every boy and girl who attends the school.

It would require a long story—too long for the space herein alloted —to give an adequate description of how the transformation of the school was brought about. Suffice it to mention only one of the steps. The step was that of bringing to the school, one at a time, individuals with whom there was good reason to think the students would *identify* and having these persons "reach out," so to speak, to the students with their great talents of music, dramatic ability, athletic skill, and so forth. Then, perhaps above all, there was a subtle and genuine *communication* to the students by these great persons that the students also could in time and with desire actualize the potentialities which they possessed within them and, individually and collectively, become "champions" (to use the youngsters' words).

Repeating, in somewhat different words, what has already been said about the changed thinking and feelings of the students about their

---

ton, D.C.: American Council on Education; English, H. B., 1951, *Child psychology,* New York: Holt, Rinehart and Winston, Inc., pages 15-32; or Prescott, D. A., 1957, *The child in the educative process,* New York: McGraw-Hill, Inc., especially page xii and Chapter 13.

school, let us summarize with the remark that there occurred in this school an evolving of healthy desires, urges to creativity, strong drives toward commonly shared aspirations and values, and a sense of membership in a society that helped sustain one's sense of pride in himself.[5]

The Seventh Condition: *Extensive information about the interests and abilities of every child in the school.* Only when such information is available and *used* can the best in every child be brought out and developed. Only under such circumstances can it be known that little Mary, age nine, plays the piano well (many like her have gone unnoticed and unappreciated through a year of discouraging neglect). Only under such circumstances will Tommy's energy be known and also his talent in painting. And only under such circumstances will every child have a chance to develop all his potentialities and to learn what a priceless adventure going to school can be.

The Eighth Condition: *Mutual respect between parents and the teacher.* For many teachers this is a hard order to fill. One takes heart, however, upon hearing a veteran principal declare, "One of my main responsibilities is to know the homes from which our pupils come. A person can't know the psychological needs of children if he doesn't know their homes. And he won't know the homes if he doesn't get into them." This principal had been in every home represented in her school and, except in a very few instances, she had been accompanied on these visits by one or more of her teachers. A thriving PTA was one consequence of this policy, and a generally friendly attitude toward the school by its patrons was another, with good "climate" a definite result.

This same principal was heard on another occasion to say "I make it a practice to learn as soon as possible something praiseworthy about each child in my school. Then I call this child's parents and tell them about it. Thus my first contact with the parent is a pleasant one. If later I must discuss a disagreeable subject with the parent I won't be so likely to encounter hostility and resistance."

The prevailing philosophy expressed in the eight conditions requisite to good psychological climate finds expression in the following:

Many classroom incidents provide creative opportunities for inculcating positive values. When students challenge you on your facts or raise questions about your interpretations, you have a splendid chance to demonstrate your

[5] Some of the description of this school appeared in an article by Baller (1965). It was stated in the article that the school being described was an actual one. There would seem to be something significant in the fact that after the publication of the article the author received a number of letters from high school principals wanting to know whether by chance it was *their* school that had been thus portrayed. The reader who has grasped the meaning and implications of the *New Focus on Education* as discussed in *Perceiving, Behaving, Becoming* must conclude that more than one school has made the ideas therein presented actually work.

own respect for inquiry and truth, your own openness to new ideas or new interpretations. When things go wrong, in science and homemaking, you can lead your students to pursue and analyze the cause of the difficulty. When you make a mistake, whether in marking a student's paper, in reporting a fact in science, or in correcting the behavior of students, you have an opportunity to demonstrate the values of honesty and moral responsibility. Your human mistakes give you an opportunity to demonstrate moral virtue. Teaching failures can be turned into exciting learning challenges which are rewarding for all.[6]

These are at least some of the very important conditions that influence the psychological climate of the school. Psychology has a great deal to tell about the makeup of these conditions.

DIFFERENT PERCEPTIONS OF SCHOOL BY DIFFERENT INDIVIDUALS

Much of an individual's behavior is affected not directly by his surroundings but by his perceptions of his suroundings. The influence of a given situation on a child or a youth is dependent upon what that situation means to him; that is, upon the way he perceives it. His perceptions, as we learned in Chapter 5, are governed in part by the conditions of his "inner environment"—the state of affairs pertaining to his bodily functions. And they are influenced by the feelings, attitudes, and persistent beliefs which are so much a part of him.

Each child views and interprets each moment in the on-going procession of school activity from the only vantage point accessible to him —his own needs and background of experience.

The children who comprise a class have come from many different kinds of backgrounds. Some have not outgrown the need for considerable supervision and direction. Others know how to use freedom and are considerably more advanced in self-control and self-reliance. How a teacher deals with them must be determined by such factors. Some bring to the class situation an experience of frustration and defeat which they have experienced elsewhere in their school endeavors. For others school has been largely a succession of triumphs. For certain children school represents something the entire family looks upon with disfavor and even intense dislike. For still others the school holds the promise of many good things. Certainly the satisfactoriness of the relationship between a pupil and his teacher will depend greatly upon the teacher's ability to keep the importance of individual differences in mind and his ability to see the school situation through the eyes of the individual child.

[6] McCreary, E. R., "You teach what you are," in Robinson, D. W., ed., *Professional growth for teachers.* New London, Conn.: Croft Educational Services.

A teacher must never fail to consider how a given situation will be interpreted by the child, and especially how it will affect his sense of personal significance. An illustration was given in Chapter 2 that may well be brought back to mind in this connection. The reader will recall the way in which a teacher and pupil misinterpreted each other's motives in what should have been a friendly skirmish of opinions about a lesson topic, and how the situation became tense largely because each one (teacher and pupil, respectively) felt that he dare not lose face in the presence of the other pupils. The opposite effect from the one just alluded to was the result of a different tactic employed by a teacher.

George, an eighth-grader, took exception to Mary's assertion that tornados and cyclones were the same thing. The teacher and most of the class tended to support Mary's statement.

In this instance, the teacher sensed an impending clash of opinions which might lead to some hurt feelings and possibly to alienation of George's respect for her. She seized the moment to structure a desirable learning experience. She suggested that here were the makings of an experience that could have more than one kind of gain in it. She explained that not only would it be desirable to settle the issue on the basis of fact rather than debate alone, but it would also be desirable to learn the useful role that is played in discussion by an informed and well-intentioned opposition. This class benefited in their understanding of the function of constructively critical debate as well as in their knowledge of the topic under discussion. And furthermore, they learned a valuable lesson in the psychology of their own interpersonal relations.

In the illustration just given, the teacher demonstrated the highly important quality of being able to see a situation through another person's eyes. It was relatively unimportant to her whether she proved to be on the winning or losing side of the debate. For her, it was more important to understand the ideas and feelings of her pupils as they engaged in a learning experience.

A very revealing description of the importance of a pupil's perception of his status in school is furnished by a wise teacher who tells of the problems related to reshaping a boy's hostile feelings and attitudes.

Paul had got off to a bad start at school. Reading was simply beyond him. It was an intolerable task. As with many other first graders sitting still and working on meaningless symbols in books was virtually impossible. Paul resorted to making a nuisance of himself which, he learned, would result in his being "excused" outdoors. But this did not make for progress in reading. Matters went from bad to worse, and Paul's parents transferred him to a private school for "discipline."

Finally, under the pressure and corporal punishment of the private school, Paul refused to do any work whatsoever, and after school he fought with everybody. This led to his expulsion from the school and to his being branded as a failure and an "incorrigible."

Paul deserved a better fate, and got it in the second grade under a teacher who, though she eyed this big, strong boy "with mixed emotions" could, nevertheless, say, "I welcomed him, and as the day wore on, my heart warmed to him as I perceived that under this 'knock'em down and kick'em' exterior was a scared and unhappy seven-year-old."

The teacher and her class had been studying rocks, some of which could best be examined only when they were broken open. Here was a job for Paul. He was set to work with a borrowed hammer at the useful task of breaking up the rocks. With the shattering of one large rock, Paul was suddenly surrounded by classmates eager to study the beautiful crystals.

This was a moment of surprise to Paul. He was for the first time a contributor rather than a disorganizer in his classroom.

More constructive experiences followed. But there were disturbances too, in one of which the teacher had forcibly to separate him from another boy who was being threatened with great bodily harm at Paul hands. Paul's damaged personality was not easily or quickly repaired.

Even reading ceased to be a dreaded ordeal. The teacher knew she had achieved her goal when one day Paul accepted her invitation to help teach some of the children how to throw and catch a ball. Quickly he assumed the role of a capable, sympathetic "coach" whose mental image of himself doubtless changed when his classmates unanimously elected him captain of the team. (Hunter, 1958) [9]

TEACHERS' CONCEPTS OF DESIRABLE AND UNDESIRABLE PUPIL BEHAVIOR

A study which is now a classic in psychology was conducted approximately forty years ago by Wickman (1928) [25], who was interested in determining what kinds of pupil behavior teachers considered to be desirable, what kinds they considered to be undesirable, and how they would rank various behaviors in terms of their importance. Wickman's method in this study was to ask teachers to rank a list of pupil behaviors in the order from most serious to least serious. He then asked mental hygienists to give their ranking of the same behaviors. The behaviors are shown in Table 16.1, the second and third columns.

It is clear from the Wickman findings that teachers tended to rate pupils as being well adjusted in their general behaviors according to the degree of success they had in their school work. Traits that teachers thought to be out of harmony with pupils' close application to their studies were deemed to indicate poor adjustment. They rated as most serious such behaviors as disregard for authority, dishonesty, immoralities, lack of orderliness, breaches of rules, and, as already stated, failure to apply themselves to their school work.

In contrast with the teachers' ratings were those of the mental hygienists, who in general looked upon the behaviors which disturbed the teachers most as being relatively unimportant. They ranked as most serious cruelty, temper tantrums, and truancy. Interestingly, these last named were considered by the teachers to be among the least serious behaviors.

Teachers in Wickman's study of four decades ago looked with much concern upon pupils' profanity, disobedience, smoking, and their writing of obscene notes. Mental hygienists, on the other hand, considered marked suspiciousness, hypercritical attitudes toward others, prolonged day dreaming, sensitiveness, and shyness to be important symptoms of unfavorable personal adjustment.

Change in Teachers' Judgments of Pupil Behavior

Mitchell (1942) 16] repeated the Wickman study fourteen years later, with different groups of teachers and mental hygienists. The evidence indicated that teachers had made appreciable, though not pronounced, changes in ratings in the direction of those of the mental hygienists and that the latter had also altered their judgments toward a somewhat more conservative position. Whereas teachers in 1926 had not shown much concern, relatively speaking, for traits of fearfulness, withdrawal, sullenness, resentfulness, easy discouragement, and hypercritical attitude toward others, the teachers of 1940 looked upon these as being serious. In the main, however, it appeared from Mitchell's findings that teachers and mental hygienists still held significantly different ideas about the relative seriousness of various behavior traits in children. It was apparent that teachers still considered behavioral conformity and amenability to authority as of first-order importance.

Still another inquiry into the possibility of changes in teachers' attitudes toward pupil problems was reported by Stouffer (1952) [22]. There were 481 male and female teachers included in the study. There were also 70 mental hygienists. The over-all sampling was very similar to the one used by Wickman.

As compared with Wickman's teachers, those of Stouffer's study showed greater concern for withdrawing behavior, unhappiness, and depression. In these respects they were in closer agreement with the mental hygienists than were Wickman's teachers. But there was in their thinking, as in that of Wickman's teachers, an inclination to regard as most serious the kinds of problems that relate to truancy, dishonesty, sex adventurers, and lack of order in the classroom.

Reflection in Ratings of Different Orientation of Teachers and Clinicians. Stouffer directs attention to the fact that teachers and mental hygienists do indeed have different responsibilities toward children. Behavior traits that are harmonious with the smooth running of the school

TABLE 16.1
Rank-order Comparison of Ratings by Teachers in 1955 and by Teachers and Mental Hygienists in 1926 of the Relative Seriousness of Fifty Behavior Problems

308 Teachers (1955) Hunter	511 Teachers (1926) Wickman	30 Mental Hygienists (1926) Wickman
1. Stealing	Heterosexual activity	Unsocial, withdrawn
2. Destroying school materials	Stealing	Suspiciousness
3. Truancy	Masturbation	Unhappy, depressed
4. Cruelty, bullying	Obscene notes, talk	Resentfulness
5. Unhappy, depressed	Untruthfulness	Fearfulness
6. Impertinence, defiance	Truancy	Cruelty, bullying
7. Untruthfulness	Impertinence, defiance	Easily discouraged
8. Unreliableness	Cruelty, bullying	Suggestible
9. Disobedience	Cheating	Overcritical of others
10. Heterosexual activity	Destroying school materials	Sensitiveness
11. Resentfulness	Disobedience	Domineering
12. Impudence, rudeness	Unreliableness	Sullenness
13. Lack of interest in work	Temper tantrums	Stealing
14. Quarrelsomeness	Lack of interest in work	Shyness
15. Easily discouraged	Profanity	Physical cowardice
16. Cheating	Impudence, rudeness	Selfishness
17. Carelessness in work	Laziness	Temper tantrums
18. Temper tantrums	Smoking	Dreaminess
19. Unsocial withdrawing	Enuresis	Nervousness
20. Selfishness	Nervousness	Stubbornness
21. Laziness	Disorderliness in class	Unreliableness
22. Disorderliness in class	Unhappy, depressed	Truancy
23. Obscene notes, talk	Easily discouraged	Untruthfulness
24. Suggestible	Selfishness	Cheating
25. Domineering	Carelessness in work	Lack of interest in work
26. Inattention	Inattention	Heterosexual activity
27. Nervousness	Quarrelsomeness	Enuresis
28. Masturbation	Suggestible	Obscene notes, talk
29. Profanity	Resentfulness	Tattling
30. Fearfulness	Tardiness	Attracting attention
31. Sullenness	Physical cowardice	Quarrelsomeness
32. Attracting attention	Stubbornness	Impudence, rudeness
33. Stubbornness	Domineering	Imaginative lying
34. Overcritical of others	Slovenly in appearance	Inattention
35. Physical cowardice	Sullenness	Slovenly in appearance
36. Thoughtlessness	Fearfulness	Laziness
37. Tardiness	Suspiciousness	Impertinence
38. Slovenly in appearance	Thoughtlessness	Carelessness in work
39. Sensitiveness	Attracting attention	Thoughtlessness
40. Shyness	Unsocial, withdrawing	Restlessness
41. Suspiciousness	Dreaminess	Masturbation
42. Enuresis	Imaginative lying	Disobedience

308 Teachers (1955) Hunter	511 Teachers (1926) Wickman	30 Mental Hygienists (1926) Wickman
43. Interrupting	Interrupting	Tardiness
44. Inquisitiveness	Inquisitiveness	Inquisitiveness
45. Dreaminess	Overcritical of others	Destroying school materials
46. Restlessness	Tattling	Disorderliness in class
47. Tattling	Whispering	Profanity
48. Imaginative lying	Sensitiveness	Interrupting
49. Smoking	Restlessness	Smoking
50. Whispering	Shyness	Whispering

Hunter, E. C., 1957, Changes in teachers' attitudes toward children's behavior over the last thirty years. *Mental Hygiene, 41:* 3–11.

are understandably of practical consequence to the teacher and of less concern to the clinician. Even if a teacher, in his own view, were inclined to be unperturbed over such behaviors as disobedience, truancy, destroying school property, and heterosexual activity, the general public would not accept this as a desirable teacher attitude. The inference is that teachers more than clinicians feel compelled to judge the importance of behaviors by cultural demands. Stouffer, in emphasizing this point, remarked, "Teachers are undoubtedly aware of the dire consequences for the child, the school, and the teacher, if community opinion is outraged by a violation of conventional sexual taboos. Similarly, their concern about truancy is understandable. How can you reach the goals of education, largely community prescribed, if the pupils fail to attend classes?"

This fact of the different positions of relationship which teachers and clinicians hold toward children was reflected in the way in which Wickman worded his instructions to the two groups respectively, when they made their ratings of problems. The phrasing of the directions to the teachers was such as to lead them to respond to problems as *present* problems; the phrasing did not necessarily invite consideration for the long-run development (future development) of the child. The phrasing employed in the directions to the clinicians was exactly reversed, and it may be assumed that they inferred that they were expected to give their responses with the child's *future* development in mind.

To make a satisfactory comparison of reactions of present-day teachers and clinicians to those of Wickman's groups it is necessary to use the same sets of directions that were given in the original investigation. A study which followed this procedure was conducted with a group (119 respondents) of elementary and high-school teachers in San Diego and a comparison group of 37 mental hygienists employed by the public schools of San Diego and Long Beach (Schupp and Gjerde, 1953) [19].

The results of this study indicated that the teachers of 1951 (in San Diego) agreed much more closely with their comparison group of mental hygienists than did Wickman's teachers with their comparison sample of mental hygienists. But the investigators found, nevertheless, that, "Teachers, when compared with clinicians, still appear to be less concerned about behavior traits associated with withdrawal and more concerned about those which appear to be transgressions against orderliness and, perhaps, morality." The investigators then added:

> Disagreements between attitudes of teachers and the criterion attitude established by clinicians, though not as pronounced as in 1927, still exist, and these disagreements are of the same nature as those pointed out by Wickman. Those responsible for teacher education, both pre-service and in-service, evidently need to continue to emphasize what might be called "a mental-hygiene viewpoint." (Schupp and Gjerde, 1953) [19]

Possible Differences with Varying Teacher Backgrounds

A study that introduced several new queries into the pattern of the Wickman investigation is a comparatively recent one by Hunter (1957) [9]. Not only did Hunter determine the relative seriousness with which teachers in 1955 looked upon the various problems of children, and how their views compared with Wickman's teachers and mental hygienists, but he also looked into the differences of attitudes that were held by teachers of different sex, race, marital status, education, and teaching experience. The comparisons between Hunter's respondents and those of Wickman are shown in Table 16.1.

It is apparent from the table, as Hunter concluded, that teachers of today "are showing more concern about non-aggressive traits and behavior suggesting mental health problems than did the teachers in 1926." Hunter found the teachers of his study to be closer to the mental hygienists in their thinking about children's behavior problems than the teachers of 1926 (Wickman's study) and 1950 (Stouffer's study).

Hunter's study showed that teachers with advance degrees tended to be more in agreement with the clinicians in their ratings of problems than did teachers with less education. Men in Hunter's report showed less concern than women for problems related to sex; women were more concerned than men for pupils' disregard for personal appearance, their destruction of school materials, and sexually suggestive behaviors. Negro teachers, more than white teachers, ranked tardiness, laziness, and carelessness as serious; they looked with less concern than white teachers upon cruelty-bullying, impertinence-defiance, and temper tantrums. For 47 of the 50 problems, the ratings which married teachers and unmarried teachers gave were not appreciably different.

Some conclusions which Hunter reached as a result of his study are especially pertinent:

> Teachers today are dealing more effectively with the whole child now and over the long span. The more highly trained teachers especially are better able than teachers were formerly to analyze and interpret the significance of recessive and withdrawing forms of behavior.
>
> At the same time the need for continued effort and more specific training in the study of complicated patterns of behavior is apparent. Through formal and informal means teachers need to be helped to understand the basic patterns of children's lives. Mental hygiene should occupy a larger role in undergraduate and graduate work, in both pre-service and in-service education of teachers. Academic study should be supplemented by abundant observation and realistic experience with children in and out of school. Mutual exchange of ideas and experiences between teachers and mental hygienists with regard to behavior problems should be encouraged. Continued cooperative research in the dynamics of child behavior should be carried on in order to increase our knowledge and understanding of how to deal more effectively with the child and his education. (Hunter, 1957) [9]

THE MENTAL-HYGIENE VIEWPOINT

During the forty years since Wickman's study, many different circumstances have combined to inject into teacher education what has been called the mental-hygiene point of view about behavior problems of children and youth.

The emphasis of this point of view is on the healthy development of boys and girls considered to be "normal children." The concept is that every child has problems associated with growing up and that some of these problems can have a crippling influence even on children who are thought to be emotionally quite stable.

The essential meaning of *mental hygiene* as a concern of the school was clearly expressed by Tryon:

> In our thinking about good mental health, or even good physical health, our tendency is to think in terms of the *absence* of pathological symptoms. This attitude stems from the fact that historically our research has been in the area of mental and physical disorders. Much of what we know about the "normal" has come by way of studying the diseased, the deviate, the abnormal. The field of medicine, concerned with the physical aspects of the human organism, however, has long since gone beyond this step of "curing." There are extensive programs of "prevention" for both individual patients and the general public.

Preventive mental health programs lag behind. Most of our time, energy, and financial resources are still allocated to the job of "picking-up-the-pieces" in psycho-social disorders, to the "cure" of the emotionally and socially disabled. Psychiatrists, clinical psychologists, social workers, and others are currently trained to diagnose what is wrong and to rehabilitate the mentally ill in our society. Little has yet been done in working out guide lines to create the conditions for *good* mental health.

Mental health is certainly more than the mere absence of emotional disorder or maladaptive behavior. Nor is mental health to be defined as the achievement of such control over our emotional life that we do not show our feelings. There are times when it is right and appropriate to be angry, to be afraid, to be happy or joyous, to be ecstatic. Mentally healthy persons are characterized by a vital, postitive emotional approach to living, both in day-to-day experiences and in long-range terms. (National Education Association, 1950) [18]

Tryon further called attention to the fact that traditionally the school's function had been deemed to be that of training individuals to *think.* From this traditional position the school came relatively late to accept a second idea. This idea was that there is importance in an individual's knowing how to *act* as well as how to think. This means knowing how to do, and how to behave when confronted with new situations. But, as Tryon explained, it was not enough for educators and teachers to have realized the importance of the individual's learning to do and to act. Individuals must also learn how to *feel.* This third aspect of living, according to Tryon, is not automatically a result of successful doing and thinking. "We are finding," said Tryon, "that this does not happen quite so automatically. Every child must have help in growing toward the goal of an emotionally mature adulthood. After these long years, we are recognizing our responsibility for helping children to learn to feel in certain ways."

CLASSROOM CONTROL AND DISCIPLINE

To what extent have the concepts that comprise the mental-health emphasis been infused into the control and discipline practices of teachers? How much has the present-day emphasis upon knowing and accepting the individual child influenced the teacher in his ways of dealing with the day-by-day situations of the school?

Some part of the answer is suggested in a study reported by Stendler (1949) [21]. Teachers were asked in the study to complete twenty-five free response statements related to various behavior patterns in children. The statements were such as "I think the child who never finishes on time should. . . ." The teacher was instructed to "finish the statement by describing what you think would be the best way of treating this particular problem. . . ." Other sample statements from the list of twenty-five are "I think the child who daydreams most of the time should. . . ." and "I think the child who is disliked by other children should. . . ."

The answers the teachers gave to indicate how they thought the behavior problems should be handled were classified into six categories. These categories and the percentage of responses falling under each category are shown in Table 16.2. Stendler takes note, in her interpretation of the tabulated findings, of the fact that the teachers in this study were not so prone as were teachers some decades ago to refer problems of behavior to a medical doctor. She recalls that it was customary practice not many years ago for parents and physicians as well as teachers to expect to find in physical conditions—diseased tonsils, for example—the explanation for almost any kind of behavior difficulty.

It is not to be inferred from Stendler's interpretation that today's teachers fail to recognize that certain unfavorable behaviors may stem from physical disorders. Rather, today's teachers, being better informed, recognize the range of conditions that may lead to a given behavioral problem. Although today's teachers do not rule out the possibility that a physical illness accounts for the problem, their approach is to examine the total situation of the child and try to identify those circumstances about which they personally can do something.

The teachers in Stendler's study considered it important in dealing with the problems of some children to adjust the work load. More than half the teachers indicated that they would do this for the dependent child, the timid child, the daydreamer, and the child who never finishes what he is doing. Adjustment of the work load meant making changes of various kinds in it depending upon what seemed to be most needed by a given child. In this, according to Stendler, teachers appeared to have "accepted the responsibility for changing the environment so that the child might be helped." This sort of procedure is obviously in contrast with the less analytical attitude behind the inclination to punishment that was characteristic of many teachers of the past.

Stendler asked three experts in the field of mental hygiene to complete the same set of twenty-five sentences which had been used for recording the teachers' responses. The mental hygienists' choice of the best means for changing the behavior patterns of children was that of Category 6, "Study him to find the cause of his behavior." Apparently the mental hygienists expected to gather considerable information about any behavior problem before proceeding with treatment. Although the teachers did show some concern for the case-study approach, the situations in which they advocated the use of such an approach were largely limited to stealing, truancy, and tardiness. Stendler pointed out that it was not possible to tell whether the teachers felt that stealing, truancy, or tardiness were the most serious types of behavior listed, or whether these situations were the type which could be understood only through a study of the out-of-school life of the pupils. Nevertheless, the teachers did not advocate extensive "study" or such behaviors as suspiciousness and withdrawal.

The conclusion which seems tentatively to be warranted from such studies is that teachers are increasingly more accepting of the idea that on their own resources they can hope to find some of the causes for some

TABLE 16.2
Percentages of Responses for Six Categories on Twenty-five Items Describing Pupil Behavior Made by 157 Elementary Teachers in a Midwestern Public School System

Category	Percent of Responses
1. Take punitive measures	13.9
2. Talk to the child	33.4
3. Send him to a doctor	2.7
4. Adjust the work	22.5
5. Praise or encourage	9.1
6. Study him to find cause of behavior	14.6
7. No answer	3.8

Stendler, Celia B., 1949, How well do elementary school teachers understand child behavior? *J. educ. Psychol.*, 40: 489–498.

of the kinds of problems children show; that they can also help some children solve the problems behind their troubled behaviors; that they are more and more inclined, with the mental hygienists, to look for explanations in the emotional-social network of child experience.

Methods of Discipline in the School

The concept of discipline in today's psychology of education is that discipline is not separable from the total pattern of interpersonal relationship in the school. Constructive discipline consists of more than threat-laden tricks by which to outwit pranksters and uncooperative learners. Mutual trust is at the heart of constructive discipline. Properly conceived it is not something which operates externally to the purposes and actions of the child; it is a pattern of controls which he learns and internalizes as he grows in the ways of self-direction.

Furthermore, today's educational psychology emphasizes the importance of the relationship between the discipline of the classroom and the behavioral controls to be exercised beyond the boundaries of the school. "Classroom discipline is important," says Symonds (1949) [23], "not only because it is an ever-present concern of teachers but also because methods of classroom control are closely related to the whole problem of training for democratic living and action." We define democratic living and action in terms of mutual helpfulness and cooperativeness, individual and group creativeness, mutually agreed upon purposes and procedures, and a sense of personal worth and responsibility. We should, therefore, expect to incorporate these same elements into the methods of control employed and learned in the school.

Under the heading, "Responsible Freedom," Wilhelms (1964) [26] devotes some pages (of a bulletin) to the relationship of freedom and *responsibility*. Freedom, as has been repeatedly emphasized in this book, is a *sine qua non* of the growth of selfhood.[7] The following lines from Wilhelms' statement will convey the cogency of his discussion:

> An essential ingredient of freedom is *responsibility*. Without it freedom is meaningless. And responsibility is *not* the negative side of the coin of freedom. We betray a misconception of the human organism when we call responsibility the cost one pays for freedom; when half-punitively, having yielded some freedom to a child, we threaten him with, "But you'll have to take the responsibility if your choice goes wrong."
>
> Responsibility is good in itself. The growing human organism—perhaps especially at adolescence—intuitively yearns for it. In truth, our society may be short-changing its young people more by denial of responsibility than by crimping of liberty. For growing responsibility is essential to self-testing, to a developing sense of capacity, to a toughening of inner fiber. A person rises to full stature only as the demands upon him challenge him to rise. And without responsibility growth can never be complete.

The importance of a developing sense of responsibility as the child becomes a youth and the youth becomes an adult cannot be overemphasized. Every agency of society must thoroughly and critically assess its ideas about what responsibility *is* and also its practices related to the inculcation of inner controls and strong social fidelity.

In a thought-provoking discussion of responsibility, Harris (1958) [8] addresses four summarizing statements to teachers—statements that underscore the functions of teachers. He states that responsibility should be viewed "as a developing process, not as a preconceived ideal by which all behavior of all children is measured." He then emphasizes the impor-

[7] The student will find stimulating discussion of this idea and related ideas in Erikson, E. H., 1964, *Insight and responsibility* [6], New York: W. W. Norton & Company, Inc. Also highly recommended for related reading is May, R., 1967, *Psychology and the human dilemma* [14], Princeton: D. Van Nostrand Company, Inc., especially pages 176–181.

tance of differentiating between true responsibility and passive acquiescence on the part of children and youth with whom teachers work. In this connection, Harris cautions teachers against the inclination to equate children's conformity to routines and teacher expectations with a real sense of responsibility.

Harris' third point deals with the tendency of teachers to think of boys as being less responsible than girls. He suggests that teachers may be judging on the basis of norms (their own norms) that fail to take into account the different maturity rates of boys and girls.

Finally, Harris notes that when they identify responsible children, teachers and children themselves are ahead of parents in the acceptance of psychological criteria. He feels that parents must be helped "toward realistic standards for their children and toward an increased understanding of cause and effect relationships in child behavior."

Democratic vs. Other Methods of Control

There has been considerable discussion—in Chapter 14 especially—of the effect of different home atmospheres on children's behavior. Psychologists have been interested in creating social group atmospheres experimentally in order to study the results on behavior. An experiment in this area was conducted some thirty years ago by Lewin, Lippitt, and White (1939) [13] with groups of ten-year-old boys.

Studies of Democratic Leadership. In this classical study by Lewin and his associates, the subjects were members of an interest club that met after school. They were divided into three groups or sections; the leader of one group handled the meetings in an autocratic and authoritarian manner, the leader of the second group relaxed and let nature take its course in a laissez-faire approach, while the third handled his group in a democratic fashion. These different "atmospheres," as anticipated, produced markedly different behaviors in the three groups.

In the authoritarian atmosphere the boys either manifested aggressive domination toward each other or they became apathetic and submissive. They soon lost interest in their activities, they looked for ways to escape from the situation, and their displays of hostility toward one another were forty times those which were shown by boys in the democratic situation.

The laissez-faire situation, which was characterized by complete freedom, led to confusion, feelings of uncertainty and insecurity, considerable aggression, much silliness, and a general tendency to run wild. Not much work was accomplished.

In contrast with the authoritarian and laissez-faire groups the boys in the democratic groups showed real interest in their tasks, took much individual responsibility made numerous constructive suggestions about how the work should be carried on, and were able satisfactorily to go ahead with their activities when the leader was absent. Their relationships with each other were consistently satisfying.

We may draw the conclusion that in general the democratic method of control, while at times noisier and harder to "oversee" than the authoritarian one, will result in more constructive activity and more cooperation and will afford greater opportunity for youngsters to develop their own habits of control and organization. A related conclusion is that avoidance of authoritarian methods of control does not of itself assure democratic methods. To allow leadership to lapse into extreme permissiveness, absence of direction, and general disregard for standards of accomplishment is to produce laissez faire—a pretty poor substitute for democracy.

There is an additional, important conclusion to be drawn from the study just described. It is that different kinds of leadership *can be* learned. This may be inferred from the fact that the participating leaders were not selected because they were thought to possess the characteristics of this or that kind of leader. Each one learned the behaviors which he was required to manifest in a given role. The indication is that a person can learn to be a particular kind of leader—a democratic one, let us say—if, first, he clearly understands the distinguishing behaviors of that kind of leader, and second, he has *practiced* these behaviors under conditions that provide a basis for objective evaluation of his performance.

In a study that involved training in democratic leadership, Bavelas and Lewin (1942) [3] demonstrated that the essence of "retraining" consisted of a combination of "changing the attitudes of the leaders and changing their techniques." And their study further emphasized the need for what was referred to above as critical, on-the-job evaluations by means of which the participant leaders could objectively judge their performance.[8]

The studies which have been mentioned were conducted in nonschool situations. Thought-provoking as the findings are, it is fair to question whether the situations of a school classroom might not test somewhat differently the relative effectiveness of the several methods of control and the benefits that derive from them.

In one study (Cunningham *et al.*, 1951) [5] an effort was made to determine to what extent pupils in school respond differently to differ-

[8] For descriptions of methods by which the members of a group can be mutually helpful in learning to improve their leadership performance, see Cartwright, D., and A. Zander, eds., 1953, *Group dynamics: Research and theory,* New York: Harper & Row, Publishers; and Jenkins, D. H., 1948, "Feedback and group self-evaluation," *J. soc. Issues,* **4:** 50–60.

ent *patterns* of teacher-pupil interactions. The results of the study, though a bit difficult to assess because of the complexities in it, suggest first, that there are numerous variations of what may be considered desirable teacher-pupil relationships in the classroom and that there are times and places where certain of these work better than others, and second, that teachers need to know how to perform in the various roles which the *variable situations* of the school present. The point which was made in the discussion of the studies by Lewin and his associates bears re-emphasis: knowing clearly the behaviors that exemplify the different methods of leadership (how the methods differ *basically*) is an important prerequisite to being effective in a leadership (teacher) capacity.

HELPING THEM STAND ON THEIR OWN TWO FEET

This book has given much emphasis to understanding children and helping them to understand themselves. Is there the possibility that someone has read into this emphasis the suggestion that teachers should never be critical of what youngsters do or say? Or the suggestion that being understanding of children means being forgiving of their every fault and failure? Has there been the inference that "you have to win them all"—at any price—to be a successful teacher? The authors of this book hope the emphasis upon *understanding* has not been so construed. Actually, to help youngsters know themselves and accept themselves we must teach them to face situations—and themselves—realistically. To be honest in appraising *with them* their faults as well as their virtues is the only firm basis for building the confidence we want our pupils to place in us.

Among our major responsibilities as teachers is that of helping children and youth to recognize that life *does* have its hardships, its disillusionments, and its heartaches as well as its triumphs and its pleasures. Our task—and our privilege—is to help boys and girls to achieve the moral courage and intellectual discipline that make it possible for a person to move ahead under his own power and with his own sense of direction. Stated a bit differently, this means helping them to gain increasing maturity of personality with every gain in size and age.

> Child, I would cherish you,
> Not for my own, but for yourself,
> Helping you to grow,
> Holding your dreams
> In the face of the world,
> Helping you not to grow callous
> And cold to the unseen.

I would not come too close
And stifle you with anxious care,
Merely be by
When life becomes too quiveringly real,
To give an understanding smile,
That you may build about your dreams
No higher wall
Than you may leap with ease and frequency.
I would that life should hurt you
And you be unafraid of pain.
Then having watched, unwatched,
I would draw quietly aside,
Happy that you had grown
To need me no more.[9]

TEACHERS' SELF-UNDERSTANDING AND SELF-DEVELOPMENT

The authors of this book have tried in many places to communicate to the reader a very personal suggestion. It is that each individual who reads the book should attempt through psychology to improve his insight *into his own behavior*. Certainly, every principle which has usefulness in his work with other individuals should have significance also for his own personal growth and development.

Self-understanding and self-acceptance is a goal of education that has importance for the teacher as he faces himself just as it does in his teaching of younger persons. In the book, *When Teachers Face Themselves,* Jersild (1955) [12] states, "The teacher's understanding and acceptance of himself is the most important requirement in any effort he makes to help students to know themselves and to gain healthy self-acceptance."

Perhaps it would be of considerable benefit to the reader when he has reached the end of this chapter to do two things. First he would reread the last section of Chapter 1: "Objectives of Psychology for Teachers." Then he would seriously consider the extent to which psychology as presented in this book has clarified the objectives and made them meaningful in his own personal life.

A FINAL WORD

Teaching should be fun. It is also, of course, hard work, sometimes stressful and wearing, but still fun. The thing that makes teaching fun is daily contact

[9] From A Credo for Parents, by E. H. McCormack, *Indiana Journal of Social Work,* December, 1948, quoted in Allen, F. H., Dilemmas of growth for parents and children, *Child Study,* 1948, **35:** 4–7.

with young lives—with people who are vital, growing, and developing (and, it must be admitted, sometimes annoying and confusing). The stimulation of contact with youth is felt most when the teacher is interested, informed, and eager to learn more about growing persons. The pupil who is fortunate enough to share a classroom with such a teacher will have a good chance of realizing the potentialities inherent in him.

Suggested Collateral Readings

A healthy personality for every child—A fact-finding report: A digest, 1951, Mid-Century White House Conference on Children and Youth. Raleigh, N.C.: Health Publications Institute.

Bruner, J. S., *The process of education.* Cambridge: Harvard University Press, 1961. Chapter 5.

Cunningham, Ruth, *et al., Group behavior of boys and girls.* New York: Teachers College, Columbia University, Bureau of Publications, 1951.

American Council on Education, *Helping teachers understand children.* Washington, D.C.: American Council on Education, 1945.

Jenkins, Gladys G., Helen Shacter, and W. W. Bauer, *These are your children.* Glenview, Ill.: Scott, Foresman and Company, 1953.

Jersild, A. T., *When teachers face themselves.* Teachers College, Columbia University, Bureau of Publications, 1955.

Johnson, C. J., and G. R. Medinnus, *Child psychology: Behavior and development.* New York: John Wiley & Sons, Inc., 1965. Chapter 12.

Klausmeier, H. J., and W. Goodwin, *Learning and human abilities,* 2d ed. New York: Harper & Row, Publishers, 1966. Chapter 6.

Lindgren, H. C., *Educational psychology in the classroom,* 2d ed. New York: John Wiley & Sons, Inc., 1962. Chapter 12.

National Educational Association, Department of Supervisors and Directors of Instruction, *Fostering Mental Health in Our Schools,* 1950 Yearbook. Washington, D.C.: National Education Association, 1950. Chapters 11 and 18.

Prescott, D. A., *The child in the educative process.* New York: McGraw-Hill, Inc., 1957. Especially page xii and Chapter 13.

Pressey, S. L., F. P. Robinson, and J. E. Horrocks, *Psychology in education.* New York: Harper & Row, Publishers, 1959. Chapters 14 and 17.

Redl, F., and W. W. Wattenberg, *Mental hygiene in teaching,* 2d ed. New York: Harcourt, Brace & World, Inc., 1959. Chapter 13.

Strang, Ruth, *The adolescent views himself.* New York: McGraw-Hill, Inc., 1957. Part Three.

Wickman, E. K., *Children's behavior and teachers' attitudes.* New York: The Commonwealth Fund, 1928.

References

1. Association for Supervision and Curriculum Development, *Perceiving, Behaving Becoming,* A New Focus on Education, Yearbook 1962. Washington, D.C.: National Educational Association. Page 238.
2. Baller, W. R., 1965, Characteristics of adolescents and their implications for the classroom. *The High School Journal,* XLVIII, 7. Pages 419–426.

3. Bavelas, A., and K. Lewin, 1942, Training in democratic leadership. *J. abnorm. soc. Psychol.,* **37:** 115–119.
4. Bruner, J. S., 1965, *On knowing—Essays for the left hand.* New York: Atheneum Publishers. Page 78.
5. Cunningham, Ruth, *et al.,* 1951, *Group behavior of boys and girls.* New York: Bureau of Publications, Teachers College, Columbia University.
6. Erikson, E. H., 1964, *Insight and responsibility.* New York: W. W. Norton & Company, Inc.
7. Gardner, J. W., 1961, *Excellence: Can we be equal and excellent too?* New York: Harper & Row, Publishers. Page 148.
8. Harris, D. B., 1958, *Let's take a look at responsibility.* Washington, D.C.: National Education Association. Pages 10–11.
9. Hunter, E. C., 1957, Changes in teachers' attitudes toward children's behavior over the last thirty years. *Mental Hygiene,* **41:** 3–11.
10. *Ibid.*
11. Hunter, Madeline C., 1958, Paul. *N. E. A. Journal,* **47:** 164–166.
12. Jersild, A. T., 1955, *When teachers face themselves.* New York: Bureau of Publications, Teachers College, Columbia University. Page 3.
13. Lewin, K., R. Lippitt, and R. K. White, 1939, Patterns of aggressive behavior in experimentally created social climates. *J. soc. Psychol.,* **10:** 271–299.
14. May, R., 1967, *Psychology and the human dilemma.* Princeton.: D. Van Nostrand Company, Inc. Pages 176–181.
15. McCreary, E. R., You teach what you are, in Robinson, D.W., ed., *Professional growth for teachers.* New London, Conn.: Croft Educational Services. October, 1964. Published by permission of Croft Educational Services.
16. Mitchell, J. C., 1942, A study of teachers' and mental hygienists' ratings of certain behavior problems in children. *J. educ. Res.,* **36:** 292–307.
17. Murphy, G., 1966, What can youth tell us about its potentialities? in *Re-assessing human potential, Bulletin of the National Association of Secondary-School Principals.* Washington, D.C.: National Association of Secondary-School Principals. Pages 14–15.
18. National Education Association, 1950, Association for Supervision and Curriculum Development, *Fostering mental health in our schools,* 1950 Yearbook. Washington, D.C.: National Education Association. Page 1.
19. Schupp, M. H., and C. M. Gjerde, 1953, Teacher growth in attitudes toward behavior problems of children. *J. educ. Psychol.,* **44:** 203–214.
20. ———, page 214.
21. Stendler, Celia B., 1949, How well do elementary school teachers understand child behavior? *J. educ. Psychol.,* **40:** 489–498.
22. Stouffer, George A. W., Jr., 1952, Behavior problems of children as viewed by teachers and mental hygienists: A study of present attitudes as compared with those reported by E. K. Wickman. *Mental Hygiene,* **36:** 271–285.
23. Symonds, P. M., 1949, Classroom discipline. *Teachers College Record,* **51:** 147–158.
24. Taba, Hilda, 1962, *Curriculum development: Theory and practice.* New York: Harcourt, Brace & World, Inc. Page 84.

25. Wickman, E. K., 1928, *Children's behavior and teachers' attitudes.* New York: The Commonwealth Fund.

26. Wilhelms, F. T., 1964, Using the curriculum to build personal strength. The *Bulletin of the National Association of Secondary-School Principals.* Washington, D.C.; The National Association of Secondary-School Principals, Vol. 48, Number 288 (January).

AUTHOR INDEX

SUBJECT INDEX